Nazi Spymaster

Nazi Spymaster

The Life And Death of Admiral Wilhelm Canaris

MICHAEL MUELLER

Introduction by Gerhard Weinberg

Skyhorse Publishing

Skyhorse Publishing books may be purchased in bulk at special discounts for sales promotion, corporate gifts, fund-raising, or educational purposes. Special editions can also be created to specifications. For details, contact the Special Sales Department, Skyhorse Publishing, 307 West 36th Street, 11th Floor, New York, NY 10018 or info@skyhorsepublishing.com.

Skyhorse® and Skyhorse Publishing® are registered trademarks of Skyhorse Publishing, Inc.®, a Delaware corporation.

Visit our website at www.skyhorsepublishing.com.

10 9 8 7 6 5 4 3 2 1

Library of Congress Cataloging-in-Publication Data is available on file.

Cover design by Rain Saukas

Print ISBN: 978-1-5107-1774-9
Ebook ISBN: 978-1-5107-1777-0

Printed in the United States of America

Contents

List of Illustrations		vii
Acknowledgements		ix
Abbreviations		xi
Introduction		xiii
Foreword		xv

PART I: OFFICER OF HIS MAJESTY   1

1	A Naval Cadet from the Ruhr	3
2	The Epic Last Voyage of the *Dresden*	10
3	Agent on a Special Mission	19
4	U-boat War in the Mediterranean	26

PART II: THE STRUGGLE AGAINST THE REPUBLIC   35

5	Servant of Two Masters	37
6	The Murderers' Helpers' Helper	43
7	On the Side of the Putschists	49
8	Agent of the Counter-Revolution	56
9	Military-Political Secret Missions	63
10	The Shadow of the Past	73

PART III: RISE UNDER THE SWASTIKA   85

11	Hitler's Military Intelligence Chief	87
12	The Duel with Heydrich	94
13	Between Führer, Duce and Caudillo	102
14	Ousting the Generals	112
15	A Double Game	120
16	Between Obedience and Conscience	127

PART IV: FINIS GERMANIAE   141

17	The Will for War	143
18	The Madness Unfolds	152
19	The War of Extermination – Act One	159

20   The Spirit of Zossen   170
21   'Now There is No Going Back'   178
22   Operation Felix   186

     PART V: THE TRIUMPH OF THE BARBARIANS   197

23   The War of Extermination – Act Two   199
24   The Struggle for Power with Heydrich   209
25   With His Back to the Wall   220
26   The Undoing of Canaris   234

     PART VI: HITLER'S REVENGE   249

Notes   259
Sources and Bibliography   336
Index   360

Illustrations

Illustrations appear between pages 208 and 209

1   Fregattenkapitän Wilhelm Canaris, late 1920s
2   In a circle of classmates after obtaining his school-leaving certificate
3   As U-boat commander with his officers
4   Amongst his crew, 1918
5   Kapitän zur See and commander of the battleship *Schlesien*, 1934
6   A leisurely stroll to the beach with friends
7   An enthusiastic horseman
8   In the air
9   Relaxing as a 'civilian' during a sea cruise
10 A beer evening in honour of Himmler in Berlin, 1935
11 In conversation with Himmler and Goebbels during the 1936
    Nuremburg Rally
12 At a military reunion with with General der Flieger Karl Eberth and
    SS-Gruppenführer Reinhard Heydrich
13 Werner Best, an important confidant for Canaris, 1933
14 With the Spanish Civil War hero General Jose Moscardo at a
    reception in Berlin, 1939
15 A visit to the Eastern Front with counter-espionage chief Franz-
    Eccard von Bentivegni
16 Assembly of the Abwehr and SD heads at Hradshin Castle, Prague,
    May 1942
17 Canaris in a circle of Abwehr colleagues
18 Hans von Dohnanyi with Karl Ludwig von Guttenberg and Justus
    Delbrück, colleagues, about 1942
19 Anti-Hitler conspirators Heinz and Oster with an unidentified officer
20 Hans Bernd Gisevius, 1933
21 Foreign Minister Joachim von Ribbentrop announces to the world
    press the invasion of the Soviet Union, 22 June 1941
22 SS-Brigadeführer Walter Schellenberg being sworn as a witness at the
    principal War Crimes Trials at Nuremberg

23   Wilhelm Keitel, Erwin Lahousen, Wilhelm Canaris and Franz-Eccard
     von Bentivegni, 1941
24   With the former head of Abwehr II, Erwin Lahousen, at Voronice,
     Ukraine, Summer 1942
25   On the occasion of the funeral of former Kaiser Wilhelm II at Doorn,
     Netherlands, June 1941
26   Canaris during one of his frequent visits to Spain
27   Relaxing in Bavaria, 1942
28   The Canaris family home at Berlin-Schlachtensee, built in 1936
29   Abwehr headquarters, Tirpitzufer, Berlin
30   The barracks at Flossenbürg concentration camp where Canaris, Oster,
     Bonhoeffer, Gehre, Sack and Strünck were executed, 9 April 1945

PICTURE CREDITS

Ullstein pictures   1, 2, 5, 10, 13, 16, 20–22, 28, 29
SV-Bilderdienst   30
Bundesarchiv Militärarchiv Freiburg   3, 4, 6–9, 17
Bundesarchiv Militärarchiv Koblenz   11, 12, 14, 15, 25
Sean E McGlynn   18
Archiv Michael Heinz   19
Stefanie Lahousen   23, 24, 26, 27

Acknowledgements

I rather fear that readers are happy to pass over the Acknowledgements section in books. I hope that it will be different in this case, for nobody writes a book alone.

First of all, my thanks go to my wife Daniele who, during the tough years of this project, gave me unconditional support, watched my back and warded off the worst of the unpleasantness which occurs when writing a book of this kind. My friend and collaborator Ingke Brodersen helped me through a number of critical situations with her endless patience and technical expertise. Without the efforts of Daniele and Ingke this book would not have been completed.

For his help in various difficult situations during the project I would like to give a special mention Rüdiger Damman. My friend and colleague Peter F Müller was to have co-authored this volume but stepped aside for personal reasons. I am therefore all the more grateful to him for his research efforts on my behalf in London, Washington and Freiburg.

The help of our friend and assistant Jacqueline Williams, who supported the project with her enthusiasm and expertise, and, above all, obtained outstanding results from her searches at the London and Washington national archives, was indispensable. I am equally indebted to Erich Schmidt-Eenboom, head of the Research Institute for Peace Politics at Weilheim, who not only placed his comprehensive archive and library at my disposal, but was always on hand to answer my numerous enquiries and solved many problems with his technical knowledge and counsel.

Significant help was rendered by Helmut Lorscheid's research at the Bundesarchiv in Berlin and in the political archives at the German Foreign Ministry, for which my heartfelt thanks, and the same goes for Annette Hauschild. For a last-minute mission to the Institut für Zeitgeschichte at Munich, my old friend Thomas Wedmann merits a mention. I thank my friend Dr Peter Kurth for his patient help in translating the old Sütterlin handwriting.

Most especial thanks for their help and information are owed to Stefanie Lahousen, Inge Haag and Michael Heinz; a number of the illustrations in this book originate from the latter's private album.

A volume of this kind is not possible without the help of domestic and foreign archives whose staffs deserve the most unstinting praise. I am especially indebted in this regard as follows: Dr Edgar Büttner (Bundesarchiv-Militärarchiv Freiburg), who gave me access to the Wilhelm Canaris literary collection, only recently available at the military archive and containing previously unknown letters and documents relating to Canaris; at the same office Kurt Erdmann smoothed the way for me and always had the answer to my questions; an immense help for me was the insight afforded by Dr Tillmann Koops (Bundesarchiv Koblenz) when I was allowed to see the then partially completed manuscript of the comprehensive Bundesarchiv documentation for OKW office Amt Ausland/ Abwehr. This saved me much fruitless searching, and moreover supplied clues to unsuspected fresh lines of inquiry. The Bundesarchiv's important work on Canaris and the Abwehr had not been published at the time my own manuscript was completed, but I include it in the bibliography.

For an important clue I thank Dr Klaus A Lankheit of Institut für Zeitgeschichte Munich. Of great help once again in research at the Washington national archive were Paul B Brown, a staff member of the Interagency Working Group, and also John Taylor, who rendered tangible help and advice.

For his wise advice, pointing me in the right direction for my research, and his corrections, especially in the early phase of the project, I am greatly indebted to author Heinz Höhne, who set the standard for the *genre* with his book on Canaris thirty years ago.

For important groundwork I also have to thank Dr Winfried Mayer, whose study *Unternehmen Sieben* belongs amongst the most quoted works in my bibliography, and to all authors and researchers in whose works over the decades this book has its roots, my collective thanks.

Last but not least I signal my appreciation to Christian Seeger of Propyläen Verlag, the German publishers, for his patience and understanding over the last two years.

I am solely responsible for all errors, omissions and inadequacies in this book.

Michael Mueller

Abbreviations

AA	Auswärtiges Amt
Abw	Abwehr
ADAP	Akten zur Deutschen Auswärtigen Politik
ADM	Admiralty
AFK	Ausfuhrgemeinschaft für Kriegsgerät (Export Association for War Equipment)
AMC	armed merchant cruiser
AWA	Amtsgruppe Allgemeine Wehrmachts-angelegenheiten (Combined Office for General Wehrmacht Affairs)
BAK	Bundesarchiv Koblenz
BA-MA	Bundesarchiv-Militärarchiv Freiburg
BGH	Bundesgerichtshof
BS	Seetransportabteilung (Naval Transport Division)
d.R.	der Reserve
DRZW	*Das Deutsche Reich und der Zweite Weltkrieg,* published by Militärgeschichtlichen Forschungsamt, Stuttgart, 1979 onwards
DDI	Documenti Diplomatici Italiani
FA	Forschungsamt (Research Bureau)
FdU	Führer der U-boote (Regional Commander of U-boats)
FHQ	Führerhauptquartier (Führer headquarters)
FO	Foreign Office (British)
FS	Freiwilliger Deutscher Schutzdienst (Voluntary German Protection Service)
GFP	Geheime Feldpolizei (Wehrmacht police corps, secret field police)
GKSD	Gardekavallerie-Schützendivision
HAPAG	Hamburg Amerika Linie
HO	Home Office (British)
HWK	Handelskrieg und Wirtschaftliche Kampfmassnahmen (Anti-Shipping and Economic Warfare)
IfZ	Institut für Zeitgeschichte München
IMG	Verhandlungen und Beweisdokumente des Prozesses gegen die Hauptkriegsverbrecher vor dem Internationalen Militärgerichtshof in Nürnberg, 14.11.1945 bis 1.10.1946 (International War Crimes Tribunal, Nuremberg)
K-Org	Kampf-Organisationen (Kommandotrupps der Abwehr II)
KPD	Kommunistische Partei Deutschlands (Communist Party of Germany)

KTB	Kriegstagebuch (War diary)
MSg	Militärgeschichtliche Sammlung
MSPD	Mehrheits-Sozialdemokratische Partei Deutschlands (Majority Socialist Party)
NA	National Archives Kew/London
NARA	National Archives and Records Administration Washington
NKVD	Narodnyi Komissariat Vnutrennikh Del (Soviet – People's Commissariat for Internal Affairs)
OKH	Oberkommando des Heeres (Army High Command)
OKM	Oberkommando der Marine (Naval High Command)
OKW	Oberkommando der Wehrmacht (Wehrmacht High Command)
Org C	Organisation Consul
OSS	Office of Strategic Services
OUN	Organisation Ukrainischer Nationalisten
PA/AA	Politisches Archiv des Auswärtigen Amtes
RG	Record Group
RM	Reichsmarine
RSHA	Reichssicherheitshauptamt
SA	Sturmabteilung (Brownshirts, Hitler's huge force of political stormtroopers)
SD	Sicherheitsdienst (Security Service)
SDF	Sudeten-Deutsches Freikorps
SdP	Sudetendeutsche Partei
SHA	Sicherheits-Hauptamt (from 1939 SS-RSHA – the SS administrative headquarters)
SIPM	Servicio Informacion Policia Militar (Spanish – secret service under Franco)
Sipo	Sicherheitspolizei (Security Police)
SIS	Secret Intelligence Service
SKL	Seekriegsleitung
SOVO	Seeoffizier-Vereinigung Ostsee (Naval Officers' Association, Baltic)
SPD	Sozialistische Partei Deutschlands (German Socialist Party)
Stapo	Staatspolizei
UAK	U-Boot-Abnahme-Kommission (U-boat Acceptance Commission)
UNL	Union Naval de Levante
USPD	Unabhängige Sozialdemokratische Partei Deutschlands (Independent Social Democratic Party)
VMD	Volksmarinedivision (People's Naval Division)
WO	War Office
ZS	Zeugenschrifttum

Introduction

This new study of a highly controversial figure in the history of Nazi Germany provides a look at both the subject, Admiral Canaris, and the sources and literature about the head of the German military intelligence for most of the years that Adolf Hitler ruled the country. The reader has an opportunity to obtain a very clear picture of the early career of Canaris in the German navy, his involvement in intelligence matters, and his acquaintance with Spain—all matters central to his subsequent career.

The author leaves no doubts about the vehement opposition of Canaris to the Weimar Republic as well as his early support for the Nazis, major aspects of his life that some have downplayed because of his disillusionment with the regime, his abhorrence of the cruelties of the regime both before and during World War II, his efforts to save some individuals (including some Jews) from persecution, and his involvement in plots to overthrow the Hitler regime beginning in 1938, if not earlier. On all of these subjects, the author brings together information from a wide variety of sources, some of which have hitherto been inaccessible or ignored by the literature.

This book offers important insight into an interesting duality in Nazi dissent that is all too easily ignored or minimized in both the literature on the Third Reich as a whole and in the published accounts of the resistance against Hitler; these government officials who took part in resistance efforts often spent the bulk of their time actually serving the policies and interests of the regime. The author presents a detailed picture of the way in which Canaris served the regime in peace and in war, carrying out his officially assigned duties as head of the Abwehr. There were occasions when he actively sabotaged the efforts of Adolf Hitler, such as hinting to Spanish dictator Francisco Franco that he would be best advised not to officially enter the war on Germany's side; but on the other hand, there was his steady provision of accurate intelligence to a government that needed to be informed about the world, in which it lived first in peace and then in war.

At times, the two types of activity intersected with each other. The German leadership obviously needed intelligence on the Soviet Union before invading that country, a task that fell to Admiral Canaris. He gathered extensive information that advised against invading the country and discouraged a breaking of the Nazi-Soviet nonaggression treaty; his advice was, of course, disregarded by a leader who was determined to take over "living space" for Germans from people he imagined to be racially inferior and, hence, incapable of effective resistance (a view quite widely shared in both the German public and among the leaders of the country's military).

It is conceivable but unlikely that important new sources might become accessible in the future, but although ignoring some English-language literature, this author has both exhausted the archives in Germany, England, the United States, and some private collections. An especially important and helpful facet of the book is the way in which the activities of Canaris are embedded in a full account of the context of the time and in relation to the personalities involved, both those inside the organization that Canaris headed and those in the other portions of the Nazi leadership with which he interacted, especially Heinrich Himmler and Reinhard Heydrich. The general reader will find this thoughtful, detailed, and fair textual account fascinating, while specialists and scholars generally will appreciate that the book not only cites the sources in extensive notes but also reviews numerous criticisms and controversies about them.

Gerhard L. Weinberg
November 2016

Foreword

From our mistakes we reap the richest harvest. Seen against the reality, they show who we were and why.

Heinrich Mann, *Zur Zeit von Winston Churchill*

Admiral Wilhelm Canaris headed Adolf Hitler's military intelligence service for nine years. His contemporaries could hardly have differed more in their appraisal of his role. Former Reich Chancellor Heinrich Brüning called him one of the most complicated and inscrutable men he had ever known; as with all secret service men, Canaris had never revealed the whole truth nor voiced his true feelings and opinions. On the other hand, Foreign Office Secretary of State Ernst von Weizsäcker trusted him to the extent that Canaris was one of the few people with whom he chose to discuss affairs unreservedly.

Canaris's long-serving colleague Inga Haag remained adamant that her chief accepted the office of Abwehr head in 1935 with the express intention of using the position to organise the resistance to the National Socialist regime, but she could not deny the friendly and even cordial nature of the relationship that existed between Canaris and Heydrich until the death of the latter in 1942. To other eyes Canaris ranged from being the devious operator, master of the conspiratorial game and secret diplomacy, to being the bureaucrat who bloated the Abwehr apparatus with his mediocrity and then steered it with a flood of edicts. He was also thought to be a convinced servant of the Nazi regime, an unscrupulous opportunist and a brilliant tactician who to the end deceived Hitler and his lackeys as to his true goals. After his execution one side saw him as a traitor who had betrayed German attack plans to the enemy and thus sent German soldiers to their deaths, while from the outset the other side adopted him as a leader of 'The Other Germany' who had done everything he could to prevent a war that he foresaw as leading to the country's destruction, and once it was careering down that road, worked towards bringing it to an end as quickly as possible.

Today, sixty years on, two things are certain: none of the foregoing conclusions can be trusted, and for virtually no other personality of the Hitler epoch is an approach to a consistent and true appraisal more difficult. So, what kind of man was Canaris, how did he think? The historian will find that there are no private diaries, few letters, only vestiges of his service diary, which allows for no conclusion to be formed as to his personal outlook on affairs, and, except for a politically motivated item on the eve of the Second World War, there is no published material. I have treated postwar evaluations with great circumspection, resisting the temptation, where facts are thin on the ground, to mythologise Canaris's role by the use of circumstantial evidence. The paucity of documentation also prevents any realistic attempt at a psychological evaluation.

In postwar Germany it became desirable to identify a stream of 'blameless' senior Wehrmacht officers who had acted with rectitude within the framework of the possibilities open to them. Canaris came to the forefront through the biography by Karl Heinz Abshagen, authored with the help of Canaris's close colleague and friend, Erwin Lahousen, and published in Germany in 1955. In the mid-1970s a dimmer view of his activities was taken in Heinz Höhne's detailed volume *Canaris – Patriot im Zwielicht* (Canaris – Twilight Patriot).

To the present day, the wealth of material covering the Wehrmacht period, particularly from British archives, is so enormous that little of it has yet been assessed. In the Federal German military archive at Freiburg a Canaris 'legacy' has become available, containing many previously unknown documents and photographs. Much of the material we have available demonstrates that Canaris did not truly fit the image of the legend, but was a typical officer of his time: the son of Westphalian gentry attracted to a career in an imperial navy whose aim was to control the world's oceans. After the Armistice, robbed of his illusions, he found the imposed democratic system incomprehensible, and was repelled by Socialism and Communism. An enemy of the Weimar Republic, he watched the rise of National Socialism with interest, and fell prey to the error shared with the majority of his conservative contemporaries in believing that the regime could be controlled. Once he saw that Germany was on the slippery slope towards the abyss, Canaris's upbringing and personal weakness made it impossible for him to confront Nazism whole-heartedly. He remained a careerist and fellow-traveller. Plagued by guilt once he had seen the horrors, he made desperate attempts here and there to steer against the current and prevent the worst. Canaris was also a respected global player who prepared the way for Hitler from Tibet to Northern Ireland yet somehow managed to be the voice of 'The Other Germany' as he did so. He also tempered his opposition to the regime by participating in the war machine and the extermination processes; this kind of contradiction is what the historian encounters time and again in researching him.

As little is known about Canaris's family as about the man himself. He was no Hitler or Himmler, but also no Dohnanyi or Bonhoeffer. He was a workaholic who often preferred the camp bed in his office to his bed at home, and kept himself distant from his daughters. He could be brusque and unjust to people, and he would speak his mind vociferously. His service assessments, though speaking of a shy and reserved personality with a weak constitution, also relate his adroitness for diplomacy, his command of languages and his untiring preparedness to work. He would be away from home for weeks on end and drove himself to the point of exhaustion. The 'tendency towards melancholia' to which he was reportedly prone would perhaps be recognised today as depression resulting from exhaustion. He was fond of animals, though, as is shown by his affection for the two dachshunds that shared his arrest and exile at Burg Lauenstein.

The Abwehr, and particularly Abwehr-Abteilung II under Erwin Lahousen Edler von Vivremont, responsible for insurrection and sabotage, extended from South America to South Africa, to the Near and Middle East, Eastern Europe, Central Asia and India. Most of its operations were aimed at supporting local uprisings and national movements against the British Empire and the Soviet Union; it collaborated closely with the Irish Republican Army. The thinking and strategy behind it all make an exciting tale, but that is another story. Despite the ever-increasing flow of new material from national archives, the documentation regarding Wilhelm Canaris remains incomplete, and this portrayal of his life neither answers all the questions, nor resolves all the contradictions.

Michael Mueller,
Cologne,
December 2005.

PART I

OFFICER OF HIS MAJESTY

A Naval Cadet from the Ruhr

Wilhelm Canaris was born on 1 January 1887 'with a silver spoon in his mouth', as his biographer Abshagen wrote, to an upper-class, wealthy family in Dortmund Applerbek.[1] His father was technical director of the Applerbek metal plant and became later a board member of a large foundry at Duisburg, part of the Rheinisches Bergbau- und Hüttenwesen A.G. Metallurgy. Mining was the family tradition, going at least as far back as a maternal great-grandfather.

The Canarisi family itself can be traced back to fourteenth-century Como. In the seventeenth century several branches of it left Italy for the Kur-States of the Rhine.[2] In 1880, Wilhelm's father Carl Canaris married Auguste Amelie Popp, daughter of a senior forester at Altershausen in the Duchy of Saxony, and brother Carl and sister Anna were born in 1881 and 1883 respectively, after which the family moved to Dortmund. (Carl graduated in mining at Berlin and was eventually director-general of the August-Thyssen metal plant at Duisburg, and of Krauss-Maffei at Munich. Anna Canaris married engineer Rudolf Buck, later head of the Buderusschen ironworks).[3]

The political ideas of the technical elite in nineteenth-century Germany were invariably national-liberal or conservative and loyal to the monarchy. Kaiser Wilhelm II saw himself as a 'naval emperor' whose destiny was to make Germany into a world naval power.[4] Shortly after ascending the throne, the twenty-nine-year-old Kaiser assured naval officers that his 'last thought would be with the Navy just as grandfather had once said that his dying thoughts would be for the Army'.[5] Naval propaganda infiltrated 'all political forces, from the conservatives to the liberal left to the social democrats'.[6] In 1897 when Admiral Alfred Tirpitz became state secretary at the Reich Admiralty, he coordinated a naval building programme aimed primarily at matching the British Royal Navy. This enforced build-up of a High Seas Fleet robbed German foreign policy of its freedom to manoeuvre and led Germany into that encirclement by Britain, France and Russia so feared by Bismarck. Ultimately, it would bring about the First World War in 1914.[7]

The Kaiser's enthusiasm for the sea lured an increasing number of the sons of middle- and upper-class families, including Wilhelm Canaris, into careers as naval officers. In April 1898 after three years in pre-secondary school he passed the acceptance examination for the Steinbart-Real High School Duisburg, and the next day took his place in a class of thirty-six pupils.[8] His fellow students remembered him as calm, reserved, even occasionally taciturn, but well liked.[9] He was amongst his own kind, sons of the upper class, whose fathers were judges, doctors or businessmen. A high point of the first two school years was the annual sports festival at Kettwig. A contemporary report evinces the militaristic character of the institution:

> At six in the morning the headmaster would face his troop of scholars, paraded in two military files, for 'Appell'. The 'platoon leaders' would deliver their reports and then came the order 'Off caps for prayer'. Accompanied by the impressive town band, hundreds of strong, youthful voices would then sing the hymn of the day. After terse military commands, the squad of fresh, happy young men marched off . . .[10]

The festivals were discontinued in 1900, probably replaced by 'terrain games' on set afternoons when the military spirit would be encouraged by orienteering, map-reading, distance estimation and bivouac-making.[11]

Canaris was the only pupil of his class with ambitions to be a career officer, although many boys who obtained their *Abitur* (matriculation certificate) at the Steinbart High School later joined the Navy as officer cadets. The Ruhr with its trade and heavy industry had always had close links to the Navy and shipbuilding. In an age of great technical strides the demand was now for naval applicants with a good education in science. This was in contrast to the Army officer corps, where noble origins or a family tradition of service was more important than education, but even in the Army the modern military – though opposed by the traditionalists – had begun to recruit *Abituriente* with good technical and scientific backgrounds. Between 1898 and 1905, the year when Canaris began his naval career, the percentage of *Abituriente* of each annual intake rose from 21 per cent to 55 per cent, and by 1909 75 per cent of the officer entry was *Abitur*-based.[12] Kaiser Wilhelm II supported this new development. By his Cabinet Order of 29 March 1890, those of 'noble mind' in addition to 'noble birth' were eligible to be 'officer aspirants'. As 'bearers of the future', sons of such 'honourable bourgeois houses in which love of King and Fatherland, a warm heart for the soldierly profession and a Christian upbringing and education' prevailed were now to be admitted.[13]

Wilhelm Canaris was a prototype of this future naval officer, but his family did not approve, for there had never been a career officer in the family before. His father attempted to force the boy to abandon his naval dreams by making him apply for entry to the Bavarian 1st Heavy Cavalry Regiment at Munich.[14] Fate took a hand, though, when Carl Canaris died unexpectedly, aged fifty-two, on 26 September 1904 while on vacation at Bad Nauheim.[15] In March 1905 Wilhelm obtained his *Abitur*. His good grades in English, French, Latin and Greek laid the foundations for his future intelligence career but he also did well in Natural Science, Geography and History; his form-master laid emphasis on his enthusiasm for laboratory work. In German he obtained a 'satisfactory', in Art 'unsatisfactory'.[16]

On 1 April 1905 Canaris went with his certificate to the old Deck-Officers' School at Kiel, one of 159 members of 'Crew 05', as the naval cadet entry was designated in the training ship tradition. His mother had yielded to her son's wishes and taken him before the Sea Cadet Acceptance Commission even before he had matriculated, and she agreed to foot the not inconsiderable cost of the first four years' naval training, a social safeguard to keep undesirable elements out of the naval officer corps.[17]

After completing the initial course of infantry training, Canaris was drafted with fifty fellow cadets aboard the Imperial Navy training ship SMS *Stein* (2,850 tonnes, a fully rigged three-master with steam auxiliaries) and made voyages to Skagen, Iceland and the Mediterranean.[18] The ship's complement was twenty officers, 449 NCOs and ratings, fifty naval cadets and 210 boys. *Stein* was notorious for its harsh regime.[19] Before breakfast the cadets had to climb to each of the three topmasts. They were required to scrub the decks with sand and stone like common mariners, learned to ward off sleep in standing night watches, were instructed in reefing, furling and generally handling the ship's rig in all states of wind and weather.[20] Young Canaris's will to master the fatiguing training routine met with approval from one of his instructors, Richard Protze,[21] who in later years became his subordinate at the Abwehr, and found him reserved and adaptable with a dry sense of humour.[22]

At the beginning of 1906 *Stein* completed her voyage and Canaris was promoted to *Fähnrich zur See*, midshipman.[23] On 1 April 1906 at the Kiel Naval College[24] he began the twelve-month course in which 'Training as an Officer and a Gentleman' was very important.[25] As future representatives of the military and social elite, the midshipmen were introduced to the rigorous code of honour of the naval officer corps and the strict caste system: deck officers at the bottom, above them torpedo and ordnance officers, then the engineers and finally at the top were the navigators. The officers' course included gunnery, torpedo and infantry training.[26] Finally in the autumn of 1907 came the passing-out ceremony in which the cadets swore the oath of allegiance to the Kaiser in the courtyard of the Naval College.[27]

On 1 November 1907 Canaris shipped out on the steamer *Cap Frio* to report twenty-four days later aboard the small cruiser SMS *Bremen* on the East American Station where its duty was to protect German interests in the Central and South American region. In his first service assessment signed on 10 June 1908 by Kapitän zur See Alberts, the opinion was that 'he had trained his seamen well and treated them correctly, but could be more energetic. Towards superior officers Canaris is always tactful and modest. He integrates well into the officers' mess and has made an earnest and composed social impression. He has good qualities of character and is a well-liked member of the mess.' This assessment shows the value placed on social integration in ships of the Imperial Navy. Alberts continued: 'He is good at Theory, talented in Practice and during the shipyard lay-up delivered a well-prepared address to his platoons. Speaks fairly good English ... leadership very good. Knowledge of ship very good. Navigational calculations sure and conscientious, very reliable support for the navigation officer. Gunnery very good, nautical knowledge good.'[28] On relinquishing command of *Bremen* to Kapitän zur See Albert Hopman at Punta Arenas, the retiring captain wrote of Canaris: 'He had been trained as captain's adjutant and promises to become a very good officer as soon as he gains more self-confidence. Military and social forms blameless. Despite a certain shyness socially very well liked for his modest manner.'[29] This may not have fitted the desired image of daring and Prussian impetuosity but accurately summed up Canaris, of whom it was generally said later that despite having gained the soldierly attributes, there remained something unsoldierly about him. He was promoted *Leutnant zur See* on 28 September 1908.[30] Kapitän Hopman, who had accepted Canaris as his adjutant, agreed with his predecessor's opinion and spoke of Canaris's 'iron industry and unconditional reliability'.[31] He seemed destined for a glittering career.

From Punta Arenas *Bremen* rounded the Horn and showed the flag at Buenos Aires, receiving the typical fanatical welcome accorded to German warships by the patriotic and nationalistic expatriate community of those pre-First World War years. At the time there were 10,000 Germans in Buenos Aires and 30,000 in Argentina as a whole; they were mostly business people, engineers, technicians and farmers, and German instructors trained the Argentine Army. 'The German colony gave us a wonderful welcome,' Hopman recalled, 'quite apart from invitations to the officer corps from leading personalities of the colony, the German Soldiers' Union and various other associations threw a huge garden party for the *Bremen* crew, which drew thousands together. Although the most varied elements were represented, it was saturated with the spirit of true love for the homeland and national pride.'[32] Hopman, who credited the twenty-two-year-old Canaris with 'far more understanding and intelligence than was to be expected for his junior status in the Service',[33] had his adjutant accompany him on visits inland to friends in Brazil and Argentina.[34] During this period Canaris became involved in intelligence work for the first time when he assisted in setting up networks of informers in Brazil and Argentina for the Etappendienst, the German naval intelligence service. It was thus on the *Bremen* voyages that Canaris began to acquire the Spanish language and became familiar with the countries of Central and South America that had inherited the Ibero-American and Spanish culture.

At Rio de Janeiro the Brazilian war minister Hermes da Fonseca came aboard to observe naval manoeuvres;[35] off Trinidad the gun and torpedo crews exercised before the ship proceeded to Venezuela.[36] On 23 November 1908 the Venezuelan state president and dictator Cipriano Castro had left for Berlin to undergo surgery and in mid-December his vice-president, Juan Vicente Gomez, took the opportunity to stage a coup. During the *Bremen*'s four-day stay in February 1909, Gomez awarded Canaris his first military decoration, the Medal of the Bust of the Liberator, Fifth Class. The reason for the award remains unknown, although it is speculated that Canaris might have been involved the previous year in talks with Gomez on President Castro's visit to Germany.[37]

After calls at the Dutch Antilles, Panama, Costa Rica and Guatemala,[38] *Bremen* spent the next three months off the North American coast. During this time Hopman instructed his young adjutant in the procedure for mobilisation for war and he was impressed by Canaris's grasp of detail.[39] In September 1909 the cruiser took part in the celebrations to mark the 300th anniversary of the founding of the city of New York. Delegations from 'all seafaring nations' were invited; Imperial Germany was represented by four warships. A naval review of 1,000 ships passed down the Hudson River before the vice-president, the governor and the mayor. A historical festival, banquets and a ball followed. 'Dazzling', Hopman found it:

> We were inundated with invitations, ate at tables covered with the most glorious mantles, adorned with the rarest orchids, the finest porcelain, silver plate and golden dessert spoons, were seated next to stylish ladies who wore expensive perfume and metre-long necklaces of pearls: we made trips in automobiles and dog-carts, danced the new two-step and generally 'had a good time'.[40]

It was the glorious twilight of an era fast approaching its end; the splendid lull before the storm.

In November 1909 Hopman and Canaris shipped for home aboard the steamer *Sachsenwald*. As watchkeeper aboard various torpedo boats, Canaris endured the ritual of autumn and spring naval exercises in the cold North Sea and was recommended by his superiors for future command of a torpedo boat.[41]

But he had contracted malaria in Central America, and the recurrent bouts he suffered over the years weakened his constitution. In the raw climate of northern Germany he contracted a severe bronchitis that kept him on the sick list for months.[42]

After being promoted *Oberleutnant zur See* at the end of August 1910 and obtaining a 'very good' classification in a sea-mines course,[43] in December 1911 Canaris joined the small cruiser SMS *Dresden* with which he would remain until her sinking.[44] In 1911/12 the 3,600-tonne cruiser won the coveted Kaiser's Prize for Small Cruisers of the High Seas Fleet in gunnery, and visited neighbouring Baltic and North Sea states and Norway. The outbreak of the First Balkans War between Germany's ally Turkey and the Balkan Federation of Serbia, Bulgaria, Greece and Montenegro in October 1912 required German interests to be protected, and the Kaiser ordered a Mediterranean Division formed under Konteradmiral Trummler. The new battlecruiser *Goeben* and the small cruiser *Breslau* were sent to the eastern Mediterranean to reinforce existing units[45] and on 6 April 1913 *Dresden*, commanded by Fregattenkapitän Fritz Emil Lüdecke, joined them.

It was a voyage fraught with difficulties. Released prematurely from a refit, much maintenance work remained uncompleted. Excessive fuel consumption forced *Dresden* to make an unscheduled coaling stop at Gibraltar, then turbine damage slowed her down and finally more engine damage left her virtually unmanoeuvrable, drifting before the Dardanelles minefields. She limped into Constantinople to join an international gathering of European warships that were monitoring the local situation closely. At embassies and aboard flagships the pressing question was how to secure the Foreign Quarter and its inhabitants in the event of a siege of the city. Turkey's enemies held back, however, the Peace of London was signed and the tension evaporated for a few months.[46] Canaris's biographer, Abshagen, reported that over this dramatic period off Constantinople Canaris studied the complex implications of politics in the 'Golden Horn' and held numerous conversations with Germans working on the Baghdad Railway, which was financed by the Deutsche Bank and was being built by German firms.[47]

Dresden returned to Germany via Malta, Sicily, Gibraltar and Cadiz. At Kiel, Fregattenkapitän Lüdecke relinquished command to Fregattenkapitän Erich Köhler, with Canaris continuing as captain's adjutant. On 27 December 1913 *Dresden* sailed for Central America to relieve *Bremen* on the East American Station, arriving off the Mexican naval base of Veracruz on 21 January 1914, greeted by two Mexican gunboats and various international warships.[48] Civil war had broken out in Mexico. The previous year, with the help of the military, Victoriano Huerta had overthrown the elected president, Francisco Madero, and seized power. Now Huerta was facing a revolt led by the legendary bandit Pancho Villa, amongst others. In early February a large oil harbour on the banks of the Rio Panuco at Tampico came under threat from the rebels. Köhler had received a plea for help from the German consul and had sailed to assist,[49] but as soon as he saw the ruined waterworks, disease and general chaos there he put back to Veracruz to solicit the help of British and US warships for a general evacuation of refugees – even the stock of cash at a bank was brought aboard to deny it to the rebels.[50] After the kidnap of two men from a naval cutter, on 22 April 1914 US troops occupied Veracruz. US citizens at Tampico, mostly oil workers and their families, took up arms and barricaded themselves in the town's two hotels. One of the oil workers came aboard *Dresden*, which was already crammed with refugees, to request help. Nieden, the first officer, and Burchardi, gunnery officer, brought the women and children aboard and later ensured the safety of the other Americans. Some time previously the American naval squadron had retired offshore, out of the range of rebel artillery.[51]

Because of his knowledge of languages, it was Canaris who conducted negotiations with the foreign delegations and groups and undertook a number of potentially dangerous shore excursions on behalf of his captain. He and Nieden advised the commander during this difficult military and diplomatic mission; it was Canaris's baptism by fire. When Tampico fell to the rebel forces on 14 May 1914, President Huerta stepped down. Diplomats worked out an Anglo-German evacuation operation in which *Dresden* would take Huerta and his war minister; the cruiser *Bristol* would take their families. Huerta and his entourage arrived at Puerto Mexico by special train in mid-July[52] by which time the British Government had withdrawn its support. Eventually everybody was accommodated aboard *Dresden* and taken to Jamaica, where Huerta expressed his thanks to the Kaiser and distributed gifts, giving Canaris his revolver.[53] On 24 July 1914 news was received of the Austrian ultimatum to Serbia, and at Port-au-Prince Fregattenkapitän Fritz Lüdecke took over command again with orders to sail the cruiser home.[54]

2

The Epic Last Voyage of the Dresden

On the evening of 31 July 1914 Lüdecke received the signal 'Do not return home. Prepare to carry out anti-shipping warfare according to mobilisation orders.'[1] Lüdecke and Canaris examined the contents of the blue envelope containing the secret instructions. Canaris summoned senior officers to the wardroom to form the prescribed 'ship's committee'.[2] The Admiralty Staff required *Dresden* and other ships in the region to hunt for enemy merchant vessels along the eastern seaboard of the American continent in order to disrupt trade routes and lines of supply. Lüdecke was short of coal and requested a rendezvous with a supply ship at the small Brazilian island of Rocas-Riff before proceeding to the River Plate to prey on Allied shipping as it left Uruguay and Argentina.[3]

Senior radio-telegraphist Hermann Heil monitored the US radio station Sayville, which received reports from Europe for the press of the neutral USA, and from these transcripts Canaris and Signals Officer Leutnant Otto Schenk constructed a gloomy situation report.[4] By 5 August 1914 Germany was at war with Great Britain, France and Russia. The Imperial Navy had as an opponent the world's strongest naval power, and *Dresden* would soon face hostile warships, the ships with which she had been cooperating shortly before in Mexico. Lüdecke was well informed about the latter situation: they were listening in to the wireless traffic of the cruisers *Suffolk, Berwick* and *Bristol*.[5]

In 1898 naval attachés in German embassies and consulates had begun setting up a secret web of *Etappenstationen* – naval intelligence posts – recruiting foreign shipping agents, ships' chandlers and coal suppliers in an attempt to guarantee at least a basic availability of provisions and coal for German warships in the event of war. Such a post would normally be run by a naval officer who kept the links oiled[6] and who would receive intelligence from pro-German agents. In 1908 Canaris had helped set up such espionage units in Brazil and Argentina. In times of war it was crucial that the *Etappe*-system functioned smoothly and secretly, for the British secret service operated a worldwide network in which all British brokerage firms and most ships' captains and consular officials were involved.[7]

On 6 August 1914 near the Amazon Delta, *Dresden* stopped the British steamer *Drumcliffe*. This ship had sailed before the general mobilisation and her captain swore that he knew nothing of any war, even though he had a wireless installation aboard. Lüdecke chose to believe his British colleague and allowed the freighter to proceed under a clause of the 1907 Hague Treaty that forbade the seizure or sinking of an enemy merchant ship if her captain was unaware that a state of war existed. After this encounter, Lüdecke addressed his crew as to the 'gravity of the situation' and warned them: 'So long as we can move through the water, no enemy will tread our decks. We will never strike the flag! Therefore – at the enemy! Either we shall win, or we will die.'[8] Everybody knew the overwhelming strength of the enemy, and that the way home was cut off.

The Rio de Janeiro *Etappe*, which Lüdecke had contacted, had ordered him to coal at Rocas and use the cover-name of the Norddeutsche Lloyd steamer *Sierra Salvada*. Bad weather and adverse currents compelled Lüdecke to ask the *Etappe* to advance the time for the rendezvous, and he then signalled the collier *Corrientes* under Kapitän Mehring to sail and recoal *Dresden* at sea. Mehring refused; he did not know what ship the *Sierra Salvada* was and suspected a British warship was attempting to lure him out of port. Eventually the identification problem was solved when correct answers were given to questions about *Dresden*'s officers in 1911 – *Corrientes*' first officer, Julius Fetzer, was a boatswain in the Naval Reserve and had served on *Dresden* that year.[9] *Dresden* coaled 515 tonnes in a small bay on the Brazilian coast near Jericoacoara. This was not much, for the cruiser needed 170 tonnes daily, and coal would remain the major problem.[10] Fetzer was taken aboard *Dresden* as an 'auxiliary *Leutnant*' and appointed prize officer. He knew Patagonian waters well and on the basis of his knowledge of the terrain would become a close colleague of Canaris in helping set up the network of *Etappe* agents.[11]

In company with *Corrientes*, *Dresden* criss-crossed the steamer tracks east of Brazil, but the British were sailing other routes. Lüdecke returned to Rocas to coal from the Hamburg America Line (HAPAG) steamer *Baden* with 12,000 tonnes in her bunkers. During the operation both ships sustained minor damage while coming alongside in the rough seas and provisions and coal in sacks had to be transferred over by launch.[12] Later, the colliers *Persia* and *Prussia* also arrived at Rocas to assist. On 14 August 1914 *Dresden*, *Baden* and *Prussia* headed for the Brazilian island of Trinidade in search of the vanished British trade route. The next day they came across the British steamer *Hyades*, which made a dash for safety after seeing the German flag, but the ship was sunk after the crew had been removed to *Prussia*. Stoker Stöckler wrote:

> I could not forget that dismal scene. I could see that other crewmen felt the same. We had come to know the inexorable face of war. Perhaps one day *Dresden* would

also twist and turn like a wounded animal before she disappeared into the deep
... nobody believed he would ever see Germany again. The sinking of *Hyades* was
for us a premonition of our own sinking.[13]

Prussia went directly to Rio to land the crew of the *Hyades*, who immediately
told the British about *Dresden*. On 24 August *Dresden* sank the British collier
Holmwood after removing the crew. British masters became uneasy about
sailing from the River Plate and their Admiralty brought heavy pressure on the
shipping companies to prevent the sea trade of the region becoming paralysed.
They also sent to South American waters two armoured cruisers, *Good Hope* and
Monmouth, as well as an armed passenger ship, *Otranto*, to search for *Dresden*.[14]
Lüdecke needed a sheltered anchorage to repair *Dresden*'s structural damage,
but the eastern Patagonian coast had no suitable hiding place. Only twenty-four
hours were possible in an Argentine port before the British would know the
whereabouts of the cruiser they had been feverishly seeking. An officer from the
collier *Santa Isabel* was sent to Punta Arenas at the tip of Patagonia to arrange
for food, clothing and other requirements, to obtain shipping intelligence and
forward reports to the *Etappe* and the Admiralty Staff in Berlin.

Canaris had the necessary contact addresses, not only in Brazil and
Argentina, but also in Chile. He expanded the circle of agents and set up an
offshore message re-transmission system[15] using ships of Norddeutsche Lloyd,
HAPAG and the Kosmos Line fitted with wireless telegraphy. Their task was to
make night-time calls at Corall, Coronel, Talcahuano and Valparaiso to collect
telegrams ashore and to signal the contents from offshore to German warships
at sea, a device to side-step the laws of neutrality. The system worked, and later
the entire cruiser squadron operating in South American waters relied on the
network of Canaris's spies and report ships.[16]

On 5 September 1914 *Dresden* and her collier *Baden* put into Orange Bay at
Hoste Island near False Cape Horn for a ten-day stay to repair. On 11 September
the collier *Santa Isabel* arrived. Leutnant Neilung brought news that the British
cruisers *Good Hope*, *Monmouth* and *Glasgow* were operating off the western end
of the Strait of Magellan, probably searching for *Dresden*. The Admiralty Staff
in Berlin recommended that *Dresden* should pair up with *Leipzig* in the Pacific,
and on 16 September *Dresden* sailed alone to make the rendezvous.

Lüdecke had received information from agents ashore that the Pacific Steam
Navigation Company ship *Ortega* was proceeding south towards Cape Horn.
She had thirty French reservists aboard and was intending to sail through the
Strait of Magellan into the South Atlantic. Upon sighting *Dresden*, *Ortega* made
an audacious escape by heading into the Nelson Channel, which had never been
surveyed; Lüdecke could not attack the transport because she was in neutral
waters. *Ortega* reported the presence of *Dresden* by wireless and the Chilean

naval station at Talcahuano repeated the alarm. Since it was now known that two German cruisers, *Dresden* and *Leipzig*, were at large off the coast of Chile, the Allies curtailed their shipping severely. Lüdecke also received the text of an enciphered top-secret telegram advising that the East Asia Cruiser Squadron of Vizeadmiral Maximilian Reichsgraf von Spee, of which nothing had been heard since the outbreak of war, was heading for the Chilean coast and was expected there at the end of October.

Lüdecke steered north to meet *Leipzig* after sending *Santa Isabel* into Valparaiso where Leutnant Neilung was to arrange for the future supply to von Spee's squadron and develop Canaris's espionage system.[17] On the night of 30 September, when it was reported that a British naval force under Admiral Christopher Cradock consisting of the armoured cruisers *Good Hope* (his flagship) and *Monmouth*, the small cruiser *Glasgow* and the AMC *Otranto* were heading for the west coast of Chile, both *Dresden* and *Leipzig* turned westwards to link up with von Spee's squadron.

Dresden anchored at Easter Island on 11 October and von Spee with the armoured cruisers *Scharnhorst* and *Gneisenau* arrived the next day; when *Leipzig* put in with her three colliers, there were twelve German ships in the neutral islands.[18] The commanders of *Leipzig* and *Dresden* informed Admiral Spee as to the situation on the Chilean coast. A strong British force was searching for them, and Canaris's spies had just signalled that *Monmouth* and *Glasgow* had coaled and reprovisioned at Valparaiso. 'The presence of strong enemy naval forces along the coast makes it impossible for the cruisers to carry out their original orders, the pursuance of commerce warfare,' Graf Spee wrote in his war diary. 'This therefore no longer applies and the destruction of the enemy force takes its place.'[19] His objective was now to strike before the British task force increased in size and prevented his break-through into the South Atlantic.[20]

Leipzig was detached eastwards as a lure, sending out radio signals to give the impression that she was acting alone and seeking contact. *Glasgow* monitored the transmissions and Admiral Cradock formulated a plan to ensnare *Leipzig*, sending *Glasgow* into the small port of Coronel south of Valparaiso to gather further intelligence. By chance the British cruiser was identified by two German spies who reported her to the *Etappe* at Valparaiso, and on the morning of 1 November 1914 Admiral Spee received a signal: 'British small cruiser anchored in Coronel roadstead 31 October at 0700hrs.'[21]

Admiral Cradock was looking for *Leipzig*, and Admiral Spee was bearing down on *Glasgow*: at 1617hrs on 1 November 1914 the *Scharnhorst* lookouts sighted the leading two ships of the British squadron,[22] *Good Hope* and *Monmouth*, and a few minutes later the third, *Glasgow*, came into sight.[23] During the next two hours, in Force 7–8 winds, the two squadrons assumed their respective battle lines, the Germans gaining the favourable inshore position for gunnery where they were difficult to distinguish against the Andes while the British ships were silhouetted against the setting sun. Firing began at ten kilometres' range, with one salvo every fifteen seconds. Around 1920hrs *Good Hope* received a salvo amidships from *Scharnhorst*, as a result of which she caught fire, sinking an hour later, taking with her all aboard, including Admiral Cradock; no rescue efforts could be made because of the sea conditions. The cruiser *Monmouth* was severely damaged by *Gneisenau* and drifted away to be sunk later with all hands by the small cruiser *Nürnberg*. Though hit by shells from *Dresden* and *Leipzig*, *Glasgow* and *Otranto* escaped.

The Battle of Coronel was an unexpected victory for the Imperial Navy and inflicted on the Royal Navy its first major defeat since the days of Nelson. The British lost 1,700 men, German casualties were two minor injuries and light damage to the two armoured cruisers. The three small cruisers emerged unscathed,[24] and the victory ensured von Spee temporary naval supremacy along the west coast of South America, of which he planned to take immediate advantage. On 2 November Canaris wrote to his mother: 'I was very pleased at the conduct of our crew. I never saw the slightest excitement amongst any of them. They were calmer than for inspections or exercises in peace time.' The words were phrased to set his dear mother's mind at rest, for Canaris saw the situation more realistically: 'Certainly a fine success which gives us a breathing space and perhaps also has some influence on the overall situation. Let us hope it continues like that.'[25] He feared, so he told Lüdecke, that the jubilation over the unexpected victory 'might blind people to the fact that the Royal Navy will not allow the world to enjoy its defeat under any circumstances. Whoever understands Great Britain correctly knows its will to resist, its tenacity and even its lust for vengeance out of hurt pride.'[26] A battle had been won, but not the war. The circumstances could quickly turn against them.

Von Spee entered Valparaiso on 3 November to gain information about the war situation and contact the German diplomatic authorities. *Scharnhorst*, *Gneisenau* and *Nürnberg* anchored inshore; *Dresden* and *Leipzig* remained outside the harbour since only three warships of a belligerent could be present simultaneously in a neutral harbour. Eventually they visited the harbour on 13 November, mainly to dispel the British claim that they had been sunk at Coronel. It resembled a State visit; the German consul-general travelled up from Santiago and – in dress uniforms, blue trousers with a gold stripe, cocked hat, sabre and full medal decorations – Lüdecke and Canaris met the Chilean Fleet commander and then, followed by a great crowd, went on to be presented to the naval governor, the commander-in-chief of the Chilean Navy and finally the consul. That evening a great ball was held at the Deutscher Verein in Valparaiso.

After this short visit the squadron headed for Cape Horn.[27] At Picton Island at the eastern end of the Beagle Channel, von Spee made a three-day stop, a delay that was to prove decisive for the fate of the squadron. Shortly before departing the island on 6 December, he allegedly made a surprising declaration to his commanders: 'After leaving Picton the squadron will sail for the Falklands. On the night of 7 December, *Gneisenau* and *Nürnberg* will form the vanguard. At o8oo on 8 December they must be at the entrance to Port Stanley, disembark the landing troops, destroy the telegraph station, set the coal dump afire and take the British governor hostage.'[28] Rumours that the British naval units covering the Falklands had sailed to put down a new Boer uprising in South Africa had led von Spee to believe that the islands were undefended. The commanders of *Dresden*, *Gneisenau* and *Leipzig* protested at the plan, pleading that he should give the Falklands a wide berth on the grounds that his intelligence about the British was faulty, but von Spee was not to be dissuaded.[29]

He had underestimated the British desire to avenge Coronel. The navy minister, Churchill, and the first sea lord, Fisher, had sent Vice-Admiral Sturdee, former chief of staff at the Admiralty, south with the battlecruisers *Invincible* and *Inflexible* to destroy the German cruiser squadron.[30] On the evening of 7 December 1914 they arrived at Port Stanley together with the armoured cruisers *Carnarvon*, *Kent* and *Cornwall*, the light cruisers *Glasgow* and *Bristol*, and the AMC *Macedonia*.[31]

Towards o9oohrs on 8 December 1914, as they approached Port Stanley from the south, Kapitän Maercker of *Gneisenau*, forming the vanguard with *Nürnberg*, reported the presence of a British squadron, with capital ships among them.[32] The sky was cloudless, visibility unlimited, and unless the weather changed the German ships had no hope of escape. A general chase ensued to the south, the British eventually opening fire at 1255hrs with a salvo close to *Nürnberg*. The three small cruisers were ordered to run while *Scharnhorst* and *Gneisenau* fought the capital ships. At 1617hrs *Scharnhorst* sank with all hands, including Admiral von Spee, and the squadron staff; *Gneisenau* went down at about 1800 with all but 187 men of her crew; *Nürnberg* went under at 1927hrs leaving ten survivors; *Leipzig* sank at 2035hrs with eighteen survivors.[33] Altogether Germany lost six ships and 2,200 men at the Falklands. Of the warships committed, only *Dresden* escaped, a nuisance and potential threat to the British that remained to be erased.

Despite difficult conditions, *Dresden* rounded Cape Horn on 9 December, and with only 160 tonnes of coal aboard, her engines and boilers in need of urgent repair, dropped anchor in Sholl Bay, 60 miles south of Punta Arenas the next afternoon. When the Chilean naval representative arrived to advise the twenty-four-hour rule, Canaris explained to him that wood was needed to fire the boilers for the run to Punta Arenas, and a further twenty-four hours were granted.[34] At Punta Arenas, Lüdecke and Canaris met Admiral Cuevas, head of Strait of Magellan Naval Station and the German consul. Fifty hours' stay was granted, in the face of French objections, but *Dresden* left after only thirty-two hours.[35] On 12 December the British consul cabled London, and the cruisers *Glasgow* and *Bristol* were sent south from the Falklands.[36]

Lüdecke had anchored in Hewett Bay, southwest of the Barbara Channel, to await a collier. Canaris kept in touch with events through the *Etappendienst* at Punta Arenas under Oberleutnant zur Helle. His work was difficult because the town was small and the British had their own espionage station there to watch the Germans. In Hewett Bay the *Dresden* crew chopped down trees for fuel, salted fish and boiled mussels to eke out the provisions while carrying out repairs. On 24 December a small coaster manned by two French spies was stopped by *Dresden* but later released; when the boat reappeared next day and loud wireless traffic was heard from the cruisers *Carnarvon*, *Bristol* and *Glasgow*,[37] Lüdecke sought a more remote anchorage at Christmas Bay on the west side of Santa Ines island, where he was recoaled with 1,600 tonnes on 19 January 1915 by the collier *Sierra Cordoba*.

In several telegrams the Berlin Admiralty had advised Lüdecke to attempt to break back into the Atlantic and make for home,[38] but he doubted that his ship was up to such a voyage and preferred 'so long as it remains possible, to continue warfare on commerce in a sea area favourable for the ship'.[39] At the beginning of February he cabled Berlin: 'On 3 February will attempt to break out with *Sierra Cordoba* to South American west coast. Intend transfer to East Indies if coal allows . . . .'[40] On 10 February, Berlin cabled to Punta Arenas: 'Admiralty Staff to *Dresden*: recommend try return home sailing-ship route Atlantic Ocean. I will send collier to 5 degrees south, 36 degrees west.'[41] Lüdecke decided he would rather search for his own coal from Allied colliers on the commerce routes and telegraphed through Punta Arenas that he needed a collier off the Chilean west coast by 5 March at the latest. He sailed before receiving a reply and on 27 February sank the barque *Conway*.

On 8 March *Dresden* was adrift in thick fog with engines stopped and unsure of her position.[42] At 1400hrs, when the visibility improved suddenly, the British armoured cruiser *Kent* was spotted at a distance of fifteen miles.[43] Neither ship had steam up,[44] but *Dresden* reacted more quickly and in the ensuing five-hour chase eventually gave her pursuer the slip at 2030hrs.[45] The run reduced the bunkers to the minimum and overtaxed the machinery. Following an inspection Lüdecke decided that he had no alternative but to intern in neutral waters. This would be a complicated proceeding, however, for he required the Chilean Government to despatch warships to protect *Dresden* against seizure or destruction by enemy units.

At daybreak on 9 March 1915, *Dresden* dropped anchor in Cumberland Bay at Mas-a-Tierra Island. The local population was about three hundred, mostly lobster fishermen. When the Chilean harbourmaster came aboard, Canaris, acting as interpreter, informed him that *Dresden* was no longer battleworthy by reason of engine damage and lack of coal, and therefore requested internment.[46] The harbourmaster promised to request instructions and warships.[47] The anxiety of the German officers that *Kent* would appear at any moment was unfounded; she was also short of fuel and had put into Coronel on 8 March.[48]

On the night of 10 March *Dresden* received the re-transmission of Berlin's message: 'His Majesty the Kaiser gives you freedom to lay-up',[49] which amounted to permission to intern. As so often before, Lüdecke kept steam up in only one boiler in order to save fuel. This meant he would not be able to sail at once should enemy warships arrive. Lüdecke had posted lookouts at the entrance to the bay and allowed three officers and the surgeon to leave the ship and attempt a return to Germany.[50] He and Canaris expected that the British would intervene sooner or later and disregard the laws of neutrality.[51]

On Sunday 14 March 1915 at 0830hrs Leutnant zur See Böker, patrolling in the steam pinnace, reported the approach of the British cruisers *Kent* and *Glasgow*. The plight of *Dresden* was now hopeless. Lüdecke sent all non-essential crew ashore and signalled that he was *hors de combat*.[52] As the harbour launch flying the Chilean flag set out towards *Glasgow*, the British cruiser opened fire on *Dresden*.[53] Lüdecke could not turn his ship away from broadside in the current and the afterdeck was soon aflame. Two ammunition chambers had to be flooded, dead and wounded were strewn across the deck.[54] He decided that before scuttling the ship to prevent her falling into enemy hands he had to get the dead and wounded ashore. He raised the flag signal 'Am sending negotiator' and despatched Canaris to parley with the British captain, John Luce, but the British continued firing over the steam pinnace bearing Canaris to the *Glasgow*.[55] In desperation Lüdecke ran up the white flag to induce the ceasefire, this was not a surrender because he had not struck the war ensign. When the British ship stopped shooting, Canaris went aboard her and protested at the bombardment of *Dresden* in neutral waters as a breach of international law, particularly since the ship and crew had been provisionally interned by the Chileans. Luce replied that he had his orders, diplomacy would sort out the rest.[56] He could only negotiate with *Dresden* for an unconditional surrender. If the Germans would not agree he would resume firing.[57] Britain had already informed Chile through diplomatic channels of a breach of neutrality should *Dresden* be found in Chilean waters.[58] Luce asked Canaris whether the flag had been struck. Canaris pointed out that it still flew at the foremast[59] and with that returned to the German cruiser where everything had been prepared meanwhile to scuttle the ship by opening the sea cocks and setting explosive charges. Lüdecke was the last man to leave.

From the shore the surviving crew members watched the death of their ship. After a violent explosion *Dresden* settled by the head, and disappeared at 1115hrs to the usual 'Hurrah!' for the Kaiser.[60] Eight men were dead, twenty-nine wounded, fifteen seriously. For most of the crew the war was over. For Canaris, however, the loss of his ship and the associated internment was a mere interlude.

3

Agent on a Special Mission

The responsibility for the care of the *Dresden* crew at Mas-a-Tierra fell on Canaris's shoulders. First Officer Nieden had been released earlier, Navigation Officer Schultz, gravely wounded, was aboard the British warship *Orama* and the captain was in shock and temporarily unfit to resume his duties.[1] The dead were interred in the local cemetery and then, while the cruisers *Glasgow* and *Orama* patrolled offshore, the survivors held out for five days under trying conditions in the hope that another German ship would materialise to take off the survivors. Instead, two Chilean warships arrived to ship the *Dresden* crew to Valparaiso[2] for internment aboard a Norddeutscher Lloyd passenger ship. As the result of a successful British protest to the Chilean foreign minister,[3] the *Dresden* crew was brought to the small island of Quiriquina, north of Coronel Bay on 24 March.[4] The island would be home for most of the crew for the next four years. The German colonies at nearby Talcahuano and Concepcion, together with German associations and naval clubs, catered for the internees' material needs. German envoy Merckert reported after his visit to Quiriquina that the men were showing their best side: 'Gardening, poultry-farming etc . . . the island was soon improved by the Germans.'[5]

The idea of an idyll of many years on a Chilean island did not appeal to Canaris, and he was not the only one with ideas of escape. Stoker Christian Stöckler recounted later: 'One escape attempt after another was made. Some were successful, but most men were caught and brought back. The officers used to rant and rave about not escaping, but Chilean fishermen would take you to the mainland for 20 pesos and all the shouting in the world couldn't combat that.'[6]

Canaris was determined to get home to Germany and was confident that the spy network in Chile would assist him. Escapes were problematical because they compromised the Chilean authorities in their relations with the British.[7] The escape of an officer from the island might therefore affect the conditions of internment for the remaining crew,[8] and it was some time before he obtained Lüdecke's permission while Lüdecke himself had to have the backing of the German consulate.

Canaris absconded on 5 August 1915. The next two months belong to the mythology of his life and his escapade has been exaggerated beyond reason in the absence of documentation. Many biographies have an eight-month odyssey,[9] in others his disguise held so well that he is portrayed assisting the British naval and port authorities at Plymouth in their examination of his fellow steamer passengers.[10]

The sober words of the official file entry made on 5 October by the Admiralty Staff in Berlin give no real impression of the stress and danger Canaris underwent in those two months on the run:

> Oberleutnant Canaris of SMS *Dresden* has reported. He absconded from the island of Quiriquina on 4 August 1915 with the consent of the commander and envoy, travelled to Osorno disguised as a peasant, from there crossed the Cordillera on horseback to Neuquen where he took the train to Buenos Aires. Arrival in Buenos Aires 21 August. Reported to attaché, shipped aboard Dutch steamer *Frisia* under false Chilean passport, via Montevideo, Santos, Rio, Bahia, Pernambuco, Lisbon, Vigo, Falmouth, Pile, Amsterdam. On 30 September returned home from Amsterdam.[11]

The dangerous journey across South America, the transit of the mountain passes over the Andes and the gruelling passage across Alpine-type highlands for the two hundred miles to Neuquen, all on horseback and in the dead of winter, a thousand miles in a local train from Neuquen to Buenos Aires via Bahia Blanca, the voyage from Argentina to Holland under a false Chilean passport in the name of Reed Rosas, a Chilean widower supposedly travelling to claim an inheritance in Holland left by his English-born mother;[12] all this shows him as an intrepid wanderer and master of disguise.

On 11 November 1915 Canaris was promoted to Kapitänleutnant[13] and resumed homeland duty with the Naval Inspectorate at Kiel. On 30 November he was transferred to the Intelligence Section at Admiralty Staff, his special mission being to set up the *Etappe* system in Spain for German U-boats and to create a network of informers to report the movements of enemy shipping there. On 4 January 1916 the Madrid embassy confirmed to Berlin that Canaris had arrived and would communicate in future under the cover-name 'Carl'.[14]

Neutral Spain was a battleground for the intelligence services of the belligerents: 'The secret invisible threads ran from the embassies and consulates and the bureaux of the military attachés not only to the luxury hotels of Madrid and Barcelona, but also into the hovels of the Spanish anarchists, conspirators and the Catalan separatists.'[15] Spanish society was split between Allied sympathisers and the Germanophiles: 'the Conservatives, the clergy, the nobility, the army, a large part of "cultured society" and, after the early German victories, the navy', wrote Canaris.[16]

The military attaché responsible for German espionage was Major Kalle, a 'young, charming and spirited cavalier' who quickly befriended the Spanish king.[17] Canaris's direct superior was retired Korvettenkapitän Hans von Krohn, who handled naval intelligence and maintained an excellent relationship with Spanish and international society in Madrid.[18] The pre-requisites for espionage were in place, and Canaris seems to have been highly successful in creating a adequate network of supply bases for German Mediterranean U-boats. After the war a British secret service agent recalled how he had often noticed the Spanish king in company with the German military attaché, probably discussing with him secrets he had learned from other military and naval attachés. He had warned of the steadily deteriorating situation in Spain because German U-boat commanders were apparently at liberty to behave as they pleased in Spanish waters and harbours.[19]

Only von Krohn's closest circle knew about Canaris. Although he changed his Madrid address frequently and did most of his work from von Krohn's house,[20] enemy spies soon had scent of him. The British and French had broken the German codes and were reading the radio traffic between Berlin and the three espionage units in Madrid, Barcelona and San Sebastian.[21] From this they knew that Canaris was operating against Britain from Spain and that he urgently required secret cover addresses in Holland and Scandinavia.[22] Whether he actually made these foreign trips is not certain but the tempo he set with the *Etappe* organisations in Spain and Spanish Morocco can have left him little time for travel. By the end of January 1916 Canaris could inform his colleagues that 'information centres' had been installed in Santander, Seville, Cadiz and Melilla, while those at Algeciras, La Linea, Tripoli, Huelva, Tangiers, Barcelona, Vigo and Corunna were in preparation.[23]

A few weeks earlier, 'Carl' had caused tension between the German embassy in Madrid and the Admiralty Staff. Military attaché Kalle had plans to establish a network of agents in southwest France, working from offices in the Spanish Basque towns of Irun and San Sebastian, with couriers carrying the most sensitive material.[24] Kalle was told by Berlin that the suggested espionage service in Bordeaux was 'Carl's province'.[25] Kalle cabled a protest to the Admiralty chief of staff personally. 'Kapitänleutnant C.' had been proposed by him for the work against Britain, but as he was 'a young officer' C did not 'possess the necessary qualifications for an intelligence officer'. Kalle thought that Berlin's instruction deprecated his own work and he threatened to resign.[26] A simple transmission error was responsible for the misunderstanding – a question mark had been omitted at the end of a sentence in the message to Madrid. Berlin had not *ordered* that Canaris should take over the Bordeaux office but had *enquired* if the Madrid embassy would transfer it to him.[27] While that was all being smoothed over, Canaris was back in Germany, possibly with a bout of malaria,[28] or perhaps because Spain was becoming too dangerous for him. British naval specialists in the Admiralty's Room 40 were decrypting signals traffic between Berlin and Madrid, and there was a source at the embassy leaking information to the French.

On 20 February, Madrid notified the Admiralty Staff in Berlin that Canaris was leaving for Genoa the next day using a Chilean passport in the name Reed Rosas.[29] After contact was lost, the Madrid embassy discovered days later that Canaris had been arrested in Genoa on 24 February. Since he held a Chilean passport, the Italians had asked the Chilean chargé d'affaires whether Canaris, or rather Reed Rosas, was a Chilean subject, which had been confirmed.[30] The German Admiralty Staff expected Canaris's early release,[31] but it was not until 19 March that Madrid cabled Berlin to inform the Navy that he was back in Spain. The Italians, Britain's ally, had refused to allow him entry into Switzerland.[32] Canaris complained later about the 'very harsh time under arrest', which had included 'long interrogations and foul treatment'.[33]

Canaris was now trapped in Spain. It seemed impossible, particularly for men of military age, to leave Spain by the overland route. In desperation the Admiralty Staff enquired if it would not be possible to bring him home through Holland, the USA or Norway,[34] but decided finally to extract him secretly by U-boat.[35] This operation required careful preparation and above all absolute secrecy.

On 28 April 1916, the Madrid embassy cabled Berlin with the news that French spies had received information regarding various top-secret telegrams between the embassy and Berlin. 'The cipher and key are therefore compromised, if we accept that the information was not betrayed by embassy staff, which seems unlikely. The ambassador desires that important secret reports should be sent in naval cipher in the period before the new cipher is received.'[36] After talks between the Admiralty Staff and the Foreign Ministry it was 'considered desirable' that the Spanish king should be aware of the activities to extract Canaris so that he could appoint an adjutant and have his confidant watch over the secret mission.[37] This amounted to protection against a plot by the British and French to kidnap Canaris.

The need for such precautions was confirmed on 2 May when the ambassador notified Berlin that Paris had the German ciphers.[38] The Canaris affair now threatened to bring diplomatic developments in its wake, for the French would not hesitate to put the Spanish king under pressure by threatening to expose his secret talks with the Germans. The Germans for their part had to keep secret their knowledge that the French had their codes, for now they could mislead the French with false material.

Canaris remained bottled up in Spain. When he arranged to escape by Swedish steamer[39] Berlin forbade it and ordered him to wait.[40] Even when U-35, commanded by the most famous U-boat ace in the Reichsmarine, Kapitänleutnant Lothar von Arnauld de la Perière, put into Cartagena on 21 June and requested a stay of twenty-four hours, Canaris was forbidden to sneak aboard. His superior officer von Krohn considered it too dangerous because of the level of enemy surveillance. The French naval attaché and secret service chief were both staying in Cartagena, and the British ambassador had made a strong but unsuccessful protest to the Spanish prime minister at U-35 being allowed the stopover. U-35 left port protected by a Spanish warship. On 3 August the British noted in their files, 'After leaving Cartagena, U-35 sank fifteen ships. A large bill which Spain has to pay.'[41]

Although Canaris was limited in his movements, he still managed to contact important circles in Spanish industry and high finance to place orders for small auxiliaries and supply ships to be built for Germany in Spanish yards. A key intermediary was the banker Ullmann, who had German ancestry, and to whom Canaris had been introduced by the German ambassador, Prince Ratibor. It was probably Ullmann who brought Canaris together with the Spanish multi-millionaire and shipyard owner Horacio Echevarrieta. Both Ullmann and Echevarrieta would become close partners with Canaris once rearmament began after defeat in the First World War.[42]

Canaris stayed away from Madrid to avoid enemy agents and awaited his chance to flee from Spain by submarine. The first attempt failed because of bad weather.[43] On 12 September he went aboard the German steamer *Roma* since he 'no longer felt safe on account of numerous British and French spies'.[44] From *Roma* he contacted a German agent and asked for his help to get him aboard a U-boat.

On 14 September, Kapitänleutnant Arnauld had sailed on the orders of the Admiralty Staff to bring Canaris out.[45] He had been given a window of three days, between 30 September and 2 October. With the help of the German agent, Canaris had chartered a fishing boat. The urgency was explained to him by Leutnant zur See Sievers, who was to accompany him on his escape: the head of French espionage in Cartagena was looking for Canaris. The latter felt secure, however: 'My sudden disappearance from Madrid had caused a stir and enemy spies had begun to look more closely at the usual ports. As I had not been spotted in Cartagena and my hideout aboard *Roma* was holding, these searches did not alarm me.'[46]

On 29 September Arnauld headed towards his rendezvous point with Canaris off the Spanish coast. He approached the bay with caution. No boat with the arranged masthead light could be seen. Arnauld decided to wait until

1100hrs, when he would have to retire offshore to recharge the batteries. He was seen by two fishing boats and at midday there was an enemy submarine, on the latter occasion he remained undetected. Canaris had not turned up because the charter had been cancelled, the owner fearing arrest if he tried to sail. With German help, Canaris hired a small sailing boat instead with which he passed through the Spanish patrols unseen and reached Salitrona Bay on the evening of 30 September. Here he spotted an enemy submarine submerging. At midnight, Leutnant Sievers came out with a larger sailing boat to which Canaris transferred, the smaller craft being sent back while Sievers began to flash the agreed lamp signal out to sea.

That evening Arnauld in U-35 had cruised the rendezvous line looking for Canaris. He saw two dark forms without navigation lights and ran towards shore at high speed to elude them. At 0200hrs a third darkened vessel materialised blinking a light message seawards. Arnauld thought he had been discovered and dived. He wrote in his report later:

> At 0354hrs I surfaced in the bay and noticed a sailing vessel with a top lantern flashing our recognition signal three times over. I laid off this boat about 300 metres away for two hours and gave my recognition reply at least ten times. Nothing happened. Later the top-lantern was extinguished . . . I did not want to approach her for fear of betraying myself.[47]

Towards five that morning, Canaris's boat headed for the open sea. Arnauld followed it to the rendezvous line and was then forced to dive when an enemy submarine appeared. The two suspicious trawlers were also drifting in the area. Shortly after sunrise one trawler approached Canaris's boat. Canaris and the other two German officers hid themselves below deck in the sand ballast.[48] The trawler stopped close by the stern and mariners wearing French naval uniform looked into the boat. Seeing only the Spanish crew, the trawler then left.

Arnauld wrote: 'I followed the boat, gradually overtaking her. The trawler remained in sight astern. The boat hoisted a red pennant abaft the sail. I surfaced fifty metres away, a couple of sea-miles offshore and within five minutes Kapitänleutnant Canaris, Leutnant zur See Sievers and his aide Badewitz were aboard and I had dived again.'[49] This transfer had been fraught with danger, for the trawler on the rendezvous line had been sounding her fog-horn persistently, from which Arnauld inferred that the enemy submarine was very close by and for some reason had been unable to attack him.[50]

On 9 October 1916 U-35 arrived at the Austrian naval base of Cattaro with its passengers, and a few days later Canaris was describing the operation to the Admiralty Staff in Berlin, proving how well informed was the enemy secret service regarding German operations. Arnauld was also convinced: 'The fact that on the first morning, before I had made my presence known, the trawlers were on the rendezvous line with a submarine ... prove clearly that the time and location of the operation had been betrayed. From this, and the fact that the first scheduled time of the Cartagena voyage was compromised, one must accept that it will be impossible to arrange similar operations if our representatives in Madrid know.'[51]

Canaris's superiors at the Admiralty Staff praised his work in the most glowing terms: 'Kapitänleutnant Canaris ... has performed the special mission awarded him with such extraordinary industry, skill and prudence that I have recommended him to the All-Highest Office for a decoration.'[52] The Kaiser agreed and on 24 October 1916 Canaris received the award of the Iron Cross First Class.[53]

4

U-boat War in the Mediterranean

In December 1916 the Marineleitung – Naval High Command – pleaded in a memorandum for the introduction of unrestricted U-boat warfare. They had calculated that it would only take five months to force Britain to sue for peace. The measure was opposed by Reich Chancellor Bethmann-Hollweg, who feared that it would provoke the entry of the United States into the war, but finally he gave in.[1] 'Unrestricted U-boat warfare' meant that enemy merchant shipping could be attacked and sunk without warning. This was an apparent breach of the rules of 'cruiser warfare' whereby the crews of merchant vessels had to be given the opportunity to leave their ship in the lifeboats before it was sunk.[2] On 1 February 1917 unrestricted U-boat warfare began, and two days later the United States broke off diplomatic relations with Germany.

At first the policy appeared to be 'paying off': by the end of April 1917, 841,000 net register tons of shipping space had been destroyed, exceeding the prognosis of the Marineleitung. 'Those spring weeks of the year 1917 provided perhaps the only period of the First World War in which, six months before the first American units arrived, the defeat of Britain seemed possible.'[3]

Canaris now entered the fray in this U-boat war. He passed the U-boat commanders' course at Eckernförde, served for two months in training aboard U-16 and took command of the boat in mid-September. His superior officer wrote of him: 'Reserved by nature, he has proved himself to be of sterling character and inspires confidence in officers and men. A well-loved comrade. Especially well suited to command a large U-boat or U-cruiser.'[4] Canaris was seconded to the Führer der U-boote (FdU) Mediterranean, Kapitän zur See Theodor Püllen, where he received the coveted command of a Front U-boat on 28 November 1917.[5]

Three weeks later he took UC-27 out of Cattaro on his first patrol, his orders being to mine the entrances to the Algerian harbours used by the Allies and to operate against enemy merchant vessels between Algiers and the Straits of Sicily.[6] Things began badly with technical problems: the gyro-compass failed and the sealing rings of the engines leaked. He frequently had to dive the boat on sighting enemy warships or fishing vessels that often operated as scouts;[7] no torpedo attacks were possible because of the heavy seas encountered.

On 29 December 1917, UC-27 entered Philippeville (now Sakidah) Bay. In his war diary Canaris wrote: 'In order to remain unseen, I will come into the coast by day, surface after dark to approach the harbour entrance and then dive to release the mines four to six miles out.' Two of the eighteen mines he laid exploded prematurely directly astern. 'Boat heavily shaken. No damage, will continue laying,' he noted.[8]

At the beginning of 1918 he steered for Sardinia but sank nothing – it was difficult to angle UC-27 into position for an attack because she was too unwieldy in the heavy swell. The Allies watched the sea from dirigibles and U-boats were forced to dive very frequently. The routine of endless repairs, alarms and unsuccessful attacks was very wearing. On 14 January 1918, UC-27 returned to Cattaro[9] and, although Canaris had no successes to report, he received a positive assessment of the voyage[10] except for the clear criticism of his tactics. Flotilla-Chief Püllen wrote: 'If the commander has no success in commerce warfare, then apart from the unfavourable weather conditions the reason is to be found in his lack of experience and that in his known frenzy for activity he did not remain sufficiently calm to make systematic observations of the enemy sea traffic.'[11]

Three days after his return, Canaris was given command of U-34.[12] Escorted out of Cattaro harbour by two Austrian torpedo boats and an aircraft, he headed once more for the North African coast,[13] but engine failure forced his return the next day.[14] Finally, off the Algerian cost on 29 January 1918 he sighted a heavily laden steamer escorted by a cruiser and a trawler. He fired, the torpedo struck the freighter amidships – his first success as a U-boat commander. The next day, while heading for the Straits of Gibraltar, he came across a convoy of five large cargo ships escorted by two Foxglove-Class sloops and several destroyers. The convoy was zig-zagging with a 45-degree turn every fifteen minutes. Canaris put U-34 between the merchant ships and awaited his chance to attack. Just before the next turn was due he torpedoed the 7,000-GRT British *Maizar* amidships. He dived at once to fifty metres, survived the resultant depth-charge attack and surfaced an hour later. The crippled steamer was about eight sea miles away; of her crew and the escort vessels there was no sign. Canaris noted: 'Sank steamer with deck gun.'[15]

Over the next two nights he had the area to himself; the moon was very bright. Canaris headed for Cap Palos, north of Cartagena, an area he knew well.[16] On 4 February a large convoy of about eighteen ships materialised on the horizon. He put U-34 into the attack position, fired at an armed transport, missed, and turned and ran to escape two avenging destroyers, failing to see his torpedo hit the British steamer *General Church*. Another boat, UB-35, saw the cloud rise after the explosion. *General Church* made port but was severely damaged.

North of Cartagena on the night of 6 February Canaris torpedoed the French steamer *Ville de Verdun*, which was going from Dakar to Marseilles loaded with wheat and peanuts. She was the last victim of U-34 on this voyage; the Allies were now routing their ships away from Spanish waters. A few days later Canaris returned to Cattaro. He had learned the trade of a U-boat commander quickly, and avoided repeating the errors of his first cruise. Moreover, he had convinced his superiors: his personal file reads 'He has the ability to be a Front U-boat commander. If he applies himself after further practice, good results are to be expected from him.'[17]

While U-34 was in the German shipyard at Pola for overhaul, Canaris found time at last to write home. The archives have little of his correspondence, but one of the few letters to his mother that has survived is dated a few days after his first voyage in U-34.[18] It was his second letter within a week:

> As I wrote earlier, this time I had a much better voyage. I was also really pleased with the fine, big boat. On 26 January I got my first steamer, not far from Algiers. A few days later a big British transport and then a brand new French steamer on her maiden voyage. I took the captain aboard. The run home was quite pleasant. Just before entering harbour I had some difficulties because of bad weather. I have quite a lot of free time here just now, there was a lot of office work to do but only in the first few days; on the whole one can take it nice and easy. At the moment we have glorious weather again.

That Canaris wrote like a holidaymaker was no doubt because he did not wish to distress his mother, whose health was causing him concern. His only mention of the political situation was brief and laconic: 'I heard about the peace agreement in a radio signal while at sea. It certainly is good news. Now we are a good step further forward.'[19] Canaris was also certainly thinking here of the 'Special Peace' that was due to be concluded between Germany and Ukraine on 9 February 1918. Unfortunately for Germany, though, the Russian negotiator at the Brest-Litovsk talks, Leon Trotsky, broke off discussions on 10 February without the treaty having been signed.[20] The rest of Canaris's two-page letter was dedicated to his brother and sister and things at home. Only once did he allow his personal sensitivity to show through: 'I am still very depressed over the news about Rudi. From several other close friends I had heard how affected they are. It is depressing and deprives one of the joy of living.'[21] In conclusion he asked to be remembered to his brother and sister and promised to write again within a few days.[22] The depressed and resigned mood apparent in the letter was often detected in the course of his career by his superiors, despite his blameless military conduct and appearance. His general health was affected by the bouts of malaria, and his tendency to drive himself unremittingly, to the extent that he frequently gave the impression of being 'under the weather'. Years later this would lead to a career crisis.[23]

In the unrestricted U-boat warfare originated by Admiral Tirpitz, Chief of the Admiralty Staff Reinhard Scheer, appointed in July 1918, had immediately shown his mettle. His first act was to create an enormous U-boat-building project known as the 'Scheer Programme'.[24] This title must have been intended to pair his project with the Army's 'Hindenburg Programme' of 1916, involving enormous production demands by the Army High Command to the German war industry.

In March 1918 Canaris was ordered back to Kiel by the U-boat Acceptance Commission[25] to work up another boat, UB-128, before sailing it down to Cattaro. As he prepared to cast off from the Blücher Bridge on 1 August, Frau Else Lüdecke, wife of the *Dresden* commander, who had written him a 'very pleasant' letter, brought him flowers, cake and fruit for the voyage. He noted a few days later that it had been an unusually enjoyable eve to his departure.[26]

The start of his U-boat voyages always seems to have been influenced by a dark star. UB-128 had to turn back to hospitalise an appendicitis case. Near Kiel the rudder machinery failed and UB-128 ran aground. At times like this Canaris would indulge in the luxury of a black mood of despair: 'It is an ugly morning, rain and gale. I am depressed by the latest events',[27] he wrote in his war diary, particularly preoccupied by the mechanical failure. After he had 'confessed' to a superior who took it 'less tragically' than he did, Canaris became 'noticeably calmer'.[28] This sensitive and somewhat uncertain side of his personality is in strong contrast to the picture of the skilful and intrepid secret diplomat that is painted in the literature.

On 3 August 1918 UB-128 sailed again. Canaris wrote: 'Carry out commerce warfare as far as possible without deviating off route.'[29] Very recently it had become too dangerous to sail through the Kattegat by day. 'Today we spent seventeen hours on the bottom. The air got gradually more foul. We were all gasping for breath. Impossible to sleep. Personally I found this long period submerged very unpleasant, but there was nothing else for it.'[30] Norwegian territorial waters presented a very grave danger, for the British had set up a new minefield with netting, which was lethal for U-boats.[31] While negotiating the waters between the Norwegian cliffs and the minefield the gyro-compass failed: 'It is a very evil situation. I cannot go back now. I have to try to get through. I manage, steering by the stars.'[32] Between Norway and the Atlantic, Canaris might have hoped for a few hours' undisturbed sleep, but he narrowly avoided a torpedo[33] – 'Escaped by a hair's breadth,' he confessed.[34] The next disaster occurred on 14 August when the boat lost trim in very heavy seas. The crew was feeling the strain and Canaris had to urge them to concentrate, for mistakes were multiplying. The boat was spending as much time as possible submerged below the hurricane. Water entered the inner hull when a valve sheered off, and crew error was suspected. When the damage was repaired, Canaris gave his officers and men a sermon. What had begun as a simple delivery voyage had turned into a life-and-death saga, the boat had been eight days without radio contact and they had no knowledge of the current situation ashore. Because of the adverse weather too much fuel had been consumed and they could only reach Cattaro if they had favourable weather and with the utmost economy.[35] 'All our calculations and predictions are useless. The situation looks very dismal,' he wrote.[36]

On 21 August UB-128 came across an enemy steamer. *Champlain* was headed for Dakar with 5,300 tonnes of coal. Canaris let her have a torpedo and then opened fire with the deck gun. 'Got the range with the fourth round. Ten hits. Four lifeboats seen some distance from steamer. Took the captain prisoner from a boat.'[37] Canaris sent a demolition party aboard the stricken freighter and sank her with explosives. There were no further attacks; the bunkers were too low and the U-boat was seriously damaged. In the end, on 4 September, he reached Cattaro by running on his lubricating oil, thus rounding off a harrowing thirty-three-day voyage.[38]

So ended Canaris's last U-boat war patrol. While UB-128 was under repair, the war situation changed dramatically. Canaris had written to his brother advising him of a three-week lay-up and expressing his hopes of receiving good news at Cattaro,[39] but what the Mediterranean U-boat commanders heard was anything but good. Martin Niemöller, U-67 commander, wrote later:

> In mid-October the Western Front was pulled back and the coast of Flanders evacuated. We understood that this was a major strategic measure to fight for peace on a new shortened front, possible peace for Germany, cost what it might! We no longer had confidence in our allies, but that the suicidal discord was nourished at this moment amongst the German people – that was the crime of 1918.[40]

The dominant emotion amongst the Imperial Navy officers, watching the war being lost from afar while the Reich for which they had fought fell apart in the Red insurrections, was a feeling of bitter helplessness that would haunt them through the chaos of the postwar years, affecting Canaris in particular. The consciousness of being an elite, which was especially true of the naval officer corps, was shaken to its foundations. With the abandonment of unrestricted U-boat warfare, Scheer and the senior officers involved in the founding of the Commerce War Command – Seekriegsleitung – were 'cut down in their ambitious plans and hopes for active naval politics and war policy'.[41]

At the end of October 1918 came the order: 'All navigable U-boats return home soonest for the final battles: boats unable to sail within twenty-four hours are to be scuttled.'[42] The installations at Cattaro and Pola were blown up and the last sixteen U-boats – amongst them Canaris's UB-128 – set off for Kiel. There were to be no final battles, but the way home for the U-boats of the Mediterranean flotilla was long and dangerous enough. On 2 November Canaris headed at full speed through the Malta Channel, narrowly avoiding an enemy destroyer, after which his boat encountered engine trouble, requiring him to throttle back.[43] After zig-zagging past a sailing ship, an enemy convoy escorted by destroyers in the Straits of Sicily and keeping a sharp watch for enemy submarines he reached the Straits of Gibraltar, and was forced to watch from a distance as another U-boat was depth-charged to destruction.[44]

He approached the Narrows on 8 November. From the Spanish side strong searchlight beams illuminated the waters to the North African coast throughout the night, creating a lit area patrolled by numerous small warships and a submarine lurking in the shadows. Canaris wrote: 'Under the Moroccan coast are many patrol boats. They present the greatest danger. Basically they are large American motor boats and small torpedo boats that are very difficult to make out in the darkness.'[45] The situation was not promising. At midnight he confided to the war diary: 'Boat is blinded in powerful searchlight beam, we do not see a silent destroyer until within 200 metres. Turned away at full revolutions, hard astern, emergency dive. Trimmed at forty-five metres.'[46]

Canaris bet everything on a single card: he attempted to run submerged below the light barrier. A steamer followed him and seven depth charges tumbled down; both electric dive rudders failed, but Canaris got UB-128 steady at sixty metres and coupled in the hand machinery. It was the most dangerous moment of his U-boat career. Now he got lucky; when the screws of the enemy ships became inaudible he surfaced; a destroyer was so close that it screened him from the patrol boats searching the waters. He remained unseen and in the early hours slipped unnoticed through the last light barrier.[47]

The Armistice conditions for the Navy were made known on 11 November 1918. All U-boats were to be handed over within fourteen days, the High Seas Fleet was to intern or disarm within seven days. Vizeadmiral Hopman wrote in his diary: 'The blackest day in German history. Consequence of the last thirty years of Wilhelm II. Servility.'[48] Two days before the Armistice agreement, General Groener had declared frankly to the Kaiser in his Great Headquarters at Spa that the Army would 'march back calmly and in good order under its leaders and commanding generals, but not under the command of Your Majesty, for it no longer stands behind Your Majesty'.[49]

The Kaiser abdicated and accepted exile in Holland the next day. Groener, a 'political' military man of the new type with an awareness for social change, which in his view made social compromise and a policy of egalitarianism essential, saw himself as a liberal-conservative, above politics, who had recognised that the Hohenzollern dynasty had outlived its usefulness. In pro-monarchical circles, however, he was considered a traitor.

The Armistice and the handover of power in Germany destroyed the political ambitions of the naval leadership. Admiral Scheer and other senior officers resigned from active service; the Admiralty survived but lacked the strength of the Prussian War Ministry or the Army High Command.[50] In future it would be controlled by the newly formed parliamentary Council of Deputies, whose chairman was the Social Democrat Friedrich Ebert, who was himself controlled by an executive formed from workers' and soldiers' councils handling the work of the government. Ebert co-opted Ewald Vogtherr of the Independent Social Democratic Party (USPD) – a leftist group that had splintered in April 1917 from the Social Democrats (SPD) – and Gustav Noske, governor of Kiel, to supervise the Admiralty. Noske, sent to Kiel to quell the Revolution there, would be an important figure for Canaris.

News of the dramatic events in Germany since 3 November and the rebellion of major elements of the armed forces, which had spread across the Reich, reached Canaris in fragmented form through telegraphed signals to the Mediterranean U-boat flotilla. The Revolution came as a shock to pro-monarchist loyalist officers, while the hate of the revolutionaries was aimed primarily at this class and the world image for which they had struggled all their lives.

On 12 November Canaris received the signal advising him of the Armistice. The following day he noted in his war diary the 'abdication of His Majesty the Kaiser' and the 'Proclamation of the Republic in Germany'.[51] Having assembled his crew, he made the sensational announcement. The last day of the voyage home was spent gloomily imagining what awaited them on their arrival. Their families had no information about the boat; Canaris's brother Carl received news from the Admiralty on 19 November 1918 that Canaris had sailed from Cattaro[52] and on 27 November confirmation that Canaris had reached Norway and was waiting for a pilot to make the run to Kiel.[53]

On 25 November eleven U-boats, escorted by Norwegian warships, headed for the Kattegat. Martin Niemöller wrote: 'We simply could not believe that the newspaper reports we read really provided a true picture of the circumstances in Germany and the mood of the German people, and we had the faint hope that perhaps very soon a counter-revolution would wash away the shame of 9 November.'[54]

Most Imperial Navy commanders thought in the same way. To the defeat was added the disgrace of the Revolution; to the military failure was added the poison of the alleged betrayal in the homeland. The U-boat men who headed for Kiel Harbour that day were neither potential pacifists nor future democrats. Neither Niemöller nor Canaris had the least desire to be welcomed home to red flags and soldiers' councils. The eleven commanders agreed to enter harbour flying the Imperial ensign and the home-coming pennant, and swore that the red flag would never be hoisted on their boats.[55]

PART II

THE STRUGGLE AGAINST
THE REPUBLIC

5

Servant of Two Masters

On 29 November 1918 the remnants of the U-boat flotilla led by Canaris entered Kiel Harbour; Noske, governor of Kiel, came down to meet them.[1] Crewmen disembarked by the landing stage 'black, from gruelling service'[2] and through Noske's address of welcome were given a broad picture of the events that had come to pass in Germany in their absence. As midday struck, the last act began; Canaris noted: 'Decomissioning. Commander's address. With three hurrahs, ensign and pennant hauled down.'[3]

Later, the crews gathered in a small hall at Kiel Castle to hear Noske again. 'They were on tenterhooks: crammed together, courageous, well disciplined men,' Noske wrote. The mood at Kiel was tense, rumours of a putsch were circulating. Halfway through Noske's address a warning was given that naval artillerymen were on the march, intent on his life. The report was false, but not inopportune: 'When I finished my speech, the commander [Canaris] mentioned the event briefly and asked who amongst the men was prepared to stand by the governor. Like a pistol shot several hundred tough young mariners stood up. They promised me loyal support.'[4] That Noske would succeed in claiming the U-boat crews for his cause[5] was by no means certain; most U-boat men were negative or indifferent towards the Revolution, but not the men from Kiel. The revolt had begun in the High Seas Fleet, where the social conflicts and the gulf between the officer corps and the men had intensified after the 1917 mutinies. Martin Niemöller related later that on entering Kiel none of the U-boat crews had been interested in who was governor,[6] yet in the next few months it would be Noske who played the decisive role in defeating the revolutionary forces. He saw himself as 'Germany's saviour', while for others he was 'the bloodhound' and 'the slaughterer of the workers'. 'Noske', according to his biographer Wolfram Wette, 'can claim to have been the most controversial politician of German social democracy and he remains so today.'[7]

As governor of Kiel, Noske made it his primary task to restore discipline and to work as a moderating influence on the hostile groups. While Ebert sought cooperation with the Army High Command, Noske addressed the disempowered and beleaguered naval officers, in his opinion the only group with the skill to end the chaos. In this early phase he mediated between the officers and the new powerholders and was recognised by both sides as the 'integration figure'.[8] To realise his plans he was forced to forge some unlikely alliances. When the Soldiers' Supreme Council at Kiel demanded the setting up of a 'revolutionary security force', Noske opposed it by creating his own mobile defence squads. Holding the council at bay with his own demands, he talked to Emil Alboldt, chairman of the Deck-Officers' Federation, and Obermaat Hirschmann, chairman of the Association of Active NCOs; they were both in favour of social democracy, but bitterly opposed to the naval officers.

Noske made clear at a session of the Soldiers' Council that no good would be served by the setting up of a 'Red troop' since 'enough career soldiers were available who could achieve the same thing'[9] and with the support of Alboldt and Hirschmann he created the 'Iron Brigade', generally seen as his own house troop. The brigade was the first unit intended for the internal struggle in Germany, to protect the government and oppose the radical-left councils.[10]

Two days after Noske's speech, Canaris was appointed to the U-boat Inspectorate and acted a little later as liaison officer between the Baltic Command and Noske.[11] Korvettenkapitän Wilfried von Loewenfeld was another senior naval officer who saw himself as a fighter 'for the national tradition and the national future',[12] and considered Noske to be a man of action who 'simply had more initiative than all the senior officers in influential positions at the time'.[13] Soon Loewenfeld would form his own Freikorps.[14] He had ended the war as No. 1 general staff officer at the German Admiralty. On 17 November 1918 he was detached to Baltic Station Kiel and became one of the most active committee members of the Naval Officers' Association, Baltic (SOVO). The main objective of this circle of naval officers was to oppose the Revolution. Supported by the Station Command at Kiel, SOVO had recruited 'probably every naval officer in the vicinity';[15] it was the nucleus for the later 3rd Naval Brigade 'Loewenfeld', in the formation of which Canaris played a leading role. Loewenfeld used his position in the committee to undermine the Soldiers' Council and the Deck-Officers' Federation, which made decisions on military issues. This enabled the naval officers to reassert their original position.

The assault battalion of the Loewenfeld Brigade was commanded by the legendary U-boat ace Lothar von Arnauld de la Perière, who had smuggled Canaris out of Spain in a cloak-and-dagger operation in 1916.[16] Canaris was one of Loewenfeld's first and closest collaborators and setting up within his naval brigade an 'outstanding intelligence bureau',[17] he liaised between Noske and Loewenfeld, but neither Loewenfeld nor Canaris was anxious to involve Noske in secret plans to form an independent naval brigade because Noske would not have been able to obtain official support for the idea and Canaris did not want to risk deceiving the deck officers and NCOs and thus provoking the resistance of the Soldiers' Council.[18]

At the beginning of December 1918, Loewenfeld sent Canaris to Berlin to contact groups 'possibly preparing a kind of counter-revolution'. The Reich Admiralty was not interested, but he was successful at the Garde-Kavallerie-Schützen-Division (GKSD), a royal elite troop commanded by Generalleutnant Heinrich von Hoffmann. In March 1918 on Ludendorff's order Hauptmann Waldemar Pabst joined GKSD as its chief of general staff to convert it from a cavalry into a rifle division.[19] Under Pabst, GKSD became the strongest counter-revolutionary unit in Germany, the 'backbone of all troops deployed' upon which Noske relied.[20] Pabst's main aim was to overthrow the Republic and its Socialist leaders. He gathered like-minded men around him, and amongst the GKSD staff were, Kapitänleutnant Horst von Pflugk-Harttung and his younger brother Heinz. All were fanatical militarists, anti-Communists and enemies of the Republic.[21] This contact brought Canaris into the shadowy circles of the most determined opponents of the new Republic.[22]

Loewenfeld, Pabst and Canaris were intent upon disbanding the Deck-Officers' Federation and building a Freikorps to replace Noske's Iron Brigade.[23] Loewenfeld later noted with satisfaction that 'in his very skilful manner' Canaris succeeded in maintaining the relationship with the Federation intelligentsia, receiving daily reports as to the intentions of the Spartacists,[24] a radical-left circle around Rosa Luxemburg and Karl Liebknecht. Although Canaris, Pabst and Loewenfeld were amongst 'the most active counter-revolutionary military figures in Kiel and Berlin',[25] Noske did not suspect that they were in collaboration at this time.

In Berlin a conflict was simmering between the government and the revolutionary VMD (People's Naval Division), which had 1,800 men quartered at three locations in the capital.[26] Initially the VMD was controlled by the police chief of Berlin, Emil Eichhorn, a member of the USPD, with which the Spartacists were allied. The political leanings of the VMD – a militia formed to protect the government – were variable. When the Berlin City Commandant Otto Wels (SPD) requested from Noske a battalion of pro-government troops as reinforcements, he received on the orders of the government leader, Ebert, and USPD-member Haase 600 radical naval ratings from Cuxhaven, who integrated into the VMD 'with difficulty'. Thus 'reinforced', the VMD drifted ever more to the left as the Social Democrats became less revolutionary. As it was loyal to Eichhorn and in the parliament supported Haase against Ebert, the VMD became increasingly drawn into politics. When the deputies refused the VMD demand for pay, and two of their men were killed in a violent affray with a pro-government unit, the VMD occupied the Reich Chancellery on the night of 23 December 1918[27] and held the city commandant, Wels, hostage.

Realising that Wels was in serious danger, Ebert asked the Prussian War Ministry for help the same night, and towards eight next morning troops of General Arnold Lequis attacked under Pabst's leadership.[28] USPD Deputy Emil Barth informed Pabst that the government had given permission to fire if necessary,[29] and a bloodbath ensued with numerous casualties. Once Eichhorn's security militia, the Red soldiers' militia and armed workers joined the fray on the side of the VMD, Lequis was ordered by Ebert to retreat.[30] On Christmas night 1918 the VMD thus had the upper hand and inflicted a bitter defeat on the Social Democrat majority in the parliament and on pro-government troops. Wels resigned, and the USPD contingent threatened to resign from the government because it had used force without informing them beforehand. On Boxing Day Ebert summoned Noske,[31] who arrived with Konteradmiral von Trotha and spoke his mind at the crisis session in the Reich Chancellery: 'In the Reich one looks with disgust upon this intolerable Berlin government,' he said. Every effort had to be made to bring about some order;[32] if the USPD faction resigned, the Social Democrats would have to rule alone and in the event of further disturbances he offered his reliable Kiel sailors to rescue the Berlin government. The adjutant to the Prussian War Ministry reported that Noske was very much in favour 'of shooting, should this seem necessary to restore order, and at anybody who crossed the sights of the troops' weapons. Without bloodshed there can be no solution.'[33] At that the USPD deputies had resigned and Noske was co-opted to the council,[34] taking over the 'Army and Navy portfolio' from Ebert.[35] The Reich president warned of Noske's 'evil etiquette'; everyone who went into that witches' cauldron was in danger of becoming a 'bloodhound'.[36]

Noske's military position was precarious. 'In early January 1919, of the 20,000 armed men in Berlin, 4,500 were security militia, several thousand VMD, 12,000 Republican People's Militia plus many thousands of disgruntled soldiers lounging in barracks, and there were not 100 soldiers upon whom the deputies could rely.'[37] In Noske's own estimation, the most powerful man in Berlin was not himself but Pabst,[38] who, after the defeat at Berlin Castle, withdrew his troops to the city limits, purged all 'pro-Spartacist elements' and set about building an elite.

Pabst had often met with Karl Liebknecht and considered him a dangerous enemy. One of his officers requested that Pabst should allow Rosa Luxemburg to address the troops, but after hearing her, Pabst recognised 'the real danger of Frau Luxemburg. She was more dangerous than all the others, even those with weapons.'[39]

The danger of a Socialist republic on Soviet lines was represented by Liebknecht and Luxemburg. Two days after the collapse of the Social Democrat–USPD coalition, the Communist Party of Germany (KDP) held its inaugural session. The Spartacus faction broke with the USPD to join the Communists. Although KPD leaders were in favour of participating in the elections for the new National Assembly, Liebknecht and Luxemburg supported the majority of the delegates in their 'appeal for a putschist adventure'.[40]

The first opportunity soon presented itself. Police President Eichhorn, a USPD leftist, had supported the VMD against the government in the Christmas fighting; his position was obviously now untenable, but he was refusing to resign. On 4 January 1919 he was ejected from office by the Prussian minister-president, creating a furore that was to go down in history as the 'Spartacus Uprising'.[41]

On Sunday 5 January more than 100,000 soldiers and civilians demonstrated against the government.[42] Noske, watching the columns of protesters in Unter den Linden remembered later the 'nice call for change' of the demonstrators: 'Liebknecht, Haase, up! Ebert, Scheidemann, down, down!'[43] Towards evening it was reported that the SPD newspaper building and other publishing houses had been occupied by the Spartacus League. Fired up by propaganda, all Berlin regiments supported the call for the violent overthrow of the Ebert–Scheidemann government and Liebknecht also agreed that it was necessary. The revolutionary committee at KPD headquarters called for a general strike.[44] At the Reich Chancellery the government discussed the situation with the military in Cabinet. Noske suggested the use of military force against the insurrectionists; ultimately it was unavoidable. 'Then you deal with it,' somebody said – nobody knows who. Noske did not hesitate: 'Someone has to be the bloodhound – I am not frightened of the responsibility.'[45] War Minister Reinhardt gave his consent and appointed Noske commander-in-chief with wide-ranging powers to restore order in Berlin.[46] The same afternoon Noske set up his provisional headquarters at Berlin Dahlem. One of his 'most active' officers was Pabst of the GKSD,[47] whose adjutant was Canaris.[48] Immediately after being appointed, Noske asked Kiel for help, and within a few days two regiments of deck officers and senior NCOs, a force of about twelve hundred men, was ready to leave for the capital.[49]

In Berlin, Canaris and Pabst had agreed to form a Freikorps to take over from Noske's 'Iron Brigade', so ridding themselves of the deck officers. Canaris convinced Loewenfeld to lead it. Loewenfeld, unaware that Pabst and Canaris were behind the idea, sent Canaris to see Noske and, with the help of Emil Alboldt, chairman of the Deck-Officers' Federation, obtained from Noske on 3 February official permission to set up 'Brigade Loewenfeld'.[50] Over the next ten days, Canaris and Loewenfeld commuted between Berlin and Kiel and, at Noske's request, also went to Weimar to 'remove the last obstacles' with the support of Pabst and the GKSD.[51] These obstacles were the retrospective approval for the drawing of weapons, uniforms, equipment and rations for 2,000 men, which Noske had appropriated without the military apparatus being aware of it.[52]

The Iron Brigade arrived from Kiel on the night of 9 January 1919, its departure having been delayed by opposition and the protests of the Soldiers' Council at Kiel when they had learned what the brigade's mission in Berlin was.[53] Noske was wavering about using military force against the demonstrators, but on 10 January he ordered 'a number of formations, the Kiel Brigade at its core, to march during the night'.[54] On Saturday morning, after a bombardment of several hours, the Spartacists vacated the SPD *Vorwärts* newspaper building. Five intermediaries, who had negotiated the surrender of the building, were summarily tried and executed; three couriers of the occupiers were murdered. Major Stephani, who was responsible for the action, was acquitted after a thirteen-month inquiry.[55]

Noske marched his 3,000 men through the city centre and government district to demonstrate the military strength and resolve of the government. There was no resistance and the other occupied publishing houses were taken before nightfall. The same day a Freikorps commanded by General Lüttwitz marched towards Berlin on Noske's orders, but before it arrived the insurrection had already been put down.

6

The Murderers' Helpers' Helper

The GKSD under Pabst set up its new headquarters in the luxury Hotel Eden in Berlin on the morning of 15 January 1919. Luxemburg and Liebknecht, who had been on the run from the police, Freikorps and civilian militia for several days,[1] were apprehended the same evening by the civilian militia at Wilmersdorf. The Reich chancellor was informed, and the militia brought Liebknecht before the 'senior authority' of the GKSD at Hotel Eden; Rosa Luxemburg was brought in half an hour later.[2] A naval detachment under Kapitänleutnant Pflugk-Harttung was sent for to 'look after' the prisoners. When the 'volunteer squads' arrived at the Hotel Eden they already knew the task ahead: Luxemburg and Liebknecht were to be eliminated.[3]

At about 2245hrs, to a barrage of insults from soldiers and hotel guests, Liebknecht was taken to a waiting car. He sat in the rear of the open vehicle flanked by the Pflugk-Harttung brothers. Rifleman Otto Runge was standing guard at the revolving door of the main entrance. When Liebknecht took his seat between the two officers, who for some reason were wearing ratings' uniform, Runge 'thought he [Liebknecht] was being released', ran forward and struck Liebknecht a savage blow with the butt of his rifle. Liebknecht collapsed bleeding and the car drove off.

Meanwhile, Rosa Luxemburg had been brought before Pabst. An odd dialogue followed: Pabst started by asking, '"Are you Rosa Luxemburg?" She replied, "Please decide for yourself." I said, "by the photo it must be you." She responded, "If you say so". I was therefore just as crafty as before.'[4] The two Spartacists had not seen each other at Hotel Eden; while the murderers were finishing off Liebknecht elsewhere, Pabst waited with Luxemburg. She darned the hem of her coat and then read *Faust* in the WC.[5] When Pabst received the report from the naval officers that Liebknecht was dead, his body being left as an unidentified corpse at the Berlin Zoo, he had Luxemburg taken outside by Oberleutnant Kurt Vogel, where Runge struck her twice on the head with his rifle, after which she was thrown into the waiting car.[6] When the car was about forty metres from the hotel, a man jumped on the running board and shot Rosa Luxemburg dead.

Towards 0300hrs Pabst called his commanding officer, Generalleutnant von Hoffmann, and told him the correct version of events. Hoffmann said that he had not ordered it, but would 'take responsibility' for Pabst's action.[7] Pabst enlisted the help of GKSD propaganda-chief Grabowsky to write up the 'official GKSD report', published by the Berlin press next day,[8] in which Liebknecht had been shot while escaping and Luxemburg killed by a mob, and her body removed. Four months later her corpse was found in the Landwehr Canal: Oberleutnant Kurt Vogel had lost his nerve and dumped her there.

When Pabst rang his superior officer von Lüttwitz, Hauptmann Kurt von Schleicher – later Reichswehrminister and the last Reich chancellor before Hitler – took the call, congratulated Pabst on his work but then informed him that Hindenburg had ordered his presence next day before the deputies at the Chancellery. To be on the safe side, Pabst took along fifty of his best men, all armed to the teeth, with orders to take the Chancellery should he fail to re-emerge.[9] Present at the Chancellery meeting were five deputies plus General von Lüttwitz and a State attorney, Kurtzig. Deputy Scheidemann demanded the immediate arrest of the murderers, but Ebert and Noske dissented. Finally, at Lüttwitz's suggestion, a judicial inquiry was decided upon, to be handled by the GKSD military court; the friends of the alleged murderers opposed this decision.[10] The same day Oberleutnant Vogel and Kapitänleutnant Pflugk-Harttung were arrested. While Pabst worked the strings behind the scenes, Kurtzig was replaced as presiding official of the inquiry by Kriegsgerichtsrat Paul Jorns, who ordered the release of the principal defendants from custody. Press, politicians and activists of the workers' and soldiers' councils followed the 'proceedings' with ever-growing criticism.[11]

In reality there was no mystery as to who had done what and in what sequence. Next day one of the murderers went to the Admiralty and confessed to a young naval officer, Ernst von Weizsäcker, who handled officers' discharges and found work for them:

> Kapitänleutnant von Pflugk-Harttung was at the Personnel Office today and, having sworn me to strictest secrecy, confessed that while transferring Liebknecht to the prison he faked a puncture at the Zoo, took Liebknecht by the arm, deliberately released him to give him a chance to flee, and then once he was a short distance away shot him from behind. Liebknecht was hit and then killed by several more shots. I advised Pflugk to flee.[12]

Where was Canaris during the Spartacist murders? It seems unlikely that he played a central role alongside Pabst during the fighting in Berlin or was directly involved in the murders,[13] but he certainly touched up the evidence and played a leading role in 'reducing the burden' of the murderers. At the time of the killings he was probably at Weimar, where he had been seconded by GKSD as liaison officer and lobbyist for the citizens' militia of the embryonic National Assembly.[14]

A military concept for the Republic was under discussion: the new Prussian war minister, Oberst Reinhardt, wanted a break with the past, but Quartermaster General Wilhelm Groener was in favour of 'bringing the officer corps into the new Army, if possible in its old form and composition'.[15] Central to the problem were the Freikorps and civilian militia for which Canaris was lobbying. The 'Law for the Formation of a Provisional Reichswehr' of 6 March 1919 attempted to satisfy everybody and so to stabilise the situation. The legislation aimed at restoring the status and influence of the officer corps within a democratic framework. The Reichswehr would thus be formed from existing volunteer units and possibly civilian and other militia,[16] all such organisations being strangers to the democratic ideal.

In October 1919 Reichswehrminister Noske promoted Reinhardt, Prussian war minister, to Generalmajor and made him chief of Army Command.[17] The majority of the volunteer units were amalgamated into the regular Army while their pro-Republican counterparts were either disbanded or merged with formations having a conservative orientation.[18] Brigade Loewenfeld, which Canaris had helped build, and 2nd Naval Brigade at Wilhelmshaven under Kapitän Hermann Ehrhardt were merged into the GKS-Corps with Pabst at its head on 1 April 1919.[19] The wheel had come full circle.

In the early hours of 8 May 1919, the Landgericht courthouse at Berlin Moabit resembled an army depot. Units of GKSD were stationed at all entrances, on the streets patrols broke up large gatherings, the whole east wing of the courthouse swarmed with soldiers and visitors, reporters and witnesses were searched for weapons. Hundreds wanted to watch the trial and see the accused in the Liebknecht and Luxemburg murders. British and American visitors were offering up to 5,000 Reichsmarks on the black market for a ticket.[20]

Charged with the premeditated murder of Karl Liebknecht were Otto Runge, naval officers Horst von Pflugk-Harttung, Ulrich Ritgen, Heinrich Stiege, Bruno Schulze and Rudolf Liepmann. Former Oberleutnant Kurt Vogel alone was accused of murdering Rosa Luxemburg. Kriegsgerichtsrat Paul Jorns was prosecuting counsel, and Chairman of the GKSD panel of military judges was Kriegsgerichtsrat Ehrhardt, assisted by three lay judges chosen by GKSD. One of these was Kapitänleutnant Canaris, who had been attached to the personal staff of Reichswehrminister Noske and active as liaison officer to GKSD since 15 February.[21] When Canaris was requested to speak on this affair ten years later, he stated that he had been invited to sit as judge because 'those involved had faith in me'.

The proceedings were organised by Pabst, who had even taken part in the questioning of the witnesses; his two trusted supporters in court were the prosecutor Jorns and the judge Canaris. For Pabst the trial had come about as a kind of accident.[22] In a letter to publisher Heinrich Seewald in 1969, he wrote that neither Noske nor Ebert had wanted a trial; Noske had even promised him that there would not be one, but the pressure from the left wing of the SPD had become too strong.[23] Pabst said in 1969: 'My brave subordinates, who had stepped forward willingly to do what had to be done, were now indicted instead of praised. I was not given a free hand, for 50,000 soldiers ... under General Hoffmann ... had we used them, that would have been an end to the glory of Weimar. Noske knew I would have done it.'[24]

The accused had been arrested after pressure from SPD politicians and the public. Pflugk-Harttung had been Jorns's clerk until his arrest. Rifle-wielding Runge had been smuggled away personally by Pabst to the Danish border as 'Male Nurse Dünnwald' and was only arrested there in April.[25] Vogel had been the first to lose his nerve – he had admitted throwing Luxemburg's body into the Landwehr Canal and lying about it afterwards. One of the accused related later that they had been very confident and comforted themselves with the knowledge that as long as Canaris was on the bench, having gone over their statements with them in role play,[26] nothing could happen to them;[27] Canaris had explained his visits to Pflugk-Harttung on remand as 'discussions about the civilian militia problem'.[28] The accused stuck to their false stories and Pflugk-Harttung, Stiege, Schulze and Ritgen were all acquitted. The Rosa Luxemburg case was more complicated; the 'offical version' of a mob and unknown assassin on the running board of the car was difficult to verify. Vogel, principal accused,[29] and all other witnesses indicated the killer to be the mysterious person who had been variously riding in the car, had jumped on the running board, had been dressed in civilian clothes or was a naval officer wearing a rating's jacket. Beyond any doubt this was the man who fired, but Vogel refused to name him.[30] On 14 May 1919 the GKSD court found Vogel guilty of offences against military discipline, making a false statement and the unauthorised disposal of a body. He was sentenced to twenty-eight months' imprisonment and to be discharged the service.[31] Vogel was cleared of murder; Runge received two years' imprisonment, two weeks' arrest, four years' loss of honour and was dismissed the service. The other defendants were acquitted.

Pabst stated later that he had attempted unsuccessfully to obtain Noske's authority for the two killings; Noske said that Pabst should approach General von Lüttwitz for approval. When Pabst retorted, 'I will never get it,' Noske replied, 'Then you must answer yourself for what has to be done.'[32] From Noske's own observations later it may be inferred that he at least knew about the murders before they happened and they were not inconvenient for him.[33] He considered Liebknecht and Luxemburg to be the prime movers of the January unrest and bloodshed and remarked that 'in those days of terror thousands had asked if nobody could stop those responsible'.[34] Pabst had undertaken the mission. In 1929 when the affair came again to the attention of the courts, the editor of the liberal-democrat *Berliner Volkszeitung* wrote:

> Herr Noske recruited men of the GKSD, reactionary officers with very dubious leanings ... the knaves of the GKSD took their own kind of steps to restore the peace, which was the peace of the graveyard ... Herr Noske was the prisoner of his office. He devised the system whereby the freedom of the young Republic was to be defended by the thugs of the old Army. A dreadful mistake! For Rosa Luxemburg and Karl Liebknecht were the first to be murdered by these thugs, but not the only ones.[35]

That Canaris had long been entangled in Noske's system would become evident soon after the scandal.[36] Three days after the sentences had been handed down, a 'Leutnant Lindemann' went to Moabit prison with a document purporting to be signed by Kriegsgerichtsrat Jorns, bearing a GKSD stamp. It read: 'The sentenced prisoner Oberleutnant Vogel is to be handed into the custody of the bearer for transfer to Tegel penitentiary.'[37] Vogel and 'Lindemann' got into a car and disappeared; 'Lindemann' was Canaris, the Jorns signature a forgery. An immediate scandal erupted.[38] The press was doubtful that they could have got far because of the numerous GKSD traffic controls and street barriers. On 28 May, however, *Freiheit* reported that Vogel was in Holland using a passport in the name Kurt Velsen, issued to him by the War Ministry. The vehicle had been purchased by GKSD from Hermann Janschkow, the driver of the car in which Rosa Luxemburg had been murdered. Behind the escape plot were Pabst and his press chief Grabowsky.[39]

After enquiries to the German embassy in Holland bore no fruit, the press reported further that, on 13 May, a man had gone to the Foreign Ministry and produced a passport issued by Police Headquarters in the name of Kurt Velsen, to identify himself, stating that he was employed by the Armistice Commission of Matthias Erzberger and required to enter Holland in the execution of his duties.[40] The Dutch consul-general had already issued him with an entry visa. The passport was a perfect forgery. The German ambassador to Holland denied all responsibility – the passport had been presented by a person 'who appeared perfectly genuine'.[41]

The Dutch press considered that only the General Staff in Berlin had the technical equipment to forge perfect passports, and former USPD deputy Haase informed the Reich chancellor that in his opinion the criminal mind behind the operation was Noske's adjutant Canaris. Canaris was then detained on Scheidemann's orders; he was not held in prison but at the City Castle controlled by Naval Brigade Loewenfeld, and was freed three days later by General von Lüttwitz for lack of evidence, backed up by an undisguised 'threat of a putsch' to Scheidemann.[42]

The inquiry into the affair was conducted by State attorney Spatz of the GKSD after Jorns was relieved. Canaris maintained that on the day of Vogel's escape he had not been in Berlin but in Pforzheim where he was celebrating his engagement to Erika Waag. (She was the daughter of factory-owner Carl-Friedrich Waag, who had died 1913. Canaris had met his future wife at Kiel in 1917 while on U-boat training. The engagement was announced publicly in May 1919 and the couple married on 22 November 1919.) In the third litigation in 1931 regarding the Jorns intrigues, the extent of Canaris's help to the murderers of the Spartacist became evident: 30,000 Reichsmarks had been made available to assist the flight of the Pflugk-Harttung brothers, the intermediary being their sister Elli, assisted by Canaris.[43]

The murderer of Rosa Luxemburg was never satisfactorily identified. Pabst stated later that he had personally ordered Leutnant zur See Souchon to do it.[44] In 1969 Souchon won an action for defamation against the radio station Süddeutscher Rundfunk and director Dieter Ertel for representing him as the murderer in a television drama. In two other investigations in the West German Federal Republic, judges decided on the basis of the GKSD trial in 1919 that it was probably Vogel who fired the gun.[45]

Despite all this, Canaris remained on Noske's personal staff and, along with chief adjutant Major von Gilsa, was his most important assistant. The Reichswehrminister therefore tolerated in his close entourage men whose commitment to the Republic was more than doubtful. It is hardly surprising that as the Weimar Republic was gradually pulled apart, plans for a military dictatorship were openly discussed within Noske's entourage. Canaris maintained a close contact to Pabst, perhaps the most vehement advocate of a dictatorship.

7

On the Side of the Putschists

On 7 May 1919 the conditions for peace of the victorious powers were made known, but the German Government had not prepared the public for their harshness. A treaty based on the fourteen points offered by US President Woodrow Wilson was believed to be the foundations for a just peace, and the German people reacted with shock. Particular outrage was caused by the 'blame paragraph' which attributed to Germany sole guilt for the war. On 12 May in an address to the National Assembly in the lecture hall at Berlin University, Reich Minister-President Scheidemann cried out: 'Who would not shrink from putting himself and us into those shackles?'[1]

The reduction of the German Army to 100,000 men and the handing over of alleged war criminals to the victorious powers were unacceptable to the majority of senior military officers. Led by the Prussian War Minister Reinhardt, many of them considered the possibility of refusing the conditions, which would have led to a resumption of hostilities. General Groener was vehemently opposed to such an idea, and even Noske warned of the 'desperado politics' of the military.[2]

The Cabinet session of 3 June found a majority in favour of signing the Treaty, but 'under protest to avoid force'.[3] Even Noske went along with this, although Scheidemann refused to sign while the victorious powers were unwilling to make substantial changes. On 16 June the Allies rejected the German counter-proposals and gave the Reich Government an ultimatum either to accept the terms within seven days or face a resumption of the war. The German peace delegation led by Foreign Minister Graf Brockdorff-Rantzau recommended to the Reich Government that the peace treaty be declined; Scheidemann and the DDP threatened to leave the Cabinet if it were signed.

On 19 June 1919 Noske and Reinhardt convened a meeting of thirty-three generals and senior officers at Weimar to discuss the military situation. Noske's adjutant, von Gilsa, attended and Canaris was also probably present. The generals considered themselves 'a political force of the first rank'[4] but for Noske the meeting was primarily a means to gauge their mood.[5] He informed them that a majority of the National Assembly was in favour of accepting the peace treaty. Since Scheidemann would not sign, a change of the Cabinet would be necessary; it had been suggested that he, Noske, might be Scheidemann's successor as minister-president. This question, of whether the Army would support the government in such a situation, asked for a vote of confidence from the generals and would decide Noske's political future – a 'somewhat shadowy proceeding for a Republic but, in view of the political power constellation, a not entirely misconceived approach by the Reichswehrminister'.[6]

Reinhardt, von Lüttwitz, von Trotha and others declared that under no circumstances would they accept the 'blame paragraph'; the cautious Groener, while pleading 'for politics to run its course', agreed, even though it contradicted his pledge of loyalty to Noske. Groener declared he would stand by Noske through thick and thin, but the other generals chose their words more circumspectly. Once Noske had left, the officers discussed openly the counter-measures the Army might take should the politicians accept the peace treaty.[7]

On his departure, Groener said to Noske, 'The salvation of Germany lies in the hands of the Reichswehrminister.'[8] 'Best of all as dictator,' General von Below added, as Oberstleutnant von den Bergh noted in his diary that evening.[9] Previously, Noske – speaking of his possible elevation to minister-president in personal union with the office of Reichswehrminister – had said that this would be a development 'which introduced a sort of dictatorship'[10] and Pabst had urged Canaris 'to keep Noske thinking along those lines'.[11]

It was Major von Gilsa, speaking against accepting the peace treaty immediately before the National Assembly session of 23 June who, with the support of the leader of the Volunteer Landjägerkorps, Generalmajor Georg Maercker, made a final appeal to Noske. Maercker encouraged him to 'take the destiny of the fatherland in his strong hands, declare himself dictator and decline to sign the treaty'.[12] If he did so, the Reichswehr would stand behind him to the last man.

Noske reflected for a while before slapping the table: 'Herr General, I am sick of this crap', and Maercker left him with a feeling that he might be prepared to seize power as dictator if the circumstances demanded. Majors von Gilsa and von Feldmann (liaison officer between Army High Command and the Reich Government) also approached Noske; a military revolt might topple the government should it accept the Allied ultimatum. General von Lüttwitz had sent similar warnings to Noske, but the latter would not allow himself to be pinned down.

It was finally Groener's intervention that brought the solution. During the session of 23 June 1919 the National Assembly had to decide whether to sign the Versailles Treaty. Groener stated that the military weakness of Germany precluded any other course, and he combined his assessment with an appeal to Ebert: 'Minister Noske must take over the leadership and the responsibility for the peace treaty.'[13] The same day Noske advised the Reichswehr that together with War Minister Reinhardt he had voted against the imposed peace, but had been outvoted. His letter of resignation had been declined by the Reich president, the minister-president, the Cabinet and the majority parties of the National Assembly. That day there followed a turbulent discussion involving all 'senior Army commanders, regimental commanders etc from Berlin and its environs',[14] von Lüttwitz, Pabst and Ehrhardt leading the confrontation; whether Canaris was present is not known. The next day, 24 June, may be regarded as the day when the first deep rift appeared in the relationship of trust between Noske and the Army leaders.

On 5 June Pabst made another attempt to induce Noske to seize power; the Army would support him to the hilt.[15] At his refusal, Pabst threatened him: 'It would be a misfortune, Herr Minister, if the national tide did not find you on the side of the officers.'[16] Noske replied, 'I suspect, Herr Hauptmann, that one day you will have the entire government, myself included, rounded up and imprisoned.' Pabst answered, 'Yourself under no circumstances, Herr Minister.' Noske elected to treat the reply as a joke, but used a serious undertone when he told him, 'You must see, Herr Hauptmann, that there is a considerable difference between us both. I cannot guarantee that one day I shall not have you arrested.'[17]

Noske was now alert to the danger of having 60,000 GKS-Corps troops stationed close to Berlin, and after his talk with Pabst ordered the corps to be split up and spread across the remotest garrisons of the Reich. Pabst responded by planning the putsch; he sought the support of Staff officers of Berlin Reichswehrgruppenkommando 1, which formed part of GKS-Corps. While the new Chief of the General Staff Hans von Seeckt was strongly opposed to a coup and threatened to have Pabst arrested, Generals von Lüttwitz, von Lossberg and von Below all agreed to discuss Pabst's proposal at a 'conspirators' conference' on 9 July. Using the pretext of a threatened Communist coup, Pabst had the GKS-Corps advance to the Berlin suburbs on 21 July. Although General von Lüttwitz sympathised with the scheme, he did not dare oppose Noske's order, and with General Maercker aborted Pabst's operation at the last minute.[18] Pabst was neither punished nor arrested.

Shortly afterwards, Pabst left the Reichswehr[19] and in August 1919 founded the Nationale Vereinigung, attracting to it various personalities who shared his political outlook, including von Lüttwitz, Ludendorff, former Chief of Staff Max Bauer, Korvettenkapitän Erhardt, General-Municipal Director Wolfgang Kapp, author and 2nd Naval Brigade member Friedrich Heinz and Wilhelm Canaris.[20]

Its purpose, according to Heinz, was 'to prepare the counter-revolution'. Heinz, later an Abwehr-man under Canaris, stated that Canaris played a key role in the Nationale Vereinigung by having 'leading men in German industry, and politicians of rank and standing approached or shadowed' by himself and his intelligence service.[21] This is one of the few indications that Canaris was running a spy network inside the Naval Brigades and GKS-Corps. Noske discovered the coup plans in the autumn and wanted von Lüttwitz pensioned off, but he was opposed by General Reinhardt, the new chief of Army Command.[22] This resulted in a sharpening of the conflict between Noske and von Lüttwitz.

In February 1920 the Inter-Allied Military Control Commission demanded the disbanding of the Naval Brigades Ehrhardt and Loewenfeld; after a fierce argument with Lüttwitz, Noske ordered this to be done by 10 March.[23] On the first anniversary of the founding of Naval Brigade Ehrhardt on 1 March, von Lüttwitz spoke to five thousand Freikorps men about the Reichswehrminister's order: 'I will not tolerate having such a hardened force broken up in such an unhealthy climate,' he vowed. Other sources have him adding, 'We will not allow ourselves to be disbanded, we would rather bring down the government.'[24] Even in the face of this defiance, Noske did not discharge Lüttwitz, nor did he punish Admiral von Trotha and other senior officers who had heard Lüttwitz speak at Döberitz and had failed to report it.[25]

Five days later Noske insisted again that Lüttwitz disband the Naval Brigades.[26] When Lüttwitz refused, von Seeckt, who had drafted the dissolution orders, Reinhardt and Admiral von Trotha suggested that Noske relieve Lüttwitz of command of the Naval Brigades and subordinate them instead to Admiral von Trotha. Noske went along with this idea, issued the order and informed Reich President Ebert,[27] who invited Noske and Lüttwitz to talks on the evening of 10 March. Here Lüttwitz demanded the immediate dissolution of the National Assembly, the dismissal of General Reinhardt as chief of Army Command, his own appointment as Commander-in-Chief Reichswehr and the retraction of the disbandment orders. Noske brushed all this aside, informed Lüttwitz that he was relieved of command of the Naval Brigades and warned him against fomenting a military revolt.[28] Lüttwitz was dismissed, but never arrested. The same day, as rumours of an imminent coup became current, Noske ordered Kapp, Bauer, Pabst, Schitzler and Grabowsky to be arrested. The first three were warned in advance from within police headquarters and went to ground, Pabst was sheltered by Ehrhardt at Döberitz, and Canaris hid out in Berlin. The suspicion that Ehrhardt had ideas of a putsch, so Canaris maintained during later trials and inquiries, was not apparent in his contacts with Ehrhardt.[29]

At that time, Canaris was on Noske's staff and responsible for all Naval Brigade affairs. Accordingly he saw Ehrhardt regularly and discussed with him the threatened disbandment of his brigade. Canaris stated in evidence: 'He often discussed with me the difficulties of the present times, but never said anything which might have led me to think that he was involved in any kind of political activity'; since everybody in the Naval Brigades was involved in political activity, the statement was absurd. Ehrhardt had also been summoned by von Gilsa to allay the latter's suspicions, and even he could inform Canaris that Ehrhardt was simply running a bona-fide military unit and following orders.[30]

Towards evening on 12 March 1919 during the Cabinet meeting at the Reich Chancellery, rumours began to accumulate that Brigade Ehrhardt would march on Berlin that night. Admiral von Trotha offered to go to Döberitz to see Ehrhardt but feared that if a putsch was actually planned he would be detained, and so requested that Noske detail a Staff officer to accompany him; Noske appointed Canaris.[31] It was dark when they got to Döberitz, and von Trotha warned Ehrhardt against an unwise military action,[32] but Ehrhardt denied such an intention and Canaris swore that during his inspection of the camp and his conversations with officers he saw and heard nothing to raise his suspicions.[33]

Noske was informed accordingly, although von Trotha and Canaris thought it wise to add that such an elite troop could be on the march at very short notice. It could not be proved that their report to Berlin was incorrect, although neither mentioned their sympathies and open collaboration with the putschists. Within a few hours, the brigade was marching on Berlin.[34]

Despite von Trotha's report, Noske had taken steps to stop Ehrhardt by force should he come; government buildings were secured but no units positioned away from the centre.[35] Officers of the Reichswehr and security police (Sipo) had declared meanwhile that they would not fire on Naval Brigade Ehrhardt, while Reichswehrgruppenkommando 1 and the Naval Brigade had agreed not to shoot at each other under any circumstances: 'Our troops do not fire on our troops.'[36] Naval Brigade Ehrhardt was well informed about the defensive measures, and towards midnight while the brigade was on its way into Berlin, on Noske's orders generals von Oldershausen and von Oven were negotiating with Ehrhardt at Döberitz. Since Ehrhardt was not prepared to make any concessions, Noske and General Reinhardt wanted to meet force with force but were uncertain whether they had the loyalty of their military commanders and so they called a conference of officers for 0100hrs at the Reichswehr Ministry.

Von Seeckt, von Oldershausen, von Oven and Hammerstein considered resistance useless in view of the strength of the brigade and feared a split in the Reichswehr since leftist insurrections were also possible.[37] Von Trotha stated that he supported the opinion of the four generals. Noske told him, 'Herr Admiral, your Navy will hurl Germany into misfortune for the second time.'[38] Only Reinhardt and Adjutant von Gilsa supported Noske, who abandoned the session 'with a feeling of the deepest disgust' and asked the Cabinet to meet at once.[39]

Towards 0400hrs the minister and members of the Prussian Government met in the Reich Chancellery. When von Trotha – who as chief of the Admiralty had constant access to Cabinet sittings – attempted to enter the chamber, Noske blocked his path: this 'highly political sitting made it necessary to limit the participants to those gentlemen who had the unquestioned confidence of the government'.[40] Von Trotha no longer had this support. The final decision of the Cabinet was to return troops to barracks, and General Reinhardt, who held out for resistance to the Naval Brigade, requested that Ebert and Noske relieve him of his duties forthwith.[41]

On the early morning of 13 March 1920, Ebert, Noske, Max Bauer and von Gilsa flew to Dresden. Shortly afterwards, Ehrhardt's troops entered the government quarter. Kapp proclaimed himself head of the government and appointed Lüttwitz Reichswehrminister; Canaris had remained in Berlin with Trotha and the Naval Brigade.[42] Under questioning later, Canaris would only confirm that he had spoken to Ehrhardt several times in Berlin after the government had fled and he stuck firmly to his story that Ehrhardt had known nothing of Lüttwitz and Kapp's intentions, and that he himself had been able to draw no other conclusion from what Ehrhardt had told him.[43] Faced with the choice between Noske and 'the troops', Canaris had decided in favour of 'the troops' without hesitation.[44] One must doubt, however, that by this he meant anything other than Kapp's troops, or that his loyalty extended any further than to a definite caste of the most reactionary officers.[45]

General Maercker, to whose Wehrkreis (military administrative district) Noske had fled, believing Maercker absolutely reliable, was also faced by a conflict of loyalty. Ordered by the new Reichswehrminister, von Lüttwitz, to take Noske and his escort into custody, he decided to sit on the fence and favoured negotiation, which was refused outright by Ebert and the other deposed ministers, who demanded the overthrow of Kapp unconditionally.[46] On 14 March in a communiqué to the Reichswehr, Ebert and Noske described the coup as a 'criminal proceeding by a small bunch of reactionary political adventurers.[47] The deposed government now travelled to Stuttgart, where the president of the National Assembly, Fehrenbach, summoned a meeting for 18 March.

At first it appeared that the putsch would be successful. On 14 March, after a conference with senior naval officers, Admiral von Trotha cabled subordinate naval stations: 'I have placed myself at the disposal of the new government and expect that as before the Navy will continue to obey my orders.'[48] The responsible chiefs of the Wilhelmshaven and Kiel naval stations fell in behind von Trotha, claiming political neutrality and military subordination, in stark contrast to the lower ranks under their command.[49] Their opposition, the general strike in all large German cities and the unyielding attitude of the deposed government and the president of the National Assembly brought the Kapp–Lüttwitz putsch to its end and both men surrendered on 17 March. Trotha was deposed as Naval commander-in-chief and arrested at home.[50] Canaris was also detained and questioned at Berlin police headquarters[51] but gave nothing away; he remained in the Navy, his reputation untarnished. Noske was dismissed by Reich president Ebert, and von Gilsa his adjutant went too. At the end of May 1920, the new Reichswehrminister Gessler appointed Konteradmiral Adolf Zenker new commandant of the Wilhelmshaven Naval Station and Kapitän zur See Ernst Freiherr von Gagern to head the Baltic Station at Kiel.

By edict to the Reichsmarine on 15 June, Ebert proclaimed the restoration of military order in the Navy and in August an amnesty was promulgated to annul all proceedings against officers compromised in the putsch.[52] By then, Canaris had a new post; on 24 July 1920 he had been appointed Admiralty Staff Officer to Freiherr von Gagern.[53]

8

Agent of the Counter-Revolution

The situation of the Reichsmarine in the summer of 1920 was desolate, distrusted by left and right. At the beginning of August, Konteradmiral Michaelis, chief of the Admiralty Staff, stated to senior commanders that nobody was interested in naval rebuilding: 'Right-wing factions blame the Navy alone for the November-Revolution . . . Democrats and the Majority-Socialists (MSPD) say the Kapp putsch was Navy inspired; the far left has fundamentally no interest in strengthening any of the military.'[1] Many considered the Navy as a superfluous independent branch in the armed forces; Reich President Ebert actually appealed for the Navy to be abolished on the grounds of expense. An interim compromise was agreed whereby the Navy High Command was re-established in October, headed by Admiral Paul Behncke.[2]

Canaris would help resurrect 'a functioning apparatus of the Navy'[3] by restoring discipline and obedience to orders, ensuring the technical competence of the officers and laying the material foundations for future naval rebuilding. He must have completed the task swiftly and well, for Korvettenkapitän Meusel, chief of Staff, Naval Station Baltic, wrote in his assessment of Canaris a year later: 'Tireless and objective, perceptive and clear in his judgement, energetic yet of modest demeanour, with his sure-footed and forward-looking gift of organisation he has played an outstanding part, under the most difficult circumstances, in the successful restoration of discipline and the resolution of all military tasks and aims of the Station Command.'[4]

Canaris had quickly realised that under the conditions of the Versailles Treaty not only were special organisational skills required to fulfil the 'principal task', but one had to be prepared to act 'unconventionally' and if necessary cross the legal boundaries. Many former Freikorps men found their way back into the Navy – a sixth of German naval personnel had been members of the Naval Brigade Loewenfeld.[5] There were those who rejected the new State, the Republic, while hoping to find room in the Reichswehr for their private political ideas. 'Others said that every vacancy in the new armed forces was better filled by a Freikorps man than a November revolutionary. The first group was mostly scattered to the winds,' Loewenthal wrote later; each member of the second group became 'a fighter for the national revival ....'[6] Fregattenkapitän Loewenfeld himself re-entered the Navy and commanded the training cruiser *Berlin*. He helped speed the integration of the former Freikorps men but he had trouble with those from Naval Brigade Ehrhardt, whose politics were more extreme.[7]

Many Ehrhardt supporters left the Navy to join the secret organisations that succeeded the Brigade, such as the Federation of Former Ehrhardt Officers, led by Ehrhardt himself. He had gone underground in Munich under the cover-name 'Consul Eichmann', and the federation formed the core of the later 'Organisation Consul' (Org-C),[8] whose members would not shrink from murder. In 1921 they murdered the centrist politician Matthias Erzberger,[9] one of the signatories to the Versailles Treaty; they were involved in the plot to kill Minister-President Scheidemann, and in the assassination of Foreign Minister Walther Rathenau in June 1922.[10] Canaris was at least indirectly involved in the activities of Org-C.

On 23 August 1927 *Weltbühne* printed an article entitled 'Canaris's Secret',[11] in which the author quoted a police statement by former Rittmeister Kurt Lieder, head of Org-C in Schleswig-Holstein, who knew Canaris well. Lieder identified Canaris as the chief activist at Naval Station Baltic, supporting the 'radical right-wing putsch movement' there with financial and material help.[12] Lieder and other prominent Org-C men such as former deck officer Werner Voss received from Canaris regular large payments to expand the Mecklenburg branch. The Gauleiter for Org-C in Holstein, Mecklenburg and Pomerania was former Kapitänleutnant Kurt Wende, whose adjutant Leutnant Erwin Kern was later convicted of the murder of Rathenau, while Voss was also implicated in Org-C killings; he was charged in the Rathenau affair but acquitted.[13]

The money distributed by Canaris helped set up the Ehrhardt terror organisation, whose aim was a 'black' Reichswehr or Navy, to assist the rise of Hitler's SA and his putsch of November 1923.[14] Lieder alleged that Canaris supplied to him weapons, uniforms and equipment for Org-C, and Lieder even had a key to the secret, unguarded entrance into the Naval Station building.[15] Canaris maintained secret stores to hoard weapons and misappropriated military equipment for Org-C under the very noses of the Allies, and Naval High Command knew and tolerated it. In 1937, Oberkommando der Marine (OKM) prepared a memorandum, 'The Navy's Battle Against Versailles',[16] in which it reported: 'After the war, false accounting for firearms, to keep firearms that were required to be destroyed on the orders of the enemy alliance, was practised on a wide scale with success at all naval depots, especially at Kiel, where there was a substantial cache. This activity resulted in a real addition over and above the stock of weapons we were allowed.'[17] Kapitän (Ordnance) Jung set up a secret dump at the Kiel naval arsenal for several thousand rifles, hundreds of machine guns, mines and optical equipment; money for maintenance and security was obtained by selling superfluous gunnery equipment overseas; and sales were made through Copenhagen to Finland, Sweden and even China, all the proceeds going to the Navy, less 40 per cent for transport and commissions. Everything was done above board by contract.

By the summer of 1922 the stock of weapons was so enormous that a larger dump had to be opened in the naval installation at Kiel-Wik. The new store was betrayed to the Allied Naval Control Commission responsible for the observance of the Versailles Treaty;[18] the arsenal employee who sold the information was convicted of treason and imprisoned. Although the commission subsequently became more vigilant and warned Reich President Ebert against attempts to undermine the treaty, most of the weapons had been smuggled away in time and the losses replaced.

Another star at Kiel was former deck officer Leutnant Richard Protze, one of Canaris's instructors when he was a sea cadet.[19] Protze headed the counter-espionage section at the Naval Station, to where numerous spies and informers reported on the mood amongst the crews and shipyard workers.[20] The Navy, particularly the Naval Stations at Wilhelmshaven and Kiel, was closely linked to radical-right, anti-Republican organisations: 'In the confusion of the time it was important to support those men who thought as soldiers beyond their own duties and by so doing ensured that the principle of self-reliance against all internal political forces, and resistance to enslavement by the enemy alliance, was not only maintained, but also fortified,'[21] the naval bulletin explained in 1937.

Naval Station Baltic pampered the developing 'pro-Fatherland' groups at Kiel – the Stahlhelm, Student Weapons-Circle and Org-C, as well as the pro-Fatherland trade unions at the naval arsenal, Germania shipyard and other Kiel technical installations. It was all probably orchestrated by Canaris, and later by Korvettenkapitän Otto Schuster.[22]

The support for radical-right movements by the Kiel Naval Station, which strengthened after the Allies occupied the Ruhr in 1923, was finally revealed publicly and brought Canaris to the attention of the press three years later. On 1 December 1926 a number of Social Democrat Reichstag deputies complained to Reichswehrminister Gessler about the involvement of the military in a series of illegal activities and SPD deputy Eggerstedt accused the Kiel Naval Station of having links to pro-Fatherland groups and of implication in the attempted murder of General von Seeckt.[23] A few days later, Gessler received documentary evidence assembled by the SPD and a six-page synopsis of the accusations against the Baltic station prepared by Eggerstedt.

On 16 December 1926 in the Reichstag, Scheidemann made a violent attack against the Reichswehr and demanded a general reckoning with the military,[24] mentioning in particular the links between the Reichwehr and Org-C, and its involvement in the Hitler-putsch of 1923 when it supported Org-C throughout. He named the 'mole', Kurt Lieder, and alleged that his successor, former Leutnant Hans-Ulrich Klintzsch, a founder member of the SA,[25] was being financed now as before by Naval Command. 'After the Hitler putsch was frustrated', Scheidemann continued, 'their rage was turned on General von Seeckt', who had helped put down the putsch as Army chief. At Kiel a 'useful man' had been found, an Oberleutnant von Bergen, real name Günther, who with an accomplice set out to kill General Seeckt. 'As you know, happily this assassination was not carried out. But you probably do not know that this Günther is being paid to the present day by the Naval Station at Kiel.'[26] Scheidemann was thus accusing the officers at Kiel, of which Canaris was one, of having supported the failed Hitler putsch and having subsequently planned the murder of the Army commander-in-chief as a reprisal.

Deputy Eggerstedt published his accusations in the *Schleswig-Holsteinische Volkszeitung*. The main witnesses were two former agents of the Kiel station – Lieder and a certain Berndorff. In their depositions they implicated a number of Kiel officers including Canaris and Loewenfeld. Accusations of high treason, illegal sale of Reich property and conspiracy to murder to Seeckt were made.[27]

Naval Command ordered its own inquiry to determine whether the collaboration with radical right organisations had been ordered or approved by Kiel Station Command or if it was merely a matter of individual officers acting independently. A friend of Canaris at Kiel, Otto Schuster, had accompanied Ehrhardt during the Kapp putsch,[28] and in a report to Naval High Command in November he had admitted that in the summer and autumn of 1923 the Naval Station had dealings with various right-wing organisations, amongst them Org-C, for the supply of weapons and military leaders 'in an emergency'. Several agents had been sent on spying missions in Denmark and were remunerated out of secret 'pots'; the counter-espionage section at Kiel Naval Station had two agents involved in the Seeckt murder plot, and Schuster thought it very likely that the Prussian police knew all this.[29]

Kiel Station Command, under Admiral Raeder since 1925, was forced on the defensive. Raeder asked the Wehrmacht Department at the Reichswehr Ministry to protect the officers under investigation for fear that the police, under SPD direction, would have no regard for national security. Raeder said that although there had been collaboration with 'formations outside the Reichswehr', these were under Wehrmacht or naval control and strictly supervised. The Reichswehr had simply not been strong enough to handle internal unrest; weapons were available to defend the borders or for civil unrest but remained in the hands of the naval authorities. Military equipment had gone to Denmark not to be sold, but to protect it against seizure by the Allied Control. Raeder denied any complicity by Station Command in the Seeckt plot[30] and when he was accused of having links to radical-right organisations after 1923, he responded by saying that such accusations could only serve 'to undermine confidence in the reliability of the Reichswehr as the proven foundation of the State and Constitution'.[31] The accusations of Deputy Eggerstedt were hearsay made public without the Navy having had the opportunity to make its case.

In his report to Naval Command, Raeder emphasised that he did not tolerate paramilitary units in his command. That Lieder was an undercover agent he had only discovered by accident in connection with the defence measures against an anticipated Communist putsch on New Year's Eve 1925, and he had ordered the immediate severing of all links with both Lieder and also Ehrhardt, even after the latter was awarded amnesty.[32]

The official inquiry lasted into 1927; Lieder, Berndorff and others were interrogated at Leipzig. During the questioning of Schuster, Canaris's name came up once when Schuster mentioned him about secret plans to set up a 'Regiment Kiel' in 1921, and again in connection with arming troops with the weapons at Wik in case of civil unrest. The plan had been dropped as being 'unfeasible' and Schuster had destroyed the secret files.[33] Attorney Werner advised the Reichswehr Ministry that no solid evidence had been found against the naval officers and he doubted whether there was even a link between the Naval Station and Org-C. Although letters from members of the Wiking-Bund, the successor to Org-C, had been found and showed that Ehrhardt had used the Bund in an attempt to infiltrate spies into Naval High Command in Berlin and the Kiel station, the new Reichswehr minister, Groener, stated in February 1928 that he considered the internal watchdog powerful enough to combat the problem. Attorney Werner had therefore decided not to proceed with the accusations against the Kiel officers.[34]

Three years before this had boiled over, Canaris had returned to sea; on 18 June 1923 he was serving aboard the training cruiser *Berlin*, commanded by his old friend Loewenfeld. Station Chief von Gagern had recommended Canaris in his personal file for 'an early promotion'.[35] In November 1923, at the time of the Hitler putsch in Munich, Canaris was in Norway aboard *Berlin* and on 1 January 1924 he was promoted to Korvettenkapitän.[36] The same month, the cruiser left for a long overseas cruise, the first by a German warship since the war;[37] Canaris met his future fellow-traveller and rival Reinhard Heydrich aboard, who between July 1923 and March 1924 was an officer cadet on *Berlin*. Heydrich led a difficult existence there; a loner and very much disliked by his colleagues, he was described as arrogant and smug, a moderate scholar but unhealthily ambitious, soft, a poor gymnast and possessed of a voice that earned him the nickname 'Goat'. He had a reputation as a lady-killer, which was considered bad form, and although he had been a member of the anti-Jewish 'Deutsch-Völkischer Schutz und Trutzbund' he was suspected of having a Jewish forebear and was therefore friendless aboard *Berlin*.[38] One thing in which he excelled was the violin, which he was wont to play in some solitary place aboard ship and Canaris, noticing this, built up a friendship with Heydrich, inviting him to his home and introducing him into Kiel society once *Berlin* returned to port. Erika Canaris, who seldom saw her husband, used to invite a string quartet to play at her home; the seat of second violin was vacant and Heydrich played within the group at weekends[39] while Canaris was in the kitchen, cooking.[40] Heydrich had been a despatch runner for Freikorps Maercker at Halle. Canaris made no secret of his own anti-Republican nationalism, and an acquaintance of Heydrich said later that Heydrich had been 'thoroughly indoctrinated' by Canaris.[41] 'If we finally get a respectable government, then we can make miracles,' Canaris told him repeatedly.[42] Even if such openness from the militarily correct and diplomatic Canaris seems unlikely, it summarises what he felt, and Heydrich's decision to specialise in naval signals may have been at Canaris's suggestion.

Canaris's hopes for swift political change in Germany and new military greatness were soon dashed. Hitler and the string of extreme-right officers from Ludendorff to Ehrhardt had all underestimated the Republic's propensity for survival. The National Revolution was postponed and Org-C dissolved. On 15 January 1924, only two weeks after his promotion to Korvettenkapitän, Canaris tendered his resignation to the commanding officer of Naval Station Baltic: 'As I no longer feel able physically to meet the demands of service in the Reichsmarine, I request my departure at the end of March . . . .'[43] The certificate of a naval surgeon attesting to his unfitness was attached: 'A state of physical exhaustion and mental lassitude' was diagnosed, describing '. . . mood swings, irritable, easily excited over trivialities and exaggerates them unreasonably. Additionally lacks energy and ability to concentrate, tends to interpret minor symptoms as the onset of a serious condition . . . looks worn out, far older than his years.' This medical opinion must have been devastating for a man of thirty-seven years. The conclusion drawn was that Canaris was 'unfit for any kind of military service by reason of chronic, severe neurosis as a consequence of deteriorating in service'.[44]

Wülfing von Ditten, Naval Station chief of Staff, wrote on Canaris's application to resign: 'On the basis of the attached medical certificate there is scarcely any prospect of retaining this previously valuable officer in the Service. His departure is extraordinarily regretted.'[45]

With that the career of Wilhelm Canaris appeared to have come to an abrupt end, but Station Commander Freiherr von Gagern was not prepared simply to accept the resignation and medical report, and he wrote a very personal five-page letter to Canaris:

I cannot and will not discuss with you by letter whether you are doing the right thing in your decision: it is probably an impossibility in a letter. I would first like to make two points. You believe you would be of more use to your Fatherland, and would find greater personal satisfaction, in occupation other than the Navy; I am an optimist (in contrast to you, dear Canaris) but on *that* point I am sceptical ... I freely admit that the field of activity within the framework of the present Navy is not great, I admit further that Naval High Command is committed to developing its forces unduly narrowly, to clip its wings. The first will probably remain so for some time, that cannot be changed, but as regards the latter on the other hand I believe that it will change in the not-too-distant future. And the second point, quite simply, I want to *retain* you for the Navy, your understanding, your energy, your work ... and for that reason I would like to ask you to reconsider your step yet again, go over it all in your mind in *peace*.[46]

Von Gagern's observations show that he knew exactly where Canaris's problem lay:

It is quite clear to me that in the last few years more has been asked of you, your abilities, your health and your self-denial than from anybody in the Navy and that it cannot – I am thinking here of our political affairs at Kiel – go on. You can be sure that I will try – and I believe that the attempt will be successful – to change that. It is clear to me that you must get away from the current circumstances, for the time being *completely* away, and that can be done.[47]

Von Gagern explained that the 'Russian mission' – here he meant secret weapons and military-political cooperation with the Soviets for the purpose of the prohibited rearmament – had been postponed for political reasons, but he gave Canaris the prospect of a mission to East Asia that would become available in the summer of 1924. He closed his letter with the request 'to consider this letter as written only for you personally, and to destroy it'.[48]

Canaris did not destroy the letter, but he acceded to the request of his superior and on 22 March 1924 – probably after a personal interview with von Gagern – withdrew his resignation.[49]

9

Military–Political Secret Missions

On 17 May 1924 Canaris shipped aboard the steamer *Rheinland* for Japan, on a mission connected with naval rearmament, in particular the U-boat Arm.[1] Under the terms of the Versailles Treaty, Germany had been required to surrender all U-boats, lifting ships and U-boat docks, and to destroy all U-boats under construction: 'The building and acquisition of all submarine craft, even those for commercial purposes, is prohibited in Germany.'[2] In January 1920 Naval High Command took the first steps to get round the Treaty; with the approval of Naval High Command, the Germania shipyard at Kiel and the Vulcan yard at Hamburg sold project sketches of German U-cruisers and minelaying U-boats to Japan with the intention that they should be built there under the supervision of German naval architects. Orders for all material supplies were to be placed with German firms.[3] In 1922, with the approval of Navy Commander-in-Chief Admiral Behncke, the shipyards Germania, Vulcan and Weser set up an office in The Hague known as 'Ingenieurskantoor voor Scheepsbouw' (IvS). Its purpose was to develop new plans for U-boats, to train crews and to organise and develop cooperation with foreign navies.[4]

After the war the Naval Transport Section at Naval High Command under Kapitän zur See Walter Lohmann handled the return of prisoners of war and prize ships. This led to many overseas contacts. After the occupation of the Ruhr in the spring of 1923, the German Government budgeted ten million gold marks to the Navy, which passed directly to Kapitän Lohmann, who became the *éminence grise* of German secret rearmament. His eventual fall dragged down Reichswehrminister Otto Gessler and the head of the Naval High Command, Admiral Zenker, while Canaris also did not survive his proximity to Lohmann unscathed.[5]

There had been complications in the U-boat negotiations with Japan and the aim of Canaris's mission was to improve the exchange of information between the respective Naval High Commands.[6] He was given only the most rudimentary briefing on the state of German–Japanese relations and had no written guidelines. On his arrival at Kobe he was received by a distrustful

Japanese officer, and only after convincing him of the serious nature of his mission did he obtain an interview with Navy Minister Takarabe, the Japanese Naval Command, and a visit to the submarine yards. The impression he gained of German–Japanese cooperation was one of discord; the intention, so he wrote in his report, 'seems to be to make use of German experience and developments' but without 'any feelings of sympathy or common interest with Germany'.[7]

Even before Canaris had returned home, Admiral Zenker had summarised it thus: 'With Japan, we are always the giver. What we get in return does not justify a pro-Japanese stance,'[8] and, in the hope of some alleviation of the terms of the Versailles Treaty, he wrote, 'An inclination towards the Anglo-Saxons is, for the time being, urgently necessary.'[9]

At the beginning of October Canaris took over a planning section in the Fleet Division at Naval High Command to organise mobilisation,[10] but it was soon apparent to his superiors that he had no love for office work, and at the end of January 1925 they sent him on a secret mission to the country closest to his heart. Naval High Command and the head of the Naval Transport Section, Lohmann, had transferred the major part of their U-boat and other naval planning to Spain. In the summer of 1922 Canaris had revived old contacts there for the Marineleitung, gauging what was on offer in the way of war material and ores for steel production.[11] He had an agent in Madrid to liaise between himself and the Marineleitung, German industrialists and important Spanish institutions and personalities: former Kapitänleutnant Mayrhofer had accepted an offer from AEG to work in their telegraphic section. 'Salary is enough to live on. But he has to have a place to manoeuvre for his real work,' Canaris noted in his report to Marineleitung.[12]

Spain, entangled in a colonial war in Morocco, wanted an independent naval armaments industry in which submarines, torpedoes and fire direction equipment played a major role.[13] This coincided perfectly with German aims to win neutral cooperation partners for the design, building and testing of precisely those armaments.

What Germany found in Spain, however, was a complicated mixture of State, private enterprise and naval–political interests.[14] Two large rivals competed for the Spanish Government's contracts – the Spanish State yard, Constructora Naval, which worked with Vickers to build Spanish submarines to British designs,[15] and Union Naval de Levante (UNL), founded in 1924, with shipyards at Valencia, Tarragona and Barcelona, and in which German armaments firm Krupp had been heavily involved. The German engineering office in Holland, IvS, had entered into partnership with UNL and could not negotiate directly with the Spanish Government or its yards.[16]

A third Spanish player was industrialist Horacio Echevarrieta, who owned shipyards at Cadiz and El Ferrol and was also tendering bids to the Spanish Government to build submarines. Echevarrieta was 'a political force of the first rank,' Canaris informed Berlin, 'Basque by birth, extremely ambitious and proud, Spain's richest industrialist. Although his yard at Cadiz is not presently competitive, he is determined to found a home-grown war industry in Spain. In this he is resolved to take on both Constructora and UNL.'[17]

The German yard Blohm & Voss had also tendered to build Spain's submarines and had submitted torpedo designs.[18] The Marineleitung was unhappy with this, fearing that the Spanish would choose to abide by the existing relationships with England and Italy if the competition was enlarged by infighting German firms. Accordingly, Germania-Werft in Kiel, a partner in IvS, sent Korvettenkapitän Blum, an IvS director, with Canaris to Spain to assess the chances for German submarine designs there.[19] Upon arrival in Madrid on 31 January 1925, they conferred with UNL technical director Ziegelasch and Spanish director-general Ernesto Anastasio. Canaris met the head of the Cartagena submarine base, Capitan Don Mateo Garcia and Capitan de Corbeta Don Manuel Medina y Morris, a candidate for the post of naval attaché to Germany.[20]

The German agent in Madrid, Mayrhofer, had prepared useful contacts for Canaris,[21] who was also using this visit to reactivate his espionage network.[22] Two old comrades with intelligence experience were Carlos Baum, who ran an export business in Barcelona, and Carlos Fricke, later consul at Valencia, both of whom had worked for German intelligence in the First World War.[23] Canaris 'made contracts' with them as spies, but neither of them would run the organisational network as this involved sending agents abroad – mainly to France – the creation of a spy network in the ports and setting up reporting centres and a sabotage organisation.[24] French espionage was very active in Spain and so the risk of compromising newly recruited agents was too great, but in any case Baum and Fricke feared that their innocent commercial activities might be prejudiced. The solution was found in twenty-eight-year-old Conrad Meyer, who had been an officer during the war and a member of Brigade Loewenfeld up to the time of the Kapp putsch. He had fallen on hard times and was willing to take over the organisational work. This was 'the beginning of the legendary intelligence network that Canaris supported later in Spain'.[25]

For Canaris, the most important Spanish official in submarine questions was Capitan Don Mateo Garcia. He wanted the design of a submarine 'of about one thousand tonnes, with high speed and a large radius of action',[26] Canaris wrote in his report. Garcia was planning to visit Germany for talks with MAN Diesel and also Blohm & Voss, hoping to use them as intermediaries to obtain torpedo designs from the Marineleitung in Berlin to be built at a new Echevarrieta factory in Cadiz.[27] Canaris was against using Blohm & Voss and convinced Garcia to approach the Marineleitung directly.

Garcia was accompanied to Germany by Capitan de Corbeta Sacro-Lirio, chamberlain to King Alfonso XIII, a member of the Spanish Commission to the League of Nations and Echevarrieta's naval expert. Canaris had been told by an agent that Baron del Sacro-Lirio was very pro-German, and 'if things were done right' it would probably be possible to influence Echevarrieta in his naval plans through that source.[28] At this time, Canaris seems to have had no direct contact to Echevarrieta; Sacro-Lirio would become an important go-between for Canaris and he made Echevarrieta the German favourite in the field of naval cooperation.

Of UNL, Canaris had obtained an unfavourable picture: technical director Ziegelasch made an 'uncertain, one-sided impression',[29] while the UNL financial base was too weak. UNL lacked channels to the Spanish Navy, not even to Don Mateo Garcia, while the value of the royal contact which it did have was not to be overestimated.[30] Canaris also took note of private assertions made by Ziegelasch that appeared to be against German naval interests, and even Ziegelasch's warning that Echevarrieta's credit was exhausted and that as a Republican he was unlikely to exercise much influence over the king or dictator Primo de Rivera[31] could not dislodge Canaris in his belief that Echevarrieta was the man for Germany.

This decision created a major problem. The Spanish Navy wanted German submarines, and the best shipyard, the favourite of the Marineleitung, was Germania-Werft of Kiel, which formed part of the IvS partnership in Holland. Echevarrieta could not negotiate for submarines in Germany with anybody because of the Versailles Treaty, nor with IvS in Holland, because its partner UNL was a direct competitor in Spain. The Spanish also wanted MAN diesels, and MAN was in the Blohm & Voss camp, with whom Echevarrieta was negotiating torpedo plans. It was in the German national interest to support IvS, since it worked in cooperation with the Marineleitung, but the latter could be compromised by a multi-national IvS;[32] German diplomats in Madrid and Barcelona were also opposed to the direct cooperation between Blohm & Voss and Echevarrieta since it could produce difficulties with the Entente.[33] The only solution to get Echevarrieta negotiating for everything through IvS was to remove UNL from the IvS partnership, and this was Canaris's recommendation to Berlin in mid-February.[34]

UNL was suspicious that something underhand was being plotted and refused to release IvS from the partnership. Berlin gave UNL a verbal assurance of a major submarine contract, which was so convincing that, at Ziegelasch's request, Navy chief Zenker had a memorandum drawn up confirming his support for the IvS project, but he did not give it to Ziegelasch before he left.[35] Meanwhile, Garcia had visited Germany as planned and was given by the Marineleitung their personal guarantee that German support for the Spanish Navy would be given 'independently'.[36]

On 20 April 1925 Canaris returned to Spain[37] carrying the Zenker memorandum. He met Almirante Marqués de Magaz, the regime's deputy and rival to dictator Primo de Rivera. He also saw for the first time Oberst Max Bauer, a political fellow-traveller with Ludendorff, who had fled to Spain after the Kapp putsch failed and was now military adviser to King Alfonso XIII.[38]

Almirante Magaz complained to Canaris that a few days earlier, UNL had tendered an unsolicited submarine project, indicating that the Marineleitung was involved, which contradicted the assurance given to Capitan Mateo Garcia in Berlin that the Marineleitung would treat with Spain independently. Canaris now played his trump by producing the memorandum supporting IvS, which he had orders to hand personally to Spanish Naval Command.[39] Once the document was in the hands of Mateo Garcia and Spanish Navy Minister Cornejo, Ziegelasch and UNL were cut adrift. Canaris assured Mateo that the Spanish Navy minister could elect any Spanish yard of his choice to build the submarines ordered by IvS, but it was important to the Marineleitung that 'German know-how, which will be communicated without reservation by IvS, should not be made known to Vickers'.[40] Canaris also guaranteed that all German torpedo designs were at the disposal of the Spanish Navy through IvS. Mateo reported that Echevarrieta had a contract to build a German-designed torpedo factory and was now anxious for twelve submarines to German blueprints; Echevarrieta confirmed personally to Canaris that he wanted to build 'German-type submarines and in close cooperation with the German Navy. Corresponding to the wishes of Marineleitung he would use German personnel in submarine and torpedo construction.'[41]

At the beginning of August 1925, Echevarrieta arrived in Kiel. Shortly before, Max Bauer had advised Canaris: 'It is really important that he is well received and gets to see everything without our giving him the impression that it is being forced on him. He would very much like to be received by Hindenburg. One should emphasise that as a Spanish patriot he is especially welcome amongst us Germans.'[42]

Spanish politics now intervened in all the careful plans; Almirante Magaz, opponent of Primo de Rivera, was ousted. The Marineleitung lamented:

> The submarine building programme of the Spanish naval leaders has been postponed in the first instance, probably until the autumn. The reason is that at the moment there is nobody as supportive of it as Magaz was. The programme will be revived, first, as soon as the Moroccan war finishes (expected this coming

spring), second, as soon as Magaz replaces Primo de Rivera at the helm. According to information from Herr Canaris, this turn in politics can be counted on in the near future.[43]

Canaris was wrong, Magaz was out of the picture for good and the submarine programme never got into its stride. Instead, the Spanish went ahead with torpedo manufacture. On 26 January 1926, Echevarrieta signed a ten-year contract with the Marineleitung for the torpedo factory and guaranteed that he would appoint a German national as manager. He also agreed to supply German-designed torpedoes only to the Spanish and German navies and to make available to the Marineleitung all test material and observations; Marineleitung experts were to be involved in all trials.[44]

A few weeks later Britain interceded,[45] putting favourable credits on the table knowing that Echevarrieta was having difficulty in paying for the overall project, which amounted to around eight million pesetas (five million Reichsmarks).[46] The Marineleitung responded by asking Lohmann to negotiate credit for Echevarrieta with the Deutsche Bank.

The explosive political nature of the Echevarrieta affair revealed itself at a session of the Reich Economy Ministry on 13 April 1926,[47] at which Admiral Zenker emphasised how vital it was for the Marineleitung that 'the designs could be tried and tested in practice and the technical personnel kept informed. If that is not possible, U-boat and torpedo science will be lost for ever.'[48]

Zenker came up against hefty criticism. The state secretary at the Finance Ministry, Ernst Trendelenburg, feared that Echevarrieta would need rather more than the eight million pesetas credit, and this would never be approved.[49] In any case, in view of the political and economic risks, his ministry had 'no interest in concluding a contract with Echevarrieta, since to do so could have catastrophic consequences for German industry'.[50] The Foreign Ministry was concerned that the arrangement might infringe the Versailles Treaty; if British competitors brought pressure on the government, Secretary of State Carl von Schubert suggested, it would prejudice the German position at the Ambassadors' Conference currently being held in Paris, in which concessions to the Versailles Treaty were being sought. Furthermore the British were very sensitive about U-boat building and it might be advisable to avoid for the moment anything in this area that might upset them.

When fresh loan negotiations for Echevarrieta began the following year, Legation Secretary Wagenmann noted: 'Kapitän Canaris has apparently attempted, knowing the reservations of the Foreign Ministry, to finance the procedure and to achieve this by approaching private rather than official sources just as he did when he arranged finance for the torpedo and U-boat factories and the fire direction installations.'[51] These private sources were principally representatives of the Deutsche Bank and Banco Alemán Transatlántico, which was founded in 1904 by the overseas agency of the Deutsche Bank.[52] A week after Reich Chancellor Luther had delivered his criticism of the Echevarrieta affair, everything had been concluded, and in Madrid on 17 May Echevarrieta received a credit of 240,000 British pounds sterling for which the Reich was to act as guarantor.[53] Echevarrieta contracted to place his material requirements for the factory and the manufacture of one thousand torpedoes that the Spanish Government had ordered with German firms wherever possible, and to appoint a German national as manager of the factory for a period of ten years.[54]

General Primo de Rivera thanked Canaris personally 'for the great support which the German Navy lent to the Spanish Navy through the office of Señor Echevarrieta'; Canaris informed Berlin, 'he explained that this grand rapprochement had given him cause to conclude a favourable trade agreement with Germany.'[55] During an audience on 20 May, Canaris told the Spanish king of the German–Spanish naval cooperation; Alfonso XIII appeared to be well informed and posed 'some very searching questions about the matter'.[56] Canaris's mission was a complete success; he reported on his commercial and armaments activities to the German ambassador in Madrid, Johannes Graf von Welczeck, and the consul-general in Barcelona, Ulrich von Hassell (whom he would meet frequently in future years). The ambassador described his own position vis-à-vis the Spanish Government as being much stronger as a result of the progress in naval cooperation.[57]

Canaris was still in Barcelona on 26 May when he received news of the visit of a German naval squadron commanded by Vizeadmiral Mommsen; Baron del Sacro-Lirio brought the 'unofficial' advice that the king 'would be pleased to receive the admiral and a deputation of officers in the capital'.[58] At the request of Welczeck and Mommsen, Canaris was invited to accompany them on the royal visit. At the banquet, Canaris discussed with the king all details of the military planning,[59] the highpoint of the visit. Admiral Mommsen reported later to the Foreign Ministry how the king had emphasised that 'German warships were welcome at any time, and anywhere, in Spain.' He had shown special interest in weapons developments 'for which the Spanish Navy would gladly play guinea-pig for German designers'. Mommsen also noted the special praise the king reserved for Canaris 'whom he has appointed his "unofficial naval attaché"'.[60]

A second official visit to Spain followed in August 1926 after Alfonso XIII expressed the desire to inspect the new German rotor-ship *Barbara* on her first foreign cruise,[61] and Canaris was given the job of making the preparations. In the saloon of *Barbara*, Lohmann had the opportunity to discuss with the king the latter's plans 'to build a Spanish national armaments industry with German help'[62] and to interest him in German E-boats (motor torpedo boats) and dual-purpose naval tankers that could double as aircraft mother-ships,[63] although for these future projects Lohmann would require prior Marineleitung approval. After King Alfonso's visit to *Barbara*, he sent an enthusiastic telegram of thanks to Reich President Hindenburg; Lohmann noted, 'It was certainly one of the best opportunities to take advantage of the enthusiasm for German abilities and technology.'[64]

After the Marineleitung agreed to 'surrender to Spain our expertise in the field of aircraft mother-ship tankers and E-boat construction[65] Canaris was sent to Spain with the corresponding files, and addressed the Secret Defence Council, which included the king, the dictator Primo de Rivera, the war minister and the navy minister. The outcome was that it was decided to commission the construction of two tankers and eight E-boats, but problems were encountered from the pro-British Navy Minister Cornejo, who obstructed the award of contracts, while the German Foreign Ministry cast a baleful eye on these activities by the Marineleitung and Canaris, considering the danger of political complications too high: 'This has also been made absolutely clear to Herr Canaris together with the observation that the Foreign Ministry declines any responsibility whatsoever for any difficulties that may arise from the liaison between German official agencies and Echevarrieta.'[66] Not even the privately funded projects met with Foreign Ministry approoval: 'In any case we have no reason – despite the wishes of Herr Canaris – to advocate them to the Reich finance minister.'[67]

In October, Echevarrieta signed a far-reaching contract during a visit to Berlin. With Deutsche Lufthansa he agreed to the founding of a German–Spanish airline. The foreign minister observed in a confidential telegram to the Madrid embassy that the Reich transport minister would support it as the monopoly concern for German air traffic with Spain and if possible between Spain and South America.[68]

Canaris and the Marineleitung, meanwhile, forged ahead with the projects disparaged by the Foreign Ministry. At the instigation of Canaris, who since 1 October 1926 had been adviser to the Marineleitung Chief of Staff Kapitän Peter Donner,[69] former Oberleutnant Messerschmidt[70] was installed in Madrid as liaison officer between the Marineleitung and Echevarrieta.

Canaris had the particular support of ambassador Welczeck, who mentioned the political advantages of German–Spanish cooperation in letters and telegrams to his superiors and pressed for a decision of the Reich Government: 'As you know, it is the exclusive merit of the Navy, especially Herr Canaris, to have led the most important and influential financier Don Horacio Echevarrieta from the French camp into our own.'[71] The mood in Berlin had finally tipped in favour of Canaris. who once again had succeeded in his goals without the help of official agencies. He had convinced Deutsche Bank to take over the financial aspects of the project and to negotiate with Foreign Minister Stresemann and Secretary of State Schubert. On 1 February 1927 the Foreign Ministry reiterated its reservations, but following a conference at the Reichswehr Ministry eight days later everyone had fallen in line behind Canaris. The Deutsche Bank would negotiate the five million Reichsmark loan with the Reichs-Kredit-Gesellschaft.[72]

In mid-February Canaris discussed with King Alfonso XIII the ever more ambitious plans he was developing with Echevarrieta. Besides the torpedo factory at Cadiz there would be others for torpedo-carrying aircraft, general aircraft and for engines; these sites would also double as test-beds for the E-boats for which Echevarrieta was negotiating with Weser shipyard and the Travemünder Yachthaven AG, part of the Lohmann group. Canaris was also thinking of the Lufthansa project in which Echevarrieta would attempt 'to penetrate Spanish air travel at the earliest' and was already in talks with Junkers regarding the aircraft factory at Cadiz.[73]

The list of projects grew steadily, and extended from negotiations with Mercedes to build a car plant, a planned Spanish oil monopoly and the joint exploitation of mineral wealth and farming in areas in Spanish Morocco and Guinea.[74] Much of this was wishful thinking: radical political change in Spain overturned Primo de Rivera's dictatorship, replacing it with a republic and bringing all these wonderful ideas crashing down. For all the enormous financial investment of the Marineleitung, the Cadiz torpedo factory never began production, while the Echevarrieta shipyard managed to turn out only a single completed U-boat for testing by German personnel.[75]

The long-term value of Spanish–German cooperation for those states cannot be underestimated, however. The Spanish Navy placed modern submarines at the disposal of German naval forces for testing and manoeuvres. For the future German production of U-boats, these preliminary steps and the fact that Spain helped Germany keep up with new developments in submarine technology would prove of decisive importance.[76]

In an appraisal, Chief of Staff Donner wrote of Canaris:

> In the exercise of his duties, he has created and developed valuable overseas contacts, in his clever, objective and tenacious manner mastered the most delicate tasks. In difficult situations for Reich and Navy he has demonstrated that he can combine caution and correctness with a bold approach. Modest, on first impression almost shy, intelligent and perceptive, people – including foreigners – are swift to recognise his good character and energy, and trust him.[77]

As with others before him, Donner was concerned that Canaris's tireless pursuit of his goals could overtax his strength:

Care will have to be taken to ensure that this valuable officer is not ruined for a seagoing career by exclusive employment in internal or foreign political service and on special missions; there is also a danger that he is being overstretched physically and mentally ... there will always be missions of which it will be said that only he can solve them fully and that accordingly he should postpone returning to sea a little while longer.[78]

Worries about the health of his subordinate may not have been the only reason for Donner's attempt to have Canaris removed from the naval-political scene. That summer there had been progress in U-boat construction and air transport affairs,[79] which had resulted in the autumn in a contract between Echevarrieta and IvS for the construction and testing of a 600-tonne U-boat and possible ancillary agreements.[80] But soon the name Canaris was to make headlines once more, headlines which were anything but welcome even if it would not be Canaris personally who unleashed the greatest scandal for the German Navy since the Kapp putsch.

10

The Shadow of the Past

Under titles such as 'Captain and Businessman' and 'The Film Scandal in the Armed Forces Ministry', from 8 August 1927 the *Berliner Tageblatt* began running a series of articles about the connection between Kapitän zur See Walter Lohmann and the Phoebus Film Company, the second-largest film producer in Germany. Eight days later the *Weltbühne* joined in. The 'Lohmann Affair' would plunge the Navy into crisis.[1]

The background to the scandal was simple: Lohmann, head of the Naval Transport Division (BS), imbued with a mixture of too much zeal, arrogance and false patriotism, had become involved in a number of 'madcap' schemes. He had continued to expand his 'armaments empire' and had so lost sight of what he was doing that it finally collapsed.

Canaris had suspected as much and warned his superiors:

> As acting chief of staff of the Marineleitung for several months this year, I gained the impression that BS was undertaking operations unknown to us and in particular to the head of the Marineleitung. Upon his return from furlough, I advised the chief of staff, Kapitän zur See Donner accordingly, and suggested that he order Kapitän zur See Lohmann to account for all his operations. A few days before the publication of the Phoebus affair, the head of Marineleitung gave Kapitän zur See Lohmann the said order. The intention was to consolidate all the operations and then relieve the Naval Transport Division of all enterprises that could not be justified.[2]

Exactly what Canaris knew about Lohmann's improprieties is not known for certain,[3] but the warnings came too late. Phoebus went bankrupt and the financial backing Lohmann had provided on his own behalf but using the name and money of the German Navy now came to light. It had been his aim to gain influence over the growing film industry, which he thought could be made useful for military propaganda purposes. He wanted to make his own films to combat foreign productions with a pacifist message such as the Soviet release *Battleship Potemkin*;[4] even Admiral Zenker saw the 'distribution of pro-Fatherland and culturally valuable films' as a suitable way 'of correcting the false impressions nourished by injurious films made at home and abroad'.[5] Lohmann feared that the German film industry was too heavily dominated by foreign ideology, as had already happened – so far as he could see – with Germany's leading film producer Ufa, which was half American-owned.[6]

Phoebus had come into being in 1922 through the merger of various small filmmakers.[7] Director Sally Isenberg had sought Lohmann's support at the beginning of 1923 knowing that he had good contacts with the Soviet Union, where she wanted to try her luck with her films, which were no longer performing so well in Germany.[8] During 1924 Lohmann made credits to Phoebus of 870,000 Reichsmarks from secret naval funds without informing Admiral Zenker and Reichswehrminister Gessler;[9] subsequently he decided to become a major Phoebus stockholder. It was agreed that in exchange for recapitalising the company, he would receive stock with a nominal value of 1.3 million Reichsmarks plus old stock worth 320,000 Reichsmarks, an inclusive capital investment of almost 1.75 million Reichsmarks, made up of the 870,000 Reichsmarks he had already credited, leaving 850,000 Reichsmarks to subscribe.

By the beginning of 1926 Phoebus needed a fresh injection of cash. An audit showed that three million Reichsmarks was needed to avoid liquidation,[10] and Lohmann requested a meeting with Reich Finance Minister Peter Reinhold in the hope of obtaining a Reich guarantee for the loan, this guarantee being the precondition of the Deutsche Girozentrale before they would bail out Phoebus. Reinhold declined to help but was then tricked into signing. Lohmann told him that if he guaranteed the loan, his guarantee would be backed by the re-guarantee of Lignose AG, a supplier of explosives and raw film material, one of Lohmann's jungle of companies. He had obtained the re-guarantee by assuring Lignose AG that the Reich was legally bound to pay if Phoebus found itself in difficulties.[11] That the Reich might then call on the re-guarantee to liquidate its loss does not seem to have occurred to Lignose AG. Reinhold, Reichswehrminister Gessler and Admiral Zenker signed the Reich guarantee on 26 March 1926 in the belief that the re-guarantee covered it,[12] the two ministers having been misled by Lohmann that the other had agreed, and the signature was purely a formality.[13] Unfortunately, Phoebus's run of bad luck continued and Lohmann had to continue to pump cash into the enterprise to prevent the Deutsche Girozentrale calling on the Reich guarantee for its three million Reichsmarks. Since Lohmann could not approach Zenker or Gessler again personally, he obtained more credit on the basis of guarantees in the name of the Reichswehr Ministry,[14] and in 1927 Phoebus received another 4.4 million Reichsmarks.

The press campaign that brought about the collapse and set the scene for the explosive budget debate in early 1928 was fuelled by major interests inside the German film industry. Sally Isenberg, who remained in dispute with Phoebus after her departure from the company, had passed information about Lohmann's involvement with Phoebus and the Berliner Bankverein to staff at publisher Ullstein. Here the scoop was attributed to the liberal-left press, and not to *Berliner Tageblatt*, which they owned, for as co-owners of Terra Film, the proprietors of Ullstein were rather hoping to acquire Phoebus's cinemas at a knock-down price.[15]

Reichswehrminister Gessler and Canaris as Marineleitung deputy chief of staff admitted later that they were aware at the beginning of 1927 of the financial disaster looming with Phoebus and Lohmann,[16] Canaris adding that steps had been taken to disentangle the trust and extricate Lohmann by promoting him.[17] Gessler appears not to have grasped the extent of the problem; immediately after the press made the first revelations, Canaris was ordered to Sylt to explain the situation to Gessler, but he seemed 'little perturbed',[18] and when Canaris furnished the guarantee document Gessler had signed in early 1926, he took the view that by co-signing it the finance minister had accepted sole responsibility. Gessler did not return to Berlin from vacation until 17 August 1927, by which time the affair had become much uglier.

Two days after the first article appeared in the *Berliner Tageblatt*, Admiral Zenker was ordered to explain the matter to Reichswehrminister Wilhelm Marz. He brought up not only Phoebus and the Reich guarantee, but also reported on the cover operations 'Navis' (E-boat construction) and 'Trayag' (training and trials) which Lohmann had initiated with the approval of the Marineleitung for the purpose of secret naval rearmament.[19] Marx realised at once that no cover-up was going to hide all this and, in order to avoid a committee of inquiry, ordered Friedrich Saemisch, president of the Reich Audits Bureau, to investigate and report.[20]

The Naval Honour Court that examined Lohmann found him free of personal corruption but guilty of exceeding his area of competence, and of irresponsibility in financial matters.[21] Gessler considered this irrelevant since Lohmann was bound to have exceeded his area of competence[22] by the nature of his appointed job.[23]

The result of Saemisch's audit was so serious for financial, naval and political circles that on 8 November 1927 he published only a part of his report and delivered the rest orally to the Reich chancellor.[24] A full publication was impossible politically and it was essential to withhold the matter from the Reichstag before the 1928 Reichswehr Estimates, and the 1927 Supplementary Budget debates, since seven million Reichsmarks was required to cover Lohmann's deficiency.

In order to draw off the opposition, Gessler resigned on 19 January 1928, the day before the debate. He was succeeded as Reichswehrminister by General Groener, an independent.[25]

The affair could not be swept under the carpet. At a session of the Budget Committee on 13 March 1928, KPD Reichswehr expert Ernst Schneller read extracts from a certain report that the government, Reichswehr and party leaders wanted kept secret, after which the matter was referred to a committee of inquiry sitting in camera. Here the delicate questions of German–Spanish cooperation in the area of secret naval rearmament, and those projects that had so occupied Echevarrieta and Canaris, were discussed, while Admiral Zenker explained the circumstances of German support for Spanish warship building and dismissed as untrue Schneller's allegations that U-boat commanders were trained there.[26]

The Reichstag voted on the closing report on 27 March 1928; the most awkward political implications were avoided and the Reich Government kept to itself the question of reimbursement by those implicated. At the beginning of May, Ulrich Fritze, former secretary of state at the Prussian Justice Ministry, began the inquiry in civilian law within very restricted terms of reference.[27] Since it was feared that the public would not tolerate Lohmann going unpunished, he had been retired from the Navy on 31 March 1928 after the Marineleitung held him liable to repay 120,000 Reichsmarks as compensation. After all adjustments he was left with a pension of 396 Reichsmarks a month; he emigrated to Rome and died there on 30 April 1930.[28]

At the end of May 1930 the Fritze Report presented the appalling statistics: Lohmann alone was adjudged responsible for the loss of thirteen million Reichsmarks and liable for its return; Gessler, Zenker and former Finance Minister Reinhold, all of whom had put their signatures to a Reich guarantee favouring the Phoebus Film Company, had each incurred with Lohmann liability to repay 1.1 million Reichsmarks.[29] In conclusion, Fritze recommended an amnesty for those responsible 'on political grounds'.[30]

All of this – not least because of the exposure of Zenker and Gessler – decided Reichswehrminister Groener to draw a veil of silence over the scandal. In Cabinet he refused to reveal the details, nor refer them to the Reichstag, and neither was he inclined to demand compensation from those four personalities implicated; the affair should be 'killed off',[31] he thought, not least so that the rearmament programme could go ahead untouched.

Canaris had nothing for which to reproach himself; in a memorandum he described his collaboration with Lohmann regarding the Spanish projects and obtaining loans for Echevarrieta. 'I had nothing to do with any of Kapitän zur See Lohmann's other enterprises. Recently I did discover the Trayag link, and

I knew of the existence of Navis, von Mentor[32] and the involvement of IvS. I had heard nothing about the film operations, the Bankverein[33] or the numerous other involvements of which I became aware during the inquiry.'[34] His superiors also vouched that Canaris 'not only had nothing to do with the things that came to be grouped together as the "Lohmann Affair", but on the contrary worked intelligently and energetically at clearing them up and therein rendered great service'.[35]

Nevertheless, the affair had unpleasant consequences for Canaris and brought him once more into the spotlight of the anti-government and anti-rearmament press. 'Canaris's Secret',[36] 'Canaris in the Baltic',[37] 'Canaris Films and the League of Nations Theatre'[38] and 'The Canary Islands Fairy Tale'[39] followed in quick succession in the *Weltbühne*. His past was put under the microscope: his contacts with Org-C, links to the Hitler putsch, allegations of knowledge after the fact relating to the murder of Foreign Minister Rathenau were all placed at his door. Worst of all for the Marineleitung was the 'Canary Islands Fairy Tale' whose anonymous author related the relationship between 'The Canary Islander' (obviously Canaris) and 'Esche' (Echevarrieta):

> Now Esche had many slaves, mines, furnaces and built ships that could swim underwater like fish. The Canary Islander came and promised him a lot of the money which his people had given him if only the Esche would build him such ships too. The Spaniard agreed and the Canary Islander promised to send him lots of money.[40]

The well-informed author of the article knew that Lohmann had brought the pair together in Madrid:

> Here he received sacks of money, went off at once and built the ships which do what fish do, for the Canary Islander. At the request of the latter he kept the building work secret and hid the finished vessels away from the gaze of other people, for he probably knew that the Canary Islander had had to swear a holy oath to other nations not to do that.[41]

The likely consequences were painted in apocalyptic terms: 'The other people saw through the tricks of the Canary Islander, showed us his lack of faith and breach of promise and killed all his people.'[42] The knowledge of *Welbühne* about the allegedly secret efforts to rearm must have alarmed the Marineleitung, and the next scandal followed hot on the heels of the first.

On 15 December 1927, at a Reichstag Committee of inquiry into the 'Causes of the German Collapse in 1918',[43] SPD deputy Dr Julius Moses stated that: 'The charges we are proposing to make are so grave that a refusal to accept Korvettenkapitän Canaris as the representative of the Marineleitung before the Committee of Inquiry is more than justified. One must express renewed surprise that the Admiralty would dare to present as its official representative to the Committee of Inquiry a person of such qualities.'[44]

Thus came to a head a dispute that had begun two years previously in the committee investigating the 'Stab in the Back' legend and the 1917 Red Revolution in the Fleet. The spokesman for the critics of the Navy was former USPD party secretary and present SPD deputy Wilhelm Dittmann. The actions of the Marineleitung and naval justice at issue were those directed against the ringleaders of the Fleet mutineers of 1917 and the death sentences handed down for treason. In 1917 the Navy had accused the USPD of incitement and causing unrest and it was still demanding that USPD leaders Haase, Dittmann and Vogtherr be handed over to stand trial.[45] The USPD took the view that the death sentences were excessive since internal circumstances in the Navy had given rise to the mutiny; these battle lines remained unchanged. After all efforts in the preliminaries to the inquiry to 'remove' Dittmann had failed,[46] and to prevent his testifying,[47] Canaris was nominated as the Marineleitung representative to rebut the opposition case. On 23 January 1928, after Dittmann had held the floor for six hours, Canaris was called: 'Deputy Dittmann has attempted to supply proof that the breakdown in the Fleet cannot be attributed to revolutionary influences, but to a combination of circumstances, in particular the failure of the officers. He has made grave accusations against the officer corps and has spoken of officers mocking the men; I have to refute these grave charges.'[48]

Canaris made an honest attempt to place the USPD in immediate proximity to 'the ringleaders of the mutiny'. At the end of the first part of his speech he summarised: 'The Fleet was inwardly sound. The virus for the unrest was brought in from outside.' He was interrupted repeatedly by laughter and indignant catcalls, but continued by alleging that the mutineers in the Fleet had had 'close contacts to the USPD' and 'groups further left of it' who were working towards 'a Revolution after the Soviet example'. 'It is certain that radical-left groups conspired to bring about the events in the Fleet, used them to the full and distributed many leaflets of a revolutionary character ... an exact division between the USPD and the radical-left groups with regard to their effect on the crews in the Fleet cannot be found.'[49]

For Canaris and the Navy in the years after the war, the enemy was the left. Therefore Canaris defended the death sentences meted out to the ringleaders, and Committee Chairman Albrecht Philipp had difficulty in controlling 'minutes-long storms of protest'.[50] KPD deputy Emil Höllein shouted: 'What about the murderer Leutnant Vogel, whom you let run for it?'[51]

After Canaris had finished speaking, SPD deputy Julius Moses said: 'I consider it my duty at this point to ask the previous speaker if he is the same

Kapitänleutnant Canaris who sat in judgement on the murderers of Liebknecht and Rosa Luxemburg, and of whom it is said that he did more than most to ensure that Vogel escaped ... if that were the case, we would view it as an affront to this inquiry by the Reichswehrminister.'[52]

Canaris attempted to side-step that attack: 'I am here as the representative of the Marineleitung and not personally,' but this only further infuriated his opponents, and shouts of 'Rubbish! Coward!' were hurled at him and a chant of 'Murderers' helper's helper!' resounded across the chamber. Finally KPD deputy Arthur Rosenberg declared:

> It is an occurrence without parallel ... that here in the inquiry into such a difficult and historical legal question Herr Reichswehrminister Dr Gessler finds it acceptable to send here a representative against whom the most serious accusations of a criminal nature have been raised ... I propose that the session be suspended, for in my opinion the majority of the committee cannot find it compatible with their dignity to dally with a government representative of the ilk of Kapitän Canaris.

The chairman brought the session to an end by offering Canaris the opportunity to speak in his defence, but he kept to the script: 'The completely unjustified allegations against me will be clarified without delay upon application to my superior office, the Marineleitung. Therefore I have nothing to add. I will not defend myself, the answer will be supplied by the Reichswehrminister.'[53]

Minister Gessler issued a declaration to the Committee at once, denying the involvement of Canaris in 'the flight of the suspect in the Luxemburg murder'.[54] In the press campaign that followed, every kind of accusation was aimed at Canaris, and he was soon the no. 1 whipping-boy of the leftist anti-military press. Gessler was obliged to issue another communiqué to back up the first:

1. Neither as First Officer of the cruiser *Berlin* nor in any other office did Korvettenkapitän Canaris make available to the leader of Organisation Consul either money, weapons or uniforms in any manner whatsoever.
2. There is no link between Korvettenkapitän Canaris and the assassination attempt on General von Seeckt.
3. There was no financing of the Schleswig-Holstein pro-Fatherland groups including the Wikingbund ... The revelations at that time in *Weltbühne* were not refuted because basically I do not react to reports in periodicals like *Weltbühne*. Accept the expression of my esteem. Gessler. [55]

It was not easy to keep Canaris out of the headlines. The recommendation in his personal file not to use him for the time being on military-political secret missions was ignored. His contacts to the heads of Spanish politics and economy overrode any idea of disengaging him from the outstanding projects, while even at the height of the press campaign in the later summer and autumn of 1927 he had been on visits to Spain[56] and was involved in attempting to set up the joint air-traffic monopoly, an anti-aircraft system for the Spanish military and plans for the manufacture of sea mines and depth charges.[57]

At the end of the year the Marineleitung arranged for Canaris to visit Spain for several months after Baron del Sacro-Lirio considered making him a 'quasi-official naval attaché'. This was unusual, for Germany had had no military attachés abroad since the end of the war, but Sacro-Lirio himself was hoping to acquire the position of naval attaché in Berlin.[58] The Foreign Ministry had not decided on the military attaché question despite pressure from the Marineleitung to appoint naval attachés to London, Paris, Rome and Madrid.[59]

In Madrid, Ambassador Welczeck was opposed to 'any quasi-official or even official appearance of Kapitän zur See Canaris';[60] support for Canaris from the embassy was limited exclusively to economic and not military matters. Baron del Sacro-Lirio had been imprudent enough to inform the ambassador of the necessity to have Canaris come to Spain to found a secret military mission but Welczeck was uncertain whether the king's chamberlain wanted to make himself appear important or knowingly compromise the embassy by 'letting it in on the secret', but in any case Welczeck considered the idea 'derailed'.[61]

Canaris arrived again in 1928 and spent most of his time in negotiations about the lagging torpedo, submarine and tanker projects. Then the Spanish interior minister, General Severiano Martinez Anido, introduced him to the head of the Spanish security police,[62] who made Canaris aware of the joint treaty between Spain, Italy and France to combat Communist influence, a treaty to which it was hoped that Germany would also subscribe. Since ambassador Welczeck was in favour of it, Canaris and the Spanish police chief worked on a draft[63] binding the two countries to a mutual exchange of intelligence about those suspected of being 'devoted to the Cause', and provided Canaris with committal warrants for several persons implicated in a plot to murder dictator Primo de Rivera and the interior minister. He also drew Canaris's attention to certain Italians living in Argentina who liaised between Spanish and German Bolshevist activists.[64]

Early in 1928 Echevarrieta finally received from Alfonso XIII and the Spanish dictator the contract to build a 750-tonne submarine to a German design. Because Berlin had grown concerned whether the Spanish armaments industry was up to the job, Canaris was sent to Argentina in May 1928[65] to see if a stronger collaboration with Spain were possible. He had met the leader of the Argentine naval mission in 1927 while the latter was touring European shipyards[66] to study ship types and prices. Canaris brought the Argentine admiral, Echevarrieta and the Weser shipyard together,[67] but the hoped-for U-boat deal never materialised.[68]

Immediately after his return from South America, the first era of Canaris's secret missions came to an end. The Marineleitung wanted him out of the public spotlight and the Foreign Ministry probably shared their view. On 22 June 1928 Canaris was appointed first officer aboard the old battleship *Schlesien*. Chief of Staff Donner noted in his personal file: 'To avoid the creation of a legend, it is as well to mention that Canaris is not the kind of person who does things in the dark of his own volition, but is always careful to inform his superiors and the competent Reich office, and seeks their approval,'[69] but the Foreign Office did not quite see it the same way.[70] Donner recommended – since Canaris's name had often been 'mentioned in connection with operations of a discreet nature ... and recently in anti-military periodicals etc mostly with the addition of completely misleading links – that all proposals to involve him in special missions should be rejected out of hand, and he should only be used on routine naval duty'. It was best to hide him away from the public gaze; even his trip to South America had been noted by *Weltbühne*.[71]

In April 1928, the naval secret service, until then an independent office of the Marineleitung, was merged with the Army Abwehr section to form the new Abwehr section at the Reichswehr Ministry.[72] The German-Spanish journalist Dr Ritter von Goss reported on military affairs, while the secret links to the Spanish Navy remained the province of Canaris's agent Messerschmidt.[73] The same month a ministerial adviser to the Reichswehr Ministry returned to Berlin from a 'fact-finding mission' to Spain and reported doubts within German industrial circles in Spain as to the reliability of Echevarrieta and Canaris's other Spanish partners,[74] which von Goss set down in a letter shortly afterwards:[75] 'Canaris's trusted people were almost exclusively in circles ... whose German-ness had not always withstood trial by fire,' and who 'in the case of a call from the home country would hardly be likely to answer it, even if it were serious.' Goss was especially critical of Canaris for his alleged inability to conspire properly and keep secrets secret: 'Herr C. is an open book. He is rumoured to be a secretive personality, with a nod and a wink: you know, the naval man, looks for and has contacts, information, important man.'[76]

Canaris had surrounded himself with an assortment of people who were only interested in money. Echevarrieta especially was a thorn in Goss's side; he had used German financial help to pay off his debts and otherwise had achieved nothing.[77] The complaint was to no avail; Canaris's successor as Marineleitung chief of staff noted at the foot of the letter: 'The allegations received against C. contradict the facts. Not the merest shadow of an accusation falls on C.'[78]

After the SPD election victory of May 1928 and the departure of Gessler and Zenker, the wind at the Reichswehr Ministry changed. The new commander-in-chief, Vizeadmiral Erich Raeder, and the new Reichswehrminister, Groener, were opposed to using Canaris any further in Spain. Raeder particularly, long committed to Germany's second rise to being a naval power, had good reason to come to an accommodation with the Weimar system;[79] he needed to keep his distance from Canaris, particularly since, after taking office, he had been under fire for his role in the Kapp putsch.[80] When in May 1929 Echevarrieta and Sacro-Lirio begged the Marineleitung to return Canaris to Spain for fear that without him the negotiations would founder, Groener and Raeder remained firm. When ambassador Welczeck appealed for Canaris to spend a few months in Spain, a conflict developed between the Foreign Ministry and the Reichswehr Ministry, and Groener complained of Welczeck's attitude. Finally Groener had the last word – Canaris was under attack in Germany and sending him abroad was out of the question;[81] after that Groener was promoted to Fregattenkapitän with effect from 1 June 1929.[82] Having completed a thirty-month stint as first officer of *Schlesien*, Canaris was appointed chief of staff, Naval Station North Sea,[83] a post that he found gave him little joy. No. 1 Admiralty Staff Officer Karl Dönitz recalled: 'We used to say of him that he had several souls in his breast. And we were not wrong.'[84]

In 1931, Canaris's past caught up with him. Once again it was his role as judge in the Luxemburg–Liebknecht murder trial and the accusations of complicity in the escape of Vogel that brought him back into the public eye. In 1928, journalist Berthold Jacob had made revelations about the Reichswehr and the radical-right, and a State attorney had claimed that his writings were treasonous.[85] Jacob avenged himself with an anonymous article in the 24 March 1928 edition of the magazine *Das Tagebuch*, in which he accused Jorns of having perverted the course of justice in his inquiries into the murders of Luxemburg and Liebknecht, and assisting in the escape of Vogel. Jorns sued the editor of *Das Tagebuch*, Josef Bornstein, for defamation, but lost;[86] the case was reinstated on appeal.

Georg Löwenthal, Bornstein's defence lawyer, suspected that he was likely to lose the second trial. He called a fresh witness, Paul Bredereck, president of the National Union of German Officers, who testified that before the Luxemburg–Liebknecht murder trial, he had collected money from the officers'union to assist in the escape of the accused. Bredereck stated that he had passed on a portion of the money, the rest was to be forwarded to the escapees once abroad. He had often visited the principal defendant, Pflugk-Harttung in prison in company with the latter's sister. Here Bredereck's testimony became less sure; he stated that in the end he had given the money to Fräulein von Pflugk-Harttung and an escort. Attorney Löwenthal asked, 'Who was the escort?' Bredereck replied, 'Kapitänleutnant Canaris.' Löwenthal asked him if Canaris knew for whom the money was intended. Bredereck said yes, but that Jorns, on the other hand, was ignorant of it. Only the anonymous donors, the officers' union, Canaris and Bredereck had been informed.[87]

On the witness stand Canaris stated that the money was for the financial support of the Pflugk-Harttung family, which had fallen on hard times, but in a written statement for the Marineleitung he had another explanation, the deadly Communist threat to the accused and their families: 'Under these circumstances a sum of money had to be held available so that in the case of a Communist takeover of the country, they would have the chance to save themselves from the ruthless terror towards all political opponents which is openly a point of their programme.' A precaution of this kind in the interest of the personal security of the accused officers was not without precedent, he went on; Minister Erzberger as leader of the Armistice Commission had issued courier passports in assumed names for the same humane reasons.[88] This was not very convincing, even when Canaris emphasised that the proceedings had nothing to do with the trial or his being one of the trial judges. After talks with Canaris and the Marineleitung, Bredereck changed his story. Now he remembered that Canaris had not been present when the first amount was paid to the prisoners, but only when the second amount was paid. He added that he had never discussed the purpose of the money with Canaris; he had merely assumed that Canaris knew what it was for.[89] At last it was all perfectly clear, and the Reichswehr Ministry supported Canaris; with the approval of Reichswehrminister Noske, Canaris had paid over the money for the Pflugk-Harttung family so that they could leave Berlin.[90]

On 1 October 1931, Canaris was promoted Kapitän zur See.[91] The character assessment of 1 November was unsparing of the accustomed superlatives for this 'most talented officer' with 'pronounced leadership qualities' who could be 'warmly recommended for a position of command'.[92]

PART III

RISE UNDER THE SWASTIKA

11

Hitler's Military Intelligence Chief

The year 1932, the last year of the Weimar Republic, would be decisive for Germany's future. Five great electoral campaigns took place, keeping the population saturated with political propaganda, and heightening the political crisis.

The battle for the Reich presidency began in the spring; on 22 February, to the jubilation of thousands of supporters in the Berlin Sportspalast, Joseph Goebbels announced that Hitler was standing as a candidate. Under the motto 'The Führer over Germany', Hitler flew from city to city in a chartered aircraft, emulating the American example, addressing a million people from the hustings.[1] Before the provincial elections in Prussia, Bavaria, Württemberg and Saxony-Anhalt and the municipal elections in Hamburg, Hitler spoke across the entire Reich. Never had the electorate been exposed to such an electoral organisation. The effort was well rewarded. In Prussia, the NSDAP became the strongest party; in Bavaria it ran almost neck-and-neck with the Bavarian Volkspartei, and in Saxony the NSDAP had their first provincial minister-president. Goebbels recognised that the highpoint of the mobilisation had been reached, now the National Socialists had to seize power before they burnt themselves out electioneering.[2]

Immediately after the presidential election, Reich Chancellor Brüning and Reichswehrminister Groener, who was also acting as minister for the interior, convinced Hindenburg to order the dissolution of 'all paramilitary NSDAP organisations'. The 400,000-strong SA had kept up a violent presence in the election campaign, and the counter-reaction had worsened the crisis for the Brüning government. On 28 April, Hitler spoke secretly with Generalmajor Kurt von Schleicher, leader of the Wehrmacht section at the Reichswehr Ministry. Schleicher was opposed to the ban on the SA, which he considered a cadre organisation for an enlarged Reichswehr whose ultimate aim would be a military dictatorship created from the people.[3] He may have advised Hitler that Reich Chancellor Brüning no longer had the support of the Reichswehr leaders;[4] Schleicher was close to Graf von Helldorf, leader of the Berlin SA and later Berlin police chief.[5] On 8 May, Goebbels noted in his diary:

Brüning will probably fall within the next few days ... the Reichstag will be dissolved, all the prohibitions will be swept away, we will have freedom to agitate and then deliver a masterpiece of propaganda. When the SA marches again in its brown shirts, we will have overthrown the Depression, and the enemy will soon sink to the ground under our blows.[6]

Hitler had agreed to tolerate a right-wing Cabinet under Reich Chancellor Franz von Papen if he lifted the ban on the SA and guaranteed new elections.[7] Schleicher wanted to oust his superior, Reichswehrminister Groener, and in the Reichstag sitting of 10 May, Goering, presumably supplied by Schleicher with confidential information from the Reichswehr Ministry,[8] launched a violent barrage against Groener. Feverish and unwell, confronted by the double-pronged attack of Nazis and generals, Groener defended the ban on the SA but made a poor impression. Next day Schleicher, after canvassing support, advised Groener that the Reichswehr was no longer behind him; upon being so informed Groener stepped down and Schleicher became Reichswehrminister.[9] On 30 May 1932 Reich Chancellor Brüning resigned,[10] succeeded by Fritz von Papen. His 'Cabinet of barons' had no parliamentary majority and he was obliged to rule by decree, tolerating the NSDAP.[11] Goebbels wrote in his diary: 'The Reichstag will be dissolved. That is the most important thing of all. Von Papen is seen as Reich Chancellor, but that is now of no interest. Vote! Vote! To the people! We are all very happy.'[12]

Canaris had never been a friend of parliamentary democracy, but was he a friend of National Socialism? The few indications of how he felt about Hitlerism date from a period when the Nazi State had already become established.[13]

On 23 May 1932 Hitler visited Wilhelmshaven. The *Völkischer Beobachter* noted that 'thousands upon thousands' gathered on the open field in front of the Schützenhof assembly hall at Rüstringen, as it was filled to capacity, Hitler's speech was relayed by loudspeaker to those outside. Afterwards Hitler went aboard the light cruiser *Köln*; he was not a naval enthusiast, and neither naval rearmament nor naval politics had any priority with Hitler or the NSDAP.[17] His priority was a modern Luftwaffe, although he wanted it to be understood that his rejection of a Fleet was political and only temporary.[15] Hitler's visit aboard *Köln* probably resulted from Raeder's suggestion that he make known his intention to stand as candidate for Reich Chancellor.

To the officers of *Köln*, Hitler promised: '1. I will eliminate all treason. 2. I will expand the Fleet within the terms of the Versailles Treaty. 3. If I say that a ship displaces 10,000 tonnes, then it displaces 10,000 tonnes irrespective of how large it actually is.'[16] This declaration must have been very satisfying for the officers, signalling as it did that he was planning to abide by the number of ships allowed under the Versailles Treaty, but not the size. He wrote in the guest book: 'Hoping to assist in the rebuilding of a Fleet worthy of the Reich,'[17] but enthusiasm for the new 'Navy-friendly' Hitler did not last very long. In October he criticised the von Papen government harshly when it demanded capital ships, a call that in Hitler's eyes was likely to damage Anglo-German relations.[18]

Meanwhile, Canaris was serving aboard the old battleship *Schlesien* on which he had once been first officer[19] and of which he had been commander since 30 September 1932. In January 1933, *Schlesien* was made the flagship of Commanding Admiral Battleships, Konteradmiral Max Bastian. Canaris spent the last dramatic weeks of the Weimar democracy aboard his ship in Kiel Bay, where gunnery and torpedo practice preceded the entry of *Schlesien* into the Kiel yards for a refit. On 30 January 1933 Hindenburg appointed Hitler Reich Chancellor. Werner Best, senior Gestapo ideologist and later Heydrich's representative working closely with Canaris, wrote after the war: 'Undoubtedly Canaris stood on Third Reich ground out of conviction into the war and was – as were most naval officers – free of the doubts of certain other officer circles.'[20] And again: 'As an old nationalist, he was convinced that the new regime was far, far better than anything that had gone before, and that so far as he could see there was no other way.'[21] Conrad Patzig, Canaris's predecessor as Abwehr chief, made a statement to the effect that Canaris was recognised as an enthusiastic National Socialist.[22] Even if such judgements after the event are to be treated with some caution, they do nevertheless correspond to the official assessments. Thus the Commanding Admiral Battleships, Bastian, wrote in a report of 1 November 1934: 'I must emphasise the untiring striving of Kapitän zur See Canaris, through personal addresses, to acquaint the ship's complement with the ideas of the national Movement and the principles of how the new Reich will be restructured.'[23] Also noteworthy of Bastian's assessments of Canaris in 1933 and 1934 is that under the formula headings 'For Which Office Specially Suitable', after the first recommendation – 'Naval attaché' – he put 'Reichswehr Ministry (initally as section leader, Abwehr section).'[24] Canaris's superiors kept his special talents in mind and repeatedly recommended an appointment for him in the secret service.

During the early days of radical political and social change in Germany, Canaris commanded *Schlesien* in the major spring naval manoeuvres. On 22 and 23 May 1933 at Kiel, Hitler, Goering and the new Reichswehrminister Werner von Blomberg arrived to observe the exercises. Goering came aboard *Schlesien*, but he did not like ships and was seasick, and so, pale and drawn, he made his way to the wardroom, where a junior lieutenant made a flippant remark. At this Goering left and later made an official complaint to the Admiralty, asking that the young officer be punished, but since the latter had already been reprimanded officially by Canaris, there was no second punishment. This was supposed to be the reason for Goering's deep and abiding aversion for the Navy[25] although whether any of it really happened is not certain.

For *Schlesien* there followed more manoeuvres: in the North Sea, then Kiel Week, Fleet gunnery practice, and in the autumn of 1933 the 1906-built pre-Dreadnought, said to be held together by her paintwork, entered the yards for another overhaul. In 1934, after more rounds of independent and squadron manoeuvres, visits to Norway, Sweden and Heligoland, as well as a period on moorings at Kiel, Canaris's superiors were full of praise for his nautical prowess and for his skill in binding together ship, crew and particularly the officer corps. Frequent references were made to his introversion, mood swings and irritability, however, leading to recommendations in appraisals that he would be better suited to work in the military-political environment rather than a purely military command.

On 29 September 1934, Canaris was given command of the fortress at Swinemünde and responsibility for coastal defence in the Baltic,[26] but this was merely an intermission, for three months later he was appointed to head the Abwehr section at the Reichswehr Ministry. It was the last segment of his career, and led to the gallows, but it also made Canaris a legend.

Upon taking up the post at Swinemünde, he was forty-seven years of age. In the literature this appointment to the Baltic fortress has been identified as the end point of his career, a banishment to the provinces, because the Admiralty, and above all the commander-in-chief, Admiral Raeder, had no better idea of what to do with the politically compromised officer.[27] Yet, in view of the overall outstanding assessments, the recurrent favourable comments on his political abilities and his nationalist past, none of which would have been disadvantageous for him under Nazism, this interpretation seems questionable. In particular the references to Admiral Raeder's personal dislike of Canaris are extremely vague and originate principally from Conrad Patzig, Canaris's predecessor as Abwehr head.[28] When one recalls that as early as 1933 Canaris had been suggested by Bastian, his flag admiral, as a candidate to head the Abwehr, it seems likely that he was 'parked' at Swinemünde until the opportunity arose for him to return to Berlin. A letter from Raeder to Canaris dated 11 October 1934, six weeks after his being drafted to Swinemünde, appears to confirm this:

> Dear Canaris, I would like to inform you as early as possible of an impending change in your service circumstances since it will soon involve your relocation. It has always been my intention to place you in the position of Abwehr head when that became possible. Unfortunately the circumstances for this were not clear before 1 October, but now they have developed in such a way that a change of head during the winter half-year, probably around 1 January, has been authorised by the minister. The minister has approved my suggestion that you should take

over the position ... I ask you to consider this information as confidential. In the hope that the new position will correspond fully to your desires, I am, with a comradely greeting, your faithful Raeder.[29]

The confidential tone of the letter does not lead one to conclude – contrary to what Conrad Patzig maintained – that there was a deeply rooted aversion between Canaris and Raeder.[30] In 1928 on the orders of Reichswehrminister Groener, the Abwehr group at Army High Command and the naval intelligence offices were transferred to the Abwehr section at the Reichswehr Ministry and consolidated into a single unit under Groener's personal control. This arrangement provoked a storm of controversy, particularly from naval quarters, but in vain. More restructuring took place in 1929 when the Wehrmacht office at the Reichswehr Ministry was replaced by a ministerial office headed by Generalmajor Schleicher, now state secretary, and the Abwehr was accordingly directly responsible to him.

Oberst Ferdinand von Bredow was appointed to head the Abwehr, but the friction between the Army and Navy groups persisted, and finally Raeder installed Fregattenkapitän Patzig to head the naval group.[31] He had no training in intelligence work and was appointed simply to give the Navy more weight in the Abwehr.[32] In June 1932, Schleicher became Reichswehrminister in the von Papen Cabinet and Patzig, an absolute novice,[33] was made Abwehr head. He succeeded in overcoming the opposition of the General Staff – which since 1870 had considered intelligence work its exclusive prerogative – and also in transforming the Abwehr from an internal political instrument of the Reichswehr Ministry into a truly military and therefore a political intelligence service with a foreign orientation.[34]

Following Hitler's seizure of power, there was no immediate change at the head of the Abwehr. Earlier, Reich President Hindenburg had elevated the head of the German military delegation at the Geneva International Disarmament Conference, Generaloberst Werner von Blomberg, as the new Reichswehrminister; the National Socialists had had nothing to do with this decision but probably welcomed it, for Blomberg was a long-term Nazi sympathiser. He assured Hitler of his unconditional loyalty at the first Cabinet session on 30 January 1933 and agreed that the Reichswehr would hold training courses for the SA and salute all uniformed NSDAP members (assimilated to officers) and their banners. Soldiers in civilian clothes were to salute by use of the word 'Heil' and on their uniforms they would wear the stylised eagle and Nazi swastika. Blomberg strove from the beginning for a clear cooperation between regime and fighting forces with the aim of elevating the Wehrmacht to a truly national body with the help of the German people.[35]

In this he received the support of his former chief of Staff in East Prussia, Oberst Walther von Reichenau, one of the first and most capable officers to sympathise with National Socialism, and he exercised an intellectual influence on Blomberg from the outset. At the beginning of 1932, Reichenau took over the ministerial office at the Reichswehr Ministry. Blomberg, naive, prone to spontaneous outbursts of enthusiasm, and Reichenau, intelligent, ambitious, a man who despised 'class-conscious aristocratic and bourgeois conservatism', now angled the Wehrmacht along the path of National Socialism. Reichenau's catch-phrase was: 'Our way is ahead, which means therefore into the new State and there maintain our rightful position!'[36]

At first Patzig remained head of the Abwehr. His authority was increased after Hitler took power and in the course of the rearmament programme he expanded the Abwehr structurally and increased staffing levels. In every active corps and Wehrkreis (military administration district) an Abwehr centre was set up, designated officially Ic/AO.[37] Patzig noticed the efforts of the party to undermine the Reichswehr monopoly of intelligence operations by the creation of its own organisations; the Foreign Office, the NSDAP Overseas Organisation, the SD under Heydrich and Goering's monitoring service, the so-called Research Bureau, all began to compete with the Abwehr, a situation in which, in Patzig's view, discretion was lost, confusion reigned and amateurism triumphed. Patzig approached Blomberg to obtain from Hitler an order making the military Abwehr the only legitimate intelligence service of the Reich, but Blomberg refused Patzig his support.[38]

Ernst Röhm, whose SA numbered 4.5 million men in 1934, saw the organisation as the 'spearhead' of the revolution and party. It was 'the support column for the coming National Socialist State' and stood 'side by side with the armed forces, not as a part of them', being an independent 'third power factor of the State' alongside the Reichswehr and police.[39] Perceiving the revolution to be in danger, he declared that the SA and SS would not allow themselves to be betrayed 'at the halfway house of being non-combatants'. In the course of 1933 the difficulties came to a head[40] and at the beginning of 1934 Hitler found it necessary to consider action against his 'over-powerful subordinates'.[41]

In the spring the SA had bought weapons, mainly in Danzig, and had them sent to Munich. Patzig notified Army High Command, which dithered,[42] while Heydrich informed the party security service, the SD. On 26 June 1934 a forged document of unknown provenance appeared on Patzig's desk; it purported to be an order signed by Röhm,[43] instructing all SA groups to arm urgently. Patzig passed the paper to Reichenau, who told Blomberg: 'Now the time is ripe;'[44] the next day Hitler had the 'proof' of the SA plot to revolt.

On Hitler's orders, between 30 June and 2 July 1934 Heydrich's SD carried out the 'Röhm putsch', which claimed up to two hundred victims, including Röhm, Schleicher, Patzig's predecessor von Bredow and other leading SA figures. On 1 July Blomberg congratulated Hitler on his 'soldierly determination', the Wehrmacht giving thanks 'through devotion and loyalty'.[45] The allegation[46] that Blomberg demanded that Himmler sack Heydrich for his part in the 'Night of the Long Knives' therefore seems improbable;[47] Patzig could recall nothing of the sort.[48]

Army Commander-in-Chief Generaloberst von Fritsch had nothing against Patzig but the SS wanted Patzig replaced, and Blomberg obliged them,[49] using as an excuse Blomberg's discovery that the Abwehr had given orders for high-altitude reconnaissance photographs to be taken of the Maginot Line without informing him. The Reichswehrminister felt that Patzig had gone over his head, so to speak, and saw in that a disregard for the wishes of the Führer. Blomberg summoned Patzig and received him with the words: 'I cannot use an Abwehr chief guilty of such escapades.'[50] Although Fritsch accepted responsibility and stated that he had actually ordered the reconnaissance himself, Blomberg had made up his mind and Patzig was relieved of office on 31 December 1934. In a letter written in 1953, Patzig asserted that at the termination of the interview with Blomberg, he had urged the Reichswehrminister 'to act today against the crimes of the party organisations and the SS';[51] the SS was 'a sink of uprooted entities and criminals who would not shrink back from anything, including murder'. Blomberg retorted that the SS was 'one of the Führer's organisations', and that he saw the future with great optimism.[52]

According to Patzig, it was he who suggested to Raeder that Canaris should succeed him as Abwehr head to prevent control of the Abwehr devolving to the Army General Staff, and on 12 December Canaris was ordered to Berlin to 'learn the ropes' at the Tirpitzufer offices.[53] Patzig claimed to have warned him that: 'I attempted to play all the strings of the violin but ... the SS is a law unto itself and will not hold back from murder if necessary.' He hoped that Canaris would succeed in combating the excesses and not become 'a traitor to the Wehrmacht'. 'Today may be the beginning of your personal end,' Patzig concluded, to which Canaris said only: 'You can rest assured, I will soon see these boys off.'[54]

12

The Duel with Heydrich

On 3 January 1934 Hitler summoned the heads of party and Wehrmacht to the State Opera House in Unter den Linden[1] for a meeting behind closed doors, aimed at restoring the shattered faith of many senior officers in the Wehrmacht leadership.[2] As new Abwehr head, Canaris sat in third row behind Hitler's adjutant Friedrich Hossbach. Hitler spoke of the 'two equally important columns' of party and Wehrmacht, emphasising his 'immovable will' that 'a strong Wehrmacht should lead Germany to new world importance and national security', which demanded 'unshakeable unity';[3] he appealed to party leaders for their loyalty and devotion, for only then could he rebuild Germany. The military men were impressed, and at the end of his speech Hitler received deafening applause.[4]

Army Commander-in-Chief von Fritsch, who had recently complained to Patzig of a Gestapo slander campaign against himself, wrote three years later: 'The Führer delivered an address that was a unique appeal for the loyalty of the Army and its leader, myself.[5] General Kurt Liebmann reported to his commanders: 'Probably nobody who was present will have been able to shake off the impression . . . that a trust is being placed in us which no man of honour can mistake.'[6] The Wehrmacht heads of service described the event as 'a glorious success', as Hitler's adjutant Hossbach later observed.[7]

Ten days later, Blomberg invited Canaris to a social evening at the Kaiser Wilhelm Academy where Reichsführer-SS Himmler, whom Canaris had met at Kiel in 1932/33, spoke on the tasks of the SS.[8] Afterwards, at Blomberg's suggestion, Canaris discussed with Himmler the future cooperation and division of work between the Abwehr, Gestapo and SD; the problem of competition between the various 'intelligence services', which plagued Canaris to the end of his career, was anchored structurally in the new regime.

The totalitarianism of Nazism manifested itself especially in the expansion of the police apparatus. In Nazi ideology, the police would protect the 'body of the Volk' (Volk as opposed to the inhabitants of Germany as a whole) against the 'arch enemy', 'parasites', 'offenders against moral decency' and later also 'asocials' who placed themselves beyond 'the community of the Volk'. The Reich saw itself in a permanent state of emergency, and the fight against its enemies extended beyond legal frontiers. This general empowerment was transferred to the police.

The police 'chief ideologist' was SD lawyer Werner Best. From late summer 1934 he had been employed in the Secret Prussian State Police and was also organisational head of the Party SD and SD Senior Section leader South and South West. On 1 January 1935 in Berlin he took over Hauptabteilung I (Law, Personnel, Administration) of the Gestapo bureaux (Gestapa). Head of Gestapa and Hauptabteilung II (Political Police) was Reinhard Heydrich. The initially insignificant Hauptabteilung III (Police Abwehr) was run by SD official Günther Patschowsky. Himmler presided over it all as inspector of Gestapo. Although, as Prussian minister-president, Goering was technically Himmler's superior, Goering had relinquished practically all authority to Himmler. Best, as Heydrich's deputy, was the third most important man in the Gestapo and held a key position 'as organiser, head of personnel, arbiter and Gestapo ideologist'.[9]

Hitler's edict for the 'Combination of all police under the Reichsführer-SS' in October 1935, and the appointment of Himmler as 'Reichsführer-SS and the head of the German Police' in June 1936 led inevitably to demarcation and difficulties between the political police and the military Abwehr, especially since the political police also had an Abwehr division whose main concern was internal dissent.[10]

The rivalry between Hauptabteilung III (Police Abwehr) under Patschowsky, and Patzig (Military Abwehr) resulted in Patzig's departure and the appointment of Canaris.[11] The first conference between the Gestapa and Military Abwehr was held at the Reichswehr Ministry on 17 January 1935. Canaris and General Staff Officer Rudolf Bamler, an NSDAP member in charge of Abwehrgruppe III (Counter-Espionage), represented Abwehr; Heydrich, Best and Patschowsky represented the Gestapa; and Jost the SD.

By a Reich Government decision of 17 October 1933, 'the Reichswehrminister will take all measures necessary for the protection of national security and military-political interests in Abwehr and propaganda. He will draw up the guidelines by which the Reich jurisdictions and provincial authorities concerned will be bound',[12] and at the January 1935 conference, Canaris and Heydrich signed an agreement defining the respective Gestapa and Abwehr spheres of competence. The 'Duties of the Wehrmacht' were:

1. Military espionage and counter-espionage.
2. Intelligence operations within the Reichswehr and its wholly owned enterprises.
3. Supervision and imposition of all anti-espionage regulations.

4. Control and vetting of all new officers admitted to the Wehrmacht.
5. Administration and directives in all cases affecting internal defence.
All Gestapo and SD officers . . . including frontier police posts are duty bound to
the closest cooperation with the competent Abwehr offices.

The Gestapo was responsible for all 'Duties of the political police, the only competent bureau for the executive, resistance to all enemies of the State, and the duties of frontier police and the frontier intelligence service, the anti-espionage police and Abwehr Intelligence Service within the Reich borders'. The competence of the SD, as well as internal political duties, consisted of 'cooperation with intelligence work'. Canaris for the Abwehr and Heydrich for Gestapo and SD were to hold the sole monopoly for all future intelligence activities: 'Other non-official intelligence services will not be recognised and will be suppressed by all available means.'[13]

Canaris had secured for the Abwehr undisputed sole jurisdiction for military intelligence and had imposed on all others the obligation to cooperate. The phrase 'responsible for resistance to all enemies of the State' could be interpreted very generously by the Gestapo, however.

Canaris and Heydrich met frequently thereafter; the 17 January conference was probably their first meeting for eleven years.[14] By coincidence they lived in the same south Berlin street – Canaris's family with two small daughters at Doellestrasse 48, the Heydrichs at No. 34,[15] and the personal relationship between Canaris and Heydrich was 'utterly correct, outwardly almost friendly'.[16] But within the regime they were rivals, different in character, but both adept in conspiracy and falsehood, and thus below the apparent friendship there lurked suspicion. SS lawyer Walter Huppenkothen recalled Heydrich's description of Canaris as 'the old fox one must be careful of'. Later, Huppenkothen, who read Canaris's diaries in 1944, stated that after his first official meeting with Heydrich, Canaris had emphasised that 'it would probably be hardly possible to work together with Heydrich because he is a brutal fanatic'.[17] Heydrich made the effort to keep the agreement and warned his subordinate officers to heed the wording strictly and cooperate with the Abwehr, and sacked his own Abwehr chief, Patschowsky, so as not to prejudice the accord.

Best took over as commissar of the Police Abwehr. Until the end of 1939 he was the 'civilian counterpart to Canaris'[18] and one of his most important conversation partners outside the Abwehr. There were times when they met daily to exchange political and organisational views; they took morning horseback rides in the Grunewald and Canaris became the most frequent visitor to the Best household.[19] Best wrote that, 'In serious matters', he had 'rarely known a negotiator who was more open-handed in his dealings and kept his promises more honourably than Canaris; in service he was completely the correct officer whose word was his bond. Moreover I got to know and value him as an utterly honourable, well-intentioned and morally sensitive character.'[20] Best was more critical of the relationship between Canaris and Heydrich; the latter, who had been discharged from the Navy in 1931 as being 'unworthy to be an officer', apparently held a grudge against the Navy henceforth.[21] During their service travels together Canaris and Heydrich would reassure each other of their fullest possible mutual agreement and honest collaboration.[22]

The Reichswehr leaders were engaged with the question of rearmament; for political and diplomatic reasons the subject had been kept on hold in recent months to avoid prejudice to the forthcoming plebiscite to return the Saar to the Reich. The previous November the Geneva Rearmament Conference had been adjourned because Germany wanted the result of the plebiscite before considering any further international armaments treaties. On 13 January 1935 the Saar electorate voted overwhelmingly for reunification into the Reich and the Reichswehr leaders determined to capitalise on this as a reason for rearmament.[23] On 6 March General Ludwig Beck, head of the Army Office, set out 'the least demands for an armaments treaty' in a memorandum:[24] the peacetime Army of 300,000 men in twenty-one divisions of December 1933 had now risen to twenty-three and would be sixty-three by the outbreak of war. He also wanted the return of the demilitarised zones either side of the Rhine, the lifting of the ban on mobilisation exercises and the recognition of Germany's right to determine for itself the size of the Reichswehr and questions of organisation, conscription, length of service and armaments. In the previous year, foreign powers had 'rearmed to the greatest degree' and thereby created a completely new situation for Germany.[25] The potential threat came from 'France, Czechoslovakia, Belgium and Poland' (despite the Non-Aggression Pact signed with Poland the previous year). The neutrality of the other nations bordering Germany could probably be accepted, while the immediate danger from less amicably inclined powers of Europe – Russia, Italy and Britain – was less likely and therefore could be left out of the considerations.[26] The goal of German rearmament was 'to secure our living space'. That the act of unilateral German rearmament might itself represent a danger to security was not considered.[27] Beck explained to Army Commander-in-Chief Fritsch in a letter a few days later that the twenty-three divisions were an interim solution for three or four years only, by which time the strength of the peacetime Army would have grown to thirty-six divisions. Blomberg and Fritsch both saw the foreign policy dangers of rearming too quickly,[28] but the Reich policymakers were adamant, with regard to foreign policy, that a conscripted Army was to be the rule by the summer of 1935.

Hitler himself determined the tempo. On 7 March the British Foreign Minister Sir John Simon and the Lord Privy Seal Anthony Eden had been expected to visit Berlin but Hitler, irritated at the British Government's statement that it was increasing military spending, cancelled the meeting.[29] On 10 March Goering announced the abrogation of the Versailles Treaty by Germany and the existence of the Luftwaffe. France and Belgium had meanwhile renewed their mutual military agreement and five days after Goering's announcement France extended the period of military conscription.

The following day Hitler told his Wehrmacht adjutant Hossbach that he had decided to introduce conscription and draft a legal framework for the Army.[30] When asked for his opinion on how large he thought the new Army should be, Hossbach gave a figure of 400,000, which Hitler accepted immediately. At Hossbach's urging, Hitler informed Blomberg and Fritsch, who both told him that his decision was irresponsible at the present time, although the Foreign Ministry did not oppose him,[31] and by the Cabinet meeting next day Blomberg and Fritsch were also in favour, Blomberg praising the Führer and swearing 'unbreakable loyalty'.[32]

On 16 March, when foreign diplomats were notified of the framework, their reactions were varied; only the United Kingdom made an official protest, and even this was accompanied by an enquiry as to whether Hitler was still interested in meeting Simon and Eden. After Hitler informed the German public, the newspapers printed special editions claiming that 'the shame of defeat' had been expunged and Germany's military reputation restored, giving rise to cheering crowds assembling before the Reich Chancellery.[33] On 25 March, when the talks with the two British politicians were held in Berlin, the British showed their willingness to meet Hitler halfway, even if this impinged on their solidarity with France; the international front against Germany began to crumble and this was the point where 'the policy of appeasement' began.[34]

At an international conference on 11 April 1935 at Stresa on Lake Maggiore, Britain, France and Italy confirmed the 1925 Locarno Treaty guaranteeing the frontiers of western Germany and the independence of Austria. Before the conference, Canaris wrote to Abwehrstellen that it was 'especially important to establish what, if any, military preparations were in hand in neighbouring states'. In the run-up to the conference, they should get their informers' reports in early and keep enough people ready for timely deployment. 'Times of foreign policy tension are a trial for the intelligence service, its organs and utility. I expect all Abwehr members to use their talents to the full for the good of the Fatherland.'[35]

Canaris himself visited the Hungarian intelligence service in Budapest with which Germany had been cooperating for fourteen years. The political mood 'was enthusiastic, and they admire our advances in military-political questions and rearmament' but doubted that 'we would fight together in a future war'.[36] As regards the international situation in Europe, 'Hungary cannot be expected to make a clear decision for or against Germany. Such a small country, surrounded by dangerous enemies, must pursue caution. If their statesmen can work out something with Italy is uncertain but possible.'

The search for allies was difficult in view of the various international constellations, and Canaris realised the need for great circumspection when approaching the intelligence communities of potential allies. Budapest had admitted to exchanging information with Rome, and Canaris began his quest by seeing Colonel Mario Roatta, head of Italian military intelligence.[37]

During his travels to inspect Abwehrstellen inside the Reich to determine the state of the organisation and its efficiency, Canaris saw that the apparatus was poorly equipped and that the network of agents at home and abroad needed to be made more comprehensive;[38] he was especially interested in Gruppe III (Counter-Espionage). The reintroduction of general conscription was bound to result in increased foreign espionage against the Wehrmacht and German industry, particularly in the field of armaments. Canaris needed the Gruppe III network 'at all levels of society' and 'on the broadest basis',[39] but did not want to use Gestapo people.[40] He and Bamler recommended that people with access to secret information should be subjected to closer controls – briefcases searched on leaving work, socialising reduced to a minimum 'since it can lead to treasonous acts',[41] private telephone lines tapped. Thus the Abwehr began a process of constant expansion. Best wrote: 'By the way he built up the apparatus, Canaris proved that – contrary to legend – he was just a typical German officer who organised everything along military lines. The Abwehr became a gigantic State apparatus that employed more clerks than agents.'[42] Best's colleague Karl Schäfer thought that the Abwehr 'swelled up overnight',[43] and Heydrich expanded the SD proportionately, which Best considered must lead eventually to jurisdiction disputes with the Abwehr, but in comparison with the Gestapo (in 1934 600 officials plus 2,000 in Prussian State Police offices[44]) the SD was small, having only 201 members that year and 269 in 1936, few of them salaried. The tally of informers was probably no more than a thousand in 1935.[45]

There was an Abwehrstelle for each of fifteen Wehrkreise by mid-1937 plus non-territorial sub-stations in the frontier regions, each staffed by two to four officers. By the end of 1937 the Abwehr employed 327 officers, officials and clerks in Berlin, and 629 elsewhere. Counter-espionage head Bamler urged more non-Reich sub-stations as 'very urgent'[46] and Canaris created Sub-Gruppe IIIF under Richard Protze with the purpose of infiltrating opposing intelligence services, identifying their agents and disseminating false information.[47] Abwehrstellen outside a Wehrkreis had to recruit agents from within the nearest Wehrkreis unless authorised otherwise by Abwehr headquarters. The 'Hauskapelle' (house orchestra) system was set up for this purpose: each house was headed by a leader, often a retired police official, with a senior agent (Kapellmeister) and three to six agents. They had always to be near a telephone, be permanently mobile and available for 'special assignments' such as shadowing suspected persons, establishing identities and hunting down suitable future agents. Hotel porters, receptionists and auditors were often agents of the Hauskapelle, and their main task was to be aware of guests who might be potential recruits.[48]

In 1936 Himmler had set up two police central headquarters: Hauptamt Ordnungspolizei (general uniformed police) under Kurt Daluege, and Hauptamt Sicherheitspolizei (SS security police) under Heydrich; the SS now controlled the entire German police corps.[49] Best wrote: 'After the SD began its amateurish foreign work, it often rubbed up against the military Abwehr, particularly counter-espionage, while exploring for intelligence services.' When Canaris protested at this 'infringement', Heydrich disputed the right of the Abwehr to handle foreign political intelligence, for which he claimed the monopoly. His actual aim was to take over counter-espionage and usurp the Abwehr completely.[50]

Canaris refused to close down the Hauskapellen, but agreed to discuss counter-espionage. On 19 October 1936 Best stated: 'Active espionage was exclusively the preserve of the military. Agreement was also reached about counter-espionage, where the Gestapo remained subordinate.'[51] On 21 December, Best and Canaris signed the 'Principles for Cooperation Between the Gestapo and the Wehrmacht Abwehr Office', which became known as 'The Ten Commandments'.[52]

Gerhard Heinkel criticised his chief Canaris for always being prepared to go too far in search of a compromise, although later he corrected his opinion about the 'Ten Commandments',[53] while Best's colleague Schäfer saw it as 'a severe setback for the police ... the Police Abwehr is practically under the control of the military Abwehr. In a conflict of jurisdiction between a State police office and an Abwehr office, the State police office could not call on Gestapa support.'[54]

It was an Abwehr victory. Best had not wanted to sour the close relationship with Canaris and the Wehrmacht High Command(OKW). 'The position of the Wehrmacht within the National Socialist regime was so strong and autonomous at the time that for the Sipo to be recognised as an equal negotiating partner was a success even if here it had to take a back seat.'[55] Best reported:

Canaris met my trust with trust. He allowed me an extensive look inside his organisation and its work. He invited me to meetings, introduced me to heads of Abwehrstellen, all of which I visited eventually. I did the same within the framework of the Police Abwehr: I invited Canaris and his section leaders to my meetings and ensured a friendly relationship[56]

Best brought together Heydrich and Canaris horse-riding at the Berlin Zoo so that service matters could be discussed in a relaxed atmosphere,[57] but the truce could not last for ever.

13

Between Führer, Duce and Caudillo

Canaris and his Meldedienst (secret reports service) had their first major foreign policy test in the spring of 1936. On 7 March Hitler broadcast to the nation from the Berlin Kroll Opera House before the Reichstag deputies. He drew attention to the French–Russian mutual assistance treaty that had rendered the Locarno Treaty meaningless: 'Germany therefore sees herself no longer bound by this defunct pact . . . by the primitive right of a people to secure its frontiers and defend itself, the German Government as from today has restored the full and unconditional sovereignty of the Reich in the demilitarised zone of the Rhineland.'[1]

The deputies sprang to their feet, shouts of 'Heil' rang through the hall. The American journalist William Shirer wrote: 'Their hands are extended in the slavish salute, their faces etched with hysteria, their mouths wide open and shouting, their eyes, burning with fanaticism, staring towards the new god, the Messiah. The Messiah plays his role superbly.'[2] At about the same time, German troops, accompanied by two planeloads of selected journalists, reached the Hohenzollern Bridge in Cologne to be received with great emotion, women throwing flowers, priests blessing them. After three years, Hitler declared, the struggle for German equality and rights could now be considered won.

Hitler's abrogation of the treaties of Locarno and Versailles was the most serious provocation yet for the Western democracies. It made no difference to his wide-ranging proposals 'to secure peace in Europe' – including Germany's readmission to the League of Nations – because he knew that they were unacceptable,[3] but whether the West would merely look on while this revolution in the European foreign policy and treaty situation proceeded was less certain.[4]

The decisive discussions had taken place in late February between Foreign Minister Neurath, Blomberg, Fritsch, Ribbentrop, Goering and Ulrich von Hassell, ambassador to Rome. Mussolini had indicated in January that he would not object to Austria becoming a German satellite; his invasion of Abyssinia had destroyed the Stresa front and the fact that he had only been punished by economic sanctions and a League of Nations resolution convinced Hitler that neither Britain nor France was interested in military intervention. Mussolini had told von Hassell that if there were further sanctions he would leave the League of Nations and tear up the Locarno Treaty, and in any case he would not support Britain and France against Hitler if Germany reacted to the French–Soviet pact. That was the go-ahead to march into the Rhineland, and from France itself came the signal that its ministers and Army were opposed to unilateral action there.[5] In London, Foreign Minister Eden stated that since the demilitarised zone had been created for the security of Belgium and France, it was up to them to maintain it;[6] Hitler knew therefore that in re-occupying the Rhineland he was running no great risk. Nevertheless, between December 1935 and March 1936 Canaris probably visited Hitler at the Reich Chancellery on seventeen occasions[7] while a former Abwehr official stated that Gruppe I (Espionage) officers had been active on the left bank of the Rhine since 1935; they were to report from Trier to Generalkommando XI Kassel Abwehrstelle on the French military response, if any, to the re-occupation.[8]

On 13 March when a telegram from the London military attaché reached Berlin, advising of a worsening of the situation, Blomberg panicked and asked Hitler to pull troops out of Aachen, Trier and Saarbrücken, but Goering had already informed Hitler of the attaché's report[9] and criticised Blomberg for his lack of nerve. Blomberg than advised the attaché that in difficult situations 'it was important for people to keep their nerve'[10] while General Beck, chief of the General Staff, wrote to the military attaché, Geyr von Schweppenburg: 'My personal opinion is that it was not you who lost his nerve, but quite different people.'[11]

Canaris took a dim view of von Schweppenburg's intervention in the Rhineland situation[12] because the attaché considered all espionage activity discreditable and had warned Canaris not to ask him to make auxiliary services available. That Schweppenburg had been admonished by Blomberg but supported by Beck highlighted the rivalry between the Reichswehrminister and the Army General Staff. In 1934 Beck had succeeded in having the military attachés transferred from the jurisdiction of the ministerial office to the Army office, a forerunner of the General Staff.[13] If the attachés were now supplying the General Staff directly with intelligence reports and assessments, it could only damage further the fragile relationship between the 'Foreign Armies' section at General Staff and the Abwehr.

Beck had had for some time his own channels for foreign political information[14] from Britain, Italy and its colonies, and Belgrade, where he encouraged the military attaché Moritz Faber du Faur to run a critical eye over Canaris's analyses.[15] Du Faur appreciated that the warnings of the military attachés were not welcome at the Reich Chancellery: 'Hitler did not want us, he wanted only Ribbentrop and Canaris, and began to want Himmler, and they silenced a military attaché from the outset.'[16.]

On 17 July 1936 Canaris was as surprised as anybody else by the revolt of the Spanish generals against the far-left People's Front government elected the previous February; the leader of the insurrection was former Chief of the General Staff Francisco Franco y Bahamonde,[17] who had been thought to be no danger in the Canary Islands. Despite the legends there is no evidence that Germany was in any way involved.

Richard Claassen, a long-term agent at Cadiz, and Gustav Draeger, German consul at Seville, were both out of Spain at the time; agent 'Bremen' at Barcelona had prior knowledge but the coup had begun before he transmitted his report to Berlin.[18] Canaris was then engaged in reinforcing 'operational measures' and enlarging the Abwehr base in Europe, Scandinavia and South America, and had no special plans for Spain,[19] although in 1935 the Gestapo had signed the international secret protocol against Communist infiltration based on the 1928 police treaty to trade information referred by Canaris.

After the People's Front took power, the Gestapo and SS obtained permission from the Foreign Ministry to place an agent in the Madrid embassy to monitor leftist activities. In May 1936 SS/SD Oberinspektor Paul Winzer started work in Madrid but was surprised by the generals' revolt even though the visit of General Sanjurjo to Berlin in the spring to buy weapons for an uprising had been reported in the Moscow newspaper *Pravda*.[20] No documents can be found to suggest Canaris as an intermediary,[21] and although in July 1936 rumours reached the Foreign Ministry regarding negotiations between Spanish conspirators and a German arms dealer, Josef Veltjens, to deliver weapons to the Falange by U-boat, Canaris's name was not mentioned.[22] The secret statistics of the Export Association for War Equipment (AFK) indicate the sale of only 150 light machine guns as at July 1934.[23]

Sanjurjo was killed in an air crash on 20 July 1936, and General Mola became the liaison officer to Germany. On 22 July the German military attaché, Kühlenthal, received a telegram from General Franco, in Spanish Morocco from where he was running the government,[24] requesting 'completely secretly' and 'very urgently' the supply of ten aircraft for ferrying troops, to be flown to Spanish Morocco by German personnel.[25]

On 24 July, when General Mola asked Berlin if the Reich would supply aeronautical material to a Nationalist counter-revolutionary government in Burgos,[26] Berlin already had firm indications that the French Government was planning to deliver bombers, bombs and field guns to the Republican government in Madrid.[27]

The following day, an aircraft arrived at Berlin-Tempelhof from Tetuan in Spanish Morocco. Two members of the NSDAP Overseas Branch, Adolf P Langenheim and Johannes E F Bernhardt,[28] alighted with Franco's envoy Capitan Francisco Arranz;[29] the envoy carried Franco's report for Hitler. No State department would receive Arranz, but eventually Rudolf Hess, acting for the NSDAP Overseas organisation, arranged for the delegation to meet Hitler at the Bayreuth Music Festival[30] where he accepted the document.[31]

A report from the Madrid embassy had warned of the danger of a Spanish Soviet if Republican Spain joined the French–Soviet bloc, and that German interests would be prejudiced if the Republic won a civil war.[32] It is not certain that Canaris was at Bayreuth at the time although Gauleiter Bouhle, head of NSDAP Overseas, mentioned 'an admiral' being there,[33] and Wolfgang Kraneck, head of NSDAP Overseas legal department, told his deputy that the possibility of shipping German war materials to Morocco by sea had been discussed, which has led to the assumption that Canaris was the anonymous admiral.[34] Hitler supplied Franco with twenty Ju 52 transport aircraft and six Heinkel biplane fighters, with the proviso that they were not to be used in hostilities unless attacked first. The aircraft flew to Spanish Morocco and then Cadiz, which was held by Franco,[35] enabling him to receive troops for the Falangists.[36]

Canaris had a network of agents in place, set up in the Echevarrieta epoch in the late 1920s. One of these, Kapitän Lietzmann, had unofficial links to the Spanish Nationalists and sent information about French weapons deliveries for the Republicans; the reports were sent by courier to Berlin.[37] Even the flow of information between General Mola, operating in the north of Spain, and General Franco, commanding the troops in the south, passed to some extent through Franco's Berlin contact. Full details became more important as the civil war became of greater importance in Europe.[38]

In mid-August 1936, Canaris received a report that the leftist French Government was sending volunteers into Spain to support the Republicans: '100 to 170 men daily, total 30,000, mostly trained reservists'.[39] Germany and Italy now decided to collaborate in support of the Nationalists. This was the beginning of the Berlin–Rome Axis that Mussolini announced on 1 November 1936. Franco was already being unofficially supplied by Italy, which the Germans learned only on 30 July when Hitler sent Canaris to Rome a few days after two Italian aircraft destined for Franco crashed in French North Africa. His mission was to discuss with General Roatta, head of Italian military intelligence, how to share the cooperation with Franco.

In mid-August OKM complained: 'At the moment, we are the only ones reaping the hate of Spain and the world, while others harvest the political fruits (Italy!). If Franco wins, they will not be so burdened as we will be if the Republicans win.'[40] Canaris and Roatta agreed to supply Franco in equal proportions in exchange for foreign currency or goods; political allegiance was not to be demanded.

Italian Foreign Minister Ciano informed Canaris that the Italian aviators – in contrast to Luftwaffe officers, who were limited to the warehousing and transport of materials and training of Spanish personnel – were at liberty to take part in aerial operations, and he asked Canaris to obtain permission to release German pilots to fight. This had also been requested by von Scheele, leader of the German volunteers in Spain, after it became apparent that Spanish pilots could not handle German bombers, and two of the Heinkel fighters had gone down; Hitler agreed on 28 August. On 12 September, War Minister Blomberg became convinced of the need to send panzers to Spain because Franco had no armour and the situation was deteriorating on account of Soviet military assistance to the Republic. The first German units came ashore on 1 October, a single panzer squadron with orders to train Franco's tank crews and gather battle experience.[41]

In October at Berchtesgaden Hitler met Foreign Minister Ciano and promised him 'that every effort was being made to guarantee that the road to Moscow will not be left open'.[42] On 30 October the decision was taken in Berlin to help Franco with Luftwaffe units. On 6 November, Canaris and Generalmajor Hugo Sperrle, leader of German troops in Spain, head of Legion Condor with direct responsibility to Goering and Wehrmacht Plenipotentiary to Franco's Staff,[43] gave Franco Hitler's conditions, which called for 'the swift capture of Madrid' to provide 'the foundation for energetic measures of support'.[44] Moreover, 'the command of the German units in Spain'would be the responsibility of 'a German commander' who would be 'responsible solely to General Franco personally for all measures', but Spanish command would be maintained outwardly. In so far as 'General Franco acknowledges these requirements unconditionally, further German assistance is in prospect'; Hitler took this decision alone and against the advice of his diplomats.

Canaris and Sperrle received Franco's agreement to the German conditions on 14 November, and three days later the first steamer left Stettin for Seville[45] with 697 German soldiers aboard. Canaris's role in these first months of the Spanish Civil War was that of a chief negotiator handling difficult diplomatic missions in Burgos and Rome.[46]

On 6 December he arrived in Italy for talks on increasing German military assistance to Spain,[47] in response to Franco's having sent what the Political Department at the Foreign Ministry described as 'a call for help' in a letter pleading for two complete divisions, one Italian, the other German. Hitler was not prepared to commit a large Army group and Canaris was obliged to inform the Italians that the Reich wanted to actually reduce its support in proportion to Italy's. Mussolini promised three thousand Blackshirts for Cadiz.[48] Ambassador von Hassell reported to Berlin in December: 'Since at the next meeting meaningful decisions have to be taken, Mussolini would welcome it if Canaris or whoever comes is not sent as observer, but has full powers;'[49] Mussolini had sent officials and specialists for two more brigades and wanted Germany to match it.[50] Goering went to the meeting instead of Canaris and agreed material support but declined any more units.[51] Canaris appointed Korvettenkapitän Wilhelm Leissner as head of the Legion Condor Abwehr, and sent out personnel, including instructors to train Franco's secret service, the Servicio Informacion Policia Militar (SIPM).[52] Head of Abwehr-III Legion Condor (Counter-Espionage) was Major Joachim Rohleder.[53]

The principal interest of the Abwehr, soon joined by members of a new Wehrmacht police corps Geheime Feldpolizei (GFP),[54] was the activity of Soviet agents in Spain and the routes by which the Republican Army received its arms shipments. Stalin had installed a large contingent of Soviet spies in Madrid, directed by the head of Red Army intelligence, General Jan Bersin. He and Michael Kolzow, editor of *Pravda*, had quarters in the Spanish War Ministry. Of the three thousand Soviets in Spain, only about forty were actually fighting, the rest were political or military advisers who kept an eye on opponents of Communism and the Soviet regime within the Republican camp.[55]

At the end of September 1936 General Kriwitzi, head of the Soviet People's Commissariat for Internal Affairs (NKVD) overseas service and operating from The Hague, received instructions to set up an organisation to buy weapons from anywhere in Europe, and the first deliveries were soon on the way from Czechoslovakia, France, Poland, Holland and even Germany. These German sales were arranged by Canaris and consisted of poor-quality and ill-repaired weapons that passed through Communist hands to the Spanish Republic. In 1938, the Nationalists protested to Berlin that weapons of German manufacture were captured from Republican and International Brigade soldiers.[56]

At the heart of a group of active Resistance workers in Germany opposed to Nazi policy in Spain was the later legendary 'Rote Kapelle' (Red Band) organisation headed by married couple Harro and Libertas Schulze-Boysen. Harro spent his childhood on the Kiel naval base; the son of a Fregattenkapitän, he came from proud naval origins, being a great-nephew of Admiral Tirpitz. But he was an opponent of National Socialism, and when his newspaper *Der Gegner* was blacklisted by the regime in 1933 he allied himself with the Communist underground movement. In April 1934 he infiltrated the Reich Aviation Ministry with the unwitting assistance of Goering, for whom he wrote articles based on photographs, cuttings and secret documents to which he was allowed access.[57]

Amongst the spies in the Rote Kapelle ring was United Press journalist Gisela von Pöllnitz.[58] In 1937 she prepared leaflets about the Spanish Civil War, using information obtained by Schulze-Boysen, hand-posted by her employer Elfriede Paul through letter-boxes across Berlin. The risk was great because the Gestapo, SA and police were alert to many members of the circle. The same year, when Schulze-Boysen was put together with a Communist spy, Werner Dissel, at Gestapo Headquarters in the hope that something incriminating would be said, Schulze-Boysen passed a message in a cigarette packet to Dissel telling him that the Gestapo did not suspect Dissel of having passed information about troop movements in Spain, and nothing further came of it.[59]

Schulze-Boysen collected all the information he could about 'Sonderstab-W', which coordinated German aid measures to Franco, and Gisela von Pöllnitz posted it into the letter-box at the Soviet Trade Mission in Berlin,[60] enabling the Soviets to focus their efforts against the German Abwehr in Spain. Eventually Pöllnitz was arrested by the Gestapo in the act of posting a document, but she kept quiet and nothing incriminating could be found during police searches. Schulze-Boysen escaped with a reprimand at the Reich Air Ministry, although the Gestapo had demanded his dismissal.[61]

In 1936 Canaris concluded with Estonia a reciprocal intelligence agreement against the Soviet Union[62] and consolidated the link with Hungary. In 1935, the Foreign Ministry, Blomberg and Goering all wanted a Sino-German alliance to secure raw materials for the armaments industry, but the driving force for a Japanese–German pact was Ribbentrop, who headed Dienststelle Ribbentrop, an NSDAP office founded in 1934 with jurisdiction in foreign policy matters and employing 160 staff.

Friedrich Wilhelm Hack was an arms lobbyist active for Heinkel in Japan.[63] The Japanese military attaché in Berlin, Hiroshi Oshima,[64] an ardent pro-German, saw in German–Japanese cooperation the opportunity to weaken German influence in China and so gain for Japan a powerful ally against the Soviet Union.[65] Hack and Oshima were introduced by Ribbentrop and after discussing ideas for cooperation on 17 September, advised Canaris and Blomberg.[66] Oshima wanted an anti-Soviet front embracing Britain, Germany, Poland and Japan; Blomberg was concerned that such a pact would prejudice Germany's position in China.[67] In November, Ribbentrop received Hitler's agreement to such a pact, but directed against Komintern for diplomatic reasons, not against the Soviet Union directly,[68] and after Hitler informed Neurath the Foreign Ministry abandoned its objections. The German ambassador to Tokyo, von Dirksen, wrote to Berlin on 1 January 1936: 'The Oshima negotiations were not begun as the result of a massive initiative but correctly and clearly by two senior German officials, Canaris and Ribbentrop. It is impossible to overstate the achievement of the two gentlemen ... others wanted to conduct the negotiations in such a way that they would collapse.'[69]

The diplomats ridiculed the draft treaty as 'the private adventure of amateurs',[70] but the Komintern Pact was signed on 25 November 1936;[71] a defensive alliance,[72] it provided for the exchange of information on Komintern activities, and resistance to them. Within a year, Italy, Hungary and Franco's Spain also signed. In a secret protocol, Germany and Japan agreed to remain neutral in the case of unprovoked attack or threat of attack by the Soviet Union, and to make no political treaty with the Soviets.[73] The 'two strongest militarist and expansionist world powers had found each other'.[74]

In December 1936 when Oshima proposed a 'German–Japanese Military Convention' that would turn the pact into an offensive alliance against the Soviet Union, the idea was successfully opposed by the Foreign Ministry, the Reich War Ministry and industry in favour of Chiang Kai-shek's China, which had supplied 'speculative shipments of war material'[75] the previous year, and whose modern Army was being trained by German generals. Canaris received open encouragement from Blomberg and Keitel to continue the cooperation with Japan and to agree 'an exchange of intelligence information and infiltration methods'.[76] He was also appointed an intermediary to the Japanese military attachés, and in future the three Wehrmacht branches of service had to pass all questions of German–Japanese cooperation through Canaris and the Wehrmacht Office. A year later, Abwehr officers in Tokyo assisted at the interrogation of the captured NKVD chief in the East, General Lyushkov, who had been brought to Japan.

From 1937 the German and Austrian military attachés began to exchange secret service reports, and following the increased cooperation desired by Hitler, Generalmajor Böhme, head of Austrian intelligence, appointed Generalmajor Erwin Lahousen Edler von Vivremont to 'prepare the reports on Czechoslovakia wanted by the German side'.[77] Lahousen was to become one of Canaris's closest confidants, although this remained the only meeting of the two men until the German annexation of Austria.

Friedrich Heinz alleged that in the winter of 1936, Canaris obtained Himmler's agreement to organise for Abwehr and selected OKW officers for a sightseeing visit to Sachsenhausen concentration camp,[78] with the purpose of showing the excursionists 'the total inhumanity of the Hitler regime'. Packed coaches rolled north from the Bendlerstrasse for the tour of the camp, led by the commandant. The methods of torture and maltreatment employed were freely explained by the Inspector of Concentration Camps and men of the SS-Totenkopf units; on the journey home not even the most enthusiastic Nazis in the contingent were able to speak.

Heinz's assertion cannot be verified. His biographer points out that in the Bendlerstrasse, Heinz spoke 'repeatedly and vehemently about the horrors in the concentration camps',[79] and Heinz insisted that he only mentioned the visit in 1945 after a large number of generals argued that they knew nothing about the atrocities.[80]

On 11 June 1937 the Soviet news agency *Tass* reported that the vice-commissar for Defence, Marshal Mikhail Tukhachevsky, and seven other generals had been condemned to death for espionage and treason,[81] the sentences being carried out the same month.[82] This marked the beginning of Stalin's Great Terror against the officers of the Red Army. By September 1938, 35,020 had been arrested or discharged the service; the number executed remains unknown.[83]

After the war there emerged an absurd legend attached to these events, when memoirs pinpointed Heydrich as being the originator of forged documents linking Tukhachevsky to high-ranking German military officers in a conspiracy to unseat Stalin. These documents were allegedly fabricated with the help of double agent Nikolai Sklobin, a White Russian former general living in Paris, and then passed to Czech President Benes, who forwarded them to Stalin.

It would be impossible to set out here all the variations of the story. Heydrich had broken into the Abwehr filing rooms to steal the papers he needed after Hitler had ordered the action;[84] or Heydrich had asked Canaris for certain handwritten documents dating from the time of German–Soviet cooperation in the 1920s;[85] or it was Sklobin who had put Heydrich up to the plan to destroy the Soviet officer corps by a purge or bloodbath.[86] The end result was always the same: Heydrich had fooled Stalin and achieved the desired objective.

The only certainty is that in January 1937, in the course of secret German–Czech talks, Benes heard from three sources rumours of an imminent coup in the Soviet Union.[87] Contrary to legend, it now appears to be the case that Benes said nothing to Moscow. Stalin, of course, already knew, but once Tukhachevsky had been executed, Benes expressed his satisfaction that Stalin had liquidated the plotters. It was Stalin who circulated the rumour through Paris for the purpose of justifying his purge; Heydrich had been used, although he did not see it that way himself.[88]

Freidrich Heinz wrote after the war that once the affair became common knowledge, Canaris confronted Heydrich and asked why he had become involved, to which the SD chief replied that Hitler had ordered it with the intention of weakening the Red Army.[89] According to Heinz, Hans Oster and the 'Hauskapelle' had made their own enquiries and confirmed the forgeries.

Perhaps Canaris really was appalled at the disdain of the regime for human life. When his predecessor Patzig, head of the Naval Personnel Office, met him in Berlin in 1937, he recalled that Canaris said at the very beginning of their conversation: 'From top to bottom they are all criminals who will bring Germany down.' Patzig asked him how he could remain head of the Abwehr if he thought that; Canaris answered: 'It is my destiny. If I go, Heydrich takes over and then we are all lost. I must sacrifice myself.'[90]

14

Ousting the Generals

On 4 February 1938 Hitler dismissed War Minister Generaloberst von Blomberg and the Army C-in-C Generaloberst von Fritsch, and assumed personal command of the Wehrmacht. He had held this position nominally as head of state since the death of Hindenburg in 1934, but now he abolished the office of Reich War Minister and replaced it with the OKW. This was decisive in the struggle for power between the NSDAP and SS, and the Wehrmacht.

From this point in time onward, many military officers and commanders took a more critical view of the regime. For Canaris, it marked the watershed in his attitude to Nazism:[1] 'That was the time when Canaris began to turn away from Hitler,' his friend Richard Protze related later. 'If one can point to any incident as the crisis of loyalty between Canaris and Hitler, then this was it.'[2] Canaris knew nothing of the developing scandals surrounding Blomberg and Fritsch; he had been in Spain and only returned to Berlin on 22 January, by when the events were already running their course.

On 12 January 1938, von Blomberg, a widower of many years standing, married Margarethe Gruhn, a woman of modest origins thirty-five years his junior. Hitler and Goering were witnesses at the ceremony.[3] On 21 January the Berlin Vice Squad reported that Gruhn was known to them; at the age of eighteen, she had posed for pornographic photographs that had subsequently fallen into police hands, and so she was then catalogued as a prostitute. By the military code and contemporary standards of military honour this was a scandal that 'caused the greatest political crisis in the Third Reich since the Röhm affair in 1934'.[4]

Blomberg's marriage had been publicised only by a small announcement in a newspaper, but a rumour originating on the street came to the attention of Werner Best, and the same evening Reichsmarschall Goering confirmed from a photograph that Frau Blomberg was the prostitute Margarethe Gruhn.[5]

On 24 July 1938 Goering discussed the matter with Hitler. The Führer was not so concerned about the photographs but that Frau Blomberg had posed to help out with the household budget at the suggestion of her boyfriend, a Czech engineer of Jewish origin.[6]

Blomberg refused Hitler's request to have the marriage annulled immediately, and the next day he was asked to resign. On 27 January Goebbels noted in his diary: 'Blomberg must go. The only way out for a man of honour is the pistol. The Führer was a witness at the ceremony; it is unthinkable. The worst crisis for the regime since the Röhm affair. I am completely distraught. The Führer is as grey as a corpse.'[7]

Hitler's military adjutant Hossbach was shocked when Hitler told him that Generaloberst von Fritsch also had to go since he was a homosexual; there had been evidence of it for several years. Hossbach rejected the accusation against Fritsch, whom he had known for years, believing him to be 'a pure and noble person', and he refused to be convinced when Hitler showed him the file. He considered the material 'poorly put together',[8] a pretext to oust the unsettled general. Although forbidden to do so by Hitler,[9] Hossbach ignored the instruction and late that evening informed Fritsch that Hitler had a file 'from which it would appear that a recidivist presently serving a long prison sentence' had 'blackmailed you on account of your homosexual activities'.[10]

Fritsch swore to Hossbach that he had never been a homosexual nor been blackmailed in connection with homosexuality, and begged Hossbach to arrange an early interview for him with Hitler.[11] He was received by Hitler at the Reich Chancellery on the evening of 26 January, and greeted with the accusation that he had been blackmailed for his homosexual activities, and that if he admitted the matter he would be sent on a long journey and not be disciplined.[12] Goering added that 'there can be no doubt as to the truth of the allegations since the blackmailer has always spoken the truth in over one hundred cases',[13] but when Fritsch asked the identity of the accuser this was parried by Hitler asking 'if even somewhere there lurked the slightest possibility of suspicion'.[14] At that he was shown a Gestapo file from 1936 containing a blackmailer's confession that in November 1933 he had surprised a gentleman engaged in a homosexual act at the Potsdam Wannsee Railway Station and had blackmailed him for 2,500 Reichsmarks. The blackmailer had identified himself as a commissioner of detectives while the victim had said he was 'General der Artillerie von Fritsch', and provided an identity document.

Whilst Fritsch read through the file, the blackmailer Otto Schmidt, who had been brought from prison, was escorted into the room and, feigning surprise, identified Fritsch as his victim. Fritsch gave Hitler his word of honour that it was a case of mistaken identity. Hitler was not satisfied and ordered Fritsch to report to Gestapo Headquarters the next morning for questioning.

At home Fritsch informed his General Staff officer and the chief of the General Staff, Beck; in reply to his question, both of them advised him not to shoot himself, since this would amount to an admission of guilt.[15] That same evening he wrote to Hitler: 'Until the restoration of my impugned honour, it will not be possible for me to discharge any official obligations. For the sake of appearances I consider it opportune to report sick ... I further request that all the accusations made against me be investigated by the competent judicial process.'[16]

Fritsch suspected that a plot involving Himmler, Heydrich and the Gestapo lay behind the charges because he had stubbornly resisted party political influences on the Army. He considered Himmler as his greatest enemy since he, Fritsch, was the major opponent to Himmler's plans for a permanent increase in the SS fighting corps.[17]

On 15 January 1933, three days after Blomberg's marriage, Fritsch had been warned against Himmler 'by a party not to be taken lightly' that Himmler and the NSDAP had decided it was time for him to go.[18] The same day, the Gestapo identified the real blackmail victim as the former Rittermeister Achim von Frisch, as Commissioner of Detectives Friedrich Fehling deposed on oath; Generaloberst von Fritsch had therefore been the victim of a deliberately planned case of mistaken identity by the Gestapo,[19] and was unaware that he had been investigated in 1936. When Hitler had seen the file at the time, he ordered it destroyed but a few pages had survived in case they should be needed in the future.[20]

On 26 January Canaris was at the War Ministry to hear Keitel announce the dismissal of Blomberg, and the next day was given better particulars by Abwehr subordinates Hans Oster and Hans Gisevius. The latter was a former Gestapo official who had been transferred out to the Interior Ministry;[21] he had known Oster since 1933 and kept him supplied with confidential Gestapo information. Gisevius was also friendly with Reichs-Kriminaldirektor Arthur Nebe; in a conversation with Keitel about the Blomberg affair, Keitel had told him, 'and there is something not right about Fritsch, either'.[22] The following day Keitel informed Canaris and other departmental heads at the War Ministry that Hitler would replace the Army commander-in-chief since there was material alleging violations of Paragraph 175 currently in the hands of the minister of justice, and Keitel had been given the job of investigating it.[23] Soon afterwards Gisevius received from his confidant Nebe information that 'a major blow was being prepared against the Wehrmacht. Fritsch would also be sacrificed, he had come to the notice of the Gestapo on several occasions and stood accused.'[24]

After his arrest following the 20 July 1944 plot, Oberstleutnant Oster allegedly told the SD that it was as a result of the Fritsch affair that the first intentions to stage a coup developed amongst circles opposed to the regime. He had 'esteemed Fritsch highly as a soldier and a person'; 'I made the Fritsch business my own. Our intentions were initially to remove Himmler and the Gestapo because we believed that their influence was against the common good.'[25] At this time Canaris began to intensify his association with Chief of the Staff Ludwig Beck, whose support for a move by the Wehrmacht against the Gestapo would have been decisive;[26] The liaison to Beck was Oster, 'who often spent the whole morning with Beck in his study'.[27] Another convinced anti-Nazi was Hans von Dohnanyi, assistant to Justice Minister Franz Gürtner. In the war years he played a central role in the Resistance to Hitler in proximity to Canaris.

At the end of January, Hitler passed the Fritsch file to Gürtner in the strictest secrecy for a legal opinion;[28] Gürtner handed it to Dohnanyi 'with a sardonic smile'.[29] Dohnanyi's opinion included the statement that Fritsch had 'so far not decisively refuted the charge, the alibi evidence he speaks of has not materialised ....' Gürtner concluded: 'One cannot and ought not speculate on the guilt or innocence of the subject ... which remains a matter for judgement.'[30]

Dohanyi's opinion read like a pre-judgement by inverting the burden of proof and is widely considered to have been a disaster for Fritsch.[31] Apparently the aim of Dohnanyi and Gürtner's report was to deflect Hitler from convening a special court on the basis of the Gestapo file, and on 30 January Gürtner obtained Hitler's agreement to court-martial Fristch before the Reich War Court, this being the only way he was likely to get a fair hearing and acquittal.[32]

Frau Christine Dohnanyi (née Bonhoeffer) recalled later that Gürtner released her husband from nearly all other duties so that he could work day and night on 'disproving the foul slander against this politically mishandled general'.[33] It was through the Fritsch affair that Dohnanyi got to know Oster, Gisevius and Canaris, linking up the various groups who supported Fritsch and conspired against the regime.[34] Oster was the most active and important link between the military and civilian threads of the web.

The plan of Oster and Gisevius at that time was to occupy Gestapo Headquarters in Berlin, arrest Himmler and Heydrich, present all the captured evidence to Hitler and simultaneously publish it. Confronted by the full facts, the Führer would then be forced by the pressure of public opinion and the expected drop in support, to remove the Gestapo terror.[35]

Reichsbank Director Hjalmar Schacht failed in his attempt to persuade Raeder and General von Rundstedt to intervene against the Gestapo; one of them stated it was outside his jurisdiction, while the other provided a cryptic explanation to justify avoiding his responsibility. Carl Goerdeler, former Oberbürgermeister of Leipzig, former Reichs commissioner for price control, was similarly unsuccessful with Justice Minister Gürtner. Neither General List (Wehrkreis VI) nor von Kluge at Münster wished to become involved[36] after hearing Gisevius, and Oster – without consulting Canaris – approached General Ulex (commanding officer, XI Armeekorps, Hannover), but Ulex doubted that a unified front of generals was possible.[37]

Meanwhile Beck had been taken over by 'a peculiar restraint';[38] he issued a strict prohibition at General Staff and Army High Command (OKH) against discussing the Fritsch affair, leading to sharp criticism from many officers at the Bendlerstrasse. When Halder saw Beck on 31 January, calling on him to place himself at the head of his generals and occupy Gestapo Headquarters, a fierce argument started; Beck said that the idea was mutiny, and 'mutiny and revolution are words that do not exist in the vocabulary of a German officer'.[39] Canaris's attempts to influence Fritsch's successor Brauchitsch were also to no avail; both Brauchitsch and Beck were of the opinion that the result of the hearing must come first.

On 5 February, pale and visibly shaken, Hitler addressed his generals, explaining the sequence of events, quoting from the police reports and then reading the Dohnanyi legal opinion. The effect was depressing, and Curt Liebmann wrote: 'We all had the feeling that the Army – in contrast to the Navy, Luftwaffe and Party – had received a devastating blow.'[40] Hitler seized his opportunity – besides Blomberg and Fritsch, twelve generals were removed and fifty-one other senior officers relieved of their posts. Walther von Brauchitsch was appointed the new commander-in-chief of the Army, and Foreign Minister von Neurath was replaced by Ribbentrop.[41]

Two days later Keitel published the new edict affecting the provisional organisation of the new OKW. Canaris became head of the new Combined Office for General Wehrmacht Affairs (Amtsgruppe Allgemeine Wehrmachts-angelegenheiten – AWA) in addition to his existing role as head of the Abwehr, making him now chief of three departments, Abwehr, Inland and Supply[42] and responsible for OKW contacts to press, party and police, a central role in the OKW political structure. Below him at AWA were General Georg Thomas (Military Economy and Armaments) and Generalleutnant Max von Viebahn, both critics of the regime and trusted by Beck. Especially in the case of von Viebahn, whom Canaris had known when they served together as Noske's adjutants,[43] the General Staff had succeeded in planting a spy into the OKW.

In order to shore up their case against Fritsch, the Gestapo scoured the Reich for his former valets, chauffeurs and Hitler-Jugend boys who lunched at his house sometime in 1933 or 1934; they also cross-examined his housekeeper.[44] Fritsch stated:

Never in history has a nation treated its Army commander-in-chief in such an offensive and shabby manner. I am making this declaration in order that later historians will know how the commander-in-chief of the German Army was treated in 1938. Such a proceeding is not only in the highest degree undignified for me, it is also dishonourable towards the entire Army.[45]

In his closing address to the Reich War Court on 17 March 1938, Fritsch emphasised 'how reprehensible and offensive' he had found it to be that people 'who trust me, who have always, even in these unhappy days, provided me with proof of their loyalty and support, should be rounded up by the Gestapo for questioning about me'.[46]

On 10 February, Canaris and Keitel went to Karinhall to discuss the case with Goering; the latter gave the impression that he was prepared to listen, at which point Canaris presented the material proving Fritsch innocent.[47] The Reich War Court, meanwhile, had shelved the proceedings until 1 March and Fritsch's defence team succeeded, after an extensive search, in finding the 'Doppelgänger' and true victim of the blackmail,[48] whose identity the Gestapo had known all along. There are various versions as to how the search eventually bore fruit: the judge working with the Abwehr and Nebe made the breakthrough,[49] or Walter Biron, leader of the research team, was tipped off by Fritsch's lawyer Rüdiger von der Goltz as to the possibility of a confusion over names, and the name of Rittmeister Frisch came up.[50]

Canaris, Beck, Oster and Gisevius fed Brauchitsch, the new Army commander-in-chief, with information about the Gestapo inquiry as they received it, hoping to recruit him to their conspiracy, but he ignored Canaris's plea to intervene when Fritsch was summoned to Gestapo Headquarters for more questioning, although he did manage to secure the release from custody of Fritsch's valet and his housekeeper.[51]

Outwardly, Canaris remained a good National Socialist, and on 3 March at OKW he addressed the heads of the Abwehrstellen and Abwehr officers at Wehrkreis commands.[52] As the expansion of Abwehr jurisdiction involved 'an internal restructuring of the Wehrmacht[53] he requested comprehensive reports on all political measures 'affecting the Wehrmacht and its prestige', and in cases of dispute with NSDAP heads it was to be made clear that 'we front-soldiers of the State belong amongst the best, least self-seeking and selfless National Socialists.'[54] Regarding the Blomberg and Fritsch affairs he cautioned them:

As to the events leading to the dismissal of the Reich Minister for War and Generaloberst Freiherr von Fritsch, you have been advised by the commanding generals on the basis of a discussion with the Führer. In the first place we have to be content with that. It is very important that you answer in this sense everything you are asked. You must not give anybody anything more, even if you are in a position where you ought to know more.[55]

Canaris was concerned about the Nazi press, like the *Völkischer Beobachter*, which spoke of 'the melting process between Wehrmacht and party',[56] and he instructed his officers: 'Should other statements in the press, in speeches or elsewhere in public, talk of the events of 4 February 1938 in such a manner as if those events represent a victory by the party over the Wehrmacht, or place the Wehrmacht under the guardianship of the party, you must report it immediately.'[57]

The previous evening, Rittmeister Frisch had admitted under interrogation to having been the true victim of Schmidt the blackmailer. He even produced the receipts for his 2,500 Reichsmarks, signed by Schmidt. Frisch swore an affidavit there and then; after weeks of tireless searching and the struggle with the Gestapo, this was the breakthrough the defence had been seeking. Lawyer von der Goltz then hurried, beaming with joy, to present his client with a bouquet of roses, but Fritsch held back his jubilation until the official verdict. The case began on 10 March, but was adjourned the same day because of the German invasion of Austria.[58] Under the weight of the defence evidence, the prosecution case collapsed; the judges, who included the three heads of the Wehrmacht services, Goering, Raeder and von Brauchitsch, acquitted Fritsch on 18 March on the grounds of 'his proven innocence'.[59] Even Goering, who had made it known often enough that he was glad to be rid of Fritsch, assented to the acquittal.[60]

The blackmailer Schmidt remained in custody. Fristch speculated that Himmler might extract him for use as a witness against Goering, who was involved in the scandal,[61] but a few years later the SS executed him instead.[62]

On 31 March Fritsch received a letter from Hitler confirming the acquittal but containing no expression of regret nor apology. Fritsch wrote to a friend: 'I can neither forgive the Führer nor forget that he considered my word of honour to be worthless against the testimony of a blackguard.'[63]

Canaris and others considered that the rectification fell far short of that which honour demanded, and they attempted to do what they could for his rehabilitation. Together with Hitler's former adjutant Hossbach, who had meanwhile been dismissed, Canaris drew up some proposals for Brauchitsch, which were shown first to Beck,[64] in which it was observed: 'The conclusion of the proceedings is thoroughly unsatisfactory from the point of view of the restoration of the honour of Generaloberst Freiherr von Fritsch, for the prestige of the Army as well as the whole Wehrmacht, and to liberate him from this Cheka nightmare.' They demanded a 'special gesture' by 'the Supreme Commander of the Wehrmacht' (Hitler), the public rehabilitation of Generaloberst von Fritsch 'in an impressive manner', preferably through 'a personal visit by the Führer at the earliest opportunity' and deemed 'intolerable' any 'further thriving collaboration of the Wehrmacht with those leading personalities of the Gestapo responsible for the defamation of Generaloberst Fritsch and the damaging and demeaning attack on the Army.'[65] Neither Brauchitsch nor Beck wished to embrace such a far-reaching demand – no basis existed amongst the generals, nor elsewhere in the Wehrmacht, for a revolt against the Gestapo, the SS or even against Hitler. On the contrary, in Hitler's policy planning, the Wehrmacht was destined to have a star role.

15

A Double Game

In February 1938 there was growing tension between Germany and Austria. During a house search the Austrian police had found evidence that Austrian Nazis were planning to simulate an assassination attempt on von Papen[1] to provide the Wehrmacht with a pretext for invasion.[2] The government published the documents and attempted to win over the lawyer and Nazi sympathiser Arthur Seyss-Inquart as an ally, but the latter was a loyal follower of Hitler and reported the details of Schussnigg's approach to Berlin, adding that he was prepared to come to Germany to help in any inquiry.

On 12 February Schussnigg went to the Obersalzberg hoping to defuse the situation, but he found instead an elaborate theatre laid on for his benefit. When Hitler received the Austrian Chancellor in company with his military adjutants, he was also in the company of Ribbentrop and Keitel, the strongly Nazi General Reichenau, and the former commander of Legion Condor, Sperrle. In his study Hitler unleashed a tirade about Austria's betrayal of the German people and culminated with the threat:

> And I tell you, Herr Schussnigg, I am utterly determined to put an end to it. The German Reich is a world power, and I will not tolerate others suggesting otherwise when I am putting the frontiers in order. Do you honestly think you could hold us up for even half an hour? Do you want to make Austria into another Spain?[3]

Austria was required to fulfil the German demands by 15 February: the lifting of all restrictions on Nazi activities in Austria, an amnesty for Nazis in custody, the appointment of Seyss-Inquart as minister of the interior, with control of the police, the appointment of Nazi sympathiser Edmund Glaise-Horstenau as minister of war, Austrian foreign and economic policy to fall in line with that of the Reich, dismissal of chief of General Staff Jansa, an opponent of Nazism, and regular consultations between the respective General Staffs.[4] If these conditions were not met, Hitler would march in.

When Schussnigg demurred and asked to consult his Foreign Minister Guido Schmidt, this was allowed while the intimidation continued, until the farce succeeded and the Obersalzberg Agreement was signed.[5] General Jodl wrote in his diary: 'Schussnigg with G. Schmidt are put under the heaviest military and political pressure. At 2300 Schussnigg signs the protocol.'

The next day, at Keitel's flat in Berlin, Canaris, Keitel, Jodl and Goebbels discussed the implementation of military exercises ordered by Hitler for 15 February, the suggestions being agreed by Hitler by telephone the same night.[6] Canaris then flew to Abwehrstelle VII at Munich with his adviser for southeast Europe, Erich Pruck;[7] Jodl wrote: 'In Austria the impression is developing of serious military preparations in Germany.'[8] The measures planned by Canaris and Keitel involved the dissemination of false, but credible reports – VII Armeekorps had cancelled all leave; in Munich, Augsburg and Regensburg wagons and railway coaches were to be prepared for the transport of troops and supplies; all frontier police posts had received reinforcements; mountain troops had announced exercises and the German military attaché in Vienna had been recalled to Berlin for talks. The Canaris–Keitel proposals made it expressly clear that 'no actual preparations were to be made by Army or Luftwaffe', nor were there to be any 'troop movements or advances towards the frontier',[9] but opinion was divided about whether all this actually deceived anybody, and Austrian intelligence officer Erwin Lahousen declared to Keitel and Jodl when in Abwehr service later, 'We were not deceived by this bluff.'[10]

Canaris was active on many fronts at this time. The Fritsch affair was still smouldering and he was involved in talks about Wehrmacht restructuring with Jodl and General Viebahn.[11] On 15 February the Austrian problem seemed resolved when Schussnigg met all Hitler's demands, while the new Austrian Security Minister Seyss-Inquart was already in Berlin, ready for orders. He was convinced that annexation could proceed only on the further threat of force.[12]

On 9 March Schussnigg announced a referendum on the question of Austrian independence,[13] a hopeless attempt to recover what he had signed away at Berchtesgaden and a clear rejection of unification with Germany. He had not consulted beyond his own borders and did not expect support from Italy, or France, where the government had just been dissolved, nor from Britain, which had signalled that it would not oppose annexation. The transparent attempt to disenfranchise the supporters of a Greater German Reich and the Nazis by raising the voting age to twenty-four played into Hitler's hands,[14] and that same evening, probably at the instigation of Goering, he decided to invade.[15]

Next morning Keitel and Jodl arrived at the Reich Chancellery with 'Fall Otto', some old theoretical plans for an invasion of Austria.[16] Chief of Staff Beck was desperate: 'We had absolutely nothing prepared, nothing had been done, nothing.'[17] He had been told by Blomberg to draw up plans for 'Sonderfall Otto' in 1937, but the General Staff had not wanted to take on the task then,[18] and now found itself having to improvise something within a few hours. Hitler wanted to enter his former homeland on Saturday, the day before the planned referendum; already it was Wednesday, and so the plans were needed by the same evening.[19]

On Thursday 11 March 1938 Canaris informed his Abwehrstelle leaders that the Führer had decided to resolve the Austrian question by force if necessary. Hauptmann Paul Leverkühn, later Abwehr chief in Instanbul disguised as a consul and head of the war organisation Naher Osten, recalled: 'The seriousness of the situation and the Admiral's deep concern were unmistakable for everybody at the discussion.'[20]

That morning Hitler gave Schussnigg an ultimatum demanding the postponement of the plebiscite for two weeks, Schussnigg's resignation and the appointment of Seyss-Inquart as federal chancellor. In the afternoon Schussnigg deferred the plebiscite but refused to step down; Goering gave him a second ultimatum. That evening, after receiving a telegram from London in which the new Foreign Minister Lord Halifax made it clear that he could not count on British support, Schussnigg resigned, but Austrian President Wilhelm Miklas refused to appoint Seyss-Inquart chancellor and a third German ultimatum followed. During the night Hitler received Mussolini's assurance that he would accept the intervention. Since Hitler had already ordered his troops to march, the invasion proceeded even when Miklas gave in towards midnight and made Seyss-Inquart chancellor. Goering had convinced Hitler some time previously that he had to act.[21]

When Canaris received the report in the early hours that Heydrich and Schellenberg were on their way to Vienna, he flew at once to the Austrian capital. While the other two proceeded to the Interior Ministry, Canaris went with Oberst Graf von Marogna-Redwitz, the new head of Austrian intelligence, to the Defence Ministry where Generalmajors Ronge and Lahousen had spent the night sorting and burning papers. Canaris retrieved a number of important files including personal dossiers on Hitler, Himmler, Heydrich and Goering. Schellenberg came a few hours later as Heydrich's envoy, but Ronge and Lahousen both declined his invitation to join the SS.[22]

Canaris spent the night of 13 March on the campbed in his study while Pruck waited in an ante-room for reports from Abwehr spies outside Germany;[23] the messages gave no grounds for concern. The Foreign Office had been informed that evening that France would not act 'unless Czechoslovakia was attacked'[24] and British ambassador Henderson wrote to Goering on 13 March that he had passed to the British Government Goering's assurance that the troops would be withdrawn from Austria as soon as the situation was stable, after which there would be free elections.[25] The German business attaché in Rome reported that the Italian press had fallen into line: 'Invasion by German troops and visit by the Führer are being reported cordially in all details.'[26]

On 14 March 1938, Hitler arrived in Vienna to a jubilant reception; the archbishop had the bells rung and swastika flags adorned the church towers and the next day Hitler addressed 'an almost deliriously happy crowd'[27] from the Heldenplatz. Some weeks before the invasion, Best and Canaris in close cooperation had arranged for mobile police units to follow the troops into Austria in order to implement 'police security measures'. The Abwehr, SD, Sipo and NSDAP had been gathering information on political opponents for some time previously and now the joint Gestapo–SD Detective Force struck; the operations were 'sharp, brutal and accompanied by excesses and atrocities kept out of sight'.[28] Six months later in the Sudetenland these units were called *Einsatzgruppen* for the first time and behaved in such a manner that Heydrich had to order them to moderate their activity.

On 14 March in Vienna Canaris accepted Generalmajor Marogna-Redwitz's suggestion that Lahousen might be useful at Berlin headquarters.[29] In the presence of Major Helmuth Groscurth, head of sabotage sub-group and later, as head of the Abwehr Overseas Office to OKH, one of the most important liaison men to the early military Resistance,[30] Canaris said to Lahousen: 'Don't bring any Nazis with you, especially not to Berlin headquarters. Bring Austrians, not *Ostmärker*'.[31] Lahousen recalled that the annexation of Austria 'was one of the few foreign policy actions of which Canaris did not disapprove ... the Admiral was opposed only – and here vehemently – to the manner, namely the invasion, which brought about the fusion of the two states'.[32] Hitler called for elections on 10 April and received a 99 per cent approval rating for the annexation from the electorates in the Old Reich and Austria, voting for 'The List of Our Führer Adolf Hitler'.

Canaris, promoted to Vizeadmiral on 1 April, addressed the 1938 new entry to the Wiener Neustadt War Academy:[33] 'We are all now standing under the heart-lifting experience of the development of Greater Germany. It was dreamed of, worked for, fought for and found its fulfilment in the plebiscite of the 10 April in the slogan "Ein Volk, Ein Reich, Ein Führer!" For us soldiers this slogan extends further to "Ein Volk, Ein Reich, Ein Führer, Eine Wehrmacht!"'[34] Canaris informed his listeners that this new Wehrmacht must be: 'a model for the realisation of the National Socialist world-view', for the 'realisation of the unadulterated idea of the Führer' and the 'great training school for the young men of the State', incorporating 'the Volk-community in exemplary form'.[35] The officer corps had to lead, 'that is the only way to preserve its position as destined by the Führer and achieved by virtue of its earlier efforts'. He went on: 'Just as the officer before the World War was obviously monarchist, just as he obviously laboured after that war to keep alive the legacy of his experience at the front, so obviously he desires today, when all our front experience finds its realisation in the National Socialist State, to be a National Socialist.' A non-political attitude on the part of the soldier in the National Socialist State was 'sabotage and a crime'.[36] Canaris thus appeared before the Austrian cadets as a dyed-in-the-wool Nazi who had mastered perfectly the partially impenetrable political rhetoric of the regime.

At the end of June 1938 the Abwehr counter-espionage section led by Rudolf Bamler issued his 'Circular on Espionage, Counter-Espionage and Internal Treason'. The latter was defined as 'the murder of comrades'; this offence could be committed premeditatively by act, or negligently by speech. 'Whoever dares to raise his hands against the Fatherland, he is Death's.'[37] By mid-1938, more and more officers in Canaris's Abwehr were ready to commit this 'treason'.

The central figure was Hans Oster. He had experience of intelligence work from service as Ic (No 3 Staff officer, Counter-Espionage) at Münster in the 1920s, spying in the demilitarised Rhineland;[38] Canaris knew him from his naval detachment in 1931.[39] As an artillery major in 1932, Oster had been forced to resign after an affair with a married woman,[40] but following a brief period in Goering's 'Research Bureau' in 1933 he entered the Abwehr in a civilian capacity under Patzig on 1 October 1933, his passage having been smoothed by General Halder, Hossbach and Canaris.[41] Once Canaris took over the Abwehr, Oster was reactivated as a serving officer in the rank of Oberstleutnant at the end of 1935.[42] He had been sceptical at the rise of National Socialism and was soon disillusioned by Nazi terror methods.[43] In 1938 Canaris appointed him Head of Abwehr Headquarters, responsible for administration and organisation. In wartime, he would become Abwehr chief of Staff.[44]

Canaris knew Friedrich Wilhelm Heinz from the GKSD. He was a former member of Brigade Ehrhardt, Org-C and the Wiking-Bund.[45] He had become a journalist and author whose books were on the Proscribed Index and was considered politically unreliable, with adverse dossiers on him held at the Army Personnel Office. Contrary to expectations, however, he passed a Gestapo tribunal to obtain entry to the Abwehr, and passed his probationary period with the help of a false assessment from Canaris.[46] Heinz began at Referat III C3, becoming its head in May 1937;[47] his immediate superior was Hans Oster.

Lawyer Franz-Maria Liedig, a former naval officer, had been Ehrhardt's ordnance officer and had been known to Canaris since 1919 when he acted as liaison between Canaris and Ehrhardt. Liedig was employed at Referat I M (Naval Reconnaissance) and was introduced by Canaris and Heinz to Oster.

Helmuth Groscurth had been a courier for Org-C and, after a period in farming, joined the Abwehr in 1935 and in June 1938 was appointed to Abteilung II (Sabotage). Groscurth was not an opponent of Nazism from the outset, but became disillusioned at the racial theory, its policy towards the Church (he was a member of the Evangelical Church), the overthrow of the Constitution and the rule of terror by party and SS.[48] It was Groscurth who brought Lahousen into Oster's Vienna circle in 1938, and later suggested him as his successor at Abteilung II 'to maintain the continuity of Resistance activity'.[49] On Lahousen's arrival in Berlin on 1 June 1938, Oster had told him: 'There is a criminal at the head of the Reich.'[50]

Canaris knew the former Stahlhelm leader Theodor Duesterberg briefly after the war. In the spring of 1936 Canaris warned him that he was being watched by the Gestapo[51] and guaranteed him emergency sanctuary at Abwehr Headquarters should a dangerous situation arise. His son Georg, until 1935 at Stahlhelm, who had Jewish ancestry and could not find work, was recruited by the Abwehr; by 1940 he was working for Oster as head of finance, setting up secret foreign exchange funds in Switzerland for resistance groups around Oster and Dohnanyi.[52]

Another ex-Stahlhelm leader at Abwehr was Werner Schrader, whom Canaris had met at the 1936 Olympic Games. He was installed at Abwehrstelle Munich under Marogna-Redwitz as a Hauptmann (E) in a specially created Referat office.

The Abwehr became the destination for many ex-Naval Brigade, GKSD and Stahlhelm personnel who had fallen foul of the regime. Canaris even managed to extract the Jewish Fritz Grabowsky, a confidant of Pabst, the press chief at GKSD Staff, from Oranienburg concentration camp in 1938. In Denmark Grabowsky worked with Horst von Pflugk-Harttung to set up a network of Abwehr agents, and when his activities were discovered at the end of 1938, Canaris sent him to France.[53] Hans von Dohnanyi, the part-Jewish lawyer who had joined Oster's circle during his work in the Fritsch case, joined the Abwehr in August 1939.[54]

The Abwehr was by no means a refuge for the Resistance or an asylum for opponents of the regime, however. Of the 13,000 officers, officials and clerks working for the wartime Abwehr, fifty at most could be considered active conspirators[55] and as a convinced anti-Communist Canaris would never accept former KPD, SPD or other Marxist activists.[56]

Oster was relentless in his efforts to unify the opposition to Hitler. After failing to coerce the Wehrmacht generals to act during the Fritsch crisis, he next set out to expand the circle around Canaris and himself with men such as Army judge Karl Sack, Berlin Police-President Graf Helldorf and his deputy Graf von der Schulenburg,[57] a specialist in constitutional law appointed at the end of 1937 who favoured an Army uprising against the SS and party.[58] General Erwin von Witzleben, the first senior military commander to work consistently for the removal of Hitler, had been admitted to a Dresden sanatorium during the Fritsch crisis, and Schulenburg did not met him until March 1938. Schulenburg was probably introduced to Heinz by Oster; on his first visit to Heinz's house he spoke out volubly against the regime. Earlier both had men been supporters of the Strasser clique within the NSDAP and were oriented towards conservative leading personalities such as Oswald Spengler; it was through Schulenburg that the so-called 'Graf Group' of opponents to the regime, including Yorck von Wartenburg, Graf Üxküll and Adam von Trott zu Sulz came into contact with Heinz.[59] Schulenburg had no qualms about taking people such as Hermann Maass from illegal trade unions or the SPD.

On 1 June 1938 after Keitel had restructured the OKW, Canaris now headed Ausland/Abwehr. The former Abwehr Gruppen were rearranged into Abteilungen such as Abwehr-Abteilung II (Sabotage, Psychological Warfare, Incitement and German Invasions).[60]

Head of Abteilung Ausland was Kapitän zur See Leopold Bürkner, who had worked with Ribbentrop on the London Naval Treaty in 1935 and was now liaison officer to the Foreign Ministry. His responsibility was to keep Keitel, the Wehmacht Command Staff through Jodl and the chiefs of the General Staffs of the three Wehrmacht services informed and to instruct the German overseas attachés. He was also liaison officer to the Wehrmacht Plenipotentiary of the Triple Power Pact and accompanied their representatives in meetings with Hitler. Bürkner recounted later how Canaris had given him a free hand to run the combined offices and protected him in awkward situations.[61] The next foreign policy crisis would be the first test of character for the growing opposition movement.

16

Between Obedience and Conscience

On 28 March 1938, Hitler received at the Berghof Foreign Minister Ribbentrop together with leaders of the Sudetendeutsche Party (SdP), Konrad Henlein and Karl Hermann Frank. Henlein had informed Hitler in a letter the previous November that an understanding between Germans and Czechs was practically impossible and that a solution to the Sudeten question, 'the incorporation of the Sudeten-German region, even the entire area of Bohemia, Moravia and Silesia into the Reich'[1] could only come from the Reich. Hitler let Henlein know that he intended 'to resolve the Czech problem in the not-too-distant future',[2] by making unacceptable demands to Prague 'so as to avoid the Czech Government giving in at some stage to British pressure to make concessions to the Sudeten Germans'.[3] Within a month, at the SdP rally in Carlsbad, Henlein announced the demands of his party to the Prague Government, extending to autonomy for the Sudetenland and a cancellation of the Czech mutual assistance treaties with France and Soviet Russia.[4] This was an open confrontation with Prague, and within four weeks Europe was on the verge of war.[5]

The Sudeten situation was a knock-on effect of the annexation of Austria. In 1938 there were about 3.2 million Czech citizens of German blood, of whom at the end of March 770,000 were SdP members; the traditional German parties left the Czech Government and joined with the SdP after the annexation. With the entry of other organisations, by July 1938 the SdP had 1.3 million members, about 41.6 per cent of the German population of Czechoslovakia,[6] and the hope was that the Sudetenland was next on the Wehrmacht list.

Since 1935, when Henlein had won a spectacular election victory, the Abwehr had operated a large network of agents directed mainly from Abwehrstellen at Breslau and Dresden.[7] They had competition from the SS and SD attempting to extend their influence to the pro-Nazi sections of the Sudeten Germans and the radical elements in Henlein's SdP. The Abwehr supported the 'traditionalists' and Henlein, who had had been agitating for an autonomous Catholic region and not necessarily for a war to satisfy Sudeten interests.[8]

According to former Abwehr officer Erwin Stolze, it had been Abwehr II that in 1937 had arranged for Henlein's deputy and SdP propaganda chief, Karl Hermann Frank, to infiltrate the Czech armed forces with SdP help, with the aim of setting up Resistance cells and an organisation that could offer effective support to the Wehrmacht if it invaded.[9] Since 1935 Frank had had links with the SS-led Volksdeutsche Mittelstelle, and on discovering this Canaris relieved him of his operational duties in 1937, replacing him in 1938 by former Austrian officer Richard Lammel.[10]

Around the end of 1936 'an upright man of the people', Oskar Schindler, entered the Abwehr; he was held and interrogated by the Czech secret police in the summer of 1938 during an attempt to recruit an informer for the Abwehr, the Czechs concluding in a highly confidential report that Schindler was 'a high calibre spy and additionally very dangerous'.[11] After the war his name was on a list of nine people who had been involved in especially daring activities – sabotage and commando operations – in connection with the invasion of Poland.[12]

Keitel had ordered plans to be drawn up for the military intervention in Czechoslovakia, 'Fall Grün', although no date for the attack existed at this point. Meanwhile, chief of the General Staff, Beck, warned in a memorandum of 5 May that Germany, by reason of its 'poor economic and military situation' was not 'capable of fighting a long war'. Moreover everything must be done 'to prevent Britain entering a war on the side of our enemies. That is, however, to be expected if Germany tries to force a solution of the Czech problem against British wishes.'[13]

Hitler reacted angrily to this memorandum, parts of which Keitel and Brauchitsch had forwarded him without Beck's knowledge.[14] 'A Foreign-Political Assessment of the Situation Following the Annexation of Austria', authored by Oster and Heinz, recommended an accommodation with Britain because a war against Czechoslovakia at this time would involve too high a risk. They pleaded for an agreement with the Soviet Union to avoid a war on two fronts.

From 2 to 10 May Hitler surrounded himself with an enormous entourage of five hundred diplomats, officials, party functionaries, security men and journalists on a State visit to Italy in order to sound out Mussolini's response if Germany invaded Czechoslovakia. Ernst von Weizsäcker, secretary of state at the Foreign Office, considered: 'Our intentions towards Czechoslovakia are not of interest to Mussolini. He sees our intentions there as "arms by foot". Is that an encouragement or a warning? The Führer believes it is the former. He is thinking of resolving the Sudeten-German question this year since the constellation could worsen.'[15]

On the night of 20 May 1938 Czech President Benes ordered a partial mobilisation of the Army and called up 180,000 reservists,[16] beginning a weekend of hectic diplomatic consultations. Canaris watched the measures for mobilisation and recommended by cable: 'I consider it essential that the Führer advise the commander-in-chief as to his intentions soon.'[17] The situation intensified when two Sudeten Germans were killed in a minor incident with Czech police, which Hitler took as a personal humiliation.[18]

On 30 May, the revised Plan Grün was on the table, regarding which Hitler declared: 'It is my unshakeable resolve to overcome Czechoslovakia in the near future by military action.' The political leadership would await, or bring about, the politically and militarily suitable situation;[19] Hitler had now decided on war even if the Western Powers intervened, and the Abwehr played a central role in the preparations. Primarily it was Groscurth's Abteilung II which was to ensure the smooth running of the planned operation through propaganda, infiltration, cooperation with deserters, acts of sabotage and occupation of the border fortifications.[20]

Beck warned Brauchitsch in a letter of 15 July 1938 that 'a military intervention by Germany against Czechoslovakia will automatically lead to a European, or World War, which from the human perspective will end not only in a military, but also a general catastrophe for Germany',[21] and in a memorandum to Brauchitsch the next day Beck remarked that 'these decisions gamble with the nation's existence; history will condemn these leaders with a debt of blood if they fail to act according to the principles of expert and State political knowledge and conscience. Your soldierly obedience has its limits where your knowledge, conscience and responsibility forbid you to carry out an order.'[22]

At this time, Hans Oster was with Beck almost daily asking his support for the planned coup attempt, and even Quartermaster-General Halder urged Beck to be more active in opposing Hitler's plans – memoranda alone were not sufficient. Beck responded with a memorandum containing ideas propounded during the Fritsch crisis by Canaris and Hossbach or Oster;[23] the document urged the self-assertion of the Wehrmacht against the SS and demanded a basic reform of the Third Reich. 'Probably for the last time,' Beck wrote on 19 July,

Fate offers us the opportunity to free the German people and the Führer himself from a Czech nightmare and the omens of a tyranny that will destroy the existence and welfare of the Reich:

1. There can and must be no doubt but that this struggle will be fought for the Führer.
2. There must never be even the slightest suspicion of a plot, yet the determination of the most senior military leaders must be manifest at every step ... Brief, clear expressions: for the Führer! Against war! Against tyranny! Peace with the

Church! Freedom of speech! An end to the methods in Czechoslovakia! The rule of law again in the Reich![24]

Was Beck aiming for a programme of reform in which the Third Reich would be purified,[25] or was this the agenda for a revolution which, had it been successful, would have destroyed the existence of National Socialism?[26] The programme was illusory, for it proceeded from the false assumption that if only one could destroy the SS and SA, the State would come back to a sober course. Yet it was palpably Hitler himself who was steering, and Beck was speaking decisively to those power-holders upon whom Hitler was relying.[27] In another memorandum on 29 July Beck wrote declining all responsibility of the generals for a war against Czechoslovakia and suggested the mass resignation of the generals and senior commanders should Hitler insist on going ahead with war.[28] On 4 August Brauchitsch summoned a conference of the senior generals at the Bendlerstrasse but preferred Halder's significantly more moderate memorandum of 16 July in which he expressed doubts about war, in regard to the current state of preparations. Beck gave up, and retired on 18 August.[29]

On 6 August, the head of Amtsgruppe Ausland, Bürkner, informed Canaris and Oster of a statement by the British ambassador Henderson that Britain would agree to any sensible solution of the Sudeten crisis provided no force was used.[30] The Foreign Office recorded: 'As Kapitän Bürkner noted in conclusion that we too would welcome a peaceful solution, the ambassador expressed by means of a gesture that he probably doubts it. The conversations then ended.'[31] Canaris informed Hitler of what Henderson had said, which fortified Hitler in his resolve for war. In his diary entry for 10 August Goebbels said: 'In Czechoslovakia terror against Germans blooms again. Another death. We will now strike massively against those bush-rangers. The Führer is hesitant about the Prague question; he has already solved it mentally and divided it into Gaue.'[32] Goebbels noted with satisfaction that propaganda companies were even being set up in the Army, and the preparations for the worst case scenario were therefore being made at full speed.[33]

Keitel's adjutant, Eberhard, recorded a violent outburst by Canaris: 'I cannot go along with this any longer. We will not allow ourselves to be used as propagandists of fables of atrocity.'[34] Instructions for the Army propaganda units were set out by Groscurth's Abteilung II, which was also responsible for the production of leaflets to intimidate the Czech population and provide the Sudeten Germans with their guidelines; Hitler reserved the right to edit these fly-bills.[35]

Canaris attempted to counteract Hitler's warmongering by manipulating the flow of intelligence reports and gave Lahousen, who was responsible for

reports from the east, secret orders for the handling of material from the Czech
Republic:

> Prioritise and OVERVALUE all reports and signals which mention the strength of the
> Czech land fortifications, the determination of the Czech people and government
> to resist as well as the probability of the intervention of the Western Powers and
> the Soviet Union (Russian air force). This will counteract the optimistic reports of
> the SD and similar party centres based on National Socialist ideology.[36]

On 15 August, just before Beck's resignation, Ribbentrop accused the Army
and General Staff of disseminating false information, insisting that 'Britain and
France will not come into the war.'[37] Canaris and Oster were searching for a way
to convince the British that a strong attitude towards Hitler was essential and
accepted the offer of the Pomeranian landowner Ewald von Kleist-Schmenzin
to travel to London as emissary. Shortly after the annexation of Austria, Kleist
had confided to the Central European correspondent of the *News Chronicle*,
Ian Colvin, that Hitler had more far-reaching plans and his next objective was
Czechoslovakia,[38] and had asked for an interview with Lord Lloyd of Dolobran,
president of the Navy League and chairman of the British Council.

Beck had told Kleist: 'Bring me definite evidence that Britain will fight if
we attack Czechoslovakia and I will make an end of this regime,'[39] but Kleist's
mission was difficult because he was being watched by the Gestapo. Canaris and
Oster procured a passport for him while Colvin contacted the British embassy
and sources in London,[40] and on 18 August, Kleist travelled to London, where
he met the permanent under-secretary of state at the Foreign Office, Sir Robert
Vansittart, opposition politicians and also opponents of appeasement, Lord
Lloyd and Winston Churchill.

Meanwhile the Hungarian regent, Admiral von Horthy, had planned a State
visit to Germany for 22 August 1938, and with the agreement of Secretary of
State von Weizsäcker, Canaris and Groscurth travelled to Budapest to stir up
concern in Hungary at Hitler's warmongering; Groscurth noted in his diary:
'The regent is determined to protest to the Führer against war.'[41] The regent
obviously changed his mind once in Germany and von Weizsäcker concluded:
'(a) Hungary is happy to expect to receive no final advices from us and (b)
Hungary believes it will probably be able to join in the fighting fourteen days
after the conflict begins.'[42]

On 22 August, twenty-six Sudeten Germans trained by the Abwehr were
captured while arms smuggling, which Karl Hermann Frank took as an
opportunity to call upon SdP supporters 'to find in these Marxist terror acts
their right to defend themselves'.[43] He had previously declared to the German
commercial envoy in Prague that the Czech State could not protect Sudeten

German citizens, and this would provide the foundation for a German invasion.[44] The same day Frank saw Hitler: 'Führer is determined for war,' he reported, and Groscurth noted: 'orders creation of incidents in CSR. Insulted Benes, will capture him alive and string him up himself.'[45] Canaris was attempting meanwhile to motivate the more moderate Henlein, who was not happy about war, to intercede with Hitler.[46]

Kleist returned from London on 24 August after a disappointing outcome to his mission; Vansittart had commissioned a speech of warning by Lord Simon, chancellor of the Exchequer, and there would be naval manoeuvres should the situation deteriorate further. This was hardly likely to convince the German generals that the British were going to fight. Churchill sent a letter to the British embassy in Berlin of which Kleist received a copy, one of the rare encouraging signs ever given to the German Resistance from abroad. Churchill wrote:

> I am certain that if German troops cross the Czech border by force . . . it will bring about a World War. As at the end of July 1914 I am sure that Britain will march with France. Do not let yourselves be deceived, I beg you. Such a war would, once begun, be fought to the bitter end as was the last. All of us should think less about what could happen in the first few months and more about where we will all find ourselves at the end of the third or fourth year of war.[47]

Canaris was said to have mentioned this letter in a report he delivered to Hitler, Weizsäcker included an extract of it in a memorandum quoting overseas opinion on a possible conflict between German and Czechoslovakia, naming Churchill as author but not stating where he had obtained the letter.[48]

On 30 August the British Government advised the Czechs to accept Henlein's Carlovy Vary programme and guarantee Sudeten German autonomy within the Czech State.[49] That evening Canaris discovered that when the Navy warned Hitler that it had only one pocket battleship and eight U-boats operational, he replied: 'That is not important, I know that Britain will stay neutral.'[50]

On 2 September 1938 Hitler told Henlein that he would move within the month. Henlein informed his British contact, a colleague of the 'neutral' negotiator Lord Runciman, that Hitler was interested in a peaceful solution, which was untrue, and supported the efforts at appeasement, but the next day Hitler set the date for the attack as 1 October.[51] On 2 September Canaris had been in Rome,[52] where he met the chief of the Italian General Staff, Pariani,[53] who informed Hitler on his return that Italy would not fight and strongly urged Germany against war. Hitler was unimpressed, believing that Mussolini had differences of opinion with his General Staff similar to those that Hitler had with his.[54]

Keitel gave Canaris strict orders not to forward any more political reports and alarming signals to the Army or Luftwaffe; Goering had sent Hitler a file

'Reports Advising Against War' and garnished the cover with the words 'This is how OKW (Keitel) works against you.'[55] Meanwhile, Frank was working to set up the incidents in Czechozlovakia ordered by Hitler. On 7 September an SdP commission had travelled to Mährisch-Ostrau to investigate the legality of the arrest of eighty-three Sudeten Germans on charges of arms smuggling and espionage, and Sudeten German deputies and police had clashed during an organised demonstration outside the court building;[56] Groscurth believed 'Incidents in Mährisch-Ostrau are doubtless provoked.'[57] Frank's handiwork had the desired effect. He and Henlein broke off the negotiations with Benes that had been underway since the latter caved in to British pressure and stated that he was ready to concede the demands of the Carlsbad programme. When Canaris returned from the Nuremberg Rally on 11 September, he told Groscurth that Henlein had now completely fallen in line behind Hitler and Frank. One day later Hitler delivered his long-awaited speech of warning should the Sudeten Germans be denied self-determination.[58]

On 13 September Keitel addressed departmental heads. 'Wild complaints against the Army,' Groscurth wrote, 'Admiral protests about it.'[59] Jodl noted in his diary:

> People have begun complaining to the Führer about alarmism and are implicating OKW as well. Abwehr reports – conversation between Canaris and Pariani, and a memorandum from military-economic Staff about the strength and invulnerability of British armaments industry give unjustified cause ... General Keitel emphasised that he will not tolerate any officer at OKW who involves himself in criticism and alarmism ... there was a cold and frosty atmosphere at Nuremberg and it is very sad that the Führer had the whole country behind him but not the senior Army generals.[60]

Since May 1938, the SdP had been building the Voluntary German Protection Service (FS) from their military trained forces, to function as a kind of security and police service, gathering information about political opponents, spying on the border fortifications, arranging provocative actions and raids and organising general chaos. Its members were trained in Germany and the Abwehr recruited from amongst them.[61] During the Nuremberg Rally the time came for the FS; up to 9 September the number of arranged incidents had been small, but on 11 September the first injuries were reported on both sides.[62]

Radiosender Breslau broadcast a provocative speech by Hitler to the Sudeten Germans on 12 September and marches and mass demonstrations followed. On 13 September when Prague imposed emergency rule in the disputed region there were casualties, and on 15 September the SdP leaders broke off all negotiations with Prague, closed down their office and flew to Germany.[63] On 17 September Hitler ordered the formation of a 'Sudeten German Legion' to guarantee the protection of the Sudeten Germans and maintain the unrest and disturbances; terror squads were to be formed from the Freikorps's sub-unit to create constant unrest in the border region and the Führer himself would arrange major actions through the OKW.[64]

The Freikorps Staff was billeted at Schloss Donndorf in Bavaria. OKW, SS and SA sent liaison officers. Groscurth was responsible for the link with the Abwehr[65] and saw the arrangement as 'the politics of adventure' but ordered the support of the Freikorps. This resulted in a violent argument with Canaris, but the next day, after receiving an OKW directive, Canaris ordered 'the fullest support of the Freikorps',[66] Groscurth noting with horror in his diary on 20 September that 'the Freikorps, entering behind the Army', would 'mop up',[67] and take its orders from Himmler instead of the Army, contrary to the OKW directive.

Beck's successor as chief of the General Staff was Franz Halder, whose aversion to Hitler occasionally drove him to 'primitive outbursts of hate'.[68] He was prepared to participate in a coup d'état, and at the beginning of September he sounded out Schacht, president of the Reichsbank, von Weizsäcker and General von Witzleben; the latter confirmed his readiness to handle the military preparations for a coup if Oster and Gisevius assisted him, and he had the orders of Halder or Brauchitsch to proceed.[69]

On 2 September Halder despatched former Stahlhelm leader retired Oberstleutnant Hans Böhm-Tettelbach to London to urge Vansittart to make no further concessions to Hitler.[70] He failed to obtain an appointment to meet Vansittart and saw instead an old friend, together with a major in the British intelligence service of the General Staff, who promised to forward the message to Vansittart; that was the only success of his visit.[71]

Von Weizsäcker at the Foreign Office had co-workers conspiring against Hitler, amongst them members of the 'Graf Group' and the Kordt brothers, Erich and Theo, who were senior civil servants with contacts in London;[72] Weizsäcker, Canaris and Oster thus held the key positions in a complicated web of connections. Although Halder considered Canaris 'by nature a difficult person to converse with'[73] and often complained that much of Weizsäcker's information came to him incomplete because of the peculiar manner Canaris had of expressing himself, he developed a close relationship with the Abwehr chief, while the contact between Canaris and von Weizsäcker was also close. In his memoirs the latter wrote of Canaris with a mixture of admiration and respect: 'One cannot pass over this phenomenon ... Canaris had the gift of getting people to talk without giving anything away of himself. His watery blue eyes gave nothing away. Very rarely, and only through a small chink, one saw his character, clear as a bell, the ethical and tragic depths of his personality.'[74]

Canaris was one of the few people to whom von Weizäcker spoke 'without reservations'.[75]

If it served the interest of the conspiracy, Weizsäcker would reveal it and his links to Canaris and potential allies. On 1 September he secretly met the High Commissioner of the Danzig People's League, Professor Carl Jacob Burckhardt, in a remote corner of the Berlin Zoo. When he explained to Burckhardt the efforts being made in London, the professor recognised that 'the whole thing was a conspiracy with a potential enemy to preserve peace, a double-game of the most extreme danger'. Weizsäcker spoke with the openness of the desperate man gambling all on the last card; he mentioned a secret mission that Theo Kordt had undertaken with Neville Chamberlain and Lord Halifax:

> He pleaded with me to go to Switzerland to inform the British Foreign Office that one must speak to Hitler unequivocally, only then would he back-track. Even then Weizsäcker made no secret of the fact that he believed it was only possible to save the general peace and Germany if the one human figure in whose hands all power resided were to disappear. He indicated to me that he was in contact with Canaris.[76]

In fact, the planned mission of the Kordt brothers did not take place until after he had gone back to Switzerland;[77] Burckhardt sought out an intermediary to Chamberlain, and Theo Kordt met Lord Halifax, to whom he made himself known as a member of the 'internal German Resistance' and asked that the BBC 'broadcast a warning to the German people' that they should get 'their Army leaders' to 'intervene against Hitler's policies by force of arms'.[78]

These missions were all fruitless, for the British Government had long since decided to surrender the territorial integrity and sovereignty of the Czechs for the sake of peace.[79] A few weeks after the Munich Conference Lord Halifax told Kordt: 'We are not in the position to be as frank with you as you were with us. At the time when you gave us your message, we were already considering sending Chamberlain to Germany.'[80]

At about this time there began to form 'a conspiracy in a conspiracy',[81] or 'a plot within the plot'.[82] Doubts as to the resolve of Halder and Canaris decided Witzleben, Oster, Schacht, Gisevius and Heinz to carry out a coup without Halder's order. Witzleben believed he could count on his long-standing contacts with commanders and officers, above all General Walter Graf von Brockdorff-Ahlefeldt – commanding officer of the 23rd Division at Postdam – who had indicated the previous autumn his readiness to move against the SS and Gestapo with force. Other conspirators in this group were Henning von Tresckow, Graf Bandissin,[83] Paul Hase, later commandant of Berlin, and probably also Erich Hoepner.[84] In early September Gisevius and Brockdorff discussed which ministries, barracks and strategically important installations in and around Berlin were to be occupied when Hitler was seized, and Gisevius spoke to Nebe and Helldorf regarding the police measures. The conspirators wanted to capture Hitler by means of a stormtroop operation using experienced soldiers and Freikorps men under Witzleben's command. Canaris, Witzleben, Schacht and Gisevius were not in favour of assassinating Hitler; they felt he should be forced to resign and then either be put on trial or certified insane and confined in a security hospital. Attornies Dohnanyi and Sack had begun the preparations to try him as a common criminal using the evidence Dohnanyi had accumulated at the Ministry. The psychiatric opinion would be obtained from a medical team led by Dr Karl Bonhoeffer, Dohnanyi's father-in-law.[85]

The assault troop in this plan would be made up of courageous, unscrupulous, motivated but politically unambitious men prepared, after the coup, to step back into the shadows.[86] Heinz was asked by Witzleben and Oster at the beginning of September to head a unit of about thirty men,[87] comprised of old street-fighters such as Liedig and Ludwig Gehre[88] alongside Abwehr officers Groscurth and Döhring and with Heinz's friend, Abwehr official Hans-Wolfram Knaak, as the tactical leader. Former members of the Stahlhelm and student ring were involved, as were Hans-Albrecht Herzner of Abwehrstelle Breslau, who one year later would lead the first commando operation of the Second World War, and journalist and military writer Albrecht Günther.[89]

The group around Halder and Canaris wanted a military dictatorship under Beck, leading eventually to civilian government, while Heinz and others preferred a kind of constitutional monarchy on the British model and had obtained from Prince Wilhelm of Prussia an assurance that he would step in should there be 'a change in government circumstances'.[90] Canaris knew little about these plans, and nothing of Heinz and Oster's schemes to eliminate Hitler, even though it was he alone who gave the order to procure weapons and explosives for the conspirators.[91]

The date for Hitler to be arrested was apparently originally mid-September. On the evening of 14 September, Groscurth, his wife Charlotte and brother Reinhard waited at their Berlin flat; Groscurth seemed nervous and excited, once exclaiming, 'Can't you be quiet? Tonight Hitler will be arrested!' Next morning he told his brother tersely that there had been an intervention.[92] By this he can only have been referring to Chamberlain's dramatic plea for a meeting with Hitler; the British prime minister arrived at Obersalzberg on 15 September to speak with Hitler.[93]

In Munich Chamberlain was greeted by cheering masses, but he, his aides and ambassador Henderson saw one troop transport after another pass them towards the Czech frontier. Nevertheless Chamberlain held firm to his belief that the Sudeten question was not worth war because his negotiator, Lord Runciman, considered Czech policy towards the national minorities as discriminatory and had suggested that Germans in the border regions should have the right to self-determination. Later Chamberlain put it in a nutshell: 'It was like a long neglected disease. A surgical operation was necessary to save the life of the patient.'[94]

At the first meeting with Hitler, Chamberlain said he would leave immediately if Hitler had the definite intention to use force, but Hitler assured his visitor that in negotiating the Sudeten question the important thing was to recognise the right of the Sudeten German population to self-determination; if that were conceded then talks could follow. Chamberlain needed to consult his Cabinet colleagues and suggested another meeting, obtaining Hitler's agreement not to use force in the meantime, unless he was provoked.[95] After diplomatic discussions, Chamberlain returned to Germany on 22 September and met Hitler at the Dreesen Hotel in Bad Godesberg.[96] He brought with him an attractive package: the agreement of the London, Paris and Prague governments to the principle of self-determination, a plan for the annexation of Sudeten German territory to Germany, transfer deadlines, border guarantees and a Non-Aggression Pact between Germany and Czechoslovakia. Hitler refused: 'I am very sorry, Herr Chamberlain, but I can no longer discuss these things. After developments in recent days the solution is no longer valid.'[97] By this he meant new Polish and Hungarian claims on Czechoslovakia, requiring prior clarification. Hitler then demanded agreement to his immediate occupation of the Sudetenland. At this Chamberlain left the discussion, and instead of appearing for the scheduled meeting the following morning sent a letter refusing Hitler's demand. Two hours later Chamberlain suggested that he would put the new German demand to the Czechs and asked for it in writing. The German memorandum wanted the evacuation of the Czech Army from an area sketched on a map by 28 September – four days hence. Despite a report that Czechoslovakia had mobilised, Hitler stated that despite the provocation he would make no move while Chamberlain remained in Germany. The next morning the prime minister returned to London.[98]

On 19 September Canaris had visted Abwehrstelle VIII Breslau to discuss demarcation lines with Sudeten-Deutsches Freikorps (SDF) leaders. Together with Groscurth on 21 September at the Reichsschule Donndorf in Bavaria they obtained a negative impression of Henlein, 'nervous with dictator-allure'.[99] Himmler's representative SS Oberführer Gottlob Berger had set up his headquarters in the SDF Staff quarters[100] and after the war he stated that Canaris came every other day for talks with Henlein.[101] On 21 September Groscurth noted in his diary, with an exclamation mark, that he had seen Henlein at the Bellevue Hotel where Heinz Jost had his headquarters. Jost would become head of Amt III (SD) of the SS administrative headquarters (Sicherheits-Hauptamt – SHA) and, as head of the Dresden Einsatzgruppe, he would be active during the invasion of Czechoslovakia with the Einsatzstab Prag.[102] Contrary to the situation when Austria was annexed, SD Amt III under Jost would control affairs instead of Gestapa because it involved an action 'abroad', but in fact the task was more than SD could handle because it lacked structure and personnel. The typical structure of an *Einsatzgruppe* was Sipo, Ordnungspolizei (uniformed civilian police) and SD.[103]

On 24 September Heydrich and Kurt Daluege, Ordnungspolizei chief, paid a visit to the Bellevue Hotel at Dresden. Two days later, after it became known that Prague had turned down the German demands, Hitler delivered a strong speech to an audience of twenty thousand in the Berlin Sportspalast in which he gave Benes a final ultimatum.

Canaris went to Keitel and drew his attention to Heydrich's preparations to eliminate the German Communists in the Sudeten German region, 'which do not coincide with our mobilisation directive'.[104] He pointed out that Army High Command had the unlimited right to operate militarily in operational areas beyond the Reich without the need to have 'the Sipo and SD mopping up after it'.[105] Daluege received orders immediately to ensure that his preparations coincided with those of OKW. Groscurth wrote with surprise that Heydrich had threatened his Gestapo people with 'the strongest measures for criminal acts – extraordinary!'[106]

Although there were high-priority arrest lists in existence, Canaris's counterpart Best promised in his 'Guidelines for the Activities of Gestapo Einsatzkommandos in the Sudeten German Regions' that 'under no circumstances are innocent people to be molested about trifling matters', 'the maltreatment and killing of prisoners is strictly forbidden.'[107]

The SDF, however, was neither under the control of the SD, the Einsatzgruppen or the Abwehr. 'The SDF has three days' freedom to hunt down all unwanted elements in Frank's initiative for the Führer! Cleansing!'[108] noted Groscurth on 28 September, the day when the ultimatum to Czechoslovakia expired.

The conspirators had meanwhile recovered from the Chamberlain intervention. Heinz wrote later that around the 20 September,[109] after a meeting at Oster's house attended by Witzleben, Heinz and Liedig, Oster asked Heinz privately afterwards why he seemed dissatisfied with the coup plan. 'I answered that it did not seem to me that the stormtroop would find Witzleben's method of committing suicide particularly original.' Oster understood immediately and issued the order: 'Hitler's study is to be taken by force. Should the SS not resist, an incident is to be provoked in which Adolf Hitler and the greatest number possible of his staff are gunned down.' This made it clear that there was no way back for the generals and that Hitler, even out of power, would still represent a deadly danger for any new government.[110] On the afternoon of 23 September, however, when Oster was informed by Erich Kordt and Albrecht von Kessel about the most recent meeting between Hitler and Chamberlain, he said: 'Now, thank God, we finally have the clear evidence that Hitler wants war no matter what. Now there can be no going back.' He urged Kordt and Kessel: 'But do everything you can to bring Hitler back to Berlin. The bird must come back to the barn.'[111] Then he ordered Heinz to lead his stormtroopers to their waiting positions.

On 26 September Schulenburg advised Kordt that he should expect the coup within forty-eight hours;[112] Halder had heard from Brauchitsch that he would probably take part. Kordt and Schulenburg agreed to open the doors of the Reich Chancellery to admit the stormtroopers at the given time,[113] but again events intervened at the last moment.

Groscurth learned from Canaris that Hitler had agreed to receive Daladier, Chamberlain and Mussolini in Munich; Goering had intervened with Henderson to win over the British to a negotiated settlement within the framework of a conference of the major powers. This led to the signing of the notorious Munich Agreement on the night of 30 September. War had been avoided; Hitler had won without a shot being fired. The agreement resembled the Godesberg Memorandum with a few minor changes; German troops would occupy the Sudeten German region within ten days. Hitler's popularity reached new heights among the German public, and ironically he was now 'the preserver of a peace he had not wanted'.[114]

As for the Resistance, Chamberlain and Daladier pulled the carpet from under the conspirators' feet. The disdain shown for them by the Western nations, and the way the classical military command structure functioned run through the story of the German Resistance movement from 1938 onwards like a red thread.[115]

British ambassador Henderson wrote to Foreign Minister Halifax on 6 October that 'by keeping the peace, we have saved Hitler and his regime ....'[116] The frustrated plotters regrouped 'willingly into the mechanism of the German occupation machinery';[117] Canaris, Oster and Groscurth followed the Führer into the Sudetenland, where they saw the images of 'real freedom' and heard 'a sigh of relief from the people after the lifting of heavy pressure'.[118]

In Hörsin the Abwehr greeted Hitler's entry: 'The band of the SS Leibstandarte broke into the Badenweiler March when the Führer arrived. We cleared the street ourselves and waited on the outskirts of the village. When the Führer saw us, he called out, "There's Canaris!" and ordered his chauffeur to stop the car. He spoke a few words with the Admiral, gave us a friendly wave and then drove on.'

Groscurth was annoyed that Canaris had not introduced his Staff to the Führer but the pleasant evening that followed with the Bad Elter spa manager cheered everybody up. It seemed odd how quickly yesterday's plotters adjusted to the new situation: 'We observed an enormous amount, had gained great and solemn impressions, but also saw that everywhere the SS and Gestapo appeared, all the crockery which could be destroyed, was destroyed.'[119]

PART IV

FINIS GERMANIAE

17

The Will for War

On the morning of 22 August 1939 Canaris reported to the Berghof just before noon. Present were Raeder, Goering and Brauchitsch, the three Wehrmacht commanders-in-chief and about fifty senior commanders of the three services.[1] All wore civilian dress 'as the conference should be kept secret as far as possible in the tense political atmosphere',[2] with Goering turning up in an old hunting suit.[3] The lecture was to be delivered in the Great Hall, whose giant windows gave onto an impressive view of the Bavarian mountain range.[4] At midday Hitler began his speech; his listeners were expressly forbidden to take it down in writing or make notes,[5] but not all respected this injunction, and even Canaris secretly scribbled down the main points and Halder and General Boehm both copied down the speech from memory the same day.[6] Its purpose was to prepare the generals for the attack on Poland.[7]

Hitler mentioned Germany's economic difficulties and gave his best analysis of the international constellation of powers before speaking of the central importance of his own person for Germany's destiny:

> Really it depends on me, on my being, on account of my political abilities. The fact is that probably nobody but me has the confidence of the whole German people ... but I can be eliminated at any time by a criminal, by an idiot.[8] ... We have nothing to lose, only to gain. Our economic situation is such that we can only hold out for a few years ... All these happy circumstances will no longer exist in two to three years; nobody knows how long I have to live. Therefore the dispute is best now ... The relationship with Poland has become intolerable ... we must accept the risk with ruthless resolve ... We have the harsh alternatives of either hitting, or sooner or later being annihilated for sure.[9] ... Our opponents are small worms; I saw them at Munich ... My only fear is that at the last moment some swinehound will give me a plan for negotiation.[10]

The monologue continued for ninety minutes; in response Goering, as senior officer present, thanked and assured him: 'The Wehrmacht will do its duty. Quite obviously, if called upon, it must do its duty.'[11] The company then dined on the terrace of the Berghof[12] and, upon resumption, Hitler spoke of 'the most iron resolve amongst ourselves ... the life and death struggle ... a long period of peace will do us no good ... Qualitatively, we have the better man. The destruction of Poland is in the foreground ... the objective is to eliminate living forces, not to reach a certain line.'[13] There has been much debate over whether this last sentence was put that way and so could be interpreted as a hint of the planned war of extermination in the East.[14] He continued:

> I will supply a motive through propaganda to start this war, irrespective of whether it is credible; nobody will ask the victor afterwards whether he told the truth or not. At the beginning and in the execution of the war it is not about right, but about victory. Hearts closed to compassion; brutal proceedings. Eighty million people must have their rights, their existence must be guaranteed. The stronger party has right on his side, the greatest harshness.[15]

What Canaris took down in hasty shorthand left nothing to be desired in terms of clarity. After the speech nobody spoke;[16] even von Brauchitsch, who was most likely to raise an opinion or protest on some point, remained silent. The officers did not discuss the speech, and Generalmajor von Sodenstern noted 'an atmosphere of suspicion'.[17]

Hitler's adjutant Nicolaus von Below summed up in his memoir: 'We were confronted by the fact that in a few days Germany would find itself in a war which Hitler considered inevitable and desired, without having trust in his generals and which his generals considered a catastrophe, although they made no move against him.'[18]

Canaris returned to Berlin the next day and informed his senior staff of the Berghof speech, and the probable date for the attack on Poland,[19] reading his notes to his closest confidants. Gisevius remembered later: 'His voice trembled; he felt he had been witness to something huge. We were both of the opinion we must preserve for the world this document and therefore we made a copy that Oster added to his document collection,'[20] referring to Oster's collection of files and documents relating to the misdeeds of the National Socialist regime.[21] Groscurth noted in his diary on 24 August 1939: 'On the 26th the war against Poland starts up. The chief spent two hours showing me his diaries and the Führer's speech to the commanders-in-chief, which he had taken down in brief phrases. We are flabbergasted. Everything is lies and deception, nothing true. It is right to say of it, "It lacks any decent basis".'[22]

It was very probably Oster who passed the document forward; on 25 August the prominent American journalist Louis P Lochner, chief of the Associated Press office in Berlin, passed a report on Hitler's Berghof speech to Ogilvie-Forbes, adviser to the British ambassador, who forwarded it immediately to London. Lochner received the speech from another source, as the note of an unnamed officer who had been present at the Berghof.[23]

Lochner stated that he took the paper first to the American envoy Alexander C Kirk, but he refused to accept it, saying: 'Oh, take this out of here. It is dynamite. I won't touch it, I don't want to get involved.'[24]

This particular copy differed substantially from the text of Canaris's stenographed version, and it seems likely that Oster doctored the text to make it more lurid.[25] Daladier and Chamberlain were now the pitiful 'little worms' too cowardly to venture a counter-strike:

What the weak Western European civilisation says about me is irrelevant. I have given the order – and I will have anyone shot who says a word in criticism of it – that the war is not to reach certain lines, but the physical annihilation of the enemy. Therefore I have, initially only in the East, drawn up my SS-Death's Head units with the order to send to their deaths, ruthlessly and without compassion, every man, woman and child of Polish extraction and mother tongue. Only in that manner will we win the living space that we need. Who talks today of the extermination of the Armenians?[26]

At the Obersalzberg meeting Hitler had not said this, but it demonstrates that the presumed author of the adulterated version, Hans Oster, understood that the planned attack was linked to genocide. The document ended with Hitler's fear that

Chamberlain or some other such filthy swine would arrive at the last moment with suggestions and upsets. He will fall down the stairs ... the attack and the destruction of Poland begin early Sunday morning. I am having a couple of companies in Polish uniform in Upper Silesia or in the Protectorate attacked. Whether the world believes it or not I don't give a shit. The world believes only in success.[27]

That the author of the falsified pamphlet assessed the situation correctly is proved by two details that Hitler had not mentioned in his address but which corresponded to his plans: the setting up of the SS-Death's Head units and the provocateurs in Polish uniforms. Canaris made clear to Halder the same day that he knew, or at least suspected, this, and Halder noted in his diary that Canaris had expressed 'his worries about the role of SS-Death's Head units in the impending war'.[28] The Abwehr had been involved for months in the preparations for 'Fall Weiss' – the attack on Poland – in both the operational planning and the provocations agreed by Hitler, Himmler and Heydrich as justification of the invasion for propaganda purposes.

Despite assurances to the contrary by Hitler and Ribbentrop, OKH expected the involvement of the Western Powers and war on two fronts, and it was for this reason that the original final plan of 15 June was shelved in favour of overcoming Poland in as short a time as possible, so that the greater part of the Wehrmacht could be transferred to the Western Front at the earliest opportunity.[29] The Polish Army would have to accept battle as close as possible to the German frontier since the area west of the Vistula River was home to their vital industrial centre and the base for their mainstream mobilisation. To withdraw their troops east of the Vistula in the hope of absorbing a German surprise attack and then using the tactic of trench warfare was not possible because of the tension existing between Poland and its eastern neighbour, the Soviet Union. Accordingly, the Polish plan in the case of a German invasion would be an attempt to intercept and hold the first waves quickly in order to concede the least amount of terrain possible until British and French support arrived, and to inflict upon the enemy the maximum casualties. At the same time, the Poles would have to either protect or destroy strategically important lines of communication and industrial installations before the Germans could capture them.[30]

The German Army planners were aware of these considerations. Two precarious bottlenecks in the path of the Wehrmacht were the Vistula bridges at Dirschau in the operational area of Army Group North, and the Jablunka Pass in the western Beskid in the area of Army Group South. Both were strategically important transport communications points that the Poles had prepared to destroy with explosives. Lahousen (Abwehr Abteilung II) had the task of preventing the destruction and so to smooth the advance of the German invasion forces;[31] both of these commando operations involved great risks since the units had to infiltrate the target area in civilian clothes 'in peacetime', ahead of the invasion.

The area around the Dirschau bridges had been watched by the Abwehr for months. It was suspected that the wires to the Polish explosives ran below the carriageway but it was not known where the actual explosives were located.[32] On 11 July, OKH decided that 1 Armeekorps was responsible for capturing the Dirschau bridges, and Lahousen's Abteilung was ordered to make the necessary preparations.[33]

The task of securing the two tunnels through the Jablunka Pass and the occupation of Mosty Railway Station was given to Leutnant (R) Herzner, who a year earlier had been a member of the stormtroop proposing to take the Reich Chancellery. His team would have to succeed in its objective at Jablunka a few hours before the scheduled time for the invasion, with the support of special units formed by the Abwehr, made up of street-fighters who for ideological or materialist reasons had joined one or other of the Abwehr battle or sabotage organisations. These units were trained along Abwehr lines and wore civilian clothes or enemy uniforms, and had been deployed during the Sudeten crisis to operate behind the Czech lines in the event of hostilities.[34] After some forethought,

Canaris had approved such K(ampf)- and S(abotage)- Organisations;[35] now it would be their job to prevent the Poles denying the invasion army possession of strategically important targets well back from the Front.

On 30 June Abwehrstelle Breslau reported a complement of two thousand men for the planned K-Organisations in the Olsa area and at Pless.[36] In the majority of cases these would be Volksdeutsche – foreign nationals of German blood – and Polish Ukrainians as well as Czechs, Slovaks and Sudeten Germans;[37] they had no military status, which often caused complications in matters of discipline.[38]

On 10 August 1939, Canaris dined with the Ribbentrop family at Schloss Fuschl near Salzburg;[39] the main topic of conversation there was the imminent war. The Reich foreign minister spoke about the 'Pact of Steel' signed with Italy on 22 May, the ten-year treaty that provided for regular consultations between Berlin and Rome, mutual support if threatened and an immediate alliance in the event of war, subject to a three-year opening period of peace before risking any adventure.[40] Ribbentrop was confident that Italy would stand beside the Reich and deny the British access to the Mediterranean, and the following day he entertained the Italian foreign minister, Count Ciano, who had come to convince the Germans that the time for an invasion was not ripe.[41] It was an icy encounter; neither exchanged a word at dinner.[42]

Next morning Ciano saw Hitler at Obersalzberg. Interpreter Schmidt remembered that Ciano 'went to the point very energetically',[43] but Hitler responded by saying that the major war against the Western Powers had to be fought while he and the Duce were still young.[44] When Ciano objected that Italy was not equipped for war,[45] Hitler explained that the Polish campaign would not lead to a general war, and therefore he would not need to request Italy's military support. Ciano returned to Salzburg the same evening and discussed the matter with Italian ambassador Bernardo Attolico, who had been advising him to break with Germany even during the negotiations with Ribbentrop, but Ciano knew that Mussolini would never agree to this.[46] On 13 August, after a second visit to Obersalzberg, he recognised that 'nothing more can be done. He is determined to strike, and he will strike.'[47] Ciano returned to Rome feeling deceived by the leaders of the Third Reich, and he envisaged Italy being dragged into an adventure with an uncertain outcome.[48]

Hitler's iron resolve had been fortified during the discussions with Ciano when information was received from Moscow that the Soviets were prepared to negotiate on matters, including Poland. That same day Hitler fixed the prospective date for the attack on Poland for Saturday 26 August.[49]

Canaris mobilised his Italian contacts and on 11 August in Berlin he met Roatta, the military attaché at the Italian embassy, and warned him that Germany was 'not equipped for a general war'. Many German senior commanders were convinced that in the event of war with Poland, Britain and France would not intervene, and therefore the attitude of Italy in the present situation was decisive.[50] Four days later Canaris told Roatta that Hitler's intention was not only to re-annexe Danzig, but to destroy Poland; the military operation would begin in about two weeks.

Canaris expected the Western Powers to become involved and that a long war would result. Germany would be victorious in the East but as in 1917/18 defeated in the West, 'and that will be the end of Germany':[51] Canaris continued that it was known that the Italian Government considered the time for a European war inopportune, but this would not shift the Führer in his resolve. Perhaps Hitler would decide otherwise if the Italians declared expressly that they were against it. Roatta relayed the message at once to an envoy at the Italian embassy in Berlin, Massimo Magisatrati, and Ciano received the report by courier, Canaris having warned expressly of the danger of telephone conversations being tapped and cables being decrypted. Magistrati made a marginal note: 'Please do not give the name of the admiral as the source of this information under any circumstances.'[52]

For some time, Ernst von Weizsäcker, secretary of state at the Foreign Office, had been attempting to influence Mussolini through ambassador Attolico, and through secret channels from London, but apparently he did not mention his link to Canaris.[53] Weizsäcker was kept informed of the discussions between Ribbentrop, Hitler and Ciano[54] by Interpreter Schmidt and a colleague of his confidant Erich Kordt.[55]

On 15 August 1939 Attolico pleaded with British ambassador Sir Neville Henderson that the British Government should approach Mussolini for a new peace initiative. Weizsäcker informed Halder of this the same day, while Theodor Kordt, an adviser to the German ambassador in London, warned the British Government.[56]

On 12 August Lahousen recorded in the Abteilung II diary: 'In view of the overall political situation, the Amtsgruppenchef [Canaris] has ordered the Abwehr to yellow alert (*Spannungsdienst*).'[57] Plans for the Dirschau and Jablunka Pass operations had been in hand since mid-June, together with a series of other sabotage missions for Abteilung II in Poland,[58] and negotiations were proceeding with Ukrainian nationalists settled in Poland who were prepared to foment an uprising. Lahousen kept Canaris regularly informed of this.[59] At some point, by mid-August at the latest, Canaris was drawn into the intrigues of Himmler and Heydrich providing the pretext for war.

SS-Gruppenführer Heinz Jost, head of the SD foreign espionage service (originally Amt III Abwehr at SD, now Amt VI-SD-Ausland[60]), brought the Führer's order that the Abwehr was to assist the Reichsführer-SS in an operation:[61] 150 Polish uniforms, weapons and soldiers' paybooks were to be procured, and Himmler would provide the necessary personnel; two days later a list of 364 names had been made available for 'most secret missions'.[62] Jost was one of the oldest party members at SS-RSHA and a close friend of Werner Best, the two having met while in the Hesse police when Jost had been Best's deputy, but nevertheless Canaris apparently did not discover the purpose to which the men and material were to be put.[63] Lahousen and Oster suspected 'something really evil' behind it,[64] Lahousen noting in the service diary on 17 August:

> To my question of why the request of General Manstein regarding deployment of three assault battalions with Polish uniforms was refused while in the same area an operation of SS-Reichsführer Himmler will be carried out, he replied that it was at the order of the Führer, who wishes under all circumstances to keep the Wehrmacht distant from all operations having a pronounced illegal character.[65]

Heydrich's plan was that, on the night before the German invasion, SD and Sipo troops disguised as Polish auxiliaries and soldiers would simulate raids on German installations and their occupants, put there by the SD. The radio station in German Gleiwitz would be occupied and anti-German propaganda broadcast. Other squads would raid the forestry house in Pitschen woods near the border (then Kreuzburg in Upper Silesia) and destroy the German customs post at Hochlinden (near Ratibos).[66] The essential point of the plan – to prove Polish culpability for the attacks – was to have bodies lying around, these being previously murdered concentration camp inmates. Gestapo chief Müller labelled this plan 'Operation Jam',[67] and these 'Polish attacks' would become immediate propaganda for the allegedly provoked German response, and provide the British and French Governments with a last opportunity to renounce their treaty pledges of support for Poland.[68]

The plan was no great secret; on 17 August, Oberst Warlimont, head of Abteilung L at OKW, informed Lahousen of the request for Polish uniforms and equipment.[69] The same day Halder made a reference to the affair in his diary[70] and Canaris notified Keitel that SS-Brigadeführer Jost had ordered uniforms, weapons and paybooks for the 'operation ordered by the Reichsführer-SS'. Canaris observed later in a note that has been preserved: 'I reported to Keitel my discussion with Jost ... he says that he does not think much of the operations but that there is no alternative if the Führer has ordered them. He was not able to ask the Führer how he thought these special operations should be carried out.'[71] Keitel sheltered behind the Führer's orders, as was his wont, even though Canaris tried to convince him that Italy would not enter the war on the side of the Reich; King Vittorio Emmanuel had declared a few days previously that he would not sign a mobilisation order from Mussolini under any circumstances.[72] Keitel now thought it pretty certain that Britain and France would not intervene in support of Poland, for if a dictatorship such as Italy was not willing to participate, then how much 'worse' would it appear to the democracies? He rejected any attempt to have him represent other views to the Führer.[73]

Groscurth wrote in his diary on 24 August: 'The basis for the war is to be provided by 150 concentration camp inmates, who will be dressed in Polish uniforms and sacrificed! This is Heydrich's doing. WC [Canaris] has done everything he can to stop it, Army completely declines, etc.'[74] Even the head of the Military Economics Office, General Georg Thomas, who prepared memoranda on the subject for Keitel, was waved away brusquely. The memoranda had been put together in collaboration with prominent members of the 'civilian opposition' such as minister Johannes Popitz, ambassador Ulrich von Hassell, Carl Goerdeler, Hjalmar Schacht, Hans Gisevius, Generaloberst Beck and Hans Oster, the intention being to show Keitel that 'Hitler's plans for conquest' would lead to 'World War' and to a long struggle that Germany could not survive without powerful allies; a lost war would mean the disappearance of Germany.[75] Keitel, General Thomas noted, had interrupted him during his discourse to tell him that 'Hitler would never fight a World War. There was no danger, in Hitler's opinion, since the French were a completely pacific people and the British far too decadent to offer Poland any useful help, and the United States would never again send a single man to Europe to pull British or even Polish chestnuts out of the fire.'[76]

Everything during the August crisis revolved around the question of whether Britain and France would stand by their treaty obligations to Poland and force Germany into a war on two fronts. While the generals prepared plans for mobilisation and invasion, on 23 August they awaited the call from Ribbentrop, who had travelled to Moscow the previous day with about thirty assistants to conclude the long-prepared pact with the Kremlin.

Towards one o'clock that afternoon Hitler received British ambassador Henderson bringing a letter from Prime Minister Chamberlain saying that war between Britain and Germany would be the worst catastrophe. As to the expected agreement between Berlin and the Kremlin, Chamberlain said that even a German–Soviet alliance would not change Britain's obligation towards Poland, and he renewed his offer for talks if it would lead to the restoration of an atmosphere of trust and peace. He proposed direct talks between Germany and Poland over the treatment of minorities by both sides, the goal being a treaty guaranteed by the major powers.[77] This was Hitler's worst scenario – the resurrection of the Munich Agreement – and he responded by accusing Britain of having stimulated 'the excesses against Volksdeutsche in Poland'. 'We were under the impression', his adjutant von Below wrote, 'that on that day he was especially outraged by Britain.'[78]

In his letter of reply to Chamberlain, Hitler's purpose was to persuade London to abandon its treaty obligations to Poland.[79] He would attack Poland if a single German there should be mistreated. Great Britain would then be responsible for the war, just as it was responsible for forcing him into his pact with the Soviets; Henderson assured Hitler 'that a war was probably unavoidable if Hitler insisted on direct action against Poland'.[80] The letter also contained a veiled threat of a general mobilisation if Britain and France mobilised. Once Henderson had left the room, Hitler slapped his leg and laughed: 'Chamberlain will not survive this conversation, his Cabinet will fall this evening.'[81] It did not, though, and the same day France reaffirmed its pledge to Poland, eclipsing one of the main aims of the forthcoming German–Soviet Pact; Poland was not isolated and the pact might not be enough to prevent Britain and France from entering the hostilities.[82]

Shortly afterwards Ribbentrop reported from Moscow that the negotiations were very promising, but questions remained to be resolved regarding Soviet influence in Lithuania, Estonia and Latvia, and their claims to the seaports of Libau and Windau. Within thirty minutes they had conceded the point, after poring over a map,[83] and Ribbentrop and Molotov signed the treaty after midnight; Ribbentrop telephoned Hitler the news within the hour. Hitler congratulated him: 'That will come as a bombshell!'[84]

In the ten-year Non-Aggression Pact, Berlin and Moscow had pledged themselves mutually not only to neutrality in the case of unprovoked attack on either, but even if either partner were involved in hostilities with a third party. A secret protocol set down the respective spheres of interest in Eastern Europe from Finland to Bessarabia. Poland was to be divided between them. With this 'Aggression Pact'[85] Stalin had given Hitler a free hand for his attack on Poland and Hitler had sealed a union with his worst ideological opponent – one of them 'wanted war, and the other, wanting to do nothing to prevent it, united in negotiating a business of life and death'.[86]

For many such as Canaris, who was still hoping to stop Hitler by means of a strong international alliance, the Hitler–Stalin Pact was a catastrophe: 'The signing of the Moscow pact paralysed all those who just a year before had been ready to stop Hitler.'[87] The last psychological barrier to Hitler's leap into the abyss had been removed. Canaris and Beck were both of the opinion that Stalin had signed this pact with cold calculation; the Kremlin could now bide its time until Europe had bled to death, and their own hour struck.[88]

18

The Madness Unfolds

According to plan, OKH removed from Berlin to a new headquarters at Zossen, south of the capital, and on 24 August 1939 Major Groscurth, who had headed Abteilung II before Lahousen, returned to Berlin to take charge of the Abwehr liaison group at OKH, from October renamed 'Abteilung zbV' of the Army General Staff. This made Groscurth the most important liaison officer between Canaris and OKH.[1] He reported to Canaris and the chief of Abteilung IV at Army General Staff (Ober-QM IV), and General Major von Tippelskirch, to whom Foreign Armies East and Foreign Armies West, responsible for situation reports on enemy dispositions at Army General Staff reported directly to Groscurth.[2]

The Army's secret field police (GFP) was under Abwehr control. Its primary function was anti-sabotage and to prevent disaffection amongst the troops, under the new leader Wilhem Krichbaum, who came from the Gestapo, where he had been frontier inspector southeast at Dresden.[3] He was a close friend of Heydrich, who had inveigled him into the new position,[4] and as a former member of the Hesse-Thuringia Freikorps, Brigade Ehrhardt and Org-C, he was an old street-fighter.[5] On his first day in Berlin, Groscurth noticed the tension existing between the Abwehr, the General Staff and the GFP. He noted in his diary: 'What a day! . . . [Tippelskirch] opportunist, aiming high. Enemy of the Admiral [Canaris]. Combining with my group impossible. Krichbaum told me at once he was an Oberst! Will have difficult times!' After Canaris had apprised him of recent developments, Groscurth concluded his diary entry: 'God grant me soon a fast, graceful end! And to everybody close to me!'[6]

Those in the know were now convinced that Hitler would strike. At the 'Kolonne', the daily morning situation conference of Abwehr chiefs in Canaris's office, mobilisation was discussed, with Lahousen noting: 'Italy: unknown. No visible signs of mobilising, mood in France and Italy not very enthusiastic.'[7] An increased watch was ordered on the Ukraine nationalists in Germany to prevent the leaders going abroad to stir up unrest against the Warsaw and Moscow Governments.[8] That kind of disturbance was no longer opportune.

When Groscurth expressed concern about the GFP, fearing interventions from convinced Nazis like Krichbaum, Canaris reassured him that he would act against the GFP if they would not follow orders. Canaris was more preoccupied with his commando units to operate behind enemy lines; some of them were already in position on the border awaiting the signal to move.

On 24 August 1939 the attack order was issued by Hitler at 1502hrs.[9] During the afternoon movement orders were distributed to the various troop commanders, telephone connections between Berlin, Paris and London were disconnected and accredited military attachés in Berlin were forbidden to leave the capital without the permission of the War Ministry. The airspace over Berlin was closed to civilian aircraft, and all airports were ordered to shut down next day.[10] At 1605hrs Abwehr headquarters was notified of the orders. Groscurth noted: 'Finally, after an hour and a half delay, the order to march for 0430hrs. First X-Day. A relief!'[11] For the Abwehr this was the signal for the K- and S-Organisations to move: Leutnant Herzner would lead the attack on the Jablunka Pass railway tunnels at the scheduled time,[12] and the attack to avert the destruction of the Dirschau bridges would coincide with the crossing of the Polish frontier.[13] Other Abwehr units, such as that formed for Operation Hornisse, in which so-called 'Corridor people' would arrive in Dirschau from areas of southwest Poland to sow confusion, were brought to a state of readiness[14] as were Heydrich's *agents provocateurs*.

The postponement of the attack order came about for the following reasons. The previous day in a letter to Mussolini, Hitler had insisted on his keeping to the terms of the pact, and was now awaiting the response. At 1400 hrs the British ambassador had called again at the Reich Chancellery; if he received a free hand to resolve the German–Polish problem, Hitler told Henderson, then he would be ready to come to an understanding with Britain that 'would not only guarantee for the German part the existence of the British Empire under all circumstances, but also, should it become necessary, provide the British Empire with German help irrespective of where such help was required.'[15] Henderson had scarcely closed the door behind him when Hitler issued his orders, not wishing to tarry longer for Mussolini's response. There now came two setbacks: Foreign Minister Ribbentrop brought Hitler news that Britain had finally signed the agreed military alliance with Poland, and a little later the French ambassador, Robert Coulondre, gave Hitler his word of honour as an officer that France would stand at Poland's side and fight.[16] The Italian ambassador Attolico then came with Mussolini's answer: 'It is for me one of the most painful moments of my life to have to inform you that Italy is not ready for war.'[17] The fuel and raw material stocks of his army and air force would last barely three weeks of war, and only the navy was ready; the Duce asked the Führer for understanding for his situation. Interpreter Schmidt observed that Hitler, with an icy demeanour, dismissed the ambassador; the treaty ally had been believed secure, but now was not. Keitel was told to call the Army commander-in-chief,[18] and Brauchitsch confirmed that there was still time to stop the attack going ahead – to gain time to win 'the political game' – and towards 1945 hrs that evening Halder received the order to abort the invasion.[19]

The main conspirators – Oster, Gisevius, Reichsminister Schacht and General Thomas – planned to use the short period between the issue of the order and the invasion for a last attempt to unseat Hitler. Pressure was to be brought to bear on Halder and Brauchitsch to arrest him on the grounds that a declaration of war without the assent of the Reich Cabinet was unconstitutional. Should they refuse, the conspirators would then threaten to reveal their secret contacts to the Gestapo.[20]

When General Thomas arrived at Abwehr headquarters, Oster told him that the attack had been postponed; Oster was now not thinking of a coup d'état – a supreme warlord forced to rescind such an order was finished: 'The Führer had brought it to a head.'[21] For Gisevius, this was the abiding memory of that unforgettable 25 August: '. . . how Oster, this man who since 1933 had fought the Gestapo thugs, this officer who had committed himself uncompromisingly and with great resolution to a coup, was now thinking, under the fresh expectation of Hitler's fall from power, no longer on this side, but already on the far side of the goal.'[22]

Canaris had also allowed himself to be ensnared by this deceptive hope. When Gisevius arrived at OKW next morning, Canaris beamed: 'What do you say now? He will never recover from this setback. Peace has been preserved for twenty years.'[23] But Gisevius, 'made to look a fool by circumstances',[24] was not convinced and warned: 'Only if we strike at him! Otherwise Himmler and Ribbentrop will use their influence and we will have the same situation within a week.'[25] If he actually said this, then Gisevius was a prophet, yet even if 'the idea of the avoided war was illusory and Gisevius was absolutely right',[26] nobody listened to him that day. His Resistance colleagues believed that a coup had become superfluous. Even Canaris was unwilling to undertake anything – Hitler had been eliminated. Erich Kordt recalled later these fateful hours and the attitude of the admiral: 'Not only Oster and the younger opponents to the regime but even a man like Wilhelm Canaris, who deliberated so cautiously, believed that Hitler had dug his own grave. A horse that refuses a fence for the second time will not jump!'[27]

In the euphoria of their collective delusion, the conspirators let the last opportunity to avert war elude them. 'Their incomprehension of political realities was breathtaking,' wrote Ian Kershaw in his biography of Hitler.[28]

That evening, unexpected complications arose for the Abwehr as the result of the recall order. When instructions were transmitted to Abwehrstellen at Königsberg, Breslau and Vienna to halt the K- and S-Organisations' operations in Poland, Hauptmann Ernst zu Eickern of Abwehrstelle VIII Breslau reported that he could not guarantee to stop it.[29] The twenty-four commandos under Leutnant Herzner had already set out, could not be contacted by radio and had crossed the Polish border at 0030hrs;[30] later, Eickern reported hearing heavy machine-gun fire from the Jablunka Pass area.[31] Not until 0830hrs on the morning of 26 August was contact established with Herzner,[32] and three hours later the signals office at Striegau morsed Abwehrstelle Breslau that Herzner was still in Poland and had two men wounded.[33] Herzner and his men had succeeded in occupying Mosty Railway Station and defusing the explosive charges in the Pass tunnels;[34] around midday the squad reached the safety of Slovakia under police fire.[35] The incident – as others on the German–Polish border that night – was explained away through diplomacy.

As head of Abwehr-Abteilung II, Lahousen was blamed, with the Foreign Ministry asserting that he had endangered 'the Führer's peace policy'. Canaris and Keitel were incensed that Herzner's commando had not been equipped with radio. Lahousen made a sober entry in the service diary on 26 August that the mobilisation was proceeding since the resumed negotiations could collapse again.[36] Unlike Canaris and Oster he anticipated that only a brief respite had been obtained.

Canaris and his fellow plotters were exposed that day to a constant flux of belief, hope, illusion and self-deception. Convinced in the morning that Hitler had shot his bolt, Canaris informed General Thomas only a few hours later that 'the attack date had been postponed for a few days'.[37] On 26 August Canaris had informed the Italian military attaché Roatta that the attack order had been cancelled, and Roatta had telephoned the information immediately to the chief of the Italian General Staff, Pariani, but the line was tapped and the conversation recorded in Berlin. Hitler summoned Canaris and confronted him with the evidence. Groscurth noted: 'Chief is worried . . . I try to calm him, but don't succeed.'[38]

The 'Eleventh Hour Show'[39] continued. French ambassador Coulondre brought to Hitler Daladier's appeal to settle the crisis by negotiation, offering himself as intermediary. Hitler replied by raising the stakes; it was no longer Danzig and an extraterritorial route through the Polish Corridor that he wanted, but the whole Corridor as sovereign German territory.[40] Swedish businessman Birger Dahlerus, an acquaintance of Goering who had often acted as intermediary and courier, was sent to London with a new offer.

The atmosphere was feverish, 'rich in apparent dialogue, transparent confusion and occasionally grotesque pretence'.[41] Groscurth learned from Berlin Police Chief Helldorf that

> a man close to Heydrich has fears that H–H [Himmler and Heydrich] have a chance to act against ambushed generals . . . advise generals to attempt something at once and demand the removal of the criminals who had brought the Führer and us into this situation. A stone would fall from the heart of the Wehrmacht if the Führer finally took steps.[42]

When Groscurth first drew this to Canaris's attention, he rejected it: 'Chief not interested,' Groscurth noted,[43] but in the end Canaris sent him to Zossen to Ober-QM I von Stülpnagel with the latest messages prophesying doom from von Helldorf, who, fearing unrest, was asking for troops and wanted direct contact to the Berlin Wachregiment.[44] Perhaps he was hoping to motivate the generals to move against the SS and even Hitler,[45] but upon his return to Berlin, all he had for Canaris was the Führer's thanks to Brauchitsch that the Army 'had done a good number'.[46] Canaris showed Groscurth other extracts from his diary about Keitel, and he was apparently shocked to discover that Hitler's adjutants were working against Keitel. 'Finally!' Groscurth wrote.

Back at Zossen, Groscurth saw Krichbaum, head of the GFP, in the latter's private suite: 'He has attempted to make himself influential, not successful. Strange company. They listen to every word in the bunkers. Stülpnagel took me into the gardens! . . . What goings-on!'[47]

The next day all hopes of a peaceful solution to the crisis were finally shattered. On the morning of 27 August, Groscurth and Canaris discussed the absurd demands Mussolini had made the day before for weapons and materials to make his participation in a war possible – the Duce had a shopping list so long that he obviously knew that there was no chance of it being met. Daladier's appeal and his preparations to fight were considered, together with Japan's protest against the German–Soviet Non-Aggression Pact, which was diametrically opposed to Japanese interests. Groscurth noted: '6th Mob[ilisation Day] is new attack date.[48] Two to three days before, the Führer will notify ObdH [Brauchitsch]. K[eitel] already talking of possibly earlier date. Halder explained no question of it. Either a surprise or invasion to plan. No half-measures are possible.'[49]

General Thomas – presumably with Canaris's knowledge – undertook one last desperate mission to Keitel, presenting him with a memorandum that Oster, Gisevius, Schacht, Beck and Goerdeler were hoping might convince the OKW chief, by the use of many statistics, that the military–economic efficiency of Germany was no match for the alliance of the major powers. Thomas reported that Keitel had shown the document to Hitler, who read it and said that he did not share the generals' fears now that 'he had the Soviet Union in his pocket'. The treaty with Russia had been the greatest political success of a German politician in recent decades. Thomas said later: 'I have never been sure whether Hitler, under the influence of Ribbentrop, really believed that Britain would not come into the Polish war, or if Keitel deceived me.'[50]

On 28 August Oster and Groscurth arrived for discussions with Halder and Stülpnagel at Zossen. Oster was apparently still hoping to drive a wedge between the Army and Hitler. He carried an 'official' warning from the Prussian finance minister to the Wehrmacht, in which Hitler had threatened: 'I can also be a Communist and apply Bolshevist methods,'[51] a clear reference to the 1937 purge of the Soviet officer corps by Stalin in which thousands of officers had been killed. In his diary, Halder noted that the warning was addressed to everybody who wanted to stab Hitler in the back.[52] Oster and Groscurth also reported on the conversations involving Hitler, the Reichstag deputies and party chiefs, including Himmler, Heydrich, Bormann, Goebbels and the Gauleiters at the Reich Chancellery the previous afternoon. Military officers had not been invited but Oster and Groscurth were told about it by security men.[53]

Groscurth summarised the content of Hitler's speech:

> Situation very grave. He [Hitler] was determined to resolve the Eastern question one way or the other. He had made certain suggestions to Henderson and was now awaiting the answer. Least demands: Danzig and Corridor. Greatest demands: depending on military situation. If least demands not met, then war. War by the most brutal and inhuman means . . . war would be difficult, perhaps even lacking any prospect of success, but an honourable defeat was preferable to capitulation. He said, 'So long as I live, I will never use the word capitulation.'[54]

Hitler seemed nervous and weak and gave the impression of being firmly in the grip of his SS advisers;[55] Mussolini had come up with a hurried idea for a compromise which proposed the immediate return of Danzig to Germany in return for German participation in a European conference. Late on the evening of 28 August Henderson came to the Reich Chancellery bringing a letter from the British Government confirming that it would stand by its pact with Poland but had reached an agreement with the Poles for direct talks with Berlin. This forced Hitler on the defensive diplomatically and from the aspect of propaganda; he appeared to consider the British offer and told Henderson that he was ready for direct talks with Poland provided a Polish negotiator presented himself within twenty-four hours in Berlin. Henderson interpreted the condition as an ultimatum to gain Hitler time in order to keep to his schedule for war,[56] but London kept the usual diplomatic channels open and the German Foreign Ministry responded with a thoroughly moderate memorandum signalling a readiness for compromise. It provided sixteen points, a mixture of demands and suggestions to resolve the conflict, which Interpreter Schmidt translated with incredulity: 'It was a real League of Nations type of thing.'[57] It was also merely a delaying tactic. Shortly before midnight on 30 August Ribbentrop received the British ambassador, read him the sixteen points but refused to let Henderson have them in writing, which made it clear that the proposal was not meant to be taken seriously. When Henderson asked in disbelief what was going on, Ribbentrop tossed the paper on the table and said: 'It has all fallen through because the Polish negotiator did not come.'[58]

Secretary of State von Weizsäcker wrote next day

> Since the evening of 30 August one is determined to have a war, come what may. I guess that Ribbentrop's advice was decisive, for he cut all strings which still offered something. Why the Führer is starting the war without Italy and against the Western Powers, which he avoided before, is not clear to me; I had understood his aim until 30 August to be a very tense bluff with the intention of eventually falling back in line. I will write nothing further about my unending attempts to avert this development, since they lack interest because ultimately they were unsuccessful. A new stage is now beginning. It remains to be seen if my life still has a purpose.[59]

Groscurth noted in his diary on 31 August: '1700hrs: orders to march given for tomorrow at 0430hrs!!! So, the madness unfolds.'[60] Late that afternoon Gisevius received a call from Oster asking him to come to OKW headquarters at the Bendlerstrasse; although Oster spoke in veiled terms, Gisevius inferred from it at once that Hitler had given fresh orders to attack Poland. In the porch leading to the Abwehr offices, he saw a group of officers approaching, amongst them Canaris. He wanted to avoid a meeting with the admiral so as to keep their friendship secret, but Canaris hung back and drew Gisevius into a dark corner. 'What do you say now?' Canaris asked. When Gisevius made no reply, Canaris sobbed: 'It is the end of Germany.'[61]

Canaris was convinced that Hitler's order would plunge Germany into the final disaster, having long anticipated it and discussed it continually amongst his closest circle.[62] To prevent war had been the primary goal of the various circles of conspirators; to the bitter end, even in the chaotic last days of peace, they had wavered between euphoria and despair. Now they were thwarted by Hitler and Ribbentrop's will for force, their own weakness and that of the Wehrmacht heads. The war on Poland signalled the defeat of the military and civilian opposition to Hitler.[63]

19

The War of Extermination – Act One

In the hours before the attack, both despair and stoic application to duty reigned amongst Canaris and his entourage. General Erich Hoepner, a member of the Resistance, commented on 1 September: 'The Polish question has to be resolved,'[1] and even Halder and other generals were of the opinion that a correction of the borders in the East was unavoidable and von Brauchitsch saw it as his duty to adhere to Hitler's political guidelines. When von Weizsäcker explained to Brauchitsch on 31 August that the intervention of France and Britain was now to be expected, and history would judge that the responsibility for it lay with the military commanders, Brauchitsch merely shrugged; the Führer did not think so, he replied.[2] But even von Weizsäcker, a severe critic of the regime, saw in the 'Danzig Question' and the 'North East Problem' political aims that needed to be settled – Danzig and the overland bridge to East Prussia were important territorial claims of the Reich[3] – so nobody condemned the attack on Poland out of hand.[4]

On the morning of 1 September 1939, Hitler went to the Reichstag wearing an SS jacket made for him by his aides. He addressed the deputies – one hundred of whom had been conscripted into the Wehrmacht, the remainder of the seats being filled by party functionaries – with a delivery that seemed forced and was not received with the customary storm of applause when he justified the attack on Poland as a necessary defence: 'In the early hours Polish regular troops fired on us for the first time on our national territory. We fired back at 0545 [actually 0445]. And from now on we shall retaliate bomb for bomb.'[5]

Groscurth, who heard the speech at Zossen, commented: 'Reichstag speech, fearsome impression everywhere;'[6] he had been called several hours before by Canaris, to tell him the latest news, but there was little information to hand from the front so early. The commando mission to take the Vistula bridges at Dirschau intact had failed; Königsberg Abwehr reported that the bridges were demolished after Polish units took the bridgeheads. Dirschau was not captured until the following day.[7]

The same morning, Canaris addressed his senior staff at the Tirpitzufer, demanding their loyalty to Führer and Reich and an 'unconditionally positive attitude',[8] afterwards listening to Hitler's broadcast speech in silence. When Hitler spoke of the fourteen border incidents that had already occurred the previous night,[9] Hans Piekenbrock, leader of Gruppe I Secret Report Service stated: 'Now we know why we had to supply the Polish uniforms.'[10]

Although Hitler had not mentioned the raid on Gleiwitz radio station, Canaris repeated Piekenbrock's observations to Lahousen and other Abteilung heads;[11] in fact, the Polish uniforms had not been used at Gleiwitz,[12] only at 'other theatres' that night. Concentration camp inmates were murdered by the SD, Sipo and SS to play their allotted roles.[13]

The same day, Brauchitsch appealed to the Polish people: 'The Wehrmacht does not see the people as its enemy. All provisions of international law will be respected. Industry and public administration will continue working, and will be expanded.'[14] What such assurances were worth would be seen in the first days of the military campaign, when the Poles were given a foretaste of the 'orgy of atrocities'[15] to come.

Army Quartermaster-General Oberst Eduard Wagner, Heydrich and Werner Best agreed to the arrest and incarceration in concentration camps of 10,000 Poles in a 'first stage', and 20,000 more in a 'second stage'.[16] The arrestees were catalogued on SD and police-Abwehr priority-capture lists, a method which had been used in the invasions of Austria, Sudetenland and Czechoslovakia; they were Poles identified as 'anti-German': clerics, Communists and so-called insurgents who had taken part in the Polish revolts in Upper Silesia in the early 1920s.[17] The mass arrests were primarily the responsibility of Einsatzgruppen attached to each of the five invading armies and would follow close behind their advance, with each Einsatzgruppe consisting of one Gestapo, Kripo (criminal police) and SD unit with specific police and intelligence missions. In Berlin a special office codenamed 'Tannenberg' was set up under Best's direct control for contact to the Einzsatzgruppen, whose aim was 'to combat anti-German and anti-Reich elements in enemy territories behind the fighting troops'.[18] Enemies of the Reich were all those who resisted the German occupation, Communists and leftist Social Democrats, including those active before the invasion, and all Jews. Halder expressed 'some doubts about Himmler's proposed measures'[19] in a conversation with Goering's liaison officer, but this was the sum total of the protests.

In principle, there was agreement between Sipo and the Wehrmacht regarding the action against the 'anti-German' elements,[20] open to individual interpretation. Although the military commander-in-chief controlled the police and there was no talk of shootings and deportations, the Einsatzgruppen demonstrated from the start that the SS leadership thought otherwise. The events of the so-called 'Bromberg Bloody Sunday' of 3 September 1939 were the decisive excuse for the dramatic 'intensification and radicalisation'[21] of their activities.[22]

That day, Canaris, Piekenbrock and Oster toured the front[23] from Neisee to Breslau via Tschenstochau and Oppeln.[24] On his return, Canaris related to Groscurth the favourable impression he had gained:[25] morale at the front was good.[26]

Speaking of the British and French declarations of war on 3 September 1939, Groscurth wrote: 'I was correct in my pessimism. Frightful!',[27] believing that the protests against false propaganda reports of alleged Polish atrocities[28] were justified, and annoyed that OKH deliberately understated German casualty figures.[29] On the other hand, he noted – not without satisfaction – 'good progress in the East'[30] and the success of the K-Organisations, one of which had captured the industrial city of Kattowitz before regular troops arrived, a feat expressly recognised as an achievement.[31]

Best remembered that shortly after the war began,[32] he had invited Canaris, Lahousen, Pieckenbrock and von Bentivegni for wine at his Berlin flat:

> My wife and I were horrified and depressed about the British and French declarations of war. The Abwehr officers were surprisingly optimistic, however, and thought it would last only a few months. When with my approval my wife said 'The war will last five years', Oberst Bentivegni smiled and told her that she did not understand and was wrong. Canaris made no comment, although in this situation he could easily have shared our fears.[33]

In any case, this incident is noteworthy for the mood that prevailed in Canaris's closest circle after the outbreak of war.

German propaganda about Polish tactics involving fifth columnists, snipers and partisans, which had led to disproportionate reprisals in the First World War, was now rife in the press.[34] This resulted from the outset in heightened aggression especially towards irregulars and civilian militia,[35] and in turn members of the German minority in Poland were held liable for German acts of sabotage and espionage. Despite grave warnings against the practice from the Foreign Ministry the previous year, numerous Volksdeutsche had been recruited as spies by the military Abwehr and police-Abwehr, and 'used for illegal operations',[36] and Poles had been asked to keep vigilant for German spies and saboteurs.[37]

Although the events are still unclear, it seems likely that, around noon on 'Bromberg Bloody Sunday', members of the German minority fired on Polish soldiers, which led to reprisals by the Polish military, militia and civilians against the Volksdeutsche. Between the departure of Polish troops from Bromberg on the evening of 3 September, and the arrival of the first German units on 5 September, the Polish 'citizen's army' had taken their revenge on the Volksdeutsche insurgents, leaving a trail of murders, rapes and beatings;[38] no figure had been given of the exact number of German victims of this 'local pogrom'[39] and the original estimate of 140 rose to one thousand the next day.[40] As similar measures had been taken in other Polish towns, the events later became known as 'the September murders' and claimed around 5,400 victims of German stock, a figure that in February 1940 became 54,000, apparently on Hitler's personal order for propaganda purposes.[41]

Ignorant of the events at Bromberg,[42] on 3 September Himmler ordered the Einsatzgruppen that all 'Polish insurgents caught red-handed or carrying a weapon'[43] were to be shot on the spot without trial. In a telex the same evening he appointed SS-Gruppenführer Udo von Woyrsch as Special Police Commander and authorised him to set up an Einsatzgruppe zbV (special purposes) whose purpose was 'the radical destruction of the burgeoning Polish insurgency in the occupied regions of Upper Silesia, by all means at their disposal, above all the overwhelming and disarming of Polish gangs, executions and arrests'.[44] Von Woyrsch had orders to work closely with the Wehrmacht and 'civilian centres' and was formally subordinate to the commander, 8.Armee, Army Group South.

When an advance Einsatzkommando of Einsatzgruppe IV arrived at Bromberg, it immediately started massive reprisals; the members of the civilian militia, which initially offered resistance but then surrendered after negotiations, were brutally mistreated by German soldiers and police. Next day, Wilhelm Bischoff, leading the Einsatzkommando, ordered the execution in the market place of fifty hostages selected by police units as retribution for a German lorry being fired on by snipers.[45]

On 6 September OKH forwarded to 4.Armee, which was operating in the Bromberg area, an 'instruction from the Führer' to take the strongest measures in the occupied territory against saboteurs and insurgents. Captured partisans could be shot immediately whereas previously there had had to be some kind of legal proceeding. The shooting of hostages was allowed if there was an urgent need for it. Himmler ordered five hundred hostages to be taken immediately by the Bromberg Einsatzgruppe; the order reached the town on 10 September, by which time many brutal reprisals had already been taken.[46] Even Generalmajor Walter Braemer, the competent commander of Bromberg since 8 September, was unable to estimate how many people had been murdered there, and he allowed it to continue.

The Einsatzgruppe killed in breach of all local and international law, without reporting what they had done and without judicial hearings. In a raid ordered by Braemer in the allegedly most dangerous district of Bromberg, 'Swedish

Heights', 120 people were shot by two Einsatzkommandos, while the nine hundred or so Poles that were in custody were taken to a wood on the outskirts of town on 12 September and shot on the orders of Einzsatzgruppe leader Lothar Beutel.

On 7 September Heydrich informed the Gestapo, Kripo and SD heads of Hitler's further instructions:

> The top layer of the Polish population is to be rendered harmless as far as possible. The remaining lower layers will not receive special indoctrination, but will have to be suppressed in one form or another … the top layer will not be permitted to remain in Poland under any circumstances, and will be brought to German concentration camps, while provisional concentration camps will be established behind the Einsatzgruppen along the border.[47]

Canaris was requested to discover exactly what had been discussed at this session and how far Heydrich was prepared to go in the concrete implementation of this decision, and informed Groscurth and Oster the next day. Groscurth noted: 'Heydrich is stirring it up in the wildest way against the Army. Everything is going ahead too slowly!!! There are two hundred executions daily. He wants to change it. People must be shot or hanged without trial immediately.' Canaris reported Heydrich's outburst as being: 'We will spare the small people, but the nobility, the clergy and Jews must be killed. After we have taken Warsaw, I will agree with the Army how we will separate all these people out.' Resignedly, Groscurth summed up the situation: 'Keitel is completely helpless,'[48] and Chief of the General Staff Halder told Groscurth: 'The butchery of the Poles behind the front is increasing so substantially that probably they will be operating with even more energy very soon.'[49] Halder confirmed that it was the intention of Hitler and Goering 'to exterminate the Poles'; Groscurth wrote: 'The rest cannot be written down.'[50]

The events at Bromberg were the catalyst for an increasingly brutal war of extermination, about which the German administrative centres involved were only informed piecemeal, as it took place. For some time the Einsatzgruppen had been developing their own initiative and Hitler's orders to Himmler merely gave the nod to the proceedings in the eyes of the SS and police leadership. Accordingly, during the first two weeks of war, Himmler was able greatly to extend his jurisdiction with regard to policy in the occupied sectors of Poland, at the expense of the Army.[51]

At this time Canaris was occupied with other matters. The Abwehr agenda listed talks ranging from the planned operations in the West to cooperation with the IRA and the proposed forays against the British on the Afghan border. Meanwhile he also kept a close watch on Ukraine nationalists, who were poised awaiting the signal from Berlin to create havoc in Polish Galicia.

On 12 September Canaris travelled with Lahousen to Illnau in Upper Silesia, where the Führer's train was in sidings. Here Canaris had the opportunity to find out from Hitler and his immediate entourage of advisers how the war was progressing and the future intentions of the leadership and Wehrmacht. He spoke with Ribbentrop, Keitel, Jodl and Hitler himself, and ordered Lahousen to keep a note of everything.[52]

From Ribbentrop Canaris learned of the planned formation of a legion of Ukraine nationalists to fight beside the Wehrmacht, and of possible support for a Ukrainian insurrection in Galicia, both under the direction of the Organisation of Ukrainian Nationalists led by Ryko Jary, Andrej Melnyk and Stepan Bandera, who already had close contact with the Abwehr. Preparations for this operation, codenamed 'Bergbauhilfe', had been in hand for some time at Abteilung II under Lahousen, but were frequently stopped or amended by political developments and Hitler's fluctuating instructions.[53] Lahousen heard Ribbentrop tell Canaris that during the insurrection 'all Polish villages had to go up in flames and all Jews killed'; he found on reflection that the idea of burning villages was 'to some extent new' since previously there had only been talk of 'liquidating or removal of people'.[54]

Keitel then supplied details of Ribbentrop's proposals for the 'solution' of the Polish war. There were, he said, various options – to 'quarter Poland', in which the 'region east of the Narev–Vistula–San line' would pass to the Soviet Union; or an 'independent remainder of Poland' (a solution to which the Führer was sympathetic because he could then negotiate peace in the East with a 'Polish' Government); or Hitler could carve up the remainder of Poland so that the Vilna region would become Lithuanian and Galician, and Polish Ukraine would become independent.

Canaris received orders to 'make preparations with the Ukrainians' so that 'a revolt will break out in Galician Ukraine which has as its goal the destruction of everything Polish and the Jews',[55] but he protested against the planned 'shootings and measures for extermination'.[56] Lahousen set it down for his chief: 'I [Canaris] made Generaloberst Keitel aware that I had received information that mass shootings were planned in Poland and that in particular the nobility and clergy were to be exterminated. For these methods the world would eventually hold the Wehrmacht responsible, since these things would have happened under their noses.'[57]

Keitel pointed out 'that this matter had already been decided by the Führer, who had made it clear to ObdH [Brauchitsch] that if the Wehrmacht wanted nothing to do with it, they would have to accept the SS and Gestapo alongside them', and so a civilian administrator would be appointed in each military region to work in parallel with the military commandant, with the former taking care of 'the exterminations amongst the local populace'.[58] Lahousen remembered at the Nuremberg Trials after the war that Keitel used a term coined by Hitler: 'political floor cleaning'.[59] His unconditional surrender to 'the will of the Führer' signalled that the Wehrmacht was not likely to win the struggle against the SS and Gestapo for control and administration of the occupied territories, and probably did not really want to. Their tactics helped them to avoid doing 'the dirty work' themselves, but capitulating to the plans for murder had the consequence that civilian control of the occupied territories and military participation in the murdering was not excluded.[60] Lahousen also noted down at Canaris's dictation comments regarding the bombing of Warsaw: 'To my observation about the unfavourable foreign policy consequences of this measure Generaloberst Keitel replied that these matters had already been settled directly between the Führer and Generalfeldmarschall Goering. The Führer often rang Goering. Sometimes he [Keitel] gained knowledge of the content of the conversation, but not always.'[61] Canaris phrased his objections to the plans for murder and extermination in such roundabout language that Keitel asked Oberstleutnant Nikolaus von Vormann, who had been present during the discussion, what Canaris had really wanted, but Vormann could only confirm that he did not know either.[62]

Canaris next met Hitler, accompanied by Jodl,[63] to report on the situation in the West, in particular the activities of the French Army at the Westwall. Hitler was emphatic in his dismissal of the Abwehr theory that the French were planning a major offensive concentrated on Saarbrücken; Jodl was sure that such preparations would take three to four weeks, which prompted from Hitler a typically optimistic assertion:

> Yes, and in October it will already be really cold, and our people will be in their protected bunkers while the French will have to attack from the field. But even if the French were to get through some weak point in the Westwall, we will by then have transferred our divisions from the East, which will give them such a roughing-up that they will not be able to see or hear afterwards. The only route they have is through Belgium and Holland, which I do not believe, but since it is not impossible we should take care.

Canaris had therefore received a rebuff and was also advised by Hitler 'to keep a sharp watch on all goings-on in these neutral countries'.[64]

The same day Brauchitsch issued an order that all Polish resistance was to be 'put down ruthlessly';[65] in his service diary Groscurth noted: 'Call of ObdH to all Poles: occupied territory is not a war area. Possession of weapons is punishable by death. Surrender of all weapons [and] ammunition within twenty-four hours to the nearest centre,'[66] and Halder wrote: 'Execution by military tribunal'.[67] When Canaris voiced his doubts regarding the exterminations, Major Rudolf

Langhaeuser, Army Group South Abwehr, told him that 180 civilians had been transferred from a camp at Czestochova to Einsatzgruppe II under Emanuel Schäfer,[68] and were rumoured to have been shot. Next morning Langhaeuser engaged in a violent altercation with an SS-Oberstrumführer, who was demanding the hand-over of prisoners, which Langhaeuser refused and went immediately to Einsatzgruppe leader Schäfer, who explained that he had orders from the Reichsführer-SS to shoot all Polish insurgents. The commander-in-chief of Army Group South, Generaloberst von Rundstedt, had no knowledge of this order, and even the Gestapa in Berlin denied knowledge of it. Heydrich's representative Werner Best informed Krichbaum, head of GFP, by telephone that 'orders have only been issued to act against insurgents. I will look into the matter,'[69] and came back the same morning with the information that the order to shoot insurgents immediately 'had originated from the Führer's train to Gestapo Einsatzkommandos and Ordungspolizei commanders'.[70] Whether Best was lying when he said he knew nothing about the shooting order, or if Hitler, Himmler and Heydrich issued these instructions on the spot without reference to Berlin while visiting Einsatzgruppen in Poland is not known.[71]

Groscurth wrote: 'Reichsführer-SS had given immediate instructions to all police commanders etc in the operational area to shoot all members of the Polish insurgent bands. Commanders-in-chief have no knowledge of it. Instead of an energetic investigation by ObdH, the order is being carried out.'[72]

Also on 17 September, the Soviet Army began rolling into the areas of Ukraine and White Russia that had been allotted to Stalin as his spheres of interest in the secret protocol to the German–Soviet pact. German military commanders were surprised by the initial Russian move and were uninformed as to where the demarcation line was to run between the respective armies. In order to avoid fighting between German and Soviet troops, territory that had been gained at the cost of German lives had to be relinquished to the Soviets, and OKW re-called the most advanced units the same day.[73] A number of officers were outraged at this development; for Halder it was 'a day of disgrace for the political leadership'[74] and Groscurth summed up: 'German blood helped the Russians and Bolshevism in an effortless advance.'[75]

Again on 17 September, Groscurth and Hauptmann Werner Fiedler of Abteilung II,[76] the latter being a strongly anti-Nazi protégé of Canaris,[77] dined with the family in Berlin. Canaris had just received news that his nephew Leutnant Rolf Buck, son of his sister Anna, had fallen in the field; Groscurth observed how profoundly the death affected everybody. The members of the circle present that night needed to make no secret of their personal feelings, with Canaris and Lahousen relating the 'devastating impression' they had obtained after their recent visit to the Führer. Groscurth noted that the admiral saw 'everything rightly very black' while at Zossen headquarters an 'unjustified and frivolous optimism' prevailed.[78] This optimism was fuelled by the quick victories in Poland; by the second week the first units had reached the outer suburbs of Warsaw and the siege of the Polish capital was being prepared.[79]

The murders in Poland continued unabated, and Canaris's secret field police under Krichbaum were willing accomplices, the GFP units giving the Einsatzkommandos so many arrestees for execution that Heydrich was forced to intervene: 'The chief of Sipo requests that the GFP be instructed to carry out their own executions.'[80] Of the 764 known executions between 1 September and 26 October 1939, 311 were undertaken by the Wehrmacht, and an estimated further 20,000 persons murdered.[81]

When Heydrich's request was received, Canaris was with Piekenbrock, Lahousen and retired Rittmeister Jary with 14.Armee at Rzeszow, where Abwehr officer Major Erich Schmidt-Richberg informed him of reports of 'unrest' that had been 'caused in the Army area through the, in part, illegal measures of Einsatzgruppe Woyrsch (the mass shootings, especially of Jews)'; 'The troops are especially upset that young men, instead of fighting at the Front, have been showing their prowess against unarmed people.'[82]

The growing pile of complaints, perhaps including the reports of Canaris and his staff, had at least a cosmetic effect on 22 September, when Brauchitsch and Quartermaster-General Wagner, the 'Wehrmacht negotiator in questions relating to the Einsatzgruppen',[83] met Heydrich.[84] Brauchitsch 'wished' that the Army might in future be informed promptly about all SS orders and that 'economic needs would be met according to priority. Therefore no getting rid of the Jews too soon,' and no measures 'which would go down unfavourably abroad'.[85] This meant that the murder of Jews was to be slowed down while they remained useful for stripping the country and providing the Army; deportations and resettlement should not begin until the Army had finished its work. Although this did not appreciably restrict Heydrich's apparatus for murder, a long argument ensued, at the end of which Heydrich agreed to make known all SS orders and to rescind the orders to shoot all members of insurgent gangs without trial.

However, during a conference with Hitler two days previously, Brauchitsch had made a concession that would have serious consequences. Courts with jurisdiction to try the illegal possession of arms had been exclusively the prerogative of the Wehrmacht, but now they would in future be presided over by the commanders of police regiments or battalions sitting with the heads of Einsatzkommandos and two members of the Army region; their judgments were to be examined only by Himmler. Therefore, before opening his discussions with Heydrich, Brauchitsch had surrendered the exclusive full powers of the military to police units and Einsatzgruppen[86] and accordingly there was no reason for Heydrich to compromise; it was already out of his hands. On the planned deportations of Jews, Brauchitsch came out of his shell and insisted that these measures should be handled by the military 'with no involvement of the civilian administration ... so that there might be no friction'.[87] Heydrich took a frosty view of the commander-in-chief's distrust, and complained afterwards to Brauchitsch's adjutant, Major Radke, about Brauchitsch's attitude.[88] He then made a concession to Oberst Wagner to withdraw Einsatzgruppe Woyrsch from the operational area of 14.Armee, and ordered it back to Kattowitz.[89] In bad humour he complained about Brauchitsch to Canaris too, saying that he had been unfriendly; all of this had been documented.[90]

The protests of the Wehrmacht heads against mass arrest, deportations and the murder of whole sections of the population remain vague and restrained, and gradually the way opened, step by step, for further radicalisation in the policies of resettlement and extermination.[91] The military men were anxious to maintain their authority, and worried about foreign reaction. They wanted the 'political mopping up' deferred until after they had tendered responsibility to the German civilian administration, and so prevent the Wehrmacht itself becoming involved in the mass murders.

Upon returning from Königsberg to Berlin on 22 September, Canaris learned of the death of Generaloberst von Fritsch. After the scandal, to preserve his honour he had been rehabilitated by Hitler to command 12.Artillerie-Regt.[92] That morning, in company with his ordnance officer Leutnant Rosenhagen, he was returning from a reconnaissance mission in the Warsaw suburb of Praga when he came under fire and was hit in the thigh by shrapnel. As Rosenhagen tried to apply a tourniquet, Fritsch told him: 'Leave it.' He bled to death within a minute.[93] Rumours soon began to circulate: while some people, such as General Beck, thought he had deliberately sought a soldier's death,[94] there were others who suspected SS involvement.[95] At the State funeral in Berlin ordered by Hitler for 26 September, Brauchitsch read the litany. 'Wonderful music; Last Post and Halali; well-fired salvoes. A great experience,' enthused Groscurth.[96] But many mourners must have considered it a mockery that Goering laid Hitler's wreath, and even Himmler was present.[97]

The Wehrmacht began the assault on Warsaw on 25 September; German forces quickly broke down the Polish lines, and on the morning of 27 September the city commandant offered the unconditional surrender of Warsaw. On 2 October Hitler arrived to accept the 'official' march-past of the German troops that had taken part in the fighting.[98]

On 28 September, the German–Soviet Treaty of Friendship was signed in Moscow. Lithuania came under Soviet influence; the Germans were granted

Warsaw and Lublin. Stalin made it clear that he had no interest in what happened to the remainder of Poland, leaving the decision to Berlin.[99]

That day Canaris travelled to Warsaw, and had leaders of the Abwehrstelle drive him round the ruined city. The devastation appalled him: 'It is dreadful. Our children's children will have to bear it.'[100] On 2 October he spoke to Groscurth about his trip to the East; Generaloberst von Rundstedt, the commander-in-chief of Army Group South and East,[101] and Generaloberst Blaskowitz, commander-in-chief of 8.Armee, had expressed concern about 'the lack of discipline and looting by troops under the leadership of officers' as Groscurth noted.[102] Writing to his wife the next day he was more forthcoming: 'C[anaris] told me about Warsaw and other things. Horrible! . . . very serious signs amongst troops in East, looting. No wonder after the years of training. But everything has now been amnestied!'[103] This closing remark referred to Hitler's edict of 4 October, which provided an amnesty for excesses by the SS and police units. Some members of the murder squads had been court-martialled,[104] but on 17 October the SS and police units were exempted from military and any other kind of justice, although Hitler authorised the setting up of a 'special justice' for persons on 'special operations'.

The half-hearted attempt of the senior military commanders to prevent the worst had done little to impede the policy of extermination; the military–civilian Resistance began to regroup in the late autumn of 1939.[105] In Berlin, Canaris was outspoken on his impressions of the Front and other matters, and Goerdeler informed Ulrich von Hassell that many generals' nerves were in very bad shape, and some, amongst them Canaris, had returned from Poland broken men.[106]

In Halder's letter of congratulation of 12 October 1939 awarding Canaris the clasps to his Iron Cross I and II, the chief of Staff concluded: 'Additionally I have the duty to express to you my thanks for the valuable cooperation of your departments. The chief of the Army General Staff received files of information valuable towards achieving the great victories in Poland and for the correct assessment of the organisation and intentions of our Western enemy and neighbour. With best wishes and Heil Hitler! Your devoted, Halder.'[107]

20

The Spirit of Zossen

On 17 October Hitler summoned Himmler, Hess, Bormann, Hans Frank, the ministers Lammers and Frick, Secretary of State Stuckart and OKW Commander-in-Chief Keitel to an urgent meeting at the Reich Chancellery.[1] His aim was to move from military to a purely civilian administration to further his objectives, avoiding the moral scruples of the generals and their subordinates who had continued to resent and criticise the activities of the SS and police units on the ground in Poland.[2] The Army should be happy to free itself of responsibility for Poland. The future General-Governor Hans Frank must be able to act independently of the Army commanders; the harsh racial struggle permitted no due process of law; 'its methods were irreconcilable with our principles'.[3] Even Keitel put two exclamation marks after his notes at this point. Affronted by not having been invited to the meeting, left in the dark as to Hitler's plans, Brauchitsch surrendered his office as military governor of Poland to Frank. By this 'apparently comfortable solution'[4] the Wehrmacht rid itself of responsibility for 'the devil's work', as Hitler himself called it, but military men such as Groscurth felt strengthened in their resistance to the regime by this decision. While a number of officers resorted to a kind of opposition of memoranda to force Brauchitsch to take some action against the war of extermination in Poland and the military response to France, Canaris used his office as Abwehr head in an increasing degree to bring individual victims of the regime and its opponents out of the firing line.

A spectacular success was accomplished at the end of September. The internationally renowned Jewish professor and Chief Rabbi Joseph Isaak Schneersohn, who had a large following in the United States, had left it too late to flee Warsaw after ensuring the safety of his students at the Rabbinical Academy, its library and art treasures. In a complicated cooperation between the Abwehr, Jewish organisations in the United States and the US State Department, Canaris succeeded, with the help of Jewish Major Ernst Bloch, leader of the Abwehr Gruppe for economic espionage, in locating Rabbi Schneersohn in Warsaw and smuggling him to safety in a neutral country.[5] Previously, during his Warsaw visit Canaris had learned that the wife and children of the former Polish military attaché to Berlin, Szymanski, were in an internment camp, and was again successful in having the family transferred to neutral Switzerland; he also made possible the escape of many Polish churchmen from certain death.[6] The saving of Rabbi Schneersohn and the Szymanski family was a useful diplomatic indication[7] that there were people and groups in Germany with whom communication could be valuable.[8]

Lawyer Hans Dohnanyi had been employed at the Reich Justice Ministry in 1933, but had been unable to prove full 'Aryan lineage' under the new laws affecting career civil servants in the Reich. Justice Minister Gürtner had obtained permission from the Führer to resolve the problem, but in Martin Bormann, Dohnanyi had a powerful enemy who was intent that he would not be retained indefinitely as Gürtner's assistant. Gürtner found him a new post at the Leipzig Reich Court, from where Canaris promised that he would be able to enter the Abwehr in the event of war. From March 1940 Dohnanyi was given the rank of major on the basis of his professional qualifications and appointed to the Central Department (Z) run by Oster. The Group for Information (ZB) was probably created for him,[9] and Oster ensured that Dohnanyi remained where Oster or Canaris could keep an eye on him. His job was to supply reports on policy situations – a cover role behind which he could continue his work on an anti-Hitler coup. For this purpose he had contacts with civilian Resistance circles around his brother-in-law Klaus Bonhoeffer, with Otto John, Ernst von Harnack and with Social Democrats and union men such as Wilhelm Leuschner, who would support a coup by calling a General Strike.

For possible use in the future, the Abwehr opposition circle kept a political chronicle and a catalogue of crimes committed by party leaders and National Socialist organisations. These included material compiled by Dohnanyi at the Justice Ministry between 1933 and 1938[10] and the information system set up by Oster in 1936/37;[11] these records would prove fatal.

At Canaris's request, Dohnanyi liaised with Ernst von Weizsäcker. Officially the regular meetings were for the purpose of exchanging information between Abwehr-Foreign and the Foreign Ministry, but unofficially Dohnanyi kept von Weizsäcker informed about the actions of the opposition group at Abwehr.[12] In Dohnanyi, Canaris and Oster had gained a colleague of inestimable value.

The rapid victory in Poland had enabled Hitler by mid-September to consider an offensive in the West. Germany would now seize the opportunity to end the 'enforced' war by defeating France and inducing Britain to negotiate peace, he told the Wehrmacht commander-in-chiefs on 27 September; he was thinking of October preferably, or at least before Christmas. The Army commander-in-chief should therefore prepare plans for 'Fall Gelb', the attack in the West. On

6 October in a speech to the Reichstag, Hitler proposed a conference of leading nations to discuss the regulation of peace in Europe, but kept his options open by issuing on 10 October the 'Instruction No 6 for Warfare'.[13]

Quartermaster-General I, von Stülpnagel, had previously warned in a memorandum of 24 September that nothing would be available for an attack within the next two years against the French and Belgian fortifications, while the panzer and motorised units worn down during the Polish campaign would not be battle-worthy. Five days later General Thomas, head of OKW Military-Economic Staff, advised that the Reich could not hold out in a long war from either an economic or military standpoint; Brauchitsch too was dubious when speaking to Keitel about the prospects for an offensive. Ritter von Leeb, commanding officer of Army Group 'C', considered Hitler's 'peace speech' to the Reichstag to be 'a fraud on the German people' and attempted to interest the commanding generals of the other two Army Groups, Generaloberst Feder von Bock, who was also doubtful about the chances of a successful attack on France, and Generaloberst von Rundstedt, to join him in a mass resignation.[14]

On 9 October Canaris spoke again to Groscurth about his meetings in the East with von Rundstedt and Blaskowitz, and also von Reichenau, with whom he had discussed the undisciplined conduct of German troops in the East and Hitler's attack plans in the West. Groscurth wrote to his wife on 10 October: 'C. was enthusiastic about v. Rundstedt. Even Reichenau turned out better.'[15] Canaris can only have meant Reichenau's reaction to his criticism of the policy of extermination and his rejection of a Western offensive; Reichenau considered the plans for the offensive flawed for tactical reasons and too early – his Chief of Staff Friedrich Paulus even stated, however, that Hitler's arrangements in Poland were necessary given the circumstances. On balance Canaris's trip was disappointing but had the result at least that Reichenau, previously loyal to the regime, in a memorandum now distanced himself from the plan to attack France, and shortly afterwards he voiced his doubts to Hitler personally.[16]

On 13 October, von Weizsäcker advised Halder that Chamberlain had turned down Hitler's 'offer'. Next day, in a private talk with Brauchitsch,[17] Halder no longer ruled out the need for an active intervention against Hitler and the previous day he had discussed with Wezisäcker the idea of arresting Hitler at the moment when he gave the order to attack in the West.[18] Brauchitsch was unwilling to go down this road – Hitler would allow himself to be convinced by the expert arguments of esteemed generals such as von Rundstedt and Reichenau.

On 16 October he had his answer when Hitler informed Brauchitsch of his 'unalterable decision' to undertake the offensive – an understanding with the Western Powers was not possible. The same day, Canaris returned shaken after visiting Halder and finding him at the end of his tether; Groscurth noted: 'Complete nervous breakdown. Brauchitsch also does not know where to turn. Führer demands attack. Firmly against all expert advice. Another rush of blood to the head ... What a situation! These are Prussian officers. A chief of the General Staff is *not supposed to* collapse.'[19]

The 'unwavering activists in the Abwehr, and above all Oster, Dohnanyi and Groscurth'[20] now collaborated more closely with the support of Canaris and Oster.[21] Groscurth played a key role in linking the opposition groups at Abwehr, the Foreign Ministry and OKH Zossen.[22] A memorandum, 'The Threatened Disaster', was 'hurriedly'[23] composed by Groscurth, Erich Kordt and Hasso von Etzdorf, Foreign Ministry liaison official at Zossen, and given to Beck on 19 October for forwarding to Halder via Stülpnagel.[24] Hitler would not allow the initiative to be wrested from himself, however, and came up with 12 November as the day for the attack.

Tactical delays dominated the conversations of many who were ready at the time to stage a coup. Within OKH were two Resistance groups: the Abwehr group around Oster and Groscurth, and the Halder–Stülpnagel group, which increasingly favoured the idea of a coup,[25] unsuspected by the first group. The Abwehr group did not particularly trust Halder's attitude, and kept applying pressure to OKH military leaders they believed approachable, but without success, and on 25 October Canaris and Oster failed with Stülpnagel. The mood in both camps was one of despair;[26] Stülpnagel had urged Halder to act, even suggesting the arrest of Brauchitsch.

On 29 October 1939, OKH issued its second 'Fall Gelb' instruction to move. While Canaris seemed resigned,[27] Oster, Dohnanyi and Gisevius, recalled from Switzerland, prepared another memorandum opposing the Western offensive, which General Thomas was to take to Halder, still thought to be unconvinced of the need to act. Both Stülpnagel and Halder were on visits to commanders-in-chief in the West, already convinced by the negative attitude of individual officers. Halder found only Leeb and Witzleben prepared to collaborate in a coup; Bock, von Rundstedt and General Fromm, commander-in-chief of the Reserve Army, declined.[28] When Halder returned to Zossen, he was at last determined to act, and surprised the memorandum writers who were still attempting to persuade him. On the evening of 31 October he sent for Groscurth and made an astounding announcement,[29] opening the one-hour talks by saying that certain people had to become 'the victims of accidents' – he named Ribbentrop and Goering, but not Hitler. Groscurth warned that a 'concerted operation' was necessary, which probably meant that a coup would not succeed if it aimed to get rid only of second-rank figures. Both men were agreed that 'there is no man in place',[30] presumably not meaning an assassin but somebody who could take over at the top. Groscurth mentioned Beck and Goerdeler, and received from Halder the job 'of securing Goerdeler'. Halder had at last declared himself in favour of a coup to members of the active opposition. Groscurth noted: 'With tears in his eyes H[alder] says that for weeks he had been going to see Emil [ie Hitler] with a loaded pistol in his pocket in order eventually to gun him down.'[31] Groscurth was now becoming the 'central figure of the coup planning' and a kind of 'chief of Staff' to the conspirators,[32] even though Halder had stated that it was Canaris who since October had belonged amongst the most insistent advocates of a coup to remove Hitler.[33]

On 2 November Groscurth received from Stülpnagel instructions to prepare the ground for the coup. Groscurth was apparently planning to supply weapons, fuses and explosives for a future assassination attempt by Lahousen's Abteilung II, which had an explosives laboratory at Quenzgut in Brandenburg. Lahousen recalled later that Oster had asked him at Abwehr headquarters if he were able to supply explosives and fuses for an attempt on Hitler's life. Lahousen enquired if Canaris knew about this idea, Oster framing his answer 'more or less' in these words: 'No, the Old Man has completely lost his nerve without adding this as well.'[34] Lahousen wanted to know if Oster had an assassin, to which Oster said yes, and by this meant Erich Kordt, who had been living at his house since 1 November and had agreed 'to throw the bomb'. Oster had told him he would have the explosives within ten days, before 11 November,[35] but between now and then a lot could happen.

Meanwhile Halder and Brauchitsch had embarked on a tour of the Army Staffs in the West. Bock and von Rundstedt remained negative, since they could not guarantee that their officers would follow them. In common with the activists amongst the conspirators, Halder had no set timetable – a fundamental error shared by both groups.[36] Brauchitsch wanted to take the 'final' opportunity to intercede with Hitler, and upon entering the Reich Chancellery on 5 November he was resolved to challenge Hitler over his plan to attack in the West. Halder waited in the ante-room during the discussion, which lasted twenty minutes. When Brauchitsch eventually came to the point and said that a Western offensive threatened to end in disaster because of a lack of preparation, Hitler raged that the Army was not ready because it did not want to fight; he knew 'the spirit of Zossen' and would exorcise it. Then he slammed the door behind him as he stormed out, leaving Brauchitsch trembling and pale.[37] Shortly afterwards Hitler ordered the attack for 1330hrs on 12 November 1939. This date was put back on 7 November because of bad weather, but Hitler's threat to destroy 'the spirit of Zossen' made Halder panic. He hurried back to Zossen and ordered the immediate destruction of all incriminating files that had any connection to Resistance plans.[38]

This order was only partially carried out and would seal Canaris's fate. Halder sent for Groscurth, who again witnessed the nervous collapse of a senior commander – this time Brauchitsch.[39] Halder stated that the offensive would proceed: 'There is nobody to take over, Volk and Army are not united,' Groscurth wrote in his diary. Halder continued: 'The forces that were counting on us are no longer bound together. You understand what I mean.'[40] Halder told him to inform Canaris that Canaris was to act, by which Groscurth understood that Canaris was to organise the assassination of Hitler, and in indignation he refused.[41] It is not agreed unanimously what Halder actually meant by his remark: Inga Haag, a close colleague of Groscurth and Canaris remembered later that Groscurth returned 'totally distraught' from the conversation with Halder and told her that he was faced by a riddle. Halder had declared with tears in his eyes that he could not assume the responsibility and had given Groscurth the task of putting it to Canaris 'that he should act off his own bat'.[42] Gisevius wrote in his memoirs:

> There remains a doubt whether Halder was talking about plans which he would execute himself or would at least be responsible for, or if he passed on the proposal in an indiscreet way as a transfer of jurisdiction. Canaris reacted angrily and forbade Oster or me to take on the task. We regretted it but somehow we cannot say that Canaris was wrong to decline. The Admiral informed the Chief of Staff that whenever he wanted to discuss that kind of high-political subject, he should do him the favour of seeing him personally. Moreover he insisted that Halder assume responsibility unequivocally and that all possibility of a straightforward military coup had been exhausted beforehand.[43]

That Groscurth actually believed he had been invited to carry out the assassination is proved by his diary entry for 14 February 1940 when, on the occasion of an argument between Canaris and Halder, he wrote: 'He [Halder] asked me to carry out a murder and maintains that he has been putting a pistol in his pocket with which to kill Hitler.' Did Groscurth understand Halder correctly? Halder denied this after the war, but admitted that he might have said: 'If people in the Wehrmacht want an assassination, then it is up to the admiral to arrange it.'[44] This would suggest that Groscurth might have misinterpreted or misunderstood what Halder said,[45] for why would Halder suggest an assassination and at the same time abandon all ideas of a coup? Groscurth knew Canaris's attitude and it seems against this background improbable that he deliberately misunderstood and repeated Halder's statement.[46]

However one looks at it, 5 November marked a turning point in the history of the preparations for a coup in the winter of 1939. It is significant that although Oster had in Erich Kordt a man prepared to carry out the assassination attempt, he did not play this 'trump card'.[47] The next day, Oster supplied Wagner and

Stülpnagel with the old plan of getting the Army to move by staging a pretended coup by Goering, Himmler and the Gestapo. Groscurth wrote: 'New proposal: occupy the Gst. But it is all too late and totally spent. These indecisive leaders make you sick.'[48] Canaris had been with Hitler previously to inform him about the preparations for the Western offensive – the principle tried and tested in Poland would be repeated, and assault troops clad in enemy uniforms would be infiltrated through the frontier to occupy strategically important bridges, sections of railway or buildings before the main force invaded. Groscurth reported that Canaris returned from Hitler depressed and asked if it would not be better if he stepped down, but Gisevius was used to such outbursts from the 'vibrating bundle of nerves' that Canaris was. After he had spent an hour in gloomy contemplation of the prognosis, Canaris went home.[49]

After Oster was told of Halder's alleged remark that he was ready, but without von Witzleben commanding 1.Armee in the West he was powerless,[50] he decided to visit von Witzleben at his Bad Kreuznach headquarters. Since he required a written approval and an order to do this, which he did not think Canaris was likely to issue in his present frame of mind, Groscurth rang von Witzleben and suggested he should telephone Canaris asking him to send Oster. When Witzleben rang, Canaris was wary, but finally acceded, enabling Oster and Gisevius to meet Witzleben on 7 November.[51]

It was a sobering session, for Witzleben commenced by telling them that he no longer believed the offensive could be stopped. He was particularly unhappy about the younger officers' attitude, which he described as 'infatuated with Hitler'. The only possibility he could see was if all three Army Group commanders-in-chief refused to carry out the attack order. He was subjected to a long period of persuasive talk before agreeing to speak to Halder, and in addition Witzleben wanted the approval of his commander-in-chief, Ritter von Leeb, whose headquarters was in Frankfurt; Oster should make an intermediate stop there to prepare Leeb. At the end of their conversation, Witzleben lost his temper when Oster brought from his pocket copies of the two appeals that Beck was to make to the German people and the Wehrmacht: 'What? You had that on you in the car? Then I will not receive you again,' he is alleged to have said to Oster.[52]

At Frankfurt Oster spoke to Oberst Vicenz Müller, whom Witzleben had recommended. Müller listened attentively before warning that the circle of accomplices must be kept as small as possible, and asked whether Oster was carrying any incriminating papers on his person, making him burn them at once in a large ashtray. Although Müller promised to speak to Witzleben again, Oster took his leave knowing that he had failed. In the officers' mess at Frankfurt Oster and Gisevius began drinking heavily and Oster had to be taken out into a side-room for safety once he began to speak out volubly against the regime. There he left copies of Beck's appeal, which he had failed to burn at Müller's request, and a list with the names of the members of a provisional government. These were discovered by a well-disposed officer.[53]

Next morning Gisevius was the first to learn the sensational news – 'Hey! They tried to bump Emil off yesterday!'[54] The previous evening a lone assassin, Georg Elser, attempted to kill Hitler by leaving a home-made bomb at the Bürgerbräukeller in Munich, but Hitler had left the hall immediately after delivering his speech, ten minutes before the bomb exploded. The official version accused the British secret service of the attempt. In the framework of an SD operation led by Walter Schellenberg, successor to SS-Brigadeführer Best as head of the Polizei-Abwehr, RHSA Amtsgruppe IV, the British SIS agents Major R H Stevens and Captain S P Best were captured next day in no-man's land in a café between the German and Dutch borders at Venlo; the Propaganda Ministry used this coup to support their version of events at Munich.[55]

Gisevius feared that the attempt on Hitler's life might have been staged in order to strike against the Resistance, upon his arrival in Berlin, he discovered that the Abwehr had no knowledge of the background nor the culprits. Canaris was increasingly more nervous and urged his circle to be more cautious. Gisevius and Oster wrote another memorandum for Halder, accompanied by a personal letter from Groscurth. Halder passed it to Brauchitsch and gave vent to his annoyance at Gisevius's hectic activities, particularly the endless conferences with Beck, Schacht, Helldorf and Goerdeler. Canaris had become more wary for the same reason and warned against close contact with Gisevius.[56] Additionally Witzleben had passed to Halder through Oberst Müller his concerns about Oster's behaviour on 7 November; Halder was beside himself with rage and advised Groscurth to report the matter to Canaris officially, but Groscurth would not do this because Oster was a friend.[57] Oster escaped with a reprimand from Halder, but by now Canaris had had enough of the game and forbade all further conspiratorial activities, and now, without the dynamic Oster, the circle of plotters threatened to break up, since he had told Gisevius that 'he would definitely not do any more'.[58]

Leeb's meeting with the three Army Group commanders-in-chief bore no fruit, and Leeb resigned.[59] Stülpnagel paid a last visit to Witzleben and learned of the refusal of the Army Group commanders-in-chief to resign en masse. Groscurth noted: 'No more talk of resistance,'[60] and one day later, he wrote: 'Generals therefore will do nothing.'[61]

21

'Now There is No Going Back'

The two-month-long conspiracy thus came to an end. Canaris was not only deeply depressed but found the attitude of the Army leaders incomprehensible; he was certain that through them Germany could avoid certain disaster.[1] Although the attack date continued to suffer regular postponements, up to May 1940 almost thirty times, the Resistance did not revive, and Hitler delivered the 'coup de grace' personally.[2]

On 23 November 1939, nearly two hundred commanding generals and senior officers of all Wehrmacht branches were ordered by Hitler to assemble in the Conference Hall of the New Reich Chancellery; Canaris was amongst them.[3] In view of the conflicts with the Army leadership in recent weeks, Hitler now went onto the counter-offensive and for Brauchitsch in particular: 'If, as in 1914, senior commanders have nervous breakdowns, what can one expect from the simple rifleman? . . . I will not cower before anything and I will destroy everybody who is against me. I will stand or fall in this struggle. I will not survive the defeat of my people. Outwardly no capitulation, inwardly no revolution.'[4] Groscurth remarked later: 'Tragic impression of a mad criminal',[5] but nobody dared protest, not even the most infirm of the Army generals. That evening Hitler accused Halder and Brauchitsch of being responsible for the failure of the Army leadership and repeated his threat to exorcise the 'spirit of Zossen'. Brauchitsch offered his resignation, which Hitler declined to accept, saying that the commander-in-chief must do his duty.[6]

Two powerful tirades[7] from Hitler had reached out to stifle a possible military uprising. The commander-in-chief of the East, Generaloberst Blaskowitz, sent a memorandum to Brauchitsch on 27 November 1939 which left nothing to be desired in clarity: 'The troops reject identification with the Sipo atrocities' and refused 'all cooperation with these Einsatzgruppen working almost exclusively as execution commandos'. This 'rush of blood' represented for the Wehrmacht 'an intolerable burden . . . since almost everything is done in a field-grey uniform'.[8] The memorandum was shown to Hitler, who retorted: 'One cannot prosecute a war with Salvation Army methods. Also confirms a long held aversion. He had never trusted Gen. Bl.'[9] By his protest, Blaskowitz had forfeited the Führer's trust – he was the only Generaloberst of the Polish campaign not to be promoted to Feldmarschall and was recalled from Poland six months later.[10]

By now Brauchitsch was 'a lonely and melancholy man'[11] and Halder had abandoned his plotting against Hitler and was advocating that 'time was not yet ripe'. On the morning of 30 November 1939, recalled ambassador von Hassell paid Canaris a visit. After their conversation Hassell recorded of him: 'He has abandoned all hope of resistance from the generals and believes there is no point in trying anything further in that direction.'[12] Only Blaskowitz had not yet given up and in Groscurth he had a helper who was ever tireless; on 18 December Groscurth travelled with a new report by Blaskowitz for the Western Front where it provoked 'great excitement'.[13]

In satisfaction, after his return he noted: 'We have worked up the most important sections of the Western Front for a putsch. With success I hope!'[14] But there was no success and barely a month later Halder criticised him, and all 'who were thinking of a putsch, but were disunited, even fighting amongst themselves, and were mostly only reactionaries who wanted to roll back the wheel of history'.[15] He inveighed most strongly against Groscurth for his trip to the Westwall – one ought not to burden the Front unnecessarily with worries – but to Groscurth this was water off a duck's back. At his request Canaris informed Halder[16] of Blaskowitz's opinion that the officers lacked courage: 'No human intervention for those unjustly persecuted'.[17]

Halder was visibly annoyed over Groscurth's stubbornness and a little later Groscurth was removed from the Abwehr and transferred to the field as a punishment.[18] The news was given to him by his immediate superior, Generalmajor Tippelskirch, but Groscurth was convinced that Brauchitsch and Halder had 'cooked it up between themselves' and that his close relationship with Canaris was a reason to wish to be rid of him, as Tippelskirch 'openly told' him: 'Halder said to Canaris on the evening of the day before yesterday, everything was in order. A fine game! But I go willingly according to honour and I have nothing to reproach myself for.'[19] On 15 February 1940 Groscurth was transferred into the OKH Führer-Reserve and took part in the French campaign as a battalion commander. His spirit of resistance remained unbroken, however; during the war of extermination in Russia he opposed the indescribable atrocities, and at Stalingrad, under the greatest difficulties, he still managed to maintain contact with the Berlin Resistance in the attempt to prevent the senseless sacrifice of 6.Armee. After the defeat there he was taken into Soviet captivity and died of typhus at Frolov camp on 7 April 1943.[20]

On 13 February there occurred a violent argument between Canaris, Tippelskirch and Halder in which the admiral emphasised how important it was 'to have officers unobjectionable in character who said what they thought even if it might be unpleasant for them and risked their position'.[21] Oster and Groscurth had dealt on his behalf and the plans for Berlin had been worked out with Etzdorf at Zossen; by this he can only have meant the plans in preparation for the coup, of which Halder denied all knowledge, putting everything on Stülpnagel. Groscurth wrote: 'A strong piece of work. He urged me to commit murder and asserts that for some time he had carried a pistol in his pocket to gun Hitler down.'[22] In the violent exchange Halder – according to Groscurth's account – distanced himself in every respect from the coup plans and he even went so far as to say 'the circumstances in the East would be forgotten later – they were not so bad.'[23] Groscurth noted: 'It is deplorable and incomprehensible. I cannot believe in any way in the decency of Halder any more.' He went on: 'Canaris told Halder that he was ready to act at once, he made it clear that he had a large unified officer corps behind him that would take on the struggle against H[itler] and H[immler].' Was Groscurth exaggerating here, or did Canaris really threaten that his resignation might have unsuspected consequences? The Abwehr chief belonged to the more cautious breed of men and often reined in his intrepid and uninhibited subordinates. But perhaps today the angered and embittered admiral was less careful in his choice of words than usual – and Halder followed suit. Groscurth reported: 'Halder suddenly identified his great confidant and schoolfriend Etscheit as an SS man and informer, he wants to have nothing more to do with him. Canaris should unload him at once. And how he protected him to the last!'[24] The lawyer Alfred Etscheit had excellent contacts in diplomatic circles. He had been sent to Switzerland in the autumn of 1939 as an Abwehr spy on a fact-finding mission. Here he endangered one of the most intricate operations of the Resistance circle, set up by the Abwehr.

The aim of Josef Müller's activities at the Vatican was to make contact with British Government circles to obtain their support for a coup attempt;[25] one of the objectives of this was to convince Halder and Brauchitsch that the Allies would become involved in such plans.[26] The plan had been developed in 1939 by Dohnanyi and Oster after discussions with Beck and Canaris,[27] as both of the latter allegedly knew the pope from his time as nuncio in Berlin.[28] Beck told Oster to restore the liaison with Pope Pius XII and to obtain through him an introduction to the British ambassador to the Vatican, Sir Francis d'Arcy Osborne. Oster entrusted this delicate mission to Catholic lawyer Josef Müller, who then arranged personal connections to the pope's staff.[29]

Since the outbreak of war it had been very difficult to obtain approval for trips abroad, but the espionage work of the Abwehr was an exception, being seen as important for the war effort.[30] In 1942 Ernst von Weizsäcker wrote in a file note for Ribbentrop that 'persons entrusted by the leader of the Abwehr with missions abroad have the freedom to travel abroad using true or false passports, whenever necessary and without special permission. To have to request special permission for such journeys would frustrate or even cripple the Abwehr in the timely and convenient execution of its duties.'[31] Canaris explained to the dubious Keitel that Müller had to use his Vatican contacts in order to observe how things were developing in Italy, whose attitude the OKW chief had been following with suspicion for some time.[32]

For safety's sake, Canaris informed Heydrich when asking for 'play material' to string the British along about the internal political situation in the Reich, but Heydrich declined because he could not take the decision alone and an enquiry to Himmler was inopportune.[33] In October 1939 Müller left on his first Vatican trip; the operation and the Vatican contacts of Canaris and Oster were directed by Abwehrstelle Munich; Dohnanyi was responsible at the Tirpitzufer.[34]

Müller succeeded in making indirect contacts to the British Foreign Office through the pope's private secretary, Pater Robert Leiber, the former presiding prelate of the centre, Ludwig Kaass, and the general abbot of the Premonstratensian Order in Rome, Hubert Noots.

On 20 October Groscurth wrote in his service diary: 'The pope himself is very interested and considers an honourable peace possible, giving his personal guarantee that Germany will not be deceived as it was in the Compiegne Forest. In all peace negotiations one finds the categorical demand for the removal of Hitler and the definite return of Czechoslovakia. Disarmament will not be required since a strong Germany is seen as a protection against Bolshevism.'[35] Müller was in Rome again from 6 to 12 November, but as a result of the Venlo incident, the contacts dried up[36] and he had to leave Rome because Heydrich was watching him.[37] On 12 January 1940 Pope Pius XII spoke on the matter to British ambassador d'Arcy Osborne for the first time, and in a further audience on 7 February more broadly about the aims and intentions of the German Resistance. Müller stated later that Canaris was not informed as to the details of the conversation and its results,[38] but in view of the fact that he covered Müller's mission with Keitel and Heydrich it is to be inferred that he knew exactly what was in progress. From the autumn of 1939, Müller's so-called espionage reports were drafted and supplied into Abwehr everyday business to legitimise Canaris's approach to Heydrich.

In the run-up to the Venlo incident, Schellenberg had used the method of 'counter-play' to test British readiness and commitment for an 'understanding' and Bürkner, head of Abteilung Ausland, requested from the Foreign Ministry 'play material' and true reports 'to use in discussions with intelligence services of neutral nations as well as exchange material for our own agents'.[39]

At the end of January, after talks between Dohnanyi and Müller, the first version of the so-called 'X-Report' appeared in the summary of the exploratory soundings through the Vatican, Müller being identified only as 'X' for security reasons. This report, discovered amongst Dohnanyi's files found at Zossen after 20 July 1944, is no longer extant. He did not receive this final version until mid-March 1940, after Müller submitted an assurance from the British Government transmitted by the pope, in which 'the will for a just peace' was guaranteed, provided that Hitler was toppled.[40] On 4 April the ailing General Thomas, believing the X-Report to be a true Abwehr document, himself took it[41] to Halder together with a covering letter authored by Dohnanyi. Halder passed the papers to Brauchitsch;[42] they had been doctored beforehand with certain amendments that the conspirators considered valid in the campaign to convince Halder and Brauchitsch.[43]

Dohnanyi did not believe that the X-Report would actually convince anybody and he was proved right. While Halder was doubtful about the material, did not like its anonymity nor certain contradictions in the content, Brauchitsch stated categorically that treason against the State was impermissible for a soldier in wartime, and urged the arrest of the X-Report author for treason, which Halder resisted with the words, 'If anyone should be arrested, then arrest me.'[44]

Hans Oster, with Beck's knowledge, now warned the British Government of the imminent German attack on Denmark and Norway through Müller's Vatican contacts, having already informed the Netherlands. On the evening of 8 October 1939, while driving through Berlin with Franz Liedig, Oster asked his friend to drop him outside the house of the Dutch military attaché Lt-Colonel Gijsbertus Jacobus Sas and wait. Sas and Oster had met during the 1936 Olympics, and Sas knew Oster's attitude to the regime. When Oster returned, he told Liedig: 'Now there is no going back;' he had just committed treason against the State by promising to give Sas timely warning of the German attack date. Liedig noted Oster's remarks:

> It is much simpler to take a pistol and shoot somebody, it is much simpler to run into a spray of machine-gun bullets than to do what I have resolved to do . . . I beg you, to remain even after my death the friend who knows how it was with me and what motivated me to do things which others perhaps can never understand or at least would never have done themselves.[45]

Was Oster correct in this assessment? A weak man like Brauchitsch would never consider treason against the State under any circumstances, but even Canaris would probably not have followed Oster down this road, despite knowing that the contacts through the Vatican verged on treason. In the following months Oster kept Sas informed about the repeated postponements of the attack date;[46]

although Müller, von Weizsäcker, the later General Warlimont and even the supposedly Nazi General Reichenau passed on the attack dates to potential enemies variously between 1938 and 1940,[47] Oster's act was nevertheless unparalleled.[48]

At the end of January 1940, Admiral Raeder ordered a plan for the possible occupation of Denmark and Norway, apparently after a warning by Canaris that the British might be thinking of landings in Norway[49] under the pretext of British 'Finland Volunteers'.[50] On 24 January 'Sonderstab Nord' was set up at OKW, renamed 'Sonderstab Weserübung' by Keitel on 5 February. A few days previously Canaris had given Oberstleutnant Pruck the task of reporting on the activities of the enemy powers in Norway, the strength and disposition of Norwegian armed forces and to reconnoitre the port installations at Oslo, Stavanger, Bergen, Kristiansand, Trondheim and Narvik. At the end of February the German ambassador in Stockholm warned of an imminent major British and French action in Scandinavia. On 3 March Hitler decided to proceed with Operation Weserübung – with Korvettenkapitän Liedig as Abwehr representative – well before the Western offensive.[51] On 31 March Canaris went personally to Abwehrstelle Oslo to see how things were progressing,[52] he and Liedig informing Oster regularly: 'It is impossible to understand how the British can be so blind. It is obvious that it would be possible to unleash a demonstration of British sea power. I am certain that the whole operation will be called off if it is seen that the Home Fleet is sailing.'[53] Two days later Oster told his friend Sas that Denmark and Norway would be invaded 'in the first half of next week',[54] that is, the first week of April. Sas informed The Hague immediately and requested that the British secret service be informed too.

When Sas told the Norwegian ambassadorial assistant Ulrich Stang at Hotel Adlon, his advice was rebuffed as nonsense; Sas was not aware that Stang was a supporter of the Fascist leader Vidkung Quisling and welcomed a German invasion. The Danish naval attaché Kolsen reported Sas's warning to Copenhagen, but no armed resistance was prepared.

On 7 April 1940 the heavy cruiser *Admiral Hipper*, fourteen destroyers and the battleships *Scharnhorst* and *Gneisenau* sailed for Narvik and Trondheim with a total of 3,700 German troops. The armada was detected by British air reconnaissance covering British naval units mining Norway's coastal waters and the first minor clashes occurred.[55] By 22 May Germany had lost eighteen warships, including three cruisers and the ten destroyers sent into Narvik, while the Luftwaffe lost 242 aircraft, but the strategically important ports and aerodromes in southern and central Norway were in German hands.

On 1 May Josef Müller was again in Rome and passed a letter authored by Oster, Dohnanyi and himself to Pater Leiber warning of an imminent

German attack in the West.[56] On 6 May the later Pope Paul VI informed the representatives of Britain and France. Osborne, however, was sceptical and in a cable to London reported: 'The Vatican expects a German offensive in the West at the beginning of next week – on account of previous similar expectations – however I have no great confidence in the present prediction.'[57] Abbot-General Noots visited the Belgian ambassador Nieuwenhuys and asked him to inform Brussels, but after the Venlo incident all information from apparent German Resistance sources was being treated as a possible plot to disseminate disinformation by German intelligence, and Nieuwenhuys also mentioned his doubts.

Meanwhile, Müller had left Rome, but finding that he had a new attack date to pass on used his friend Hauptmann Wilhem Schmidhuber, consul in Portugal, who was in Rome on 6 May and from then on remained in telephone contact with Müller. Oster was meeting Sas every day in Berlin, often at the latter's flat. The German conspirators were running a high risk because the constant flow of telegrams, telephone calls and meetings left a trail that the eavesdropping crews of Goering's Forschungsamt – Research Bureau (FA) – did not overlook. In the run-up to Operation Weserübung they had already recorded the conversations of the Danish military attaché Kjolsen without knowing where his information originated. On 7 May Jodl wrote in his diary: '... the F very upset about another postponement, as danger of betrayal, esp in Brown Sheets. Conversation of Belgian ambassador at Vatican to Brussels which leads to conclusion of treason by German personality who travelled from Berlin to Rome on 29 April.'[58] The FA decrypts were prepared on brown folios, ridiculed in the Abwehr as 'brown birds' because of the giant Reich eagle at the head.[59] The FA had also intercepted two cables from Nieuwenhuys on 1 and 4 May 1940, while the script of the telephone conversations between Sas and the Dutch war minister in The Hague were shown to Hitler on 9 May.

On 10 May 1940, 136 German divisions entered Holland, Belgium and France. Holland gave in after five days; the Dutch queen and her government fled to exile in Britain. Belgium held out until the 18th of the month before capitulating, and after less than five weeks German soldiers were in Paris. The new French Government under Marshall Pétain sued for peace, and on 21 June 1940 at Compiègne the armistice was signed in the same railway coach that had been used to stage the German surrender in 1918. Hitler had achieved his great goal; 'The symbolic liquidation of the old debt was completed.'[60]

At the beginning of June Hitler ordered Canaris and Heydrich to find the traitor who had betrayed his attack plan; the task was given to Joachim Rohleder, responsible for counter-espionage at Abwehr headquarters, and to Schellenberg at SS-RSHA. According to SS-Standartenführer Huppenkothen, Canaris and

Heydrich agreed to a mutual exchange of information,[61] but the relationship between them cooled very quickly because the Abwehr did not keep to its side of the bargain. At Schellenberg's complaint, Heydrich took over,[62] thus putting Canaris in an awkward position, as the investigation could fatally expose the organisation.[63] Rohleder was bound quickly to identify Oster, simply by checking the dates of departure of all persons who had gone to Rome at the time in question, and moreover Rohleder had his own source at the Vatican.[64] Rohleder discovered everything, and also the connection between Sas and Oster, but put aside the file codenamed 'Palmenzweig' – 'Palm branch' – when Canaris decided not to proceed with the matter 'for lack of evidence'. Eventually, however, he requested a copy and said that the relationship between Oster and Müller was being terminated. Rohleder reminded his chief of the danger that the Gestapo might also know everything, but Huppenkothen confirmed later that Gestapo inquiries had fallen on fallow ground: a 'circle of travellers to Italy' had been identified, but no significant name was forthcoming.[65] Canaris had succeeded once more in saving Oster, Dohnanyi and Müller.

22

Operation Felix

After the triumph in the West, Hitler and his generals had a dilemma, for Britain remained to be defeated and was unwilling to negotiate. Hitler wanted a quick solution to this, for Germany did not want to be forced to the defensive in the near future, and so on 30 June 1940 Generalmajor Jodl presented his memorandum 'The Continuation of the War against Great Britain',[1] which recommended determination 'to break the British will to resist' if 'political means' were inadequate.[2]

Either England had to be invaded or the war extended peripherally, by which Jodl meant extending towards 'the lucrative inheritance' of states that Germany would control once the British Empire gave in. Besides Russia and Japan, it was principally from Italy and Spain that Jodl was hoping for military support to bring about this desired end, by mining the Suez Canal or helping in the capture of Gibraltar.

On 1 July 1940 Hitler spoke to Italian ambassador Alfieri, and a week later with Foreign Minister Ciano[3] about the possibilities of attacking Gibraltar, which the German Staffs were thinking about 'very seriously'. 'Special weapons' would be used, but the actual occupation would be done by Spanish troops, and the problem lay in obtaining Franco's agreement; Italy should request air bases in Spain, Spanish Morocco and the Balearics in order to attack Gibraltar.[4] It speaks volumes for the confusion on one hand and the readiness to keep all options open on the other that it was not until 12 July that OKW issued the order to prepare the attack operation or, in support of a Spanish *coup de main*, set up an Intelligence Staff Gibraltar. Four days later 'Instruction No 16 – Preparation of Landing Operations in England', also known as Operation Seelöwe, appeared.[5] When Hitler announced to his generals at the Berghof on 13 July that he was intending to draw Spain into the war 'in order to consolidate the front against Britain from the North Cape to Morocco',[6] Canaris was already working on the plans. At the end of June he had made it clear to Franco, the Minister for Air Juan Vigón and Foreign Minister Beigbeder that Germany was not currently interested in having Spain enter the war, but was requesting permission to move German troops across Spanish territory. Franco was cautious – an attack by Spanish troops on Gibraltar would only be possible if Germany supplied aircraft and artillery.[7]

Canaris arrived in Spain on 23 July 1940 in order to see for himself the prospects for the operation locally. In his entourage were Piekenbrock, Oberst Mikosch, the commanding officer of 51.Pionierbatallion, Major Langkau from the Staff of Jüterbog Artillery School, paratrooper Hauptmann Rudolf Witzig and Hauptmann Osterecht. These officers represented the essential technical branches for an attack on the Gibraltar,[8] and arrived singly by different routes, in civilian dress and with false passports. On 23 July Canaris and Piekenbrock met in Madrid and visited the head of K-Organisation Spain, Fregattenkapitän Wilhelm Leissner. K-Org was the Abwehr apparatus in neutral countries, usually structured around the German embassy, and its network of agents spread out across the country. The K-Org heads not only kept in touch with the important civilian and military offices of the 'host' and collated the available information, but also courted the secret services of the various belligerent states. In this way during the course of the war Stockholm, Berne, Istanbul, Lisbon and Madrid became meeting points for the international intelligence communities and enabled conspiratorial contact across the frontlines. Shortly after seeing Leissner, Canaris and Piekenbrock met Vigón, the new chief of the Spanish General Staff Campos, and Lt-Coronel Pardo, the latter presumably an intelligence officer from the Army Ministry.[9] Canaris stated frankly that the purpose of his visit was to discuss a possible operation against Gibraltar and to obtain the fullest information about the Rock, and he requested the help of his Spanish hosts for their maps of the British defence system in order to assess the military conditions for the attack.

Vigón reacted evasively; he considered a surprise attack out of the question since only one road led there, it would take time to position the artillery, and the Spanish railway gauge differed from the French. Shortly afterwards there was a meeting with Franco, who did not dismiss the German plans out of hand but spoke of his manifold reservations. He feared the British naval strength and thought they might retaliate against the Canary Islands. He pointed to Spain's economic difficulties, which Canaris had often described himself,[10] and was especially concerned at the shortage of oil caused by the American refusal to meet his needs.[11] The meeting, though warm, ended without any concrete result, but three houses in Algeciras were placed at the disposal of the Germans, one as a residence while the other two looked across the Bay of Gibraltar and were useful as observation posts.[12]

During the next two days Canaris's commando squad had a closer look at Gibraltar, and did not like what they saw. The steep slopes and unpredictable winds ruled out gliders and paratroop drops. The access over the isthmus that connected Gibraltar to the mainland was apparently mined and the defenders had a good field of fire from all positions. All troop and material transports had to change trains at the French–Spanish border and the Spanish did not have the resources to support the troops in transit with signals technology, supplies and security. An attack would succeed only at the cost of high casualties.[13]

On 27 July Canaris held a concluding conference in which the results were discussed. The outlook was not appealing; a surprise attack was out of the question, the Spanish degree of commitment was uncertain and even if an attack were undertaken, the Spanish would need to make immense preparations to support a German Expeditionary Corps. Despite these sobering difficulties, Canaris and his team were not deterred, and on their return to Germany work started immediately on a plan of attack.[14]

On 31 July 1940, Brauchitsch, Halder, Jodl, Keitel and Raeder met at the Berghof to discuss the invasion of England with Hitler, but found the Führer preoccupied with his plans to destroy 'the life force of the Soviet Union' in the spring of 1941. The increase in size of the Army from 120 to 180 divisions in the middle of August was a signal to those in the know that he did not expect to defeat Britain in 1940 and was calculating for the entry of the United States into the war with the change in the German–Soviet relationship. Operation Seelöwe was not discarded but the Luftwaffe had first to win air supremacy over England, and the subsequent invasion by sea had serious troop transportation problems and problematic weather. That Franco knew this had prompted Canaris to make his fact-finding mission to Spain.

An offensive in the East and the destruction of the Soviet Union would 'show Britain the mainland sword' and, if Russia could be overwhelmed quickly, strengthen Japan sufficiently to deter the United States from entering the war against such an Axis. The conquest of Gibraltar, the support of the Italian adventure in Libya, even the preparations against England, were now little more than diversionary moves to disguise the real direction of the main activity, as Halder wrote in his diary on 31 July 1940.[15]

On 2 August Canaris reported on his findings in Spain to Keitel and General Warlimont, chief of the Land Defence Department, Abteilung L, at OKW.[16] Building on this knowledge, the Army and Navy Groups of Abteilung L weighed the operational possibilities of an expedition to North Africa consisting of one or two panzer divisions, provided that Operation Seelöwe fell by the wayside permanently and the troops became available. Warlimont was of the opinion that if Gibraltar were captured, the British could probably be driven out of the Mediterranean theatre in the winter.[17] Canaris warned against such speculations: Franco would not act against Gibraltar on his own and Spain's catastrophic economic situation would make it difficult for Hitler to lure Spain into the war.[18] Nevertheless Hitler wanted the 'great solution' in four steps:

1. A binding agreement with General Franco that Spain under a fully camouflaged German participation would resist a British attack or landings in the Campo de Gibraltar on the mainland.
2. A surprise attack by massed German Luftwaffe groups operating from Bordeaux against the British Fleet in Gibraltar harbour, and at the same time the transfer of Stukas and coastal artillery batteries to Spain.
3. Destruction of the harbour and harassment of British Fleet by Stukas and coastal artillery.
4. Capture of the Rock by attack from the landward side and possibly also from the sea under Spanish supreme command, although the command of the operation as a whole should remain in German hands through the force of personality of the German commander.[19]

Canaris was under strict instructions to undertake no further reconnaissance missions to the Iberian Peninsula[20] to ensure that the British remained unaware of the German interest in Gibraltar, and he drove to Paris and Abwehrstellen in Occupied France to collect information before meeting Vigón in Madrid.[21] The Spanish air minister had just come from a meeting with the former Legion Condor commander, Luftwaffe-General Wolfram von Richthofen, and was concerned at the progress of the German plan. Franco was very interested in accelerating the operation because of his worsening fuel and food situation, although this would not improve appreciably if he captured Gibraltar. Vigón then voiced Franco's demands; Spain would only become involved if it were supplied with goods and weapons. These amounted to two hundred heavy guns, over one hundred flak guns, three squadrons of naval reconnaissance aircraft and many other items.[22] Apparently no detailed discussions were held on the hundreds of thousands of tonnes of fuel, wheat, oil and coal that the Caudillo urgently needed.[23]

On 24 August, Hitler approved the operational plan Felix. Franco had agreed to participate, provided that his massive material demands were satisfied,[24] and Canaris notified Halder of the quantity and types of weapons, the amounts of fuel and food the Spanish leader thought he could make do with.[25] Canaris remained pessimistic about the whole endeavour and tried to bring Halder round to his way of thinking. Franco had the generals and the clergy against him, his only supporter being Serrano Suñer, his brother-in-law and the future successor to Foreign Minister Beigbeder, and even he preferred the Italians to the Germans. One assumes that Franco would not have 'got involved' until Britain was already on its knees. Ultimately, as Canaris advised, it would need a personal visit of the Führer to 'work it'; Hitler was keen, as he told Brauchitsch and Halder on 14 September, 'to promise the Spanish all they want, even if we can't deliver in full'.[26]

On 16 September Ribbentrop met Suñer in Berlin; Suñer was friendly towards the Berlin–Rome Axis, but he was also a Spanish Nationalist, a lawyer and a pious Catholic, and could not stand Ribbentrop. He began by refusing the German request for a naval base on the Canary Islands, and avoided all other suggestions by detailing again all Franco's material demands. Franco wanted Gibraltar, French Morocco and Oran, but Hitler was only ready to let him have French Morocco if he allowed a German naval base there and mining rights. Franco refused, and so the Ribbentrop–Suñer meeting ended without accord except for Franco's offer to meet Hitler personally at the Spanish border with France.[27]

On 23 September Hitler agreed to meet Franco's demands, but his conversation with Mussolini on 4 October 1940 at the Brenner Pass, in which he described these demands, changed the situation. Hitler wanted bases in Morocco from where he could strike at British colonies in West Africa; Mussolini wanted Nice, Corsica, Tunis and Djibouti. As it now appeared certain that Hitler would abandon Operation Seelöwe, Mussolini was hoping, as was his Foreign Minister Ciano, to bring France in on the side of an anti-British coalition. Regarding the situation in Spain, there was agreement[28] on the basis of Canaris's advice that very little military assistance was to be expected from Spain[29] and therefore Mussolini should now take over the job of manoeuvring Franco into the Berlin–Rome Axis, as Halder later confirmed.

The Duce went on the defensive, considering that great caution was advisable, for Spain was unreliable and Franco was demanding too much; it would be best to hold back.[30] The relationship between Hitler and Mussolini was harmonious at this point, but when Mussolini was surprised by a report that a German military commission was in Bucharest preparing the defence of the Romanian oilfields, he reacted by ordering the invasion of Greece at the end of the month in order to present Hitler with his own *fait accompli*.

During the first fortnight of October 1940 there was increasing disquiet at Franco's delaying tactics and the General Staff was considering an attack on Gibraltar without Spanish help. In an earlier meeting between Hitler and Suñer, Hitler had offered Spain the opportunity to extinguish the civil war debt, and in response, according to Halder, Suñer had given Hitler a sermon: 'Suñer replied, "Such a combination of materialism and idealism is incomprehensible for the Spanish." The Führer seemed like "a small Jew".'[31] Franco had requested a document granting his demands for Gibraltar, Morocco and Oran, but Hitler had declined to sign it, worried that if France learned of these demands, it would not defend its colonies but hand them over to Britain.

On 12 October Operation Seelöwe was shelved and the preparations for Operation Felix accelerated.[32] Halder even thought it possible that the Rock might be taken without a fight, but if that was not the case it would be costly. 'Gibraltar is just a prestige thing. I do not rule it out that the British will abandon it when they see that we are preparing an attack, for it is less harmful to prestige to abandon something voluntarily than lose it. If they hold it, however, then we must have the whole peninsula down to the southern end in our hand, otherwise it will become an Alcazar'[33] (Alcazar was the minor fortress that Franco had sworn to relieve as a debt of honour and which cost him the early capture of Madrid in 1936).

Travelling in the Führer's train towards the Spanish frontier and his meeting with Franco on 23 October, Hitler was already forewarned by Canaris that he would be disappointed by Franco, who was basically a hard-bitten diplomat.[34] The dictatorial pair were thus well matched. Franco was intent on tightening the screw to the fullest as the price for Spain's entry into the war, while Hitler knew that many of his leading military men placed little value on Franco because of the underlying situation in Spain.[35] State Secretary von Weizsäcker wrote three days previously: 'My vote is that Spain should be left out of the game ... Gibraltar is not worth that much to us ... Today Spain is starving and has a fuel shortage ... even the entry of Spain (together with other vassal states) has no practical value.'[36]

The meeting with Franco took place in Hitler's saloon coach at the border station of Hendaye, and lasted almost nine hours. Franco wanted much, and Hitler had almost nothing to offer[37] and in the end the talks were fruitless.[38] As Hitler left the meeting he murmured: 'We cannot do anything with this guy.' Halder noted later, after hearing from Hitler's Army adjutant Engel that in the Reich Chancellery Hitler had raged wildly about the 'Jesuit swine' and 'the false pride of the Spaniard'.[39] At the German border on his return he was told of the impending Italian attack on Greece, at which he erupted in rage.[40] From then on, Hitler planned to solve the Gibraltar problem with Spain, cutting Italy out.

On 2 November Canaris had several conversations with Halder, to whom he had offered the role of negotiator in the dealings with Spain.[41] Halder asked him to summon his representative at Algeciras, Major Fritz Kautschke, to Berlin; Kautschke had been recruited into the Abwehr by Canaris after being required to relinquish his post with the artillery for 'non-Aryan racial descent'. Together with Coronel Pardo, General Campos and other Spanish General Staff officers, he had made a detailed analysis of the Gibraltar area and the British defence measures, and he now presented a long report accompanied by photos, maps and sketches. He was enthusiastic, even if the situation in Spain was assessed as very bad indeed. He wrote: 'Total collapse of the internal [apparatus of] administration: for food and fuel totally dependent on Britain, which receives ore in exchange. Difficult position for Franco who has nothing behind him and therefore cannot risk anything. His position is being weakened rather than strengthened by Suñer, who can be considered the most hated man in Spain.'[42]

Of the new foreign minister it was said that his 'arrogance and excessive sensitivity were not justified by his achievements' and combined with 'Franco's stubbornness' he was becoming a problem. Canaris was to hold himself in readiness for the preparation of further negotiations[43] and to ensure that the Abwehr shielded the military survey of Gibraltar from British intelligence.

The preparations for the actual attack proceeded to plan. As soon as the first German troops had crossed the Spanish border, the Luftwaffe would strike at the ships in Gibraltar harbour. 22.Infanteriedivision was completely fitted out, and leave restrictions had been imposed, additional troops were at readiness in order to invade Portugal if necessary and it was being calculated how quickly artillery units could be stationed on the North African coast of the Strait. Lahousen now set in motion the preparations of Abwehr II;[44] the operation was codenamed 'Felsennest' ('Nest on the Rock'), later changed to 'Basta' (Spanish: 'Enough'). Lehrregiment *Brandenburg* would have 150 men ready for a commando mission shortly to start up in southern France.[45]

In the first half of November, a series of secret operations began around Gibraltar. Canaris sent Kapitän Hans-Erich Voss to Algeciras to determine where best to place the heavy coastal batteries to support the German attack and Abwehr Hauptmann Hermann Menzel cooperated with K-Org chief Leissner in supplying reports for the naval intelligence on Gibraltar's weak points. From 12 November, Canaris was in Spain,[46] but when he returned to Zossen a fortnight later and informed Halder of his conversations with Vigón and other generals, it was still not known when or even whether Spain would enter the war on Germany's side;[47] Franco was still playing for time.

The significance of having Spain in the Axis was primarily to cover the situation in the Mediterranean and North Africa against the background of the planned war in the East, and at the same time to relieve the pressure on Italy; Mussolini's refusal to become entangled in Operation Felix was final. Meanwhile, Felix was now competing in logistics and dates with the planned operations in the Balkans and in Greece. Disguising the operation precluded a Blitzkrieg because the troops now needed thirty-eight days to move down to Gibraltar from the French border. The first advance commandos would move into the Iberian Peninsula on 6 December, the main force would attack early in 1941.[48]

Canaris watched the hectic preparations in November with some concern, particularly Halder's zealous plans calling for two numerically large advance commandos driving through France in civilian clothing in French vehicles and entering Spain under false identities; these advance commando stormtroops consisted of eleven officers for Seville in addition to sixteen artillery spotters and twelve other artillery officers for Cadiz, and sixteen supply officers. Canaris was sure that such large groups of officers were bound to be detected by British intelligence. He intervened, and at the end of November Halder's plans were toned down.[49] Halder noted: 'The decision for Felix is firm [statement of Hitler]. Pummel every square metre of British ground. Therefore many mortar bombs needed. Disregard quantity used. Twenty to thirty munition trains through Occupied France or by sea to Malaga.'[50]

On the evening of 7 December, Canaris had an audience in Madrid with Franco to confirm his agreement to the passage of German troops through Spain,[51] with Vigón taking down the notes of the meeting. Canaris conveyed Hitler's desire to begin the attack very soon, and requested approval for the transit of German troops on 10 January, when the German aid package would also begin arriving. Franco was aware that the Luftwaffe did not have air supremacy over England and that the Italian position in the Balkans grew worse day by day, and he knew his own problems only too well. Accordingly, as he told Canaris, he could not fight a long war without the Spanish people having to make intolerable sacrifices. Vigón noted: 'Generalissimus explained to admiral that it was impossible for Spain to enter the war on the date set for the reasons given, namely: the threat of British naval retaliation, his lack of armaments, and the supply situation did not permit an early entry into the war.'[52] To Canaris's enquiry of when the transit of German troops would be possible, the Caudillo was unable to provide a date. Canaris returned to the German embassy from where he cabled Bürkner the same night. Keitel took the telegram to Hitler, conveying Franco's unequivocal message. His demand that Germany should make the preparations for the conquest of Gibraltar under conditions of the strictest secrecy and disguise was no more than a diplomatic smoke-screen. On 10 December, Canaris spelt it out: 'The Caudillo has given us clearly to understand that he cannot enter the war until Britain is on the verge of defeat.'[53]

Hitler reflected on the 'extreme consequences' resulting from this information. If Operation Felix were cancelled, so must be the next step into French Morocco, and this would make it possible for General Weygand with his army in French Morocco to set up his own government to oppose the occupation of the remainder of France.[54]

The abandonment of the Gibraltar plan led the Eastern Mediterranean theatre to come into focus. Ambassador Alfieri had painted a very gloomy picture of the Italian Army's predicament in Albania, and German preparations for Operation Marita, the occupation of Greece, continued apace. This was a prelude to the attack on the Soviet Union, for as Instruction No 20 made clear, at the conclusion of Marita the units involved would be withdrawn for other purposes.[55]

There has been much speculation as to Canaris's real role in the negotiations with Franco and the eventual rejection of the plan to attack Gibraltar. Was he the tireless intelligence officer, planner and motivating force whose purpose was to lure Spain at any cost into the Axis and the war against Britain? Although the journeys to talks seem to support it, there is nothing to suggest that in his meetings with Franco, Vigón, Campos or Suñer he was especially convincing. He conveyed the German requests, probably aware that Franco neither wanted to, nor could, meet them. Keitel concluded in his memoirs that Canaris made no serious attempt to win Franco over for Operation Felix, and may even have advised his Spanish friends against it.[56] More cautiously, former Legion Condor commander von Richthofen expressed the suspicion in his diary that Canaris might have helped contribute to Franco's negative attitude[57] while State Secretary von Weizsäcker put it more boldly: 'After consulting me Canaris would not allow himself to be misused in a fraudulent business against his Spanish friends. He advised them against it, and that had plausible reasons.'[58] In a note on 12 December 1940 he added: 'It gives little satisfaction to have seen the Spanish in their true light. They say they can only join the Axis in the last moments before victory – but what else would they be for us than guests at the table?'[59] A few days later he had harsher words to say: 'Spanish disorganisation and Franco's inability to run a state at peace makes it our fortune not to have to drag this cripple along with us. There are people starving in Spain.'[60]

This sounded like relief and corresponded completely to the strategy employed by Canaris to make Franco's refusal palatable to Hitler and his generals. Even Ulrich von Hassell noted in October 1940 after the meeting between Hitler and Franco at Hendaye that Canaris had advised against getting too involved in Spain since the situation there was unstable and Franco was weak.[61] Despite all the intelligence activity and diplomatic verve he displayed, Canaris seems to have had a foot on the brake and to have provided nothing persuasive to bring Hitler and Franco together.

It is significant that British writers on the Abwehr have interpreted Canaris's first report at the end of July 1940 on the poor prospect for a surprise attack on Gibraltar as 'a masterpiece of calculated discouragement'.[62] There were, however, other personalities involved in the plans for the conquest of the Rock whom Canaris would not have influenced with negative assessments. In the early months of diplomacy Canaris would not have risked warning his Spanish friends. Lahousen recalls that Canaris had not been able to warn his friend

Vigón because the old general would not have understood the political message at that stage of the negotiations.[63] Suñer was of a different calibre; on his visit to Berlin in September 1940, he had wondered at the confused ideas of Hitler, to whom the geographical and technical difficulties of capturing Gibraltar did not seem at all clear.[64]

Suñer had gone from there to Rome to hear Ciano's opinion on Spain entering the war and – as alleged – had there met Canaris's confidant Josef Müller, who had informed him: 'The admiral asks you to inform the Caudillo that he would like Spain to stay out of the game. It may appear to you that we are currently in the stronger position – in reality it is hopeless, we have hardly any hope of winning the war. The Caudillo can rest assured that Hitler will not invade Spain.'[65]

Apparently it was also Canaris – eventually in unison with Richthofen – who had convinced Franco to demand ten 38-cm guns for the bombardment of Gibraltar knowing that Hitler did not have them. And it was also Canaris who advised Martinez Campos quite openly to preserve and protect Spanish neutrality. Although there is only the evidence of the eye-witnesses and inferences to rely on, everything points to Canaris having been more disposed to keeping Spain out of the war than expanding it into Hitler's bastion in southwest Europe.

PART V

THE TRIUMPH OF THE BARBARIANS

23

The War of Extermination – Act Two

Operation Felix was finally discarded in February 1941.[1] On 19 February Lahousen recorded in his service diary the first discussion with the Army General Staff on the involvement with Abwehr II in Operation Barbarossa.[2] On 22 February Halder and Canaris discussed the preparations for measures in the Ukraine and Baltic States[3] and as a result Canaris ordered Abwehrstelle Cracow to resume contact with the Ukrainian Nationalist leader Andrej Melnyk, which had been discontinued at the end of 1940;[4] he was to provoke civil disorder once the Red Army began to crack.

Reports were collated by Oberquartiermeister IV of the General Staff, von Tippelskirch, respecting the military situation in the Soviet Union and the strength of the Red Army. These originated primarily from the Abwehr and the attachés, both Halder and Canaris attaching special importance to the information sent by General Köstring, military attaché in Moscow,[5] while the material that the Abwehr had confiscated during the attack on Poland regarding the 1939 Russo-Finnish winter war was also considered valuable. Radio transmissions in the Soviet Union were monitored at the Königsberg and Warsaw monitoring stations. The Lyck and Lancut companies sent their reports directly to the Tirpitzufer.

Canaris and Halder realised that the shortages that afflicted the Red Army in its early operations were being overcome and obsolete equipment replaced, but its great weakness was a lack of trained officers at the intermediate and higher command levels to replace the officers murdered in Stalin's purges of 1937–8. Although the deficiency had not yet been made good, Halder recognised that the transfer of command out of the hands of the political commissars to the military commanders had strengthened the Red Army.[6]

Canaris assessed the Soviet General Staff to be

bold in its plans and adequately trained technically in the leadership and deployment of large army masses . . . the Russian soldier is hard and self-sufficient, tough and unyielding on the defensive. His fighting technique is primitive to some degree, but with his obedience and natural instinct, after brief battle experience he quickly adapts to everything in which the European soldier at present has the advantage. Especially in winter warfare this toughness and primitiveness will turn the Russian soldier into a dangerous enemy.

Canaris also recognised how crucial the time factor would be in such a war:

In the first year of an attack on the Soviet Union, Germany will have the advantage. If Russian strength is not crushed, in the second and third years the forces on either side will be counter-balanced. From the third year onwards and by the latest in the fifth year the nationalist-fanatic masses of at least 25 million Russian soldiers will be in a position to overwhelm any army with an unstoppable impetus. An attack on the Soviet Union will therefore only succeed if one destroys the command centre for the centrally controlled Russian armed forces from the outset, or unleashes a strong freedom movement opposed to Communism. Since neither possibility exists, any war of aggression against the Soviet Union will not only terminate in defeat but turn into a deadly threat towards the attacking nation.[7]

Hitler, Heinz remembered, had dismissed these assessments with contempt. This was a war of world views, at the end of which the enemy would not merely be defeated but exterminated, and what the Führer meant by that was explained in a speech to 200 senior commanders at the Reich Chancellery, lasting two and a half hours: 'It will be a war of extermination. If we do not see it as such, then we may defeat the enemy, but in thirty years the Communists will confront us again.' Hitler called for the 'extermination of the Bolshevist commissars and Communist intellectuals ... this is not a question of military courts ... commissars and GPU personnel are criminals and must be treated as such.' Hitler required the commanders to suppress all personal scruples: 'In the East, ruthlessness is a lenient way to the future.'[8]

From the beginning, Canaris and his staff were deeply involved in planning the war of extermination; starting in January, von Brauchitsch had been discussing with Heydrich the deployment of Sipo units 'after the occupation of enemy territory'.[9] Before the French campaign, OKH had successfully prevented the installation and operation of such units following the experience in Poland, but there had been a major area of agreement since March 1941 regarding the Einsatzkommandos behind the front. On 6 and 7 March Oster and Bentivegni conferred with the representative Abwehr officer, Army Group Centre, Rittmeister Schack von Wittenau, to clarify the remaining details. The summary of this meeting confirmed the agreement that the Wehrmacht must be notified of all orders from Reichsführer-SS, and that to 'avoid disturbing operations' if possible, they should 'allow orders setting out boundaries' while 'executions should be undertaken if possible away from the troops'.[10] Before a final conference between OKH and officers of the Reichsführer-SS at the highest level, the competent OKH and SS-RSHA departments agreed that under certain conditions, Sipo and SSD units could operate in Army areas: 'Einsatzgruppen and kommandos are authorised within the framework of their mission to take execution measures against the civilian population on their own responsibility. They are duty-bound to cooperate as closely as possible with the Abwehr.'[11] Canaris was given a copy of this order for his information, which he accepted without changes.[12]

While the preparations for Barbarossa were in hand, diplomatic efforts were also proceeding to attract more Balkan States into a pact with Germany. In November, Hungary, Romania and Slovakia had joined the Tripartite Pact, and Bulgaria joined the Axis on 1 March 1941. The Yugoslav Minister President Cvetkovic and his Foreign Minister Cincar-Markovic signed the pact in Vienna on 25 March, but several hours later the Cvetkovic government was overthrown in a coup by Serbian officers.[13] Canaris, who since the cancellation of Operation Felix had expended much energy in negotiations between Greece and Italy to end the war between them and strengthen the Italians in their rearguard action against the British in North Africa[14] was now obliged to recognise that Operation Marita, the invasion of Yugoslavia and the occupation of Greece, could no longer be stopped. Hitler set the date for the invasion of Yugoslavia for 6 April 1941 at 0520hrs.

On 16 April 1941 Canaris flew to Belgrade with his Abwehr heads. Since all bridges over the Danube and Save rivers had been demolished, the group and its luggage were crammed into a Fieseler-Storch aircraft that set them down in the centre of a city ruined by air attacks, lacking water, electricity and gas; Lahousen noted seven thousand dead and the stench of decomposing bodies hovered over the area. Late that afternoon 'a totally dejected and battered Yugoslav division' passed Canaris and his colleagues. Their general wanted to negotiate a surrender but he was sent away – the full surrender of the Yugoslav Army was being sought. The Abwehr party spent the night at Semlin, where talks were held the next day with the German embassy officials and resident Abwehr officers. Later they crossed the Donau aboard a makeshift ferry for a meeting with the Armistice Commission and Luftwaffe General Loehr, who reported on the destruction caused by air attacks under his orders.[15]

During April the orders were formulated for the war in the East. On 13 May Keitel signed the order for the 'Exercise of Military Law in the Barbarossa Region and Special Measures by the Forces', the so-called Military Law Order (Kriegsgreichtsbarkeiterlass), which laid down that crimes committed by enemy civilians no longer came within the jurisdiction of military law, and it was not obligatory to prosecute for crimes committed by Wehrmacht members against civilians. Partisans were to be shot immediately, and collective reprisals were permitted if an individual offender could not be identified sufficiently quickly. At the beginning of June at the request of OKH the notorious 'Commissar Order' followed, by which all Red Army political commissars and all personnel working for the Communist Party or administration, and anybody else of significance who fell into German Army hands, were to be shot.[16]

On 30 May 1941 Canaris discussed with Reichsleiter Alfred Rosenberg, designated Reichsminister for the Occupied Eastern Territory, the tasks that fell to the Abwehr during the planned attack on the Soviet Union. Rosenberg explained his geopolitical plan 'by which the historical moment will be used to free Germany once and for all from the nightmare of a possible threat from the East, by dividing Russia into four States,' Canaris wrote. Rosenberg's concept was a Finland extended eastwards, a German Baltic Protectorate reaching into White Russia, an independent Ukraine and the Caucasus as a Federative State with a German head. To control and administer these territories the Reichsleiter would need the cooperation of 'suitable personalities, above all of unobjectionable character' who 'have a knowledge of the region, or come from minority groups with which the Abwehr Overseas Office has cooperated militarily (Ukrainians, Caucasians, etc)'. Canaris should make a list of such persons and forward the names to the Reichsleiter:

> I have assured Reichsleiter Rosenberg of the full support of my office in this direction, and mentioned to him especially that I can name personalities from Estonia known to me through my Abwehr contacts. Furthermore I would also have people in Lehr-regiment *Brandenburg* zbV 800 and the Ukraine Volunteer Groups who at the appropriate time can be placed at the disposal of the Reichsleiter as interpreters, administrative officials, commissioners, etc.[17]

Four days after this conversation Canaris gave exact instructions for the special employment of Abteilung I in Operation Barbarossa and described in detail the armament, clothing and use of agents and fifth columnists whose task would be to procure and relay reports from the operational area of the front and up to fifty kilometres in advance of it.[18]

On 5 and 6 June a conference was held in Berlin involving Heydrich, Schellenberg and SS-Standartenführer Hans Nockeberg, head of Amt II, SS-RSHA, and to which were invited all Ic officers of OKH and Abwehr up to divisional level and scheduled to take part in the campaign; the officers were informed as to the purpose of the Einsatzgruppen, with whom they had to cooperate.[19] Nockeberg described their main activity as being 'the rounding up of enemy political material and politically dangerous personalities (Jews, emigrants, terrorists, political Church, etc)' and moreover 'provision for the final elimination of Communism will be made'.[20]

Executions and mass murders do not seem to have been discussed; the Abwehr officers apparently did not intend to allow the Einsatzgruppen in their operational areas unrestricted freedom to do as they pleased and OKH even wanted to direct the SD squads.[21] Until immediately before the attack on the Soviet Union, the Army was opposed to any useful cooperation between Sonderkommandos and Army Abwehr sections. No comprehensive extermination order was issued, as there had been before the Polish campaign, although it seems to have been clear to everybody that Jews, Communists, the disadvantaged and gypsies were the main targets.[22]

On 9 June the Abwehr discussed closer cooperation with the Army in the field so as to avoid delays in the campaign due to involved channels of transmission. Abwehr I, responsible for reconnaissance, had set up a forward command staff (Walli I) at Warsaw, to which the Army Group sections were subordinate. Lahousen's fifth columns, each with twenty-five men, had to reconnoitre up to three hundred kilometres inside Russia and prevent important junctions being destroyed by the Red Army. Abwehr II operations were concentrated in the former Polish regions of the Soviet Union, the Baltic States and the Caucasus with its enormous oil reserves.[23] Abwehr III, together with the Foreign Ministry's so-called Künsberg Group, had to secure certain files from Soviet government offices and foreign embassies. The Bandera and Melnyk Ukraine Nationalist groups were responsible for sabotage and the creation of diversions. Operations Tamara I and II were to foment revolts in Georgia in connection with securing the Caucasian oilfields.[24]

Two days before the attack date, Reichsleiter Rosenberg addressed a circle of representatives from the Wehrmacht, party and State. Together with ministers Lammers and Fricke were Heydrich, General Thomas and admirals Frick and Canaris. Rosenberg's aim was to obtain a 'uniform inner attitude' of the various offices required to liaise with the political leadership and administration of the region to be conquered,[25] and to explain the ideological basis for the racial battle with the Soviet Union. The division of the Soviet Union into individual states, which Rosenberg had already explained to Canaris, would free Germany forever from the nightmare of attack from the East. With regard to its purpose there were clear priorities to be set: 'The most important of all measures is the need to feed the German people, and we do not see any obligation to feed the Russian people as well. This recognition may be hard and bring the Russian people hard times, but it is necessary.' Reichsleiter Rosenberg concluded his talk by pointing out that the task in the East involved the 'most difficult colonial work and served two great goals, namely to feed the German people and safeguard the war economy'.[26]

At midday on 21 June 1941, Lahousen noted in the Abwehr II service diary: 'The codeword "Dortmund" signalled the commencement of Fall Barbarossa.'[27] The following day, Lahousen's old confidants from the Ukraine, who until shortly before had been out of favour, now saw that their hour had come: 'Rittmeister Jary, active for some time as an Abteilung II spy . . . sent a telegram to the Führer requesting the inclusion of the Organisation of Ukraine Nationalists into the German Wehrmacht to fight for a free Ukraine.'[28] On 25 June 1941 Lahousen learned that Lehr-Regiment 'Brandenburg' had succeeded in holding a series of important bridges, but with heavy losses, twenty-three dead and twenty-seven wounded, and the fighting groups in the Eastern Baltic area suffered 160 dead in the first few days while protecting strategically important objectives against the Red Army.[29] Lahousen's Lithuanian activists had not been able to take the Memel bridges held by the Russians, but managed to hold twenty-four important bridges on the line of the German advance – for the loss of four hundred men.[30]

A summary of Abwehr II operations to the end of June 1941 was submitted to Keitel shortly afterwards. Along the entire Front, sabotage troops drawn from 'foreign peoples' had been infiltrated behind enemy lines to engage the objectives ordered while the Ukraine Nationalists of the Bandera group had 'cooked up the first insurrections in cooperation with German troops'.[31] Cooperation with the Ukrainians had not been easy because elements of the movement were not prepared to subordinate themselves unconditionally to German interests – members of the group around Stepan Bandera had declared openly that they would work against the Germans if their wishes were not met.[32]

On 30 June elements of Lehr-Regiment 'Brandenburg' were involved in an assault on the Ukrainian city of Lemberg and on 3 July they were the first to reach the city centre, occupy important buildings and prevent the food warehouses from being destroyed by Soviet troops or looted by the populace. Lahousen wrote in his service diary: 'The battalion reported again on unimaginable Bolshevist atrocities committed against Ukrainian prisoners and also German prisoners of war. A number of prisoners were freed from the still-burning jail.'[33] Thousands of people murdered by the Soviets were found in other towns; the Abwehr strategy of provoking a coup in the Ukraine by fifth-columnists and Ukrainian Nationalists played their part in these murders.[34] Most of the insurrectionists were killed by the Red Army before their retreat since they did not want to take prisoners eastwards with them.[35] Freshly raised national militia, the mob and the Einsatzgruppen now took a fearful revenge on the Jews, who were seen as supporters of the Soviet system; by mid-July, Einsatzgruppe 'C' alone had shot seven thousand Jews.[36] On 8 July Canaris went with Bentivegni and Abwehr officer Major von Gamm to visit 1.Armee General Staff. He was informed of the massacre at Jasi initiated by the Romanian secret police where, by the end of June, up to five thousand Jews had been murdered in the putting-down of a non-existent Jewish rebellion; the Abwehr 'Hauskapelle' in Bucharest was involved in planning the pogrom.[37] Also on 8 July 1941, the chief of the General Wehrmacht Office at OKW, Generalleutnant Hermann Reinicke, who also ran the PoW Department there, signed an order stating the principles for the treatment of Soviet PoWs:[38] 'The use of weapons on Soviet PoWs will in general be considered lawful.' On carrying out orders, 'whoever does not make use of his weapon, or makes insufficient use of his weapon, is liable to punishment'. This order, which provided for the 'Aussonderung' (elimination), that is to say the murder of politically unacceptable prisoners by Sipo and SD, led to a conference in July to which Reinicke invited, amongst others, Gestapo Chief Müller, Canaris and staff from the PoW Department. Canaris preferred not to attend personally and sent Lahousen with instructions to oppose the order, or at least see if he could get it moderated. Lahousen stated later that the admiral detested Reinicke, whom he considered 'the prototype of the eternally obsequious Nazi general' and correspondingly 'did not wish to meet him personally'.[39] At the conference, Reinicke said that the Soviet soldier was not a soldier but the deadly enemy of National Socialism. This had to be 'made clear to the Wehrmacht and very especially to the officer corps, which gave the appearance of still having an Ice-Age mentality, and not thinking in the National Socialist present'.[40]

Lahousen explained to the conference that the order made the Abwehr role very difficult since it interfered with the recruitment of agents from within the national minorities and would render ineffective all propaganda directed towards the Red Army. This opinion caused a violent argument with Gestapo Chief Müller, who defended the measure, while Reinicke also advocated ruthless harshness. Lahousen was therefore compelled to report the total failure of his mission.[41]

Canaris lodged an official protest. Helmut Graf von Moltke, who worked in the International Law Department at Abwehr headquarters, composed with colleague Günther Jaenicke a paper signed by Canaris and addressed to Keitel stating the legal principles in international law respecting the treatment of prisoners of war as being the prevention of their further participation in hostilities: neither revenge nor punishment were lawful. All armies recognised that 'it was contrary to military concepts to kill or maim unarmed prisoners. It was in the interest of any belligerent to know that its own soldiers were protected against mistreatment in the event of capture.'[42] Keitel dismissed all objections: 'The doubts expressed correspond to the soldierly conception of chivalrous warfare! We are dealing here with the destruction of a world view! Therefore I approve the measures and support them. 23 September K[eitel]'.[43]

The atrocities committed during the German advance had precisely the effect on the enemy's will to resist that Canaris had feared.

On 20 July 1941 at FHQ Rastenburg, Canaris noted that the mood was exceptionally nervous because the campaign was not going 'according to the rules of the game'. The expected internal collapse of the Soviet Union had not occurred, but on the contrary the assault was fortifying Bolshevism. Canaris was aware of the possibility that the Abwehr might be held responsible for not having supplied sufficiently accurate estimates of the strength and fighting capacity of the Red Army. Hitler had apparently remarked that, had he known of the existence of the new heavy Russian tank (T-34), he would not have begun the war; Canaris took the precaution of having Piekenbrock, Lahousen and Bentivegni immediately assemble all material proving that the Abwehr had long before given notice of all problems now under scrutiny.[44]

From late summer 1941, ever more reports were received by Canaris and his staff regarding inhumanities committed during the German advance; the leaders of Abwehr units attached to Army Groups and armies were reporting regularly 'on the mass executions of Jews and Soviet PoWs, and the repulsive and inhuman nature of these executions, which were being carried out at the front and rearward areas of Army Groups and armies'.[45] Copies of these reports were certainly forwarded to Dohnanyi for filing in his 'Rarities Folder', the collection of documentation regarding the crimes of the National Socialist regime.[46]

According to Lahousen after the war, Brauchitsch, Goering and Raeder were kept constantly informed of the excessive party involvement and illegal measures ordered by Hitler in the areas of jurisdiction,[47] and to judge by his report dated 23 October 1941 entitled 'Observations and Facts from a Tour of the Operational Area in the East'[48] it would appear that Lahousen went to the Front and saw for himself. The lines of Russian PoWs he passed reminded him of 'herds of cattle'; prisoners who had collapsed by the wayside and could not be helped forward by their comrades were left where they fell to be shot later on the authority of a 6.Armee directive. Since this happened at the roadside and in towns and villages, the populations witnessed these murders; he also reported that cases of cannibalism had increased in PoW camps. As to the 'resettlement of Jews', Lahousen wrote:

> The Jews get an order at short notice to assemble the next night at a predetermined spots wearing their best clothes and jewellery. No distinction is made as to age, sex or position in the community. From the meeting place they are then brought to a previously selected and prepared place outside the town or village. Under the pretext of certain formalities, they have to take off their clothing and jewellery before being led away from the street and liquidated. The situation that develops is so ghastly that I cannot describe it. The effect on the German squads is intolerable.

In general the executions are carried out under the influence of drink. An SD officer ordered to witness a mass execution stated that he had the most fearsome nightmares the following night.[49]

'A nightmare of violence'[50] reigned in the conquered territories during the last four months of 1941. Coinciding with Lahousen's report, Abwehr interpreter Oberwachtmeister Soennecken gave an eye-witness report describing the mass murder of seven to eight thousand Jews between 20 and 21 October 1941 in the White Russian town of Borissov that almost certainly ended up in the 'Rarities Folder'[51] and on Canaris's desk.[52]

On 23 October 1941, returning from a trip to Switzerland to arrange intelligence contacts with the Yugoslav Government in exile in Palestine, Canaris and Lahousen visited Keitel. The latter complained bitterly that Goering behaved as though he were the real OKW chief and went constantly over his head: 'If I did not have people in my office who remain loyal to me as you do, Canaris, I would have long since shed the whole burden.'[53] The day following this outburst, the three of them travelled to FHQ Rastenburg before Canaris and Lahousen went on to visit the Army Groups in the East.

At Riga they looked over the churches and buildings of the Old Town, and also the Jewish ghetto, which the inhabitants might only leave for the purpose of work. Following a conference at Abwehrstelle Ostland, they celebrated Lahousen's forty-fourth birthday that afternoon with local fish specialities and vodka at the Hotel de Rome.[54] From Riga they flew to Pskov (Pleskau) and then joined a convoy of vehicles to visit the ruins of Novgorod, occupied by the Spanish Division under Lt-General Augustin Muñoz Grandes. Novgorod was under Russian artillery bombardment and during Canaris's stay there a Soviet attack was beaten off. Lahousen noted good morale, especially amongst the officers, despite the heavy casualty list; he also recorded that the Spanish 'took no prisoners'. They travelled at a snail's pace through woods and swamps, seated in a car with pistols cocked because of the danger from partisans, towards Korstyn, the headquarters of Armeeoberkommando 16, where the touring party dined on fish freshly caught in the Ilmensee and listened to the commanding general's high praise for his troops.[55] The next day they flew to the ruins of Smolensk, headquarters of Army Group Centre, where Lahousen saw more great streams of suffering prisoners: 'If you give one a piece of bread, he will be knocked down and the food torn from his hands. This may sometimes be fatal, for whoever falls down seldom has the strength to get up again.'[56]

The talk came round to 'the shooting of the Borissov Jews': 'Seven thousand Jews were liquidated there in the sardine-tin method. I cannot describe the scenes. Often even the SD cannot go through with it unless they are drunk. Spent the night in the Army Group sleeping car. Very nice and comfortable.'[57]

A Ju 52 next took the party on to Army Group South via Gommel and Kiev, but blizzards and fog prevented them from going any further East. After a stop at Warsaw, they presented a report to Keitel at FHQ Rastenburg; Lahousen saw Hitler stop while on the way to the map room and ask Canaris what the weather was like at the Front. 'He responded to the answer "bad" with a gesture of annoyance. Everyone there has camp fever and noises and bad smells come from all directions all day.'[58]

When Canaris finally received an eye-witness report on the shooting of the Riga Jews, he met Hitler and read him the document. Hitler replied: 'You want to be soft? I have to do it. After me, nobody else will.'[59] Canaris's reaction is not recorded. A report from the Eastern Front, discovered amongst Lahousen's collection of material, painted a dramatic picture of the plight in which the German forces found themselves; it was a disaster unique for losses of materials, insufficient fuel and a sinking morale in men who recognised how miserably led they were. As a reprisal for the killing of Russian PoWs, the Soviets took German wounded from field hospitals during the withdrawal and hung them by the feet from trees, poured petrol over them and set fire to it.[60] In January 1942, General von Sodenstern reported for the first time signs of panic at the Front, comparing it to Napoleon's Army – if the Russians did not pause for breath, but simply kept coming, a repeat of 1812 was unavoidable.[61]

On 28 January 1942 Piekenbrock and Lahousen reported to Canaris that the OKW PoW Department had ordered that in future all Russian PoWs were to be branded on the left forearm with a cross using silver nitrate, but Canaris managed to have this order rescinded.[62] When a similar idea was pursued by the head of the PoW Department a few months later, Lahousen, Piekenbrock and Bentivegni protested again on behalf of the Abwehr. The arrangement 'would lead to severe difficulties in obtaining volunteers and agents from amongst the prisoners of war'.[63] By now Canaris was probably aware that his enemies within the State were preparing to strike at him.

1 Fregattenkapitän Wilhelm Canaris, late 1920s

2 In a circle of classmates after obtaining his Abitur school-leaving certificate, (Canaris second from right)

3 As U-boat commander with his officers on the foredeck of UB-128

4 Amongst his crew, 1918

5 Kapitän zur See and commander of the old battleship *Schlesien*, 1934 (Canaris second from left)

6 A leisurely stroll to the beach with friends. A photograph from an album which Canaris (centre) gave to his No. 1 Staff Officer, Karl Dönitz, upon his departure as Chief of Staff from Wilhelmshaven naval station

7 From the same album, the enthusiastic horseman taking a hurdle

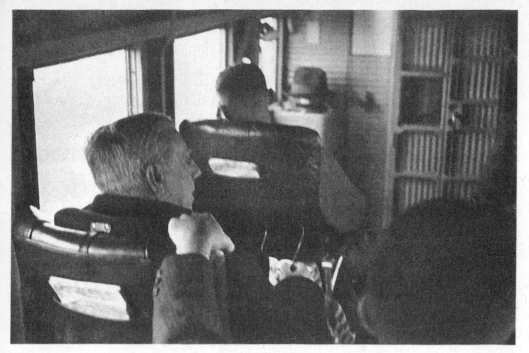

8 In the air

9 Relaxing as a "civilian" during a sea cruise

10 A beer evening in honour of SS-Reichsführer Himmler at the Old Military Academy, Berlin, in January 1935. From the left: von Leeb, von Fritsch, Himmler, von Blomberg, Secretary of State Körner, Raeder, von Rundstedt (Luftwaffe Staff officer not identified)

11 In conversation with Himmler (left) and Goebbels during the 1936 Nuremberg Rally

12 At a military reunion in Berlin with General der Flieger Karl Eberth (left) and SS-Gruppenführer Reinhard Heydrich (right)

13 Werner Best, 'senior lawyer' of the Gestapo, and an important conversation partner for Canaris, 1933

14 With the Spanish Civil War hero General Jose Moscardo at a reception in Berlin, 1939

15 A visit to the Eastern Front with counter-espionage chief Franz-Eccard von Bentivegni

16 Assembly of the Abwehr and SD heads at Hradshin Castle, Prague, May 1942, a few days before the assassination of Heydrich

17 'To our esteemed Chief, in memory of sunnier days.' Canaris in a circle of Abwehr colleagues, probably during a stay in France. From a photo album he received in April 1943

19 The lawyer and Resistance worker Hans von Dohnanyi (with spectacles) posing with Karl Ludwig von Guttenberg and Justus Delbrück, colleagues at Abwehr HQ, about 1942 for a photo to be presented to Hans Oster. The trio never wore uniform in practice

facing page:
18 Anti-Hitler conspirators: Heinz (left) and Oster (right) with an unidentified officer
20 Hans Bernd Gisevius, 1933. The former Gestapo official joined the Abwehr and became an important link to the American OSS in Switzerland

21 22 June 1941: Foreign Minister Joachim von Ribbentrop announces to the world press the invasion of the Soviet Union. From left, seated, Secretary of State Ernst von Weizsäcker, Reich Press Chief Otto Dietrich and Senior Interpreter at the Foreign Ministry Paul Schmidt

22 The former head of RSHA Amt VI (SD-Ausland), SS-Brigadeführer Walter Schellenberg, being sworn as a witness at the principal War Crimes Trials at Nuremberg

23 Wilhelm Keitel, Erwin Lahousen, Wilhelm Canaris and Franz-Eccard von Bentivegni at FHQ Felsennest, Eiffel Forest, 1941

24 With the former head of Abwehr II, Erwin Lahousen, at Voronice, Ukraine, Summer 1942

25 On the occasion of the funeral of former Kaiser Wilhelm II at Doorn, Netherlands, June 1941. Left to right: Canaris, Reich Commissar Arthur von Seyss-Inquart, Generalfeldmarschall August von Mackensen, Admiral Hermann Densch

26 Canaris (left, with hat) during one of his frequent visits to Spain

27 Relaxing in Bavaria, 1942

28 The Canaris family home at Berlin-Schlachtensee, built in 1936

29 Abwehr headquarters, Tirpitzufer, Berlin

30 The barracks at Flossenbürg concentration camp where Canaris, Oster, Bonhoeffer, Gehre, Sack and Strünck were executed on 9 April 1945

24

The Struggle for Power with Heydrich

In the spring of 1942 the struggle for power in the National Socialist intelligence apparatus escalated into a battle between SS-RSHA and the Abwehr over jurisdiction, and between Canaris and Heydrich over Canaris's personal future. Besides the pure jurisdictional struggle in which since mid-1940 Heydrich had maintained a strict division between RSHA counter-intelligence, Group IVE under Schellenberg and the Abwehr, and which was based on a 'revision of the Ten Commandments' requested in 1936 and forced through at the end of 1941[1], major conflicts arose involving the use of Jews as key Abwehr informers, and the protection of Jewish spies by the Abwehr.

Three examples of top agents of Jewish origin were Ivar Lissner, Richard Kauder and Edgar Klaus.[2] Klaus, born in Riga in 1879 of Jewish parents who had converted to Christianity, had studied geology in Russia, worked there for several banks and, after returning home, made a small fortune from an estate agency. In the First World War he had been deported to the Volga area and worked there and later in Siberia for the Russian Red Cross as an interpreter in PoW camps, where he became acquainted with German and Austrian Social Democrat activists and, as he later admitted, Stalin.[3] After the war he worked for the Danish consulate in Riga, and between April and October 1919, he used an identity document legitimising him as 'secretary of the Royal Danish Consulate at Riga', which enabled him to pass in and out of Germany, where as a courier he established contacts within the German Foreign Office.[4] The intelligence services of the Western Allies considered that he was probably an informer.[5]

At the end of 1919, in possession of a Danish passport, Klaus fled from the civil war in Latvia to Germany, to where he had already transferred his money. After the German invasion of Poland in 1939 he worked in Lithuania as an informer and liaison man for the Abwehr representative at the Germany embassy, where he was noticed by the SD. An RSHA list dated February 1940 had pinpointed him as a baptised Jew and Communist working for French and Russian intelligence, but despite these suspicions, in January 1940 the German embassy had issued him with a passport, and in March he even received an expedited 'German immigrant passport' from Himmler's Volksdeutsch agency, enabling him to flee to the Reich before the attack on the Soviet Union.[6]

On 30 March 1941 Klaus left Kovno in Lithuania and was received in Berlin by Hans-Ludwig von Lossow, a member of Abwehr I staff. A few days later he was introduced to Canaris, masquerading under the name Prittwitz von Gaffron; the two men discussed the situation in Russia and the strength of the Red Army, Klaus warning emphatically against the invasion of the Soviet Union. He was then led to a conference room where a dozen senior commanders were gathered, amongst whom Klaus thought he recognised Brauchitsch and Manstein. In a two-hour discussion he answered the generals' questions on the Soviet Union. Two years later, in Stockholm, he recalled how he had warned them against breaking the German–Soviet Pact: 'but they did not wish to hear the voice of reason.'[7] As he himself expected, Canaris's attempt to win the commanders over by using the arguments of an agent who knew the country failed.

Klaus and Canaris met again at the beginning of May when Canaris asked him if he would be confident about working with representatives of the Soviet embassy in Stockholm whose leader was Alexandra Michailova Kollantai, a Bolshevist from Lenin's entourage. When Klaus agreed, Canaris asked him to contact the important Soviet diplomats in Stockholm, and if possible as many other Russians as he could, for the purpose of collecting information about the circumstances and military situation in the Soviet Union, and relaying it to Berlin through an Abwehr man at the German embassy. This individual was Werner G Boening, officially the 'film attaché', but unofficially 'Berger' of K-Org Sweden.[8]

Klaus arrived in Stockholm a month before Operation Barbarossa; the city was considered to be an 'intelligence metropolis', like Madrid, Lisbon, Istanbul and Berne. Since 1936, Canaris had maintained relations with the Swedish General Staff head of intelligence, Lt-Colonel Helge Jung. A year later Canaris made an agreement with the long-serving Swedish attaché in Berlin, Carlos Adlercreutz – nominated as Jung's successor – that he would not work against Swedish interests on Swedish territory, and until 1944 the Abwehr exercised a strict prohibition on 'all activities against Sweden'. In September 1940 Canaris discussed with Adlercreutz in Stockholm mutual intelligence measures against Soviet aggression, and until his arrest Canaris continued secret contacts with Adlercreutz's successor, the Swedish military attaché in Berlin, Curt Juhlin-Dannfeldt.[9]

By giving Klaus his mission, Canaris now had an experienced 'expert' as a liaison man between the German military opposition and the Soviets, and he protected Klaus from the Reich-wide Gestapo hunt for him. Under the pretext that Klaus was a fraudster, forger and cheat, SS-RSHA had ordered the Gestapo to arrest him. Since RSHA knew, however, that Canaris had used Klaus to warn senior military commanders against invading Russia, it was their intention to bring him under their umbrella; Klaus was to become the ball in a power game between the RSHA and the Abwehr.[10] In the remaining four weeks until Barbarossa, Klaus established no useful contacts in the Soviet embassy in Stockholm, but after the German invasion he reported through Boening under the cover name 'General Schönemann' on the Soviet offensive capability and warned against the illusion of a quick collapse of the Soviet Union. Operationally the reports had no great value, but the assessments were generally correct and Klaus supplied details of Soviet divisions, tanks and artillery that corresponded with Boening's data. Nobody in the Reich political and military leadership wanted to believe in him and he reacted by making a satirical announcement that Alexandra Kollontai was prepared to defect to Germany if she were given guarantees, also alleging that she had a private fortune of 3 million dollars and wanted to buy a house in Germany. Klaus sent Boening with this report to Canaris, who merely shook his head but forwarded it to Hitler. After Canaris had seen him on 20 July 1942, Jodl informed the Foreign Ministry that Hitler had ordered every effort to be made to accommodate Frau Kollontai (with freedom from taxes, absolute security).[11]

Besides this kind of theatre, Klaus supported Canaris principally by reporting on the readiness of the Soviet Union to negotiate, which Canaris could use as an argument for a separate peace, irrespective of how true such information might be. The first real initiative and peace feelers put out by Canaris with Klaus's cooperation occurred in the spring of 1942, when the high point of the struggle for power between Canaris and Heydrich had already passed.

The lawyer Ivar Lissner, born at Riga, Latvia, arrived in Germany as a refugee in 1920 with his parents. Ivar and his brother Percy were NSDAP members by 1933 and later joined the SS. Well known as a travel writer, Ivar Lissner wrote leading articles and commentaries for Goebbels's broadsheet *Der Angriff*, mainly on the political and military situation in the Far East. Not until 1939 did he become aware of the Jewish ancestry of his father, who was then a successful businessman in Berlin.[12] When the head of the Soviet state security service for the Far East defected to the Japanese, Lissner was by chance in Manchuria, and offered his services to the Japanese as interpreter. Later he assisted in the interrogation of the defector in Tokyo and was the first journalist to interview him for *Der Angriff*; subsequently he had excellent contacts with Japanese intelligence and Army officers. From the spring of 1939 as Far East correspondent of the *Völkischer Beobachter* and *Der Angriff*, he followed Japan's war in China and beat the press drum for the Berlin–Tokyo Axis. When Ivar Lissner's father was denounced, the Gestapo realised the Jewish origin of the author and journalist and arrested him, causing the 'half-Jew' to lose all his offices, be expelled from the Reich Chamber of Writers and banned from having his work published. All attempts by Ivar and Percy Lissner on behalf of their father remained unsuccessful.

Canaris and Oster had been made aware of Lissner in 1938 when he addressed journalists. An initial attempt to recruit him through his schoolfriend Abwehr-Hauptmann Werner Schulz in 1939 failed, but when Schulz was sent by Canaris to set up a K-Organisation in Shanghai, where Ivar's brother Percy was living, Ivar agreed to work for the Abwehr as a spy on the condition that his father was freed and his family allowed to leave Germany. Despite the tremendous difficulties – the Gestapo 'chain of proof' was watertight – the Abwehr Overseas Office eventually succeeded in obtaining for Robert Lissner and his wife safe passage out of Germany. Their daughter Sigrid, a secretary at OKW, was obliged to remain behind; the circumstances of her death in 1943 were never clarified.

Lissner now erected for Canaris at Harbin in Manchuria an espionage network that reached to eastern Siberia. White Russian emigrants, a fascist Cossack ataman with links to senior Soviet officers in the Far East, German journalists and bar-girls were amongst his informants and complemented his good relationship with the Japanese secret service. Punctually for the invasion of the Soviet Union, Lissner supplied Canaris with reports from the eastern regions of the Soviet Union via the German embassy at Hsinking, from where they were transmitted by telegraph to the Foreign Ministry in Berlin.[13] When by the spring of 1943 Lissner had submitted more than two hundred reports, Canaris wrote of him in a signed longhand memorandum: 'Agent Ivar is the only Amt Ausland/Abwehr source who sends comprehensive information on Asiatic Russia and the Manchuria/Russia border. His reports, especially the more recent ones, are extraordinarily comprehensive and provide the only reconnaissance enabling the reserves, new installations etc, especially the Soviet Air Force in the Siberian area, to be assessed.'[14] Dohnanyi relied on the anti-Communist Lissner's information when preparing military and political situation reports or lecture notes for Canaris.

Like Klaus, Lissner came under fire from the party and SS apparatus. With the help of his immediate superior Major Friedrich Busch, he survived a party tribunal hearing to expel him in the spring of 1941; it also appears that an attempt was made to lure him to Germany to seize him. OKW drew up a document stating that Hitler had declared him to be 'assimilated to a person of German blood'[15] but further intrigues against him were continued principally by the police at the German embassy in Tokyo, SS-Standartenführer Josef Meisinger.[16]

Richard Klatt, alias 'Engineer' or 'Major', by the end of 1941 headed Meldekopf (report centre) Sofia, Abwehrstelle Vienna, and controlled from there the only direct Abwehr connections into the Soviet Union. His true name was Richard Kauder, born in 1900 of Jewish parents in Vienna. A qualified architect, he fled to Hungary in the summer of 1938 on an Austrian passport, was arrested in December and expelled into the hands of the German border police in February 1940. He escaped being sent to a concentration camp only because in the summer of 1939 at his mother's insistence he had met one of her friends from Abwehrstelle Vienna and had volunteered himself to Oberstleutnant Roland von Wahl-Welskirch for employment. The Abwehr not only prevented his incarceration in a camp, but sent him back to Hungary, from where he made service journeys on their behalf to Austria, Romania, Yugoslavia and Slovakia.

On the orders of the RSHA counter-espionage section, in September 1941 the Sipo and SD Einsatzgruppe stationed in Yugoslavia arrested a Fritz Kauders 'on suspicion of treason against the State, sending false information, falsification of documents and inter-racial sexual activity'.[17] Actually Richard Kauder[18] had brought this unwelcome attention upon himself at Agram in Croatia by posing as a journalist and offering to exchange information with a Gestapo spy. He claimed to be acting in Croatia on the instructions of Wilhelm Höttl, SD official of Vienna, and was moreover in the service of the Meldekopf Budapest. At the end of September he was given into the custody of the state police at their Vienna headquarters, who were to process the treason charge. How Kauder the remanded traitor became Klatt the head of the Abwehr Meldekopf at Sofia within the next few weeks is unknown, but he took over the remains of the espionage system, including a partial radio network built up before the war by White Russian general Anton Turkul.[19] One of these radio cells was in Moscow, and the reports from its agent 'Max' made Klatt into a legend and one of Canaris's top agents. At the beginning of November 1942, 'Max' reported on a meeting of the Soviet War Council chaired by Stalin, and also from the theatres of the planned Soviet offensives. His reports coincided with the assessment of the Foreign Army East section of the General Staff, and OKW eventually informed Canaris that the regular and punctual delivery of reports from 'Max' were of decisive importance for the war.[20] Another of Klatt's agents was 'Moritz', and this led to the results of the 'Klatt Bureau' going down in history and literature as the 'Max and Moritz Reports'.

Klatt's most deadly enemy was Otto Wagner who, as 'Dr Delius' was head of K-Organisation Bulgaria and also held the rank of SS-Hauptsturmführer. Wagner had made strenuous efforts to unmask Klatt as a Soviet double-agent and at the end of 1942 even put a member of his staff exclusively on permanent surveillance of him.[21] Klatt, known to the Abwehr as 'Jew Klatt', was also anxious to be certified 'assimilated to a person of German blood', but this could only be granted to a person of mixed blood, and not a full Jew. Canaris ordered absolute secrecy to be kept on Klatt's racial origins and had a furious encounter with Otto Wagner at the beginning of 1943 for supplying him with a dossier on Klatt. Canaris tore it up without opening it, but later he agreed that Wagner could continue to keep Klatt under observation on the strict understanding that it did not prejudice Klatt's work.[22]

Canaris used three Jews – Klaus, Lissner and Klatt – to spy on the 'Jewish–Bolshevik' Soviet Empire for Hitler. Two of them provided the constant supply of vital war information about the Soviet Union, while the third was used to extend feelers for peace towards the Soviets. Canaris's protecting these Jewish spies gave his opponents ammunition in their struggle against him for supremacy in the espionage apparatus. Another Jewish spy shielded by Canaris was the banker and race-track owner Waldemar von Oppenheim, who between the autumns of 1941 and 1942 was one of the most important informers on the American armaments industry.[23]

According to the memoir of Gerhard Engel, Hitler's Army ADC, it was Himmler who, in February 1942, on the initiative of Heydrich or Schellenberg, complained to Hitler about Canaris. Himmler had apparently been informed by one of his subordinates of the existence of a German agent in Tangiers who was 'a full Jew' under Nazi racial law. Canaris considered this agent, who supplied valuable information from the Arab world and counter-espionage material from Tangiers and Casablanca, extraordinarily reliable and thought so much of him that he met him regularly in Spain. Himmler used this information to complain to Hitler about Canaris, it being known that 'on the basis of his positive attitude to Jewry that he used numerous Jewish liaison men and intermediaries both at home and abroad'.[24] Hitler, incensed, ordered Keitel to suspend Canaris from duty immediately; Engel recalled the pathetic obedience of the OKW head in raising no word of protest. Canaris's deputy Bürkner was ordered to take over the Abwehr and for a week Canaris attempted in vain to obtain an interview with Hitler through Keitel and Wehrmacht adjutant Schmundt, but when Engel went behind their backs with the request, he was surprised to receive Hitler's consent. After the private meeting Canaris was restored to office and that evening he rang Engel and asked him who had arranged the interview. When Engel said that he had done it himself, Canaris related how Keitel had just visited him to offer his best wishes for Canaris's rehabilitation. He, Keitel, had gone to terrific lengths to convince Hitler of Canaris's innocence and had finally won the Führer's approval to receive Canaris for a talk.[25]

Since the intervention of Himmler occurred at a time when Canaris and Heydrich were involved in negotiations to review the 'Ten Commandments', it is likely that the initiative came not from Himmler, but from Heydrich. In mid-1940, Heydrich had told Schellenberg, then head of Group IVE at RSHA, to draft a 'Ten Point Programme' for the coordination of the secret services and a basic reorganisation.[26] On 20 December, significantly, Heydrich wrote not to Canaris's immediate superior Keitel, but to Jodl, pointing out that the areas of jurisdiction and responsibility between Abwehr and RSHA had to be rearranged, which in Heydrich's book meant that the Abwehr had to cede more ground to Sipo and SD.[27]

On 7 November 1940 Heydrich wrote to Canaris enclosing an endless list of queries which had been addressed from Abwehr staff or offices to SD or party offices on a wide range of subjects. Heydrich saw this overlapping of functions as a threat to his empire: 'Reporting inside the Reich is, as I mentioned in my letter of 1 April 1940, the responsibility of my bureaux, SD sections and Stapo offices. The Security Service was designated by a directive of the party dated 9 June 1934 to be the sole intelligence service of the NSDAP, its branches, and its subordinate and affiliated organisations. In equal measure it is the sole intelligence service of the State in the internal political sphere.' Since it was inappropriate, in the interests of a uniform intelligence organisation for the entire area populated by the German people, to have other independent intelligence agencies working alongside it, Heydrich said that he was 'of course willing to abandon those intelligence activities of my offices upon which the OKW lays especial importance'. Obviously, he added, this was valid only for the Reich interior.[28]

Canaris waited until 7 January 1941 before answering. He made it clear that in order to do their jobs properly, those involved in intelligence duties in industry and armaments needed to be advised continuously – not just now and then – as to morale amongst the population and the 'followers' in the factories, otherwise the war effort might run into problems. Furthermore, as regards the use of agents, who were not only needed in counter-espionage but for pre-emptive measures, he saw no possibility of withdrawing his apparatus from here in favour of the SD.[29] Canaris anticipated correctly that Heydrich would not let it rest at that and asked Bentivegni, in whose domain the problem area resided, to draft a statement of the Abwehr position as the basis for talks between Canaris and Heydrich. These talks were held on 12 January 1941[30] at Prinz-Albrecht-Strasse, where Gruppenführer Müller, Gruppenführer Streckenbach and Sturmbannführer Huppenkothen, who had been head of Gruppe IVE at RSHA since the end of 1940, welcomed them; Heydrich came later.[31] The conference began with Canaris and Heydrich speaking in private. Canaris said that he regretted that Heydrich had not come to him directly; even Keitel had been surprised at it and asked him to have the matter clarified, emphasising that 'in wartime there was no question of a change in the mutual responsibilities'.[32]

Heydrich claimed competence for security in the civilian sector of the Reich, which meant that Sipo was responsible for counter-espionage and counter-sabotage in the Reich.[33] Bentivegni objected, particularly with reference to industrial concerns with secret armaments projects for the Wehrmacht. Heydrich countered that the Abwehr claimed jurisdiction over gas and electricity installations, which had nothing to do with top secrets, and should be surrendered to RSHA.[34] And so it went on. Finally a compromise was hammered out in which Canaris made concessions in the civilian field and counter-espionage; even the 'Hauskapellen' would in future transmit their suspicions both to the Abwehr and the Stapo centre.[35] It fell to Huppenkothen to commit the revised 'Ten Commandments' to paper.

On 26 January Canaris received a paper entitled 'Basic Principles for Cooperation Between Sipo, SD and Abwehrstellen of the Wehrmacht',[36] personally dictated by Heydrich. The same day Streckenbach brought a letter from Heydrich containing suggestions for the future control of the GFP,[37] which was not well received and Müller left 'totally depressed', while Streckenbach was 'really gloomy'. When Heydrich received the Abwehr counter-proposal on 2 February he was 'bitterly disappointed and affected';[38] he wanted to transfer the GFP lock, stock and barrel in to SS-RSHA, but after speaking to Canaris by telephone he had approached Keitel and received a firm no to the idea. Heydrich finished his letter:

> Faithful to our promise in private, I would like to say that I see no sense in negotiations conducted in a gentlemanly manner in which a stenographer is needed in order to arm oneself for the next discussion. Since I continue to receive my guidelines for these basic negotiations from the Reichsführer-SS, there seems to me no possibility of arriving at a satisfactory conclusion on this basis. I therefore consider it right and proper that we keep our respective distance from the time of the next discussions until the RF-SS makes his decision. I believe you will understand my position and disappointment. I remain with Heil Hitler! Your very devoted . . .[39]

When Canaris went with Bentivegni next day to RSHA headquarters, Huppenkothen described the rebuff: 'Canaris said he would wait for Heydrich to return and sat for several hours in the ante-room. Then he gave up but told Bentivegni not to come back until he had spoken to Heydrich. SS-Gruppenführer Müller was then given the unpleasant task of speaking to Bentivegni, and sending him on his way.'[40]

Heydrich enjoyed the cheap satisfaction and wrote to Canaris the next day,

I hear that despite my letter you made the effort to visit my office. This is very distressing for me, for you could have saved yourself the trouble if you had clearly understood what my letter said; I am not in the position to have any conversations, not even of the personal kind, before seeing Reichsführer-SS at headquarters. For day-to-day business my head office and my whole staff are at your disposal now as before. It is my heartfelt request that you do not make a difficult situation any more burdensome, please, to yourself, someone years older . . .⁴¹

This was pure sarcasm, and when he answered Heydrich's two letters of 5 and 6 February Canaris must have been hard put to reply in the vein which he did, hoping 'that things between us both will soon return to what they were . . . for I am against making business matters personal, only then are they unbridgeable. We must both be clear that we . . . each to his own sphere . . . serve *one* aim. For that I ask for the same trust from you as I extend to you. Then our two offices will find it easy to resolve the questions which unsettle them.'⁴²

This did not resolve the conflict and eventually Keitel had to intervene and telegraph Heydrich before he would agree to speak to Canaris again;⁴³ previously Canaris had asked Himmler to urge Heydrich to find an acceptable solution.⁴⁴ On 12 February Heydrich and Canaris met at a villa at Klein-Wannsee to work out an agreement for the basic principles. In the civilian sphere counter-espionage would be handled by Sipo and SD. Abwehr would combat radio signals of enemy intelligence active in the Reich. The Hauskapellen would in future cooperate closely with the Sipo head, and this cooperation would extend to counter-espionage and sabotage in industry.⁴⁵ Heydrich had not succeeded in everything, but he was a winner on points, and the principles of the compromise were issued as an OKW order on 6 April.

On 18 May 1942 at the Prague Hradshin, Canaris and Heydrich, now acting Reich-Protector for Bohemia and Moravia, presided at the 'Joint Conference of the Leader of the Abwehrstellen of the Wehrmacht and the Leader of the Stapostellen and SD Sections Leaders'. There were 337 people present, including all RSHA departmental heads, all Einsatzgruppen leaders, active and former Einsatzkommando leaders and Sipo and SD commanders as well as senior Abwehr heads. The purpose of the conference was to reorganise cooperation between the Abwehr and Stapo/SD, to explain the revised 'Ten Commandments', and to allow a general exchange of experience;⁴⁶ Heydrich and Canaris delivered the main addresses. Abwehr official Otto Wagner described later an argument when Abwehr members criticised the negative effects on the civilian populations of the killings in occupied territories. Heydrich reacted angrily, saying that neither he nor the RSHA had ordered these, but Hitler personally.⁴⁷ There was also disagreement between Canaris and Heydrich after the latter accused the Abwehr chief of unreliability and inefficiency. Heydrich had been insistent that his rival accept the new arrangement,[48] but Schellenberg spoke of a long final conversation with Canaris, who gave the impression of mild resignation. Canaris said that although there seemed to be a solution, he did not feel that Heydrich had abandoned his general attack on him.[49]

This must have been the meeting that Canaris described to his nephew Constantin shortly afterwards. Constantin Canaris, an NSDAP member since 1932, had entered the Stapo on Werner Best's advice and made a career of it relatively quickly. By 1941 he was Sipo and SD attaché to the military commandant of Belgium and Northern France in Brussels before taking over the Stapo headquarters at Königsberg, and in the spring of 1942 he was promoted to SS-Obersturmbannführer as a governmental adviser.[50] Constantin Canaris reported after the war that his uncle had never disclosed to him military secrets – probably to protect his nephew – but he made no secret of his attitude towards Himmler, Heydrich and the SS, for after the Hradshin conference he had apparently told Heydrich that he would continue to fight for those people who in his opinion had been arrested unjustly by the SS and SD. This would not have improved his personal standing with Heydrich.[51]

Nine days after the Hradshin meeting, on 27 May 1942 Heydrich left his estate for the city as usual in his open-topped Mercedes limousine; he was running ninety minutes late because he had gone for a walk in the park with his pregnant wife and then played with his children. On a sharp bend a man jumped out and aimed a machine-pistol at Heydrich, but the gun jammed and Heydrich told his chauffeur to stop so that the would-be assassin could be taken in charge. This gave a second assassin the opportunity to throw his bomb.[52] Heydrich died on 4 June 1942 of internal injuries and an infected wound. Four days later, the train bearing his coffin arrived at Berlin Anhalter Station; his State funeral was held on 9 June in the Mosaic Hall at the Reich Chancellery before the carriage bearing the coffin was drawn by six black horses to the Invaliden Cemetery. Himmler's eulogy evoked 'the great SS family and the long battalions of SS dead' while Hitler's parting was more sorrowful.

Canaris was among the mourners, deeply moved. Huppenkothen remembered: 'When I spoke to him at the reception, with tears in his eyes he expressed to me his own and the sympathy of his office, and assured me that he had valued and venerated Heydrich as a great and extraordinary person, and had lost in him a great friend.'[53] Canaris wrote to Heydrich's widow Lina: 'Be sure, I have lost a true friend.'[54] Inga Haag, former secretary to Helmuth Groscurth and later Canaris's close colleague, recalled years later how the death of Heydrich affected Canaris; despite all the rivalry and professional disagreements their relationship had always been friendly and cordial.[55] When Groscurth learned of Heydrich's death, he wrote to Ludwig Beck from the Eastern Front: 'The struggle for the Church, air raids and Heydrich's death are all further causes for sorrow . . . .'[56] He did not mean sorrow for Heydrich, however, but rather for the terrible revenge which would follow.

25

With His Back to the Wall

More so than the neutral capitals Berne, Stockholm or Madrid, Istanbul was the 'capital city' of espionage. MI5 and OSS were thick on the ground there in 1943; the German Abwehr had its representatives and as in Spain or Sweden profited from the pro-German politics of the country.

The head of the K-Organisation Istanbul office was Dr Paul Leverkühn. Born at Lübeck in 1893, his first experience of intelligence work had been at German diplomatic missions in Turkey and the Middle East during the First World War. After qualifying in law he subsequently spent several years in the United States working for the German delegation of the Mixed Claims Commission, during which time he got to know the American attorney William J Donovan, with whom he remained in contact after returning to Germany in 1930. In Berlin he set up a law practice on the Pariser Platz and spent the next nine years as a lawyer and notary. For some time Adam von Trott zu Sulz worked at the practice, and in 1938 Helmuth Graf von Moltke started work there. Throughout this period Leverkühn visited Donovan, now a Wall Street attorney, on a regular basis. In 1939 Donovan came to Germany and was introduced to Moltke and the Kreisau circle, to ambassador Dr Otto Kiep, a member of the Solf Circle, a loose association of like-minded anti-Nazis grouped around Hanna Solf, the widow of the former German ambassador to Tokyo, Dr Wilhelm Solf. That summer, a few weeks before the outbreak of war, Donovan also met Secretary of State von Weizsäcker. Whether he also had contact to Canaris has not been proven but is very probable, for 'Wild Bill' Donovan, who in 1942 took over the OSS, forerunner of the CIA, attempted to contact Canaris during the war. In Turkey the paths of Donovan, Leverkühn, Moltke and Trott zu Solz would cross frequently.[1]

In January 1943 at a press conference following the Casablanca Conference in French Morocco, Roosevelt had stated that the only terms on offer for Germany were 'unconditional surrender'.[2] This had serious consequences for German Resistance circles, since it meant that there could neither be separate peace negotiations with Germany, nor negotiated cooperation to stated conditions with a German Resistance movement that hoped for the assistance of the Allies in a planned coup d'état.

Canaris played an important role in the extension of peace feelers from the German side. At the end of January 1943 he met the US naval attaché to Istanbul, Captain George H Earle, the ex-governor, friend of Roosevelt and expert on the Balkans, who had just arrived in Turkey as an observer.[3] Leverkühn had made contact with him through the former diplomat Kurt Freiherr von Lersner, who had worked at the German legation in Washington and was friendly with the German ambassador to Turkey, Fritz von Papen.

Canaris wanted to find out if there were any alternatives to unconditional surrender, perhaps an armistice in the West or common cause against Communism in the East, as the leading representatives of the National-Conservative and anti-Bolshevist opposition hoped. Earle promised to ask Roosevelt, but received a categorical denial – there was no question of withdrawing the demand for unconditional surrender.[4]

Nevertheless, the attempts at contact between Canaris and the Western Allies were continued. In Donovan's papers for February and March 1943 are several telegrams from his colleague Florimond Duke to Colonel Ulius C Amoss, who was working for Donovan in Cairo. Every move Canaris made was carefully noted by the Americans in OSS files under code number 659 or 'C':[5]

> 26 February: C is in Berne again after he visited the Balkans last week. He registered as Dr Spitz in the St Gotthard Hotel in Berne. 5 March: A short while ago he made a trip to the Balkans and also visited Turkey. He wants to contact the American secret service. If you [Amoss] consider it advisable it might be possible to arrange his return to Cairo at a convenient time for yourself. 10 March: It will need time to fulfil C's wish to meet you. He is at the moment in southern Spain. As soon as it is possible we will let you have further information with respect to this. 23 March: C was contacted in France. He says that at the moment he is under close watch by Himmler, who suspects him to be working for the overthrow of Hitler and the Party. Therefore C must be extremely careful.[6]

This caution was justified. Canaris knew that his enemies and rivals were watching his every step, waiting for a mistake.

The head of OSS at Berne, Allen Welsh Dulles, who had contact with the Abwehr man Gisevius, Eduard Waetjen and Theodor Strünk, mentioned for the first time at the beginning of April Himmler as a possible successor to Hitler; shortly afterwards he reported on Himmler's efforts to take over the entire German secret service apparatus.[7] It is noteworthy that also in Great Britain at the same time the rumours of the undermining and removal of Canaris were circulating and probably frustrated any further efforts to contact him.

A British intelligence report immediately after the war confirmed that Britain knew very little about the German Abwehr until 1941;[8] few, if any, documents had been captured, nor telegrams decoded. That changed in 1942 when the decryption experts were regularly able to present the assessors and analysts with Abwehr telegraphic material, although the picture remained fragmented. The interpretation of the decrypted material often proved difficult.

The final breakthrough came with the Allied landings in the framework of Operation Torch in North Africa in November 1942, with the capture of Abwehr officers. From then on the British secret service was able to penetrate the Abwehr so deeply that no important activity remained unknown to the intelligence service until the dissolution of the Abwehr in the spring of 1944.[9]

The decisive event occurred on 7 November 1942, immediately after the Allied landings in Spanish Morocco and Algeria, when the Abwehr staff in Algiers decamped and headed for Tunis. Passing American convoys and slipping through checkpoints as 'Frenchmen', at a crossroads they eventually met a troop of French officers whom they could not deceive and were taken prisoner. One of the Abwehr prisoners, whose name remains a British top secret, was given the cover name 'Harlequin' and became one of the most important informers of the British intelligence service. He knew the structure, work method and personnel of the Abwehr, and the British took him to the United Kingdom immediately, where they interrogated him throughout December.[10] 'Harlequin' was cooperative and expressed the convictions of a Canaris or a Moltke – the war could no longer be won, the National Socialist regime was unworthy of a cultured people and had to be eliminated, the now hopeless struggle against the Western democracies should be discontinued, for all weakening of German power with regard to the continuing fight against Bolshevism and Soviet mastery was to be deprecated. He even mentioned the idea of a European Community led by a State with a long democratic tradition, for which only Britain was qualified.[11]

'Harlequin' mentioned Canaris: 'He ['Harlequin'] is obsessed by the idea of a compromise peace. He believes that this can be achieved through the office of Admiral Canaris, himself and perhaps Prinz Hohenlohe being the liaison people,'[12] a report recorded in early April 1944.

The relationship, particularly between the British Foreign Office and MI5, was not without its complications, and 'Harlequin' was stubborn in insisting that his contacting Canaris to sound out peace had been guaranteed in his first conversations with the British;[13] he had made this a condition of his cooperation. Meanwhile, rumours were circulating about Canaris's downfall, and the negotiations with 'Harlequin' were now less useful. He had already provided a great quantity of insider information, he saw the basis for his cooperation withdrawn, and requested – plagued by conscience – his 'discharge' and transfer to a PoW camp.

The situation for Germany at this time was catastrophic. 6.Armee had just capitulated at Stalingrad and the Front in North Africa was in a state of imminent collapse. At the beginning of February 1943, in the company of Lahousen and the new 'Brandenburg' commanding officer, Alexander von Pfuhlstein, Canaris discussed the critical situation of Army Groups Centre and Don with Keitel and Jodl at FHQ Rastenburg; both generals expressed fears that the Allies would invade Portugal and Spain. Canaris countered this by explaining that K-Org Spain would report the first signs of such an operation immediately, but neither general took much comfort from this assurance.[14] At Nikolaiken, Lahousen reported on the success of Abwehr II in Gibraltar and North Africa, but otherwise Canaris had little positive to report, especially about the Tunisian Front. On 26 February 1943 Canaris conferred with Generalfeldmarschall Kesselring in Italy about the apparent discord between the Abwehr in Tunis and local units. He flew out each morning from Frascati in a bomber put at his disposal by Kesselring, and within ninety minutes landed in Tunis. Here Canaris and Lahousen saw long columns of American prisoners, exhausted, dispirited 'but well-fed, American football types'.[15]

Over breakfast with Generaloberst von Arnim and his chief of Staff, the disastrous situation of the German troops there was detailed. Only a fraction of the required fuel was getting through to Tunis, in barrels transported by aircraft because ships were unable to pass through the Allied blockade. Von Arnim said he could predict the date when it would end;[16] nobody knew who was in charge any more. In the south, Rommel was leading an attack with two divisions which was officially an Army Group but had no Staff nor Ic officers responsible for intelligence. In addition, Rommel would be returning shortly to Germany, while Kesselring and his Command Staff were running Army operations in North Africa from Frascati in Italy.

Von Arnim was also critical of the Abwehr, especially Fiedler, Canaris's appointee, who was currently at odds with the SD and everybody else and whom von Arnim considered an unsuitable leader. From Abwehr I he had received only misleading reports, while Abwehr II at least was in the position to recommend how to inflict the occasional pinprick on the enemy, while forcing him to commit forces to protect the rear. He said he would use Arabs for sabotage and commando missions in future because of the 'waste of people of high soldierly qualities, who were very difficult to replace in the desert'.[17] Canaris leapt to the defence of his men but promised to think about recalling Fiedler, although he saw the root of the problem as being in the typical jealousies between SD and Abwehr.

With an escort of three fighters he flew next day to Rome, where 'a severely wounded man, who needed an immediate operation to save his life, was stretchered aboard. He had lost both eyes and his face to a mine explosion, his head was hidden in white muslin with holes to breathe. He was set down beside Lahousen and passed the whole flight without a word of complaint.'[18] At Frascati Canaris caught the next flight out for Venice, in company with Lahousen and Bentivegni.

A person in Canaris's position at this time could no longer remain unaware that the situation was worsening daily. Total defeat in a total war was a mere question of time, and no hope existed of convincing the Allies through clandestine channels to drop their demand for unconditional surrender in favour of common cause against the Soviets. Thus the plans for a coup were revived, the initiative coming from a group of conspirators of Army Group South around Tresckow, Schlabrendorff and Gersdorff.

Since January 1943 at the Bendlerstrasse, Gisevius had been revising the 1938 coup plans in a room put at his disposal by General Friedrich Olbricht, head of the General Army Office and acting commanding officer for the Reserve Army. As before, Beck was 'Head of the Movement',[19] Oster acted as chief of Staff and liaison man, and Olbricht had the role of organiser and 'technical chief'[20] of the conspiracy, and was planning the necessary steps for the seizure of Berlin and strategic locations in Cologne, Munich and Vienna. At the end of 1942 Olbricht had assured Tresckow that he needed eight weeks for the preparations; a month later cooperation was agreed between the Berlin conspirators and Army Group Centre plotters Tresckow, Beck and Goerdeler.[21] Olbricht told Schlabrendorff: 'We are ready. You can light the first fuse.'[22] The final touches between the coup conspirators in Berlin and the 'action centre'[23] at Army Group Centre followed.

'For this purpose,' Schlabrendorff remembered, 'Admiral Canaris organised a service flight from Berlin to Army Group Centre headquarters at Smolensk. He arrived with a large entourage and, so that nobody suspected the real reason, arranged a big conference of Abwehr officers active in the intelligence service.'[24]

The aircraft touched down on 7 March 1943 and Canaris, Dohnanyi and Lahousen alighted. The cargo was explosives and a delay fuse of the newest kind intended officially for Abwehr II attached to the Army Group. In February, Oster had asked Lahousen if Abwehr II-kommando at Smolensk had enough explosives since the senior General Staff officer, Oberst von Tresckow, was interested in them in connection with an advised visit of the Führer.[25] Lahousen guessed from this ambiguous statement what the true purpose was, and was asked by Dohnanyi for the newest type of explosive and fuses.[26]

Canaris knew what the aircraft was carrying and, contrary to his decision three years before, Lahousen let him know its purpose.[27] Canaris was impressed by the work of the Abwehr group and, dining with Ic Gersdorff, a plotter, was given 'some enlightening anecdotes about the attitude of the Hungarians to the war in the East'. The Hungarians kept strictly to the orders of their vice-regent to avoid hostilities with the Red Army and only engage in security duties to the rear; Gersdorff spoke of the intention 'to spare Hungarian blood at any price'.[28] The explosives passed to the Abwehr squad via Gersdorff,[29] and that evening Dohnanyi and Tresckow agreed a code between the two groups for use after a successful assassination attempt.

The opportunity for which Tresckow and the conspirators were waiting came when Hitler arrived five days later at Smolensk with a huge retinue to discuss the Kursk Offensive. That morning, as agreed with Dohnanyi, Schlabrendorff rang Abwehr-Hauptmann Ludwig Gehre and gave the password for the imminent initial move. The original plan to shoot Hitler in the officers' mess had fallen through, and Tresckow would now explode his aircraft in the air instead.

After his conference, the company dined in the mess. As the visitors were about to depart, Tresckow asked a member of Hitler's entourage, Oberstleutnant Heinz Brandt of the General Staff operational section, to take back to OKH a package for Oberstleutnant Hellmuth Stieff; it was not an unusual request, and Brandt readily agreed. The contents of the package were ostensibly two bottles of Cointreau, but actually were two pairs of British limpet mines type 'Clam'. The timer was set for thirty minutes. It was planned that the aircraft would explode over Minsk, but a few hours later its safe arrival at Rastenburg was confirmed. It is not known why the detonators failed, although perhaps the severe cold in the cargo-hold was the reason. Tresckow rang Brandt in Berlin telling him that there had been a mistake and he should hold on to the package, and next morning Schlabrendorff arrived in Berlin and at OKH exchanged the bomb package for two bottles of cognac. The bomb was disarmed in the couchette of the train that brought Schlabrendorff to Berlin.[30] Lahousen stated after the war that the explosives and materials used for this unsuccessful attempt were not those brought aboard Canaris's aircraft.[31]

The next opportunity presented itself a few days later. Gersdorff volunteered to be a suicide bomber. His intention was to blow up Hitler and himself during the Heroes' Memorial Day celebrations on 21 March 1943 in Berlin. After the ceremony in the courtyard of the Berlin Zeughaus, Hitler was to inspect an exhibition of weapons confiscated from the Russians. Gersdorff stood at the entrance, and as Hitler passed him, Gersdorff activated the detonator of the bomb, which was concealed beneath his greatcoat. It was set for ten minutes, the shortest time possible. Unfortunately for Gersdorff, Hitler almost ran through the exhibition and left two minutes after his arrival. All that remained to be done was disarm the bomb in a toilet.[32] By chance, luck, intuition or the dark fates, Hitler had survived two bomb attempts within a very short time.

On the morning of 5 April 1943, police attorney Manfred Roeder and Gestapo Commissioner Franz Sonderegger arrived at the Tirpitzufer to arrest Hans von Dohnanyi. Canaris was shocked. When his secretary asked him if nothing could be done, he shook his head. As the two officers passed through Oster's office to make the arrest, Oster said to Roeder: 'You should arrest me at the same time, for Dohnanyi has done nothing that I do not know about.'[33]

Canaris and Oster were present at the arrest and witnessed the search of Dohnanyi's office and safe. Although he kept little incriminating material in the office, documents were found relating to 'Unternehmen Sieben' (Operation Seven), the escape of fourteen Jews to Switzerland supposedly as agents for deployment in the United States, and also material covering a journey to Rome by Bonhoeffer and Josef Müller a few days ahead, with the secret purpose to contact Western Allied sources; these papers only mentioned planned espionage activities by Bonhoeffer in Rome.[34]

There now occurred the dreadful misunderstanding that developed into the well-known 'Note Incident'. Dohnanyi whispered to Oster, 'Send my wife a note,' but in the confusion, Oster heard only the word 'note' and thought that Dohnanyi meant he should destroy a slip of paper taken from an assorted batch of documents by Roeder. This paper was innocuous and contained only instructions for Bonhoeffer's journey to Rome, but now both Oster and Sonderegger wrongly concluded that it had a more sinister significance. Roeder insisted that Oster surrender the note and ordered him out of the room.[35] The same day Roeder complained officially about Oster to Keitel, with the result that Oster was suspended from duty and placed under house arrest; nine days later he was dismissed from the Abwehr and transferred to the Führer-Reserve. Bonhoeffer and Christine von Dohnanyi in Berlin, and Josef Müller, his wife, secretary and a colleague in Munich were arrested. After the Berlin business was over, Canaris is alleged to have told Oster's secret to Dohnanyi's secretary and Freda von Knobelsdorff, adding that 'if Dohnanyi had been wearing uniform, all that would not have gone off so badly'.[36]

Dohnanyi was charged with high treason, currency offences, corruption and breaches of service regulations.[37] The investigation preceding his arrest was a complicated range of inquiries which included Unternehmen Sieben within the Abwehr, the ongoing Vatican conversations since 1939, financial transactions in connection with the 'Cash Deposit' case and the consul to Portugal, and an anti-Nazi agent attached to Abwehrstelle Munich, Wilhelm Schmidhuber.

The deadly threat for Canaris and his co-conspirators during the investigation came from two Abwehr staff members. Oberintendant Johannes Toeppen, head of Group Finances in Oster's headquarters department, and Walter Herzlieb, head of the Legal Services Group, belonged amongst the majority of those in the Abwehr who had 'no doubts about the military and political order of the Third Reich, or were fanatical Nazis'.[38]

Toeppen hated Dohnanyi and Oster, but while he subjected expense invoices from Abwehr staff and agents to the most minute scrutiny, Toeppen was very generous as to the boundaries of his own transactions. At the instigation of the alleged master spy Dusko Popoff, alias 'Ivan', he had opened a gold reserve for German agents in Great Britain. Since 1941 Toeppen had been promoting Dusko's brother Ivo, godfather to Toeppen's son, and was soon allowing Ivo Popoff to handle the major part of his financial transactions. In actual fact, Dusko Popoff, alias 'Tricycle', was head of a comprehensive British spy ring in the service of MI5's 'XX Committee'. Ivo Popoff belonged to this ring, and so did other relations and friends of Popoff. Dusko Popoff's services were so highly valued by the British that he was granted British nationality after the war and became the only overseas agent to be awarded the OBE. The gold deposit in London set up by Toeppen was controlled by MI6.[39]

Toeppen felt that he had been rumbled by Oster when the latter requested a similar foreign exchange deposit with Abwehr banker von der Heydt which was not approved by the competent authority, and this movement of Abwehr funds into Switzerland had been uncovered by Keitel's auditors. Oster and Dohnanyi, who had initiated Unternehmen Sieben at Canaris's request, had been obliged to guarantee to the Swiss authorities the financial independence of the fourteen Jewish immigrants. Accordingly, it had not been possible to avoid involving Group headquarters finances in this rescue action and Toeppen as head of finance had inevitably discovered the preparations; he saw his chance for revenge and protested to Canaris. A huge sum such as this had only ever once been approved, namely for the disastrous Operation Pastorius against the United States, in which the agents had been unmasked, tried and some of them executed.[40] Canaris ignored Toeppen's complaint but the latter subsequently kept a close watch on Dohnanyi and Oster, especially after 29 September 1942, when the Unternehmen Sieben 'agents' left for Switzerland. His persistent requests for the activities of the agents pressurised Dohnanyi and Oster to such an extent that they falsely employed reports from other sources as reports of the 'Swiss agents'.

Toeppen continued his inquiries, examining large book entries made in connection with the sale of the valuables of the Jewish refugees and the 'refinancing' of their 'spy mission'. Finally Toeppen requested an attorney,

Ludwig Ruge, to investigate how the money, which had been turned over to the alleged agents, was being used in Switzerland.

Ruge travelled to Basle on behalf of the Abwehr and interviewed all fourteen refugees during December 1942. He had not been given the background to the affair and so did not suspect that he was being manipulated by Toeppen until his conversations with those involved in Switzerland made Toeppen's motives clear. In Berlin he reported to 'some accounting centre at OKW' about his inquiries in Basle and had assured the appropriate authority that 'everything was in order'.[41] Bonhoeffer informed Dohnanyi and Oster, who told Canaris and demanded the dismissal of Toeppen. When Canaris saw that Toeppen had intrigued against him, he ordered his discharge for the year's end, probably based on the dubious movement of funds by Toeppen to the Popoffs, which Dohnanyi and Oster knew in outline at least.[42]

Danger also threatened from the Legal Services Group. Dohnanyi was appointed by Canaris to examine their legal opinions and his reports were rarely favourable. For this reason Dohnanyi was not liked and had made many attempts to wriggle out of the assignment, but Canaris had told him that 'here he gave the orders, and if he thought it correct to give to his own man things that actually came under the jurisdiction of others, that had nothing to do with those gentlemen'.[43]

The convinced Nazi Herzlieb, whose advice Canaris had often sought in the past, but who now realised he was being eclipsed by Dohnanyi, saw that a rummage into the background of Unternehmen Sieben would give him the chance to strike back. Herzlieb requested the head of administration, Archibald von Gramatzki, to allow him to research the operation, but Gramatzki, a great admirer of Canaris, informed the admiral of Herzlieb's petition and so enabled Canaris initially to fight off this attack from within his own ranks.[44]

An investigation was proceeding into suspected serious currency offences and customs fraud against Major Schmidhuber and Hauptmann Ickrath of Abwehrstelle Munich, which had come to the attention of Herzlieb's group. Schmidhuber's immediate superior at Abwehr headquarters was a friend of Dohnanyi and Oster's enemies, and he knew that when in Berlin Schmidhuber was a regular guest at the Dohnanyi household and often gossiped about Dohnanyi's suspicious activities.[45] In 1939 Schmidhuber had restored the contacts with Josef Müller, who put out feelers for peace through the Vatican. In May 1940 Schmidhuber had betrayed the date of the German attack in the West to the Vatican at Müller's instigation, and since the end of 1940 he had used Dietrich Bonhoeffer as an agent at Munich and had been useful to him in procuring visas for journeys abroad for Resistance purposes. Schmidhuber was an unstable personality who, in order to save his own skin, now put Müller and his supporters in the Abwehr in danger, even after they had got him away to Italy to prevent his arrest and interrogation.[46]

When Schmidhuber's superior officer at Abwehr headquarters, Luftwaffe-Major Walter Brede, went behind Canaris's back and obtained the assistance of Manfred Roeder to arrest Schmidhuber in Italy on 31 October 1942, the situation threatened to run out of control. Canaris appointed attorney Walter Schoen to safeguard OKW interests during the interrogation of Schmidhuber, but unfortunately Schoen was also a fanatical Nazi and one of the closest associates of Herzlieb, who was his superior, with the result that the first thing he did was to discuss the affair with Roeder,[47] and then propose the extension of the interrogation to include Dohnanyi, Oster and Müller.

Under interrogation, Schmidhuber stated that the proven currency offences had been 'ordered by his superior', describing them as 'the standard practice within the Abwehr, and are political necessities'. He continued: 'For the heads of Amt Ausland/Abwehr, Dohnanyi set up a currency account abroad for the use of Dohnanyi and Oster for special political purposes (coup d'état).' At the least the setting up of such an account for illegal purposes was planned by Dohnanyi;[48] this was how the later trial in the Reich War Court came by the term 'Cash Deposits'. Schmidhuber meant the Abwehr currency deposits set up by the Swiss banker Eduard von der Heydt, which were intended as 'funds for the putsch', but from which money for the financial support of the fourteen Jewish refugees saved in Unternehmen Sieben had been appropriated.

In mid-November 1942, immediately after the German occupation of Vichy France, Canaris was at Toulon to observe the seizure of the French warships there. This operation failed when the French managed to scuttle the fleet before the German attack. On his return, Canaris met Josef Müller in Munich and asked him how the Schmidhuber affair was progressing. Müller noticed that Canaris 'was very close to losing his nerve'; his anxiety was understandable, for before his arrest Schmidhuber had threatened 'to give away everything and everybody without exception'.[49]

At the end of November Schmidhuber was transferred from the Wehrmacht interrogation prison in Munich to Gestapo custody in Berlin, and in mid-January 1943 Franz Sonderegger took over the questioning. In the judgement of Roeder and his colleagues the focus of the inquiries should shift more and more from the currency frauds to the treason allegations surrounding the Vatican conversations in 1939 and 1940. Schmidhuber, who thought that the Abwehr had left him exposed, stated that he was prepared to talk, but he was careful not to incriminate himself. Mentioning that there had been Abwehr approaches to the British Government mediated by the Vatican, he left it open as to whether these were motivated by the Resistance or were intelligence activities to gauge the attitude of the enemy, and he pointed to the lack of interest shown by Heydrich and later Himmler in pursuing accusations against Dohnanyi and others.[50]

After extensive investigation, Sonderegger drafted his report in mid-February 1944, implicating principally Oster, Dohnanyi, Müller and Bonhoeffer, and ended with the question, 'Can Canaris have known nothing about all this?'[51] Gestapo Chief Müller and Roeder agreed that the report should be forwarded to Himmler and Keitel for instructions. While Keitel took steps to have the matter tried by the Reich War Court because the accusations had been made against an admiral, namely Canaris, Himmler returned the report in mid-March with the observation, 'Leave Canaris in peace. I will deal.'[52] Gestapo Chief Müller called off Huppenkothen and Sonderegger after a talk with Himmler, who had meanwhile agreed with Canaris to keep RSHA out of the investigation and let the matter go before the Reich War Court. Ultimately this was a manoeuvre by Himmler to avoid becoming embroiled in investigating the fraud allegation, and on 3 April 1943 the president of the Reich War Court, Admiral Max Bastian, nominated Roeder as judge of inquiry into the 'Cash Deposit' affair. Two days later Roeder arrested Dohnanyi.

Canaris and Oster did everything possible to shift the burden from Dohnanyi. The first thing was to explain away the 'Note', which Dohnanyi implored him by roundabout means from jail to identify as an official paper.[53] Canaris and Oster now supported Dohnanyi's explanation that it contained rough guidelines for what the agent appointed to the Vatican negotiations had to say. In order to justify Bonhoeffer's role, Canaris stated that he was an Abwehr spy who sent 'useful agent's reports'.[54]

As interest in Unternehmen Sieben and its prior history grew in succeeding weeks, Canaris found himself being drawn in ever deeper; Dohnanyi was pressured under interrogation to 'spill the beans' about Canaris and the Abwehr, which he would not do. On 15 June 1944, under official questioning by Roeder in the presence of attorney Alexander Kraell,[55] Canaris declared that 'with regard to the selection of agents for Unternehmen Sieben, he had not had them vetted by headquarters since he already knew some of them because they had lived in Zehlendorf and the others were recommended by Dohnanyi and were known to Oster. He had not considered an approval of the use of the foreign currency account as especially necessary because a counter-balance had been struck against money paid by the Unternehmen Sieben agents into the Reich Exchequer.'[56] None of this was very convincing, and Roeder felt certain of victory – Canaris's fall from power was only a matter of time.

Canaris advised his deputy Bürkner that the whole Abwehr apparatus was now threatened with collapse. Finally his friend Judge Sack approached Keitel and convinced him that the trial and subsequent departure of Canaris could not be in the interests of the OKW chief. Keitel was forced onto the back foot but knew it would be difficult to stop the wheels of justice once they were rolling. However, Roeder now came up unwittingly to his assistance by submitting an interim report in which he stated that crimes of a non-political nature had been committed but that the political misdeeds were difficult to prove even though more or less serious discrepancies had come to light.[57]

Ultimately it was Himmler who kept Canaris in the saddle. After a conference with the Reichsführer-SS, Keitel noted on a copy of Roeder's interim report: 'Himmler refused to read the report, he stated he was not interested in prosecuting Canaris, moreover he gave his personal consent to Canaris for the Unternehmen Sieben operation and holds to his promise: furthermore Canaris will finally purge the unreliable elements around him and work more effectively in future.'[58]

The process against Canaris was abandoned. Himmler had good reasons beyond Reich frontiers for not toppling the Abwehr chief, while Canaris knew that he was indebted to Himmler; this was going to mean his personal agreement to Himmler's appointees in key Abwehr posts, and Lahousen's removal as head of Abwehr II could not long be postponed. He also had to steer clear of the trial against the other defendants, particularly Dohnanyi. The latter's wife recalled: 'Canaris reassured my husband that he had gone to the limits of the possibilities, but his position was no longer so strong that he could pound his fist on the table. My husband had another opinion to the last.'[59] Canaris was saved, but Dohnanyi was doomed.

Although these events and investigations threatened to cripple the Abwehr and the work of its head, Canaris was not tied to his office nor restrained in his activities. Immediately after the capitulation in Tunisia on 13 May 1943 – when 250,000 German and Italian troops were taken into captivity and the southern flank of 'Festung Europa' was now exposed to Allied attack – Canaris saw his nephew Constantin, head of Sipo and SD in Brussels, for the last time. The admiral told him resignedly that he had discussed the hopeless situation with von Arnim in Tunis a week before the collapse, and been told that Tunis could not be held in the face of overwhelming Allied superiority. Three days before the surrender he had relayed this assessment to Keitel, who waved it aside with the observation that Britain would suffer a second Gallipoli far worse than the first.[60]

Canaris believed that the defeat in North Africa did not necessarily mean that the war was lost, but if it were followed by a second successful Allied landing, then defeat was only a matter of time. Constantin Canaris spoke later of a cryptic remark by his uncle that he had known where the next landings would be, but he had refused to say where.

Whether Canaris actually did have this information is unknown. Criticism of the performance of his office had led to a considerable loss of authority for Canaris and the British knew this. At the end of May 1943, the British signals monitoring service reported: 'The Abwehr in Madrid is sending commander-in-chief West their estimate of enemy intentions on the basis of reports between 16 May 1943 and 31 May 1943 – the main thrust will be in the western Mediterranean.' This confirms that the Abwehr had no clear idea of where the next major attack would come,[61] although Canaris had received a report from Madrid at the same time that General Campos saw no threat to Spain, Morocco or the Balearics, the British informer being well aware of how highly the Germans valued Campos's opinion.[62]

On 9 July British Intelligence noted the OKH complaint that no information or Abwehr reports had been received from Tunis, as a response to which Abwehr headquarters ordered Abwehr Madrid to link up all the centres in the region for intelligence purposes. The tentacles had extended as far as Spanish Morocco and Algeciras; the British SIS agent commented: 'Algeciras has no connection to Tunis, but they took note of the instruction.'[63]

With amusement the British watchers followed the trail of a German report from Algeciras about the Allies' plans for Gibraltar. The message went through the Italian representatives in Tangiers to the Italian embassy in Madrid, and then secretly to the German embassy in Madrid with the observation, 'From a Moroccan source, good up to now.' The German embassy passed it to Madrid Abwehr which, unaware that it originated from German agents in Algeciras, forwarded it to Abwehr headquarters. The Germans thus believed for some time that they had the same information from two independent sources.[64]

In the first half of June 1943, ever-more alarming reports reached Abwehr headquarters and Abwehr Rome as to Allied intentions in the Mediterranean, indicating an invasion of Sicily. While the British monitoring service knew everything with only a marginal time delay,[65] Abwehr reports generally came in too late. The British reported: 'Abwehr headquarters reports the receipt of various reports which by comparison provided precise details of the landings in Sicily. These arrived after the event because of sluggish reporting. As a result, the Abwehr in Spain and Portugal has been ordered to speed up their reports on enemy intentions.'[66] British and US forces landed in Sicily on 10 July 1943. Canaris's apparatus had been informed accurately and early, but the transmission of information lacked the required urgency; British intelligence observed that on 30 June a British informer working for an Abwehr agent in Lisbon had passed details as to troop movements for an operation against Sicily, but the information did not reach Abwehr headquarters until 12 July.[67] A source in Gibraltar had also reported that a large contingent of paratroops was expected on the Rock, with the objective of Sicily.[68] On 10 July a message dated the 9th was received in Madrid from Melilla, reporting the departure of an Allied invasion fleet from Algiers and Tunis, heading for Sicily. Not until later did Abwehr headquarters establish that correct information had been passed but had failed to reach Kesselring's staff in Rome in time.[69]

On 25 July 1943 Mussolini was arrested, Marshal Badoglio took over the government of Italy, and on 28 July the Italian Fascist Party was disbanded. On 29 July Canaris flew with Lahousen and Oberst Freytag-Loringhoven to Venice to confer with General Amé, head of Italian intelligence.[70] This journey was Lahousen's last foreign venture as head of Abwehr II, and he vacated the office to Freytag-Loringhoven on 1 August; Lahousen took over a regiment on the Eastern Front following a last visit with Canaris to FHQ.[71]

In Venice the future prosecution of the war was discussed, a subject that came very low on the list of Italian priorities, but a joint communiqué was issued nevertheless, stating the contrary. Canaris and Amé knew that the Italians were about to abandon the Axis, but Canaris did nothing to convince the Italians to reconsider; he wished them well and warned of a possible German invasion.[72]

Schellenberg maintained later that shortly afterwards he laid a dossier before Himmler alleging that Canaris had not conveyed to Berlin the true nature of his conversations with Amé. He had reminded Himmler three times about the file and his promise to show it to Hitler, but Himmler had done nothing.

Himmler advised Schellenberg that the errors of the Abwehr chief and his attitude towards the regime were 'on another page', and Schellenberg should not worry about it.[73] This was not the first occasion on which he had inferred from Himmler's reaction that currently he was no longer interested in toppling Canaris, if ever he had had such an interest in the past. The reasons for Himmler's reticence since the spring of 1943 are unknown; Christine von Dohnanyi stated that Himmler always had a surprisingly 'normal' working relationship with her husband.

26

The Undoing of Canaris

Although it seems that there was no further direct contact between Canaris and emissaries of the OSS, in Istanbul US naval attaché Earle, who had conferred with Canaris in January 1943, contacted Canaris's man, Leverkühn, who – according to his own account – reported the approach at once to the Gestapo.[1] At about the same time Archbishop Spellman of New York attempted to obtain an interview with ambassador von Papen, but was turned down by Ribbentrop.[2] On 17 June 1943, Adam von Trott zu Sulz travelled to Istanbul immediately after the third meeting of the Kreisau circle to discuss their foreign policy outlook, to sound out the terrain for Moltke and to open channels for a possible offer by the German Resistance to the United States.[3] Trott sought out Consul-General Dr Fritz von Twardowski and made contacts with German émigrés – after 1933 many university lecturers had resettled in Turkey and now taught at the University of Istanbul – and in Ankara attempted to win over von Papen to an active participation in the German Resistance. Trott also met Leverkühn, who probably used the opportunity to ask Trott's help for a young member at K-Organisation Istanbul, lawyer Erich Vermehren, son of an old friend of Leverkühn, now a legal adviser and stenographer on his staff. Vermehren's wife Elisabeth, the former Countess Plettenberg, was still in Germany and needed an exit visa to come to Turkey; Trott could help. It is not certain whether he suspected that the Vermehrens were talking to British intelligence at this time and planned to defect.[4]

On 5 July 1943 Moltke arrived in Istanbul as an Abwehr agent. His contact people to OSS Istanbul, headed by Lanning MacFarland, were the economics expert Hans Wilbrandt and the sociologist Alexander Rüstov who, using the cover names 'Hyacinth' and 'Magnolia', were part of the German Freedom Movement based in Istanbul cooperating with the US secret service. These two were also involved in the US spy ring 'Dogwood–Cereus Circle', so-called for the US agents 'Dogwood' (Alfred Schwartz) and Cereus (Archibald Coleman) active in other parts of Europe.

In the summer of 1943 all attempts to discuss peace had failed because of American lack of interest and the indifferent attitude of von Papen, who was unable to commit himself to the Resistance.[5] It was probably Moltke's efforts to convince the US Government to lift its demand for 'unconditional surrender' that had resulted in a refusal to talk and a ban on Moltke making contact with the US ambassador to Cairo, Alexander C Kirk, whom Moltke knew and was hoping to enlist as intermediary.

In the summer of 1943 Canaris may have attempted to contact his British counterpart Stewart Menzies. Through Baron Oswald von Hoyningen-Huene, the German ambassador in Lisbon, and another middleman, he made an offer to meet Menzies on neutral territory. Menzies himself confirmed the invitation after the war, but Foreign Minister Eden had forbidden the meeting on the grounds that if the Soviets found out they might suspect that Britain and Germany were negotiating a separate peace. Not all suggested attempts at contact with London and Washington are actually proven, but the OSS files at least show that during 1943 several serious attempts were made in this direction and were unsuccessful for one reason or another.

Moltke's second trip to Turkey in December 1943 had Canaris's knowledge;[6] contrary to his expectations no meeting with ambassador Kirk could be arranged, but he put out feelers to various US journalists and to Wilbrandt and Rüstow. After he left, they set out his proposals in the so-called 'Herman' Plan that they passed to William Donovan through the agents 'Dogwood' and 'Cereus'.

The primary platform of the Herman Plan was the coordination and cooperation of the German democratic opposition. The German defeat and territorial losses were declared inevitable and necessary for Germany's future. Moltke and his friends proposed to help the Allies not only win the war, but also the peace, and to avoid an Allied invasion resembling the Italian campaign.[7]

Since Moltke undertook his mission with Canaris's support, the proposals presumably coincided with Canaris's own ideas. The Herman Plan concept of a capitulation and cooperation with the Western Powers, coupled with an unconditional resistance to the peril of a Bolshevist occupation in the East, can be traced back to Canaris, and correspond to what he had stated to military attaché Earle in January 1943, although no certain proof exists.[8]

Moltke had planned a third excursion to Turkey for January 1944 but was arrested by the Gestapo on 19 January, together with Otto Kiep. The latter was friendly with the Abwehr's Erich Vermehren, whose wife had now arrived in Istanbul with the help of the German Foreign Ministry and Canaris in spite of Gestapo wishes. It may be that news of the arrests of Moltke and Kiep fortified the resolutions of the Vermehrens to change sides,[9] and on 27 January 1944 both disappeared without trace.

The telegram reporting their disappearance arrived in Berlin on the night of 3 February 1944. It was assumed that they were being hidden by the British until the chance arose to smuggle them out of Turkey, or that they were already on British territory. The K-Organisation sub-branch considered the passing of military secrets unlikely to be the primary force behind the defection but rather that Elisabeth Vermehren, as a 'Catholic activist' had decided to take up the political struggle against the Third Reich and would make radio broadcasts for the BBC. It was feared that the affair could 'involve wider circles' and that – especially as regards the defection of the wife, whose emigration from Germany had caused some misgivings on the military side – 'persons inside the Reich possibly had an interest'.

The finger of suspicion was quickly pointed at Foreign Ministry staff, who had provided Frau Vermehren with a service passport, money and a mission, and to get around the military borders the Foreign Ministry had even placed a seat at her disposal aboard a courier aircraft.[10] The telegrams, now a Reich secret, made a concrete accusation against anonymous staff in the Wilhelmstrasse without mentioning the mission for which she had come to Turkey. It was agreed that OKW and principally the SD would look into the matter further.

Adam von Trott was obliged to come up with an explanation since he had been the staff member at the Foreign Ministry who had supported Leverkühn's petition in the Vermehren case. Herr Vermehren had appeared at the Foreign Ministry in December 1943 and said that he wanted to take his wife with him to Turkey; the Abwehr was not opposed, and apparently it was very urgent. He was in Istanbul and responsible for creating connections to an 'interesting' American; he had good insight into the British–US internal relationship but his political reports had been for the most part of no interest to the Abwehr and therefore appeared seldom in the embassy reports sent from Turkey. This was why it was important to use Frau Vermehren, so as to procure political information for the Foreign Ministry through private channels. This pitiful explanation did nothing to help the relationship between the Abwehr and Foreign Ministry in the Vermehren case.[11] Canaris was alarmed because Herr Vermehren had also had 'good insight into the organisations and activities of the Abwehr in Turkey' and this gave rise to the 'danger of betrayal with all the unpleasant consequences attaching thereto'.[12]

Leverkühn suggested that OKW should take hostages in Germany and announce it in a radio broadcast to force the couple to surrender to the German authorities. Papen intervened against this plan, fearing further publicity and the revelation of Turkish secret service cooperation in the search for the absentees; under no circumstances must German–Turkish collaboration against Britain and the Soviet Union become apparent. Papen suspected that an Austrian resistance group supported in Turkey by the US secret service there had also had a finger in the Vermehren case, and he asked that none of the measures that the SD wanted should be implemented until his own inquiries were exhausted.[13] Papen was soon under suspicion himself for procuring the entry visa into Turkey for Elisabeth Vermehren and also being related to her. Her father's half-sister had married into a branch of Papen's family, but this branch had separated from the line of the former Reich Chancellor two hundred years previously, a fact he found himself obliged to explain in a telegram to the Foreign Ministry.[14]

The Vermehren case now began to draw in those wider circles as Papen had feared.[15] Together with the Vermehrens, an Abwehr agent named Hamburger, and a married couple, the Kleczkowskis, had also disappeared, the latter having been sought feverishly since 11 February. Twelve embassy staff and three other Abwehr workers were recalled for complicity in the Vermehren defection, and the entry of all new Abwehr agents into Turkey was stopped.[16]

The affair signalled extremely unpleasant consequences for Canaris, for in talks during the summer with the Abwehr, the Foreign Ministry had called Abwehr activities in Turkey 'of extremely doubtful value', and had demanded the recall of a number of staff including Hamburger and the Kleczkowskis. The Abwehr had declined to do so.[17]

The Abwehr had discovered that the Italian military attaché in Ankara had been 'very pleased' to learn on 2 February that the 'three birds had flown', which could only have meant the Vermehrens and an escort, and the British press agency Associated Press in London announced that ambassador von Papen had broken off his leave because an embassy official had been missing for several days.[18] Papen was forced to request guidelines for his replies and was told that if 'the enemy press or radio should discuss the matter publicly', he should state that Vermehren 'was not an embassy official' but 'a minor employee working at the consulate-general in Istanbul who had been seduced by the British and against the wishes of the Turkish authorities, and had been removed from Turkey by force'.[19] A week later the Germans remained none the wiser as to the whereabouts of the Vermehrens, although they thought it might be Lisbon, since Elisabeth Vermehren's mother was living there as a correspondent for the periodical *Das Reich*. All Portuguese airports were being watched by Abwehr and SD agents,[20] but in fact, the Vermehrens had actually been taken to Cairo.

A Foreign Ministry report dated 20 February presumed that 'the desertion of a married couple in high society is in the foreground for the British in their efforts for the Vermehren husband and wife, and that obtaining information about our Abwehr service plays a subordinate role'. This was wishful thinking, for the same report stated: 'Vermehren knew our Abwehr system in Turkey, including the structuring of Abwehr representatives in the authorities of the foreign service there, also the Abwehr officers in Turkey and their cover designations as well as a large number of Abwehr agents with their cover names. He has not been instructed as to Abwehr activities in the field of counter-espionage, sabotage and the Navy.'[21]

Vermehren had prepared a forty-page treatise on Abwehr personnel and embassy staff. Whether he could supply the British with the key to the ciphers was not known for certain, and it was hoped that the actual damage to the intelligence service would be slight. The Foreign Ministry may have thought so, but Canaris considered it substantial, and Kaltenbrunner presented Hitler with a report on 7 February from his SD attaché in Istanbul that put the matter in a dramatic light. The affair hit Canaris at a time that could scarcely have been less favourable; his position in the National Socialist power structure had been weak since the beginning of 1944, and his rivals were now arming for the decisive battle to oust him.

The exposure of a German spy ring in Argentina caused the government in Buenos Aires to sever diplomatic relations with the Reich. Moreover this scandal offered the German ambassador in Madrid, Dieckhoff, brother-in-law of Foreign Minister Ribbentrop, the opportunity to strike against the Abwehr, whose sabotage activities in Spain had long been a thorn in his side. On 28 January he wrote to the Wilhelmstrasse: 'The events in Argentina give me cause to take a basic stand on the whole question of using German agents in Spain.'[22] The acts of sabotage against British shipping by Abwehr II and – since the defection of Italy – also against Italian ships in Spanish ports, had severely damaged diplomatic relations between Berlin and Madrid and brought the Spanish Government under pressure. Since the 'Italian betrayal' British intelligence had been informed of many details and was in a position to lay before the Spanish authorities 'documentary and photographic' evidence about the German Abwehr apparatus. One should not overestimate the durability of personal links and confidences existing since the Civil War – here Canaris was meant; he had made a friendly visit to Spain in October 1943 and a few days later the Spanish authorities had caved in to British pressure by shutting down an Abwehr post. Dieckhoff demanded that

> all Abwehr posts should be removed from the service buildings of embassies and consulates as soon as possible so that in a given case we can give the assurance with some credibility that we have no knowledge of Abwehr activities ... everything must be done to ensure that in future the remaining Abwehr staff receive only operations that are outwardly defensive ... above all so-called active missions, as for example acts of sabotage, such as those undertaken a few weeks ago against British shipping in Spanish Mediterranean ports without sufficient camouflage or any obvious military or political purpose, will be made impossible from now on.

Ribbentrop supported his brother-in-law. The Foreign Minister wrote to Keitel and Himmler, giving his staff members Ritter and Wagner the job of contacting the SD:

In the expectation that both Keitel and Himmler will soon be issuing the instructions, it must be ensured that: (1) In Axis or neutral countries all sabotage activity ceases. If for any reason an act of sabotage is considered essential, the planning and execution can only be undertaken with the previous agreement of the Foreign Minister; and (2) that the dismantling of the Abwehr organisation, in so far as that is possible, is begun now.[23]

Ribbentrop wanted to control Abwehr sabotage work himself and reduce the organisation, discussing this with Himmler and ignoring Canaris; he also prepared a memorandum on this for Hitler.[24] On 3 February Canaris wrote to Ribbentrop: 'Chief OKW has forbidden all further sabotage against British shipping in Spanish ports. However, he considers desirable the continuation of sabotage attacks against Badoglio-tonnage [Italian ships] in Spanish ports, and attacks against those carrying contraband to the enemy remain viable.'[25]

Ribbentrop and Dieckhoff worked hand in hand. On 6 February 1944 Dieckhoff cabled to Berlin the current development in Spain; the house of Hauptmann Hummel, head of Abwehr II in Spain, had been searched, and Dieckhoff had received warnings that the Spanish were planning an operation against the entire German network of agents. The previous day the British had reported that a time-bomb of German origin had been found aboard a freighter travelling from Spain with a cargo of onions. 'The Anglo-Saxons have reacted with a fury that the whole country is feeling today (fuel blockade),' Dieckhoff reported.[26] After speaking to Hitler, Ribbentrop informed Canaris on 8 February: 'The Führer has stated that (1) all such acts of sabotage must cease absolutely; and (2) no acts of sabotage are to be made against Italian ships.'[27] In connection with the breaking-off of diplomatic relations by Argentina, the Foreign Minister called the embassies in Ankara, Lisbon, Stockholm and Berne 'without regard to special interests and internal German service posts'[28] to determine which Abwehr and SD units were still viable and which could be recommended for dismantling.

Canaris wanted to meet Dieckhoff in Madrid[29] but held back, travelling finally in company with Lahousen's successor Freytag-Loringhoven to Biarritz to confer with the head of K-Organisation Spain, Leissner, and the Foreign Ministry representative to the Abwehr, Freiherr von Grote; Dieckhoff also sent a deputy. The conversations increased the ill-feeling between Abwehr and Foreign Ministry. Canaris was forced to make major concessions, pulling out completely from embassies and consulates, and removing ten K-Organisation employees from Spain monthly, and sabotage activity in Spain and Spanish

Morocco was forbidden. Canaris was embittered that Dieckhoff had used a complaint about worthless political reporting to arrange with immediate effect restrictions that included the transmission of political reports of any kind. In the long run, apart from counter-espionage, this was the reason for the existence of the Abwehr.

The Foreign Ministry representatives Grote and Stille emphasised that 'the rectification ordered by Admiral Canaris rests on his own decision', the Foreign Ministry and embassy 'had, together with a certain physical separation, considered it politic to diminish the complement of K-Organisation Spain in order to reduce the exposure to Anglo-Saxon pressures which is sure to come'.[30]

Unusually, Canaris allowed Grote to see his resentment and resignation both on the flight and during the talks. He felt deceived by Dieckhoff, having assured the ambassador a few months before that good and reliable cooperation existed with the Abwehr. The Foreign Ministry inclined to the view, Canaris said, that 'every difficulty arising from the political or military development in the relationship with neutral States could be traced back to Abwehr mistakes. He had been accused of responsibility for the severing of diplomatic ties with Argentina, and now he was the scapegoat-in-waiting should the Spanish do the same.'[31] Grote had contradicted him, and 'pointed to undeniable ineptitude'. In his notes for the Foreign Minister, however, Grote wrote that he could sympathise with Canaris's disappointment and the admiral had asked him a number of awkward questions to which he was unable to furnish an answer.

Canaris's complaints were obviously relayed to Dieckhoff who, in his hour of triumph, used his reply to Ribbentrop for a gloating settlement of the account with Canaris. Since taking the Madrid post in February 1943, he had been dubious about Abwehr activity and, when presenting his credentials to Franco, the Caudillo had spoken confidentially about Canaris, making clear that, as far as he was concerned, it was the ambassador, and not the admiral, who was the German partner for discussions;[32] Franco had not wanted to meet Canaris on his last visit, and nobody on the Spanish side had a good word to say for him. The violent closure of Abwehrstelle Algeciras by the Spanish authorities made him doubt strongly 'the alleged friendly understanding between Admiral Canaris and Spanish offices'. As for Canaris's old friend and confidant Italian General Roatta, Franco hated him; irrespective of how firm the friendship between Canaris and Franco and other Spanish generals might have been during the Civil War, it could no longer be built on today.

The telegrams sent to Berlin by Canaris during his visit to Madrid in October 1943 spoke in different terms.[33] The correctness of the decision to close Abwehrstelle Algeciras was disputed even in Spain since, according to information from K-Organisation, it had been ordered by the Spanish Foreign Ministry without the knowledge of the Spanish secret service.[34]

Dieckhoff's offensive coincided with the political eclipse of Canaris. His conduct at Biarritz and his orders had created new enemies in the Foreign Ministry, even amongst those who were not in agreement with the suppression of the Abwehr political reports, for Spanish Foreign Ministry telegrams intercepted by K-Organisation agents were an especially important resource for the German Foreign Ministry.[35] When Leissner's negotiations with the Spanish generals fell through after the latter declared that in the current situation they had no guarantee that the Abwehr would exist in Spain beyond the German embassy, Canaris's enemies had reached their objective.

The end of Canaris was sealed. Too much had happened in recent months: the investigations of Dohnanyi and Oster, the suspicions against Canaris himself, the complaints of Abwehr incompetence over the Allied landings in North Africa and Allied plans for offensives, the diplomatic entanglements over the sabotage activities of Abwehr II, and finally the Vermehren affair, for which Hitler blamed Canaris personally – Hitler's patience was exhausted. At the beginning of March 1944, after his visit to Obersalzberg, Goebbels noted in his diary how much the Vermehren affair preoccupied Hitler.[36] Huppenkothen reported later that after an outburst of rage over the Vermehrens, Himmler's representative at FHQ, SS-Brigadeführer Fegelein suggested on 11 February 1944 that 'the Führer ought to transfer the whole box of junk to the Reichsführer-SS'.[37]

Hitler agreed and informed Himmler immediately that Canaris was relieved of office and the entire German intelligence service was being placed in Himmler's charge. The next day Hitler signed the following order:

1. A unified German secret service is to be created.
2. I appoint the Reichsführer-SS to head it.
3. In so far as it touches on military intelligence and Abwehr, the Reichsführer-SS and head of OKW will take the necessary measures in bilateral agreement.[38]

The exclusion of Canaris was now official, and the news spread quickly amongst the Military Abwehr staff. Keitel and Jodl travelled to the new Abwehr headquarters at Maybach II, Zossen, in order to inform Canaris personally that he had been relieved, and was now obliged to proceed to Burg Lauenstein in the Franconian Forest to await details as to his future employment.[39] On 23 February 1944 Keitel noted that 'the future employment of Admiral Canaris will be decided later' and until then he would be 'amongst the OKW officers at my disposal'.[40] A little afterwards at Burg Lauenstein Canaris received a message from Grossadmiral Dönitz: 'The commander-in-chief Kriegsmarine informed Admiral Canaris on 10 March 1944 that he will enter the Retired List with effect from 30 June. The welfare and care provisions apply. Admiral Canaris is at the disposal of the Kriegsmarine. A new appointment is not envisaged.'[41]

The laboratories, research equipment and workshops of the Abwehr were located at Burg Lauenstein, but how Canaris spent his time there, or received news of his enforced retirement, is not known. He was accompanied there by his chauffeur and two dachshunds, but had not been able to take leave of his family. His wife Erika had been evacuated to friends on the Ammersee to escape the bombing, his daughter Brigitte was at boarding school, and his sick daughter Eva lived in the Bodelschwingschen Institute at Bethel.[42] Oberstleutnant Albrecht Focke, who ran Burg Lauenstein, was told to treat Canaris with courtesy and respect, allowing him freedom of movement there while shielding him as much as possible from the outside world. During this time his wife visited him once; Schellenberg also came, but the substance of their long conversation is unknown.

Schellenberg cooperated with Bentivegni and the head of the Wehrmacht Central Office, Generalleutnant Paul Winter, who had received full authority from Keitel, to ensure the smooth transfer of the Abwehr into the RSHA apparatus.[43] Bentivegni's efforts to retain at least a small nucleus of the military intelligence centre paid off: Abwehr-Abteilung I and II were annexed to RSHA as 'the Military Office' (Amt Mil or Amt M). The new head of Amt Mil, Oberst Georg Hansen, a convinced anti-Nazi, became deputy to Amt VI (SD-Ausland) Chief Schellenberg, and vice versa – Abteilung III (counter-espionage) passed mainly to the corresponding office at RSHA IV (Gestapo). The front-line reconnaissance units and the competent offices monitoring the armed forces remained under OKW control together with elements of the former Abwehr II (Sabotage against Foreign Armies); civilian sabotage units passed to RSHA.[44] At a castle close to Salzburg at the beginning of May 1944, Keitel and Himmler held a conference for all senior Abwehr and RSHA officers and officials to announce the new regulations officially. Himmler praised again 'the valuable work of the military Abwehr'.[45]

By an edict of 10 June 1944, Hitler discharged Admiral Canaris from active military service with effect from the end of the month 'with permission to wear his former uniform'. Shortly afterwards he countermanded this order and appointed Canaris admiral on standby from 1 July to head the virtually insignificant Special Staff for Anti-Shipping Warfare and Economic War Measures at OKW (HWK), Potsdam-Eiche.[46] What lay behind this 'comeback' is not known, but it may have been an idea of Himmler to hold available a man with good contacts and of international renown.

According to the British secret service expert Anthony Cave Brown, the reason was the alleged contacts Canaris had to the French intelligence chiefs

Arnould and Keun in May 1944. Cave Brown refers to statements by Arnould made in an interview after the war in which Canaris had given Keun a personal message from the Resistance to the head of British Intelligence, Menzies, concerning the retraction of the demand for 'unconditional surrender'. Canaris met Arnould at a Paris convent to receive the answer, a two-page letter,[47] with the answer in the negative. This story sounds unlikely and is unproven. As head of HWK, Canaris could not have travelled to Paris at that time, but fragments that do fit the story occur in the interrogations after 20 July. Baron Kaulbars,[48] Canaris's confidant and liaison to Stockholm and Moscow, made a written statement under interrogation that he had learned in Sweden that Canaris was to be removed, and was informed of the 'attitude of foreign circles'. Kaltenbrunner observed of this statement: 'With the removal of the admiral, the chance of any kind of accord if Germany was ready to negotiate with the enemy powers about the possibility of a peace acceptable to both sides, evaporated. The report that the admiral had gone would be a signal to those abroad to sever whatever cooperation existed with Germany. Canaris was one of the few men with whom other countries would still deal and cooperate.'[49]

This contradictory report raises more questions than it answers. The German readiness to negotiate was irrelevant if the Allies refused to talk. What cooperation existed to be severed? Even the question as to who might still have been interested in peace soundings from Canaris in the summer of 1944 remains unanswered. Attention focuses finally on Himmler, who showed a complete disdain for investigating the suspicions against Canaris, but also ensured that the accusations against him in connection with the prosecution of Dohnanyi and Oster did not proceed. What was behind his attitude towards Canaris and his closest circle, which endured until the beginning of April 1945, remains one of the great mysteries.

Canaris was not personally involved in the attempted coup and assassination plot of 20 July. He was too far from the centre of events, bereft of his power base and without contact to his former staff, and so it was not until early July that he was even apprised of the basics of the planned operation by Freytag-Lovinghoven and Schrader.[50] Canaris knew Graf von Stauffenburg, the leader of the plot, from meetings since the end of 1943, when he had been chief of Staff at the General Army Office at OKH, but there had been no common ground between them, and according to Huppenkothen the relationship was so bad that sometimes Canaris's friend Judge Sack had to step in as referee.[51] Nevertheless, it was supposedly Stauffenburg who informed Canaris of the assassination attempt on 20 July 1944. According to the story, Canaris was entertaining his neighbour, the pianist Helmut Maurer, a regular guest at the Schlachtensee house, and also Baron Kaulbars and Judge-General Sack when

Stauffenburg told him by telephone that the Führer was dead; a bomb had killed him. Suspecting that his line was tapped, Canaris answered: 'Dead? For God's sake who was it then? The Russians?'[52] According to Abshagen, it came to light during the interrogation by Huppenkothen that the telephone conversation between Stauffenburg and Canaris had been monitored and documented, but this is doubtful because Stauffenburg could not have called at the time of day stated by Maurer. According to Höhne, Judge-General Sack was informed by a colleague of Olbricht in the Bendlerstrasse and hurried to tell Canaris;[53] when Canaris went to his office at Potsdam-Eiche afterwards, his adjutant was already composing a letter of loyalty addressed to Hitler.

Canaris was mistaken if he thought he could escape the immediate campaign of revenge. On 22 July he told a former subordinate he met on the street: 'Yes, my dear boy, it can't be done! Call me in a few days.'[54] It would not be long before his name surfaced in the files of 'Sonderkommission 20/7'. Canaris's successor, Hansen, who was involved in the plot and had been taken into Gestapo custody on 22 July, made a written statement:

> I see Canaris as the spiritual founder of the Resistance Movement which led to 20 July. Its beginnings are found in 1938. At that time the departure of Fritsch was used to usher in an internal revolution. Canaris himself continued substantially as the carrier of the essential contacts abroad. Canaris went to great lengths to get those people abroad who were opposed to the Nazi regime, amongst them numerous Jews, church people etc and clergy for the purpose of using them as contacts to church circles in Sweden, Switzerland or at the Vatican.[55]

Whatever was said in the Gestapo dungeons and how little it might have had to do with the events of 20 July 1944, nevertheless Kaltenbrunner included it all in his report to Martin Bormann on the foreign connections of the conspirators, and for Canaris it had catastrophic consequences.

On 23 July 1944 Schellenberg received orders from Gestapo Chief Müller to arrest Canaris. According to Schellenberg's account he proceeded to Berlin Schlachtensee with an SS-Hauptsturmführer who knew Canaris, having been formerly with the Abwehr. Canaris was in the company of Baron Kaulbar and his nephew Erwin Delbrück. Canaris asked his visitors to leave the room while he spoke to Schellenberg: 'Somehow I felt it would be you. Tell me, have they found anything in writing by that clown Oberst Hansen?' When Schellenberg nodded and said a notebook had been discovered containing a list of those persons to be eliminated, but not about Canaris himself or his participation in a coup d'état, Canaris replied: 'Those idiots in the General Staff cannot live without scribbling.' If we accept Schellenberg's account further, Canaris then made a remarkable request: 'You must make me a promise on your word of honour to obtain for me within the next three days the opportunity for an interview with Himmler. The others – Kaltenbrunner and Müller – are no more than evil killers, out for my head.'[56]

Schellenberg promised and then offered to wait in the living room while Canaris did whatever he needed. He declined; he neither wanted to run for it nor shoot himself. Schellenberg then took him to the Frontier Police School Fürstenberg where twenty other senior officers suspected of complicity in the assassination attempt were being held under house arrest. Schellenberg stated that Canaris then invited him to stay for dinner and they drank a bottle of red wine while he instructed Canaris on how he should speak to Himmler. Next day, Schellenberg alleges that he spoke at length with Himmler and obtained his promise to grant Canaris an interview.[57]

Hans Oster was arrested on 21 July at the Schnaditz estate after a list of conspirators was discovered at the General Army Office.[58] Erwin Delbrück and Karl Ludwig Freiherr von und zu Guttenberg were arrested, while Dohnanyi, Bonhoeffer and Josef Müller were transferred from Wehrmacht custody to the Gestapo. Huppenkothen led the interrogations of Canaris and Oster from the beginning of August. He was assisted by Kriminalkommissar Sonderegger, who since the 'Cash Deposits' case had been handling the available prosecution evidence against the Abwehr headquarters staff members involved.

It was above all due to the skill and resistance of Oster that Huppenkothen and Sonderegger at first made little progress. Oster talked and tried to say nothing; he spoke about the mental and political attitude of Canaris:

> Those of us of his time had a childish passion for soldiering that led us to become officers in the monarchy. That that kind of State could ever be destroyed was unimaginable for us. There was no politics. We wore the Kaiser's uniform and that was enough[59] . . . The collapse in 1918 was a hammer-blow to us, the abolition of the Wilhelminian monarchy into an uncohesive State of political parties.

Kaltenbrunner wrote

> According to Oster, the 1933 Revolution was a relief from the conflict of conscience which for them had begun in the early period of the Weimar system! The return to strong national parties, rearmament, the reintroduction of general conscription, these things were for officers a return to the earlier traditions. Whereas the soldier in the Weimar system only did what he was duty-bound to do, Oster had warmly welcomed these points of the National Socialist expansionist programme.

In a written statement Oster described the cracks which appeared in the relationship of the conservative officer towards the new regime: the murders of Schleicher and Bredow in June 1934, the Blomberg affair and Fritsch trial, the rise of the Waffen-SS to be the elite Wehrmacht branch. And it went on and on in this vein.

For a while Oster entangled his interrogators in an irrelevant political and historical analysis that had nothing to do with the criminological investigation into who was involved in the plot to kill Hitler on 20 July 1944. When he was confronted with the statements of Alexander von Pfuhlstein and Friedrich Wilhelm Heinz, in which particularly Pfuhlstein implicated Canaris, Oster came under pressure and was forced into attempting to lay on Canaris the portion of the blame that he could not shift on the dead Olbricht.[60] From the interrogations of Pfuhlstein and Heinz, the impression grew that Canaris must have played a more significant role in the revolt: 'Canaris had been, if extremely lacking in perception, totally pessimistic. He had seen the general military collapse approaching month by month, as for example Christmas 1943. Even Heinz confirmed that in the Abwehr a pronounced "tired industry" had reigned. Canaris always made on him "a melancholy impression".'[61]

Although all these statements did not connect Canaris directly with the events of 20 July, they tightened the noose about his neck. He relied on denials, reinterpretations and the devaluation of his fellow-travellers' explanations, and kept this tactic going when he was finally confronted by his accusers. His former subordinates had got it wrong, he explained; he did not implicate them, but tried to blunt the sharpness of what they said by giving their allegations a more harmless meaning. Kaltenbrunner's report sounded slightly resigned: 'Although Oster, Pfuhlstein and Hansen maintained their allegations when confronting Admiral Canaris, Canaris disputes the assertions of Pfuhlstein, for example that he predicted certain collapse for Christmas 1943.'[62] With reference to peace discussions and the necessity 'to remove the present government at least for a while',[63] Canaris admitted that such considerations had been uttered in conversations with Oster, but they had been 'only incidental' and were discussed in connection with reports received. Here Canaris played the naive man:

> I placed no value on these reports and never accepted them as serious. As far as I was concerned it was just talk to pass the time. For me there was never any doubt that a change in the government during the war would be considered a stab in the back, and would destroy the Home Front. It would be a repeat of 1918, but in a much worse form.

In a comprehensive extract from a statement during interrogation, which Kaltenbrunner added to his report of 21 September 1944, he quoted Canaris as saying:

> For me, one thing was clear above all else, and I explained it to the officers who discussed the point with me, that a war of such enormous dimensions was willed by Fate and could not have been prevented. Moreover I never doubted, and I often emphasised in conversation that the great sacrifices that our people have

made in this war at the Front and at home under a tight uniform leadership could never have been in vain, and would still turn out well even if the war does not end favourably as the optimists think it will.[64]

One day after Kaltenbrunner had completed his report on the former Abwehr chief – a report which would not have sent Canaris to the gallows – certain documents were discovered at Zossen. Hitler's revenge would now run its course, and the last chapter in the life of Wilhelm Canaris began.

PART VI

HITLER'S REVENGE

*　　*　　*

Within a few months of the failed assassination attempt and coup of 20 July 1944 Hitler's revenge machinery, operated by '20 July Special Commission' at RSHA, was running full out; hundreds had been rounded up, dozens already executed.[1] Graf von Stauffenburg, Albrecht Ritter Mertz von Quirnheim, Friedrich Olbricht and Werner von Haeften had all been shot dead on the same night in the courtyard at the Bendlerblock; others such as Ludwig Beck and Hening von Tresckow had committed suicide. Canaris was arrested on 23 July, his name having been mentioned by several of those incarcerated in connection with the plot. He had been confined initially in the Frontier Police School at Fürstenberg, then brought to the cells of the RSHA at Prinz-Albrecht-Strasse in Berlin.[2]

Although accused by former colleagues, Canaris denied any involvement in the conspiracy. Since it had not been possible to obtain documentary proof to support the oral statements, the members of the '20 July Special Commission', particularly SS-Standartenführer Walter Huppenkothen and Kriminalkommissar Franz Sonderegger – both long-term enemies of Canaris – made no further progress. Their principal interest was in his vanished diaries. During a search of Canaris's last service office at Potsdam, a portion ending at October 1942 was discovered in a safe. Huppenkothen thought that this was probably an attempted deception.[3]

As a result of this find by Huppenkothen and Sonderegger, and the statements of close colleagues of Canaris, they could be certain that such a diary existed. Only a small circle knew that he had documented his activities as Abwehr chief, and the military and political developments in Germany since 1937. The material was intended, as Canaris had explained to his co-conspirators, 'to show the world and the German people with what criminal amateurism, and with what unlimited self-overestimation this war was created from a row about trifles':[4] 'The world must know of the guilt of these people.'[5] Now the 'guilty' ones were searching high and low for evidence proving the involvement of the former Abwehr chief in the failed coup of 20 July 1944.

A hectic search began for the diaries that were believed to hold the key to everything.[6] At first all that could be established was that Oberstleutnant

Werner Schrader at Abwehr had retained the diary for later use in a history of the Abwehr.[7] The search spread, and in mid-September a member of Otto Strasser's anti-Hitler 'Black Front', Kurt Kerstenhahn, came to Prinz-Albrecht-Strasse. Known to the Gestapo, he had been Schrader's chauffeur. Schrader had committed suicide after 20 July and Kerstenhahn feared that his own name might come up during the research of the Sonderkommission into 20 July.[8] He admitted that in 1942–3 he had on many occasions driven Schrader and Friedrich Heinz to the 'Haus der Preussischen Seehandlung' run by Heinz's half-brother. In the vaults there they had lodged certain Abwehr papers, which Kerstenhahn and Hans Oster had later removed to a safe in the underground bunkers at OKH headquarters, Zossen,[9] and he told Sonderegger exactly where to find them.[10]

On 22 September, Sonderegger went to Maybach II at Zossen where he located and had the safe forced open.[11] The files, sketches, reports and notes that Sonderegger found represented 'an explosive of a quite special kind'.[12] Apart from a few copied pages, the Canaris diaries were not amongst them, but now the Gestapo had a substantial portion of the chronicle that Hans von Dohnanyi had been assembling regarding the misdeeds of the regime and the activities of the Resistance circle since 1933.[13]

Since his arrest in 1943, Dohnanyi had kept saying that the files should be destroyed: 'Every jotting about the business is a death sentence.'[14] Why Oster and other conspirators ignored him is a mystery, but it is probable that the wishes of the former Chief of Staff Ludwig Beck, who wanted to preserve the documents for posterity, played a not insignificant role. Another reason was certainly that the plotters no longer felt safe with the idea of going to Zossen to destroy the papers; after 20 July those involved and still at large were ultra-cautious. Perhaps it was simply believed that the files were somewhere else.[15]

Huppenkothen and Sonderegger had the files from the 1938–40 period proving that the plans to overthrow Nazism began earlier than previously suspected, in the spring of 1938, and that they originated not in the military circle around Stauffenburg, but with Canaris and his immediate staff. The link between the earlier conspirators and the would-be assassins of 20 July was now clear. In the loose pages of Canaris's diary found in the armoured safe there appeared – as conversational partners – names of such high-ranking military officers as von Witzleben, Halder, Brauchitsch, Thomas and Reichenau. Papers from the 1938 Blomberg and Fritsch affairs documented the first considerations for a coup, Oster's and Dohnanyi's thoughts on the consequences and discussions with Beck and Canaris, and they also included a three-page handwritten plan drawn up by Oster listing the post-coup executions and a list of persons supporting the conspiracy. Also found were Dohnanyi's notes about the negotiations that Josef

Müller had had at the Vatican to extend peace feelers to the Western Powers, including the 'X-Report', in which Dohnanyi had summarised Müller's efforts. Besides comprehensive notes to various coup plans, there was Abwehr Gruppe IIIF material betraying the attack date for the Western offensive in the spring of 1940. From the files it was clear that the liaison officer to the Vatican, Josef Müller, previously above all suspicion, was a traitor.[16] Most of those implicated by the material – Canaris, Oster, Dohnanyi, Bonhoeffer – were in custody and the new evidence against them was devastating. Friedrich Wilhelm Heinz said of the Zossen find after the war: 'When Prussian officers plot revolution, they not only keep a careful diary, but also a travel log and all bureaucratic files.'[17]

Huppenkothen and Sonderegger concur that the investigations against Oster, Dohnanyi, former Army Judge Karl Sack and Abwehr-Hauptmann Ludwig Gehre were close to completion and these persons were about to be indicted before the People's Court almost immediately.[18] Gestapo Chief Müller now ordered Huppenkothen not to mention the find to the 'circle of comrades' and to award it the classification of Reich top secret at ministerial level.[19]

In the next three weeks Huppenkothn drafted a 160-page report, of which only four copies – one each for Hitler, Himmler, Kaltenbrunner and Müller – were prepared.[20] After reading it, Hitler reserved to himself all further decisions and ordered that the People's Court was not to be informed.[21] Even when Huppenkothen considered the 'work on the treasonous complex'[22] complete, Canaris, Oster, Dohnanyi and other former Abwehr members were not indicted. Presumably the purpose envisaged was to retain the material for possible use in negotiating a separate peace with the West in the future or to stage a show trial against Canaris's group, attributing to it responsibility for a defeat that could not be avoided.[23] The clearest evidence of high treason, the betrayal of the date of the Western offensive, was not suitable as the basis for an indictment[24] because it was not certain that it might not have been 'disinformation' by the Abwehr to deceive the enemy.

In the weeks after the Zossen find, the RSHA dungeons received ever more occupants; on 26 September Josef Müller,[25] on 8 October Dietrich Bonhoeffer, on 11 October General Thomas 'for treasonous activities', and in November Korvettenkapitän Liedig. Friedrich Heinz went into hiding, but his wife and half-brother were taken into custody on racial grounds.[26]

The cells at Prinz-Albrecht-Strasse measured 1.5 x 2.5 metres and were furnished with a folding bed high on the wall, a small table and a stool. Morning and evening prisoners were given a mug of ersatz-coffee, two slices of bread with marmalade, and at midday a soup. At the end of the corridor was a small washroom with cold showers and toilets. There was no exercise yard, but short secret conversations were possible in the showers or in the so-called Himmler

Bunker where the prisoners were taken during the frequent air raids.[27] Day and night they might be brought from their cells and subjected to hours of interrogations in which they were subjected to torture and other brutalities.[28]

Canaris was spared the mistreatment but together with Müller and Oster, and certain other prisoners received only a third of the usual diet. At mealtimes and when visiting the toilet they were required to wear painful handcuffs that had been deliberately roughened inside, and were forced to perform demeaning labour. Alexander von Pfuhlstein, for some time commanding officer of Abwehr Division 'Brandenburg', stated that when he arrived in the Gestapo dungeon he could hardly recognise the prisoners, they looked so harassed and malnourished; especially of Canaris he had the impression that it was intended to soften him up by starvation.[29] Fabian von Schlabrendorff was so badly mistreated that he suffered a heart attack lying in his bloodied clothes in his cell,[30] and Karl Ludwig von und zu Guttenberg, beaten by Sonderegger with fists and a cosh during his first interrogation, considered suicide.[31]

The cries of those being tortured were audible in the cells. When Josef Müller arrived in the dungeons, Canaris warned him during a walk to the washroom that hell awaited him,[32] but instead he received special treatment. Although it was forbidden, Sonderegger allowed him to exchange letters with his wife and receive small food parcels, the contents of which he shared with Oster and Canaris. For the starving Canaris, Müller even left a sausage discreetly in the toilet. Müller was provided by Sonderegger with information about the stage the inquiries had reached and was left alone in the interrogation room with the files, which he was able to 'clean up' by removing certain documents.[33]

After the Zossen discovery the interrogations were intensified. Huppenkothen and Sonderegger were anxious to prove that Canaris was guilty of internal treason and was behind Müller's Vatican activities and the betrayal of the Western offensive. Through Gisevius, Canaris had made contact with the head of the OSS in Berne, Allen Welsh Dulles, and to the Polish Government-in-exile in London.[34]

Canaris knew now that because of the Zossen find, his former strategy of denials no longer served a purpose and he relied henceforth on mainly explaining away his complicity on the grounds of service necessity. Accordingly, he had informed Baron Vladimir Kaulbars, a Russian emigrant whom he had known since the early 1920s,[35] two weeks before the attack on the Soviet Union about Operation Barbarossa, but only because he knew that Kaulbars was an OKW spy.[36] He mentioned the 'clique of conspirators'[37] involved in the 20 July plot, but even here what concerned him most was the search for the best solution for the Reich and his original basic duty of obtaining information.

Huppenkothen and Sonderegger advanced little further in their quest for evidence, for Kaulbars's point of view was that he had frequently voiced his doubts about German policy towards the Soviet Union in reports for the OKW, and had discussed it with Canaris. His ineffectiveness in this regard had led him to offer his resignation on several occasions.[38]

Canaris was at pains to play down his role and represent himself as a secret service professional. At the same time the desperate Dohnanyi was in Sachsenhausen concentration camp trying to buy time in a situation where it was important for others that he did so, remaining faithful to the adage of Eberhard Bethges, 'keep silent by talking and lying'.[39] Meanwhile Oster confessed everything; he explained that *the intention to stage a putsch began with the Fritsch affair*[40] and went on to describe without reservations how the intention had been at first to take out the Reichsführer-SS and Gestapo, but that from the very beginning there was a defeatist attitude to the war. 'Finally he admitted that people were *not in agreement with many National Socialist measures of internal policy*, especially the handling of the *Jewish Question* and the *Church*. The treatment of the Jews and the Poles in occupied Poland was not approved in any case.'[41] Similarly Dohnanyi was quoted in a report at the beginning of December: 'Sonderführer Dohnanyi bases his rejection of National Socialism on the grounds of its having a despotic law and with *the actions of National Socialism in the Jewish and Church Questions.*'[42]

The interrogations of Canaris, Oster and the other Abwehr suspects continued, and at the beginning of February 1945, Canaris whispered to Josef Müller that 'he still did not know what he was being charged with'.[43] On 3 February the prisoners and accused were taken down into the Himmler Bunker and other air-raid shelters. In this devastating American air raid on the city centre of Berlin, the RSHA building was severely damaged and the private Gestapo prison was no longer suitable for its purpose.[44] After the all-clear, Canaris, Josef Müller and Ludwig Gehre had to scrub the prison floors. One of the guards mocked the ex-admiral: 'I say, little sailor, I bet you never thought you would have to scrub floors again.'[45]

Müller reported later in his memoirs the secret dialogue that now developed; Canaris did not react to the persistent verbal abuse of the guard, but whispered to Müller: 'If only he knew what a favour he is doing us!' Then he added quickly: 'Has Dohnanyi given me away?' Müller replied: 'I don't know, are they keeping documents from you?' After he observed that everybody, including the guard, used the informal pronoun 'Du' to him now, Müller asked: 'Have you been thrown out of the Wehrmacht?' Canaris did not know, and Müller said: 'Then you can be content. They are not putting you before the People's Court and you are winning time.'[46]

On 6 February 1945, Gestapo Chief Müller ordered Josef Müller, Bonhoeffer, Gehre, Liedig and others to be transferred to Buchenwald concentration camp.

Canaris, Oster, generals Halder and Thomas, ex-Minister Schacht and the former Austrian Chancellor Schussnigg were driven the following day to Flossenbürg concentration camp in the woods on the Bavarian–Bohemian border.[47] Here they were lodged under 'Kommandantur-Arrest' in a long cell block. On the north side of the brick barrack was an enclosed courtyard with a wooden roof at one end, and a crossways supporting beam equipped with hooks. It was here that most of the executions were carried out, and based on the sketches from memory of the Danish secret service officer Hans Mathiesen Lunding, there was also a place for executions by a shot to the back of the head.

Bound hand and foot, Canaris was locked into Cell 22. Next to him in Cell 21 was Lunding, who had been there since the summer of 1944.[48] The former Danish spy spoke perfect German,[49] having been in the Danish espionage service since 1937, where he had set up a network to spy on Germany. After the occupation of Denmark he gathered information about German units and maintained contacts with MI5 and the British and Polish embassies in Sweden;[50] he had been arrested when the Danish Army was disbanded in August 1943 and on 5 June 1944 was brought to Flossenbürg.[51] Lunding and Canaris had never previously met, but he knew Canaris's face from a photograph and a visit the Abwehr chief had made to Copenhagen. Through a crack in the cell door he could see a portion of the floor and through the window a part of the courtyard with the execution equipment. Lunding learned from an SS guard the identity of the new arrival and set out to establish contact with him. A sympathetic guard allowed him to pass Canaris a note containing a code for tapping the wall, and by this means Lunding became the witness and friend to the Abwehr chief during the final weeks of his life. They communicated almost daily but only once managed to exchange a few words face to face; Lunding reported later on the 'disgusting treatment' meted out to Canaris and the way he endured it.[52]

Perhaps there might have been a possibility for Canaris, Oster, Dohnanyi and others to have survived the approaching defeat of Germany. Dohnanyi was still planning a desperate escape attempt in Berlin at the end of March[53] when another disaster occurred. At the beginning of April 1945, when General Walter Boule was inspecting the underground bunker space allotted to Amt Ausland/ Abwehr at Maybach II, Zossen, he came across an armoured safe that until then had been overlooked, and in it the general found the diaries of Wilhelm Canaris.

Boule sent the five bound volumes and six volumes of trip reports to SS-Brigadeführer Hans Rattenhuber, head of the Reich security service, from where they were forwarded on 4 April either to Gestapo Chief Müller or RSHA Chief Kaltenbrunner. On 5 April Kaltenbrunner showed them to Hitler; after one glance at certain highlighted paragraphs the Führer ordered 'the immediate execution of the conspirators'.[54]

It was the task of Huppenkothen next day, Friday 6 April 1945, to go to Sachsenhausen concentration camp as prosecutor in the military tribunal against Dohnanyi, whom Sonderegger was to bring from the Police Hospital in Berlin to Oranienburg. The same day Huppenkothen was appointed prosecutor in the proceedings against Canaris, Oster, Gehre, Sack and Bonhoeffer for Sunday 8 April at Flossenbürg.[55]

When Sonderegger fetched Dohnanyi from the State hospital, the prisoner was under the influence of a medicinal prescription; the attending physician had given Dohnanyi a high dosage of Luminal early that morning, and it is possible that he had also been given morphine, for a number of tablets were found in his possession. He was brought – asleep or drugged – into the 'trial room' on a stretcher, where the theatre was acted out. There was no defence counsel, for he would have been superfluous, and no stenographer. The farce lasted several hours before Dohnanyi was sentenced to death on the evidence contained in the original Zossen find. The judge dictated the judgment to Huppenkothen's female secretary, and then Huppenkothen returned to Berlin.[56] When Dohnanyi was executed is unknown; his family was not informed.[57]

Huppenkothen arrived at Flossenbürg on 7 April and the trials were held the next day. Chairman of the tribunal was SS Judge Otto Thorbek, assisted by Camp Commandant SS-Obersturmbannführer Max Koegel and another person whose identity was not revealed by Huppenkothen at his own trial after the war. At four in the afternoon General Hans Oster was brought into court. According to Huppenkothen and Thorbek at their own postwar trials, Oster made a clean breast of it and implicated unreservedly all other defendants on the basis of the Zossen files.[58] He was sentenced to death by hanging, the sentence to be carried out the next morning.

Towards eight in the evening Lunding heard the adjacent cell door being opened and the customary noise of the chains being removed from the prisoner's ankles.[59] Huppenkothen recalled that Canaris either denied all accusations or put a favourable gloss on them: 'At the hearing he was very alive and disputed every point of the indictment in order to save his neck. We had great difficulties with him.'[60] When Canaris emphasised over and again that it had been his intention to foil the coup at the last minute, and this was the reason why it appeared he had made common cause with the conspiracy, Judge Thorbek interrupted the hearing and had Oster brought into court. Allegedly Oster contradicted everything in Canaris's defence strategy, swearing that Canaris had been involved in all the activities of the Resistance circle.

Canaris refuted the allegation and maintained that it had all been for appearances, to which Oster responded: 'No, that is not true. I cannot testify other than to what I know, I am not a rogue.' When Canaris, in reply to

Thorbek's enquiry if Oster was lying, gave a resigned 'No', the tribunal had reached its objective. The sentence was death by hanging.[61]

Canaris was returned to his cell towards ten o'clock; Lunding heard the steps, the opening of the cell door and the fitting of the leg chains. Once the cell block was quiet he communicated with Canaris by the knock code, and he was told that it was all over with, and then given the somewhat cryptic information that 'he' had broken his nose, or 'someone' had broken his nose.[62] There is evidence that he received beatings during the hearing,[63] but it is possible he was saying that he had fallen on his nose, meaning everything was lost.[64] Canaris indicated to Lunding that he remained convinced that what he had done was right; he had done nothing wrong, he was not a traitor, and he had done his duty by Germany, and he asked: 'If you survive, pay my respects to my wife.'[65]

Towards six o'clock on the morning of 9 April 1945 Lunding awoke and heard the cell door being opened, followed by the order 'Come with us!' A few moments later came another order: 'Undress!' A little later still Lunding heard the sound of bare feet on the stone floor of the cell block and saw through the crack in the door for a brief second the white skin and grey hair of Canaris. Shortly afterwards the other cell doors were opened and the prisoners called forward.[66] Josef Müller, who expected to be hanged at any moment, remarked that the execution yard had been lit all night with a pale glow, dogs were barking and camp inmates had dragged wooden planks along the path leading to the hilltop past the watchdogs.[67]

Huppenkothen was present as the naked prisoners were led individually to the execution shed. The judgment of the court was read out and then they had to climb to a staging. The hangman placed a noose around the condemned man's neck and then the staging was kicked away from under his feet.[68] The Flossenbürg doctor, SS-Obersturmbannführer Hermann Fischer, said he was 'shaken' to see Bonhoeffer kneeling in prayer in a room near the guardhouse as he awaited his turn to die.

Canaris was the first to go to the gallows. According to Fischer he died 'firm and like a man' and it was all over within seconds. This was possibly untrue; according to Stefanie Lahousen, widow of Erwin Lahousen, who spoke to Lunding after the war, he had noticed that they were preparing a specially long and painful death for Canaris.[69] A few hours later the bodies were brought to the crematorium and burnt on a wood pyre; soon a foul smoke wafted into the cells of the survivors.[70] When Lunding was certain that Canaris was dead, he asked an SS guard if that was how Germany always got rid of its officers. The guard replied: 'He was no officer, he was a traitor.'[71] Never for a moment of his life had Canaris wanted to be that, and he died convinced that he was not.

Notes

Canaris's personal service record exists in the Bundesarchiv-Militärarchiv, Freiburg under reference Pers. 6/105 and 2293 and in photocopy form at the Institut für Zeitgeschichte under reference 1858/56. In these notes it is referred to as Canaris-IfZ.

PART I: OFFICER OF HIS MAJESTY

1 A Naval Cadet from the Ruhr

1 Notification of birth, 3 January 1887 in BA-MA, N 812/1.
2 Gebhardt, Peter von, *Die Canaris*, Leipzig, 1938; and Gebhardt, Peter von, *Die Canaris. 1. Nachtrag: Stammtafeln und Regesten zur Genealogie der Canarisi aus Torno vom 14. bis 16. Jahrhundert*, Leipzig 1939, with a foreword by Wilhelm Canaris; both works are in BA-MA, N 812/46 and 47. See also Ronge, Paul, 'Zur Ahnentafel des Admirals Canaris', in *Genealogie. Deutsche Zeitschrift für Familienkunde*, vol VI, 11/12, pp 33–6. The well-worn legend that over the centuries various branches of the family could trace links to the Greek freedom fighter and statesman Constantin Canaris, or even Napoleon, are all anecdotal, although Canaris would frequently embrace them as true. Abshagen, Karl Heinz, *Canaris – Patriot und Weltbürger*, Stuttgart, 1955, p 25; Höhne, Heinz, *Canaris – Patriot im Zwielicht*, Munich, 1976, pp 15 and 18.
3 Ibid; Herzog, Bodo, 'Der junge Canaris in Duisburg (1892–1905)', in *Die Nachhut* 2, 1972, pp 14–21, BA-MA, MSg 3-22/1, p 16; Höhne, *Canaris*, p 16.
4 Röhl, John C G, *Wilhelm II. Der Aufbau der persönlichen Monarchie 1888–1900*, Munich, 2001, p 1109ff.
5 Ibid, p 1111.
6 Deist, Wilhelm, 'Reichsmarineamt und Flottenverein 1903–1906', in Deist, Wilhelm, *Militär, Staat und Gesellschaft*, Studien zur preußisch-deutschen Militärgeschichte Beiträge zur Militärgeschichte 43, Munich, 1991, pp 57–81.
7 Röhl, *Wilhelm II*, p 1152.
8 Herzog, 'Der junge Canaris', p 15.
9 Ibid, p 18.
10 Ibid, p 15.
11 See Saul, Klaus, 'Dokumentation "Der Kampf um die Jugend zwischen Volksschule und Kaserne. Ein Beitrag zur 'Jugendpflege' im Wilhelminischen Reich 1890–1914"', *Militärgeschichtliche Mitteilungen* 9, 1971, pp 97–143, whose main period of research lies between 1905/6 and 1914 and deals with school-leavers in industry. Contrary to so-called 'Jugendwehren', cadet corps that practised military exercises, bayonet fighting and sniping, the proceedings described were primarily designed as pre-military training for future NCOs by former senior career officers.

12 Herwig, Holger H, 'Soziale Herkunft und wissenschaftliche Vorbildung des Seeoffiziers der Kaiserlichen Marine vor 1914' *Militärgeschichtliche Mitteilungen* 10, 1971, p 89.

13 Ibid, p 86.

14 Höhne, *Canaris*, p 18, reference to Erich Ferdinand Pruck in n 35.

15 Herzog, 'Der junge Canaris', p 17, gives no cause of death: Brissaud, André, *Canaris – Fürst des deutschen Geheimdienstes oder: Meister des Doppelspiels?*, Frankfurt, 1970, p 15, says he died of a stroke: Höhne, *Canaris*, p 21, states that death resulted as the consequence of a heart attack and Abshagen, *Canaris*, p 29, speaks only of a heart condition.

16 Certificate, 16 March 1905, BA-MA, N 812/1, document 6; in this recently opened batch of papers are included originals of most nominations to positions aboard ship, notifications of promotions and decorations, some private and service correspondence, operational orders and war diaries together with files of the Committeee of Inquiry into the 1918 collapse, and photo albums. The originals correspond to microfilm collection NARA, T 84, Roll 491.

17 Herzog, 'Der junge Canaris', p 18; Höhne, *Canaris*, p 21; for the Naval Cadet Acceptance Commission and the costs of training and its function as a social barrier, see Herwig, 'Herkunft', p 85f and 93 with n 70.

18 Herzog, 'Der junge Canaris', p 18.

19 Höhne, *Canaris*, p 21.

20 Persius, Lothar, 'Erinnerungen eines Seeoffiziers II. Als Kadett an Bord der "Niobe"', *Die Weltbühne* 15, 14 April 1925, p 546.

21 Höhne, *Canaris*, p 21.

22 Herzog, 'Der junge Canaris', p 18; Abshagen, *Canaris*, p 31f.

23 Personal service record, Canaris-IfZ, folios 90 and 96.

24 Ibid, folio 90.

25 Höhne, *Canaris*, p 23ff.

26 Canaris-IfZ, folio 90f.

27 Höhne, *Canaris*, p 25.

28 Service certificate, New York, 10 June 1908 (written over 'SMS Dresden 20.11.1907' reason for alteration indecipherable), Canaris-IfZ, folio 2.

29 On occasion of changing commanders, Punta Arenas, 12 December 1908, signed Alberts, service record, Canaris-IfZ, folio 3.

30 Canaris-IfZ, folio 90.

31 Assessment report to 1 November 1909, ibid, folio 4.

32 Hopman, Albert, *Das Logbuch eines deutschen Seeoffiziers*, Berlin 1924, p 330f.

33 Assessment report to 1 November 1909, Canaris-IfZ, folio 4.

34 Diary, Albert Hopman, BA-MA, N 326/5, quoted in Höhne, *Canaris*, p 26.

35 Hopman, diary, p 336.

36 Ibid, p 338f.

37 Original of notification of award at BA-MA, 812/9; the decoration is mentioned in the personal file twice, 23 May 1909, folio 97 is crossed through. A further stay in Venezuela in May as suggested by Hopman is not possible. Höhne, *Canaris*, p 26, is equally vague as to the circumstances of the award. A connection with a naval blockade of Venezuela, as Britain, Italy and Germany had imposed in 1902 to force Venezuela to acknowledge its debts, did not exist at this time; had it done so the

European expedition would have led to confrontation with the United States as a breach of the Monroe doctrine. Heideking, Jürgen, *Geschichte der USA*, Tübingen/ Basel 2003, p 239.

38 Hopman, diary, pp 339–42.

39 Assessment report to 1 November 1909, Canaris-IfZ, folio 4.

40 Hopman, diary, p 355.

41 Handwritten assessments, 15 April 1910 and 3 September 1910, Canaris-IfZ, folio 5f; assessment report 1 December 1911, ibid, folio 11; personal sheet, ibid, folio 90f.

42 Naval medical certificate, 15 January 1924, ibid, folio 80.

43 Personal sheet, ibid, folio 90; certificate as mining officer, ibid, folio 7.

44 Assessment report to 1 December 1913, ibid, folio 11. The assessment report for December 1912 is absent, but it is obvious from the later one that Canaris had already held the position for two years at the end of 1913.

45 Parker de Bassi, Maria Teresia, *Kreuzer Dresden. Odyssee ohne Wiederkehr*, Herford, 1993, p 16. The author interviewed the last surviving members of *Dresden* and was allowed access to private papers. Unfortunately she does not indicate what information comes from whom. As her account is otherwise very painstaking and reliable, I have used it, especially where contemporary witnesses or sources are rare or non-existent. This applies particularly to details of the *Dresden* mission in the Mediterranean and for various conversations involving Canaris that are reported only in this source and are included where relevant and plausible in the context

46 Ibid, p 17.

47 Abshagen, *Canaris*, p 34; also Höhne, *Canaris*, p 27.

48 Schneider, Heinrich, *Die letzte Fahrt des Kleinen Kreuzers Dresden*, Berlin/Leipzig, 1926, p 15.

49 Parker de Bassi, *Kreuzer Dresden*, p 29.

50 Schneider, *Letzte Fahrt*, pp 16–18; Parker de Bassi, *Kreuzer Dresden*, p 28ff.

51 Ibid, p 36f.

52 Schneider, *Letzte Fahrt*, p 16ff; Parker de Bassi, *Kreuzer Dresden*, p 40ff. The dates differ in the two accounts.

53 Copy of letter, Konsul Otto to Reich Chancellor Bethmann Hollweg, 25 July 1914, BA-MA, RM 5/2228, folio 207; Parker de Bassi, *Kreuzer Dresden*, p 42.

54 Raeder, Erich (ed.), *Der Kreuzerkrieg in den ausländischen Gewässern. Vol I: Das Kreuzergeschwader*, Berlin 1927 (*Der Krieg zur See 1914–1918*, published by the Marine-Archiv, Berlin, 1920 ff), p 370f. This work, which describes the naval war between 1914 and 1918, has an English companion: *History of the Great War. Based on Official Documents by Direction of the Historical Section of the Committee of Imperial Defence*, London 1920 ff. The volumes used here are Corbett, Julian S., *Naval Operations:* vol I, *To the Battle of the Falklands*, London, 1920 and vol II, London, 1921.

2 *The Epic Last Voyage of the* Dresden

1 Raeder, *Kreuzerkrieg*, p 371.

2 Parker de Bassi, *Kreuzer Dresden*, p 47.

3 Raeder, *Kreuzerkrieg*, p 372.

4   Parker de Bassi, *Kreuzer Dresden*, p 48.

5   Raeder, *Kreuzerkrieg*, p 371f; Parker de Bassi, *Kreuzer Dresden*, p 50f.

6   Höhne, *Canaris*, p 30.

7   Parker de Bassi, *Kreuzer Dresden*, p 61.

8   For morale aboard *Dresden* see the memoir of former Unteroffizier Heinrich Schneider, *Die letzte Fahrt*, p 37.

9   Raeder, *Kreuzerkrieg*, p 374.

10 Ibid and Höhne, *Canaris*, p 29.

11 Raeder, *Kreuzerkrieg*, p 374. Obituary of Julius Fetzer in *Die Nachhut* 3, 1968, p 24, BA-MA, MSg 3-22/1.

12 Parker de Bassi, *Kreuzer Dresden*, p 65.

13 Ibid, p 67.

14 Raeder, *Kreuzerkrieg*, p 380.

15 Parker de Bassi, *Kleiner Kreuzer*, pp 80 and 128f.

16 Ibid and Raeder, *Kreuzerkrieg*, p 147f.

17 Parker de Bassi: *Kreuzer Dresden*, p 112.

18 Raeder, *Kreuzerkrieg*, p 388; Parker de Bassi, *Kreuzer Dresden*, pp 115–22; Schneider, *Die letzte Fahrt*, p 59ff.

19 Raeder, *Kreuzerkrieg*, p 147.

20 Parker de Bassi, *Kreuzer Dresden*, p 130.

21 Raeder, *Kreuzerkrieg*, p 197; Parker de Bassi, *Kreuzer Dresden*, p 130ff.

22 Ibid, p 135; for a detailed account from the British perspective, see Bennett, Geoffrey, *Die Seeschlachten von Coronel und Falkland und der Untergang des deutschen Kreuzergeschwaders unter Admiral Graf Spee*, Munich, 1980, p 27ff.

23 Raeder, *Kreuzerkrieg*, p198. For an account of the battle see pp 207–13, and Parker de Bassi, *Kreuzer Dresden*, p 137–43. For an eyewitness account, see Schneider, *Die letzte Fahrt*, p 67–74.

24 Raeder, *Kreuzerkrieg*, p 218.

25 Abshagen, *Canaris*, p 36. This letter and another of 12 November mentioned by Abshagen appear to have been in his private possession.

26 Parker de Bassi, *Kreuzer Dresden*, p 152.

27 *Translator's note:* This single sentence covers a whole month of activity. Between 6 and 15 November, the squadron coaled and refitted at Mas Afuera Island several hundred miles west of Valparaiso. On 12 November, when *Dresden* and *Leipzig* visited Valparaiso for intelligence and diplomatic purposes, Canaris went ashore with his commander. In cables from Berlin, which they brought back for the admiral, von Spee was allegedly asked what his intentions were. No documents relating to his decisions and activities over this last month of his life have ever been discovered in the German archives. Delayed by heavy weather, on 21 November the squadron put next into the secluded Bay of San Quintin in the Gulf of Penas on the southern coast of mainland Chile, where they recoaled and shipped supplies from three freighters of the German-run Kosmos Line. Here the final preparations were made for the assault on the Falkland Islands.

28 Parker de Bassi, *Kreuzer Dresden*, p 186.

29 Raeder, *Kreuzerkrieg*, p 273.

30 Bennett, *Die Seeschlachten*, p 144f; Parker de Bassi, *Kreuzer Dresden*, p 189.

31 Ibid, p 190.

32 For the exact course of the battle see the detailed accounts and analyses from the various perspectives in: Raeder, *Kreuzerkrieg*, p 269–341; Corbett, *Naval Operations*, vol I, p 414–36 and Bennett, *Die Seeschlachten*, p 166–200.

33 Parker de Bassi, *Kreuzer Dresden*, p 195f.
Translator's Note: In the absence of any official German documents, it is clear from the disposition of the German squadron that the intention was to invade, occupy and fortify the Falklands. A hit-and-run raid on islands believed undefended would have required no more than one or two small cruisers, as had been Admiral Spee's practice in the preceding four months in the Pacific. From Admiral Sturdee's Despatch (*London Gazette* 29087, 3 March 1915) it is known that the auxiliaries *Baden*, *Santa Isabel* and *Seydlitz* must have arrived during the night of 7 December and hidden up inshore at Port Pleasant. Next morning, once the five German cruisers were being pursued in perfect visibility, the cruiser *Bristol* and AMC *Macedonia* saw the three German auxiliaries 'which at first sight seemed to be probably colliers or transports' according to Captain J D Allen of HMS *Kent*, emerge from inshore at 1127hrs. *Seydlitz* fled south-west and arrived safely at San Antonio Oeste in Argentina to be immediately interned as an auxiliary warship. *Baden* and *Santa Isabel* headed east and were captured at about 1400hrs. The crews were given ten minutes to abandon ship before the British examined and sank them. If this operation involved a planned invasion and occupation of the Falklands, Canaris was certain to have known about it by reason of his closeness to the naval espionage organisation ashore.

34 Raeder, *Kreuzerkrieg*, p 390; Schneider, *Die letzte Fahrt*, p 117; Höhne, *Canaris*, p 36; Parker de Bassi, *Kreuzer Dresden*, p 205f.

35 Raeder, *Kreuzerkrieg*, p 390; Parker de Bassi, *Kreuzer Dresden*, p 208f.

36 Corbett, *Naval Operations*, vol I, p 435f and vol II, p. 241–4.

37 Parker de Bassi, *Kreuzer Dresden*, p 211.

38 BA-MA, 5/2228; Raeder, *Kreuzerkrieg*, p 395.

39 Ibid, p 396.

40 Telegram, Admiralty staff to naval attaché Buenos Aires, BA-MA, RM 5/2228, folio 33.

41 Telegram, Stockholm naval attaché to Admiralty Staff, BA-MA, RM 5/2228, folio 48.

42 Schneider, *Die letzte Fahrt*, p 128.

43 Raeder, *Kreuzerkrieg*, p 399.

44 Schneider, *Die letzte Fahrt*, p 130; Raeder, *Kreuzerkrieg*, p 400; Parker de Bassi, *Kreuzer Dresden*, p 239.

45 Log HMS *Kent*, NA, ADM 53/45610.

46 Parker de Bassi, *Kreuzer Dresden*, p 241.

47 Raeder, *Kreuzerkrieg*, p 401; Parker de Bassi, *Kreuzer Dresden*, p 241.

48 Radio log HMS *Glasgow*, NA, ADM 137/4802; Ship's log HMS *Kent*, NA, ADM 53/45610.

49 Raeder, *Kreuzerkrieg*, p 401; Parker de Bassi. *Kreuzer Dresden*, p 242.

50 Raeder, *Kreuzerkrieg*, p 402; see also correspondence, British Legation, Santiago at NA, FO 132/139 and German letters intercepted by British intelligence at NA, ADM 137/4159.

51 Parker de Bassi, *Kreuzer Dresden*, p 244.

52 Raeder, *Kreuzerkrieg*, p 403ff; Parker de Bassi, *Kreuzer Dresden*, p 246ff; Schneider, *Die letzte Fahrt*, p 133ff; Höhne, *Canaris*, p 12f.

53 Schneider, *Die letzte Fahrt*, p 132; the logs of the three British warships contain different details as to the time of the attack and the sinking of *Dresden*: NA, ADM 53/42828 (*Glasgow*), ADM 53/45610 (*Kent*), ADM 53/53455 (*Orama*); Raeder gives the time of the attack as 0850hrs, Raeder, *Kreuzerkrieg*, p 403.

54 For the action see report of Lüdecke, Juan Fernandez, 15 March 1915, to Chief of Admiralty Staff, BA-MA, RM 5/2228, folios 156–9.

55 Raeder, *Kreuzerkrieg*, p 406f.

56 Telegram, Stockholm to Foreign Office, naval attaché to Admiralty Staff, 16 March 1915, BA-MA, RW 5/2228, folio 71.

57 Ibid. The two semi-official histories of the naval war differ in their evaluation of the incident. There can be no doubt that the attack by the British warships was a serious breach of Chile's neutrality. See Corbett, *Naval Operations*, Vol II, p 249f, which emphasises the British point of view that *Dresden* had committeed numerous infringements of Chilean neutrality. This had been tolerated by Chile and the cruiser should have been interned, something which Chile had not been in a position to accomplish. For the German view see Raeder, *Kreuzerkrieg*, p 407f.

58 Letter, British envoy Francis Strong to Chilean Foreign Minister Alexander Lira, 8 March 1915, NA, FO 132/139.

59 Raeder, *Kreuzerkrieg*, p 406.

60 Ibid, p 407; Schneider, *Die letzte Fahrt*, p 139.

3 Agent on a Special Mission

1 Parker de Bassi, *Kreuzer Dresden*, p 253.

2 Ibid, p 57.

3 Report, Honorary Consul Milward, Punta Arenas, to Consul-General Maclean, Valparaiso, 19 March 1915, NA, FO 132/142, and letter, British envoy Francis Strong to Chilean Foreign Minister Alexander Lira, 8 March 1915, NA, FO 132/139.

4 Parker de Bassi, *Kreuzer Dresden*, p 261.

5 Report, Erckert, visit to Quiriquina, Santiago, 28 July 1915, BA-MA, RM 5/2228, folios 249–652.

6 Christensen, C P, *Letzte Kaperfahrt nach Quirinquina*, Berlin, 1936, p 213. The Danish novelist recounts the experiences of Stoker Stöckler from the latter's personal story.

7 The flight of three officers and an auxiliary surgeon put ashore by Lüdecke before the sinking of *Dresden* was very awkward for the Chilean government, which attempted to conceal it from the British. Originally the authorities assumed that the former had absconded from Quiriquina, an error later clarified: see reports of Imperial German Legation, Santiago, 22 June 1915, BA-MA, RM 5/2228, folio 238 and 1 July 1915, ibid, folio 245.

8 In fact similar action was taken after Canaris's escape. See letter from German envoy Erckert to Chilean Foreign Minister Lira, 28 September 1915 and his letter to Reich Chancellor Bethmann Hollweg, 9 October 1915, BA-MA, RM 5/2228, folio 286–8.

9   Abshagen, *Canaris*, p 39f; Brissaud, *Canaris*, p 17; Richard Bassett, *Hitler's Spy Chief. The Wilhelm Canaris Mystery*, London, 2005, p 142.

10 Abshagen, *Canaris*, p 40; Basset *Hitler's Spy Chief*, p 42.

11 File note Admiralty Staff, 5 October 1915, BA-MA, RM 5/2228, folio 247.

12 Abshagen, *Canaris*, p 39.

13 Canaris-IfZ, folio 92.

14 Madrid Naval Messages, vol III, 25 December–31 January 1916: German Embassy Madrid, Telegram 30, 4 January 1916, NA, ADM 223/641.

15 'Ein König im Netz', *Die Weltbühne*, 10 January 1928.

16 Papeleux, Léon, *L'Admiral Canaris entre Franco et Hitler. Le rôle de Canaris dans les relations germano-espagnoles (1915–1944)*, Brussels, 1977, p 31. Papeleux quotes a report by Canaris of 18 October 1916 on the political situation in Spain.

17 'Ein König im Netz', *Die Weltbühne*, 10 January 1928, pp 53–7.

18 Abshagen, *Canaris*, p 41.

19 'Ein König im Netz', *Die Weltbühne*, 10 January 1928, pp 53–7.

20 Abshagen, *Canaris*, p 43.

21 Madrid Naval Messages, vol III–VI, 25 December 1915–8 May 1916, NA, ADM 223/641-644. See: Derencin, Robert, 'Secret Naval Supply System of the German Imperial Navy in WWI', available at www.uboat.net/articles, 2 April 2005.

22 Madrid Naval Messages, vol III, 25 December 1915–31 January 1916: German Embassy Madrid, Telegram 41, 5 January 1916, NA, ADM 223/641.

23 Ibid, Madrid, Telegram 214, 29 January 1916, NA, ADM 223/641.

24 Ibid, Madrid, Telegram 161, 21 January 1916, NA, ADM 223/641.

25 Ibid, Admiralty Staff Berlin, Telegram 37, 26 January 1916, NA, ADM 223/641.

26 Ibid, Madrid, Telegram 198, 27 January 1916, NA, ADM 223/641.

27 Ibid, Admiralty Staff Berlin, Telegram 47, 29 January 1916, and Madrid, Telegram 232, 31 January 1916, NA, ADM 223/641.

28 Naval medical certificate, 15 January 1924, in Canaris-IfZ, folio 80.

29 Madrid Naval Messages, vol IV, 1–29 February 1916: German Embassy Madrid, Telegram 420, 20 February 1916, NA, ADM 223/642. Madrid warned that Canaris had to be issued without fail with a new passport in Zurich so that the old one should not be rendered worthless by German entry visas. In the telegram a 'new' passport is spoken of confusingly.

30 Madrid Naval Messages, vol V, 1–29 March 1916: Embassy Madrid, Telegram 108, 29 February 1916, NA, ADM 223/643.

31 Letter from Chief of the Admiralty Staff, 3 March 1916, in Canaris-IfZ, folio 61.

32 Madrid Naval Messages, vol V, 1–29 March 1916: Embassy Madrid, Telegram 656, 19 March 1916, NA, ADM 223/643. Even this 'escape' from Italian custody was embellished as if it were a novel. Canaris was put aboard ship with a fellow prisoner, a priest, for Cartagena, with a prior call at Marseilles. The Italians informed the French so that they could capture him. When Canaris boldly revealed his true identity to the ship's captain, the latter took Canaris under his protection and sailed to Spain direct. See Abshagen, *Canaris*, p 47; Brissaud, *Canaris*, p 21. There is no proof of this tempting story.

33 Naval medical certificate 15 January 1924, in Canaris-IfZ, folio 80.3.

34 Madrid Naval Messages, vol V, 1–29 March 1916: Admiralty Staff Berlin, Telegram 147, 22 March 1916, NA, ADM 223/643.

35 Ibid, Admiralty Staff Berlin, Telegram 52, 24 March 1916, NA, ADM 223/643.
36 Madrid Naval Messages, vol VI, 30 March–8 May 1916: Embassy Madrid Telegram 970, 28 April 1916, NA, ADM 223/644.
37 Ibid, Admiralty Staff Berlin, Telegram 242, 1 May 1916, NA, ADM 223/644.
38 Ibid, Embassy Madrid Telegram 992, 2 May 1916, NA, ADM 223/644.
39 Ibid, Embassy Madrid Telegram 1005, 4 May 1916, NA, ADM 223/644.
40 Ibid, Admiralty Staff Berlin, Telegram 258, 6 May 1916, NA, ADM 223/644.
41 Report on visit of U-35 to Cartagena, NA, ADM 1/8461 52ff.
42 Bassett, *Hitler's Spy Chief*, pp 54ff. Bassett's assertions are to be treated with caution. According to him, Canaris took eight months to get home from Chile, went first to Spain in the spring of 1916 and did not return to Germany for the first time until 1917.
43 Herzog, Bodo, 'Canaris wird am 1. Oktober 1916 aus Spanien abgeholt', *Die Nachhut* 1, 1973, p 21, BA-MA, MSg 3-22/1.
44 KTB U 35, Appendix 1, BA-MA, RM 97/766.
45 KTB U 35, 14 September–9 October 1916, BA-MA, RM 97/766.
46 KTB U 35, Appendix 1, BA-MA, RM 97/766.
47 KTB U 35, Appendix 2 BA-MA, RM 97/766.
48 KTB U 35, Appendix 1: BA-MA, RM 97/766.
49 KTB U 35, Appendix 2: BA-MA, RM 97/766.
50 Ibid.
51 Ibid.
52 Letter, Admiralty Staff to Naval Station Baltic, 20 October 1916, Canaris-IfZ, folio 70.
53 Canaris-IfZ, ibid, folio 96.

4 U-Boat War in the Mediterranean

1 Wehler, Hans-Ulrich, *Deutsche Gesellschaftsgeschichte 1914–1949*, Munich, 2003, p 144f.
2 Keegan, John, *Der Erste Weltkrieg. Eine europäische Tragödie*, Reinbek, 2000, p 488.
3 Wehler, *Gesellschaftsgeschichte*, p 145.
4 Letter from Head, U-boat School, Korvettenkapitän Eschenburg, 11 September 1917, Canaris-IfZ, folio 12.
5 Undated file note of CO, I. U-Boot-Flottille Mittelmeer, Canaris-IfZ, folio 15.
6 War diary, Kreigstagebuch (KTB), UC 27, BA-MA, RM 97/1785, folio. 8.
7 Ibid, folio 9.
8 Ibid, folio 10.
9 Ibid, folio 15.
10 Undated file note of CO, I. U-Boot-Flottille Mittelmeer, Canaris-IfZ, folio 15.
11 Assessment report, 25 January 1918, KTB, UC 27, BA-MA, RM 97/1785, folio 18.
12 KTB, U 34, BA-MA, RM 97/753, folio. 21; for this second war patrol see also Herzog, Bodo, 'Kapitänleutnant Canaris als U-Boot-Kommandant: Kritische Situation im Geleitzug!', *Die Nachhut*, 3, 1972, p 11, BA-MA, MSg 3-22/1.
13 KTB, U 34, BA-MA, RM 97/753, folio 26.
14 Ibid, folio 27.

15 Ibid, folio 28.
16 Ibid, folio 29.
17 Undated file note of CO, I. U-Boot-Flottille Mittelmeer, Canaris-IfZ, folio 15.
18 Letter, Canaris to his mother, Cattaro, 20 February 1918, BA-MA, N 812/41.
19 Ibid.
20 Also Wehler, *Gesellschaftsgeschichte*, p 151f; Keegan, *Der Erste Weltkrieg*, p 532ff.
21 Letter, Canaris to his mother, Cattaro, 20 February 1918, BA-MA, N 812/41.
22 His brother Carl wrote on 22 February 1918 a worried letter of enquiry, having received no further news after Canaris sailed from Cattaro, BA-MA, N 812/41.
23 His ruthless demands upon himself and the danger of mental and physical over-exertion are reflected over the years in the various assessment reports in his personal file: see Canaris-IfZ, especially personal letter from CO, Naval Station Baltic, Freiherr von Gagern to Canaris, 6 February 1924, ibid, folios 104–8.
24 Deist, Wilhelm, 'Die Politik der Seekriegsleitung und die Rebellion der Flotte Ende Oktober 1918', *Vierteljahrshefte für Zeitgeschichte* 14, 1966, p 343.
25 File note, U-boat Acceptance Commission (UAK), Korvettenkapitän Schaper, 1 August 1918, Canaris-IfZ, folio 15.
26 Canaris, handwritten memorandum, 4 August 1918, BA-MA, N 812/41, p 1f.
27 Ibid, p 5. and KTB, UB 128, BA-MA, RM 97/1648, folio 16.
28 File note, UAK, Korvettenkapitän Schaper, 1 August 1918, p 6.
29 KTB, UB 128, BA-MA, RM 97/1648, folio 16f.
30 File note, UAK, Korvettenkapitän Schaper, 1 August 1918, p 7.
31 Ibid, p 9.
32 Ibid, p10.
33 KTB, UB 128, BA-MA, RM 97/1648, folio 19.
34 Canaris, handwritten memorandum, 4 August 1918, BA-MA, N 812/41, p 11.
35 Ibid, p 18f.
36 Ibid, p 19. Here Canaris's personal notes tail off. The events of the voyage after this are to be reconstructed only from the entries in the war diary.
37 KTB, UB 128, BA-MA, RM 97/1648, folio 23.
38 Ibid, folio 32, and opinion of I. U-Bootflottille Mittelmeer, 12 September 1918, ibid, folio 13.
39 Copy letter to Carl Canaris, 3 September 1918, BA-MA, N 812/41.
40 Niemöller, Martin, *Vom U-Boot zur Kanzel*, Berlin, 1934, p 133.
41 Deist, Wilhelm, 'Die Unruhen in der Marine 1917/18', *Marinerundschau* 68, 1971, pp 325–43, here from reprint in Deist, Wilhelm, *Militär, Staat und Gesellschaft. Studien zur preußisch-deutschen Militärgeschichte*, Munich 1991, p 182.
42 Niemöller, *Vom U-Boot zur Kanzel*, p 133.
43 KTB, UB 128, BA-MA, RM 97/1648, folio 46.
44 Ibid, folio 48.
45 Ibid, folio 49.
46 Ibid.
47 Ibid, folio 50.
48 Hopman, Albert, *Das ereignisreiche Leben eines 'Wilhelminers' – Tagebücher, Briefe, Aufzeichnungen 1901 bis 1920, herausgegeben von Michael Epkenhans'*, Schriftenreihe des Militärgeschichtlichen Forschungsamtes, vol 62, Munich, 2004, p 1140 with note 121.

49   As to the origins, personality and evaluation of Groener, see Hürter, Johannes, *Wilhelm Groener. Reichswehrminister am Ende der Weimarer Republik (1928–1932), Schriftenreihe des Militärgeschichtlichen Forschungsamtes, Vol 39*, Munich, 1993, quoted at p 17; for Groener's involvement in the transition from Kaiserreich to democracy see: Rakenius, Gerhard W, *Wilhelm Groener als Erster Generalquartiermeister. Die Politik der Obersten Heeresleitung 1918/19*, Wehrwissenschaftliche Forschungen, Abteilung Militärgeschichtliche Studien, vol 23, Boppard, 1977.

50   Wette, Wolfram, *Gustav Noske. Eine politische Biographie*, Düsseldorf, 1987, p 244.

51   Ibid, p 51.

52   Letter, Admiralty Staff to industrial director Dr Canaris, 19 November 1918, BA-MA, N 812/41.

53   Letter-telegram Admiralty Staff to Herrn Canaris, 27 November 1918, BA-MA, N 812/41.

54   Niemöller, *Vom U-Boot zur Kanzel*, p. 139.

55   Ibid, p 140.

PART II: THE STRUGGLE AGAINST THE REPUBLIC

5 Servant of Two Masters

1   KTB, UB-128, entry dated 29 November 1918, BA-MA, RM 97/1648, folio 54.

2   Noske, Gustav, *Von Kiel bis Kapp. Zur Geschichte der deutschen Revolution*, Berlin, 1920, p 45.

3   KTB, UB-128, entry dated 29 November 1918, BA-MA, RM 97/1648, folio 54.

4   Noske, *Von Kiel bis Kapp*, pp 45 and 46.

5   Wette, *Noske*, p 250.

6   Niemöller, *Vom U-Boot zur Kanzel*, p 140f. See also Wette, *Noske*, p 250 with notes 255 and 261.

7   Wette, Wolfram, 'Noske-Ära: Die vertane Chance mit dem preußisch-deutschen Nationalismus zu brechen', in Butenschön, Rainer, and Spoo, Eckart, *Wozu muß einer der Bluthund sein? Der Mehrheitssozialdemokrat Gustav Noske und der deutsche Militarismus des 20. Jahrhunderts*, Heilbronn, 1997, p 27. This volume combines criticism of Noske. Wette's contribution assembles the research of his Noske biography.

8   Wette, *Noske*, p 246.

9   Noske, *Von Kiel bis Kapp*, p 52.

10   Wette, *Noske*, pp 235–43. For the creation and role of the naval brigades generally, and for their part in the Kapp *putsch*, see Dülffer, Jost, 'Die Reichs- und Kriegsmarine 1918–1939', in *Handbuch zur deutschen Militärgeschichte 1648–1939, Abschnitt VIII, Deutsche Marinegeschichte in der Neuzeit*, Militärgeschichtlichen Forschungsamt, Munich, 1977, pp 337–488, especially pp 347–53 and pp 361–8; Bird, Keith W, *Weimar, The German Naval Officer Corps and the Rise of National Socialism*, Amsterdam, 1977, pp 40–82 and pp 107–168; Forstmeier, Friedrich, 'Zur Rolle der Marine im Kapp-Putsch', in *Seemacht und Geschichte. Festschrift zum 80. Geburtstag von Friedrich Ruge*, Bonn, 1975, pp 51–80.

11   Canaris PSR, folio 92.
12   Memoir, Wilfried von Loewenfeld (1934), 'Wie die 3. (Freiwillige) Marinebrigade von Loewenfeld erstand', BA-MA, RM 122/116, folios 107–33.
13   Ibid, folio 109.
14   For the 3rd Naval Brigade Loewenfeld described herein see principally Loewenfeld's reports in BA-MA, RM 122/116 and RM 8/1013: also Wette, *Noske*, pp 243–55; Dülffer, 'Die Reichs- und Kriegsmarine', p 352f; Bird, *The German Naval Officer Corps*, pp 44–8; Forstmeier, 'Zur Rolle der Marine im Kapp-Putsch', pp 51–80.
15   Loewenfeld report: 'Wie die 3. Marinebrigade von Loewenfeld erstand', BA-MA, RM 122/116, folio 110.
16   For Loewenfeld's collaborators see ibid, folio 111; report, Admiral Siegfried Sorge, IfZ, ZS 1785; Wette, *Noske*, p 249f; Bird, *The German Naval Officer Corps*, p 46, n 30.
17   Loewenfeld report, BA-MA, RM 122/116, folio 115.
18   Wette, *Noske*, p 251.
19   Gietinger, Klaus, *Eine Leiche im Landwehrkanal. Die Ermordung der Rosa L.*, Berlin, 1919, p 16f, and ibid, p 142: Annexe, Document III: 'Gedächtnisprotokoll eines zweiten Gesprächs mit Major a.D. Waldemar Pabst' (v. 3 May 1966).
20   Letter, Noske to Austrian Federal Chancellor Seipel, 10 October 1928, BA-SAPMO NL 56/7, in: Gietinger, *Eine Leiche*, p 17.
21   See letter Pabst to SDR editor Dieter Ertel, 30 May 1967, in Gietinger, *Eine Leiche*, Annexe, Document VI, p 150 and ibid, protocol, Annexe, Document II, p 139.
22   Loewenfeld report, BA-MA, RM 122/116, folio 115.
23   Ibid, folio 116f.
24   Ibid, folio 115.
25   Wette, *Noske*, p 252.
26   Here and subseqently, see: Dülffer, 'Die Reichs- und Kriegsmarine', p 346f.
27   For the 'Christmas fighting' see the accounts in Winkler, Heinrich August, *Weimar 1918–1933. Die Geschichte der ersten deutschen Demokratie*, Munich, 1998, p 53f; Mommsen, Hans, *Aufstieg und Untergang der Republik von Weimar*, Munich, 2001, p 53f; Rakenius, *Wilhelm Groener*, p 149f.
28   Pabst's report of 25 December 1918, BA-MA, N 620/2, and Gietinger, *Eine Leiche*, pp 19 and 118, n 35.
29   *Die Regierung der Volksbeauftragten 1918/19*, Düsseldorf, 1969, 2 vols, also published as *Quellen zur Geschichte des Parlamentarismus und der politischen Parteien*, edited by Werner Conze and Erich Matthias, 1st edition, vol 6, parts I and II, part II, p 31, Document 70b.
30   Winkler, *Weimar*, p 54; even Noske, who was not present, describes how great numbers of people streamed out of the factories, and the attacking troops, on the verge of victory, laid down their arms and joined the tail of the procession: Noske, Gustav, *Erlebtes aus Aufstieg und Niedergang einer Demokratie*, Offenbach, 1947, p 82.
31   Noske's reflections on Ebert 1925, from Wette, *Noske*, p 284.
32   Noske, *Von Kiel bis Kapp*, p 63.
33   Böhm, Gustav, *Aufzeichnungen des Hauptmanns Gustav Böhm, hrsg. und bearbeitet von Heinz Hürten und Georg Meyer*, Stuttgart, 1977, quoted in Wette, *Noske*, p 285. The description of the crisis session, dismissed in a few lines in Noske's memoir of the

Revolution, is based on Wette, who draws on the notes of Böhm. Cf Wette, *Noske*, p 284 with n 107.

34 Noske, *Erlebtes*, p 82. Rudolf Wissel confirmed later that Noske had actually said he was indispensable at Kiel, but nobody was listening, see Wette, *Noske*, p 285, n 113.

35 Noske, *Von Kiel bis Kapp*, p 63.

36 Wette, *Noske*, p 287.

37 Noske, *Erlebtes*, p 83.

38 Gietinger, *Eine Leiche*, statement from memory, Annexe, Document II, p 139. See also 'Ich ließ Rosa Luxemburg richten', *Spiegel* interview with Waldemar Pabst, *Der Spiegel* 16, 1962, p 38.

39 Ibid.

40 Winkler, *Weimar*, p 56.

41 Heinrich August Winkler, p 55f, puts forward the view that the term 'Spartacus Revolt' is not apt since the KPD leaders had neither planned for nor demanded the overthrow of the government. Liebknecht (swiftly) and Luxemburg (later) bowed to the pressure of the masses. Similarly Wette, *Noske*, p 299, who sees the founding of a revolutionary committeee on the evening of 5 January as an 'act of retrospective solidarity with the occupiers of the newspaper district'.

42 Wette, *Noske*, p 299.

43 Noske, *Von Kiel bis Kapp*, p 66.

44 Winkler, *Weimar*, p 57.

45 Quotation in Noske, *Von Kiel bis Kapp*, p 68. For the discussion see Butenschön and Spoo, *Bluthund*, and for the self-styling of Noske especially, Buckmiller, Michael, 'Nachdenken über Funktion und Rollenverständnis eines "Bluthundes"', in ibid, pp 54–66.

46 Cf Wette, *Noske*, p 301.

47 Noske, *Von Kiel bis Kapp*, p 72.

48 'Ich ließ Rosa Luxemburg richten', *Der Spiegel* 16, 1962, p 39.

49 Wette, *Noske*, p 241. For this description Wette refers to the official history of the Deck Officers' Federation, *Deckoffiziere der deutschen Marine. Ihre Geschichte 1848–1933*, published by Bund der Deckoffiziere, Berlin, 1933. Rather different is the version in Höhne, *Canaris*, p 63, in which the first leader of the Naval Brigade, Kapitän zur See Bruno von Roehr, who led it to Berlin on 9 January 1919 and was obliged to hand over command to Army officer Hans von Roden next day, had personally offered Noske the help of the Iron Brigade on 3 January. Höhne follows the account in *Die Wirren in der Reichshauptstadt und im nördlichen Deutschland 1918–1920*, Berlin 1940 (= *Darstellungen aus den Nachkriegskämpfen deutscher Truppen und Freikorps*, Vol 6, published by the Army Kriegsgeschichtliche Forschungsanstalt).

50 Bericht Loewenfeld, 'Wie die 3. (Freiwillige) Marinebrigade von Loewenfeld erstand', BA-MA, RM 122/116, folio 116f.

51 Ibid, folio 129–32.

52 Report by Fregattenkapitän von Loewenfeld on the 3 Marinebrigade (von Loewenfeld), its founding and activity to disbandment, BA-MA, RM 8/1013, folio 42a. Cf also Wette, *Noske*, p 252.

53 Noske, *Von Kiel bis Kapp*, p 72; Wette, *Noske*, p 242.

54 Noske, *Von Kiel bis Kapp*, p 74.

55 Winkler, *Weimar*, p 59; Wette, *Noske*, p 305.

6 The Murderers' Helpers' Helper

1 Hannover-Drück, Elisabeth, and Hannover, Heinrich, *Der Mord an Rosa Luxemburg und Karl Liebknecht – Dokumentation eines politischen Verbrechens*, Frankfurt am Main, 1967, p 29.

2 Gietinger, *Eine Leiche*, pp 28–32, and Annexe, Document IV, p 146, provides the most extensive description and reconstruction of the events of that day.

3 Ibid, Annexe, Document IV, p 146.

4 Extracts from Pabst's interrogation during the main trial before the field-court of the Garde-Kavallerie-Schützen-Division, 8–14 May 1919, reproduced in Hannover-Drück and Hannover, *Der Mord*, p 162f. For the events in and around the Hotel Eden also: Gietinger, *Eine Leiche*, pp 32–7.

5 File note, Günter Nollau, 1 December 1959, regarding a conversation with Waldemar Pabst on 19 November 1959, extracts reproduced in *Der Spiegel* 1, 1970, p 49.

6 Gietinger, *Eine Leiche*, p 36.

7 Ibid, pp 38–42.

8 Wette, *Noske*, p 308 with n 216 and Gietinger, *Eine Leiche*, pp 38 and 40.

9 Gietinger, *Eine Leiche*, p 39.

10 Additionally the information from Pabst in the statement from memory of SDR editor Dieter Ertel in Gietinger, *Eine Leiche*, Annexe, Document III, p 143 and Document IV, p 147, and ibid, p 39; cf Wette. *Noske*, p 309 with n 218.

11 Gietinger, *Eine Leiche*, p 44f.

12 Hill, Leonidas E. (ed.), *Die Weizsäcker-Papiere 1900–1932*, Berlin, Frankfurt am Main and Vienna, 1982, p 325, entry 16 January 1919.

13 Even Klaus Gietinger has found no evidence as to Canaris's whereabouts at the time in question, but agrees that he was not in Berlin

14 Abshagen, *Canaris*, p 58f; Höhne, *Canaris*, p 69; Buchheit, Gert, *Der Deutsche Geheimdienst – Geschichte der militärischen Abwehr*, Munich, 1966, p 193; Brissaud, *Canaris*, p 23. The accounts here all vary and cannot be verified from the sources. Abshagen and after him Buchheit both have Canaris returning to southern Germany during February, which cannot be correct for on seeing Noske on 3 February he received full powers to set up Brigade Loewenfeld. Brissaud does not have Canaris in Weimar until the end of the month. Buchheit adds that there is no further material available as to Canaris's activities in Weimar, while Höhne describes him from 6 February as an extremely active propagandist and secret diplomat.

15 Ibid, p 19.

16 Carsten, Francis L, *Reichswehr und Politik 1918–1933*, Cologne and Berlin, 1964, p 39.

17 Hürter, *Groener*, p 19f.

18 Mommsen, *Aufstieg und Untergang*, p 58.

19 Forstmeier, 'Zur Rolle der Marine im Kapp-Putsch', p 52.

20 *Deutsche Allgemeine Zeitung*, 8 May 1919 (evening edition), in Hannover-Drück and Hannover, *Der Mord*, p 59.

21 Canaris PSR, folio 92.

22 Gietinger, *Eine Leiche*, Annexe, Document II, p 139.

23 Ibid, Annexe, Document VII, p 153.

24 Ibid.

25 Ibid, p 51.
26 Cf the description in Höhne, *Canaris*, p 72ff, which relies on the contemporary report of Paul Levi in Levi, Paul, *Der Jorns-Prozeß. Rede des Verteidigers*, Berlin, 1929. Extracts reproduced in Hannover-Drück and Hannover, *Der Mord*, p 144–57. Paul Levi was Josef Bornstein's defence attorney. Bornstein was co-publisher of *Tagebuch*, against which Jorns commenced litigation in 1928/29. In an anonymous article, Jorns had been named as an accessory in the murders of Luxemburg and Liebknecht. The court acquitted Bornstein, Jorns appealed and lost again. Finally the Reichsgericht at Leipzig decided that although Jorns was blameless in a subjective sense, objectively he had been deficient. Cf Gietinger, *Eine Leiche*, pp 52–4.
27 Note of a conference of the Seetransportabteilung, 31 January 1931, BA-MA, RM 6/267, folio 27.
28 Telephone note, Korvettenkapitän Fliess, 31 January 1931, BA-MA, RM 6/267, folio 38.
29 Comprehensive court files at Bundesarchiv-Militärarchiv, PH 8-V (Batch Kavalleriedivisionen 1902–1932, here GKSD). Cf Gietinger, *Eine Leiche*, pp 57–9.
30 Statement of Vogel reprinted in: Hannover-Drück and Hannover, *Der Mord*, pp 88–91. Cf Höhne, *Canaris*, p 74f; Gietinger, *Eine Leiche*, p 58.
31 Extracts from judgment of court-martial reprinted in Hannover-Drück and Hannover, *Der Mord*, pp 116–21.
32 Gietinger, *Eine Leiche*, Annexe, Document IX, letter from Otto Kranzbühler to Klaus Gietinger, 12 January 1993, p 158f; ibid, p 111.
33 Gietinger considers Noske's personal responsibility for the murders of Liebknecht and Luxemburg as proven. Noske's biographer, Wette, prefers to place responsibility on the shoulders of leading Mehrheit-Social Democrat politicians; cf Wette, *Noske*, p 313f.
34 Noske, *Von Kiel bis Kapp*, p 76.
35 *Berliner Volkszeitung*, 28 April 1929, reprinted in: Hannover Drück and Hannover, *Der Mord*, p 162f. Also quoted in Wette, *Noske*, p 315.
36 Bassett, *Hitler's Spy-Chief*, alleges that Vickers' manager and armaments lobbyist Basil Zaharoff, whom Canaris knew from 1916/17 in Spain and who worked for British intelligence, met Canaris in Berlin in January 1918. The purpose of the alleged talks was to discuss how to silence Liebknecht and Luxemburg, who were agitating against the international arms trade. Bassett cites Allfrey, Anthony, *The Life and Legend of Basil Zaharoff*, London, 1989, which in turn relies on McCormick, Donald, *Pedlar of Death*, London, 1965. The originator of this story therefore appears to be McCormick, who provides no sources. A meeting between Canaris and Zaharoff is not proven, and the National Archives in London have yielded nothing. To interpret the murders of Liebknecht and Luxemburg as a conspiracy involving the international arms lobby surrounding Canaris, Pabst, Zarahoff and their backers belongs in the realm of secret service legend rather than serious historical research.
37 Gietinger, *Eine Leiche*, p 60.
38 That it was Canaris who sprang Vogel from prison was confirmed later by Pabst. Cf Gietinger, *Eine Leiche*, Annexe, Document II, p 140. Cf Höhne, *Canaris*, p 76 with n 123. Höhne refers to the personal communication of Helmut Krausnick, to whom Vogel related the events in the 1930s. In the 1960s, Ritgen admitted forging the signature. Cf Gietinger, *Eine Leiche*, p 60 with n 157.

39 Cf here et seq Gietinger, *Eine Leiche*, pp 61–71.

40 BA-MA, RM 6/267, folio 50.

41 Gietinger, *Eine Leiche*, p 64.

42 Ibid, p 65. Cf BA-MA, RM 6/267, folio 38.

43 *Vorwärts*, 23 January 1931; BA-MA RM 6/267, folios 22ff. and 50ff.

44 File note, Günter Nollau, 1 December 1959, regarding a conversation with Waldemar Pabst on 19 November 1959, extracts reproduced in *Der Spiegel* 1, 1970, p 49. See also Gietinger, *Eine Leiche*, Annexe, Document II, p 140.

45 Cf Gietinger, *Eine Leiche*, pp 95–105. After the painstaking reconstruction of Gietinger's and Pabst's statements, confirmed by several people whom Pabst talked to, there can no longer be a serious doubt as to the immediate involvement of Souchon.

7 ON THE SIDE OF THE PUTSCHISTS

1 Winkler, *Weimar*, p 91.

2 Here et seq Wette, *Noske*, p 466ff. Also see Winkler, *Weimar*, p 92f.

3 Wette, *Noske*, p 468.

4 Ibid, p 471.

5 Ibid, p 472.

6 Ibid, p 476.

7 Ibid, pp 476 and 477.

8 Ibid, p 476.

9 Wette, Wolfgang (ed.), *Aus den Geburtsstunden der Weimarer Republik – Das Tagebuch des Obersten Ernst van den Bergh*, Quellen zur Militärgeschichte, series A, vol 1, Düsseldorf, 1991, p 101. Ernst van den Bergh was head of the Ministerial Department at the Prussian War Ministry. He was made Oberst in 1920. Ibid, p 11f.

10 Ibid, p 100.

11 Höhne, *Canaris*, p 77.

12 Here et seq Wette, *Noske*, p 483.

13 Ibid, p 484.

14 Noske, *Von Kiel bis Kapp*, p 155.

15 Volkmann, Ernst Otto, *Revolution über Deutschland*, Oldenburg, 1930, p 322. For detail, see Wette, *Noske*, p 509; Noske, *Von Kiel bis Kapp*, p 200.

16 Wette, *Noske*, p 509.

17 Noske, *Von Kiel bis Kapp*, p 200.

18 Erger, Johannes, *Die Kapp-Lüttwitz-Putsch. Ein Beitrag zur deutschen Innenpolitik*, Beiträge zur Geschichte des Parlamentarismus und der politischen Parteien, vol 35, Düsseldorf, 1967, p, 36f; Wette, *Noske*, p 551f.

19 Ibid, p 513f.

20 Meinl, Susanne, *Nationalsozialisten gegen Hitler. Die nationalrevolutionäre Opposition um Friedrich Wilhelm Heinz*, Berlin, 2000, p 28f; Wette, *Noske*, p 514; Höhne, *Canaris*, p 79.

21 Heinz, Friedrich Wilhelm, 'Von Wilhelm Canaris zum NKWD', typescript, private possession of Michael Heinz, p 2.

22 Noske, *Erlebtes*, p 178f; Wette, *Noske*, p 517.

23   Noske, *Von Kiel bis Kapp*, p 203; Erger, *Kapp-Lüttwitz-Putsch*, p 115; Wette, *Noske*, p 628.

24   Quoted in Wette, *Noske*, p 628 (quote 1) with n 5 (quote 2).

25   Ibid, p 329.

26   Noske, *Von Kiel bis Kapp*, p 204; Wette, *Das Tagebuch des Obersten Ernst van den Bergh*, p 124.

27   Wette, *Noske*, p 631.

28   Ibid, p 632; Noske, *Von Kiel bis Kapp*, p 207. For the text of the conversation see also the statements of Noske, Oven and Oldershausen to the Reichsgericht. Extracts reprinted in Erger, *Kapp-Lüttwitz-Putsch*, Document 20, p 317f.

29   Canaris's statement of 7 March 1923, Walter Luetgebrune literary bequest, BAK, N 1150.

30   Ibid.

31   Trotha, Adolf von, *Persönliches, Briefe, Reden und Aufzeichnungen*, selected and published by Bendix von Bargen, Berlin, 1938, p 19f.

32   Ibid, p 20. Cf Noske, *Von Kiel bis Kapp*, p 208.

33   Erger, *Kapp-Lüttwitz-Putsch*, p 136f. Cf the differing statements of Trotha and Canaris during the investigation: Luetgebrune literary bequest.

34   Erger, *Kapp-Lüttwitz-Putsch*, p 136f.

35   Ibid, p 137; Noske, *Von Kiel bis Kapp*, p 208.

36   Wette, *Noske*, p 635f.

37   Ernst, Fritz, *Aus dem Nachlaß des Generals Walther Reinhardt*, Stuttgart, 1958, p 62. See also Wette, *Noske*, p 638.

38   Quoted from ibid. Somewhat different is Noske, *Von Kiel bis Kapp*, p 209: 'The Navy will perhaps let the Reich have the remnants, but the officer corps will not be amongst them ...'

39   Noske, *Von Kiel bis Kapp*, p 209.

40   Wette, *Noske*, p 640.

41   Ernst, *Nachlaß Reinhardt*, p 63.

42   Noske, *Von Kiel bis Kapp*, p 211; Wette, *Noske*, p 642; Höhne, *Canaris*, p 83; Abshagen, *Canaris*, p 74.

43   Canaris, statement, 7 March 1923, Luetgebrune literary bequest, BAK, N 1150.

44   Abshagen, *Canaris*, p 74.

45   Wette, *Noske*, p 635.

46   Ibid, p 643.

47   Quoted from ibid, p 645.

48   Forstmeier, 'Zur Rolle der Marine im Kapp-Putsch', p 56.

49   Ibid, pp 61 and 65.

50   Quoted in ibid, p 59.

51   Abshagen, *Canaris*, p 74.

52   Forstmeier, 'Zur Rolle der Marine im Kapp-Putsch', p 76f.

53   Canaris-IfZ, folio 92.

8 *Agent of the Counter-Revolution*

1   Dülffer, 'Die Reichs- und Kriegsmarine', p 366.

2   Ibid and p 402f.

3   Ibid.

4   Canaris PSR, service assessment report at 1 August 1921, folio 17.

5   Dülffer, 'Die Reichs- und Kriegsmarine', p 402; Dülffer, Jost, *Weimar, Hitler und die Marine. Reichspolitik und Flottenbau 1920–1939*, Düsseldorf, 1972, p 60.

6   Loewenfeld, Wilfried, 'Das Freikorps von Loewenfeld', typescript., BA-MA, RM 122/116, folio 52.

7   Dülffer, 'Die Reichs- und Kriegsmarine', p 404 and Krüger, Gabriele, *Die Brigade Ehrhardt*, Hamburger Beiträge zur Zeitgeschichte, vol 7, Hamburg, 1971, p 71.

8   Ibid, pp 72ff. and 78.

9   Ibid, p 89.

10   Ibid, p 91; for Organisation Consul and its involvement in the contemporary political murders see especially Sabrow, Martin, *Der Rathenaumord. Rekonstruktion einer Verschwörung gegen die Republik von Weimar*, Schriftenreihe der Vierteljahrshefte für Zeitgeschichte, vol 69, Munich, 1994.

11   Oliver, 'Das Geheimnis um Canaris', *Die Weltbühne* 34, 23 August 1927, p 285–9.

12   Ibid, p 286.

13   Sabrow, *Rathenaumord*, p 112.

14   Discussed comprehensively in Krüger, *Brigade Ehrhardt*, ch V; Sabrow, *Rathenaumord*, pp 183–215.

15   Oliver, 'Das Geheimnis um Canaris', p 287.

16   'Der Kampf der Marine gegen Versailles 1919–1935', edited by Kapitän zur See Schüssler, Berlin, 1937. Reproduced in IMG, vol XXXIV, exhibit 156-c, pp 530–607. Hereafter Schüssler, 'Kampf'.

17   Ibid, p 541.

18   Ibid, p 542.

19   Ibid and Höhne, *Canaris*, p 22.

20   Oliver, 'Das Geheimnis um Canaris', p 287f.

21   Schüssler, 'Kampf', p 550.

22   Ibid.

23   Bird, *German Naval Officer Corps*, p 171.

24   Carsten, *Reichswehr und Politik*, p 277.

25   Krüger, *Brigade Ehrhardt*, p 105.

26   Ibid, p. 148, note 18.

27   Bird, *German Naval Officer Corps*, p 172.

28   Indictment of Kapitän Ehrhardt, 5 May 1923, pp 16f and 28, Luetgebrune literary bequest, BAK, N 1150/29.

29   Note on conversation with Admiral Pfeiffer regarding events at Kiel in 1923: 25 November 1926, BA-MA, RM 6/269, folio 194–6; Bird, *German Naval Officer Corps*, p 173.

30   Ibid, p 174.

31   Ibid.

32   Ibid, p 176.

33   Statement of Otto Schuster to State attorney (Oberreichsanwalt), 31 January 1927, BA-MA, RM 6/269, folio 10f.

34   Bird, *German Naval Officer Corps*, p 179.

35   Entry: »Bei Abkommandierung am 18. Juni 1923«, Canaris PSR, folio 18.

36   Bird, *German Naval Officer Corps*, personal service record at p 92.
37   Herzog, Bodo, 'Wilhelm Canaris: I. Offizier an Bord des Schulkreuzers *Berlin*', *Die Nachhut* 31, 1973, pp 18–23 (Part 1) and 1, 1974, pp 3–7 (Part 2), BA-MA, MSg 3-22/1.
38   With numerous contemporary reports: Aronson, Shlomo, *Reinhard Heydrich und die Frühgeschichte von Gestapo und SS*, Stuttgart, 1971, pp 25–34; cf: Deschner, Günther, *Reinhard Heydrich. Statthalter der totalen Macht*, Esslingen, 1977, pp 26–35; most recently, Dederichs, Mario R., *Heydrich. Das Gesicht des Bösen*, Munich and Zürich, 2005, pp 40–5.
39   Deschner, *Heydrich*, p 30.
40   Höhne, *Canaris*, p 91.
41   Dederichs, *Heydrich*, p 42.
42   Ibid, p 42.
43   Letter requesting permission to resign, 15 January 1924, longhand, Canaris PSR, folio 75.
44   Naval medical certificate, 15 January 1924, Canaris PSR, folio 79f.
45   Letter requesting permission to resign, 15 January 1924, longhand, Canaris PSR, folio 75.
46   Von Gagern's letter of 6 February 1924, photocopy, Canaris PSR, folios 104–8. Emphasis in original.
47   Ibid, folio 107.
48   Ibid, folio 108.
49   Copy file observation, 31 March 1924, Canaris PSR, folio 81.

9   Military-Political Secret Missions

1   Report by Korvettenkapitän Canaris on his visit to Japan 17 May–26 September 1924, BA-MA, RM 20/1635, folios 537–93.
2   Quoted from: Treue, Wilhelm, Möller, Eberhard, and Rahn, Werner, *Deutsche Marinerüstung 1919–1949. Die Gefahren der Tirpitz-Tradition*, Herford and Bonn, 1992, p 139.
3   Schüssler, 'Kampf', p 566; Treue, Möller and Rahn, *Marinerüstung*, p 139; Rahn, Werner, *Reichsmarine und Landesverteidigung 1919–1928*, Munich, 1976, p 173.
4   Schüssler, 'Kampf', p 566.
5   For Lohmann and a detailed and up-to-date review of the whole 'Lohmann Affair', see Remmele, Bernd, 'Die maritime Geheimrüstung unter Kapitän z. S. Lohmann', *Militärgeschichtliche Mitteilungen* 56, 1997, pp 315 and 317f. For his research Remmele initiated the first researches into forty volumes of folios containing Lohmann's correspondence which had been returned to Germany by the Moscow archive: BA-MA, RM 21/162-201. Other than these the most comprehensive material on the Lohmann case are to be found amongst the Reichskanzlei files, BAK, R 43 I 603-605, especially 'Bericht des Staatssekretärs i. R. Dr. Fritze über den durch Urkunde vom 22. Mai 1928 erteilten Auftrag, die Frage einer etwaigen persönlichen Haftung der verantwortlichen Reichsminister, Reichsbeamten und Offiziere für die sogenannten Lohmann-Unternehmungen zu klären', BAK, R 43 I 605, folios 26–295. Hereafter 'Fritze Report'. Cf Rahn, *Reichsmarine*, p 214ff; Dülffer, *Weimar*,

Hitler und die Marine, pp 90–7; Bird, *German Naval Officer Corps*, p 180–9; Raeder, *Mein Leben*, vol 1, p 229–233; Gessler, Otto, *Reichswehrpolitik in der Weimarer Zeit*, published by Kurt Sendtner, Stuttgart, 1958, pp 443–57.

6 Rahn, *Reichsmarine*, p 173.

7 Report by Korvettenkapitän Canaris on his visit to Japan 17 May–26 September 1924, BA-MA, RM 20/1635, folio 554.

8 Rahn, *Reichsmarine*, p 175.

9 Dülffer, *Weimar, Hitler und die Marine*, p 75.

10 Assessment report at 1 November 1921, Canaris PSR, folio 24.

11 Report by Korvettenkapitän Canaris on his visit to Spain of 15 June–1 July 1922, BA-MA, RM 6/48, folios 1–6.

12 Ibid, folio 1.

13 Rahn, *Reichsmarine*, p. 182.

14 Report by Korvettenkapitän Canaris on his visit to Spain of 28 January–17 February 1925, BA-MA, RM 6/48, folios 30–45.

15 Ibid, folios 31 and 35.

16 Ibid, folio 30f.

17 Ibid, folio 38f.

18 Ibid, folio 33f.

19 Ibid, folio 30.

20 Ibid, folio 32.

21 Ibid, folio 33.

22 Canaris, report, N-work [*Translator's note:* ie setting up intelligence network] in Spain during tour from 28 January to 17 February 1925, BA-MA, RM 6/48, folios 46–9.

23 Ibid, folio 46.

24 Ibid, folio 47.

25 Höhne, *Canaris*, p 101.

26 Report by Korvettenkapitän Canaris on his visit to Spain of 28 January–17 February 1925, BA-MA, RM 6/48, folio 33.

27 Ibid, folio 34.

28 Ibid.

29 Ibid, folio 35.

30 Ibid, folio 37.

31 Ibid, folio 38.

32 Ibid, folio 44f.

33 Ibid, folio 42f.

34 Ibid, folio 45.

35 Höhne, *Canaris*, p 104.

36 Canaris's report on state of U-boat and torpedo opportunity, BA-MA, RM 6/48, folio 62 (Appendix to foregoing journey report).

37 Report by Korvettenkapitän Canaris on his visit to Spain of 20 April–8 May 1925, BA-MA, RM 6/48, folios 57–61.

38 Canaris's report on the state of the Spanish opportunity (probably end July 1925), BA-MA, RM 6/48, folios 67–71.

39 Canaris's report on state of U-boat and torpedo opportunity, BA-MA, RM 6/48, folio 62 (Appendix to foregoing journey report).

40 Ibid, folio 63f.

41 Ibid, folio 66.

42 Ibid, folio 68f.

43 Situation report on the Spanish business, BA-MA, RM 6/48, folio 72.

44 Rahn, *Reichsmarine*, p 183.

45 Canaris's note of 22 February 1926, regarding torpedo manufacture in Spain, BA-MA, RM 6/48, folio 75f.

46 Ibid and report by Kapitän zur See Lohmann on his visit to northern Spain, and the calls of the rotor-ship *Barbara* at Bilbao and Santander, BA-MA, RM 6/48, folio 96.

47 Record of a session at the Reich Finance Ministry of 13 April 1926, re: Echevarrieta, ADAP, series B, vol III, no 112, p 231ff.

48 Ibid, p 231.

49 Ibid, p 232.

50 Ibid, p 233.

51 Note, Legationssekretär Wagenmann, 11 February 1927, ADAP, series B, vol IV, no 132, p 290, n 2.

52 Tortella, Teresa, *A Guide to Sources of Information on Foreign Investment in Spain 1780–1914*, published for the Section of Business and Labour Archives of the International Council on Archives by the International Institute of Social History, Amsterdam, 2000, p 12.

53 Report by Korvettenkapitän Canaris on his visit to Spain of 9 May–10 June 1926, BA-MA, RM 6/48, folio 87; Opinion of Korvettenkapitän Canaris on the Lohmann affair, BA-MA, RM 6/48, folio 183; Note of Ministerialdirektor Köpke, 10 January 1931, regarding change in the conditions of a credit in the sum of 240,000 pounds sterling paid to the Spanish industrialist Echevarrieta on military/political grounds at the request of the Naval Administration in 1926: ADAP, series B, vol XVI, no 148, pp 371–3.

54 Ibid, p 371.

55 Report by Korvettenkapitän Canaris on his visit to Spain of 9 May–10 June 1926, BA-MA, RM 6/48, folio 88.

56 Ibid, folio 89.

57 Ibid, folio 93.

58 Madrid ambassador Graf von Welczeck to Foreign Ministry, Madrid, 11 June 1926, ADAP, series B, vol III, no 149, pp 307–9.

59 Report by Korvettenkapitän Canaris on his visit to Spain of 9 May–10 June 1926, BA-MA, RM 6/48, folio 94f.

60 Madrid ambassador Graf von Welczeck to Foreign Ministry, Madrid, 11 June 1926, ADAP, series B, vol III, no 149, p 308, n 6.

61 Report by Kapitän zur See Lohmann on his visit to northern Spain, and the calls of the rotor-ship *Barbara* at Bilbao and Santander, BA-MA, RM 6/48, folio 97.

62 Ibid, folio 100.

63 Opinion of Korvettenkapitän Canaris on the Lohmann affair, BA-MA, RM 6/48, folio 184f.

64 Report by Kapitän zur See Lohmann on his visit to northern Spain, BA-MA, RM 6/48, folio 101.

65 Opinion of Korvettenkapitän Canaris on the Lohmann affair, BA-MA, RM 6/48, folio 185.

66 Note by Ministerialdirektor Köpke (regarding a conversation with Canaris), 15 December 1926, ADAP, series B, vol III, no 246, p 494.
67 Ibid, p 495.
68 Ibid, p 495, n 7.
69 Assessment report, 1 November 1927, Canaris-PSR, folio 29.
70 Schüssler, 'Kampf', p 569.
71 Note by Legationssekretär Wagenmann, 11 February 1927, ADAP, series B, vol IV, no 132, pp 289–91, quote here from p 290, n 2.
72 Ibid, p 290.
73 Canaris's report on visit to Spain, February 1927, BA-MA, RM 6/48, folio 109f.
74 Ibid and report on visit to Spain, 28 April–18 May 1927, BA-MA, RM 6/48, folio 113–42.
75 Schüssler, 'Kampf', p 570; Rahn, *Reichsmarine*, p 184.
76 Ibid, p 185.
77 Assessment report, 1 November 1927, Canaris-PSR folio 30f.
78 Ibid.
79 Report by Canaris on opportunities in Spain, 8 August 1927, BA-MA, RM 6/48, folios 150–4.
80 Report by Canaris on visit to Spain, 8–19 November 1927, BA-MA, RM 6/48, folio 215f.

10 The Shadow of the Past

1 Remmele, 'Geheimrüstung', p 317, with n 16.
2 Opinion of Korvettenkapitän Canaris on the Lohmann affair, BA-MA, RM 6/48, folio 187.
3 The Fritze Report differs from Canaris's account when it states that Canaris was not party to the Lohmann affair until the talks with Reichswehrminister Gessler which he had immediately after the press revelations, Fritze Report, p 98f, BAK, R 43 I/605, folio 79.
4 Fritze Report, p 91f, BAK, R 43 I/605, folio 76f, cf Appendix 12 to Fritze Report, ibid, folio 188f.
5 Fritze Report, p 92, BAK, R 43 I/605, folio 76.
6 Appendix 12 to the Fritze Report, BAK, R 43 I/605, folio 188.
7 Fritze Report, p 62, BAK, R 43 I/605, folio 61.
8 Remmele, 'Geheimrüstung', p 355.
9 Fritze Report, p 64f, BAK, R 43 I/605, folio 62f.
10 Ibid., folio 64.
11 Ibid., folio 65f. Cf Remmele, 'Geheimrüstung', p 356f.
12 Appendix 13 to the Fritze Report, BAK, R 43 I/605, folio 190; cf Remmele, 'Geheimrüstung', p 357, with n 308.
13 Cf Gessler's written declaration in Fritze Report, p 78f, BAK, R 43 I/605, folio 69f.
14 Ibid, folio 82f.
15 Remmele, 'Geheimrüstung', p 317.

16   Gessler, *Reichswehrpolitik*, p 452. In this later memoir Gessler wrote that he had first been made aware of the true circumstances by the press revelations and the related investigation.

17   Opinion of Korvettenkapitän Canaris on the Lohmann affair, BA-MA, RM 6/48, folios 182–7; Remmele, 'Geheimrüstung', p 318.

18   Fritze Report, p 98, BAK, R 43 I/605, folio 79.

19   Note on the conference of Navy commander-in-chief with the Reich chancellor, 10 August 1927, ADAP, series B, vol 6, no 103, p 221f.

20   Ibid and Remmele, 'Geheimrüstung', p 318.

21   Cf Canaris's report of 8 October 1928: 'Besprechung mit Hausknecht [ie Echevarrieta] am 5. und 6. X. in Bremen', BA-MA, RM 6/48, folios 310–13. Further source: Rahn, *Reichsmarine*, p 228 with n 26.

22   Remmele, 'Geheimrüstung', p 318.

23   Gessler, *Reichswehrpolitik*, p 456, insists in his memoirs that upon conclusion of the inquiries he had released Lohmann unconditionally, and that there was nothing to reproach him for morally: 'His fate seems tragic to me: the motivation and dynamism of his dealings were honourable and militarily pro-Fatherland. I repeat that this man, who had millions of Reichsmarks at his disposal, kept his hands clean. He was right in this, the things that he saw as his "general mission" could not be done "bureaucratically".'

24   Memorandum of Regierungsrat Planck, conference note re Phoebus Film Affair, 1. Preliminary Report of (former) Staatssekretär Saemisch, ADAP, series B, vol VII, no 95, pp 221–3.

25   Remmele, 'Geheimrüstung', p 319.

26   Ibid, p 320f.

27   Ibid, p 321f.

28   Ibid, p 315, note 8 and p 318f.

29   Fritze Report, p 275f, BAK, R 43 I/605, folio 166f.

30   Ibid, p 270f, BAK, R 43 I/605, folio 165f.

31   Rahn, *Reichsmarine*, p 228.

32   Lohmann had involved IvS with a 28 per cent share in Mentor Bilanz GmbH, founded in 1925. Mentor represented all U-boat interests of Naval Command. Schüssler, 'Kampf', p 566.

33   For reasons of secrecy, Lohmann considered it essential to use a small bank for the development of his business affairs, as the large banks would not accept these difficult transactions because of their overseas involvements. Therefore in 1925 Lohmann had bought a major shareholding in the Berliner Bankverein. Fritze Report, pp 151–67, BAK, R 43 I/605, folios 106–14.

34   Opinion of Korvettenkapitän Canaris on the Lohmann affair, BA-MA, RM 6/48, folio 186.

35   Asessment report at change of duties, 18 June 1928, Canaris PSR, folio 32.

36   *Die Weltbühne* 34, 23 August 1927, pp 285–9.

37   *Die Weltbühne* 36, 6 September 1927, pp 357–9.

38   *Die Weltbühne* 37, 13 September 1927, p 393.

39   *Die Weltbühne* 47, 22 November 1927, pp 775–7.

40   Ibid, p 776.

41   Ibid.

42   Ibid, p 777.
43   *Die Ursachen des Deutschen Zusammenbruches 1918: 2.Abteilung, Der Innere Zusammenbruch*, 12 vols in 14 parts, Berlin, 1925–8, here vol 9, p 423. Referred to hereafter as *Ursachen*.
44   Ibid.
45   Deist, 'Die Unruhen', p 177.
46   Letter from Canaris, 26 November 1925, no addressee, BA-MA, N 812/45, no page numbers. Further correspondence and ideas in preparation for his appearance before the committee of inquiry.
47   Ibid, conversation with Dr [Albrecht] Philipp [sub-committee chairman] and Dr [Walther] Bloch [committee secretary] in the Reichstag, 21 November 1925.
48   *Ursachen*, 9. vol 1, p 426.
49   Ibid, p 132.
50   'Mördergehilfen als Geßlers Vertreter', *Sächsische Arbeiterzeitung*, 25 January 1925.
51   Ibid.
52   *Ursachen*, 9, vol 1, p 139f.
53   Ibid, p 144.
54   Ibid, p 165.
55   *Ursachen*, 9, vol 1, p 494f.
56   Canaris, report, 'Aufenthalt in Spanien: 21. September bis 5. Oktober 1927', BA-MA, RM 6/48, folios 220–30; Canaris's report, 'Reise Spanien vom 8. 11.–19. 11. 1927', ibid, folios 215–19.
57   Canaris report, 'Aufenthalt in Spanien: 21. September bis 5. Oktober 1927', BA-MA, RM 6/48, folio 221.
58   Letter from ambassador Welczeck to Ministerialdirektor Köpke, 29 December 1927, secret, ADAP, series B, vol VII, no 242, p 587.
59   Report by Legationsrat Forster on sending German military attachés, 21 June 1927, ADAP, series B, vol V, no 251, p 575.
60   Letter from ambassador Welczeck to Ministerialdirektor Köpke, 29 December 1927, secret, ADAP, series B, vol VII, no 242, p 588. The ambassador was mistaken as to Canaris's rank.
61   Ibid, n 5.
62   Report by Canaris on his visit to Spain, 3–21 February 1928, BA-MA, RM 6/48, folio 268.
63   Draft, 'Wechselseitige Beziehungen zwischen der Polizeiverwaltung Deutschlands und Spaniens', 17 February 1928, BA-MA, RM 6/48, folio 270f.
64   Report by Canaris on his visit to Spain, 3–21 February 1928, BA-MA, RM 6/48, folio 268.
65   Unsigned memorandum, 'Zusammenstellung der in Spanien bearbeiteten Marine-Interessen', June 1928, ADAP, series B, vol IX, no 110, p 258.
66   Canaris report, 'Bericht über Reise nach Spanien vom 28. April bis 18. Mai 1927', BA-MA, RM 6/48, folio 137.
67   Canaris report, 'Reise Spanien vom 8. 11.–19. 11. 1927', BA-MA, RM 6/48, folio 217.
68   Schüssler, 'Kampf', p 568.
69   Assessment report on change of duties at 18 June 1928, Canaris PSR folio 32.

70 Thus Canaris, probably with the knowledge of Naval Command but not the Foreign Ministry, entered the discussions with the military attachés of Britain, France, Italy and the United States regarding admissible calibre sizes for naval guns. Cf note by Legationsrat Forster, 'Aufzeichnung über Marinefragen', 24 January 1928, ADAP, series B, vol VIII, no 41, p 81.

71 'Im Reichsmarineamt erscheint Herr Dillen mit einem ausländischen Rechtsanwalt', *Die Weltbühne* 21, 22 May 1928, pp 777–97.

72 Buchheit, *Der Deutsche Geheimdienst*, p 38; Höhne, *Canaris*, p 123.

73 Ibid.

74 'Bericht Ministerialrat Frerichs über Berufsbelehrungsreise', BA-MA, RM 6/48, folios 290–2.

75 Copy of a letter dated 27 September 1928, ibid, folios 304–6. In this letter mention is made of another letter dated 29 June, but other letters referred to are absent from the file.

76 Ibid, folio 304.

77 Ibid, folio 305.

78 Ibid.

79 Dülffer, *Weimar, Hitler und die Marine*, p 108f.

80 *Berliner Tageblatt*, 26 September 1928, quoted in Carsten, *Reichswehr*, p 315.

81 Höhne, *Canaris*, p 124, refers to file notes not contained in BA-MA, RM 6/48. It is interesting that the partially burned Foreign Ministry correspondence regarding the planned post abroad for Canaris are located in the Foreign Ministry secret archive at NA, GFM 33/2393.

82 Canaris PSR, folio 94.

83 Ibid.

84 Dönitz, Karl, *Zehn Jahre und zwanzig Tage*, Frankfurt and Bonn, 1964, p 299. Quote from Höhne, *Canaris*, p 125.

85 Extensively in: Hannover-Drück and Hannover, *Der Mord*, which provides comprehensive documentary material on the so-called 'Jorns-trials'.

86 Ibid, pp 158–61, here extracts from the jury trial of 27 April 1929.

87 *Vorwärts*, 23 January 1931, extracts reprinted in Hannover-Drück and Hannover, *Der Mord*, p 176f. Cf memoranda, letters, notes on conversations and press clippings in BA-MA, RM 6/267.

88 Canaris, opinion, 26 January 1931, BA-MA, RM 6/267, folio 50f.

89 Record of conversation with attorney Rechtsanwalt Bredereck in Kapitän Canaris–Jorns Case, 26 January 1931 [written by Canaris], BA-MA, RM 6/267, folio 33.

90 Statement by Reichswehrministerium, reprinted, inter alia, in *Der Abend*, 29 January 1931, BA-MA, RM 6/267, folio 40.

91 Canaris PSR, folio 94.

92 Ibid, folio 46.

PART III: RISE UNDER THE SWASTIKA

11 Hitler's Military Intelligence Chief

1 Kershaw, Ian, *Hitler 1889–1936*, Stuttgart, 1998, p 456.

2 Ibid, p 458.

3 Ibid, p 359.

4 Winkler, *Weimar*, p 461.

5 For Helldorf, one of the most 'controversial figures of the Third Reich', who followed a meandering path from the SA to the Resistance, see principally Harrison, Ted, "Alter Kämpfer" im Widerstand. Graf Helldorf, die NS-Bewegung und die OppositiongegenHitler', *Vierteljahrshefte für Zeitgeschichte* 45, 1997, pp 385–421. For the Helldorf–Schleicher–Hitler link, ibid, p 393.

6 Goebbels, Joseph, *Tagebücher 1924–1945*, 5 vols, published by Ralf Georg Reuth, Munich, 1999, here vol 2, 1930–34, p 652f. Hereafter 'Goebbels's Diaries'. See also Winkler, *Weimar*, p 462.

7 Papen, Franz von, *Der Wahrheit eine Gasse*, Munich, 1952, p 176; cf Winkler, *Weimar*, p 462; Kershaw, *Hitler 1889–1936*, p 460.

8 Brüning, Heinrich, *Memoiren 1918–1934*, Stuttgart, 1970, p 578; cf Hömig, Herbert, *Brüning. Kanzler in der Krise der Republik*, Paderborn, 2000, p 540f.

9 Brüning, *Memoiren*, p 588f; Hömig, *Brüning*, p 541f; Hürter, *Groener*, p 350ff; Winkler, *Weimar*, p 464f; Kershaw, *Hitler 1889–1936*, p 460.

10 Brüning, *Memoiren*, p 601f.

11 Kershaw, *Hitler 1889–1936*, p 461.

12 Goebbels's Diaries, vol 2, p 662.

13 'Die nationalpolitische Stellung des Offiziers in der Deutschen Wehrmacht', address by Vizeadmiral Canaris, OKW. 22 April 1938, in IfZ, FD 47; Canaris, Wilhelm, 'Politik und Wehrmacht', in Donnevert, Richard, *Wehrmacht und Partei*, Leipzig, 1938, pp 43–54.

14 Dülffer, *Weimar, Hitler und die Marine*, p 221. For Hitler's position towards the Navy see also Salewski, Michael, 'Dokumentation "Marineleitung und politische Führung 1931–1935"', *Militärgeschichtliche Mitteilungen* 10, 1971, p 121f.

15 Dülffer, 'Die Reichs- und Kriegsmarine', p 451.

16 Dülffer, *Hitler, Weimar und die Marine*, p 222.

17 Maser, Werner, *Hitlers Briefe und Notizen. Sein Weltbild in handschriftlichen Notizen*, Graz and Stuttgart, 2002, p 116.

18 Dülffer, *Weimar, Hitler und die Marine*, p 222; Dülffer, 'Die Reichs- und Kriegsmarine', p 451.

19 'Beurteilungsbericht zum 1. November 1933' in Canaris PSR, folios 50–3. See also Herzog, Bodo, 'Das letzte Bordkommando von Wilhelm Canaris', *Die Nachhut* 21, 1973, pp 10–13, BA-MA, MSg 3-22/1.

20 Best, Werne, 'Canaris, Kopenhagen 1949', manuscript reproduced in Matlok, Siegfried, *Dänemark in Hitlers Hand. Der Bericht des Reichsbevollmächtigten Werner Best über seine Besatzungspolitik in Dänemark mit Studien über Hitler, Göring, Himmler, Heydrich, Ribbentrop, Canaris u.a.*, Husum, 1988, pp 175–8. In 1948 and 1949 Best composed a series of studies on leading personalities of the Third Reich that Matlok assembled in his book. In his critical appraisal of Abwehr literature, Best's biographer Ulrich Herbert arrives at the conclusion that the 'sketching of Canaris's career by Best was far and away more accurate and sober than most other attempts in postwar literature'; see Herbert, Ulrich, *Best. Biographische Studien über Radikalismus, Weltanschauung und Vernunft 1903–1989*, Bonn, 2001, p 577, n 139.

21 Höhne, *Canaris*, p 135.

22 Ibid, p 134.

23 Assessment report to 1 November 1934, Canaris PSR, folio 56.

24 Ibid, folios 51 and 55.

25 Herzog is of the same opinion: Herzog, 'Bordkommando', p 10.

26 'Beurteilungsbericht zum 1. November 1934', Canaris PSR, folios 54–57 and personal service record, ibid, folio 94.

27 Abshagen, *Canaris*, pp 94–7; Brissaud, *Canaris*, p 40f; Höhne, *Canaris*, p 137; also Höhne, 'Admiral Wilhelm Canaris', in Ueberschär, Gerd R. (ed.), *Hitlers militärische Elite, vol 1. Von den Anfängen des Regimes bis Kriegsbeginn*, Darmstadt, 1998, p 55.

28 Conrad Patzig, letter to Walter Baum, 10 November 1953, IfZ, ZS 540, folio 4.

29 Raeder, letter to Canaris, 11 October 1934, BA-MA, N 812/1.

30 Conrad Patzig, letter to Walter Baum, 10 November 1953, IfZ, ZS 540, folio 4.

31 Buchheit, *Der Deutsche Geheimdienst*, p 38ff; Höhne, *Canaris*, p 155f.

32 Conrad Patzig, letter to Walter Baum, 10 November 1953, IfZ, ZS 540, folio 2.

33 Buchheit, *Der Deutsche Geheimdienst*, p 40; Höhne, *Canaris*, p 157.

34 Buchheit, *Der Deutsche Geheimdienst*, p 41.

35 See Mitcham, Samuel W., 'Generalfeldmarschall Werner von Blomberg', in Ueberschär. *Hitlers militärische Elite*, vol 1, p 30f.

36 Boll, Bernd, 'Generalfeldmarschall Walther von Reichenau', in Ueberschär. *Hitlers militärische Elite*, vol 1, p 196.

37 Buchheit, *Der Deutsche Geheimdienst*, p 42.

38 Conrad Patzig, letter to Walter Baum, 10 November 1953, IfZ, ZS 540, folio 2. Cf also Müller, Klaus Jürgen, *Das Heer und Hitler. Armee und nationalsozialistisches Regime 1933–1940*, Schriftenreihe des Militärgeschichtlichen Forschungsamtes; Beiträge zur Militär- und Kriegsgeschichte, 10, Stuttgart, 1969, p 68f.

39 Herbert, *Best*, p 139; cf also Kershaw, *Hitler 1889–1936*, p 632.

40 Herbert, *Best*, p 139.

41 Kershaw, *Hitler 1889–1936*, p 636.

42 Thilo Vogelsang, file note on conversation with Conrad Patzig, 16 June 1954, IfZ, ZS 540, folio 9.

43 Ibid.

44 Kershaw, *Hitler 1889–1936*, p 644.

45 Quoted in ibid, p 645.

46 Höhne, *Canaris*, p 162.

47 Letter, Helmut Krausnick to Conrad Patzig, 5 March 1955, IfZ, ZS 540, folio 18f. Krausnick asked Patzig for an opinion on this alleged reaction of Raeder and Blomberg, which had been conveyed to him by Admiral von Schubert.

48 Patzig's letter of reply to Krausnick, 21 March 1955, ibid, folio 20.

49 Letter, Conrad Patzig to Walter Baum, 10 November 1953, ibid, folio 4.

50 Buchheit, *Die Deutsche Geheimdienst*, p 50, referring to a personal communication from Patzig.

51 Conrad Patzig, letter to Walter Baum, 10 November 1953, IfZ, ZS 540, folio 5.

52 Ibid, folio 5f.

53 Ibid, letter from chief of Naval Station Baltic, 22 November 1934.

54 Conrad Patzig, letter to Walter Baum, 10 November 1953, IfZ, ZS 540, folio 5.

12 The Duel with Heydrich

1 Here et seq: Krausnick, Helmut, 'Vorgeschichte und Beginn des militärischen Widerstandes gegen Hitler', in *Vollmacht des Gewissens – Probleme des militärischen Widerstands gegen Hitler*, Frankfurt am Main and Berlin, 1960, p 254f; Müller, Klaus Jürgen, *Das Heer und Hitler – Armee und nationalsozialistiches Regime 1933–1940*, Stuttgart, 1969, p 158f; Höhne, *Canaris*, p 170f.

2 Krausnick, 'Vorgeschichte', p 251, n 44; Müller, *Heer und Hitler*, p 158, n 77.

3 Höhne, *Canaris*, p 171, from *Berliner Illustrierte Zeitung*, 10 January 1935. Quotation from Müller, *Heer und Hitler*, p 159.

4 Kershaw, *Hitler 1889–1936*, p 686.

5 Fritsch, note dated 1 February 1938, in Hossbach, Friedrich, *Zwischen Wehrmacht und Hitler*, Wolfenbüttel, 1949, p 71.

6 Liebmann, notes for a Conference of Commanders, 7 January 1935, quoted from Krausnick, 'Vorgeschichte', p 255; similarly Müller, *Heer und Hitler*, p 159.

7 Hossbach, *Zwischen Wehrmacht und Hitler*, p 47.

8 Höhne, *Canaris*, p 172, from *Völkischer Beobachter*, 14 January 1935; cf Mühleisen, Horst, 'Dokumentation: "Das letzte Duell. Die Auseinandersetzungen zwischen Heydrich und Canaris wegen der Revision der 'Zehn Gebote'"', *Militärgeschichtliche Mitteilungen* 58, 1999, p 398. Also see note by Fritsch, 1 February 1938, p 71.

9 Herbert, *Best*, p 147ff; for the theory for the political direction of the police apparatus followed the guidelines of this study.

10 Ibid, p 169f and 180ff. Over this question Himmler overcame the opposition of Interior Minister Frick, who wanted the Political Police and Gestapo under his own command. This would have contradicted the political ideology of Himmler, Heydrich and Best who wanted to expand the police jurisdiction beyond the legal norms to cover 'the health of the Volk'. Herbert points out that this was not an abstract striving for power by Himmler, but corresponded to Hitler's political view. For the resulting conflicts with the Interior and Justice Ministries and the provincial authorities see Herbert, Ulrich, and Graf, Christoph, 'Kontinuitäten und Brüche. Von der Politischen Polizei der Weimarer Republik zur Geheimen Staatspolizei', in Paul, Gerhard and Mallmann, Klaus-Michael (eds), *Die Gestapo. Mythos und Realität*, Darmstadt, 1996, pp 73–83; Tuchel, Johannes, 'Gestapa und Reichssicherheitshauptamt. Die Berliner Zentralinstitutionen der Gestapo', in Paul and Mallmann, *Gestapo*, pp 84–100. See also Wildt, Michael, *Generation des Unbedingten. Das Führungskorps des Reichssicherheitshauptamtes*, Hamburg, 2002. Wildt, and Herbert, *Best*, provide comprehensive bibliographies.

11 Herbert, *Best*, p 181.

12 Decision of the Reich Government at the Ministerial Conference of 17 October 1933, photocopy at BA-MA, RM 5/195, folio. 45. The decision laid the foundation for the jurisdictional struggle of the Abwehr against Heydrich. See eg the report signed by Rudolf Bamler 'Organisation der Abwehrabteilung', August 1937, BA-MA, RW 5/v. 207, folios 65–7; Memorandum, Oberst von Bentivegni on the conference between Admiral Canaris and SS-Obergruppenführer and General der Polizei Heydrich, 12 January 1942, BA-MA, RW 5/690, folios 28–31, reproduced in Mühleisen, 'Duell', pp 424–7. Walter Huppenkothen described the Cabinet decision

as the 'most comprehensive general authority document which a bureau had ever been given in the Third Reich', IfZ, ZS 249 I, folio 36.

13   Höhne, *Canaris*, p 177; similarly Mühleisen, 'Duell', p 399. Herbert, *Best*, p 181f describes the agreement in his own words but gives a source: 'Besprechung über Abwehrfragen im Reichswehrministerium', 17 January 1935, GstAB, Rep. 90 P/1-2, folio 203ff. (Geheimes Staatsarchiv der Stiftung Preußischer Kulturbesitz, Gestapo-Bestand.)

14   Thus in Mühleisen, 'Duell', p 400. According to an anecdote from the postwar account of Heydrich's widow Lina, Heydrich did not know of Canaris's appointment as Abwehr chief, and 'they bumped into each other by chance while out walking in early 1935'. In view of the significance of the change in Abwehr leadership, this would appear to be the stuff of legend. Höhne, *Canaris*, p 174. Deschner also relies on Lina Heydrich, but here the first conversation on the subject took place in a Berlin luxury restaurant at the end of January. This merely serves to underline the dubious nature of the material. Deschner, 'Heydrich', p 142.

15   Mühleisen, 'Duell', p 400.

16   Copy, statement by Walter Huppenkothen, Canaris and Abwehr, IfZ, ZS 249, folio 31.

17   Ibid. It is doubtful that these statements were made by Huppenkothen after the war, and that his first meeting with Canaris was in August 1941. As a source for the Canaris–Heydrich relationship they must be treated with caution, as must the diary entry alluded to. The mutual sentiments of envy are also to be found almost verbatim in Abshagen, *Canaris*, p 147f. Höhne, *Canaris*, p 174ff, reports claims by Lina Heydrich respecting 'Heydrich's superstitious fear of the apparently ubiquitous Canaris' which were the basis of her husband's deep distrust of Canaris.

18   Best, *Herbert*, p 181.

19   Ibid, p 185 and p 578, n 146 with mention of Best's calendar notes. See also Best, 'Canaris', pp 175–8.

20   Best, 'Canaris', p 172.

21   In Kiel Heydrich became acquainted with the daughter of a naval official, the father allegedly being a senior architect. The girl's identity has never been disclosed, but she considered herself engaged to Heydrich. Meanwhile Heydrich became engaged to Lina von Osten, his future wife, and announced the engagement in a newspaper, which came to the attention of the first girl, who subsequently suffered a nervous breakdown. On complaining, the matter was referred to a naval honour court where it would have blown over had Heydrich not attempted to impugn the girl's virtue. He showed no readiness to accept responsibility and was thus discharged the service as an unfit officer. Shortly afterwards he joined the SS; Himmler was advertising for a 'Nachrichtenoffizier'. The word 'Nachrichten' means 'signals' as well as 'intelligence', and as Heydrich had been in the signals branch of the Navy he applied under a misunderstanding as to the nature of the post. Himmler decided to give him a trial, and asked him to set up an intelligence section for the SS. Aronson, *Frühgeschichte*, p 34ff; Deschner, 'Heydrich', p 36ff; Dederichs, *Heydrich*, p 49ff.

22   'Reisebericht über die Reise Chef Abw mit Leiter III, Kaptn. Bartenbach und SS-Gruppenführer Heydrich zur Ast Kiel am 7. 2. 1935', BA-MA, RW 5/v. 197, folio 308f and 'Reisebericht über die Reise nach Bremen und Wilhelmshaven, 25. 3. 1935', ibid, folio 305f.

23 Deist, Wilhelm, 'Die Aufrüstung der Wehrmacht', in *Das Deutsche Reich und der Zweite Weltkrieg* (hereafter *DRZW*), 9 vols, Militärgeschichtlichen Forschungsamt, Stuttgart, 1979 ff, here *Vol 1, Ursachen und Voraussetzungen der deutschen Kriegspolitik*, p 415ff; Kershaw, *Hitler 1889–1936*, pp 686–8.

24 Müller, Klaus Jürgen, *General Ludwig Beck*, Studien und Dokumente zur politisch-militärischen Vorstellungswelt und Tätigkeit des Generalstabschefs des deutschen Heeres 1933–1938, Schriften des Bundesarchivs, vol 30, Boppard, 1980, document 24, pp 415–24.

25 Ibid, p 418.

26 Ibid, p 419.

27 Deist, 'Aufrüstung', p 416.

28 Kershaw, *Hitler 1889–1936*, p 689; Müller, *Beck*, document 25, pp 424–6.

29 Kershaw, *Hitler 1889–1936*, p 690f.

30 Hossbach, *Zwischen Wehrmacht und Hitler*, p 94f.

31 Ibid, p 96; Müller, *Heer und Hitler*, p 208f; Kershaw, *Hitler 1889–1936*, p 692.

32 Ibid, p 692.

33 Ibid, p 693.

34 Ibid, p 697.

35 Canaris, letter to all Abwehrstellen, 29 March 1935, BA-MA, RW 5/v. 197, folio 302f.

36 Note, journey of Abwehr chief and I L to Budapest, (4–7 April 1935), BA-MA, RW 5/v. 197, folio 299f.

37 Höhne, *Canaris*, p 182.

38 Note, journey of Abwehr chief to Abwehrstelle Münster 15/16 May 1935, BA-MA, RW 5/v. 197, folio 293ff.

39 Letter, Canaris to all Abwehrstellen, 29 March 1935, BA-MA, RM 5/v. 195, quoted in Höhne, *Canaris*, p 183.

40 Note, journey of Abwehr chief to Abwehrstelle Münster 15/16 May 1935, BA-MA, RW 5/v. 197, folio 296.

41 Conference note, Bamler 10 April 1935, BA-MA, RM 5/v. 195, quoted from Höhne, *Canaris*, p 184.

42 Best, *Canaris*, p 174.

43 Schäfer, Karl, report on the Abwehrpolizei, p 5, IfZ, ZS 372.

44 Wildt, Michael (ed), *Nachrichtendienst, Politische Elite und Mordeinheit. Der Sicherheitsdienst des Reichsführers SS*, Hamburg 2000; Wildt, 'Einleitung', p 14, n 23.

45 Ibid, p 11; see also, Wildt, *Generation des Unbedingten*, p 269; Wildt follows the calculations of Browder, George C, 'The Numerical Strength of the Sicherheitsdienst des RFSS', *Historical Social Research* 28, 1983, pp 30–41.

46 All statistics from report signed by Rudolf Bamler, 'Organisation der Abwehrabteilung', August 1937, BA-MA, RW 5/v. 207, folios 65–7.

47 Bamler, report on the Abwehr conference of 21 and 22 June 1935; see also Höhne, *Canaris*, p 186.

48 Mader, Julius, *Hitlers Spionagegenerale sagen aus*, Berlin (East), 1970, p 211f. The GDR author Julius Mader, roundly abused in the West, refers to statements and documents made by Franz-Eccard von Bentivegni (head of Abwehr III 1939–44) in Soviet captivity. Even if Mader's books were aimed ideologically at West German intelligence, and must be treated with great caution, in many respects they do have a

solid foundation in information. The statements attributed to senior Abwehr officials and officers – principally Piekenbrock, Bentivegni and Stolze – are comprehensive regarding the human and structural expansion of the Abwehr in the early years under Canaris. See also Höhne, *Canaris*, pp 185–202.

49 Wildt, *Nachrichtendienst*, p 14.

50 Best, 'Canaris', p 176; cf also Leverkuehn, Paul, *Der geheime Nachrichtendienst der deutschen Wehrmacht im Kriege*, Frankfurt am Main, 1957, p 11ff; Bartz, Karl, *Die Tragödie der deutschen Abwehr*, Preußisch Oldendorf, 1972, p 68ff; Höhne, *Canaris*, p 203f; finally Mühleisen, 'Duell', p 401f and Herbert, *Best*, p 184.

51 'Bericht über Stapostellen-Leiter-Besprechung am 19. 10. 36', dated 11 November 36, BA-MA, RW 5/v. 194, o.P.

52 'Grundsätze für die Zusammenarbeit zwischen der Geheimen Staatspolizei und den Abwehrdienststellen der Wehrmacht vom 21. 12. 1936', copy, 23 December 1936, BA-MA, RW 5/v. 194, o.P.

53 Henke, Gerhard, 'Bericht und Erinnerungen', *Die Nachhut* 2, 1967, p 10, BA-MA, MSg 3-22/1.

54 Schäfer, report on the Abwehrpolizei, p 5f, IfZ, ZS 372, folio 5f; see also Herbert, *Best*, p 184.

55 Ibid.

56 Best, 'Canaris', p 176.

57 Höhne, *Canaris*, p 203.

13 Between Fürher, Duce and Caudillo

1 Quoted from Kershaw, *Hitler 1889–1936*, p 738, and also Kershaw, *Hitler 1936–1945*, Stuttgart, 2000, p 15. This account follows Kershaw, who for his part relies primarily on the American journalist Shirer, William, *Berliner Tagebuch. Aufzeichnungen 1934–1941*, published by Jürgen Schebera, Leipzig and Weimar, 1991. Shirer's book is one of the most impressive and enlightening contemporary works by a foreign observer and is very frequently used as a source in historical writing.

2 Kershaw, *Hitler 1889–1936*, p 739.

3 Ibid, p 738.

4 Messerschmidt, Manfred, 'Außenpolitik und Kriegsvorbereitung', in *DRZW*, vol 1, p 606.

5 Kershaw, *Hitler 1889–1936*, p 733f.

6 Messerschmidt, 'Kriegsvorbereitung', p 604.

7 Höhne, *Canaris*, p 205. Höhne refers repeatedly to Farago, Ladislas, *The Game of the Foxes*, New York, 1971, a thoroughly controversial book that exercised a major influence on subsequent secret service literature. Farago (1906–80) worked for US Naval Intelligence in the Second World War. His anecdote that on the evening of 11 February Canaris passed to Hitler a forged secret protocol to the French–Soviet pact that influenced Hitler that night to advance the date of the invasion, seems extremely unlikely (Höhne, *Canaris*, p 205). According to Hossbach (*Zwischen Wehrmacht und Hitler*, p 97) Hitler did not return from the funeral of Wilhelm Gustloff until 12 February, after which he left for Garmisch for the Winter Olympics. While in Berlin he spent a few hours in talks, but the name of Canaris never crops up. Schmidt,

Rainer F, *Die Außenpolitik des Dritten Reiches 1933–1939*, Stuttgart, 2002, p 193, agrees that at that point in time the decision had already been taken and Hitler informed Fritsch, and next day Blomberg at Garmisch. Kershaw is of the opinion that the final decision was taken on 1 March. Kershaw, *Hitler 1889–1936*, p 736.

8   Reile, Oscar, *Geheime Westfront*, Munich and Wels, 1962, p 23ff. Buchheit follows him in *Die Deutsche Geheimdienst*, p 133.

9   Hossbach, *Zwischen Wehrmacht und Hitler*, p 98; Schmidt, *Außenpolitik*, p 200; Kershaw, *Hitler 1889–1936*, p 741; Müller, *Heer und Hitler*, p 214.

10   Hossbach, *Zwischen Wehrmacht und Hitler*, p 98; Müller, *Heer und Hitler*, p 215f.

11   Ibid.

12   Höhne, *Canaris*, pp 199 and 217.

13   Müller, *Heer und Hitler*, p 227, n 107.

14   Ibid, p 233.

15   Faber du Faur, Moritz, *Macht und Ohnmacht*, Stuttgart, 1953, p 233ff.

16   Ibid, p 200.

17   Preston, Paul, *Franco. A Biography*, London, 1995, p 140ff.

18   For German involvement at the beginning of the Spanish Civil War see, most recently, Viñas, Angel, and Seidel, Carlos Collado, 'Franco's Request to the Third Reich for Military Assistance', *Contemporary European History* 11, 2002, p 197.

19   Ibid, p 196.

20   Viñas and Seidel, 'Franco's Request', p 192.

21   Eg Höhne, *Canaris*, p 219f, who refers to Thomas, Hugh, *Der spanische Bürgerkrieg*, Berlin, Frankfurt and Vienna, 1961. In the extended English language reprint of the 2001 standard work there is no reference to a meeting between Sanjurjo and Canaris.

22   Legation Secretary von Bülow to Botschaftsrat Völckers (Madrid), 6 July 1936, in ADAP, series C, vol V, 1, no 433, p 687f.

23   Viñas and Seidel, 'Franco's Request', p 194.

24   Ibid, p 199.

25   Consulate, Tetuan to Foreign Ministry, 22 July 1936, in ADAP, series D, vol III, no 2, p 5.

26   Chargé d'affaires Lisbon to Foreign Ministry, 24 July 1936, in ADAP, series D, vol III, no 8, p 10.

27   Ambassador Welczeck, Paris, to Foreign Ministry, 23 July 1936, in ADAP, series D, vol III, no 3, p 6.

28   Viñas and Seidel, 'Franco's Request', p 191.

29   Ibid, p 201.

30   Ibid, p 204.

31   Kershaw, *Hitler 1936–1945*, p 49.

32   Ambassadorial Adviser Schwendemann, Madrid, to the Foreign Ministry, 23 July 1936, in ADAP, series D, vol III, no 4, pp 6–8.

33   Viñas and Seidel, 'Franco's Request', p 202.

34   Viñas and Seidel, 'Franco's Request', p 204, doubt but cannot rule out that this was either Raeder or Commandant Karl Coupette. There is a possibility that Canaris was staying at Bayreuth and assisted Hitler in his decision. Abshagen, *Canaris*, p 163, points out that it is not certain when Canaris and Franco were introduced, but he ascribes to Canaris an important role in the decision to support Franco, which

virtually all Franco and Canaris biographies follow. The colourful representations (Brissaud, *Canaris*, p 71, and Höhne, *Canaris*, p 223), which have Hitler, Canaris, Blomberg and Goering enjoying the music at Bayreuth is not suppoorted by the sources. Abendroth, Hans-Henning, 'Hitlers Entscheidung', in Schieder, Wolfgang, and Dipper, Christoph (eds), *Der Spanische Bürgerkrieg in der Internationalen Politik (1936–1939)*, Munich, 1976, pp 92 and 122, n 103, draws attention to the fact that Hitler sent an aircraft to Hamburg that night to enable naval expert Konteradmiral Lindau to come to Bayreuth.

35   Kershaw, *Hitler 1936–1945*, p 49.

36   Viñas and Seidel, 'Franco's Request', p 207.

37   Botschafter von Welczeck to Ministerialdirektor Dieckhoff, 2 August 1936, in ADAP, series D, vol III, no 25, p 22f.

38   Ambassador in Paris to Foreign Ministry, 8 August 1936, in ADAP, series D, vol III, no 33, p 30f.

39   Ibid, no 44, p 39.

40   Abendroth, 'Hitlers Entscheidung', p 103.

41   Ibid, p 103f.

42   Ibid, p 110.

43   Schieder, Wolfgang, 'Spanischer Bürgerkrieg und Vierjahresplan. Zur Struktur nationalsozialistischer Außenpolitik', in Schieder and Dipper, *Der Spanische Bürgerkrieg*, p 170.

44   Reichsminister von Neurath to Ambassador von Hassell, 30 October 1936, in ADAP, series D, vol III, no 113, pp 105–7.

45   Abendroth, 'Hitlers Entscheidung', p 111.

46   Schieder, 'Spanischer Bürgerkrieg und Vierjahresplan', pp 170 and 187f, n 47.

47   Ambassador in Rome to the Foreign Ministry, 1 December 1936, in ADAP, series D, vol III, no 136, p 126.

48   Note, Ministerialdirektor Dieckhoff, 11 December 1936, in ADAP, series D, vol III, no 151, p 142; Ambassador in Rome to Foreign Ministry, 17 December 1936, in ibid, no 156, p 145; cf also Thomas, Hugh, *The Spanish Civil War*, London, 2001, p 553f.

49   Ambassador in Rome to Foreign Ministry, 29 December 1936, in ADAP, series D, vol III, no 170, p 162f.

50   Jodl diaries, entries 5 and 9 January 1937, in IMG, vol XXVIII, document 1780-PS, p 346f.

51   Ibid, entry 14 January 1937, p 349.

52   Buchheit, *Die Deutsche Geheimdienst*, p 137; Höhne, *Canaris*, p 231f.

53   Ibid; see also the statement by former Abwehr III Chief von Bentivegni after the war in Soviet in Mader, *Hitlers Spionagegenerale*, p 230.

54   Höhne, *Canaris*, p 232.

55   Courtois, Stephane, and Panné, Jean-Louis, 'Der lange Arm des NKWD fällt auf Spanien', in Courtois, Stephane, Werth, Nicolas, Panné, Jean-Louis, Paczkowski, Andrzej, Bartosek, Karel, and Magolin, Jean-Louis, *Das Schwarzbuch des Kommunismus. Unterdrückung, Verbrechen und Terror*, Munich and Zürich, 2000, p 370.

56   Thomas, *Spanish Civil War*, p 337f.

57   Roloff, Stefan, *Die Rote Kapelle. Die Widerstandsgruppe im Dritten Reich und die Geschichte Helmut Roloffs*, Munich, 2002, p 100ff; Brysac, Shareen Blair, *Mildred*

Harnack und die Rote Kapelle, Berne, 2003, p 295ff; Höhne, Heinz, *Kennwort Direktor, Die Geschichte der Roten Kapelle*, Frankfurt am Main, 1970, p 130f; for a retrospective reconstruction of the so-called Rote Kapelle made by the Gestapo and long admitted by research, Coppi, Hans, 'Die Rote Kapelle im Spannungsfeld von Widerstand und nachrichtendienstlicher Tätigkeit – Trepper Report, June 1943', *Vierteljahrshefte für Zeitgeschichte* 44, 1996, pp 431–58, including a survey and review of the research. See also Coppi, Hans, Danyel, Jürgen and Tuchel, Johannes (eds), *Die Rote Kapelle*, Berlin, 1994; Roth, Karl Heinz and Ebbinghaus, Angelika (eds), *Rote Kapellen – Kreisauer Kreise - Schwarze Kapellen, Neue Sichtweisen auf den Widerstand gegen die NS-Diktatur 1938–1945*, Hamburg, 2004.

58 Brysac, *Harnack*, p 297; Roloff, *Kapelle*, p 101.
59 Brysac, *Harnack*, p 300.
60 Höhne, 'Direktor', p 142; Brysac, *Harnack*, p 299; Roloff, *Kapelle*, p 103.
61 Ibid; Brysac, *Harnack*, p 299f; Höhne, 'Direktor', p 142f; also Höhne, *Canaris*, p 233. Höhne gives the arrest as 1937, Roloff puts it at February 1938.
62 Höhne, *Canaris*, p 234.
63 ADAP, series C, vol IV, no 2, p 929, publisher's note to no 479, pp 930–8; Schmidt, *Außenpolitik*, p 210; Kershaw, *Hitler 1936–1945*, p 62.
64 Kordt, Erich, *Nicht aus den Akten*, Stuttgart, 1950, p 123.
65 Martin, Bernd, 'Die deutsch-japanischen Beziehungen während des Dritten Reiches', in Funke, Manfred (ed), *Hitler, Deutschland und die Mächte. Materialien zur Außenpolitik des Dritten Reiches*, Bonner Schriften zur Politik und Zeitgeschichte 12, Düsseldorf, 1978, p 460.
66 Ibid, p 461.
67 Ibid.
68 Ibid, p 462 with n 40; Kershaw, *Hitler 1936–1945*, p 63. Ribbentrop and Hack had already been working for months – probably with the involvement of Canaris (Schmidt, *Außenpolitik*, p 210) – towards a treaty. Canaris is mentioned in Hack's papers, assessed by Martin.
69 Ambassador von Dirksen, Tokyo, to Legationsrat von Erdmannsdorff, 1 January 1936, in ADAP, series C, vol IV, 2, no 479, pp 930–8 (with Appendix 'Aufzeichnung über die Möglichkeiten eines deutsch-japanischen militärischen und politischen Zusammenwirkens').
70 Kordt, *Nicht aus den Akten*, p 156.
71 Martin, 'Die deutsch-japanischen Beziehungen', p 462.
72 Schmidt, *Außenpolitik*, p 210.
73 Both texts reproduced in Sommer, Theo, *Deutschland und Japan zwischen den Mächten 1935–1940*, Tübingen, 1962, p 493ff.
74 Kershaw, *Hitler 1936–1945*, p 63.
75 Schmidt, *Außenpolitik*, p 211.
76 Höhne, *Canaris*, p 238.
77 Glaubauf, Karl, and Lahousen, Stefanie, *Generalmajor Erwin Lahousen Edler von Vivremont*, vol 2, Münster, Berlin, Hamburg, London and Vienna, 2005, p 25f.
78 Heinz, 'Canaris', p 59ff.
79 Meinl, *Nationalsozialisten*, p 258.
80 Heinz, 'Canaris', p 59.

81 Werth, Nicolas, 'Ein Staat gegen sein Volk. Gewalt, Unterdrückung und Terror in der Sowjetunion', in Courtois et al, *Schwarzbuch*, pp 51–295, here p 220.

82 Lukes, Igor, 'Stalin, Benesh und der Fall Tuchatschewski', *Vierteljahrhefte für Zeitgeschichte* 44, 1996, pp 527–47, here p 529f, with n 9.

83 Werth, 'Staat', p 221.

84 Schellenberg, Walter, *Memoiren*, London, 1956, p 48f.

85 Abshagen, *Canaris*, p 167f.

86 Hagen, Walter, *Die geheime Front*, Linz and Vienna, 1950, p 56f.

87 It is equally impossible here to delve into all the ramifications involved in the passing of information on the part of the interested German side during these secret negotiations. For greater detail see Lukes, 'Stalin', including discussion on the research with opinion and sources.

88 Ibid, p 541ff.

89 Heinz, 'Canaris', p 40f.

90 Letter, Patzig to Walter Baum, 10 November 1953, IfZ, ZS 540, folio 5. That it was not only Heydrich who was waiting for Canaris to throw in the towel is proved by a letter or file note – without an addressee it is uncertain which – of Gruppenleiter Rudolf Bamler, who with regard to Canaris's workload and frequent absences abroad attempted quite openly to undermine his position. Bamler told Canaris frankly that he would not be able to run the Abwehr himself. Apparently the manoeuvring had no success. Letter signed by von Bamler, August 1937, BA-MA, RW 5/207, folios 65–9.

14 Ousting the Generals

1 For the Blomberg–Fritsch crisis see primarily Müller, *Heer und Hitler*, ch VI, pp 255–99; Janssen, Karl-Heinz and Tobias, Fritz, *Der Sturz der Generäle – Hitler und die Blomberg-Fritsch-Krise 1938*, Munich, 1994; Mühleisen, Horst, 'Dokumentation: "Die Fritsch-Krise im Frühjahr 1938. Neun Dokumente aus dem Nachlaß des Generalobersten"', *Militärgeschichtliche Mitteilungen* 56, 1997, pp 471–508. Mühleisen is highly critical of Janssen and Tobias. The analysis of the Blomberg–Fritsch crisis here really follows Mühleisen and the documents edited by him in the Fritsch collection (BA-MA, N 33/19 and N 33/20) as well as Müller.

2 From Colvin, Ian, *Chief of Intelligence. Was Canaris, Hitler's Spy Chief, a British Agent?*, London, 1951, p 43.

3 Mühleisen, 'Fritsch-Krise', pp 473 and 497, n 164.

4 Kershaw, *Hitler 1936–1945*, p 93.

5 Janssen and Tobias, *Sturz*, p 45f.

6 Ibid, pp 27f and 51; Kershaw, *Hitler 1936–1945*, p 95.

7 Goebbels's Diaries, vol 3, p 1184, entry 27 January 1938.

8 Hossbach, *Zwischen Wehrmacht und Hitler*, p 125.

9 Ibid, p 126.

10 Longhand draft by Fritsch. 'Notiert von Februar bis September 1938, beendet am 27. September 1938', in Mühleisen, 'Fritsch-Krise', document 7, p 493.

11 Ibid, and p 494.

12 Ibid, p 494.

13 Letter from Fritsch addressed to commanding generals (but not sent), May 1938, in Mühleisen, 'Fritsch-Krise', document 6, p 492.

14 Longhand draft, Fritsch, in Mühleisen, 'Fritsch-Krise', document 7, p 494.

15 Ibid, p 495.

16 Letter, Fritsch to Hitler, 26 Janaury 1938, in Mühleisen, 'Fritsch-Krise', document 1, p 483.

17 Longhand draft, Fritsch, in Mühleisen, 'Fritsch-Krise', document 7, pp 495 and 496.

18 Ibid.

19 Mühleisen, 'Fritsch-Krise', p 476 and document 6, p 492 with n 125 and 126. See also statement of Gisevius in IMG, vol XII, p 222. Contradicting this, see Janssen and Tobias, *Sturz*, pp 167–70 who strongly doubt that the Gestapo was handling the Fritsch investigation before the official start to the inquiry on 24 January 1938.

20 Mühleisen, 'Fritsch-Krise', p 474. Janssen and Tobias, *Sturz*, pp 86ff and 276, n 15, agree that in the wake of the Blomberg affair, Hitler recalled the Fritsch affair in 1936 and feared a supplementary scandal. Therefore he had ordered the file reconstructed. The authors rely on the statements of General Hermann Foertsch in 1952. Kershaw, *Hitler 1936–1945*, p 96f, follows this version. Müller, *Heer und Hitler*, p 256, contends that Goering linked the Blomberg and Fritsch cases together and laid the Fritsch papers before Hitler. See also Krausnick, 'Vorgeschichte', p 286, with n 177.

21 Thun-Hohenstein, Remedio Galeazzo Graf von, *Der Verschwörer – General Oster und die Militäropposition; mit einer Einleitung von Golo Mann*, Berlin, 1982, p 44f; for Oster see also Graml, Hermann, 'Der Fall Oster', *Vierteljahrshefte für Zeitgeschichte* 14, 1966, pp 26–39; for Nebe see Rathert, Ronald, *Verbrechen und Verschwörung: Arthur Nebe. Der Kripochef des Dritten Reiches*, Münster, Hamburg and London, 2001; Gisevius, Hans Bernd, *Wo ist Nebe? Erinnerungen an Hitlers Reichskriminaldirektor*, Zürich, 1966; on the relationship between Gisevius and Nebe, see Jacobsen, Hans-Adolf (ed), *Opposition gegen Hitler und der Staatsstreich vom 20. Juli 1944 – Geheime Dokumente aus dem ehemaligen Reichssicherheitshauptamt*, 2 vols, Stuttgart, 1989, vol 1, p 245.

22 Gisevius, Hans Bernd, *Bis zum bitteren Ende, Vol 1, Vom Reichstagsbrand zur Fritsch-Krise*, Zürich, 1946, p 400f.

23 Jodl diaries, 28 January 1938, in IMG, vol XXVIII, p 359.

24 Gisevius, *Bis zum betteren Ende*, vol 1, p 404.

25 Jacobsen, *Opposition*, p 430, SD report, 2 October 1944.

26 Hoffmann, Peter, *Widerstand, Staatsstreich, Attentat. Der Kampf der Opposition gegen Hitler*, Munich, 1985, p 66f; Müller, *Heer und Hitler*, p 276f; Fest, Joachim, *Staatsstreich. Der lange Weg zum 20. Juli*, Berlin, 1994, p 65.

27 Höhne, *Canaris*, p 254, from a communication from Halder to the MGFA.

28 Draft notes, Christine v. Dohnanyi, IfZ, ZS 603, folio 4.

29 On Dohnanyi, see principally Smid, Marikje, *Hans von Dohnanyi – Christine Bonhoeffer: Eine Ehe im Widerstand gegen Hitler*, Gütersloh, 2002, p 185ff.

30 Quoted from Janssen and Tobias, *Sturz*, p 120.

31 Ibid, p 121. Janssen and Tobias put forward the argument that Gürtner helped Hitler out of his quandary by anticipating the verdict and thus accelerating Fritsch's downfall. Kershaw, *Hitler 1936–1945*, p 99, considers that the opinion inverted all standard rules of justice.

32 Smid, *Dohnanyi – Bonhoeffer*, p 186.

33 Draft, Christine v. Dohnanyi, IfZ, ZS 603, folio 4.

34 Bösch, Hermann, *Heeresrichter Dr. Karl Sack im Widerstand*, Munich, 1967, p 51; Deutsch, Harold C, *Das Komplott oder die Entmachtung der Generale. Blomberg- und Fritsch-Krise, Hitlers Weg zum Krieg*, Eichstätt, 1974, p 253.

35 Krausnick, 'Vorgeschichte', p 308; Müller, *Heer und Hitler*, p 284f; Hoffmann, *Widerstand*, p 65.

36 Thun-Hohenstein, *Verschwörer*, p 67.

37 Müller, *Heer und Hitler*, p 278; Hoffmann, *Widerstand*, p 65; Gisevius, *Bis zum betteren Ende*, vol 1, p 408ff.

38 Müller, *Heer und Hitler*, p 282.

39 Hoffmann, *Widerstand*, p 68; Müller, *Heer und Hitler*, p 283; Fest, *Staatsstreich*, p 65.

40 Quoted from Kershaw, *Hitler 1936–1945*, p 103.

41 Ibid, p 101.

42 Keitel's instruction of 7 February 1938, reproduced in Müller, *Heer und Hitler*, document 35, p 641. For the divergent plans of the Army and Navy Commands to the Wehrmacht leadership in the spring of 1938 see Dülffer, Jost, 'Überlegungen von Kriegsmarine und Heer zur Wehrmachtspitzengliederung und zur Führung der Wehrmacht im Kriege im Februar-März 1938', *Militärgeschichtliche Mitteilungen* 9, 1971, pp 145–71.

43 Abshagen, *Canaris*, p 70.

44 Letter by Fritsch addressed, but not sent, to the commanding generals, May 1938, in Mühleisen, 'Fritsch-Krise', document 6, p 492.

45 Statement dictated by Fritsch, 23 February 1938, in Mühleisen, 'Fritsch-Krise', document 3, p 487.

46 Fritsch's closing address to the Reich War Court, 17 March 1938, in Mühleisen, 'Fritsch-Krise', document 4, p 488.

47 Jodl diaries, 10 February 1938, in IMG, vol XXVIII, p 367.

48 Longhand draft, Fritsch, in Mühleisen, 'Fritsch-Krise', document 7, p 499.

49 Statement by Gisevius, in IMG, vol XII, p 222.

50 Janssen and Tobias, *Sturz*, p 164f.

51 Müller, *Heer und Hitler*, p 279.

52 'Niederschrift eines Vortrags des Chefs der Amtsgruppe Ausland/Abwehr, Konteradmiral Canaris, anläßlich einer Ic-Besprechung im OKW am 3. März 1938', printed in Müller, *Heer und Hitler*, document 36, pp 641–5.

53 Ibid, p 642.

54 Ibid, p 643.

55 Ibid, p 644.

56 Quoted from Höhne, *Canaris*, p 260.

57 'Niederschrift eines Vortrags des Chefs der Amtsgruppe Ausland/Abwehr, Konteradmiral Canaris, anläßlich einer Ic-Besprechung im OKW am 3. März 1938', p 645.

58 What transpired in the remaining days before the trial began is also disputed. Ex-Adjutant Hossbach and OKW legal expert Heinrich Rosenberger were concerned for the safety of Rittmeister Frisch and had asked Canaris to ask Gürtner to ensure his safety; Gürtner refused, saying that it was up to the Wehrmacht to do so. Canaris and Rosenberger then attempted unsuccessfully to convince Keitel to protect Frisch

(Janssen and Tobias, *Sturz*, p 171f). Another version states that Canaris did not take the fears seriously, and Frisch was then arrested by the Gestapo. Canaris had photographed the Gestapo papers, as a life policy for Frisch. Höhne, *Canaris*, p 267). Janssen and Tobias refer to the statement of Kriminaldirektor Erich Sander, in which Frisch was never arrested (Janssen and Tobias, *Sturz*, p 172). No less controversial is the alleged additional interrogation of Generaloberst Fritsch on 20 February by the Gestapo at a Wannsee villa. This neutral venue had been chosen at Keitel's suggestion because Canaris, Goltz and Oster feared for Fritsch's life (Höhne, *Canaris*, p 265). Janssen and Tobias doubt such an interrogation took place, since neither Goltz nor Fritsch mentioned it in their memoirs (Janssen and Tobias, *Sturz*, p 163). This is supported by Fritsch's longhand draft in Mühleisen, 'Fritsch-Krise', document 7, p 501, with n 179. Here Fritsch wrote that he was interrogated by the Gestapo twice (27 and 28 January) and by the Reich War Court once (23 February).

59 Mühleisen, 'Fritsch-Krise', p 475 and document 6, pp 491–3.

60 Longhand draft, Fritsch, in Mühleisen, 'Fritsch-Krise', document 7, p 500.

61 Longhand draft, Fritsch, 18 January 1939, in Mühleisen, 'Fritsch-Krise', document 8, p 506.

62 Blackmailer Schmidt, sentenced to seven years' imprisonment in 1936, was transferred to Sachsenhausen concentration camp in November 1939 and hanged there on Himmler's order on 30 October 1942. See letter from Himmler to Goering, 29 July 1942 in Müller, *Heer und Hitler*, document 32, p 637, with appendix at p 638. Goering noted in the margin of the letter: 'He should have been shot long ago.'

63 Quoted from longhand draft, Fritsch, in Mühleisen, 'Fritsch-Krise', document 7, p 501, n 196.

64 Anonymous opinion on the case of Generaloberst Freiherrn von Fritsch, reproduced in Müller, *Heer und Hitler*, document 34, pp 639–40. For the collaboration of Canaris and Hossbach, see Hossbach, *Zwischen Wehrmacht und Hitler*, p 129. For the origins of the Canaris–Hossbach relationship see Müller, *Heer und Hitler*, p 280. The Gestapo and SD were convinced after 20 July 1944 that Oster and Dohnanyi were the authors of a document entitled 'Die Wehrmacht als Machtfaktor im innerpolitischen Kräftespiel' (The Wehrmacht as a Power Factor in the Internal Political Power Game), appendix to Kaltenbrunner's letter to Bormann, 15 December 1944, in Jacobsen, *Opposition*, p 529. Janssen and Tobias consider their involvement probable and also attribute to Gisevius a hand as author or contributor, which is not to be inferred from his memoirs (Janssen and Tobias, *Sturz*, p 190f; Gisevius, *Bis zum Bitteren Ende*, vol 1, p 413. In my opinion too much weight is attached to this part. Also ibid, p 437ff.)

65 'Stellungnahme zum Fall des Generaloberst Freiherrn von Fritsch', p 640.

15 A Double Game

1 Kershaw, *Hitler 1936–1945*, p 115.

2 Schmidt, *Außenpolitik*, p 249; see also Papen, *Wahrheit*, pp 456 and 460ff.

3 Kershaw, *Hitler 1936–1945*, p 116; Schmidt, *Außenpolitik*, p 250.

4 Record of conference of 12 February 1938, in ADAP, series D, vol 1, no 294, pp 421–4; Kershaw, *Hitler 1936–1945*, p 116; Schmidt, *Außenpolitik*, p 251.

5   Statement Keitel, IMG, vol X, p 568.
6   Jodl diaries, 13 February 1938, IMG, vol XXVIII, p 367; also IMG, vol II, p 449 and Statement, Keitel, IMG, vol X, p 568.
7   Höhne, *Canaris*, p 263.
8   Jodl diaries, 14 February 1938, IMG, vol XXVIII, p 367.
9   Nuremberg document 1775-PS, IMG, vol II, p 450.
10 Statement, Keitel, IMG, vol X, p 568 and vol XI, p 28.
11 Jodl diaries, 4 March 1938, IMG, vol XXVIII, p 369.
12 Schmidt, *Außenpolitik*, p 251; Kershaw, *Hitler 1936–1945*, p 118f.
13 Ibid, p 120.
14 Schmidt, *Außenpolitik*, p 252f.
15 Kershaw, *Hitler 1936–1945*, p 121.
16 Jodl diaries, 4 March 1938, IMG, vol XXVIII, p 371.
17 Statement, Keitel, IMG, vol X, p 566; Kershaw, *Hitler 1936–1945*, p 122.
18 Müller, *Heer und Hitler*, p 236.
19 Statement, Manstein, IMG, vol XX, p 566.
20 Leverkuehn, *Der geheime Nachrichtendienst*, p 69.
21 Kershaw, *Hitler 1936–1945*, p 125.
22 Information from Stefanie Lahousen to the author, 3 January 2006; Glaubauf and Lahousen, *Lahousen*, p 26f; another version with slight differences appears in Brissaud, *Canaris*, p 154. Brissaud, who gives no sources and relies mainly on personal conversations with former Abwehr colleagues, must be treated with caution, but what he says does not contradict Pruck's recollection that Canaris spent the night of 13 March in his office. It is very possible that he flew back on the 12th to observe the foreign policy situation (Höhne, *Canaris*, p 270). Responsibility for the security measures attending Hitler's entry into Vienna on 14 March was handed to Schellenberg, who flew to Vienna on the night of 13 March (Schellenberg, *Memoiren*, p 53).
23 Höhne, *Canaris*, p 270.
24 Foreign Ministry note, 13 March 1938, in ADAP, series D, vol 1, no 372, p 482.
25 British ambassador Henderson to Generalfeldmarschall Goering, 13 March 1938, in ADAP, series D, vol 1, no 376, p 484.
26 Chargé d'affaires in Rome to Foreign Ministry, 13 March 1938, in ADAP, series D, vol 1, no 373, p 482.
27 Kershaw, *Hitler 1936–1945*, p 130.
28 Herbert, *Best*, p 234.
29 Statement, Lahousen, IMG, vol 2, p 491. According to Stefanie Lahousen, the main purpose of Marogna-Redwitz's suggestion that Canaris should take Lahousen with him to Berlin was to rid himself of an unsettled colleague in Vienna by elegantly 'pushing him upstairs'.
30 See Groscurth, Helmuth, *Tagebücher eines Abwehroffiziers 1938–1940*, edited by Helmut Krausnick and Harold C Deutsch, Stuttgart, 1970, here Introduction, pp 15–95; referred to hereafter as Krausnick, Deutsch and Kotze, *Einführung*, also 'Groscurth diaries'.
31 From Abshagen, *Canaris*, p 182. [*Translator's note:* an *Ostmärker* was an Austrian Nazi in favour of Austria becoming a German province.]
32 Letter, Lahousen to Otto Benninghoff, 23 October 1954, IfZ, ZS 658, folio 12.

33 'Die nationalpolitische Stellung des Offiziers in der Deutschen Wehrmacht', Address by Vizeadmiral Canaris, OKW, 22 April in Vienna, IfZ, FD 47. There is no indication of where this conference was held or to whom the speech was made, and after the war Lahousen could not help with this information (see letter to Otto Benninghoff, IfZ, ZS 658, folio 12). Details here from Höhne, *Canaris*, p 275. Stefanie Lahousen remains of the opinion that this was mere 'window dressing' by Canaris and in no way reflected his real attitude.

34 Address, Canaris, IfZ, FD 47.

35 Ibid, p 2.

36 Ibid, p 5.

37 'Merkblatt über Spionage, Spionageabwehr und Landesverrat', with annotation by Rudolf Bamler, BA-MA, RW 5/196 b, folios 22–6.

38 Personal service record, Hans Oster, original at BA-MA, copy at IfZ, folio 87, Thun-Hohenstein, *Verschwörer*, p 33.

39 Ibid, p 34.

40 Ibid, p 40f.

41 Ibid, pp 42 and 277, n 53.

42 Personal service record, Oster, IfZ, folio 87.

43 Thun-Hohenstein, *Verschwörer*, p 51f.

44 Ibid, p 120.

45 Meinl, *Nationalsozialisten*, p 44.

46 Ibid, p 244f. For more on Heinz see: Meinl, Susanne and Krüger, Dieter, 'Der politische Weg des Friedrich Wilhelm Heinz. Vom Freikorpskämpfer zum Leiter des Nachrichtendienstes im Bundeskanzleramt', *Vierteljahrshefte für Zeitgeschichte* 42, 1994, pp 39–69.

47 Letter signed by Canaris, 1 May 1937, regarding the restructure of IIIc on 22 April 1937, BA-MA, RW 5/196a, folio 34.

48 Ibid, p 255f.

49 Affidavit, Lahousen, Seefeld, 27 January 1948, IfZ, ZS 658, folios 50–4.

50 Glaubauf and Lahousen, *Lahousen*, p 28; Thun-Hohenstein, *Verschwörer*, pp 120 and 284, n 7. According to this account, Lahousen told Achim Oster after the war how his father had received him and how this welcome had very much surprised him.

51 From Meinl, *Nationalsozialisten*, p 253.

52 Meyer, Winifried, *Unternehmen Sieben – Eine Rettungsakton für vom Holocaust Bedrohte aus dem Amt Ausland/Abwehr im Oberkommando der Wehrmacht*, Frankfurt am Main, 1993, p 112f; Meinl, *Nationalsozialisten*, p 253.

53 Ibid, p 252.

54 Opinion of General (retd) Erwin Lahousen, 28 August 1952, IfZ, ZS 658, folio 6.

55 Höhne, Heinz, 'Canaris und die Abwehr zwischen Anpassung und Opposition', in Schmädecke, Jürgen, and Steinbach, Peter (eds), *Der Widerstand gegen den Nationalsozialismus. Die deutsche Gesellschaft und der Widerstand gegen Hitler*, Munich, 1985, p 407.

56 Letter, Canaris to OKM, OKH and OKL, 31 March 1938, BA-MA, RW 5/v. 197, folio 24.

57 Meinl, *Nationalsozialisten*, p 272.

58 Ibid, p 273.

59 Ibid, p 272.

60 Höhne, *Canaris*, p 275f.

61 Report, Vizeadmiral a.D. Leopold Bürkner, 22 August 1960, 'Die "Abteilung später Amtsgruppe Ausland" im "Amt Ausland/Abwehr" des Oberkommandos der ehemaligen deutschen Wehrmacht', BA-MA, RW 5/278, folios 1–9, here folio 4.

16 Between Obedience and Conscience

1   Schmidt, *Außenpolitik*, p 261.

2   Ibid; see also Röhr, Werner, 'Das Sudetendeutsche Freikorps – Diversionsinstrument der Hitler-Regierung bei der Zerschlagung der Tschechoslowakei', *Militärgeschichtliche Mitteilungen* 52, 1993, p 36; Smelser, Ronald M, *Das Sudetenproblem und das Dritte Reich 1933–1938*, Munich and Vienna, 1980, p 193ff; Kershaw, *Hitler 1936–1945*, p 148.

3   From Kershaw, *Hitler 1936–1945*, p 148.

4   The catalogue of demands are detailed in Röhr, 'Freikorps', p 39; cf Schmidt, *Außenpolitik*, p 261; Kershaw, *Hitler 1936–1945*, p 148.

5   Röhr, 'Freikorps', p 38; Schmidt, *Außenpolitik*, p 261.

6   Röhr, 'Freikorps', p 38.

7   See Crowe, David M, *Oskar Schindler*, Frankfurt am Main 2005, who describes the activities of German intelligence in Czechoslovakia, with special attention to Oskar Schindler, an Abwehr agent during the Sudeten crisis and who, until the invasion of Poland, played an important role. See Mader, *Hitlers Spionagegenerale*, p 150ff, who deals extensively with the recruitment of Henlein's deputy Frank by the Abwehr (probably in 1937). Höhne, *Canaris*, p 278f.

8   Crowe, *Schindler*, p 129.

9   Mader, *Hitlers Spionagegenerale*, p 150.

10 Ibid, p 151; Höhne, *Canaris*, p 279.

11 From Crowe, *Schindler*, p 32.

12 Ibid.

13 Memorandum, Beck: 'Betrachtungen zur militärpolitischen Lage im Mai 1938 vom 05.05.1938', printed in Müller, *Beck*, Document 44, p 510 and 512.

14 Kershaw, *Hitler 1936–1945*, p 149.

15 Hill, Leonidas E (ed), *Die Weizsäcker-Papiere 1933–1950*, Berlin and Frankfurt am Main, 1974, p 127f.

16 Thun-Hohenstein, *Verschwörer*, p 83; Höhne, *Canaris*, p 281; Brandes, Detlev, 'Die Politik des Dritten Reiches gegenüber der Tschechoslowakei, in Funke, Manfred (ed), *Hitler, Deutschland und die Mächte*, Düsseldorf 1978, p 516; Smelser, *Sudetenproblem*, p 201.

17 Canaris, undated telex (probably 21/22 May), IMG, vol XXV, document 388-PS, p 432.

18 Jodl diaries, account with clear date; Kershaw, *Hitler 1936–1945*, p 152.

19 Changed instruction for 'Aufmarsch Grün', 30 May 1938, IMG, vol XXV, document 388-PS, p 434f.

20 Draft for the new instruction 'Grün', 20 May 1938, IMG, vol XXV, document 388-PS, pp 422–7.

21 'Denkschrift an den Oberbefehlshaber des Heeres über die militärische Aussichtslosigkeit eines Krieges gegen die Tschechoslowakei vom 15. 07. 1938', printed in Müller, *Beck*, document 48, p 538.

22 'Vortragsnotiz Becks über mögliche innen- und außenpolitische Entwicklungen, insbesondere über das Verhalten der obersten militärischen Führung angesichts der Gefahr eines Krieges mit der Tschechoslowakei vom 16. 07. 1938', printed in Müller, *Beck*, document 50, p 552. See Heinemann, Winfried, 'Der militärische Widerstand und der Krieg', in *DRZW*, *Vol 9. 1, Die deutsche Kriegsgesellschaft 1939– 1945. Politisierung, Vernichtung, Überleben*, Stuttgart, 2004, p 756.

23 Müller, *Heer und Hitler*, p 326f; Thun-Hohenstein, *Verschwörer*, p 89f.

24 'Vortragsnotiz des Chefs des Generalstabs des Heeres vom 18. Juli 1938 mit ergänzenden Vorschlägen zur Vortragsnotiz vom 16. Juli 1938', reprinted in Müller, *Beck*, document 51, pp 554–6; cf also Müller, *Heer und Hitler*, p 327f; Reynolds, Nicholas, *Beck. Gehorsam und Widerstand*, Wiesbaden and Munich, 1977, p 145ff; Thun-Hohenstein, *Verschwörer*, p 90.

25 According to Müller, *Heer und Hitler*, p 329.

26 According to Reynolds, *Beck*, p 146.

27 Thun-Hohenstein, *Verschwörer*, p 90; Kershaw, *Hitler 1936–1945*, p 157.

28 'Vortragsnotiz Becks über innen- und außenpolitische Informationen von Hauptmann a.D. Wiedemann und eigene Vorschläge zu innenpolitischen Maßnahmen der Generalität vom 29. 07. 1938', reprinted in Müller, *Beck*, document 52, p 558.

29 For the timing of Beck's decision see Müller, *Heer und Hitler*, p 333.

30 Thun-Hohenstein, *Verschwörer*, p 91.

31 Memorandum, Legationrat von der Heyden-Rynsch (Pol. Abt.), 6 August 1938, *ADAP*, series D, vol II, no 337, p 429.

32 Goebbels's Diaries, vol 3, entry 10 August 1938, p 1250.

33 Goebbels's Diaries, vol 3, entry 13 August 1938, p 1251.

34 Quoted from Höhne, *Canaris*, p 286.

35 Groscurth diaries, p 102, entry 15 August 1938 (private diary).

36 'Bericht des Generalmajor Lahousen. Geheimorganisation Canaris', Part I, BA-MA, MSg 1/2812, p 1.

37 Groscurth diaries, pp 111 and 113, entries 2 and 4 September 1938 (private diary).

38 Scheurig, Bodo, *Ewald von Kleist-Schmenzin. Ein Konservativer gegen Hitler*, Berlin and Frankfurt am Main, 1994, pp 150 and 153ff. Scheurig points out that most documents used by Colvin for his sources are not valid in every case and that he personally only uses information confirmed by the principal witness, von Schlabrendorff, p 222, n 9; see also Klemperer, Klemens von, *Die verlassenen Verschwörer. Der deutsche Widerstand auf der Suche nach Verbündeten 1938–1945*, Berlin, 1994, p 95ff; Thun-Hohenstein, *Verschwörer*, p 93f.

39 From Scheurig, *Kleist-Schmenzin*, p 153; similarly Thun-Hohenstein, *Verschwörer*, p 93; Hoffmann, *Widerstand*, p 83.

40 Scheurig, *Kleist-Schmenzin*, p 154.

41 Groscurth diaries, p 102f, entry 20 August 1938, n 20 and 23 (private diary); for State visit see Weizsäcker, Ernst von, *Erinnerungen*, Munich, 1950, p 168f; Hill, *Weizsäcker-Papiere 1933–1950*, pp 137–9; for Canaris's Hungarian contacts also Abshagen, *Canaris*, pp 187–90.

42 Hill, *Weizsäcker-Papiere 1933–1950*, p 139.

43 Groscurth diaries, p 103, entry 23 August 1938 (private diary).
44 Ibid, n 24.
45 Ibid, p 104, entry 27 August 1938 (private diary).
46 Ibid.
47 *Documents on British Foreign Policy, 3rd Series, vol II, 1938,* London, 1949, p 688, here quoted from Scheurig, *Kleist-Schmenzin,* p 158.
48 Ibid; Hoffmann, *Widerstand,* p 86.
49 Kershaw, *Hitler 1936–1945,* p 162.
50 Groscurth diaries, p 107, entry 29 August 1938 (private diary).
51 Kershaw, *Hitler 1936–1945,* p 163.
52 Groscurth diaries, p 113, entry 4 September 1938 (private diary).
53 Ibid, n 68.
54 Kershaw, *Hitler 1936–1945,* p 163.
55 Groscurth diaries, p 114, entry 8 September 1938 (private diary).
56 Ibid, p 115, n 78; cf also Smelser, *Sudetenproblem,* p 210.
57 Groscurth diaries, p 113, entry 8 September 1938.
58 Kershaw, *Hitler 1936–1945,* p 164.
59 Groscurth diaries, p 118, entry 13 September 1938 (private diary).
60 Jodl diaries, entry 13 September 1938, p 378.
61 Röhr, 'Freikorps', p 40f.
62 Ibid, p 41.
63 Ibid, p 45.
64 IMG, vol XXV, document PS- 388, p 445, Telegram Schmundt to OKH, quoted in Röhr, 'Freikorps', p 48. Groscurth diaries, entry 17 September 1938, p 120 with n 104.
65 Röhr, 'Freikorps', p 51.
66 Groscurth diaries, p 121f., entry 19 September 1938, with n 107 (private diary).
67 Ibid, p 122, entry 20 September 1938 (private diary).
68 Müller, *Heer und Hitler,* p 348.
69 Meinl, *Nationalsozialisten,* p 281.
70 Hoffmann, *Widerstand,* p 86.
71 Ibid; Klemperer, *Verschwörer,* p 98.
72 Hoffmann, *Widerstand,* p 87.
73 Halder's communication to Krausnick, 14 July 1955, in Krausnick, *Vorgeschichte,* p 341, n 399.
74 Weizsäcker, *Erinnerungen,* p 175.
75 Ibid, p 176.
76 Burckhardt, Carl J, *Meine Danziger Mission 1937–1939,* Munich, 1980, p 181f.
77 Cf additionally Thielenhaus, Marion, *Zwischen Anpassung und Widerstand. Deutsche Diplomaten 1938–1941,* Paderborn, 1985, p 71ff.
78 Quoted from ibid.
79 Meinl, *Nationalsozialisten,* p 281.
80 Quoted from Hoffmann, *Widerstand,* p 92.
81 Müller, *Heer und Hitler,* p 357.
82 Meinl, *Nationalsozialisten,* p 282. Presumably this originated from Heinz, who meant the current plans of the inner circle of conspirators to kill Hitler. See Heinz, 'Canaris', p 96ff.

83 Scheurig, Bodo, *Henning von Tresckow*, Oldenburg and Hamburg, 1973, p 59ff.
84 Meinl, *Nationalsozialisten*, p 283.
85 Smid, *Dohnanyi – Bonhoeffer*, p 194; Bethge, Eberhard, *Dietrich Bonhoeffer – Eine Biographie*, Munich, 1967, p 710f; Chowaniec, Elisabeth, *Der 'Fall Dohnanyi' 1943– 1945. Widerstand, Militärjustiz, Willkür*, Schriftenreihe der Vierteljahrshefte für Zeitgeschichte 62, Munich, 1991, p 14f.
86 This profile originated with Heinz's biographer, Susanne Meinl, who has assembled the most detailed research to date into the various Nationalist opposition groups to Hitler. Meinl, *Nationalsozialisten*, pp 284–8.
87 Heinz spoke of two assault squads each of about fifty men, but without going into details of their composition; Heinz, 'Canaris', p 96f. Buchheit, after speaking to Heinz, wrote of an assault squad of thirty men; Buchheit, *Geheimdienst*, p 148.
88 Gehre's participation was confirmed by Josef Müller, who learned of this from Gehre at Flossenbürg shortly before Gehre's execution there in 1945. IfZ, ZS 659, vol IV.
89 Meinl, *Nationalsozialisten*, p 285f. For Herzner see the next Part.
90 Heinz, 'Canaris', p 100; see also Meinl, *Nationalsozialisten*, pp 288–90; Hoffmann, *Widerstand*, pp 117 and 122ff; Müller, *Heer und Hitler*, p 362ff.
91 Hoffmann, *Widerstand*, p 125.
92 Krausnick, Deutsch and Kotze, *Einführung*, p 35. If Reinhard Groscurth was correct in saying that it was mid-September and not the end of the month, then it must have been the evening of the 14th. His brother's observation that 'something had happened in between' presumably meant Chamberlain's first visit to Hitler. After the Munich Conference the carpet had been pulled out from under the coup d'état preparations. That would also contradict Bassett's assertion (*Hitler's Spy Chief*, p 160) that Canaris, Groscurth, Lahousen and Piekenbrock were dining together when news was received of Chamberlain's visit. Fest, *Staatsstreich*, p 98, with n 33, is of the opinion that it was more probably on the evening of 27 September, since the coup preparations were not complete by mid-September. Erich Kordt reported, however, that Oster had told him on 13 September that the coup would be carried out, the decision coming within forty-eight hours. Then came Chamberlain's suggestion to meet Hitler. Kordt, *Nicht aus den Akten*, p 258. Höhne, *Canaris*, p 294, dates Groscurth's assertion in Krausnick, Deutsch and Kotze likewise at 14 September. From the foregoing it would seem that the conspirators were ready to act in mid-September, after which Heinz and Oster's decision to kill Hitler changed. See also Meinl, *Nationalsozialisten*, p 295; Smid, *Dohnanyi – Bonhoeffer*, p 194, and above all the discussion in Hoffmann, *Widerstand*, p 697f, n 293, who quotes Kordt amongst others (but not Groscurth) and is therefore of the opinion that Kordt's dates are incorrect. The possibility that there were two dates for the coup, both frustrated by Chamberlain's activities, can probably no longer be ascertained.
93 Kershaw, *Hitler 1936–1945*, p 164.
94 From Schmidt, *Außenpolitik*, p 277.
95 Schmidt, Paul, *Statist auf diplomatischer Bühne 1923–1945*, Bonn, 1949, pp 396–8; interpreter Paul Schmidt was the only other person present at this conversation; see Schmidt, *Außenpolitik*, pp 278–80; Kershaw, *Hitler 1936–1945*, pp 165–6.
96 Schmidt, *Außenpolitik*, p 281; Kershaw, *Hitler 1936–1945*, p 167.
97 Schmidt, *Statist*, pp 400–2; cf Schmidt, *Außenpolitik*, pp 281–3; Kershaw, *Hitler 1936–1945*, p 169.

98 Schmidt, *Statist*, pp 403–6; Kershaw, *Hitler 1936–1945*, p 170f.
99 Groscurth diaries, p 122, entry 21 September 1938 (private diary).
100 Ibid, n 114.
101 Affidavit, Gottlob Berger, IMG, vol IV, p 177f (quoted extract from document US 3036–PS, US-102).
102 Groscurth diaries, p 122f, entry, 21 September 1938, with n 115 (private diary).
103 Herbert, *Best*, p 235.
104 Jodl diaries, entry 27 September 1938, p 387.
105 Herbert, *Best*, p 236.
106 Groscurth diaries, p 126, entry 28 September 1938 (private diary).
107 All quotations from Herbert, *Best*, p 235.
108 Groscurth diaries, p 127, entry 28 Septmeber 1938 (private diary).
109 Heinz, *Canaris*, p 96.
110 Ibid, p 98.
111 Kordt, *Nicht aus den Akten*, p 262.
112 Meinl, *Nationalsozialisten*, p 295.
113 Kordt, *Nicht aus den Akten*, p 270; Meinl, *Nationalsozialisten*, p 296f.
114 Kershaw, *Hitler 1936–1945*, p 181; also for previous, ibid, pp 176–80.
115 Heinemann, 'Der militärische Widerstand und der Krieg', p 756; Hoffmann, *Widerstand*, pp 125f and 132; Fest, *Staatsstreich*, p 111.
116 Quoted from Hoffmann, *Widerstand*, p 129.
117 Meinl, *Nationalsozialisten*, p 298.
118 Groscurth, 'Persönlicher Reisebericht über die Reise in die befreiten sudetendeutschen Gebiete vom 1.–7. Oktober 1938' dated 10 October 1938, reproduced in Groscurth diaries, pp 129–36.
119 Ibid, p 136.

PART IV: FINIS GERMANIAE

17 The Will for War

1 Below, Nicolaus von, *Als Hitlers Adjutant 1937–45*, Mainz, 1980, p 180.
2 Note, General a.D. Liepmann, in Baumgart, Winfried, 'Zur Ansprache Hitlers vor den Führern der Wehrmacht vom 22. August 1939. Eine quellenkritische Untersuchung', *Vierteljahrshefte für Zeitgeschichte* 16, 1968, pp 120–49. For participants, content and course of conference in detail, see Boehm, Hermann and Baumgart, Winfried, 'Miszelle: "Zur Ansprache Hitlers vor den Führern der Wehrmacht am 22. August 1939"', *Vierteljahrshefte für Zeitgeschichte* 19, 1971, pp 294–304.
3 Baumgart, 'Zur Ansprache', p 144, n 97.
4 Ibid, p 145.
5 Gisevius, *Bis zum betteren Ende*, vol 2, p 114. Cf also Baumgart, 'Zur Ansprache', p 120, n 2.
6 For the various versions of the speech, particularly for discussions on the quality and authorship of the notes, including those by Canaris, see Baumgart, 'Zur Ansprache', and Boehm and Baumgart, 'Miszelle'. The two undated and unsigned jottings found later in OKW files were used as central documents by the prosecution at Nuremberg:

IMG, vol XXVI, pp 338–46, document 798-PS (ADAP, series D, vol 7, pp 167–70, no 192) and IMG, vol XXVI, pp 523–4, document 1014-PS (ADAP, series D, vol 7, pp 171–2, no 193). For content and significance of the speech see also Müller, *Heer und Hitler*, p 409 ff and primarily Kershaw, *Hitler 1936–1945*, pp 292–6.

7 Below, *Adjutant*, p 181.
8 ADAP, series D, vol 7, pp 167–70.
9 Ibid, p 169.
10 Ibid, p 170.
11 IMG, vol 9, p 547, statement by Goering.
12 Baumgart, 'Zur Ansprach', p 135f and 149, and Below, *Adjutant*, p 181.
13 ADAP, series D, vol 7, no 193, p 171f.
14 Baumgart, 'Zur Ansprach', p 133f, n 57. Cf also Kershaw, *Hitler 1936–1945*, p 295. The Nuremberg prosecutors attached great weight to this sentence in document 1014-PS.
15 Ibid, p 172.
16 For the later reactions see Baumgart, 'Zur Ansprach', p 141, n 84 and p 146f, n 101; Kershaw, *Hitler 1936–1945*, p 296f.
17 Quoted from Müller, *Heer und Hitler*, p 411.
18 Below, *Adjutant*, p 182.
19 Copy, Abwehr II service diary, BA-MA, RW 5/497–499, photocopy at IfZ, F 23/1, hereafter 'Lahousen diaries', p 4, entry 23 August 1939, folio 7. British secret service expert and author Anthony Cave Brown, *Bodyguard of Lies. The Extraordinary True Story behind D-Day*, London, 1975, reprinted Guildford, 2002, p 176, originated the version whereby at Munich that evening the notes passed from Canaris to Oster, who gave them in his sleeping car to Berlin to his confidant, the deputy Dutch military attaché, Gijsbertus Jacobus Sas. From Sas they passed to the resident SIS agent in Berlin, Major Francis Foley, from whom they went immediately to Paris and London. This variation does not occur elsewhere in the literature and I would like to thank Heinz Höhne for pointing it out.
20 Gisevius, *Bis zum betteren Ende*, vol 2, p 119f.
21 Cf Baumgart, 'Zur Ansprach', pp 127 and 137, who indicates that Gisevius's recollections are to be 'treated with caution', but argues convincingly that this was the document that caused Louis P Lochner to make a stronger case to the British ambassadorial adviser. This item (Nuremberg document L003, ADAP, series D, vol 7, p 170f) was not admitted in evidence at Nuremberg.
22 Groscurth diaries, p 179, entry 24 August 1939.
23 Baumgart, 'Zur Ansprach', p 121f; Müller: *Heer und Hitler*, p 412f.
24 Hoffmann, *Widerstand*, p 143; cf also p 702, n 55 and communication from Krausnick to Baumgart in Baumgart, 'Zur Ansprach', p 121, n 11.
25 Baumgart, 'Zur Ansprach', p 121f; Müller, *Heer und Hitler*, p 412f.
26 All quotations from Nuremberg document L003, ADAP, series D, vol 7, p 171f.
27 Ibid, p 172.
28 Halder, war diary, vol I, p 30.
29 Cf also for detail 'Die Errichtung der Hegemonie auf dem europäischen Kontinent', *DRZW*, vol 2, pp 92–104.
30 *DRZW*, vol 2, pp 104–10.

31   Schindler, Herbert, *Mosty und Dirschau 1939. Zwei Handstreiche der Wehrmacht vor Beginn des Polenfeldzuges*, Einzelschriften zur militärischen Geschichte des Zweiten Weltkrieges 7, Freiburg, 1979. Also see Höhne, *Canaris*, p 321f.

32   Schindler, *Mosty und Dirschau*, p 108ff.

33   Ibid, p 111.

34   Leverkuehn, *Der geheime Nachrichtendienst*, p 23; Buchheit, *Geheimdienst*, p 308.

35   Ibid, pp 308–9.

36   Schindler, *Mosty und Dirschau*, p 21.

37   Ibid, p 19.

38   Buchheit, *Geheimdienst*, p 309.

39   Abshagen, *Canaris*, p 198.

40   See Schmidt, *Außenpolitik*, p 330f and Rauscher, Walter, *Hitler und Mussolini. Macht, Krieg und Terror*, Graz, Vienna and Cologne, 2001, p 316f.

41   For the background of Italian policy, of the initial determination for war – not only at this point in time – and its influence on Hitler's policies cf also 'Der Mittelmeerraum und Südosteuropa. Of Italy's "non belligeranza" until the entry of the United States into the war', *DRZW*, vol 3, Stuttgart, 1984, pp 5–8.

42   Moseley, Ray, *Zwischen Hitler und Mussolini – Das Doppelleben des Grafen Ciano*, Berlin, 1998, p 103; Rauscher, *Hitler und Mussolini*, p 330.

43   Schmidt, *Statist*, p 439.

44   Schmidt, *Außenpolitik*, p 333; Rauscher, *Hitler und Mussolini*, p 330f.

45   Schmidt, *Statist*, p 439.

46   Moseley, *Zwischen Hitler und Mussolini*, p 103.

47   Ciano diaries 1939–43, quoted in Kershaw, *Hitler 1936–1945*, p 290 and Rauscher, *Hitler und Mussolini*, p 331.

48   Moseley, *Zwischen Hitler und Mussolini*, p 107; Rauscher, *Hitler und Mussolini*, p 332.

49   Below, *Adjutant*, p 178.

50   Roatta, report to Mussolini, 12 August 1939, *I Documenti Diplomatici Italiani* (*DDI*), series VIII, vol XIII, Rome, 1953, no 10, p 11. Cf Siebert, Ferdinand, *Italiens Weg in den Zweiten Weltkrieg*, Frankfurt am Main 1962, p 252.

51   Magistrati, report to Ciano, 16 August 1939, *DDI*, series VIII, vol XIII, no 67, p 46f. Cf Groscurth diaries, p 181, n 372 to entry 24 August 1939.

52   *DDI*, series VIII, vol XIII, no 67, p 47, n 1.

53   Cf Thielenhaus, *Zwischen Anpassung und Widerstand*, p 140ff.

54   Hill, *Weizsäcker-Papiere 1933–1950*, p 181.

55   Thielenhaus, *Zwischen Anpassung und Widerstand*, p 140.

56   Ibid, p 141.

57   Lahousen diaries, p 1, entry 12 August 1939, IfZ, F 23/1, folio 4.

58   Cf additionally with examples Höhne, *Canaris*, p 322.

59   Ibid, p 323.

60   For Jost see Wildt, *Generation*, p 422, and also a short biography of Jost, ibid, p 936f.

61   See Lahousen, note: 'Unternehmen Himmler', undated, IfZ, ZS 658, folio 45; Lahousen diaries, p 2, entry 17 August 1939, IfZ, F 23/1, folio 5.

62   Ibid, and p 3, entry 19 August 1939.

63   Wildt, *Generation*, p 392f; cf Wildt, *Nachrichtendienst*, p 264f.

64 Lahousen, statement to IMG, vol II, p 496f.

65 Lahousen diaries, p 2, entry 17 August 1939, IfZ, F 23/1, folio 5.

66 Gruchmann, *Der Zweite Weltkrieg*, vol 1, p 22; Höhne, Heinz, *Der Orden unter dem Totenkopf – Die Geschichte der SS*, Munich, 1984, pp 240–5; also Höhne, *Canaris*, p 325. No Polish uniforms were used during the raid on the Gleiwitz radio station because it had already been occupied by an SS unit. Cf Runzheimer, Jürgen, '"Der Überfall auf den Sender Gleiwitz" im Jahre 1939', in VfZ 10, 1962, pp 408–26.

67 Lahousen, note, 'Unternehmen Himmler', IfZ, ZS 658, folio 47; cf IMG, vol IV, p 270f. Affidavit, Alfred Helmut Naujocks, 20 November 1945; Höhne, *Orden unter dem Totenkopf*, p 241 and Runzheimer, 'Der Überfall', p 412.

68 Gruchmann, *Der Zweite Weltkrieg*, p 22.

69 Lahousen diaries, p 1, entry 17 August 1939, IfZ, F 23/1, folio 4.

70 Halder, War Diary, vol I, p 19, entry 17 August 1939.

71 Canaris, note, 'Aussprache mit Generaloberst Keitel am 17. August 1939', BA/MA, RW 4/v. 764; reprinted in Abshagen, *Canaris*, pp 195–7; cf Höhne, *Canaris*, p 328f.

72 Ibid.

73 Cf Müller, *Heer und Hitler*, p 407ff.

74 Groscurth diaries, p 180, entry 24 August 1939 (private diary).

75 Thomas, Georg, 'Gedanken und Erinnerungen', *Schweizer Monatshefte* 25, 1945, p 542f; Gisevius, *Bis zum betteren Ende*, vol II, p 112f; IMG, vol XII, p 246, statement Gisevius. Cf Hoffmann, *Widerstand*, p 143f. Despite differing accounts it appears possible that one of the memoranda was given to Keitel before 25 August, and one on the 27th: see Hoffmann, *Widerstand*, p 702, n 61. For General Thomas see also Überschär, Gerd R (ed), *Hitlers militärische Elite, vol I: Von den Anfängen des Regimes bis Kriegsbeginn*, Darmstadt, 1998, pp 248–57.

76 Thomas, 'Gedanken und Erinnerungen', p 542. Cf Gisevius, *Biz zum betteren Ende*, vol II, p 113.

77 ADAP, series D, vol VII, no 200, p 180; Schmidt, *Statist*, p 448; Kershaw, *Hitler 1936–1945*, p 299f; Schmidt, *Außenpolitik*, p 346f.

78 Below, *Adjutant*, p 182.

79 According to Weizsäcker, *Erinnerungen*, p 252; cf Kershaw, *Hitler 1936–1945*, p 300.

80 Ibid.

81 Weizsäcker, *Erinnerungen*, p 252.

82 Cf Schmidt, *Außenpolitik*, p 346.

83 Schmidt, *Statist*, p 444; Below, *Adjutant*, p 183.

84 Ibid.

85 Ahmann, Rolf, 'Der Hitler–Stalin-Pakt: Nichtangriffs- und Angriffsvertrag?', in Oberländer, Erwin (ed), *Hitler–Stalin-Pakt 1939. Das Ende Ostmitteleuropas?*, Frankfurt am Main, 1989. For the whole complex also see Schmidt, *Außenpolitik*, p 340f; Hildebrand, Klaus, *Das vergangene Reich – Deutsche Außenpolitik von Bismarck bis Hitler*, Stuttgart, 1995, p 803ff, with rather differing interpretations; Kershaw, *Hitler 1936–1945*, p 297.

86 Hildebrand, *Das vergangene Reich*, p 806.

87 Heinz, 'Canaris', p 108.

88 Ibid, p 109.

18 The Madness Unfolds

1   Krausnick, Deutsch and Kotze, 'Introduction', p 7.

2   Ibid, p 48 and Groscurth diaries, p 179, entry 24 August 1939 (private diary).

3   For Krichbaum and the GFP see principally: Brown, Paul B, 'Forester to Feldpolizeichef: The Life and Counter-intelligence Career of Wilhelm Krichbaum', paper presented at the Conference of the International History Study Group, Tutzing, 24–6 April 1998, and Brown, Paul B, 'The Senior Leadership Cadre of the Geheime Feldpolizei, 1939–1945', *Nazi War Criminal Records Interagency Working Group, National Archives and Records Administration: Holocaust and Genocide Studies* 17, no 2, Autumn 2003, pp 278–304. I thank Erich Schmidt-Eenboom for drawing my attention to the two texts and Paul Brown for his support during my research in Washington. Krichbaum left the liaison group on 23 September 1939; cf Krausnick, Deutsch and Kotze, 'Introduction', p 48, n 147, p 128, n 140 and Groscurth diaries, entry 23 September 1939, in ibid, p 278.

4   Ibid, p 128, n 140.

5   Meinl, *Nationalsozialisten*, p 307.

6   Groscurth diaries, p 183, entry 24 August 1939 (private diary).

7   Lahousen diaries, p 7, entry 25 August 1939, IfZ F 23/1, folio 10.

8   Ibid.

9   Groscurth diaries, p 184, entry 25 August 1939 (private diary).

10   Schmidt, *Außenpolitik*, p 349; Kershaw, *Hitler 1936–1945*, p 302.

11   Groscurth diaries, p 184, entry 25 August 1939 (private diary).

12   Schindler, *Mosty und Dirschau*, p 74.

13   Ibid, p 114.

14   Ibid, p 116, n 42.

15   Schmidt, *Außenpolitik*, p 349.

16   Schmidt, *Statist*, p 452.

17   Ibid.

18   Keitel, statement, IMG, vol 10, p 578.

19   Kershaw, *Hitler 1936–1945*, p 303.

20   Gisevius, *Bis zum betteren Ende*, vol 2, p 132f; also see Müller, *Heer und Hitler*, p 413f. This attempt to prevent the war and end the dictatorship has undergone various evaluations (Ritter, Gerhard, *Carl Goerdeler und die deutsche Widerstandsbewegung*, Stuttgart, 1956, p 498, n 54; Müller, *Heer und Hitler*, p 414). For more recent opinions on the reactions of Canaris, Oster and others see Fest, *Staatsstreich*, p 114 and Kershaw, *Hitler 1936–1945*, p 316.

21   As portrayed by Gisevius, *Bis zum betteren Ende*, vol 2, p 134ff. Kershaw points out that Gisevius did not claim to report Oster word for word, but guaranteed the sense of what he said. Cf Kershaw, *Hitler 1936–1945*, p 316 and p 1153, n 309.

22   Gisevius, *Bis zum betteren Ende*, vol 2, p 135.

23   Ibid, p 136.

24   Fest, *Staatsstreich*, p 114.

25   Gisevius, *Bis zum betteren Ende*, vol 2, p 136f.

26   Fest, *Staatsstreich*, p 114.

27   Kordt, *Nicht aus den Akten*, p 329.

28   Kershaw, *Hitler 1936–1945*, p 316.

29 Lahousen diaries, p 8, entry 25 August 1939, IfZ F 23/1, folio 11.
30 Herzner, 'Bericht über das Unternehmen gegen Bahnhof und Tunnel von Mosty in der Nacht vom 25./26. August 1939', Handakte Herzner, Archive Heinz Höhne.
31 Lahousen diaries, p 8, entry 26 August 1939, IfZ F 23/1, folio 11.
32 Report, Eickern, 26 August 1939, Handakte Herzner, Archive Heinz Höhne.
33 Radio message Striegau, 26 August 1939, Handakte Herzner, Archive Heinz Höhne.
34 Cf 'Bericht vom 26.8.1939 K.O.J. Besetzung Bahnhof Mosty und Tunnel', Handakte Herzner, Archive Heinz Höhne. Cf the very divergent accounts from the German and Polish sides of the exact circumstances of Unternehmen Herzner, principally in Schindler, *Mosty und Dirschau*.
35 Herzner, 'Bericht über das Unternehmen gegen Bahnhof und Tunnel von Mosty in der Nacht vom 25./26. August 1939', Handakte Herzner, Archive Heinz Höhne, and Lahousen diaries, entry 26 August 1939, IfZ F 23/1, folio 11.
36 Lahousen diaries, p 8, entry 26 August 1939, IfZ F 23/1, folio 11.
37 Schlabrendorff, Fabian von, *Offiziere gegen Hitler; bearbeitet und herausgegeben von Gero v. S. Gaevernitz*, Zurich, 1946, p 32.
38 Groscurth diaries, p 185, entry 26 August 1939 and n 388 (private diary).
39 Fest, Joachim, *Hitler – Eine Biographie*, Munich, 1973, p 821.
40 Schmidt, Außenpolitik, p 351.
41 Fest, *Hitler*, p 821.
42 Groscurth diaries, p 185, entry 26 August 1939 (private diary).
43 Ibid, p 186.
44 See above, similar entries by Halder in his War Diary.
45 Groscurth diaries, p 186, n 391.
46 Ibid, p 186, entry 26 August 1939 (private diary).
47 Ibid.
48 That would have been 31 August; the attack occurred on 7th Mobilisation Day. Brauchitsch informed Halder on 28 August that Hitler had set the definitive attack date for 1 September: Halder, War Diary, vol I, p 40.
49 Groscurth diaries, p 187, entry 27 August 1939 (private diary).
50 Thomas, *Gedanken und Erinnerungen*, p 542f; Gisevius, *Bis zum betteren Ende*, vol II, p 113f; cf Hoffmann, *Widerstand*, p 145. It is not beyond doubt that the second memorandum reached Hitler; Schlabrendorff mentions only that Keitel dismissed all Thomas's arguments and supported Hitler.
51 Groscurth diaries, p 190, entry 28 August 1939 (private diary).
52 Halder, War Diary, vol I, p 38, entry 28 August 1939.
53 Groscurth diaries, p 190, entry 28 August 1939; similarly Halder, War Diary, vol I, p 38, following information from Groscurth and Oster. The content of the address quickly made the rounds. Reichstag Deputy Heinrich Ernst von Sybel, at breakfast on 29 August, spoke at length with Finance Minister Popitz, State Secretary Kempner, Chief of the OKW-Household Department Tischbein, Generalmajor Heinrici and Ambassador von Hassell: Hassell diaries, p 117f, entry 29 August 1939.
54 Groscurth diaries, p 190, entry 28 August 1939 (private diary).
55 Halder, War Diary, vol I, p 38, entry 28 August 1939.
56 Schmidt, *Außenpolitik*, p 353f.
57 Schmidt, *Statist*, p 456.

58 Ibid, p 459.
59 Hill, *Weizsäcker-Papiere*, p 163.
60 Groscurth diaries, p 195, entry 31 August 1939 (private diary).
61 Gisevius, *Bis zum betteren Ende*, vol 2, p 138; cf IMG, vol XII, p 247, statement of Gisevius.
62 Lahousen, statement, IMG, vol II, p 490.
63 Fest, *Staatsstreich*, p 115.

19 The War of Extermination – Act One

1 Ueberschär, Gerd R, 'Der militärische Widerstand, die antijüdischen Maßnahmen, "Polenmorde" und NS-Kriegsverbrechen in den ersten Kriegsjahren (1939–1941)', in Ueberschär, Gerd R, (ed), *NS-Verbrechen und der militärische Widerstand gegen Hitler*, Darmstadt, 2000, p 34.
2 Hill, *Weizsäcker-Papiere 1933–1950*, p 164, note of 7 October 1939.
3 Ibid, p 173.
4 Ueberschär, 'Widerstand', p 34.
5 Kershaw, *Hitler 1936–1945*, p 313.
6 Groscurth diaries, p 196, entry 1 September 1939 (private diary).
7 Ibid; Halder, War Diary, vol I, pp 50 and 52, entry 1 September 1939. Also see Schindler, *Mosty und Dirschau*, pp 120f and 150f.
8 Lahousen diaries, p 11, entry 1 September 1939, IfZ, F 23/1, folio 14.
9 Runzheimer, 'Der Überfall', p 409.
10 Lahousen, Erwin, 'Das Unternehmen Himmler', undated, IfZ, ZS 658, folio 45; IMG, vol II, p 497, statement by Lahousen. Abshagen, *Canaris*, p 207, writes – after Lahousen's statement before the IMG – that Piekenbrock made the statement after the publication of the first Wehrmacht report. This is incorrect. See Runzheimer, 'Der Überfall', p 410, n 11.
11 Interrogation of Lahousen at the Nuremberg OKW trial in Runzheimer, 'Der Überfall', p 411.
12 Ibid, p 412, with n 21.
13 Höhne, *Orden unter dem Totenkopf*, pp 241–5.
14 Browning, Christopher R, *Die Entfesselung der 'Entlösung' – nationalsozialistishe Judenpolitik 1939–1942*, Munich, 2003, p 35 and Müller, *Heer und Hitler*, p 426.
15 Kershaw, *Hitler 1936–1945*, p 334.
16 Halder, War Diary, vol I, p 44, entry 29 September 1939.
17 Herbert, *Best*, pp 234–40; Wildt, *Generation*, pp 426–8; Krausnick, Helmut, and Wilhelm, Hans Heinrich, *Die Truppe des Weltanschauungskrieges – Die Einsatzgruppen der Sicherheitspolizei und des SD 1938–1942*, Stuttgart, 1981, p 40f.
18 Quotation from Herbert, *Best*, p 238.
19 Halder, War Diary, vol I, p 44, entry 30 September 1939.
20 Herbert, *Best*, p 239.
21 Ibid, p 240.
22 For the 'Bromberg Bloody Sunday' in detail, see Wildt, *Generation*, pp 432–47; Krausnick and Wilhelm, *Truppe*, pp 55–65.

23 Groscurth diaries, p 198 (private diary) and p 257 (service diary), entry 3 September 1939.

24 Ibid, p 257, entry 4 September 1939 (service diary).

25 Ibid, p 199, entry 5 September 1939 (private diary).

26 Ibid, p 260, entry 5 September 1939 (service diary).

27 Ibid, p 198, entry 3 September 1939 (private diary).

28 Ibid, p 200f, entry 8 September 1939 (private diary); cf Wildt, *Generation*, p 433f, with n 52.

29 Groscurth diaries, p 198, entry 4 September 1939 (private diary).

30 Ibid, p 198 ff, entries 3, 4, 5, 7 and 8 September 1939 (private diary).

31 Ibid, p 199, with n 461 (private diary) and p 259 (service diary).

32 Werner Best dates the evening meal as the day of the British declaration of war, 3 September. According to the service diaries Canaris was at the Front that day. Presumably the visit occurred after his return. Groscurth's diary entries do not mention it and Lahousen refers only to journeys and conferences planned by Canaris for the following week. See Best, 'Canaris', p 177.

33 Ibid.

34 Cf the recent study by John Horne and Alan Kramer, *Deutsche Kriegsgreuel 1914*, Hamburg, 2004.

35 Wildt, *Generation*, p 436f.

36 Krausnick and Wilhelm, *Truppe*, p 55, with n 134; Herbert, *Best*, p 593, n 316; Wildt, *Generation*, p 439.

37 Ibid.

38 See for the discussion of the events Wildt, *Generation*, p 439ff; Kershaw, *Hitler 1936–1945*, p 336; Krausnick and Wilhelm, *Truppe*, p 55ff.

39 Kershaw, *Hitler 1936–1945*, p 336.

40 For the divergent details see Wildt, *Generation*, p 439f, n 71.

41 Kershaw, *Hitler 1936–1945*, p 336.

42 Wildt points out, contrary to the general interpretation, that Himmler's orders of 3 September were in reaction to Bromberg. Wildt, *Generation*, p 434, n 53.

43 Ibid, p 433 and Herbert, *Best*, p 240.

44 Ibid.

45 Wildt, *Generation*, p 414ff.

46 Ibid, p 447f, with n 96.

47 Protocol of Conference of Departmental Chiefs, 7 to 8 September 1939 in Herbert, *Best*, p 241.

48 Groscurth diaries, p 201, entry 8 September 1939 (private diary).

49 Ibid, p 202, entry 9 September 1939 (private diary).

50 Ibid, in his service diary Groscurth put the time of his appointment with Halder (1615hrs) but made no mention of the content of the conversation: ibid, p 265.

51 Cf opinions of Herbert, *Best*, p 241 and Wildt, *Generation*, pp 447 and 449.

52 File note by Oberstleutnant von Lahousen on the conference in the Führer's train on 12 September 1939 at Illnau and Vienna, 14 September 1939, BA-MA, N 104/3; Groscurth papers, reproduced in Groscurth diaries, pp 357–9, document 12; cf statement of Lahousen at Nuremberg: IMG, vol II, pp 492–5.

53 Galicia and White Russia played an important role for some time in the Abwehr plans for the war against Poland. See 'Ergebnis der Besprechung der Abwehr II-

Referenten der Abwehrstellen VIII und XVII beim Chef der Abt II der Amtsgr. Ausland/Abwehr', 3 July 1939, BA-MA, RW 5/123; 'Bericht Lahousen an Chef der IV. Abt. d. GenStH über die Ausbildung von Angehörigen der OUN für den Überfall auf Polen', 15 July 1939, BA-MA, RW 5/699; 'Direktive Lahousens zur Kampfausbildung von Angehörigen der OUN', 4 August 1939, BA-MA, RW 5/699; Lahousen diaries, entry 15 August 1923 and 8 and 25 August 1939, IfZ, F 23/1. For Abwehr planning and activities with regards to the Ukraine and Galicia, cf Höhne, *Canaris*, pp 304–9, 323f and 342ff

54 IMG, vol II, p 494, Lahousen statement.

55 File note, Lahousen, 14 September 1939.

56 IMG, vol II, p 493, Lahousen statement.

57 File note, Lahousen, 14 September 1939.

58 Ibid and IMG, vol II, p 493, statement of Lahousen.

59 Ibid, p 494. Keitel avoided recollecting any details of this conference to the Nuremberg judges, but admitted to having repeated 'frankly' what had been discussed in his presence by Brauchitsch and Hitler. IMG, vol X, p 580, statement of Keitel.

60 Cf principally Krausnick and Wilhelm, *Truppe*, p 64ff; Müller, *Heer und Hitler*, p 427ff; and Browning, *Entfesselung*, pp 34–48 and 116–29f.

61 File note, Lahousen, 14 September 1939; cf IMG, vol II, p 493, statement of Lahousen.

62 Nikolaus von Vormann, 'Erinnerungen' (unpublished, IfZ 34/2), quoted in Höhne, *Canaris*, p 349.

63 IMG, vol II, p 494, statement of Lahousen.

64 File note Lahousen, 14 September 1939.

65 Groscurth diaries, p 204, entry 13 September 1939 (private diary).

66 Ibid, p 286, entry 13 September 1939 (service diary).

67 Halder, War Diary, vol I, p 71, entry 13 September 1939.

68 Conference note, Oberquartiermeister IV for ObdH, Generaloberst von Brauchitsch, 17 September 1939, BA-MA N 104/3 reproduced in Groscurth diaries, p 360, document 13; cf here et seq principally Wildt, *Generation*, p 451ff and Browning, *Entfesselung*, p 38ff.

69 Conference note, 17 September 1939.

70 Ibid.

71 This is denied by Wildt, *Generation*, p 452.

72 Groscurth diaries, p 206, entry 18 September 1939 (private diary).

73 Cf *DRZW*, vol 2, p 126f; Hoensch, Jörg K, 'Der Hitler-Stalin-Pakt und Polen', in Oberländer, Erwin (ed), *Hitler–Stalin-Pakt 1939. Das Ende Ostmitteleuropas?*, Frankfurt am Main 1989, p 51 (with facsimile of the secret protocol, p 127f); Kershaw, *Hitler 1936–1945*, p 329.

74 Halder, War Diary, vol I, p 80.

75 Groscurth diaries, p 208, entry 22 September 1939 (private diary).

76 Lahousen, personal list of Abw. Abt. I (1938–mid 1943), NA, KV 2/173, Lahousen file.

77 Report by Generalmajor Lahousen on Canaris secret organisation, part II, p 2, PRO KV 2/173, Lahousen file.

78 Groscurth diaries, p 206, entry 18 September 1939 (private diary).

79 *DRZW*, vol 2, p 130f; Kershaw, *Hitler 1936–1945*, p 328.

80　Groscurth diaries, p 272, n 771. See also Browning, *Entfesselung*, p 55. On 15 September 1939 a corresponding order was issued by the chief of the Sicherheitspolizei to the Army chief of police OKW (Abwehr). On 20 September 1939 Heeresgruppe Süd sent a corresponding telex to AOK's 8, 10 and 14; see Krausnick and Wilhelm, *Truppe*, p 46, n 82.

81　Figures from Browning, *Entfesselung*, p 633, n 66. Browning refers to Madajczyk, Czeslaw, *Die Okkupationspolitik Nazideutschlands in Polen 1939–1945*, Berlin, 1987, p 28.

82　Groscurth diaries, p 209, n 509. See also Müller, *Heer und Hitler*, p 427, n 21; Krausnick and Wilhelm, *Truppe*, p 54f. Browning (*Entfesselung*, p 39) makes Groscurth incorrectly Ic of 14.Armee and even has him reporting to Canaris.

83　Browning, *Entfesselung*, p 39.

84　Note, Groscurth, 'Mündliche Orientierung am 22. 9. 1939 durch Major Radke', BA-MA N 104/3. Reproduced in Groscurth diaries, p 361, document 14.

85　Ibid.

86　See Wildt, *Generation*, p 453.

87　Note, Groscurth, 'Mündliche Orientierung am 22. 9. 1939', reproduced in Groscurth diaries, document 14, pp 361–3.

88　Ibid; cf Müller, *Heer und Hitler*, p 432f; Krausnick and Wilhelm, *Truppe*, p 69f and Browning, *Entfesselung*, p 39f.

89　Groscurth diaries, p 277, entry 23 September 1939 (service diary); Krausnick and Wilhelm, *Truppe*, p 54, with n 130.

90　Groscurth diaries, p 282, entry 27 September 1939 (service diary).

91　Cf the recent results of research in Wildt, *Generation*, p 452f; Browning, *Entfesselung*, p 41f.

92　Janssen and Tobias, *Sturz*, p 239.

93　'Bericht des Leutnants Rosenhagen über den Tod des Generaloberst Frhr. v. Fritsch vom 26. 9. 1939', reproduced in Groscurth diaries, Appendix 1, document 16, p 365f; cf Janssen and Tobias, *Sturz*, p 248f.

94　Cf Ludwig Beck's letter to his brother Wilhelm, 22 September 1939: 'I knew that he was looking for the opportunity to die nobly.' Reproduced in Müller, Beck, p 589, Document 58.

95　Hassell diaries, p 127, entry 11 October 1939. Also see the anonymous letter to OKH dated 27 September 1939 from NCOs and men returning to Berlin repeating the rumours surrounding the death of Fritsch and making undisguised threats to Himmler. Reproduced in Groscurth diaries, document 17, p 367. For the falsity of these rumours see Rosenhagen's statement. Also Brausch, Gerd, 'Der Tod des Generalobersten Werner Freiherr von Fritsch', *Militärgeschichtliche Mitteilungen* 5, 1969, pp 95–112.

96　Groscurth diaries, p 210, entry 29 September 1939 (private diary).

97　Cf Janssen and Tobias, *Sturz*, p 251, according to whom Hitler's participation was prevented by bad flying weather; for the same reason Keitel did not arrive until the last minute. Groscurth remarked in his diary that there were hardly any SS to be seen: 'only Goebbels, Ley, Frick, Lutze were there.' Groscurth diaries, p 210, entry 29 September 1939 (private diary).

98　From *DRZW*, vol 2, p 131.

99　Kershaw, *Hitler 1936–1945*, p 331f; *DRZW*, vol 2, p 137.

100 According to former Abwehr officer Reile, Oscar, *Geheime Ostfront – Die deutsche Abwehr im Osten 1921–1945*, Munich, 1963, p 309f; cf Höhne, *Canaris*, p 346. For Horatzek see: article in *Die Nachhut*, 11/12 and 15 February 1971, p 4, BA-MA, Msg 3/22–1.

101 On 3 October, von Rundstedt took over the entire military command in the newly erected Grenzabschnitten Nord, Mitte und Süd (3., 8. and 14.Armee) and also became military commander of Posen and Danzig–West-Prussia, *DRZW*, vol 2, p 132.

102 Groscurth diaries, p 216, entry 9 October 1939 (private diary).

103 Field letter from Groscurth to his wife, 10 October 1939, from Groscurth diaries, p 216, n 546.

104 Graml, Hermann, 'Die Wehrmacht im Dritten Reich', *Vierteljahrshefte für Zeitgeschichte* 45, 1997, p 373.

105 Cf Ueberschär, 'Widerstand', p 35.

106 Hassell diaries, p 127, entry 11 October 1939.

107 Halder, letter to Canaris, 12 October 1939, BA-MA, MSg 1/1186.

20 *The Spirit of Zossen*

1 See also Krausnick and Wilhelm, *Truppe*, pp 85–7.

2 Graml, 'Wehrmacht im Dritten Reich', p 373.

3 From Krausnick and Wilhelm, *Truppe*, p 86.

4 Graml, 'Wehrmacht im Dritten Reich', p 325.

5 Meyer, *Unternehmen Sieben*, pp 128–39.

6 Buchheit, *Geheimdienst*, p 73f; Reile, *Geheime Ostfront*, p 310f.

7 Meyer, *Unternehmen Sieben*, p 128.

8 Basset, *Hitler's Spy Chief*, pp 219, 230, 262 insinuates that Halina Szymanska was the intermediary for messages between Canaris and the British Secret Service head Stewart Menzies. The sources are not complete.

9 Here et seq Smid, *Dohnanyi – Bonhoeffer*, pp 227–30; Meyer, *Unternehmen Sieben*, pp 14–21.

10 Cf note of Christina Dohnanyi, IFZ, ZS 603 folio 35.

11 Smid, *Dohnanyi – Bonhoeffer*, p 228.

12 Ibid, p. 229; Thielenhaus, *Zwischen Anpassung und Widerstand*, p 154.

13 Umbreit, Hans, 'Der Kampf um die Vormachtstellung in West europa', *DRZW*, vol II, p 238f; Kershaw, *Hitler 1936–1945*, p 364f; Halder, War Diary, vol I, p 101, entry 10 October 1939.

14 Umbreit, 'Kampf um die Vormachtstellung', pp 237 and 242f.

15 Groscurth diaries, p 216, n 546.

16 Müller, *Heer und Hitler*, p 481; Deutsch, Harold C, *Verschwörung gegen den Krieg. Der Widerstand in den Jahren 1939–1940*, Munich 1969, p 76. Groscurth stated in his entry of 5 October 1939 that Canaris did not want 'to have anything more to do with the skinny generals. They are all talking already about the attack in the West against Holland and Belgium that is in preparation.' That Canaris had these conversations at the Western Front, as the literature asserts, mostly based on a report by Lahousen, is out of the question since the named conversational partners were in the East at

the time, as was Groscurth. Groscurth diaries, p 201f, entries 9 and 11 October 1939 (private diary).

17 Halder, War Diary, vol I, p 105, entry 14 October 1939.

18 Müller, *Heer und Hitler*, p 280, with n 59; Kershaw, *Hitler 1936–1945*, p 367; Weizsäcker, *Erinnerungen*, p 269f.

19 Groscurth diaries, p 218, entry 16 October 1939 (private diary).

20 Müller, *Heer und Hitler*, p 490.

21 Kershaw, *Hitler 1936–1945*, p 368.

22 Smid, *Dohnanyi – Bonhoeffer*, p 232.

23 Kordt, *Nicht aus den Akten*, p 358.

24 Groscurth diaries, p 219, entry 19 October 1939, with n 566; memorandum reproduced in ibid, document 70, pp 498–503 and Kordt, *Nicht aus dem Akten*, pp 359–65; Ueberschär, Gerd R, 'Militäropposition gegen Hitlers Kriegspolitik 1939 bis 1941. Motive, Struktur und Alternativvorstellungen des entstehenden militärischen Widerstandes', in Schmädecke, Jürgen, and Steinbach, Peter (eds), *Der Widerstand gegen den Nationalsozialismus – Die deutsche Gesellschaft und der Widerstand gegen Hitler*, Munich and Zürich, 1985, p 349.

25 Müller, *Heer und Hitler*, pp 494ff and p 502f.

26 Groscurth diaries, p 220, entries 22–5 October 1939 (private diary).

27 Müller, *Heer und Hitler*, p 495, indicates the error of some references to Canaris's activities during this phase.

28 Ueberschär, 'Militäropposition', p 350; Ueberschär, Gerd R, *Generaloberst Franz Halder. Generalstabschef, Gegner und Gefangener Hitlers*, Göttingen and Zürich, 1991, p 40f; Müller, *Heer und Hitler*, p 508f.

29 Groscurth diaries, p 222, entry 1 November 1939 (private diary), with n 578; cf Müller, *Heer und Hitler*, p 511, n 249.

30 Groscurth diaries, p 222, entry 1 November 1939 (private diary); for the interpretation of this entry see Müller, *Heer und Hitler*, p 511ff, with which I concur. From the entry it is not completely clear whether the objection regarding the 'missing man' came from Halder or Groscurth.

31 Groscurth diaries, p 222, entry 1 November 1939 (private diary).

32 Thus Vogel, Thomas, 'Die Militäropposition gegen das NS-Regime am Vorabend des Zweiten Weltkriegs und während der ersten Kriegsjahre (1939–1941), in *Aufstand des Gewissens. Militärischer Widerstand gegen Hitler und das NS-Regime 1933 bis 1945*, a companion volume to the open exhibition of the Militärgeschichtlichen Forschungsamtes, Hamburg, Berlin and Bonn, 2001, p 199.

33 Halder, letter to Walter Baum, 3 June 1957, IfZ, ZS 240, vol V, here from Höhne, *Canaris*, p 367.

34 Note, Lahousen, 'Zur Vorgeschichte des Anschlags vom 20. Juli 44', IfZ, ZS 658, folio 8.

35 Kordt, *Nicht aus den Akten*, p 371.

36 As it was also misunderstood, when Halder let Oster and other civilian conspirators such as Goerdeler, Schacht and Beck know, they should hold themselves in readiness *from* 5 November, not *on* the 5th. Halder had no specific action to set the coup in motion; for him it all depended on Hitler's reaction and was linked to the clarification

of several open questions such as the troop units to be involved. Cf Müller, *Heer und Hitler*, p 520.

37   Cf statement of Brauchitsch, IMG, vol XX, p 628; Kershaw, *Hitler 1936–1945*, p 370; Müller, *Heer und Hitler*, p 520; according to Müller the talks were longer and Keitel was summoned after half an hour.

38   Ibid, cf Groscurth diaries, p 224, n 589.

39   Ibid, p 224, entry 5 November 1939 (private diary).

40   Ibid, p 225.

41   Ibid, and n 590.

42   Copy note, Inga Haag, 4 April 1948, IfZ, ZS 2093, p 2f.

43   Gisevius, *Bis zum bitteren Ende*, vol II, p 159.

44   According to Müller, *Heer und Hitler*, p 527.

45   Ibid, pp 527–9 for the comprehensive talk by Müller.

46   Deutsch, *Verschwörung*, p 251; in research the discussion is either avoided or it is accepted that Halder wanted to transfer the responsibility to Canaris and the Abwehr. See Kershaw, *Hitler 1936–1945*, p 370; Ueberschär, 'Militäropposition', p 350; also Halder, War Diary, p 42; Fest, *Staatsstreich*, p 130; Thun-Hohenstein, *Verschwörer*, p 168; Hoffmann, *Widerstand*, p 179; Höhne, *Canaris*, p 375, presumes an 'act of desperation' on Groscurth's part.

47   Müller, *Heer und Hitler*, p 530.

48   Groscurth diaries, p 225, entry 6 November 1939 (private diary).

49   Gisevius, *Bis zum bitteren Ende*, vol II, p 161.

50   Ibid, p 162.

51   Ibid, p 162ff; Groscurth diaries, p 225, entry 6 November 1939 (private diary); Müller, *Heer und Hitler*, p 531f; Hoffmann, *Widerstand*, p 179f; Thun-Hohenstein, *Verschwörer*, p 170.

52   Deutsch, *Verschwörung*, p 259. The Oster–Gisevius trip is described in detail ibid, p 256ff; Müller, *Heer und Hitler*, p 532ff; Thun-Hohenstein, *Verschwörer*, p 170f. The accounts differ because of the confusion between Gisevius's and Vincenz Müller's versions as to whether they visited Witzleben or Müller first.

53   Deutsch, *Verschwörung*, p 259ff; Thun-Hohenstein, *Verschwörer*, p 171.

54   Gisevius, *Bis zum bitteren Ende*, vol II, p 165.

55   Kershaw, *Hitler 1936–1945*, p 371. Agents of the Abwehr posing as opponents of the Nazi regime succeeded in making contact with two senior MI6 officers in Holland. When Heydrich found out, he sent Schellenberg to meet them. The operation was run from Berlin by SS-Sturmbannführer Helmut Knochen. Canaris stated that he knew nothing of the Venlo affair. Undoubtedly it signalled the intention of the SD to pursue its own ambitions in foreign espionage. Among the more recent accounts are Doerries, Reinhard R, *Hitler's Last Chief of Foreign Intelligence. Allied Interrogations of Walter Schellenberg*, London and Portland, 2003, pp 11–14; Cave Brown, *Bodyguard of Lies*, pp 186–92; Cave Brown, Anthony, *The Secret Servant. The Life of Sir Stewart Menzies, Churchill's Spymaster*, London, 1988, pp 208–23. Accounts of those involved are Best, S Payne, *The Venlo Incident*, London, 1950; Schellenberg, Walter, *Memoiren*, London, 1956, pp 79–89; Schulze-Bernett, Walter, 'Der Grenzzwischenfall bei Venlo/ Holland', *Die Nachhut*, 2, 1973, pp 1–9, BA-MA, MSg 3-22/1.

56   Gisevius, *Bis zum bitteren Ende*, vol II, p 169; Müller, *Heer und Hitler*, p 536.

57   Groscurth diaries, p 228f, entries 10 and 11 November 1939 (private diary).

58 Gisevius, *Bis zum bitteren Ende*, vol II, p 171.
59 Müller, *Heer und Hitler*, p 542f; Vogel, 'Militäropposition', p 204.
60 Groscurth diary, p 230, entry 13 November 1939 (private diary).
61 Ibid, p 231, entry 14 November 1939 (private diary); differs over the content of the conversation with Gisevius, *Bis zum bitteren Ende*, vol II, p 172f.

21 'Now There is No Going Back'

1 Gisevius, *Bis zum bitteren Ende*, vol II, p 173f.
2 Vogel, 'Militäropposition', p 205.
3 See Groscurth diaries, p 234, entry 10 December 1939 (whole entry in private diary). Groscurth was also present for this address. See also Müller, *Heer und Hitler*, p 548f, with n 463. A version of the speech probably taken down by Groscurth is reproduced in Groscurth diaries, Appendix I, document 40, pp 414–18; cf Kershaw, *Hitler 1936–1945*, p 377ff.
4 Kershaw, *Hitler 1936–1945*, pp 377–80 and Groscurth diaries, p 234, n 638.
5 Groscurth diaries, p 234, entry 10 December 1939 (whole entry in private diary).
6 Halder, War Diary, vol I, p 132, entry 23 November 1939; Müller, *Heer und Hitler*, p 550; Kershaw, *Hitler 1936–1945*, p 380.
7 Graml, 'Wehrmacht im Dritten Reich', p 372.
8 From Groscurth diaries, p 426f, document 43: 'Blaskowitz ans OKH, 27 November 1939'. Cf Graml, 'Wehrmacht im Dritten Reich', p 374 and principally Browning, *Entfesselung*, p 120f.
9 Engel, Gerhard, *Heeresadjutant bei Hitler 1938–1943. Aufzeichnungen des Majors Engel*, edited and with commentary by Hildegard von Kotze, Schriftenreihe der Vierteljahrshefte für Zeitgeschichte 29, Stuttgart, 1974, p 68, entry 18 November 1939. The date may be erroneous, as suspected by the IfZ editor. Engel did not date his notes until after the war (see ibid, p 67, n 196), or possibly there was another, earlier note (see Groscurth diaries, p 80; Müller, *Heer und Hitler*, p 437f; Müller, *Vorgeschichte*, p 100, n 37, and p 101, n 43a). See also Browning, *Entfesselung*, p 121 and p 647, n 138.
10 Browning, *Entfesselung*, p 128.
11 Kershaw, *Hitler 1936–1945*, p 380.
12 Hassell diaries, p 147, item subsequent to entry 30 November 1939.
13 Groscurth diaries, p 238, entry 19 December 1939 (private diary).
14 Ibid, entry 21 December 1939.
15 Ibid, p 241, entry 13 January 1940.
16 Ibid, p 242, entry 16 January 1940; Halder, War Diary, vol I, p 159, entry 16 January 1939.
17 Halder, War Diary, vol I, p 160, entry 18 January 1940.
18 Vogel, 'Militäropposition', p 206.
19 Groscurth, letter to his wife Charlotte, 1 February 1940, BA-MA, N 104/8.
20 Krausnick, Deutsch and Kotze, *Einführung*, pp 85–95.
21 Groscurth diaries, p 246, entry 14 February 1940 (private diary).
22 Ibid.
23 Ibid, p 247, entry as above.

24   Ibid.

25   Ibid, n 688.

26   See Draft, Christine v. Dohnanyi, IfZ, ZS 60, folio 56f; Meyer, *Unternehmen Sieben*, p 21; Smid, *Dohnanyi – Bonhoeffer*, p 235 with reference to the Dohnanyi documentation.

27   Smid, *Dohnanyi – Bonhoeffer*, p 235.

28   Deutsch, *Verschwörung*, p 117, quoting conversations with Josef Müller.

29   Ibid; see also Graml, 'Fall Oster', p 34ff.

30   Meyer, Winfried, 'Nachrichtendienst, Staatsstreichvorbereitung und Widerstand – Hans von Dohnanyi im Amt Ausland/Abwehr 1939–43', in Meyer, *Verschwörer im KZ*, p 90.

31   Ibid.

32   Deutsch, *Verschwörung*, p 117, quoting conversations with Josef Müller.

33   Höhne, *Canaris*, p 372.

34   Lahousen, 'Geheimorganisation Canaris', Part II, p. 41, BA-MA, MSg 1/2812.

35   Groscurth diaries, p 299, entry 20 October 1939 (private diary), with n 862; at the conclusion of the Müller journey, per a file note by Dohnanyi found amongst the Zossen material, according to Huppenkothen. See also 'Protokoll der Besprechung mit Frau v. Dohnanyi am 1. Dezember 1952', p 7, IfZ, ZS 603, folio 17, in the 'Europäischen Publikation' publishing project, in which Müller and Lahousen took part.

36   See Müller, Josef, 'Report on Conversation at the Vatican and in Rome between November 6th and 12th, 1939', copy, IfZ, ZS 659, folios 1–130.

37   Ueberschär, 'Militäropposition', p 353. For the negotiations and strategies developed by Müller and Kaas see Müller's above-mentioned report, which should be accepted with due caution, also Ludlow, Peter, 'Papst Pius XII., die britische Regierung und die deutsche Opposition im Winter 1939/40', *Vierteljahrshefte für Zeitgeschichte* 22, 1974, pp 299–341, containing also Osborne's reports to Lord Halifax on the audiences granted on 12 January and 7 February 1940.

38   Höhne, *Canaris*, p 380.

39   See Meyer, 'Nachrichtendienst', p 92.

40   Meyer, *Unternehmen Sieben*, p 21; Meyer, 'Nachrichtendienst', p 92; Smid, *Dohnanyi – Bonhoeffer*, p 237.

41   Thomas, Georg, 'Gedanken und Ereignisse', *Schweizer Monatshefte*, 25, 1945, p 548, who used this as a part of his defensive strategy under interrogation, not knowing that the Vatican talks had been set up by Oster and Dohnanyi. Meyer, 'Nachrichtendienst', p 92.

42   See the margin entries in Halder, War Diary, vol I, p 245ff., entries of 4 and 5 April 1940.

43   Dohnanyi, Christine von, 'Aufzeichnung über das Schicksal der Dokumenten-sammlung meines Mannes', IfZ, ZS 603, folios 27–30, copy folio 30a–d; printed in Bethge, *Dietrich Bonhoeffer*, pp 1047–52; for the complicated underlying history and Halder's manoeuvres see Smid, *Dohnanyi – Bonhoeffer*, pp 238–41.

44   Hoffmann, *Widerstand*, p 212, which gives the reaction of Brauchitsch in detail.

45   Interview with Franz Liedig by Helmut Krausnick and Harold C Deutsch, IfZ, ZS 2125, folio 5f.

46 See also Thun-Hohenstein, *Verschwörer*, and also, Thun-Hohenstein, Remedio Galeazzo Graf von, 'Widerstand und Landesverrat am Beispiel des Generalmajors Hans Oster', in Schmädecke and Steinbach, *Widerstand*, pp 751–62.

47 Ueberschär, 'Militäropposition', p 355.

48 Thun-Hohenstein, 'Widerstand und Landesverrat', p 760.

49 Raeder, *Mein Leben*, vol II, p 200.

50 Maier, Klaus A, and Stegemann, Bernd, 'Die Sicherung der europäischen Nordflanke', in *DRZW*, vol II, p 196f.

51 Ibid, p 212.

52 Brammer, Uwe, *Spionageabwehr und 'Geheimer Meldedienst'. Die Abwehrstelle im Wehrkreis X Hamburg 1935–1945*, Einzelschriften zur Militärgeschichte 33, Freiburg, 1989, p 117.

53 Interview with Franz Liedig by Helmut Krausnick and Harold C Deutsch, IfZ, ZS 2125, folio 6.

54 Ibid.

55 Maier and Stegemann, 'Sicherung', p 212.

56 Thun-Hohenstein, *Verschwörer*, p 190.

57 Ibid.

58 Jodl diaries, entry 7 May 1940, IMG, vol XXVIII, p 428, document 1890-PS.

59 For the history and activity of the 'Research Bureau' – Forschungsamt – see Gellermann, Günther W, ... *und lauschten für Hitler. Geheime Reichssache: Die Abhörzentralen des Dritten Reiches*, Bonn, 1991, pp 104–11.

60 Kershaw, *Hitler 1936–1945*, p 399–405, quotation p 405.

61 Höhne, *Canaris*, p 396.

62 Copy, Huppenkothen statement, 'Verhältnis Wehrmacht–Sicherheitspolizei, II. Teil', p 2, IfZ, ZS 249, folio 18.

63 The assertion of Josef Müller that Canaris had sent him back to Rome as an intermediary in his own affair, where he then developed the tale that the informer came from amongst Ribbentrop's colleagues and had passed it to Italian Foreign Minister Ciano has nothing to commend it. Müller, *Konsequenz*, p 151f.

64 The Jewish agent was German émigrée Gabriel Ascher, who lived and worked in Stockholm as correspondent for a Swiss newspaper. Deutsch, *Verschwörung*, p 175f; Müller, *Konsequenz*, p 153f.

65 Copy, Huppenkothen statement, 'Verhältnis Wehrmacht–Sicherheitspolizei, II. Teil', p 2, IfZ, ZS 249, folio 18.

22 Operation Felix

1 Schreiber, Gerhard, 'Die politische und militärische Entwicklung im Mittelmeerraum 1939/40', *DRZW*, vol III, p 178.

2 Ibid, p 179.

3 See also Halder, War Diary, vol II, pp 31 and 45, entries re conferences of 21 and 30 July 1940.

4 Schreiber, 'Entwicklung', p 166, with n 25.

5 Ibid, p 181.

6 Halder, War Diary, vol II, p 20, entry 13 July 1940.

7 Preston, *Franco*, p 368.
8 Burdick, Charles B, *Germany's Military Strategy and Spain in World War II*, Syracuse, New York, 1968, p 24.
9 This is according to Höhne, *Canaris*, p 405; Burdick states that Pardo was a General Staff officer and Vigón Minister for War; the latter is definitely wrong. Höhne makes Martinez Campos a colonel and chief of the Secret Intelligence Service of the Spanish Army; Preston thinks he was not a colonel but a general and chief of the General Staff. Preston also has Vigón as Air Force Minister – which is questionable as to timing – while for Höhne he was a major-general and chief of the General Staff. As regards the mission of Canaris I have mainly followed Burdick, who bases his material on the basis of an exchange of correspondence with Mikosch, Witzig and Leissner, and an interview with Langkau. Burdick, *Military Strategy*, pp 25–9.
10 Ibid, p 25 and Schreiber, 'Entwicklung', p 182. See also the report of the Italian Navy Secret Service chief, Alberto Lais, following a visit by Canaris to Rome on 22 July 1939; this was after Canaris had spoken with Franco in Spain on the Gibraltar problem and the setting up of German bases for the event of war: *DDI*, series VIII, vol XII, no 638, p 485ff.
11 Burdick, *Military Strategy*, p 25.
12 Ibid, n 30.
13 Ibid, p 26.
14 Schreiber, 'Entwicklung', p 182; Burdick, *Military Strategy*, p 27. Abwehr-Hauptmann Hans-Jochen Rudloff was supposedly making a reconnaissance in Spain at the beginning of July (Höhne, *Canaris*, p 409), or perhaps at the same time as Canaris's mission, although independent of it (Burdick, *Military Strategy*, p 29), or perhaps in common with Canaris's troops (Buchheit, *Geheimdienst*, p 375), the purpose being to see if it would be possible to siphon a Brandenburger unit through Spain without anybody noticing, and to ship artillery round to Tarifa and Ceuta at the same time. The accounts seem to go back to Rudloff and Oscar Reile, *Geheime Westfront. Die Abwehr 1935–1945*, Munich, 1962, p 283ff. The idea of a secret one-man operation in parallel to Canaris has little to commend it.
15 Halder, War Diary, vol II, pp 46–50, entry 31 July 1940; Schreiber, 'Entwicklung', p 184f.
16 Burdick, *Military Strategy*, p 35, OKW War Diary, vol I.
17 Schreiber, 'Entwicklung', p 185f.
18 Halder, War Diary, vol II, p 60, entry 9 August 1940.
19 Schreiber, 'Entwicklung', p 187f, with corresponding references to the OKW War Diary.
20 Ibid, p 187, n 31; OKW War Diary, vol I, p 22 (12 August 1940).
21 Lahousen diaries, p 90, entries 16–24 August 1940, IfZ F 23/1, folio 93.
22 Burdick, *Military Strategy*, p 41.
23 Preston, *Franco*, p 372.
24 Schreiber, 'Entwicklung', p 188, n 136.
25 Halder, War Diary, vol II, p 86, entry 3 September 1940.
26 Ibid, p 100, entry 14 September 1940. But soon Canaris and the chief of the Operational Division at General Staff, General Hans von Greiffenberg, could report that the preparations for the capture of Gibraltar were in hand, see ibid, p 104, entry 17 September 1940.

27 Kershaw, *Hitler 1936–1945*, p 440.

28 Ibid, p 441.

29 Preston, *Franco*, p 387.

30 Halder, War Diary, vol II, p 128, entry 7 October 1940.

31 Ibid, p 137, entry 15 October 1940.

32 See ibid, p 134, entry 13 October 1940.

33 Ibid, p 140, entry 16 October 1940. Alcazar was the old Moorish fortification in the centre of Toledo that Franco dallied to liberate on the road to Madrid.

34 Picker, Henry (ed), *Hitlers Tischgespräche im Führerhauptquartier, ungekürzte Neuausgabe*, Berlin, 1999, p 614 (7 July 1942).

35 Kershaw, *Hitler 1936–1945*, p 442.

36 Hill, *Weizsäcker-Papiere 1933–1950*, p 221, entry 21 October 1940.

37 Full coverage of the negotiations is in Schmidt, *Statist*, pp 500–3; also Preston, *Franco*, p 395ff.

38 Kershaw, *Hitler 1936–1945*, p 444.

39 Halder, War Diary, vol II, p 158, entry 1 November 1940.

40 Kershaw, *Hitler 1936–1945*, p 445.

41 Halder, War Diary, vol II, p 157, entry 1 November 1940.

42 Ibid, p 159, entry 2 November 1940.

43 Burdick, *Military Strateggy*, p 67.

44 Halder, War Diary, vol II, pp 164–8, entries 4–6 November 1940.

45 Lahousen diaries, p 98f, entries 5 and 6 November 1940, IfZ F 23/1, folio 101f.

46 Halder, War Diary, vol II, p 175, entry 11 November 1940; Burdick, *Military Strategy*, pp 76 and 80ff.

47 Halder, War Diary, vol II, p 1192, entry 25 November 1940; Burdick, *Military Strategy*, p 80.

48 Schreiber, 'Entwicklung', p 213.

49 Burdick, *Military Strategy*, p 81ff.

50 Halder, War Diary, vol II, p 209f, entry 5 December 1940 (square brackets in original).

51 Burdick, *Military Strategy*, p 103ff, who sets the date of the journey three days too early; Preston, *Franco*, p 412f; Crozier, *Franco*, p 336; the script of the ensuing conversation between Canaris and Franco is reproduced in: Detwiler, Donald S, *Hitler, Franco und Gibraltar*, Wiesbaden, 1962, pp 123–5; Höhne, *Canaris*, p 420f; ADAP, series D, vol XII, no 500, p 852f.

52 ADAP, series D, vol XII, no 500, p 852f; Detwiler, *Hitler, Franco und Gibraltar*, p 124, quoted here from Höhne, *Canaris*, p 420.

53 Schreiber, 'Entwicklung', p 213; OKW War Diary, vol I, p 222 (10 December 1940).

54 Halder, War Diary, vol II, p 218, entry 8 December 1940.

55 See additionally Klink, Ernst, 'Die militärische Konzeption des Krieges gegen die Sowjetunion', in *DRZW*, vol 4, part IV, p 238.

56 Preston, *Franco*, p 412.

57 Papeleux, Léon, *L'admiral Canaris entre Franco et Hitler – Le role de Canaris dans les Relations germano-espagnoles 1915–1944*, Casterman, 1977, p 138.

58 Weizsäcker, *Erinnerungen*, p 297.

59 Hill, *Weizsäcker-Papiere 1933–1950*, p 228, n 13 December 1940.

60 Ibid, p 229, n 18. 12. 1940.

61 Hassell diaries, p 216.

62 Cave Brown, *Bodyguard of Lies*, p 213.

63 Thus is the inclination of Colvin, *Chief of Intelligence*, p 127ff, who relies on conversations with Lahousen and Canaris's adjutant Jenke. Stefanie Lahousen quotes her husband as saying after the war that the final report on the negotiations with Franco had already been dictated by Canaris before the talks had concluded, which strengthens the suspicion that Canaris was working towards a Spanish 'No'. Statement by Stefanie Lahousen to the author, 3 January 2006. That Lahousen accompanied Canaris to Spain is not corroborated by the service diary; Lahousen seems to have been at Besançon in France between 6 and 9 December 1940 on Operation Felix business. Lahousen diaries, p 106, IfZ, F 23/1, folio 109.

64 Ibid, p 128.

65 Quoted from ibid; and the same words in Cave Brown, *Bodyguard of Lies*, p 214. The work of the German emigrant Werner Emil Hart (actually Aron), who returned to Germany from exile in Britain in 1951, offering his services and a batch of material on the Abwehr to the publishing project Europäische Publikationen, corresponds in detail to Colvin's account. Ausarbeitung Werner Emil Hart Dezember 1953, IfZ, ZS 1984, folio 131ff. As was apparent for accompanying correspondence, those involved were not fully sure about Hart's manuscript. It is extraordinarily precise in many details but it is quite possible that Hart had seen Colvin's book. Bassett relies extensively on Hart: Bassett, 'Canaris', p 198ff.

PART V: THE TRIUMPH OF THE BARBARIANS

23 The War of Extermination – Act Two

1 Schreiber, Gerhard, 'Politik und Kriegführung 1941', in *DRZW*, vol 3, part IV, p 540.

2 Lahousen diaries, p 112, entry 19 February 1941, IfZ F 23/1, folio 115.

3 Halder, War Diary, vol II, p 282, entry 21 Feburary 1941.

4 Lahousen diaries, p 113, entry 25 Feburary 1941, IfZ F 23/1, folio 116. At the end of 1940 a dispute arose regarding the cooperation of the Abwehr with leaders of the Ukraine Nationalist Movement (OUN), who worked as Abwehr agents. Hitler had ordered that anything that might irritate or warn the Soviet Union was to be stifled. Canaris had therefore decided that he should abandon his support for OUN, of which Lahousen advised Melnyk on 3 December 1940. Gestapo Chief Müller even ordered the arrest of a leader of one of the nationalist groups, and an Abwehr man, Ryko Jary, but Canaris intervened to prevent this. In mid-December Lahousen infomed Jary that cooperation had been broken off because of the foreign policy situation. See ibid, p 105ff, entries 30 November, 3 and 14 December 1940.

5 Heinz, *Canaris*, p 158; Fleischhauer, Ingeborg, *Die Chance des Sonderfriedens. Deutsch-sowjetische Geheimgespräche 1941–1945*, Berlin, 1986, p 27f.

6 Also Klink, 'Konzeption', p 194ff.

7 Heinz, *Canaris*, p 158f.

8 From Halder, War Diary, vol II, p 337, entry 30 March 1941; similarly Kershaw, *Hitler 1936–1945*, p 473.

9   Angrick, Andrej, *Besatzungspolitik und Massenmord. Die Einsatzgruppe D in der südlichen Sowjetunion 1941–1943*, Hamburg, 2003, p 42; see also, Angrick, Andrej, 'Zur Rolle der Militärverwaltung bei der Ermordung der sowjetischen Juden', in Quinkert, Babette (ed), *'Wir sind die Herren dieses Landes.' Ursachen, Verlauf und Folgen des deutschen Überfalls auf die Sowjetunion*, Hamburg, 2002, p 108.

10   From Angrick, *Besatzungspolitik*, p 42f. This account relies on his basic research.

11   Ibid, p 49.

12   Ibid, p 46, with n 49.

13   Kershaw, *Hitler 1936–1945*, p 480.

14   Schramm von Thadden, Ehrengard, *Griechenland und die Großmächte im Zweiten Weltkrieg*, Wiesbaden, 1955; Höhne, *Canaris*, pp 414–16 and 421–6.

15   Lahousen diaries, pp 130–2, entries 15–17 April 1941, IfZ, F 23 /1, o.P.

16   See Krausnick, Helmut, 'Kommissarbefehl und ›Gerichtsbarkeitserlaß Barbarossa‹ in neuer Sicht', *Vierteljahrshefte für Zeitgeschichte* 25, 1977, pp 658–81; Graml, *Wehrmacht im Dritten Reich*, p 376f; Kershaw, *Hitler 1936–1945*, p 474f; Angrick, *Besatzungspolitik*, pp 60–8.

17   'Aktennotiz über die Besprechung mit dem Reichsleiter Rosenberg am 30. Mai 1941', Berlin, 31 May 1941, signed Canaris, BA-MA, RW 4/760.

18   Conference note, Chef A Ausl/Abw, Berlin, 4 June 1941, BA-MA, RW 4/578, folios 29–32.

19   Lahousen diaries, p 148, entry 6 June 1941, IfZ, F 23/1, o.P.; Höhne, *Canaris*, p 443, refers to the file note of Hauptmann Keunes regarding this meeting, which had set down the respective tasks of the Wehrmacht ('defeating the enemy') and Reichsführer SS ('political police combat against the enemy') as well as the duty of all GFP, SD and SP offices 'to provide the broadest support on a mutual basis'.

20   Angrick, *Besatzungspolitik*, p 105.

21   Ibid.

22   Ibid, p 111f.

23   Klink, 'Konzeption', p 276.

24   Information AST Romania to Abt II Ausl/Abw regarding sabotage and diversionary tactics for Melnyk and Bandera OUN groups in the event of war of the 12 June 1941; Instruction from Lahousen to Abw II liaison officer, Army Groups and armies, to support the non-Russian peoples of the USSR, especially those collaborating with K-Organisations, 19 June 1941; Instruction of Chief Ausl/Abw to AST Romania for the fomenting of an insurrection in Georgia in connection with securing the Caucasian oilfields ('Tamara I and II'), 20 June 1941; Plan of Abw II liaison officer to commanding officer, 11.Armee for the formation of a Ukrainian unit to support German troops ('Organisation Roland'), 27 June 1941, all BA-MA, RH 20-11/48, reproduced in: Das Amt Ausland/Abwehr im Oberkommando der Wehrmacht. *Eine Dokumentation, bearbeitet von Norbert Müller unter Mitwirkung von Helma Kaden, Gerlinde Grahn und Brün Meyer, Materialien aus dem Bundesarchiv, vol XVI*, Bremerhaven, 2005; see also the numerous entries in Lahousen's diaries on this theme, IfZ, F 23/1.

25   Notes of an address by Reichsleiter Rosenberg, 20 June 1941 (probably written up by Canaris or Lahousen, partially burnt and illegible), copy IfZ, FD 47 (formerly FO Library 1959), folios 29–32. This collection entitled 'Canaris–Lahousen Fragments' contains mainly notes by Lahousen copied from his own and Canaris's diaries,

and the 'Rarities Folder' compiled by Dohnanyi and Oster, and given to Marogna-Redwitz in 1943. After the war they were discovered by US Intelligence, acting on information from former Abwehrstelle Munich officers, in the safe of an attorney known to Marogna-Redwitz. See Lahousen's letter to Dr Anton Hoch, 12 November 1953, IfZ, F 23/1. For another version of Rosenberg's address in which he spoke of a certain autonomy for White Russia see Gerlach, Christian, *Kalkulierte Morde. Die deutsche Wirtschafts- und Vernichtungspolitik in Weißrußland 1941–1944*, Hamburg, 1999, p 94, n 351, here pointing to BA-MA, FPF 01/7855, folios 1040–51.

26 Ibid.

27 Lahousen diaries, p 151, entry 21 June 1941, IfZ F 23/1, o.P.

28 Ibid.

29 Ibid, entry 28 February 1941, IfZ F 23/1, o.P.

30 Ibid, p 154, entry 29 February 1941, IfZ F 23/1, o.P.

31 'Vortragsnotiz fuer Chef OKW ueber bisher vorliegende Ergebnisse des Einsatzes des Amtes Ausland/Abwehr im Kampf gegen Sowjet-Rußland'; Komandos Abw II/Chief, Berlin July 1941; IfZ, FD 47, folios 39–42.

32 Lahousen diaries, p 160, entry 7 July 1941, IfZ F 23/1, o.P. Hitler, who had no interest in an independent Ukraine, refused to support the nationalist leaders, and they were brought to Germany for questioning, including Bandera.

33 Lahousen diaries, p 159, entry 5 July 1941, IfZ F 23/1, o.P.

34 Lahousen's deputy Oberst Erwin Stolze stated that he had given the instruction to Melnyk and Bandera personally to foment insurrection immediately after the German invasion. In addition to weakening the Red Army, this would have influenced international opinion that an 'apparently total break-up of the Soviet hinterland' was in progress. Statement of Erwin Stolze introduced into evidence by Soviet prosecutor at Nuremberg, 25 December 1945, IMG, vol VII, p 303.

35 Angrick, *Besatzungspolitik*, p 137.

36 Ibid, p 138.

37 Ibid, pp 141–5, especially p 145, with n 59.

38 See Streit, Christian, 'Die Behandlung der sowjetischen Kriegsgefangenen und völkerrechtliche Probleme des Krieges gegen die Sowjetunion', in Ueberschär, Gerd, and Wette, Wolfram (eds), *Der deutsche Überfall auf die Sowjetunion. Unternehmen 'Barbarossa' 1941*, Frankfurt am Main, 1991, pp 159–89, Order reproduced in ibid, pp 297–300, following quotation here at p 297.

39 Lahousen, statement, IMG, vol II, p 501; Lahousen, affidavit, 8 January 1948, IfZ, ZS 658, folios 22–7.

40 Ibid, IMG, vol II, p 503.

41 Ibid, p 505; Lahousen, affidavit, 8 January 1948, IfZ, ZS 658, folios 22–7.

42 Conference note: 'Betr.: Anordnung für die Behandlung sowjetischer Kriegsgefangener, Berlin, 15. 9. 1941', signed Canaris, reproduced in Ueberschär and Wette, *Überfall*, pp 301–5 (with appendix showing Soviet order regarding PoWs), p 301.

43 Ibid, p 302, see also IMG, vol XXII, p 539f.

44 Anonymous document (author probably Lahousen) 20 July 1941, IfZ, FD 47, folio 38.

45 Lahousen, declaration, 23 January 1953, p 2, IfZ, ZS 658, folio 5.

46 Meyer, *Unternehmen Sieben*, p 27.

47 Lahousen, declaration, 23 January 1953, p 2, IfZ, ZS 658, folio 5.

48 Copy, 'Auf einer Fahrt in das Operationsgebiet im Osten gemachte Beobachtungen und Feststellungen' (author very probably Lahousen) Berlin, 23 October 1941, IfZ, FD 47, folios 54–9. As there is a gap in the Abwehr service diary before the period, and a little later similar terminology appears in another fragment of his diary, it is very probable that Lahousen was the author of this report

49 Ibid, p 3, folio 56.

50 Gerlach, *Kalkulierte Morde*, p 585.

51 Meyer, *Unternehmen Sieben*, pp 27 and p 466, n 94, for the exhaustive account of the report's history and Lahousen's role; see also Gerlach, *Kalkulierte Morde*, p 597ff; slightly abridged impression of 'Bericht über die Judenerschießungen in Borissow' in Krausnick and Wilhelm, *Truppe*, pp 576–9.

52 Krausnick and Wilhelm, *Truppe*, p 578, n 69.

53 Copy 'Aktenvermerk ueber den Vortrag bei Chef OKW am 23. Oktober 1941', Berlin, 24 October 1941, IfZ, FD 47, folio 60f.

54 Lahousen diaries, 24–30 October 1941, IfZ, FD 47, folios 62–7. These diary pages are not part of the copy of the service diary at IfZ, F 23/1.

55 Ibid, folio 64f, entry 27 October 1941.

56 Ibid, folio 65.

57 Ibid, folio 66. [*Translator's note:* the sardine-tin method involved digging a deep trench in which the bodies were layered.]

58 Ibid, folio 67, entry 30 October 1941.

59 Fleming, Gerald, *Hitler und die Endlösung. 'Es ist des Führers Wunsch ...'*, Wiesbaden and Munich, 1982, p 100f includes the eye-witness report.

60 Fragment 'Bericht über die Lage an der Ostfront, Dezember 1941/Januar 1942', IfZ, FD 47, folios 76–7.

61 Ibid.

62 Lahousen diary, p 187, entry 28 January 1942, IfZ, F 23/1, o.P.

63 Lahousen diary, p 211, entry 25 July 1942, IfZ, F 23/1, o.P.

24 The Struggle for Power with Heydrich

1 Mühleisen, 'Duell', p 402.

2 For lengthy coverage of the three cases with the most comprehensive sources: Meyer, *Unternehmen Sieben*, pp 139–77; Lissner, Ivar, *Vergessen aber nicht vergeben*, Frankfurt am Main, Berlin and Vienna, 1970. For Klaus see also Fleischhauer, *Chance des Sonderfriedens*. I have mainly followed Meyer's study.

3 For evaluation of Klaus (also Claus, Clauss and Clauß) see Fleischhauer, *Chance des Sonderfriedens*, p 30ff; Meyer, *Unternehmen Sieben*, p 163.

4 Fleischhauer, *Chance des Sonderfriedens*, p 34f.

5 Meyer, *Unternehmen Sieben*, p 163, with n 331.

6 Fleischhauer, *Chance des Sonderfriedens*, p 43.

7 Ibid, p 45.

8 Ibid, p 45f; Meyer, *Unternehmen Sieben*, p 164.

9 Fleischhauer, *Chance des Sonderfriedens*, p 51f; quoted in ibid; it would have been on this visit by Canaris to Copenhagen that the Danish intelligence officer Hans

Lunding saw him in a hotel, and was able to recognise him later at Flossenbürg camp, see Part VI, 'Hitler's Revenge'.

10   Meyer, *Unternehmen Sieben*, p 164f.

11   Ibid, p 166.

12   Ibid, p 141, see Lissner, *Vergessen aber nicht vergeben*, and Höhne, Heinz, 'Fall Lissner', an epilogue by Höhne to the reprint of Lissner's memoir entitled *Mein gefährlicher Weg*, Munich and Zürich, 1975, p 221ff. I have relied on Meyer's account, which is based to a large extent on Höhne.

13   Ibid, p 146.

14   Ibid.

15   Ibid.

16   Ibid, p 149.

17   Ibid, p 156. For Kauder's biography, if with a few differences, see also NA, KV 2/1631.

18   For a discussion on the identities of Kauder/Kauders/Klatt see Meyer, *Unternehmen Sieben*, p 498, n 287.

19   Ibid, p 156; according to which Turkul set up his espionage service for pro-monarchist Russian exile groups in the 1930s. Once the finances failed he offered it to the Italians, but eventually gave it to the Germans. Marogna-Redwitz, head of Abwehrstelle Vienna, evaluated the contacts, set up Meldekopf Sofia and appointed Kauder as its head, probably after Barbarossa. The chief of K-Organisation Bulgaria (from 1943) Oberstleutnant Franz Seubert, stated that Kauder had been a worker in Turkul's organisation and rose to take it over. A third version, in which Turkul and his intelligence chief Ilya Lang played a much greater role appears in the comprehensive Klatt/Turkul and Ira Longin dossier at NA, KV 2/1631.

20   Meyer, *Unternehmen Sieben*, p 155f.

21   Ibid, p 160.

22   Ibid, p 161f.

23   These three spies survived the war. In several other cases Canaris was personally involved in protecting less prominent Jews by appointing them as Abwehr agents. Some Abwehr men on sabotage missions, particularly to the United States, masqueraded as Jewish refugees to gain entry. See Winfried Meyer's work.

24   Gerhard Engel, letter to Helmut Krausnick, 17 October 1964, IfZ, ZS 222, vol I, folio 98ff; telephone interview with Gerhard Engel, 24 June 1970, p 1f, ibid, o.P., this was Heydrich Himmler's source. Engel is the only source for this incident accepted by scientific research. The fact that from the spring of 1943 Himmler more or less took Canaris under his personal protection may seem extraordinary, but by now, following the death of Heydrich and the major defeats, there had been a radical change in the situation for some Nazi leaders.

25   Ibid, IfZ, ZS 222, vol I, folio 99.

26   Mühleisen, 'Duell', p 402; scheme of the Ten Points from Schellenberg, *Memoiren*, p 139f.

27   Ibid, p 402f.

28   Heydrich, letter to Canaris, Berlin 7. 11. 1941, BA-MA, RW 5/v. 690, folios 3-10; reproduced in Mühleisen, 'Duell', pp 413-18, document 1.

29   Ibid, folios 13-20; reproduced in ibid, pp 419-24, document 2.

30   Bentivegni, note, 12 January 9142, BA-MA, RW 5/v. 690, folios 28–31; reproduced in Mühleisen, 'Duell', p 424–7, Doc. 3.

31   Bentivegni, notes on conversation between Canaris and Heydrich, 12 January 1942, BA-MA, RW 5/v. 690, folios 21–7; reproduced in Mühleisen, 'Duell', pp 427–33, document 4.

32   BA-MA, RW 5/v. 690, folio 21.

33   Ibid, folio 22.

34   Ibid, folio 23.

35   Ibid, folio 25ff.

36   Draft plan RSHA, 'Grundsätze für die Zusammenarbeit der Sicherheitspolizei und des SD mit den Abwehrdienststellen der Wehrmacht', BA-MA, RW 5/v. 690, folios 95–102; reproduced in Mühleisen, 'Duell', pp 433–7, document 6.

37   Draft plan Abwehr, 'Grundsätze für die Zusammenarbeit der Sicherheitspolizei und des SD mit den Abwehrdienststellen der Wehrmacht', BA-MA, RW 5/v. 690, folios 49–57; reproduced in Mühleisen, 'Duell', pp 437–43, document 7.

38   All quotations from Heydrich's letter to Canaris, 5 February 1941, BA-MA, RW 5/v. 690, folios 85–9; reproduced in Mühleisen, 'Duell', pp 443–6, document 8.

39   Ibid, folio 88f.

40   Huppenkothen, copy statement, 'Canaris und Abwehr', p 5, IfZ, ZS 249, folio 39.

41   'Abschrift eines handschriftlichen Briefes SS-Obergruppenführers Heydrich vom 6. Februar 1942 an Herrn Admiral Canaris', BA-MA, RW 5/v. 690, folio 93; reproduced in Mühleisen, 'Duell', p 446f, document 9.

42   Canaris, letter to Heydrich, [7 February 1941], BA-MA, RW 5/v. 690, Bl. 91f; reproduced in Mühleisen, 'Duell', p 447f, document 10.

43   Huppenkothen, copy statement, 'Canaris und Abwehr', p 5, IfZ, ZS 249, folio 39; Canaris letter to Heydrich, 8 February 1942, BA-MA, RW 5/v. 690, folio 90; reproduced in Mühleisen, 'Duell', p 448f, document 11.

44   Mühleisen, 'Duell', p 405.

45   'Grundsätze für die Zusammenarbeit der Sicherheitspolizei und des SD und den Abwehrdienststellen der Wehrmacht', 1 March 1942, appendix 1 to the OKW order of 6 April 1941, BA-MA, RW 5/v. 690, folios 160–4; reproduced in Mühleisen, 'Duell', pp 451–5, document 14.

46   Angrick, Besatzungspolitik, p 128; Schellenberg, Memoiren, p 255f.

47   Fleming, Hitler und die Endlösung, p 76f, for Wagner's affidavit.

48   Cave Brown, Secret Servant, p 410f, who relies on Schellenberg's statements in his postwar interrogations. This quarrel is neither mentioned in his own memoirs nor those of Doerries.

49   Schellenberg, Memoiren, p 255.

50   'First Detailed Interrogation Report on SS-Standarten-Führer Canaris, Constantin', 12 July 1945, NA, WO 204/12806, pp 1–26; also second interrogation report, 8 August 1945. At the end of the war Constantin Canaris was an SS Standartenführer and Oberst der Polizei. When the Germans withdrew from Brussels in the autumn of 1944, Himmler sent him to Croatia, and from there in April 1945 on a special mission to Italy, where he was captured on 30 April 1945 in Milan. His interrogators did not consider him a Gestapo fanatic, but on 4 August 1951 a Belgian court sentenced him to twenty years' imprisonment. Soon afterwards he was returned to Germany. The Kiel State prosecutor subjected him to inquiry proceedings with regard

to the deportation of Belgian Jews to Auschwitz, but he was not found culpable; see additionally Wildt, *Generation*, p 523, n 118. Extracts from the interrogation of Constantin Canaris appear at NA, KV 3/8.

51 Ibid, p 17. Canaris and his nephew did not cross paths in their service careers. Constantin Canaris mentioned only a single incident after the war. The comte d'Avignon, a close acquaintance of General Falkenhausen, military commander in Belgium, opened an office in Brussels to collect political information for the occupying forces. This amounted to a private intelligence service, and Abwehrstelle Brussels began an inquiry. They quickly found a top-secret document for the OKW that Falkenhausen's chief of Staff had passed to the count, probably knowing that he would let the king of Belgium know the contents. The matter was reported to Canaris as the betrayal of an official secret, but nothing appears to have come of it.

52 Haasis, Hellmut G, *Tod in Prag. Das Attentat auf Reinhard Heydrich*, Reinbek, 2002, p 97ff.

53 Huppenkothen, copy statement, 'Canaris und Abwehr', p 5, IfZ, ZS 249, folio 40.

54 Höhne, *Canaris*, p 450.

55 Inga Haag, conversation with the author, 20 September 2005.

56 Groscurth, letter to Beck, 25 June 1942.

25 With His Back to the Wall

1 For Leverkühn see primarily Jähnicke, Burkhard, 'Lawyer, Politician, Intelligence Officer: Paul Leverkuehn in Turkey, 1915–1916 and 1941–1944', *Journal of Intelligence History* 2, no 2, pp 69–87; Heideking, Jürgen, and Mauch, Christof, 'Dokumentation: "Das Herman-Dossier. Helmuth James Graf von Moltke, die deutsche Emigration in Istanbul und der amerikanische Geheimdienst Office of Strategic Services (OSS)"', *Vierteljahrshefte für Zeitgeschichte* 40, 1992, p 567–623; for Donovan's contacts with Leverkühn, Moltke and eventually Canaris in Germany see Cave Brown, Anthony, *Wild Bill Donovan. The Last Hero*, New York, 1982, pp 129f and 133; for the contacts with Weizsäcker, Hill, *Weizsäcker-Papiere 1933–1955*, p 382f, note to 26 August 1944; for Leverkühn's collaboration with Moltke see also Moltke, Freya von, Balfour, Michael, and Frisby, Julian, *Helmuth James von Moltke 1907–1945 – Anwalt der Zukunft*, Stuttgart, 1975, pp 80 and 261.

2 Winston Churchill expressed surprise, although he had already agreed to the demand, see Kershaw, *Hitler 1936–1945*, p 752.

3 Höhne, *Canaris*, p 461f; I have followed his version.

4 Ibid, p 462.

5 Heideking, Jürgen, 'Die "Breakers"-Akte. Das Office of Strategic Services und der 20. Juli 1944', in Heideking, Jürgen, and Mauch, Christof (eds), *Geheimdienstkrieg gegen Deutschland. Subversion, Propaganda und politische Planungen des amerikanischen Geheimdienstes im Zweiten Weltkrieg*, Göttingen, 1993, p 42, n 10. The so-called 'Breakers' documents are at NARA, RG 226 E 134 B 298.

6 Ibid, quoting Cave Brown, *Donovan*, p 292f; cf also Heideking, '"Breakers"-Akte', pp 14 and 42, n 10.

7 Ibid, pp 23 and 42, n 11.

8 NA, KV 3/8: 'Bibliography of the GIS' [ie= German Intelligence Service].

9   Ibid.

10   The 'Harlequin' files are at NA, KV 2/268 and also KV 2/274-277, the report of his capture at KV 2/275.

11   Harlequin's report (in German), NA, KV 2/268, document 4A.

12   Report on meeting, 8 April 1943, NA, KV 2 /267, document 59K.

13   Reports 22 April, 4 and 19 May 1943, NA, KV 2 /268, document 43B, 45A, 47A.

14   Copy, diary 8–9 Feburary 1943, IfZ, FD 47, folios 120–2.

15   Copy, 'Reise nach Tunis am 27. 2. 1943', IfZ, FD 47, pp 123–7.

16   Ibid, folio 124.

17   Ibid, folio 125.

18   Ibid, folio 126.

19   Schlabrendorff, *Offiziere*, p 68.

20   Fest, *Staatsstreich*, p 190.

21   Thun-Hohenstein, *Verschwörer*, p 222.

22   Schlabrendorff, *Offiziere*, p 69.

23   Hoffmann, *Widerstand*, p 350.

24   Schlabrendorff, *Offiziere*, p 70.

25   According to Hoffmann, *Widerstand*, p 350, Oster was also there although Schlabrendorff, *Offiziere*, p 69, maintains that Oster and Tresckow never met. The sources below only speak of Lahousen, Dohnanyi and Canaris.

26   Report by Lahousen, 'Zur Vorgeschichte des 20. Juli 44', IfZ, ZS 658, folio 9; Lahousen diary, p 247, entry 7 March 1943, IfZ, F 23/1, o.P.

27   Copy, 'Reise zur Heeresgruppe Mitte nach Smolensk' (extract from Canaris's diary 7–9 March 1943), IfZ, FD 47, folios 128–30, Canaris observed the transport of the explosives.

28   Ibid.

29   Lahousen report: 'Zur Vorgeschichte des 20. Juli 44', IfZ, ZS 658, folio 10.

30   Schlabrendorff, *Offiziere*, pp 67–82; Hoffmann, *Widerstand*, p 352f; Kershaw, *Hitler 1936–1945*, p 870f.

31   Lahousen report: 'Zur Vorgeschichte des 20. Juli 44', IfZ, ZS 658, folio 10; more recently Glaubauf and Lahousen, *Lahousen*, p 47, who write that the Clam mines had proven useless in trials and Schlabrendorff had made a bomb out of the explosive material supplied; the result looked similar.

32   Hoffmann, *Widerstand*, pp 355–60; Kershaw, *Hitler 1936–1945*, p 871f.

33   For the background of the affair leading to the arrest of Dohnanyi and Oster see Chowaniec, *Fall Dohnanyi*; Meyer, *Unternehmen Sieben*, pp 336–458; Smid, *Dohnanyi – Bonhoeffer*, pp 296–305 and 341–476; older versions dealing with it include Hoffmann, *Widerstand*; Thun-Hohenstein, *Verschwörer*. Höhne, *Canaris*, p 465–513, dedicates the affair good coverage. I have relied mainly on Meyer, which is the best in detail and from all aspects, and links the affair extensively to 'Unternehmen Sieben'. Chowaniec looks closely at the legal aspects of the proceedings and provides both the prosecution statements as well as the defence pleadings in an appendix. Oster's quote here is from Meyer, *Unternehmen Sieben*, p 383, n 274.

34   Ibid, p 383f.

35   Christine von Dohnanyi, declaration, p 8f, IfZ, ZS 603, folio 69f.

36   Meyer, *Unternehmen Sieben*, p 566, n 274.

37   Cf Chowaniec, *Fall Dohnanyi*, pp 31–43.

38   Meyer, *Unternehmen Sieben*, p 337.
39   Ibid, p 338. The comprehensive MI5 files on Tricycle's espionage ring are at NA, KV 2/845-866 (Dusko Popoff); KV 2/867–870 (Ivo Popoff). Dossiers for other ring members ('Balloon', 'Freak', 'Gelatine') are here; Dusko Popoff wrote an autobiography: *Spy – Counterspy*, New York, 1974.
40   Ibid, p 340; for Unternehmen Pastorius see Lahousens report: Unternehmen 'Pastorius', IfZ, ZS 658, folios 29–31; Thorwald, Jürgen, *Der Fall Pastorius*, Stuttgart, 1953.
41   Meyer, *Unternehmen Sieben*, p 342.
42   Ibid, p 547, note 36.
43   Christine von Dohnanyi, draft, p 2, IfZ, ZS 603, folio 63.
44   Meyer, *Unternehmen Sieben*, p 348ff.
45   Ibid, p 353.
46   Ibid, p 355f.
47   Ibid, p 360.
48   Ibid, p 363.
49   Müller, *Konsequenz*, p 166.
50   Meyer, *Unternehmen Sieben*, pp 370–5, including individual treatments of each case.
51   Ibid, p 375.
52   Ibid, p 377.
53   Christine von Dohnanyi, draft, p 12, IfZ, ZS 603, folio 73.
54   Meyer, *Unternehmen Sieben*, p 385.
55   Ibid, p 397.
56   Ibid, p 398.
57   Ibid, p 403.
58   Ibid, p 404.
59   Christine von Dohnanyi, draft, p 14, IfZ, ZS 603, folio 75.
60   NA, KV 3/8, extract from interrogation of Constantin Canaris.
61   NA, CAB 154/77, Abwehr Operational Material, no 155, 30 May 1943.
62   Ibid, no 124, 29 May 1943.
63   Ibid, no 458, 9 July19 43.
64   Ibid, no 230, 5 June 1943.
65   Ibid, no 543–550, 18–20 July 1943.
66   Ibid, no 517, 17 July 1943.
67   Ibid, no 490, 13 July 1943.
68   Ibid, no 489, 13 July 1943.
69   Ibid, no 470, 10/11 July 1943.
70   Lahousen diary, p 260, entry 29 July 1943, IfZ F 23/1, o.P.
71   Ibid, p 261, entry 1 August 1943, IfZ F 23/1, o.P.
72   Höhne, Canaris, p 507.
73   Schellenberg, *Memoiren*, p 331.

26 *The Undoing of Canaris*

1   Heideking, Jürgen, and Mauch, Christof, 'Dokumentation: "Das Herman-Dossier. Helmuth James Graf von Moltke, die deutsche Emigration in Istanbul und der

amerikanische Geheimdienst Office of Strategic Services (OSS)'", *Vierteljahrshefte für Zeitgeschichte* 40, 1992, p 572.

2 Papen, *Der Wahrheit eine Gasse,* p 568.

3 Wuermeling, Henric L, *'Doppelspiel'. Adam von Trott zu Solz im Widerstand gegen Hitler,* Munich, 2004, p 152f.

4 The version of the early contacts of the Vermehrens is primarily in: Cave Brown, *Secret Servant,* p 560 and also *Bodyguard of Lies,* pp 401 and 455, according to which the couple had attempted unsuccessfully to defect to the British in the spring of 1943 from Lisbon. Later they had direct contact through the double-agent Dusko Popoff to the British 'XX Committee' which recruited and handled double-agents. Erich Vermehren had the cover name 'Junior'.

5 Heideking and Mauch, 'Herman-Dossier', pp 569 and 573.

6 Hoffmann, *Widerstand,* p 279.

7 Heideking and Mauch, 'Herman-Dossier', p 274, for the 'Herman Plan, see pp 589–91.

8 Ibid, p 574 with note 38.

9 Moltke, Balfour and Frisby, *Moltke,* p 288.

10 Telegram Istanbul, no 68, 2 February 1944, signed Twardowski, PA/AA, R 29783, folio 41960f.

11 Document, Legationsrat von Trott, Berlin, 5 February 1944, PA/AA, R 29783, folio 41985f.

12 Letter, Legationsrat von Grote, eo Pol I M 290 gRs, Berlin, 5. 2. 1944, PA/AA, R 101883, folio 311725.

13 Telegram, Istanbul, no 77, 6 February 1944, signed Papen, PA/AA, R 29783, folio 41976f.

14 Telegram, Istanbul, no 78, 7 February 1944, signed Papen, PA/AA, R 29783, folio 41988.

15 Telegram, Ankara, no 190, 8 February 1944, signed Papen, PA/AA, R 29783, folio 41989.

16 Letter, von Papen, Ankara, 22 February 1944, Re: Cabled Instr. no 216, 9 February 1944, PA/AA, R 101883, folios 311749–311751.

17 Letter, von Papen, Ankara, 17 February 1944, Re: Vermehren, Kleczkowski, Hamburger Cases, PA/AA, R 101883, folio 311765.

18 Telegram, Ankara, no 191, 7 February 1944, signed Papen, PA/AA, R 29783, folio 41990.

19 Telegram, Ankara, no 192, 8 February 1944, signed Papen, PA/AA, R 29783, folio 41991.

20 Telegram Lisbon, 10 February 1944, signed Huene, PA/AA, R 101883, folio 311770.

21 Copy draft, envoy Frohwein, 20 February 1944, PA/AA, R 101883, folios 31788–93.

22 Telegram, Madrid, no 525, 28 January 1944, signed Dieckhoff, PA/AA R 27815, folios 359213–17. [*Translator's note:* In May 1942, Himmler and Canaris negotiated an exception to the 'Ten Commandments' Agreement whereby in Argentina the German Foreign Office, SD and Abwehr collaborated as a consortium known as 'Red Bolivar' (the Bolivar Network).]

23 Letter, Ribbentrop, 2 February 1944, PA/AA, R 27815, folio 359219.

24 Führer-note of 30 January 1944 regarding incident of the oranges in Spain, Ribbentrop, PA/AA, R 101874, vol 268526–268528.

25 Letter, Canaris to Foreign Ministry, 3 February 1944, PA/AA, R 27815, folio 359226.

26 Telegram, Madrid, no 739, 6 February 1944, PA/AA, R 27815, folios 359220–3.

27 Letter, Legationsrat Grote to OKW Amt Ausl/Abw, 8 February 1944, quoted in Höhne, *Canaris*, p 521.

28 Telegram eo Pol I M 348 gRs, Berlin 8 February 1944, signed Steengracht, PA/AA, R 101869, folio 302861.

29 Intercepted telegram, 4 February 1944, NA, KV 3/3, p 26.

30 Note of conference, 10/11 February 1944 in Biarritz, PA/AA, R 27815, folios 359254–7.

31 Note re talks in Biarritz, 10 and 11 February 1944, PA/AA, R 27815, folios 359249–53.

32 Telegram, Madrid, no 918, 14 February 1944, PA/AA, R 27815, folios 359245–7.

33 Intercepted telegram, 6 October 1943, NA, KV 3/3, p 20.

34 Intercepted telegram, 18 October 1943, NA, KV 3/3, p 21. For the forcible closure of Abwehrstelle Algeciras by the Guardia Civil cf in PA/AA, R 101874, folios 268464–88.

35 Grote, jotting, 17 February 1944, PA/AA, R 27815, folio 359262f.

36 Goebbels's Diaries, vol 5, p 2011, entry 5 March 1944.

37 Huppenkothen, copy statement, Canaris and Abwehr, p 6, IfZ, ZS 249, folio 41.

38 Hitler's order for the creation of a uniform German secret Intelligence service, 12 February 1944, BA-MA, RH 2/1929, quoted here from Meyer, *Unternehmen Sieben*, p 442, and Höhne, *Canaris*, p 528. For this order and subsequent objections and instructions see Bundesarchiv documentation 'Amt Ausland/Abwehr' mentioned elsewhere.

39 Höhne, *Canaris*, p 529.

40 Meyer, *Unternehmen Sieben*, p 442.

41 Letter, OKM, MPA I no 1454, Berlin, 21 March 1944, signed Baltzer, Canaris-IfZ, folio 99.

42 These and the details of Canaris's stay at Burg Lauenstein are from Höhne, *Canaris*, p 530f, who relies on information from Otto Wagner.

43 Huppenkothen, copy statement: Canaris and Abwehr, p 7, IfZ, ZS 249, folio 43; Meyer, *Unternehmen Sieben*, p 442f; Höhne, *Canaris*, p 531.

44 Ibid, here also are comprehensive descriptions of the negotiations between the representatives of the OKW and Kaltenbrunner. The instructions of Keitel and Himmler in BA-MA, RH 2/1929, are reproduced in Abwehr documentation at Bundesarchiv.

45 Buchheit, *Geheimdienst*, p 432.

46 Canaris-IfZ, folio 100.

47 Cave Brown, *Bodyguard of Lies*, p 595ff.; same author, *Secret Servant*, p 584ff.

48 See Part VI, 'Hitler's Revenge'.

49 Report, Kaltenbrunner to Bormann, 29 September 1944, in Jacobsen, *Opposition*, p 425.

50 Buchheit, *Geheimdienst*, p 438.

51 Höhne, *Canaris*, p 537, from a draft by Huppenkothen.

52 From Abshagen, *Canaris*, p 373. It can only be assumed from the Kaltenbrunner report of 29 September 1944 that Kaulbars and Sack were with Canaris.
53 Höhne, *Canaris*, p 540.
54 Abshagen, *Canaris*, p 374f.
55 Report, Kaltenbrunner to Bormann, 29 November 1944: 'Verbindungen zum Ausland', in Jacobsen, *Opposition*, vol 1, p 503.
56 Schellenberg, *Memoiren*, p 334.
57 Ibid, p 335f. It is not known if this conversation ever took place. That Canaris survived almost to the war's end is justification in Schellenberg's mind that it must have occurred.
58 Meyer, *Unternehmen Sieben*, p 450; Höhne, *Canaris*, p 545.
59 Appendix 1 to report by Kaltenbrunner to Bormann: 'Die geistige Haltung des Offiziers', 25 August 1944, in Jacobsen, *Opposition*, vol 1, p 302f.
60 Thun-Hohenstein, *Verschwörer*, p 263.
61 Report, Müller to Bormann, 8 September 1944, 'Das Zusammenspiel mit der Abwehr', in Jacobsen, *Opposition*, vol 1, pp 369–71.
62 Report, Kaltenbrunner to Bormann, 21 September 1944, in Jacobsen, *Opposition*, vol 1, p 406.
63 Ibid, p 407.
64 Appendix 1 to Kaltenbrunner's report to Bormann of 21 September 1944, in Jacobsen, *Opposition*, vol 1, p 410.

PART VI: HITLER'S REVENGE

1 Ueberschär, Gerd R, *Stauffenberg. Der 20. Juli 1944*, Frankfurt am Main, 2004, pp 145–67; Hoffmann, *Staatsstreich*, pp 623–58; *Aufstand des Gewissens*; Kershaw, *Hitler 1936–1945*, pp 892–907.
2 Arrest list 24 July 1944, in Jacobsen, *Opposition*, vol 1, p 49; Meyer, *Unternehmen Sieben*, p 450; Höhne, *Canaris*, p 543f; for the proceedings against the principal colleagues in the circle around Canaris and Hans Oster see also: Thun-Hohenstein, *Verschwörer*; Chowaniec, *Fall Dohnanyi*; Meinl, *Nationalsozialisten*, ch XVI; and most recently Smid, *Dohnanyi –Bonhoeffer*, ch VII.
3 Letter, Wera Schwarte to Helmut Krausnick, 24 November 1964, IfZ, ZS 2101, folio 1, Meyer, *Unternehmen Sieben*, p 451.
4 Lahousen, note, Geheimorganisation CANARIS Part II, p 1, BA-MA, MSg 1/2812; see also statement of Lahousen, 30 November 1945, IMG, vol II, p 491f.
5 Lahousen, note, Geheimorganisation CANARIS Part II, p 1, BA-MA, MSg 1/2812.
6 Interrogation Huppenkothen, 28 June 1948, copy, IfZ, ZS 249, folio 124.
7 Chowaniec, *Fall Dohnanyi*, p 120; Bartz, Karl, *Die Tragödie der deutschen Abwehr*, Oldendorf, 1972, p 214; for the fate of the diaries see Mühleisen, 'Duell', pp 395–458, here p 396f, with n 5 and 6.
8 Meinl, *Nationalsozialisten*, p 325.
9 Statement of Heinz to the Gremium der Europäischen Publikation, 11 August 1952, quoted here from Meinl, *Nationalsozialisten*, p 325. For Oster's participation see Chowaniec, *Fall Dohnanyi*, p 123.

10 Chowaniec, *Fall Dohnanyi*, p 121, with n 115, points out that the statements of Sonderegger and Huppenkothen are contradictory. Both said that Kerstenhahn led them to the files, on another occasion that a search by others had been successful. That does not nullify Kerstenhahn's treachery, although he may have had honourable motives; Christine von Dohnanyi assumed after the war that Schrader had buried some of the documents at his hunting lodge on Lüneburg Heath – a place which Kerstenhahn knew – while on Beck's orders a part containing the plans for the 1939/40 coup were left at Zossen for later use. Kerstenhahn betrayed these in order to protect Schrader's widow and others, which would explain why incriminated members of the Dohnanyi circle were never arrested. Dohnanyi, Christine von, note on the fate of the document collection of my husband, Reichsgerichtrats Dr. Hans von Dohnanyi, IfZ, ZS 603, folios 27–30, copy, folios 30a–d; printed in Bethge, *Dietrich Bonhoeffer*, Munich, 1970, pp 1047–52. According to information from Werner Wolf Schrader the Dohnanyi files, containing a copy of the Canaris diaries, were hidden at Gross-Denkte south of Wolfenbüttel. See Fraenkel, Heinrich, and Manvell, Roger, *Canaris. Tatsachenbericht*, Munich, 1978, pp 276–9, n 134–7.

11 Bartz, *Tragödie*, p 214f; Höhne, *Canaris*, p 553; see the discussion in Chowaniec, *Fall Dohnanyi*, p 120f and previous note.

12 Meinl, *Nationalsozialisten*, p 326.

13 Cf Christine v. Dohnanyi, note, IfZ, ZS 603, folio 35.

14 Dohnanyi, Christine von, Note on the fate of the document collection of my husband, Reichsgerichtrats Dr Hans von Dohnanyi, IfZ, ZS 603, folio 28.

15 Chowaniec, *Fall Dohnanyi*, p 123; Smid, *Dohnanyi – Bonhoeffer*, p 431f; Meyer, *Unternehmen Sieben*, p 451. To attribute the survival of the files to Dohnanyi, as has long been the case, is unrealistic. See the contrary arguments in: Müller, *Konsequenz*, p 216; Thun-Hohenstein, *Verschwörer*, p 264.

16 Also Chowaniec, *Fall Dohnanyi*, pp 123–6 as per the statements of Huppenkothen und Sonderegger; Meyer, *Unternehmen Sieben*, p 451f. See also copy of Huppenkothen's statement, 'Canaris und Abwehr', IfZ, ZS 249, folio 35 and copy statement, Huppenkothen, 20 July 1944, IfZ, ZS 249, folio 152–168, here folios 154–60.

17 Quoted from Meinl, *Nationalsozialisten*, p 325.

18 Chowaniec, *Fall Dohnanyi*, p 130.

19 Höhne, *Canaris*, p 555.

20 Meyer, *Unternehmen Sieben*, p 452.

21 Chowaniec, *Fall Dohnanyi*, p 130.

22 Quoted from Meyer, *Unternehmen Sieben*, p 453.

23 For the theory of the planned show trial see statement of Josef Müller, 20 October 1947, p 2, IfZ, ZS 659, vol II, folio 59. For other motives see also Chowaniec, *Fall Dohnanyi*, p 130 and Meyer, *Unternehmen Sieben*, p 453.

24 Hoffmann, *Widerstand*, p 631; for the defensive strategy to distribute the incriminating material as 'play material' see copy of Huppenkothen's deposition, 24 April 1948, p 3, copy at IfZ, ZS 249.

25 Josef Müller, statement, 20 October 1947, p 2, IfZ, ZS 659, vol II, folio 59.

26 Smid, *Dohnanyi – Bonhoeffer*, p 431.

27 Bethge, *Dietrich Bonhoeffer*, p 1015f.

28 Se the compulsive story of a survivor, Schlabrendorff, *Offiziere*, pp 164–6.

29 Statement by Pfuhlstein in prosecution of Sonderegger, Bergedorf judgment, 12 January 1949, p 9f, copy at IfZ, ZS 659. Statement of Brigitte Canaris, ibid, p 16. See also Abshagen, *Canaris*, p 377f. Karl Heinz Abshagen was a brother of the Abwehr officer Wolfgang Abshagen, who was captured by the Soviets in 1945 and died in captivity. According to Erwin Lahousen the biography was based on information from former Abwehr colleagues, one of whom was Lahousen himself, as confirmed to this author by his wife Stefanie. Unfortunately Abshagen rarely supplied his sources. See opinion of Lahousen, IfZ, ZS 658, folios 1–3. See also letter from Ernst Behrens [former Oberst at OKW Amt Ausland/Abwehr] to Karl Heinz Abshagen dated 30 August 1950 with opinion on the Canaris biography, BA-MA, MSg 1/2813. The circumstances of the arrest are portrayed similarly in Müller, *Konsequenz*, p 220.

30 Schlabrendorff, *Offiziere*, p 167.

31 Bergedorf judgment, 12 January 1949, p 13f, copy at IfZ, ZS 659; Höhne, *Canaris*, p 559.

32 Müller, *Konsequenz*, p 220.

33 Even the judges at the Bergedorf trial were unable to make sense of Sonderegger's ambivalent behaviour. On 12 January 1949 he was sentenced to seven years' imprisonment, but they mentioned the special treatment afforded by Sonderegger to Müller and Dohnanyi. See Bergedorf judgment, 12 January 1949, p 22f, copy at IfZ, ZS 659. After the war Müller interceded for Sonderegger for having saved his life, see statement of Josef Müller, 20 October 1947, p 4f, IfZ, ZS 659, vol II, folio 59 and correspondence Müller–Sonderegger, ibid. In a statement to US authorities on 23 May 1945 Müller stated that his comparatively good treatment was due to his friendship with SS-Gruppenführer Rattenhuber and SS-General Dunkern, of which Sonderegger had been informed. Statement by Müller, Capri, 23 May 1945, NARA, RG 226 E 125 B 29. For the treatment of Dohnanyi, sick with diphtheria and transferred on 1 February 1945 from Sachsenhausen camp to the Prinz-Albrecht-Strasse, see secret messages from Dohnanyi to his wife, 25 February and 8 March 1945, copies at IfZ, ZS 603, appendix, folios 4–10. For the presumption that Sonderegger was protecting his own back for postwar safety see also Chowaniec, *Fall Dohnanyi*, p 110. Apparently neither Sonderegger nor Huppenkothen mistreated Dohnanyi; it was Kriminalrat Kurt Stawitzki, responsible for his care in Berlin, who refused to continue his medical treatment and left him for weeks lying in excrement in his cell. Müller was also mistreated repeatedly by Stawitzki. See secret message of 25 February 1945; statement of Müller 20 October 1947; Smid, *Dohnanyi – Bonhoeffer*, p 440.

34 This statement in Höhne, *Canaris*, p 556f, who relies on Huppenkothen's statement.

35 Report, Kaltenbrunner to Bormann, 19 September 1944, in Jacobsen, *Opposition*, vol I, pp 424–9.

36 This statement in Höhne, *Canaris*, p 556f, who relies on Huppenkothen's statement.

37 Report, Kaltenbrunner to Bormann, 19 September 1944, in Jacobsen, *Opposition*, vol I, p 425.

38 Ibid, p 429.

39 Smid, *Dohnanyi – Bonhoeffer*, p 433.

40 Report, Kaltenbrunner to Bormann, 2 October 1944, in Jacobsen, *Opposition*, pp 430–4, here p 430.

41   Ibid, italics in original.

42   Report, Kaltenbrunner to Bormann, 9 December 1944, in Jacobsen, *Opposition*, vol I, pp 517-20, here p 519, italics in original.

43   Meyer, *Unternehmen Sieben*, p 453.

44   Schlabrendorff, *Offiziere*, p 177f; Bethge, *Dietrich Bonhoeffer*, p 1022.

45   Statement of Josef Müller, (autumn 1948), IfZ, ZS 659, folio 88.

46   Müller, *Konsequenz*, p 229.

47   Cf Judgment of Landgericht Augsburg in criminal prosecution of Walther Huppenkothen and Dr Otto Thorbeck, 15 October 1955, reproduced in *Justiz und NS-Verbrechen. Nazi Crimes on Trial. Sammlung deutscher Strafurteile wegen nationalsozialistischer Tötungsverbrechen 1945-1999*, edited and revised by Christiaan Frederik Rüter and Dick W de Mildt, Amsterdam and Munich, 1968 onwards, c 50 vols, still being completed, here vol XIII, lfd no 420a; ibid, confirmation of Court of Revision of BGH, same matter, 25 May 1956, 1 StR 50/56, lfd no 420d. Excerpts are available on Internet at: http://www1.jur.uva.nl/junsv/Excerpts/420inhalt.htm.

48   Ibid, lfd no 420a VII, see also Lunding's hand-drawn sketch in: *Die Nachhut*, 2, 1971, p 13, BA-MA, MSg 3-22/1 (between 1967 and 1974 *Die Nachhut* was the veteran's publication of AGEA, the organisation of former Abwehr members), also Lunding, Hans, 'In Memoriam Wilhelm Canaris', printed letter of eulogy on twentieth anniversary of his death, 9 April 1965, BA-MA, MSg 1/1193 and. 2172.

49   Augsburg Judgment, lfd no 420a XIII.

50   For Lunding's spell of incarceration at Flossenbürg see statement of Lunding, Capri, 12 May 1945, NA, WO 311/597.

51   Augsburg Judgment, lfd no 420a XIII.

52   Ibid, see also Lunding, 'In Memoriam Canaris', BA-MA, MSg 1/1193 and. 2172; Höhne, *Canaris*, p 562. See also a comprehensive OSS dossier on Lunding's statements of 25 February 1946, NARA, RG 226 E 125 B 29. Lunding, not always reliable on facts, stated that Kaltenbrunner and Gestapo Chief Müller were at Flossenbürg camp on 6 April to try Canaris. In the time-frame, and with the diary background this is not implausible. In one version after this conversation Lunding had an exchange of code-knocks with Canaris, who communicated his fate by this method.

53   Meyer, *Verschwörer im KZ*, p 133; Smid, *Dohnanyi - Bonhoeffer*, p 452f.

54   Buchheit, *Geheimdienst*, p 444f; Canaris, *Höhne*, p 563; Meyer, *Unternehmen Sieben*, p 456; letter from Wera Schwarte to Helmut Krausnick, 24 November 1964, p 2, IfZ, ZS 2101, folio 2.

55   Augsburg Judgment, lfd. no 420a VII.

56   Cf the extensive agreement of analysis and interpretation in Chowaniec, *Fall Dohnanyi*, pp 131-8; Meyer, *Unternehmen Sieben*, p 456; Smid, *Dohnanyi -Bonhoeffer*, p 454. For a legal appraisal of this trial against the background of perverted National Socialist law see Chowaniec, *Fall Dohnanyi*, pp 138-58; for the occasionally scandalous abuses of jurisprudence after the war: Mohr, Philipp, 'Die Verfolgung Hans von Dohnanyis durch Reichskriegsgericht, Gestapo und SS 1934-45 und ihre Aufarbeitung durch die Justiz nach 1945', in Meyer, *Verschwörer im KZ*, pp 116-44, with further literary sources. The Federal Criminal Court acquitted Thorbeck on 19 June 1956, Huppenkothen was convicted as an accessory to murder, but only for the Flossenbürg trial, and only then because he agreed to the immediate execution

of the sentence, which he attended knowing that it had not been confirmed by a Court of Revision. The Federal Criminal Court did not find grounds to criticise the conviction and sentence on Canaris. For the literature in the Huppenkothen trial see Mohr, 'Verfolgung', p 143, n 67.

57 Smid, *Dohnanyi – Bonhoeffer*, p 455.

58 See Höhne, Canaris, p 566; Thun-Hohenstein, *Verschwörer*, p 271. As to the trials themselves we have only the evidence of the proceedings at Munich (16 February 1951 and 5 November 1952) and Augsburg (15 October 1955).

59 Augsburg Judgment, lfd. no 420a XIII.

60 Höhne, *Canaris*, p 567.

61 Quotation ibid, and similarly Thun-Hohenstein, *Verschwörer*, p 271. See also Augsburg Judgment, lfd no 420a X. As to the ambivalence of Canaris's attitude to the Resistance see opinion of Erwin Lahousen, 29 August 1952, IfZ, ZS 658, folio 6 in which he says that Canaris was 'overcautious'. 'Canaris shielded the opposition activities of others but never became involved himself.'

62 Augsburg Judgment, lfd no 420a XIII.

63 Abshagen, *Canaris*, p 393; Hoffmann, *Widerstand*, p 653.

64 Höhne, *Canaris*, p 567.

65 Augsburg Judgment, lfd no 420 XIII; Höhne, *Canaris*, p 567.

66 Augsburg Judgment, lfd no 420 XIII.

67 Müller, *Konsequenz*, p 251.

68 Augsburg Judgment, lfd no 420 IX.

69 Information from Stefanie Lahousen to the author, 3 January 2006. For statement of the camp doctor see Höhne, *Canaris*, p 569; Bethge, *Dietrich Bonhoeffer*, p 1038.

70 Müller, *Konsequenz*, p 252.

71 See Höhne, *Canaris*, p 569.

Sources and Bibliography

Archives and Sources

BAK: Bundesarchiv, Koblenz

N 1150	Nachlaß Walter Luetgebrune
R 43 I 603-605	Alte Reichskanzlei/Akten zur Affäre Lohmann

BA-MA: Bundesarchiv-Militärarchiv, Freiburg

Pers. 6/105 u. 2293	Personalakte Canaris
MSg 1	Wilhelm Canaris
MSg 1/812	Erwin Lahousen
MSg 3-22/1	*Die Nachhut*
N 104	Nachlaß Helmuth Groscurth
N 326	Nachlaß Albert Hopmann
N 612	Nachlaß Gert Buchheit
N 620	Nachlaß Waldemar Pabst
N 812	Nachlaß Wilhelm Canaris
RH 2/1929	Oberkommando des Heeres/Generalstab des Heeres
RH 20-11/334	Akten AOK 11
RH 20-11/485	Akten AOK 11 Aufträge/Sonderunternehmen Abwehr II
RM 5/2228	Admiralstab Berichte/Schriftwechsel S.M.S. Dresden
RM 6/48	Marineleitung Akten betreffend Spanien
RM 6/267	Handakte Canaris/Jorns-Prozeß
RM 6/269	Untersuchungen zu den Vorgängen in Kiel 1923
RM 8/145	Bericht Reinhard
RM 8/1013	Marineleitung Kriegsakten Loewenfeld II
RM 20/1635	Akten betreffend Japan
RM 97/753	KTB U 34
RM 97/766	KTB U 35
RM 97/1648	KTB UB 128
RM 97/1785	KTB UC 27
RM 122/116	Akten Loewenfeld II
RW 4/578	Wehrmachtführungsstab Chefsachen Barbarossa
RW 4/760	Wehrmachtführungsstab Verwaltung Barbarossa
RW 4/764	Wehrmachtsführungsstab Akten Barbarossa
RW 5/123	Abwehr II
RW 5/143	Abwehr II Polen
RW 5/194	Handakten Abwehr III a Juli 1933–September 1936

RW 5/195   Handakten Abwehr III a
RW 5/196 a   Handakten Abwehr III a
RW 5/196 b   Handakten Abwehr III a
RW 5/197   Handakten Abwehr III a
RW 5/198   Handakten Abwehr III a
RW 5/207   Vortragsnotizen Abwehr III a
RW 5/278   Bericht Leopold Bürkner
RW 5/350   Außenpolitische Übersichten
RW 5/351   Ausland I
RW 5/497   Diensttagebuch Abwehr II (Lahousen diaries, part I)
RW 5/498   Diensttagebuch Abwehr II (Lahousen diaries, part II)
RW 5/499   Diensttagebuch Abwehr II (Lahousen diaries)
RW 5/690   Akten 10 Gebote

IfZ: Institut für Zeitgeschichte, München

ED 63   Berichte und Dokumente Robert Nowak
ED 92   Josef Müller Private Papiere 1947–1956
F 23/1   Abschrift Diensttagebuch der Abwehr II (Lahousen diaries)
F 87   Personalnachweis Hans Oster
FD 47   Canaris-Lahousen Fragments
ZS 222   Gerhard Engel
ZS 249   Walter Huppenkothen
ZS 303   Franz Xaver Sonderegger
ZS 372   Karl Schäfer
ZS 520   Franz Halder
ZS 540   Conrad Patzig
ZS 603   Christine von Dohnanyi
ZS 658   Erwin Lahousen
ZS 659   Josef Müller
ZS 1785   Siegfried Sorge
ZS 1986   Werner Emil Hart
ZS 2093   Inga Haag
ZS 2101   Wera Schwarte
ZS 2125   Franz Liedig

NA: National Archives, Kew/London

ADM 1/8405/459   Naval Engagement Falkland Islands, 8 Dec 1914
ADM 1/8461/155   Visit S/M u 35 in Spain
ADM 53/42828   Log HMS *Glasgow*
ADM 53/45610   Log HMS *Kent*
ADM 53/53455   Log HMS *Orama*
ADM 137/3155   War Records 1914–1918, Sinking ss *Roma*
ADM 137/4159   War Records 1914–1918, Intercepted German Letters (SMS *Dresden*)
ADM 137/4802   War Records 1914–1918, W/T War Log HMS *Glasgow*
ADM 223/641-644   Madrid Naval Messages Vol III–Vol VI
ADM 223/780   German Diplomatic, South America, 1915–1917

ADM 223/781	South American Papers (SMS *Dresden*)
ADM 233/490	Spain Naval Intelligence Directorate
CAB 41/35/63	Naval Engagement, Falkland Islands, 10 Dec 1914
CAB 146/413	OKW/Abwehr & Intelligence
CAB 154/77-79	Abwehr-Reports 1943
FO 118	British Embassy and Consulates in the Argentine, 1915
FO 132/139	Correspondence South America 1915
FO 132/141	Correspondence South America 1915
FO 132/142	Correspondence South America 1915
FO 132/143	Correspondence South America 1915
FO 162	British Consulate at Punta Arenas, Chile, 1914–1915
FO 185/1237	Consular Telegrams
FO 371/414	Foreign Office Political Western Department Spain (WWI)
FO 371/2468	Foreign Office Political Western Department Spain (WWI)
FO 371/2469	Foreign Office Political Western Department Spain (WWI)
FO 371/2761	Foreign Office Political Western Department Spain (WWI)
FO 371/9489	Foreign Office Political Western Department Spain (WWI)
FO 371/31230	Foreign Office Political Western Department Spain (WWII)
FO 372/174	Treaty Department at the Foreign Office/Spain Files
FO 372/175	Treaty Department at the Foreign Office/Spain Files
FO 372/650	Correspondence South America 1915
FO 372/753	Correspondence South America 1915
FO 372/825	Correspondence South America 1915
FO 372/85	German Ships 1916
FO 372/886	German Ships 1916
FO 445	British Embassy Madrid, 1916
GFM 33/2393	German Foreign Ministry (Geheimakten des AA)
KV 2/167	Canaris, Joachim Wilhelm Walter
KV 2/173	Lahousen, Erwin
KV 2/268	Harlequin
KV 2/275	Harlequin
KV 2/276	Harlequin
KV 2/277	Harlequin
KV 2/693	Rolland, Baron Ino von @ Ezratty; Isaac
KV 2/845	Popov, Dusko @ Trycicle
KV 2/846	Popov, Dusko @ Trycicle
KV 2/847	Popov, Dusko @ Trycicle
KV 2/1171	Molkenteller, Clara
KV 2/1391	Pescator, Hans von/Piert, Willy
KV 2/1631	Longin (Klatt) [Richard Kauder]
KV 3/3	Abwehr – History Sheets – Canaris Traffic
KV 3/8	Abwehr – General & H. Q. Organisation
KV 4/259-261	Defence of Gibraltar
WO 106/1576-1579	Directorate of Military Operations and Intelligence
WO 106/5128	Correspondence with Military Attachés 1915–1917
WO 204/12806	Interrogation Reports Constantin Canaris Col.
WO 208	Records of the Directorate of Military Intelligence (WW II)

NARA: National Archives and Records Administration, Washington

RG 226/   Records of the Office of Strategic Studies E 122 B 1/E 125 B 29, B 52/E 134 B 298/ E 171A B 2 /E 210 B 22, B 58, B 64, B 195, B 199, B 201, B 208, B 212, B 217, B 230, B 266, B 284, B 352, B 355, B 384, B 401, B 402, B 409, B 415, B 420, B 426, B 427, B 440–442 (Boston Series), E 216 B 6

PA/AA: Politisches Archiv des Auswärtigen Amtes, Berlin

R 27815   Handakten Ritter – Spanien, Sonderheft I
R 27816   Handakten Ritter – Spanien, Sonderheft II
R 27828   Handakten Ritter – Großmufti und Gailani, Japan, USA
R 29782   Büro des Staatssekretärs – Türkei, Bd. 8
R 29783   Büro des Staatssekretärs – Türkei, Bd. 9
R 29805   Büro des Staatssekretärs – USA, Bd. 8
R 101863   Pol I M Akten zu Ivar Lissner
R 101864   Pol I M Akten zu Ivar Lissner
R 101869   Pol I M Akten Schweiz
R 101883   Pol I M Akten zu Affäre Vermehren

Private Collections

Archiv Michael Heinz
Archiv Heinz Höhne

Published Sources, Editions, Documents

Akten zur Deutschen Auswärtigen Politik (ADAP), Serie A–D

Baumgart, Winfried, 'Dokumentation: "Zur Ansprache Hitlers vor den Führern der Wehrmacht vom 22. August 1939. Eine quellenkritische Untersuchung"', *Vierteljahrshefte für Zeitgeschichte* 16, 1968, pp 120–49

Berghahn, Volker R, and Deist, Wilhelm, 'Dokumentation: "Kaiserliche Marine und Kriegsausbruch 1914. Neue Dokumente zur Juli-Krise"', *Militärgeschichtliche Mitteilungen* 7, 1970, pp 37–58

Brausch, Gerd, 'Dokumentation: "Der Tod des Generalobersten Werner Freiherr von Fritsch"', *Militärgeschichtliche Mitteilungen* 7, 1970, pp 95–112

Breitman, Richard, and Aronson, Shlomo, 'Dokumentation: "Eine unbekannte Himmler-Rede vom Januar 1943"', *Vierteljahrshefte für Zeitgeschichte* 38, 1990, pp 337–48

Coppi, Hans, 'Die "Rote Kapelle" im Spannungsfeld von Widerstand und nachrichtendienstlicher Tätigkeit. Der Trepper-Report vom Juni 1943', *Vierteljahrshefte für Zeitgeschichte* 44, 1996, pp 431–58

Das Amt Ausland/Abwehr im Oberkommando der Wehrmacht, *Eine Dokumentation, bearbeitet von Norbert Müller unter Mitwirkung von Helma Kaden, Gerlinde Grahn und Brün Meyer*, Materialien aus dem Bundesarchiv 16, published by Bundesarchiv, Bremerhaven, 2005

Die Regierung der Volksbeauftragten 1918/19, *Eingeleitet von Erich Matthias, bearbeitet von Susanne Miller unter Mitwirkung von Heinrich Potthoff*, 2 vols, Düsseldorf, 1969 = *Quellen zur Geschichte des Parlamentarismus und der politischen Parteien*, published by Werner Conze and Erich Matthias, Erste Reihe, vol 6 I and II

Die Ursachen des Deutschen Zusammenbruches 1918, 2. *Abteilung: Der Innere Zusammenbruch. Im Auftrag des Vierten Unterausschusses unter Mitwirkung von Eugen Fischer, Walter Bloch und Albrecht Phillip*, 12 vols in 14 parts, Berlin 1925–8

Dülffer, Jost, 'Überlegungen von Kriegsmarine und Heer zur Wehrmachtspitzengliederung und zur Führung der Wehrmacht im Kriege im Februar-März 1938', *Militärgeschichtliche Mitteilungen* 9, 1971, pp 145–71

Ernst, Fritz, *Aus dem Nachlaß des Generals Walther Reinhardt*, Sonderdruck, Stuttgart, 1958

Geyer, Michael, 'Dokumentation: "Das zweite Rüstungsprogramm (1930–1934)"', *Militärgeschichtliche Mitteilungen* 17, 1975, pp 125–72

Gorlow, Sergej A, 'Dokumentation: "Geheimsache Moskau-Berlin. Die militärpolitische Zusammenarbeit zwischen der Sowjetunion und dem deutschen Reich 1920–1933"', *Vierteljahrshefte für Zeitgeschichte* 44, 1996, pp 133–65

Hannover-Drück, Elisabeth, and Hannover, Heinrich, *Der Mord an Rosa Luxemburg und Karl Liebknecht – Dokumentation eines politischen Verbrechens*, Frankfurt am Main, 1967

Hartmann, Christian, and Slutsch, Sergej, 'Dokumentation: "Franz Halder und die Kriegsvorbereitungen im Frühjahr 1939. Eine Ansprache des Gene-ralstabschefs des Heeres"', *Vierteljahrshefte für Zeitgeschichte* 45, 1997, pp 467–95

Hauner, Milan, 'Dokumentation: "Ein Bericht des britischen Militärattachés in Prag vom 4. April 1938 über seine Reise zur Besichtigung der tschechischen Grenzbefestigungen"', *Militärgeschichtliche Mitteilungen* 24, 1978, pp 125–36

Heideking, Jürgen, 'Dokumentation: "Westliche Geheimdienste und die nordchinesische Guerilla im Zweiten Weltkrieg"', *Militärgeschichtliche Mitteilungen* 37, 1985, pp 103–36

Heideking, Jürgen, and Mauch, Christof, 'Dokumentation: "Das Herman-Dossier. Helmuth James Graf von Moltke, die deutsche Emigration in Istanbul und der amerikanische Geheimdienst Office of Strategic Services (OSS)"', *Vierteljahrshefte für Zeitgeschichte* 40, 1992, pp 567–623

Heideking Jürgen, and Mauch, Christof (eds), *USA und deutscher Widerstand – Analysen und Operationen des amerikanischen Geheimdienstes im Zweiten Weltkrieg*, Tübingen and Basel, 1993

Heideking, Jürgen, and Mauch, Christof (eds), *American Intelligence and the German Resistance to Hitler – A Documentary History*, Boulder, CO, 1996

Herwig, Holger H, 'Soziale Herkunft und wissenschaftliche Vorbildung des Seeoffiziers der Kaiserlichen Marine vor 1914', *Militärgeschichtliche Mitteilungen* 10, 1971, pp 81–113

Hill, Leonidas E (ed), *Die Weizsäcker-Papiere 1900–1932*, Berlin, Frankfurt am Main and Vienna, 1982

Hill, Leonidas E (ed) *Die Weizsäcker-Papiere 1933–1950*, Berlin, Frankfurt am Main and Vienna, 1974

Hillgruber, Andreas, and Förster, Jürgen, 'Dokumentation "Zwei neue Aufzeichnungen über 'Führer'-Besprechungen aus dem Jahre 1942"', *Militärgeschichtliche Mitteilungen* 11, 1972, pp 109–26

Hürten, Heinz, 'Dokumentation: "Das Wehrkreiskommando VI in den Wirren des Frühjahrs 1920"', *Militärgeschichtliche Mitteilungen* 15, 1974, pp 127–56

Hürter, Johannes, 'Dokumentation: "Auf dem Weg zur Militäropposition. Tresckow, Gersdorff, der Vernichtungskrieg und der Judenmord. Neue Dokumente über das Verhältnis der

Heeresgruppe Mitte zur Einsatzgruppe B im Jahr 1941'", *Vierteljahrshefte für Zeitgeschichte* 52, 2004, pp 527–62

I Documenti Diplomatici Italiani (DDI), series VIII, vols XII and XIII

Internationaler Militärgerichtshof Nürnberg, *Der Prozeß gegen die Hauptkriegsverbrecher vom 14. November 1945–1. Oktober 1946*, 48 vols, Nuremberg, 1947 onwards

Jacobsen, Hans-Adolf (ed), *Opposition gegen Hitler und der Staatsstreich vom 20. Juli 1944 – Geheime Dokumente aus dem ehemaligen Reichssicherheitshauptamt*, 2 vols, Stuttgart 1989

Jacobsen, Hans-Adolf (ed), *Generaloberst Halder: Kriegstagebuch. Tägliche Aufzeichnungen des Chefs des Generalstabs des Heeres 1939–1942*, 3 vols, Stuttgart 1962–4

Jochmann, Werner (ed), *Adolf Hitler – Monologe im Führerhauptquartier 1941–1944, Die Aufzeichnungen Heinrich Heims*, Hamburg, 1980

Justiz und NS-Verbrechen, *Nazi Crimes on Trial. Sammlung deutscher Strafurteile wegen nationalsozialistischer Tötungsverbrechen 1945–1999*, edited and revised by Christiaan Frederik Rüter and Dick W de Mildt, c 50 vols Amsterdam and Munich, 1968 onwards; still being completed

Krausnick, Helmut, 'Dokumentation: "Denkschrift Himmlers über die Behandlung der Fremdvölkischen im Osten"', *Vierteljahrshefte für Zeitgeschichte* 5, 1957, pp 194–8

Krausnick, Helmut, 'Dokumentation: "Aus den Personalakten von Canaris"', *Vierteljahrshefte für Zeitgeschichte* 10, 1962, pp 280–310

Krausnick, Helmut, 'Dokumentation: "Hitler und die Morde in Polen. Ein Beitrag zum Konflikt zwischen Heer und SS um die Verwaltung der besetzten Gebiete"', *Vierteljahrshefte für Zeitgeschichte* 11, 1963, pp 196–209

Longerich, Peter (ed), *Die Ermordung der europäischen Juden. Eine umfassende Dokumentation des Holocaust 1941–1945*, Munich, 1989

Maser, Werner, *Hitlers Briefe und Notizen – Sein Weltbild in handschriftlichen Dokumenten*, Graz, 2002

Matlok, Siegfried (ed), *Dänemark in Hitlers Hand. Der Bericht des Reichsbevollmächtigten Werner Best über seine Besatzungspolitik in Dänemark mit Studien über Hitler, Göring, Himmler, Heydrich, Ribbentrop, Canaris u.a.*, Husum, 1988

Meier-Welcker, Hans, 'Dokumentation: "Zur deutsch-italienischen Militärpolitik und Beurteilung der italienischen Wehrmacht vor dem Zweiten Weltkrieg"', *Militärgeschichtliche Mitteilungen* 7, 1970, pp 59–94

Meier-Welcker, Hans, 'Dokumentation: "Der Weg zum Offizier im Reichsheer der Weimarer Republik"', *Militärgeschichtliche Mitteilungen* 19, 1976, pp 147–80

Mommsen, Hans, 'Dokumentation: "Der nationalsozialistische Polizeistaat und die Judenverfolgung vor 1938"', *Vierteljahrshefte für Zeitgeschichte* 10, 1962, pp 68–87

Mühleisen, Horst, 'Dokumentation: "Die Fritsch-Krise im Frühjahr 1938. Neun Dokumente aus dem Nachlaß des Generalobersten"', *Militärgeschichtliche Mitteilungen* 56, 1997, pp 471–508

Mühleisen, Horst, 'Dokumentation: "Das letzte Duell. Die Auseinandersetzungen zwischen Heydrich und Canaris wegen der Revision der 'Zehn Gebote'"', *Militärgeschichtliche Mitteilungen* 58, 1999, pp 395–458

Müller, Klaus-Jürgen, 'Dokumentation: "Zu Vorgeschichte und Inhalt der Rede Himmlers vor der höheren Generalität am 13. März 1940 in Koblenz"', *Vierteljahrshefte für Zeitgeschichte* 18, 1970, pp 95–120

Müller, Rolf-Dieter, 'Dokumentation: "Kriegsrecht oder Willkür? Helmuth James Graf v. Moltke und die Auffassungen im Generalstab des Heeres über die Aufgaben der Militärverwaltung vor Beginn des Rußlandkrieges"', *Militärgeschichtliche Mitteilungen* 42, 1987, pp 125–51

Overy, Richard, *Verhöre – Die NS-Elite in den Händen der Alliierten 1945*, Munich and Berlin, 2002

Picker, Henry (ed), *Hitlers Tischgespräche im Führerhauptquartier, ungekürzte Neuausgabe*, Berlin, 1999

Public Record Office, *Operation Foxley: The British Plan to Kill Hitler*, introduction by Mark Seaman with a foreword by Ian Kershaw, Kew, 1998

Public Record Office, *Secret History Files: CAMP 20 – MI 5 and the Nazi Spies*, introduction by Oliver Hoare, Richmond, 2000

Public Record Office, *Secret History Files: GARBO – the Spy who saved D-Day*, introduction by Mark Seaman, Richmond, 2000

Public Record Office, *The Security Service 1908–1945 – The Official History*, introduction by Christopher Andrews, Kew, 1999

Roon, Ger van, 'Dokumentation: "Oberst Wilhelm Staehle. Ein Beitrag zu den Auslandskontakten des deutschen Widerstandes"', *Vierteljahrshefte für Zeitgeschichte* 14, 1966, pp 209–23

Rothfels, Hans, 'Dokumentation: "Promemoria eines bayerischen Richters zu den Juni-Morden 1934"', *Vierteljahrshefte für Zeitgeschichte* 5, 1957, pp 102–4

Rothfels, Hans, 'Dokumentation: "Der geheime deutsch-japanische Notenaustausch zum Dreimächtepakt"', *Vierteljahrshefte für Zeitgeschichte* 5, 1957, pp 182–93

Rothfels, Hans, 'Dokumentation: "Zwei außenpolitische Memoranden der deutschen Opposition (Frühjahr 1942)"', *Vierteljahrshefte für Zeitgeschichte* 5, 1957, pp 38–397

Rothfels, Hans, 'Dokumentation: "Widerstandsrecht und Widerstandspflicht"', *Vierteljahrshefte für Zeitgeschichte* 10, 1962, pp 88–94

Salewski, Michael, 'Dokumentation: "Marineleitung und politische Führung 1931–1935"', *Militärgeschichtliche Mitteilungen* 10, 1971, pp 113–58

Saul, Klaus, 'Dokumentation: "Der Kampf um die Jugend zwischen Volksschule und Kaserne. Ein Beitrag zur 'Jugendpflege' im Wilhelminischen Reich 1890–1914"', *Militärgeschichtliche Mitteilungen* 9, 1971, pp 97–143

Schreiber, Gerhard, 'Zur Kontinuität des Groß- und Weltmachtstrebens der deutschen Marineführung', *Militärgeschichtliche Mitteilungen* 26, 1979, pp 101–71

Schüssler, Wilhelm (rev), 'Dienstschrift Nr. 15 Geheim, Der Kampf der Marine gegen Versaille 1919–1935', Berlin 1937, in Internationaler Militärgerichtshof Nürnberg, a.a.O., vol XXXIV, document 156-C, pp 530–607

Stegmann, Dirk, 'Dokumentation: "Die deutsche Inlandspropaganda 1917/18. Zum innenpolitischen Machtkampf zwischen OHL und ziviler Reichsleitung in der Endphase des Kaiserreiches"', *Militärgeschichtliche Mitteilungen* 12, 1972, pp 75–116

Vogelsang, Thilo, 'Dokumentation: "Die Reichswehr in Bayern und der Münchner Putsch 1923"', *Vierteljahrshefte für Zeitgeschichte* 5, 1957, pp 91–101

Volkmann, Hans-Erich, 'Dokumentation: "Das 'Vlasov'-Unternehmen zwischen Ideologie und Pragmatismus"', *Militärgeschichtliche Mitteilungen* 12, 1972, pp 117–55

Waddington, Geoffrey T, 'Dokumentation: "Hitler, Ribbentrop, die NSDAP und der Niedergang des britischen Empire 1935–1938"', *Vierteljahrshefte für Zeitgeschichte* 40, 1992, pp 273–306

Wilhelm, Hans-Heinrich, 'Dokumentation: "Hitlers Ansprache vor Generalen und Offizieren am 26. Mai 1944"', *Militärgeschichtliche Mitteilungen* 20, 1976, pp 123–70

Wollstein, Günter, 'Dokumentation: "Eine Denkschrift des Staatssekretärs Bernhard von Bülow vom März 1933. Wilhelminische Konzeption der Außenpolitik zu Beginn der nationalsozialistischen Herrschaft"', *Militärgeschichtliche Mitteilungen* 13, 1973, pp 77–94

Diaries, Letters, Memoires and Recollections

Bazna, Elyesa, *I Was Cicero*, New York, 1962

Below, Nicolaus von, *Als Hitlers Adjutant 1937–45*, Mainz, 1980

Böhm, Gustav, *Aufzeichnungen des Hauptmanns Gustav Böhm*, edited and revised by Heinz Hürten and Georg Meyer, Stuttgart, 1977

Bonhoeffer, Dietrich, and Wedemeyer, Maria von, *Brautbriefe Zelle 92: 1943–1945*, edited by Ruth-Alice von Bismarck and Ulrich Kabitz with a foreword by Eberhard Bethge, Munich, 1993

Brüning, Heinrich, *Briefe und Gespräche 1934 – 1945*, edited by Claire Nix with Reginald Phelps and George Pettee, Stuttgart, 1974

Brüning, Heinrich, *Memoiren 1918–1934*, Stuttgart, 1970

Bülow, Bernhard von, *Denkwürdigkeiten:* vol 3, *Weltkrieg und Zusammenbruch*, Berlin, 1931

Burckhardt, Carl J, *Meine Danziger Mission 1937–1939*, Munich 1960, 1980

Churchill, Winston S, The Second World War, 6 vols, London, 2002, first published Boston, 1948–53

Diels, Rudolf, *Lucifer ante portas . . . es spricht der erste Chef der Gestapo*, Stuttgart, 1950

Engel, Gerhard, *Heersadjutant bei Hitler 1938–1943. Aufzeichnungen des Majors Engel*, edited and with a commentary by Hildegard von Kotze, Schriftenreihe der Vierteljahrshefte für Zeitgeschichte 29, Stuttgart, 1974

Eppler, John W, *Geheimagent im Zweiten Weltkrieg zwischen Berlin, Kabul und Kairo*, Oldendorf, 1974

Faber du Faur, Moritz von, *Macht und Ohnmacht. Erinnerungen eines alten Offiziers*, Stuttgart, 1953

Felfe, Heinz, *Im Dienst des Gegners – Autobiographie*, Berlin, 1988

Gehlen, Reinhard, *Der Dienst*, Mainz and Wiesbaden, 1971

Gessler, Otto, *Reichswehrpolitik in der Weimarer Zeit*, edited by Kurt Sendtner, Stuttgart, 1958

Geyr von Schweppenburg, Leo Freiherr, *Erinnerungen eines Militärattachés*, London, 1933–1937, Stuttgart, 1949

Gisevius, Hans Bernd, *Bis zum bitteren Ende*: vol 1, *Vom Reichstagsbrand bis zur Fritsch-Krise*, vol 2, *Vom Münchner Abkommen zum 20. Juli 1944*, Zürich, 1946

Goebbels, Joseph, *Tagebücher 1924 – 1945*, 5 vols, edited by Ralf Georg Reuth, Munich, 1999

Gollwitzer, Helmut, Kuhn, Käthe, and Schneider, Reinhold (eds), *Du hast mich heimgesucht bei Nacht – Abschiedsbriefe und Aufzeichnungen des Widerstandes 1933–1945*, Munich, 1954

Groscurth, Helmuth, *Tagebücher eines Abwehroffiziers 1938–1940, mit weiteren Dokumenten zur Militäropposition gegen Hitler*, edited by Helmut Krausnick and Harold C Deutsch with Hildegard von Kotze, Stuttgart, 1970

Hassell, Fey von, *Niemals sich beugen – Erinnerungen einer Sondergefangenen der SS*, Munich, 1990

Hassell, Ulrich von, *Die Hassell-Tagebücher 1938–1944 – Aufzeichnungen vom Anderen Deutschland, Nach der Handschrift revidierte und erweiterte Ausgabe unter Mitarbeit von Klaus Peter Reiß herausgegeben von Friedrich Freiherr Hiller von Gaertringen*, Berlin, 1988

Hopmann, Albert, *Das Logbuch eines deutschen Seeoffiziers*, Berlin, 1924

Hopmann, Albert, *Das ereignisreiche Leben eines 'Wilhelminers' – Tagebücher, Briefe, Aufzeichnungen 1901 bis 1920*, edited by Michael Epkenhans, Schriftenreihe des Militärgeschichtlichen Forschungsamtes, vol 62, Munich, 2004

Hossbach, Friedrich, *Zwischen Wehrmacht und Hitler*, Wolfenbüttel and Hannover, 1949

John, Otto, *Zweimal kam ich heim*, Düsseldorf, 1969

John, Otto, *'Falsch und zu spät' – Der 20. Juli 1944*, Munich and Berlin, 1984

Kantorowicz, Alfred, *Spanisches Kriegstagebuch*, edited by Hein Kohn and Werner Schartel, with a new foreword by the author, Hamburg 1979

Kennan, George F, *Impressionen eines Lebens*, Düsseldorf, Vienna and New York 1999

Kordt, Erich, *Nicht aus den Akten . . . Die Wilhelmstraße in Frieden und Krieg. Erlebnisse, Begegnungen und Eindrücke 1928–1945*, Stuttgart, 1950

Lissner, Ivar, *Vergessen aber nicht vergeben. Erinnerungen*, Frankfurt am Main, Berlin and Vienna, 1970

Mann, Heinrich, *Zur Zeit von Winston Churchill*, edited, revised, with commentary and a foreword by Hans Bach, Frankfurt am Main, 2004

Manstein, Erich von, *Soldat im 20. Jahrhundert – Militärisch-politische Nachlese*, edited by Rüdiger von Manstein and Theodor Fuchs, Bonn, 1997

Meissner, Otto, *Staatssekretär unter Ebert – Hindenburg – Hitler. Der Schicksalsweg des deutschen Volkes 1918–1945, wie ich ihn erlebte*, Hamburg, 1950

Moltke, Helmuth James von, *Briefe an Freya 1939–1945*, edited by Beate Ruhm von Oppen, Munich, 1988

Müller, Josef, *Bis zur letzten Konsequenz – Ein Leben für Frieden und Freiheit*, Munich, 1975

Niemöller, Martin, *Vom U-Boot zur Kanzel*, Berlin, 1934

Noske, Gustav, *Von Kiel bis Kapp – Zur Geschichte der deutschen Revolution*, Berlin, 1920

Noske, Gustav, *Erlebtes aus Aufstieg und Niedergang einer Demokratie*, Offenbach, 1947

Papen, Franz von, *Der Wahrheit eine Gasse*, Munich, 1952

Popov, Dusko, *Spy/Counterspy. The Autobiography of Dusko Popov*, New York, 1974

Raeder, Erich, *Mein Leben*: vol 1, *Bis zum Flottenabkommen mit England 1935*, Tübingen, 1956, vol 2, *Von 1935 bis Spandau 1955*, Tübingen, 1957

Reile, Oscar, *Geheime Ostfront – Die deutsche Abwehr im Osten 1921–1945*, Munich, 1963

Reile, Oscar, *Treff Lutetia Paris – Der Kampf der Geheimdienste im westlichen Operationsgebiet, in England und Nordafrika 1939–1945 – Im 'Dienst' Gehlens 1949–1961*, Munich, 1968

Reile, Oscar, *Der deutsche Geheimdienst im II. Weltkrieg – Westfront*, Augsburg, 1990

Ritter, Nikolaus, *Deckname Dr. Rantzau – Die Aufzeichnungen des Nikolaus Ritter, Offizier unter Canaris im Geheimen Nachrichtendienst*, Hamburg, 1972

Rittlinger, Herbert, *Geheimdienst mit beschränkter Haftung. Bericht vom Bosporus*, Stuttgart, 1973

Schellenberg, Walter, *Memoiren*, London, 1956

Schlabrendorff, Fabian von, *Offiziere gegen Hitler*, revised and edited by Gero v. S. Gaevernitz, Zürich, 1946

Schlabrendorff, Fabian von, *Begegnungen in fünf Jahrzehnten*, Tübingen, 1979

Schmidt, Paul, *Statist auf diplomatischer Bühne 1925–45*, Bonn, 1949

Schneider, Heinrich, *Die letzte Fahrt des kleinen Kreuzers 'Dresden'*, Berlin and Leipzig, 1926

Schulze-Holthus, Bernhardt, *Frührot in Iran. Abenteuer im Deutschen Geheimdienst*, Esslingen, 1952

Shirer, William, *Berliner Tagebuch. Aufzeichnungen 1934–1941*, edited by Jürgen Schebera, Leipzig and Weimar, 1991

Soltikow, Michael Graf, *Meine Jahre bei Canaris*, Rastatt, 1982

Speer, Albert, *Erinnerungen*, Munich, 1969, 2003

Spitzy, Reinhard, *So haben wir das Reich verspielt – Bekenntnisse eines Illegalen*, Munich and Vienna, 1986

Stahlberg, Alexander, *Die verdammte Pflicht. Erinnerungen 1932 bis 1945*, Berlin, 1994

Stehlin, Paul, *Auftrag in Berlin. Diplomat in geheimer Mission. Deutschland zwischen Olympischen Spielen und Kriegsausbruch*, Berlin, 1965

Stephan, Enno, *Deutscher Agent. Geheimauftrag Irland. Agenten im irischen Untergrundkampf 1939–1945*, Oldenburg, 1961

Stieff, Hellmuth, *Briefe, herausgegeben und eingeleitet von Horst Mühleisen*, Berlin, 1991
Thomas, Georg, 'Gedanken und Erinnerungen', *Schweizer Monatshefte* 25, 1945, pp 537–59
Trotha, Adolf von, *Persönliches, Briefe, Reden und Aufzeichnungen – Ausgewählt und herausgegeben von Dr. Bendix von Bargen*, Berlin, 1938
Weizsäcker, Ernst von, *Erinnerungen*, Munich, 1950
Wette, Wolfgang (ed), *Aus den Geburtsstunden der Weimarer Republik – Das Tagebuch des Obersten Ernst van den Bergh*, Quellen zur Militärgeschichte, series A, vol 1, Düsseldorf, 1991

Research, Monographs and Essays

Abendroth, Hans-Henning, 'Hitlers Entscheidung', in Schieder, Wolfgang, and Dipper, Christoph (ed), *Der Spanische Bürgerkrieg in der Internationalen Politik (1936–1939)*, Munich, 1976, pp 76–128
Abendroth, Hans-Henning, 'Deutschlands Rolle im spanischen Bürgerkrieg', in Funke, Manfred (ed), *Hitler, Deutschland und die Mächte. Materialien zur Außenpolitik des Dritten Reiches* (Bonner Schriften zur Politik und Zeitgeschichte, vol 12), Düsseldorf, 1978, pp 471–88
Abendroth, Hans-Henning, 'Die deutsche Intervention im spanischen Bürgerkrieg', *Vierteljahrshefte für Zeitgeschichte* 30, 1982, pp 117–29
Abshagen, Karl Heinz, *Canaris – Patriot und Weltbürger*, Stuttgart, 1955
Ahmann, Rolf, 'Der Hitler–Stalin-Pakt: Nichtangriffs- und Angriffsvertrag?', in Oberländer, Erwin (ed), *Hitler–Stalin-Pakt 1939. Das Ende Ostmitteleuropas?*, Frankfurt am Main, 1989
Allfrey, Anthony, *Man of Arms. The Life and Legend of Sir Basil Zaharoff*, London, 1989
Alvarez, David, and Graham, Robert A, *Nothing Sacred. Nazi Espionage against the Vatican, 1939–1945*, London, 1997
Angrick, Andrej, *Besatzungspolitik und Massenmord. Die Einsatzgruppe D in der südlichen Sowjetunion 1941–1943*, Hamburg, 2003
Arnold, Klaus Jochen, 'Verbrecher aus eigener Initiative? Der 20. Juli 1944 und die Thesen Christian Gerlachs', *Geschichte in Wissenschaft und Unterricht* 53, 2002, pp 20–31
Arnold, Klaus Jochen, *Die Wehrmacht und die Besatzungpolitik in den besetzten Gebieten der Sowjetunion. Kriegführung und Radikalisierung im 'Unternehmen Barbarossa'*, Zeitgeschichtliche Forschungen, vol 23, Berlin, 2005
Aronson, Shlomo, *Reinhard Heydrich und die Frühgeschichte von Gestapo und SS*, Stuttgart, 1971
Aronson, Shlomo, 'Die dreifache Falle. Hitlers Judenpolitik, die Alliierten und die Juden', *Vierteljahrshefte für Zeitgeschichte* 32, 1984, pp 29–65
Aufstand des Gewissens – Militärischer Widerstand gegen Hitler und das NS-Regime 1933–1945, a companion volume to the exhibition of the Militärgeschichtlichen Forschungsamtes, edited by Thomas Vogel, Hamburg, Berlin and Bonn, 2001
Aussaresses, Général (pseud), *Pour la France – Services Speciaux 1942–1954*, Paris, 2001
Bailey, Geoffrey (pseud), *The Conspirators. An Extraordinary Story of Intrigue between Russia and Western Europe During the Years before Word War II*, London, 1961
Banach, Jens, *Heydrichs Elite – Das Führerkorps der Sicherheitspolizei und des SD, durchgesehene und erweiterte Auflage*, Paderborn, 2002
Bartz, Karl, *Die Tragödie der deutschen Abwehr*, Oldendorf, 1972
Bassett, Richard, *Hitler's Spy Chief. The Wilhelm Canaris Mystery*, London, 2005

Baum, Walter, 'Marine, Nationalsozialismus und Widerstand', *Vierteljahrshefte für Zeitgeschichte* 11, 1963, pp 16–48

Bennet, Geoffrey, *Die Seeschlachten von Coronel und Falkland und der Untergang des deutschen Kreuzergeschwaders unter Admiral Spee*, Munich, 1980

Benzing, Klaus, *Der Admiral Wilhelm Canaris – Leben und Wirken*, Nördlingen, 1973

Best, S Payne, *The Venlo Incident*, London, 1950

Bethge, Eberhard, 'Adam von Trott und der deutsche Widerstand', *Vierteljahrshefte für Zeitgeschichte* 11, 1963, pp 213–23

Bethge, Eberhard, *Dietrich Bonhoeffer – Eine Biographie*, Munich, 1967

Bird, Keith W, *Weimar, the German Naval Officer Corps and the Rise of National Socialism*, Amsterdam, 1977

Black, Peter, *Ernst Kaltenbrunner – Vasall Himmlers: Eine SS-Karriere*, Paderborn, Munich, Vienna and Zürich, 1991

Bloß, Hartmut, 'Zur Zweigleisigkeit der deutschen Fernostpolitik und Hitlers Option für Japan 1938', *Militärgeschichtliche Mitteilungen* 27, 1980, pp 55–92

Boehm, Hermann, and Baumgart, Winfried, 'Zur Ansprache Hitlers vor den Führern der Wehrmacht am 22. August 1939 (Miszelle/Erwiderung)', *Vierteljahrshefte für Zeitgeschichte* 19, 1971, pp 294–304

Bösch, Hermann, *Heeresrichter Dr. Karl Sack im Widerstand. Eine historisch-politische Studie*, Munich, 1967

Bracher, Karl Dietrich, *Die Deutsche Diktatur – Entstehung, Struktur, Folgen des Nationalsozialismus*, 4. verbesserte Auflage, Cologne, 1972

Brammer, Uwe, *Spionageabwehr und 'Geheimer Meldedienst'. Die Abwehrstelle im Wehrkreis X Hamburg 1935–1945*, Militärgeschichtliches Forschungsamt Freiburg edition, Freiburg, 1989

Brausch, Gerd, 'Der Tod des Generalobersten Werner Freiherr von Fritsch', *Militärgeschichtliche Mitteilungen* 5, 1969, pp 95–112

Breitman, Richard, *Heinrich Himmler. Der Architekt der Endlösung*, Zürich, 2000

Brissaud, André, *Canaris – Fürst des deutschen Geheimdienstes oder: Meister des Doppelspiels?*, Frankfurt, 1970

Broszat, Martin, 'Hitler und die Genesis der "Endlösung". Aus Anlaß der Thesen von David Irving', *Vierteljahrshefte für Zeitgeschichte* 45, 1997, pp 739–75

Brown, Paul B, 'Forester to Feldpolizeichef: The Life and Counterintelligence Career of Wilhelm Krichbaum', paper presented at the Conference of the International History Study Group, Tutzing, 24–6 April 1998

Brown, Paul B, *The Senior Leadership Cadre of the Geheime Feldpolizei, 1939–1945*, Nazi War Criminal Records Interagency Working Group, National Archives and Records Administration: Holocaust and Genocide Studies, vol 17, no 2, Washington, 2003, pp 278–304

Browning, Christopher R, *Der Weg zur 'Endlösung' – Entscheidungen und Täter*, Reinbek, 2002

Browning, Christopher R, *Die Entfesselung der 'Endlösung' – nationalsozialistische Judenpolitik 1939–1942*, Munich, 2003

Brysac, Shareen Blair, *Mildred Harnack und die 'Rote Kapelle' – Die Geschichte einer ungewöhnlichen Frau und einer Widerstandsbewegung*, Bern, 2003

Buchheit, Gert, *Der Deutsche Geheimdienst – Geschichte der militärischen Abwehr*, Munich, 1966

Buchheit, Gert, *Die anonyme Macht – Aufgaben, Methoden, Erfahrungen der Geheimdienste. Mit einer Einführung von Wilhelm Ritter v. Schramm*, Frankfurt am Main, 1969

Buckmiller, Michael, 'Nachdenken über Funktion und Rollenverständnis eines "Bluthundes"', in Butenschön, Rainer, and Spoo, Eckart (eds), *Wozu muß einer der Bluthund sein? Der*

Mehrheitssozialdemokrat Gustav Noske und der deutsche Militarismus des 20. Jahrhunderts, Heilbronn, 1997, pp 54–66

Burdick, Charles B, *Germany's Military Strategy and Spain in World War II*, Syracuse, NY, 1968

Burdick, Charles B, 'The American Military Attachés in the Spanish Civil War, 1936–1939', *Militärgeschichtliche Mitteilungen* 46, 1989, pp 61–77

Bussmann, Walter, 'Zur Entstehung und Überlieferung der "Hoßbach-Niederschrift"', *Vierteljahrshefte für Zeitgeschichte* 16, 1968, pp 373–84

Butenschön, Rainer, and Spoo, Eckart (eds), *Wozu muß einer der Bluthund sein? Der Mehrheitssozialdemokrat Gustav Noske und der deutsche Militarismus des 20. Jahrhunderts*, Heilbronn, 1997

Carr, Raymond (ed), *The Republic and the Civil War in Spain*, Oxford, 1971

Carsten, Francis L, *Reichswehr und Politik 1918–1933*, Cologne and Berlin, 1964

Carsten, Francis L, *Widerstand gegen Hitler – Die deutschen Arbeiter und die Nazis*, Frankfurt am Main and Leipzig, 1996

Cave Brown, Anthony, *Wild Bill Donovan. The Last Hero*, New York, 1982

Cave Brown, Anthony, *The Secret Servant. The Life of Sir Stewart Menzies, Churchill's Spymaster*, London, 1987

Cave Brown, Anthony, *Bodyguard of Lies – The Extraordinary True Story Behind D-Day*, London, 1975

Chowaniec, Elisabeth, *Der 'Fall Dohnanyi' 1943 – 1945. Widerstand, Militärjustiz, Willkür*, Schriftenreihe der Vierteljahrshefte für Zeitgeschichte, vol 62, Munich, 1991

Colvin, Ian, *Chief of Intelligence – Was Canaris, Hitler's Chief of Intelligence, a British Agent?* London, 1951

Coogan, Tim Pat, *The I.R.A.*, London, 1970, 2000

Coppi, Hans, Danyel, Jürgen, and Tuchel, Johannes (eds), *Die Rote Kapelle im Widerstand gegen den Nationalsozialismus*, Berlin, 1994

Corbett, Julian S, *Naval Operations Vol. I, To the Battle of the Falklands. History of the Great War. By Direction of the Historical Section of the Committee of Imperial Defence*, London, 1920

Corbett, Julian S, *Naval Operations Vol. II. By Direction of the Historical Section of the Committee of Imperial Defence*, London, 1921

Courtois, Stephane, and Panné, Jean-Louis, 'Der lange Arm des NKWD fällt auf Spanien', in Courtois, Stephane, Werth, Nicolas, Panné, Jean-Louis, Paczkowski, Andrzej, Bartosek, Karel and Magolin, Jean-Louis, *Das Schwarzbuch des Kommunismus. Unterdrückung, Verbrechen und Terror, erweiterte Studienausgabe*, Munich and Zürich, 2000, pp 366–86

Crowe, David M, *Oskar Schindler. Die Biographie*, Frankfurt am Main, 2005

Crozier, Brian, *Franco. A Biographical History*, Fakenham, 1967

Daniel, Silvia, '"Troubled Loyalty"? Britisch-deutsche Debatten um Adam Trott zu Solz 1933–1969', *Vierteljahrshefte für Zeitgeschichte* 52, 2004, pp 409–40

Darstellungen aus den Nachkriegskämpfen deutscher Truppen und Freikorps, 6 vols (2 series), *Die Wirren in der Reichshauptstadt und im nördlichen Deutschland*, Berlin, 1940

Das Deutsche Reich und der Zweite Weltkrieg (DRZW), published by Militärgeschichtlichen Forschungsamt, 9 vols in 11 parts, Stuttgart, 1979 onwards

Dederichs, Mario R, *Heydrich. Das Gesicht des Bösen*, Munich and Zürich, 2005

Deist, Wilhelm, 'Brüning, Herriot und die Abrüstungsgespräche von Bessinge 1932', *Vierteljahrshefte für Zeitgeschichte* 5, 1957, pp 265–72

Deist, Wilhelm, 'Die Politik der Seekriegsleitung und die Rebellion der Flotte Ende Oktober 1918', *Vierteljahrshefte für Zeitgeschichte* 14, 1966, pp 341–68

Deist, Wilhelm, 'Die Unruhen in der Marine 1917/18', *Marinerundschau* 68, 1971, pp 325–43

Deist, Wilhelm, 'Die Aufrüstung der Wehrmacht', in *DRZW*, vol 1, *Ursachen und Voraussetzungen der deutschen Kriegspolitik*, Stuttgart, 1979, pp 371–532

Deist, Wilhelm, 'Die Reichswehr und der Krieg der Zukunft', *Militärgeschichtliche Mitteilungen* 45, 1989, pp 81–92

Deist, Wilhelm, *Militär, Staat und Gesellschaft. Studien zur preußisch-deutschen Militärgeschichte*, Beiträge zur Militärgeschichte vol 34, published by Militärgeschichtlichen Forschungsamt, Munich, 1991

Delattre, Lucas, *Fritz Kolbe – Der wichtigste Spion des zweiten Weltkriegs*, Munich, 2004

Deschner, Günther, *Reinhard Heydrich – Statthalter der totalen Macht*, Esslingen, 1977

Deutsch, Harold C, *Verschwörung gegen den Krieg – Der Widerstand in den Jahren 1939 – 1940*, Munich, 1969

Deutsch, Harold C, *Das Komplott oder die Entmachtung der Generale. Blomberg- und Fritsch-Krise, Hitlers Weg zum Krieg*, Eichstätt, 1974

Dipper, Christof, 'Der Deutsche Widerstand und die Juden', *Geschichte und Gesellschaft* 9, 1983, pp 349–80

Dobbs, Michael, *Saboteurs. The Nazi Raid on America*, New York, 2004

Doerries, Reinhard R, *Hitler's Last Chief of Foreign Intelligence: Allied Interrogations of Walter Schellenberg*, London and Portland, OR, 2003

Doerries, Reinhard R (ed), *Diplomaten und Agenten. Nachrichtendienste in der Geschichte der deutsch-amerikanischen Beziehungen*, American Studies, A Monograph Series, vol 88, Heidelberg, 2001

Donnevert, Richard, *Wehrmacht und Partei*, Leipzig, 1938

Dorril, Stephen, *MI6 – Fifty Years of Special Operations*, London, 2000

Dülffer, Jost, *Weimar, Hitler und die Marine. Reichspolitik und Flottenbau 1920–1939*, Düsseldorf, 1973

Dülffer, Jost, 'Der Beginn des Krieges 1939: Hitler, die innere Krise und das Mächtesystem', *Geschichte und Gesellschaft* 2, 1976, pp 443–70

Dülffer, Jost, 'Die Reichs- und Kriegsmarine 1918–1939', in *Handbuch zur deutschen Militärgeschichte 1648–1939, Abschnitt VIII Deutsche Marinegeschichte in der Neuzeit*, published by Militärgeschichtlichen Forschungsamt, Munich, 1977, pp 337–488

Dulles, Allen W, *Verschwörung in Deutschland*, Zürich, 1948

Einhorn, Marion, 'Die ersten Maßnahmen des deutschen Imperialismus zur wirtschaftlichen Ausplünderung Spaniens (Juli-August 1936)', in Schieder, Wolfgang, and Dipper, Christoph (eds), *Der Spanische Bürgerkrieg in der Internationalen Politik (1936–1939)*, Munich, 1976, pp 147–61

Eppler, John W, *Rommel ruft Kairo*, Gütersloh, 1959

Erger, Johannes, *Der Kapp-Lüttwitz-Putsch. Ein Beitrag zur deutschen Innenpolitik*, Beiträge zur Geschichte des Parlamentarismus und der politischen Parteien, vol 35, Düsseldorf, 1967

Erskine, Ralph, 'The Admiralty and Cipher Machines During the Second World War: Not so Stupid after All', *Journal of Intelligence History*, 2, no 2, pp 49–68

Falin, Valentin, *Zweite Front – Die Interessenkonflikte in der Anti-Hitler-Koalition*, Munich, 1995

Farago, Ladislas, *The Game of the Foxes. The Untold Story of German Espionage in the United States and Great Britain during World War II*, New York, 1971

Ferguson, Niall, *Der falsche Krieg – Der Erste Weltkrieg und das 20. Jahrhundert*, Stuttgart, 1999

Fest, Joachim, *Das Gesicht des Dritten Reiches – Profile einer totalitären Herrschaft*, Munich and Zürich, 1963

Fest, Joachim, *Hitler – Eine Biographie*, Munich, 1973, Munich and Berlin, 2002

Fest, Joachim, *Staatsstreich – Der lange Weg zum 20 Juli*, Berlin, 1994

Fest, Joachim, *Der Untergang – Hitler und das Ende des Dritten Reiches*, Berlin, 2002

Fleischhauer, Ingeborg, *Die Chance des Sonderfriedens. Deutsch-sowjetische Geheimgespräche 1941–1945*, Berlin, 1986

Fleming, Gerald, *Hitler und die Endlösung. 'Es ist des Führers Wunsch . . .'*, Wiesbaden and Munich, 1982

Forstmeier, Friedrich, 'Zur Rolle der Marine im Kapp-Putsch', in Seemacht und Geschichte. Festschrift zum 80. Geburtstag von Friedrich Ruge, Bonn, 1975, pp 51–80

Fraenkel, Heinrich, and Manvell, Roger, *Der 20. Juli*, Frankfurt am Main and Berlin, 1964

Fraenkel, Heinrich, and Manvell, Roger, *Canaris. Spion im Widerstreit*, Bern, Munich, and Vienna, 1969

Fuhrer, Hans Rudolf, *Spionage gegen die Schweiz – Die geheimen deutschen Nachrichtendienste gegen die Schweiz im Zweiten Weltkrieg 1939–1945, Schriftenreihe der allgemeinen Schweizerischen Militärzeitschrift*, Frauenfeld, 1982

Fuhrer, Hans Rudolf, 'L'espionnage allemand contre la Suisse pendant la Deuxième Guerre mondiale', *Relations Internationales* 78, 1994, pp 215–39

Funke, Manfred (ed), *Hitler, Deutschland und die Mächte. Materialien zur Außenpolitik des Dritten Reiches*, Bonner Schriften zur Politik und Zeitgeschichte, vol 12, Düsseldorf, 1978

Gellermann, Günther, *. . . und lauschten für Hitler. Geheime Reichssache: Die Abhörzentralen des Dritten Reiches*, Bonn, 1991

Gellermann, Günther, *Geheime Reichssache. Geheime Kommandosache. Rätselhafte Fälle aus der Zeit des Zweiten Weltkrieges*, Hamburg, 2002

Gerlach, Christian, *Krieg, Ernährung, Völkermord. Deutsche Vernichtungspolitik im Zweiten Weltkrieg*, Hamburg, 1998

Gerlach, Christian, *Kalkulierte Morde. Die deutsche Wirtschafts- und Vernichtungspolitik in Weißrußland 1941 bis 1944*, Hamburg, 1999

Geyer, Michael, 'Die Wehrmacht der Deutschen Republik ist die Reichswehr', *Militärgeschichtliche Mitteilungen* 14, 1973, pp 152–99

Gietinger, Klaus, *Eine Leiche im Landwehrkanal – Die Ermordung der Rosa L.*, Berlin, 1995

Giskes, Hermann, *London ruft Nordpol, Abwehr III F. Das erfolgreiche Funkspiel der deutschen militärischen Abwehr*, Bergisch Gladbach, 1982

Glaubauf, Karl, and Lahousen, Stefanie, *Generalmajor Erwin Lahousen Edler von Vivremont. Ein Linzer Abwehroffizier im militärischen Widerstand*, Schriftenreihe des Dokumentationsarchivs des österreichischen Widerstands zu Widerstand, NS-Verfolgung und Nachkriegsaspekten, vol 2, Münster, 2004

Gorodetsky, Gabriel, *Die große Täuschung – Hitler, Stalin und das Unternehmen 'Barbarossa'*, Berlin, 2001

Graf, Christoph, 'Kontinuitäten und Brüche. Von der Politischen Polizei der Weimarer Republik zur Geheimen Staatspolizei', in Paul, Gerhard, and Mallmann Klaus-Michael (eds), *Die Gestapo. Mythos und Realität*, Darmstadt, 1996, pp 73–83

Graml, Hermann, 'Der Fall Oster', *Vierteljahrshefte für Zeitgeschichte* 14, 1966, pp 26–39

Graml, Hermann, *Europas Weg in den Krieg. Hitler und die Mächte 1939*, Munich, 1990

Graml, Hermann, 'Die Wehrmacht im Dritten Reich', *Vierteljahrshefte für Zeitgeschichte* 45, 1997, pp 365–84

Grose, Peter, *Gentlemen Spy – The Life of Allen Dulles*, Boston and New York, 1994

Gruchmann, Lothar, *Der Zweite Weltkrieg – Kriegführung und Politik*, 2 vols, Munich, 1969

Gruchmann, Lothar, 'Schweden im Zweiten Weltkrieg. Ergebnisse eines Stockholmer Forschungsprojekts', *Vierteljahrshefte für Zeitgeschichte* 25, 1977, pp 591–653

Güth, Rolf, 'Die Organisation der deutschen Marine in Krieg und Frieden 1913–1933', *Handbuch zur deutschen Militärgeschichte 1648–1939, Abschnitt VIII Deutsche Marinegeschichte in der Neuzeit*, published by Militärgeschichtlichen Forschungsamt, Munich, 1977, pp 263–336

Haasis, Hellmut G, *Tod in Prag – Das Attentat auf Reinhard Heydrich*, Reinbek, 2002

Hachmeister, Lutz, *Der Gegnerforscher – Die Karriere des SS-Führers Franz-Alfred Six*, Munich, 1998

Haffner, Sebastian, *Churchill*, Reinbek, 1967, Berlin, 2001

Haffner, Sebastian, *Die Deutsche Revolution 1918/19*, Berlin, 2002, first published as *Die verratene Revolution*, Bern, Munich and Berlin, 1969

Hagen, Walter [Wilhelm Höttl], *Die geheime Front*, Linz, 1950

Hamerow, Theodore S, *Die Attentäter. Der 20. Juli – von der Kollaboration zum Widerstand*, Munich, 1999

Harrison, Ted, '"Alter Kämpfer" im Widerstand. Graf Helldorf, die NS-Bewegung und die Opposition gegen Hitler', *Vierteljahrshefte für Zeitgeschichte* 45, 1997, pp 385–421

Heideking, Jürgen, 'Die "Schweizer Straßen" des europäischen Widerstands', in Schulz, Gerhard (ed), *Geheimdienste und Widerstandsbewegungen im Zweiten Weltkrieg*, Göttingen, 1982, pp 143–87

Heideking, Jürgen, *Geschichte der USA*, 3rd edn, revised by Christof Mauch, Tübingen and Basel, 2003

Heideking, Jürgen, and Mauch, Christof (eds), *Geheimdienstkrieg gegen Deutschland. Subversion, Propaganda und politische Planungen des amerikanischen Geheimdienstes im Zweiten Weltkrieg*, Göttingen, 1993

Heinemann, Winfried, 'Der militärische Widerstand und der Krieg', in *DRZW*, vol 9.1, *Die deutsche Kriegsgesellschaft 1939–1945. Politisierung, Vernichtung, Überleben*, Stuttgart, 2004, pp 743–892

Herbert, Ulrich (ed), *Nationalsozialistische Vernichtungspolitik 1939–1945. Neue Forschungen und Kontroversen*, Frankfurt am Main, 1998

Herbert, Ulrich, *Best – Biographische Studien über Radikalismus, Weltanschauung und Vernunft 1903–1989*, Bonn, 2001

Herfeldt, Olav, *Schwarze Kapelle. Spionage und Widerstand. Die Geschichte der Widerstandsgruppe um Admiral Wilhelm Canaris*, Augsburg, 1990

Heydeloff, Rudolf, 'Staranwalt der Rechtsextremisten. Walter Luetgebrune in der Weimarer Republik', *Vierteljahrshefte für Zeitgeschichte* 32, 1984, pp 373–421

Hilberg, Raul, *Die Vernichtung der europäischen Juden*, 3 vols, Frankfurt am Main, 1999

Hildebrand, Klaus, *Das vergangene Reich – Deutsche Außenpolitik von Bismarck bis Hitler*, Stuttgart, 1995, Berlin, 1999

Hill, George, *Franco – The Man and his Nation*, London, 1967

Hilton, Stanley E, *Hitler's Secret War in South America 1939–1945: German Military Espionage and Allied Counterespionage in Brazil*, New York, 1982

Hobsbawm, Eric, *Das Zeitalter der Extreme*, Munich and Vienna, 1995

Hoensch, Jörg K, 'Der Hitler-Stalin-Pakt und Polen', in Oberländer, Erwin (ed), *Hitler–Stalin-Pakt 1939. Das Ende Ostmitteleuropas?*, Frankfurt am Main, 1989, pp 43–60

Hoffmann, Peter, 'Warum mißlang das Attentat vom 20. Juli 1944', *Vierteljahrshefte für Zeitgeschichte* 32, 1984, pp 441–62

Hoffmann, Peter, *Widerstand – Staatsstreich – Attentat – Der Kampf der Opposition gegen Hitler*, vierte neu überarbeitete und ergänzte Ausgabe, Munich and Zürich, 1985

Hoffmann, Peter, *Claus Schenk Graf von Stauffenberg und seine Brüder*, Stuttgart, 1992

Höhne, Heinz, *Kennwort: Direktor – Die Geschichte der Roten Kapelle*, Frankfurt am Main, 1970

Höhne, Heinz, and Zolling, Hermann, *Pullach intern – General Gehlen und die Geschichte des Bundesnachrichtendienstes*, Hamburg, 1971

Höhne, Heinz, *Canaris – Patriot im Zwielicht*, Munich, 1976

Höhne, Heinz, *Der Orden unter dem Totenkopf – Die Geschichte der SS*, Munich, 1984

Höhne, Heinz, *Der Krieg im Dunkeln. Die Geschichte der deutsch-russischen Spionage*, Munich, 1985

Höhne, Heinz, 'Canaris und die Abwehr zwischen Anpassung und Opposition', in Schmädecke, Jürgen, and Steinbach, Peter (eds), *Der Widerstand gegen den Nationalsozialismus. Die deutsche Gesellschaft und der Widerstand gegen Hitler*, Munich, 1985, pp 405–16

Höhne, Heinz, *'Gebt mir vier Jahre Zeit' – Hitler und die Anfänge des Dritten Reiches*, Berlin and Frankfurt am Main, 1996, first published as *Die Zeit der Illusionen*, 1991

Horne, John, and Kramer, Alan, *Deutsche Kriegsgreuel 1914*, Hamburg, 2004

Hürter, Johannes, *Wilhelm Groener. Reichswehrminister am Ende der Weimarer Republik (1928–1932)*, Schriftenreihe des Militärgeschichtlichen Forschungsamtes, vol 39, Munich, 1993

Jacobmeyer, Wolfgang, 'Die polnische Widerstandsbewegung im Generalgouvernement und ihre Beurteilung durch deutsche Dienststellen', *Vierteljahrshefte für Zeitgeschichte* 25, 1977, pp 658–81

Jähnicke, Burkhard, 'Lawyer, Politician, Intelligence Officer: Paul Leverkuehn in Turkey, 1915–1916 and 1941–1944', *Journal of Intelligence History* 2, no 2, pp 69–87

Janssen, Karl-Heinz, and Tobias, Fritz, *Der Sturz der Generäle – Hitler und die Blomberg-Fritsch-Krise 1938*, Munich, 1994

Jong, Louis de, *Die deutsche fünfte Kolonne im Zweiten Weltkrieg*, Quellen und Darstellungen zur Zeitgeschichte, vol 4, Stuttgart, 1959

Jung, Otmar, '"Da gelten Paragraphen nichts, sondern da gilt lediglich der Erfolg ...". Noskes Erschießungsbefehl während des Märzaufstandes in Berlin 1919 – rechtshistorisch betrachtet', *Militärgeschichtliche Mitteilungen* 45, 1989, pp 51–79

Kahn, David, *Hitler's Spies – German Military Intelligence in World War II*, New York, 1978

Keegan, John, *The First World War*, London, 1998

Kern, Karl-Hans, *Die Geheimnisse des Dr. Josef Müller. Mutmaßungen zu den Morden von Flossenbürg (1945) und Pöcking (1960)*, Berlin, 2000

Kershaw, Ian, *Der NS-Staat – Geschichtsinterpretationen und Kontroversen im Überblick, erweiterte und bearbeitete Neuausgabe*, Reinbek, 1999

Kershaw, Ian, *Der Hitler-Mythos – Führerkult und Volksmeinung*, Munich, 1999

Kershaw, Ian, *Hitler 1889 – 1936*, Stuttgart, 1998

Kershaw, Ian, *Hitler 1936 – 1945*, Stuttgart, 2000

Kieseritzky, Wolther von, and Sick, Klaus-Peter (eds), *Demokratie in Deutschland – Chancen und Gefährdungen im 19. und 20. Jahrhundert, Historische Essays*, Munich, 1999

Klemperer, Klemens von, 'Naturrecht und der deutsche Widerstand gegen den Nationalsozialismus. Ein Beitrag zur Frage des deutschen "Sonderwegs"', *Vierteljahrshefte für Zeitgeschichte* 40, 1992, pp 323–37

Klemperer, Klemens von, *Die verlassenen Verschwörer: der deutsche Widerstand auf der Suche nach Verbündeten 1938–1945*, Berlin, 1994

Kluge, Ulrich, *Die deutsche Revolution 1918/1919*, Frankfurt am Main, 1985

Knightley, Phillip, *Kim Philby – Geheimagent*, Munich, 1989

Knipping, Franz, '"Réseaux" und "Mouvements" in der französischen Résistance 1940–1945', in Schulz, Gerhard (ed), *Geheimdienste und Widerstandsbewegungen im Zweiten Weltkrieg*, Göttingen, 1982, pp 105–42

Koch, Hannsjoachim W, 'The Spectre of a Separate Peace in the East: Russo-German "Peace Feelers", 1942–44', *Journal of Contemporary History* 10, 1975, pp 531–49

Koch, Peter-Ferdinand, *Die Geldgeschäfte der SS – Wie deutsche Banken den schwarzen Terror finanzierten*, Hamburg, 2000

König, Rudolf, Soell, Hartmut, and Weber, Hermann (eds), *Friedrich Ebert und seine Zeit – Bilanz und Perspektiven der Forschung*, Munich, 1990

Kordt, Erich, *Wahn und Wirklichkeit – Die Außenpolitik des Dritten Reiches. Versuch einer Darstellung*, edited by Karl Heinz Abshagen, Stuttgart, 1948

Krausnick, Helmut, 'Erwin Rommel und der deutsche Widerstand gegen Hitler', *Vierteljahrshefte für Zeitgeschichte* 1, 1953, pp 65–70

Krausnick, Helmut, 'Vorgeschichte und Beginn des militärischen Widerstandes gegen Hitler', in *Vollmacht des Gewissens – Probleme des militärischen Widerstands gegen Hitler I*, published by Europäischen Publikation, Frankfurt am Main and Berlin, 1960, pp 177–384

Krausnick, Helmut, 'Kommissarbefehl und "Gerichtsbarkeitserlaß Barbarossa" in neuer Sicht', *Vierteljahrshefte für Zeitgeschichte* 25, 1977, pp 658–81

Krausnick, Helmut, and Wilhelm, Hans Heinrich, *Die Truppe des Weltanschauungskrieges – Die Einsatzgruppen der Sicherheitspolizei und des SD 1938–1942*, Stuttgart, 1981

Krebs, Gerhard, 'Aussichtslose Sondierung. Japanische Friedensfühler und schwedische Vermittlungsversuche 1944/45', *Vierteljahrshefte für Zeitgeschichte* 45, 1997, pp 425–48

Krüger, Gabriele, *Die Brigade Ehrhardt*, Hamburger Beiträge zur Zeitgeschichte, vol 7, Hamburg, 1971

Kühne, Horst, 'Ziele und Ausmaß der militärischen Intervention des deutschen Faschismus in Spanien (1936–1939)', in Schieder, Wolfgang, and Dipper, Christoph (eds), *Der Spanische Bürgerkrieg in der Internationalen Politik (1936–1939)*, Munich, 1976, pp 129–46

Kurowski, Franz, *Deutsche Kommandotrupps 1939 bis 1945 – 'Brandenburger' und Abwehr im weltweiten Einsatz*, vol 1, Stuttgart, 2001, vol 2, Stuttgart, 2003

Leverkuehn, Paul, *Der geheime Nachrichtendienst der deutschen Wehrmacht im Kriege*, Frankfurt am Main, 1957

Lindgren, Henrik, 'Adam von Trotts Reisen nach Schweden 1942–1944', *Vierteljahrshefte für Zeitgeschichte* 18, 1970, pp 274–91

Loeff, Wolfgang, *Spionage. Aus den Papieren eines Abwehr-Offiziers*, Stuttgart, 1950

Ludlow, Peter, 'Papst Pius XII., die britische Regierung und die deutsche Opposition im Winter 1939/40', *Vierteljahrshefte für Zeitgeschichte* 22, 1974, pp 299–341

Lukacs, John, *Fünf Tage in London – England und Deutschland im Mai 1940*, Berlin, 2000

Lukes, Igor, 'Stalin, Benesch und der Fall Tuchatschewski', *Vierteljahrshefte für Zeitgeschichte* 44, 1996, pp 527–47

MacDonald, Callum A, 'The Venlo Affair', *European Studies Review* 8, no 4, 1978, pp 443–64

Madajczyk, Czeslaw, *Die Okkupationspolitik Nazideutschlands in Polen 1939–1945*, Berlin, 1987

Mader, Julius, *Hitlers Spionagegenerale sagen aus*, Berlin (East), 1970

Maier, Hedwig, 'Die SS und der 20. Juli 1944', *Vierteljahrshefte für Zeitgeschichte* 14, 1966, pp 299–316

Malinowski, Stephan, *Vom König zum Führer – Sozialer Niedergang und politische Radikalisierung im deutschen Adel zwischen Kaiserreich und NS-Staat*, Berlin, 2003

Mallmann, Klaus-Michael, and Musial, Bogdan (eds), *Genesis des Genozids. Polen 1939–1941*, Darmstadt, 2004

Manninen, Otho, 'Die Beziehungen zwischen den finnischen und deutschen Militärbehörden in der Ausarbeitungsphase des Barbarossaplanes', *Militärgeschichtliche Mitteilungen* 26, 1979, pp 79–95

Martin, Bernd, 'Verhandlungen über separate Friedensschlüsse 1942– 1945. Ein Beitrag zur Entstehung des kalten Krieges', *Militärgeschichtliche Mitteilungen* 20, 1976, pp 95–113

Martin, Bernd, 'Japans Weg in den Krieg. Bemerkungen über Forschungsstand und Literatur zur japanischen Zeitgeschichte', *Militärgeschichtliche Mitteilungen* 23, 1978, pp 183–209

Martin, Bernd, 'Die deutsch-japanischen Beziehungen während des Dritten Reiches', in Funke, Manfred (ed), *Hitler, Deutschland und die Mächte. Materialien zur Außenpolitik des Dritten*

Reiches, Bonner Schriften zur Politik und Zeitgeschichte, vol 12, Düsseldorf, 1978, pp 454–70

Matthäus, Jürgen, Kwiet, Konrad, Förster, Jürgen, and Breitmann, Richard, *Ausbildungsziel Judenmord? 'Weltanschauliche Erziehung' von SS, Polizei und Waffen-SS im Rahmen der 'Endlösung'*, Frankfurt am Main, 2003

Mauch, Christof, *Schattenkrieg gegen Hitler – Das Dritte Reich im Visier der amerikanischen Geheimdienste 1941 bis 1945*, Stuttgart, 1999

Meinl, Susanne, and Krüger, Dieter, 'Der politische Weg des Friedrich Wilhelm Heinz. Vom Freikorpskämpfer zum Leiter des Nachrichtendienstes im Bundeskanzleramt', *Vierteljahrshefte für Zeitgeschichte* 42, 1994, pp 39–69

Meinl, Susanne, *Nationalsozialisten gegen Hitler. Die nationalrevolutionäre Opposition um Friedrich Wilhelm Heinz*, Berlin, 2000

Messerschmidt, Manfred, 'Militär und Schule in der Wilhelminischen Zeit', *Militärgeschichtliche Mitteilungen* 23, 1978, pp 51–76

Messerschmidt, Manfred, 'Außenpolitik und Kriegsvorbereitung', *Das Deutsche Reich und der Zweite Weltkrieg*: vol 1, *Ursachen und Voraussetzungen der deutschen Kriegspolitik*, Stuttgart, 1979, pp 535–701

Metzmacher, Helmut, 'Deutsch-Englische Ausgleichsbemühungen im Sommer 1939', *Vierteljahrshefte für Zeitgeschichte* 14, 1966, pp 369–412

Meyer, Winfried, *Unternehmen Sieben – Eine Rettungsaktion für vom Holocaust Bedrohte aus dem Amt Ausland/Abwehr im Oberkommando der Wehrmacht*, with a summary by Klaus von Dohnanyi, Frankfurt am Main, 1993

Meyer, Winfried (ed), *Verschwörer im KZ – Hans von Dohnanyi und die Häftlinge des 20. Juli 1944 im KZ Sachsenhausen; Schriftenreihe der Stiftung Brandenburgische Gedenkstätten*, Oranienburg, 1998

Meyer, Winfried, 'Nachrichtendienst, Staatsstreichvorbereitung und Widerstand – Hans von Dohnanyi im Amt Ausland/Abwehr 1939–43', in Meyer, Winfried (ed), *Verschwörer im KZ – Hans von Dohnanyi und die Häftlinge des 20. Juli 1944 im KZ Sachsenhausen; Schriftenreihe der Stiftung Brandenburgische Gedenkstätten*, Oranienburg, 1998, pp 76–115

Mohr, Philipp, 'Die Verfolgung Hans von Dohnanyis durch Reichskriegsgericht, Gestapo und SS 1943–45 und ihre Aufarbeitung durch die Justiz nach 1945', in Meyer, Winfried (ed), *Verschwörer im KZ – Hans von Dohnanyi und die Häftlinge des 20. Juli 1944 im KZ Sachsenhausen; Schriftenreihe der Stiftung Brandenburgische Gedenkstätten*, Oranienburg, 1998, pp 116–52

Moltke, Freya von, Balfour, Michael, and Frisby, Julian, *Helmuth James von Moltke 1907–1945 – Anwalt der Zukunft*, Stuttgart, 1975

Mommsen, Hans, *Alternative zu Hitler – Studien zur Geschichte des deutschen Widerstandes*, Munich, 2000

Mommsen, Hans, *Aufstieg und Untergang der Republik von Weimar 1918–1933*, Berlin, 1989, Munich, 2001

Mommsen, Wolfgang J, *War der Kaiser an allem schuld? Wilhelm II. und die preußisch-deutschen Machteliten*, Munich, 2002

Mommsen, Wolfgang J, *Der Erste Weltkrieg – Anfang vom Ende des bürgerlichen Zeitalters*, Frankfurt am Main, 2004

Moon, Tom, *This Grim and Savage Game – The OSS and U.S. Covert Operations in World War II*, New York, 1991

Moseley, Ray, *Zwischen Hitler und Mussolini – Das Doppelleben des Grafen Ciano*, Berlin, 1998

Müller, Klaus Jürgen, *Das Heer und Hitler – Armee und nationalsozialistisches Regime 1933–1940*, Stuttgart, 1969

Müller, Klaus Jürgen, 'Ludwig Beck. Probleme seiner Biographie', *Militärgeschichtliche Mitteilungen* 11, 1972, pp 157–75

Müller, Klaus Jürgen, *Armee, Politik und Gesellschaft in Deutschland 1933–1945. Studien zum Verhältnis von Armee und NS-System*, Paderborn, 1979

Müller, Klaus Jürgen, *General Ludwig Beck. Studien und Dokumente zur politisch-militärischen Vorstellungswelt und Tätigkeit des Generalstabschefs des deutschen Heeres 1933–1938*, Schriften des Bundesarchivs, vol 30, Boppard, 1980

Müller, Klaus Jürgen, and Dilks, David N (eds), *Großbritannien und der deutsche Widerstand 1933–1944*, Paderborn, Munich, Vienna and Zürich, 1994

Müller, Peter F, and Mueller, Michael, *Gegen Freund und Feind – Der BND: Geheime Politik und schmutzige Geschäfte*, Reinbek, 2002

Newman, Bernard, *German Secret Service at Work*, New York, 1940

Niedhart, Gottfried, 'Der Bündniswert der Sowjetunion im Urteil Großbritanniens 1936–1939', *Militärgeschichte* 10, 1971, pp 55–67

Oberländer, Erwin (ed), *Hitler-Stalin-Pakt 1939. Das Ende Ostmitteleuropas?*, Frankfurt am Main, 1989

Overy, Richard, *Die Wurzeln des Sieges – Warum die Alliierten den Zweiten Weltkrieg gewannen*, Stuttgart and Munich, 2000

Paine, Lauran, *The Abwehr – German Military Intelligence in World War Two*, London, 1984

Papeleux, Léon, *L'admiral Canaris entre Franco et Hitler – Le rôle de Canaris dans les Relations germano-espagnoles 1915–1944*, Paris, 1977

Parker des Bassi, Maria Teresa, *Kreuzer Dresden – Odyssee ohne Wiederkehr*, Herford, 1993

Paul, Gerhard, and Mallmann, Klaus-Michael (eds), *Die Gestapo. Mythos und Realität*, Darmstadt, 1995

Paul, Gerhard, and Mallmann, Klaus-Michael (eds), *Die Gestapo im Zweiten Weltkrieg. 'Heimatfront' und besetztes Europa*, Darmstadt, 2000

Petersen, Jens, 'Deutschland und der Zusammenbruch des Faschismus in Italien im Sommer 1943', *Militärgeschichtliche Mitteilungen* 37, 1985, pp 51–69

Peukert, Detlev J K, *Die Weimarer Republik*, Frankfurt am Main, 1987

Pfaff, Ivan, 'Prag und der Fall Tuchatschewski', *Vierteljahrshefte für Zeitgeschichte* 35, 1987, pp 95–134

Porch, Douglas, *The French Secret Services – a history of French Intelligence from the Dreyfuss Affair to the Gulf War*, New York, 1995

Portner, Ernst, 'Koch-Wesers Verfassungsentwurf. Ein Beitrag zur Ideengeschichte der deutschen Emigration', *Vierteljahrshefte für Zeitgeschichte* 14, 1966, pp 280–98

Powers, Thomas, *Intelligence Wars. American Secret History from Hitler to Al-Qaeda, Revised and Expanded Edition*, New York, 2004

Preston, Paul, *The Spanish Civil War 1936–39*, London, 1986

Preston, Paul, *Franco*, London, 1993

Querg, Thorsten J, 'Spionage und Terror. Das Amt VI des Reichssicherheitshauptamtes 1939–1945', PhD thesis, Berlin, 1997

Quinkert, Babette (ed), *'Wir sind die Herren dieses Landes'. Ursachen, Verlauf und Folgen des deutschen Überfalls auf die Sowjetunion*, Hamburg, 2002

Raeder, Erich (rev), *Der Kreuzerkrieg in den ausländischen Gewässern. Erster Band: Das Kreuzergeschwader*, Berlin, 1927, published as *Der Krieg zur See 1914–1918*, by Marine-Archiv, Berlin, 1920

Rahn, Werner, *Reichsmarine und Landesverteidigung 1919–1928, Konzeption und Führung der Marine in der Weimarer Republik*, Munich, 1976

Rakenius, Gerhard W, *Wilhelm Groener als Erster Generalquartiermeister. Die Politik der Obersten Heeresleitung 1918/19*, Wehrwissenschaftliche Forschungen, Abteilung Militärgeschichtliche Studien, vol 23, Boppard, 1977

Rathert, Ronald, *Verbrechen und Verschwörung: Arthur Nebe. Der Kripochef des Dritten Reiches*, Münster, 2001

Rauscher, Walter, *Hitler und Mussolini – Macht, Krieg und Terror*, Graz, Vienna and Cologne, 2001

Reese, Mary Ellen, *Organisation Gehlen – Der Kalte Krieg und der Aufbau des deutschen Geheimdienstes*, Berlin, 1992

Remmele, Bernd, 'Die maritime Geheimrüstung unter Kapitän z.S. Lohmann', *Militärgeschichtliche Mitteilungen* 56, 1997, pp 313–76

Reuth, Ralf Georg, *Goebbels. Eine Biographie*, Munich, 1990

Reynolds, Nicholas, *Beck – Gehorsam und Widerstand. Die authentische Biografie des deutschen Generalstabschefs 1935–1938*, Wiesbaden and Munich, 1977

Richelson, Jeffrey T, *A Century of Spies – Intelligence in the Twentieth Century*, New York and Oxford, 1995

Ringshausen, Gerhard, 'Hans-Alexander von Voß (1907–1944). Offizier im Widerstand', *Vierteljahrshefte für Zeitgeschichte* 52, 2004, pp 361–407

Ringshausen, Gerhard, 'Erwiderung auf Johannes Hürter: Der Aussagewert von Paraphen und der Handlungsspielraum des militärischen Widerstandes', *Vierteljahrshefte für Zeitgeschichte* 53, 2005, pp 141–7

Ritter, Gerhard, *Carl Goerdeler und die deutsche Widerstandsbewegung*, Stuttgart, 1956

Röhr, Werner, 'Das Sudetendeutsche Freikorps – Diversionsinstrument der Hitler-Regierung bei der Zerschlagung der Tschechoslowakei', *Militärgeschichtliche Mitteilungen* 52, 1993, pp 35–66

Roloff, Stefan, with Mario Vigl, *Die Rote Kapelle. Die Widerstandsgruppe im Dritten Reich und die Geschichte Helmut Roloffs*, Munich, 2002

Ronge, Paul, 'Zur Ahnentafel des Admirals Canaris', *Genealogie. Deutsche Zeitschrift für Familienkunde* VI, no 11/12, pp 33–6

Roon, Ger van, 'Wilhelm Staehle. Ein Leben auf der Grenze (1877– 1945)', *Militärgeschichtliche Mitteilungen* 6, 1969, pp 69–93

Roon, Ger van, 'Graf Moltke als Völkerrechtler im OKW', *Vierteljahrshefte für Zeitgeschichte* 18, 1970, pp 13–61

Roon, Ger van, *Widerstand im Dritten Reich – Ein Überblick, vierte neu bearbeitete Auflage*, Munich, 1987

Roseman, Mark, *Die Wannsee-Konferenz – Wie die NS-Bürokratie den Holocaust organisierte*, Munich and Berlin, 2002

Roth, Karl Heinz, and Ebbinghaus, Angelika (eds), *Rote Kapellen – Kreisauer Kreise – Schwarze Kapellen. Neue Sichtweisen auf den Widerstand gegen die NS- Diktatur 1938–1945*, Hamburg, 2004

Rothfels, Hans, *German Opposition to Hitler*, Illinois 1948; German: *Die deutsche Opposition gegen Hitler. Eine Würdigung*, Krefeld, 1949

Rothfels, Hans, 'Zerrspiegel des 20. Juli', *Vierteljahrshefte für Zeitgeschichte* 10, 1962, pp 62–7

Ruhl, Klaus-Jörg, 'Die Internationalen Brigaden im Spanischen Bürgerkrieg 1936–1939', *Militärgeschichtliche Mitteilungen* 17, 1975, pp 212–24

Runzheimer, Jürgen, 'Der Überfall auf den Sender Gleiwitz im Jahre 1939', *Vierteljahrshefte für Zeitgeschichte* 10, 1962, pp 408–26

Sabrow, Martin, *Der Rathenaumord – Rekonstruktion einer Verschwörung gegen die Republik von Weimar*, Schriftenreihe der Vierteljahrshefte für Zeitgeschichte, vol 69, Munich, 1994

Schafranek, Hans, and Tuchel, Johannes, *Krieg im Äther. Widerstand und Spionage im Zweiten Weltkrieg*, Vienna, 2004

Scheurig, Bodo, *Henning von Tresckow – Eine Biographie*, Oldenburg, 1973

Scheurig, Bodo, *Ewald von Kleist-Schmenzin – Ein Konservativer gegen Hitler*, Berlin and Frankfurt am Main, 1994

Schieder, Wolfgang, and Dipper, Christoph (eds), *Der Spanische Bürgerkrieg in der Internationalen Politik (1936–1939)*, Munich, 1976

Schieder, Wolfgang, 'Spanischer Bürgerkrieg und Vierjahresplan. Zur Struktur nationalsozialistischer Außenpolitik', in Schieder, Wolfgang, and Dipper, Christoph (eds), *Der Spanische Bürgerkrieg in der Internationalen Politik (1936–1939)*, Munich, 1976, pp 162–90

Schindler, Herbert, *Mosty und Dirschau 1939. Zwei Handstreiche der Wehrmacht vor Beginn des Polenfeldzuges*, Einzelschriften zur militärischen Geschichte des Zweiten Weltkrieges, vol 7, 2nd edition, Freiburg, 1979

Schmädecke, Jürgen, and Steinbach, Peter (eds), *Der Widerstand gegen den Nationalsozialismus – Die deutsche Gesellschaft und der Widerstand gegen Hitler*, Munich and Zürich, 1985

Schmidt, Rainer F, *Die Außenpolitik des Dritten Reiches 1933–1939*, Stuttgart, 2002

Schöllgen, Gregor, *Ulrich von Hassell – Ein Konservativer in der Opposition*, Munich, 1990

Schramm, Wilhelm Ritter von, *Geheimdienste im Zweiten Weltkrieg, Fortgeführt von Hans Büchler*, 6th edition, Munich, 2002

Schreiber Gerhard, 'Politik und Kriegführung 1941', in *DRZW*, vol 3, *Der Mittelmeerraum und Südosteuropa, Vierter Teil*, pp 515–87

Schulz, Gerhard (ed), *Geheimdienste und Widerstandsbewegungen im Zweiten Weltkrieg*, Göttingen, 1982

Schulze, Hagen, *Weimar – Deutschland 1917 – 1933, durchgesehene und aktualisierte Ausgabe*, Berlin, 1994

Schwengler, Walter, 'Marine und Öffentlichkeit 1919–1939', *Militärgeschichtliche Mitteilungen* 46, 1989, pp 35–59

Schwerin, Detlef Graf von, *Die Jungen des 20. Juli 1944 – Brücklmeier, Kessel, Schulenburg, Schwerin, Wussow, Yorck*, Berlin, 1991

Sebag-Montefiore, Hugh, *ENIGMA – The Battle for the Code*, London, 2000

Seidel, Carlos Collado, 'Zufluchtsstätte für Nationalsozialisten? Spanien, die Alliierten und die Behandlung deutscher Agenten 1944–1947', *Vierteljahrshefte für Zeitgeschichte* 43, 1995, pp 131–57

Seidel, Carlos Collado, 'In geheimer Mission für Hitler und die bayerische Staatsregierung. Der politische Abenteurer Max Neunzert zwischen Fememorden, Hitler-Putsch und Berlin-Krise', *Vierteljahrshefte für Zeitgeschichte* 50, 2002, pp 201–36

Sereny, Gitta, *Das Ringen mit der Wahrheit – Albert Speer und das deutsche Trauma*, Munich, 1995

Singer, Kurt D, *Spies and Traitors of World War II, New York 1945*; German: *Spione und Verräter des Zweiten Weltkrieges*, Zürich, 1946

Smid, Marikje, *Hans von Dohnanyi – Christine Bonhoeffer: Eine Ehe im Widerstand gegen Hitler*, Gütersloh, 2002

Smith, Bradley F, 'Die Überlieferung der Hoßbach-Niederschrift im Lichte neuer Quellen', *Vierteljahrshefte für Zeitgeschichte* 38, 1990, pp 329–36

Smith, Michael, *The Spying Game – The Secret History of British Espionage*, London, 2003

Speidel, Helm, 'Reichswehr und Rote Armee', *Vierteljahrshefte für Zeitgeschichte* 1, 1953, pp 9–45

Spindler, Arno (rev), *Der Handelskrieg mit U-Booten. Dritter Band: Oktober 1915 – Januar 1917*, Berlin, 1934, also published as *Der Krieg zur See 1914–1918*, by the Marine-Archiv, Berlin, 1920

Stafford, David, *Churchill and Secret Service*, London, 1997

Stegemann, Bernd, 'Hitlers Ziele im ersten Kriegsjahr 1939/40. Ein Beitrag zur Quellenkritik', *Militärgeschichtliche Mitteilungen* 27, 1980, pp 93–105

Stein, Georg H, and Krosby, H Peter, 'Das finnische Freiwilligen-Bataillon der Waffen-SS: Eine Studie zur SS-Diplomatie und zur ausländischen Freiwilligen-Bewegung', *Vierteljahrshefte für Zeitgeschichte* 14, 1966, pp 413–54

Streit, Christian, 'Die Behandlung der sowjetischen Kriegsgefangenen und völkerrechtliche Probleme des Krieges gegen die Sowjetunion', in Ueberschär, Gerd R, and Wette, Wolfram (eds), *Der deutsche Überfall auf die Sowjetunion. Unternehmen 'Barbarossa' 1941*, Frankfurt am Main, 1991, pp 159–89

Summers, Anthony, *Official and Confidential – The Secret Life of Edgar J. Hoover*, London, 1993

Thamer, Hans-Ulrich, *Verführung und Gewalt – Deutschland 1933–1945, durchgesehene und aktualisierte Ausgabe*, Berlin, 1994

Thielenhaus, Monika, *Zwischen Anpassung und Widerstand – Deutsche Diplomaten 1938–1941*, Paderborn, 1984

Thies, Jochen, *Die Dohnanyis – Eine Familienbiografie*, Berlin, 2004

Thomas, Hugh, *The Spanish Civil War*, London, 1961, London, 2003

Thorwald, Jürgen, *Der Fall Pastorius*, Stuttgart, 1953

Thoss, Bruno, 'Nationale Rechte, militärische Führung und Diktaturfrage in Deutschland 1913–1923', *Militärgeschichtliche Mitteilungen* 42, 1987, pp 27–76

Thun-Hohenstein, Remedio Galeazzo Graf von, *Der Verschwörer – General Oster und die Militäropposition; mit einer Einleitung von Golo Mann*, Berlin, 1982

Thun-Hohenstein, Remedio Galeazzo Graf von, 'Widerstand und Landesverrat am Beispiel des Generalmajors Hans Oster', in Schmädecke, Jürgen, and Steinbach, Peter (eds), *Der Widerstand gegen den Nationalsozialismus – Die deutsche Gesellschaft und der Widerstand gegen Hitler*, Munich and Zürich, 1985, pp 751–62

Treue, Wilhelm, Möller, Eberhard, and Rahn, Werner, *Deutsche Marinerüstung 1919–1942 – Die Gefahren der Tirpitz-Tradition*, Herford, 1992

Tuchel, Johannes, 'Gestapa und Reichssicherheitshauptamt. Die Berliner Zentralinstitutionen der Gestapo', in Paul, Gerhard, and Mallmann Klaus-Michael (eds), *Die Gestapo. Mythos und Realität*, Darmstadt, 1996, pp 84–100

Turner, Henry A, *Hitlers Weg zur Macht – Der Januar 1933*, Munich, 1996

Ueberschär, Gerd R, 'Militäropposition gegen Hitlers Kriegspolitik 1939 bis 1941. Motive, Struktur und Alternativvorstellungen des entstehenden militärischen Widerstandes', in Schmädecke, Jürgen, and Steinbach, Peter (eds), *Der Widerstand gegen den Nationalsozialismus – Die deutsche Gesellschaft und der Widerstand gegen Hitler*, Munich and Zürich, 1985, pp 345–67

Ueberschär, Gerd R, *Generaloberst Franz Halder – Generalstabschef, Gegner und Gefangener Hitlers*, Göttingen and Zürich, 1991

Ueberschär, Gerd R (ed), *Hitlers militärische Elite*: vol 1, *Von den Anfängen des Regimes bis Kriegsbeginn; Bd. 2 : Vom Kriegsbeginn bis zum Weltkriegsende*, Darmstadt, 1998

Ueberschär, Gerd R (ed), *NS-Verbrechen und der militärische Widerstand gegen Hitler*, Darmstadt, 2000

Ueberschär, Gerd R, 'Der militärische Widerstand, die antijüdischen Maßnahmen, "Polenmorde" und NS-Kriegsverbrechen in den ersten Kriegsjahren (1939–1941)', in Ueberschär, Gerd R (ed), *NS-Verbrechen und der militärische Widerstand gegen Hitler*, Darmstadt, 2000, pp 31–43

Ueberschär, Gerd R, *Stauffenberg – Der 20. Juli 1944*, Frankfurt am Main, 2004

Uberschär, Gerd R, and Wette, Wolfram (eds), *Der deutsche Überfall auf die Sowjetunion. 'Unternehmen Barbarossa' 1941, überarbeitete Neuauflage*, Frankfurt am Main, 1991

Uberschär, Gerd R, and Bezymenskij, Lev A (eds), *Der deutsche Angriff auf die Sowjetunion 1941. Die Kontroverse um die Präventivkriegsthese*, Darmstadt, 1998

Ullmann, Hans-Peter, *Das Deutsche Kaiserreich 1871–1918*, Frankfurt am Main, 1995

Umbreit, Hans, 'Der Kampf um die Vormachtstellung in Westeuropa', in *DRZW*, vol II, *Die Errichtung der Hegemonie auf dem europäischen Kontinent*, Stuttgart, 1979, pp 235–327

Valenta, Jaroslav, 'Addenda et Corrigenda zur Rolle Prags im Fall Tuchatschewski', *Vierteljahrshefte für Zeitgeschichte* 39, 1991, pp 437–45

Vanwelkenhuyzen, Jean, 'La Belgique et la menace d'invasion, 1939–1940: les avertissements venus de Berlin', *Revue Historique* 535, 1980, pp 377–98

Viñas, Angel, and Seidel, Carlos Collado, 'Franco's Request to the Third Reich for Military Assistance', *Contemporary European History* 11, 2002, pp 191–210

Vogel, Thomas, 'Die Militäropposition gegen das NS-Regime am Vorabend des Zweiten Weltkriegs und während der ersten Kriegsjahre (1939–1941)', in *Aufstand des Gewissens – Militärischer Widerstand gegen Hitler und das NS-Regime 1933 – 1945*, a companion volume to the exhibition of the Militärgeschichtlichen Forschungsamtes, edited by Thomas Vogel, Hamburg, Berlin and Bonn, 2001, pp 187–222

Volkmann, Ernst Otto, *Revolution über Deutschland*, Oldenburg, 1930

Vollmacht des Gewissens – Probleme des militärischen Widerstands gegen Hitler I, published by Europäischen Publikation, Frankfurt am Main and Berlin, 1960

Wehler, Hans-Ulrich, *Deutsche Gesellschaftsgeschichte 1914–1949*, Munich, 2003

Wentker, Hermann, 'Der Widerstand gegen Hitler und der Krieg. Oder: Was bleibt vom Aufstand des Gewissens?', *Geschichte in Wissenschaft und Unterricht* 53, 2002, pp 4–19

Werth, Nicolas, *Ein Staat gegen sein Volk – Schwarzbuch Kommunismus – Sowjetunion*, Munich, 2002

Wette, Wolfram, *Gustav Noske. Eine politische Biographie*, Düsseldorf, 1987

Wette, Wolfram, 'Noske-Ära: Die vertane Chance, mit dem preußisch-deutschen Nationalismus zu brechen', in Butenschön, Rainer, and Spoo, Eckart, *Wozu muß einer der Bluthund sein? Der Mehrheitssozialdemokrat Gustav Noske und der deutsche Militarismus des 20. Jahrhunderts*, Heilbronn, 1997, pp 27–37

Wette, Wolfram, *Die Wehrmacht – Feindbilder, Vernichtungskrieg, Legenden*, Frankfurt am Main, 2002

Wette, Wolfram (ed), *Zivilcourage. Empörte, Helfer und Retter aus Wehrmacht, Polizei und SS*, Frankfurt am Main, 2004

Whealy, Robert H, 'Foreign Intervention in the Spanish Civil War', in Carr, Raymond (ed), *The Republic and the Civil War in Spain*, Oxford, 1971, pp 213–38

Wheeler-Bennet, Paul, *Der hölzerne Titan. Paul von Hindenburg*, Tübingen, 1969

Whymant, Robert, *Richard Sorge. Der Mann mit den drei Gesichtern*, Hamburg, 1999

Wildt, Michael, *Generation des Unbedingten – Das Führungskorps des Reichssicherheitshauptamtes*, Hamburg, 2002

Wildt, Michael (ed), *Nachrichtendienst, politische Elite und Mordeinheit. Der Sicherheitsdienst des Reichsführers SS*, Hamburg, 2003

Winkler, Heinrich August, *Weimar 1918 – 1933 – Die Geschichte der ersten Deutschen Demokratie*, Munich, 1993, 1998

Winkler, Heinrich August, *Der lange Weg nach Westen*: vol 1, *Deutsche Geschichte vom Ende des Alten Reiches bis zum Untergang der Weimarer Republik*, Munich, 2000

Winkler, Heinrich August, *Der lange Weg nach Westen*: vol 2, *Deutsche Geschichte vom 'Dritten Reich' bis zur Wiedervereinigung*, Munich, 2000

Witt, Peter-Christian, 'Zur Finanzierung des Abstimmungskampfes und der Selbstschutz-organisationen in Oberschlesien 1920–1922', *Militärgeschichtliche Mitteilungen* 13, 1973, pp 59–76

Wohlfeil, Rainer, 'Zum Stand der Forschung über Hauptprobleme des Spanischen Bürgerkriegs', *Militärgeschichtliche Mitteilungen* 6, 1969, pp 189–98

Wohlfeil, Rainer, 'Heer und Republik', in *Handbuch zur deutschen Militärgeschichte 1648–1939, Abschnitt VI Reichswehr und Republik*, published by Militärgeschichtlichen Forschungsamt, Frankfurt am Main, 1970, pp 11–303

Wright, Jonathan, and Stafford, Paul, 'Hitler, Britain and the Hoßbach Memorandum', *Militärgeschichtliche Mitteilungen* 42, 1987, pp 77–124

Wuermeling, Henric L, *'Doppelspiel' – Adam von Trott zu Solz im Widerstand gegen Hitler*, Munich, 2004

Wunderlich, Dieter, *Göring und Goebbels – Eine Doppelbiografie*, Regensburg, 2002

Young, A P, *Die X-Dokumente. Die geheimen Kontakte Carl Goerdelers mit der britischen Regierung 1938/1939*, edited by Sidney Aster, translated and with a foreword by Helmut Krausnick, Munich and Zürich, 1989

Zaun, Harald, *Paul von Hindenburg und die deutsche Außenpolitik 1925–1934*, Cologne, Weimar and Vienna, 1999

Zee, Nanda van der, *'Um Schlimmeres zu verhindern . . .' – Die Ermordung der niederländischen Juden: Kollaboration und Widerstand*, Munich and Vienna, 1999

Zeidler, Manfred, *Reichswehr und Rote Armee 1920–1933. Wege und Stationen einer ungewöhnlichen Zusammenarbeit*, Munich, 1993

Index

Abwehr 5, 19, 52, 89, 91, 93,
　99, 107–8, 117, 122–4,
　126, 138, 146, 152, 154,
　156–7, 160–1, 171, 173–
　4, 179, 181–2, 187, 192,
　199–206, 208–14, 220,
　222–5, 227, 229, 231–3,
　236, 238, 252–3, 255
contacts with Allies 234–8,
　253
employment and protection
　of Jews 170–1, 209–14
organisation 81, 91–2,
　95–6, 99–100, 104, 124,
　126, 146–7, 171, 187,
　215–16
　'Hauskapelle' system 100,
　110, 216–17
　K-Organisation 161,
　239–41
　'Ten Commandments'
　100, 209, 215, 217
penetration of by Allies
　222, 235–8
relations with Foreign
　Ministry 236–41
relations with Gestapo 94,
　96, 100, 154, 210–11
relations with OKH 152,
　203, 205–6, 223, 232
relations with OKW 100
relations with RSHA 211,
　215, 242
relations with SD 96,
　99–100, 127, 215–17,
　223, 236–7
relations with Sipo 215–17
relations with SS 94, 127–
　8, 184–5, 200–1, 203,
　209–14, 216, 221
relations with Wehrmacht
　109, 126, 134, 216

resistance to Hitler 124–6,
　144, 154, 170–7, 182–3,
　224–5
dissolved and set up in
　RSHA 222, 242
Abyssinia 102–3
Adlercreutz, Carlos 210
Admiral Hipper (Ger) 183
Albania 193
Alberts, Kapitän zur See 6
Alboldt, Emil 38, 41
Alfieri, Ambassador 186, 193
Alfonso XIII, King of Spain
　21–2, 66, 69–71, 80
Algeria 26–7, 222, 233
Amé, General 233
Amoss, Colonel Ulius C 221
Anastasio, Ernesto 65
Argentina 6–7, 10, 12, 20,
　80–1, 238–9
Arnauld de la Perière, Lothar
　von 23–5, 38
Arnim, General von 223, 231
Arranz, Captain Francisco
　105
Attolico, Bernardo 147–8,
　153
Austria 9, 24, 27, 98, 102,
　109, 213, 236–7
　Anschluss 98, 120–3, 138,
　160

Baden (Ger) 11–12
Badoglio, Marshal 233
Bamler, Rudolf 95, 99, 124
Bandera, Stepan 164, 204
Barbara (Ger) 69–70
Barth, Emil 40
Bastian, Admiral Max
　89–90, 230
Bauer, Max 51–2, 67
Beck, General Ludwig 97,
　103, 114–19, 121–2,

128–31, 151, 156, 168,
　173–4, 176–7, 180, 218,
　224, 251–2
Behncke, Admiral Paul 56,
　63
Beigbeder, Juan 186, 189
Belgium 97–8, 103, 172, 184,
　218, 231
Below, General von 50–1,
　144
Benes, President 110, 129,
　133
Bentivegni, Eccard von 161,
　200, 204–5, 206, 208,
　215–16, 242
Bergh, Oberstleutnant von
　50
Berlin (Ger) 57, 60–1, 79
Bernhardt, Johannes EF 105
Bersin, General Jan 107
Berwick, HMS 10
Best, Captain S P 177
Best, Werner 89, 95–6, 99–
　101, 112, 123, 138, 149,
　160–1, 166, 177
Bethmann-Hollweg,
　Theobald von 26
Blaskowitz, General 169,
　172, 178
Blomberg, General Werner
　von 89, 91–3, 97–8,
　102–3, 108–9, 122
　marriage and dismissal of
　112–14, 245, 252
Bock, General Feder von
　172–3
Böhme, General 109
Bonhoeffer, Dietrich 226,
　228, 230, 245, 253, 255,
　257–8
Bonhoeffer, Dr Karl 136
Bonhoeffer, Klaus 171

Bormann, Martin 157, 170–1, 244
Braemar, General Walter von 162–3
Brauchitsch, General Walther von 116–19, 128–30, 134, 139, 143–4, 154, 156, 159–60, 164–5, 167–8, 170–5, 177–80, 182, 188–90, 200, 210, 252
Bredereck, Paul 82–3
Bredow, Ferdinand von 91, 93, 245
Bremen (Ger) 6–8
Breslau (Ger) 8
Brest-Litovsk, Peace of 28
Bristol, HMS 9–10, 15–16
Britain 3, 9, 12, 16, 20, 65, 68, 97–8, 103, 108, 121–2, 128, 135, 139
and Sudeten crisis 128, 130–2, 134–5
in WW I 10, 21–3, 29
in WW II 145–51, 153, 155, 157, 159, 161, 163, 171–2, 177, 180–4, 186, 188–9, 191–3, 201, 221–2, 225, 227, 232, 234, 236, 238–9, 243, 256
Brockdorff-Ahlefeldt, General Walter 135–6
Brockdorff-Rantzau, Graf 49
Brüning, Heinrich 87–8
Buck, Anna (sister) 3, 166
Buck, Lt Rolf (nephew) 166
Buck, Rudolf (brother-in-law) 3, 28
Bulgaria 8, 201
Burckhardt, Carl Jacob 135
Bürkner, Captain Leopold 126, 130, 181, 193, 230
as head of Abwehr 214
Busch, Major Friedrich 212

Campos, General Martinez 191, 194–5, 232
Canaris, Admiral Wilhelm 56–7, 59–61, 63, 70, 103, 109–10, 114–15, 117, 134, 138, 140, 145, 152, 155–6, 160–1, 166–7, 180–1, 183–7,
189–92, 195, 201–3, 205–6, 208, 210–16, 218, 224, 231, 233, 237, 255
birth, family and education 3–5
naval career 4–38, 48, 56–83, 89–90
in naval intelligence 7, 63–73
abortive resignation 61–2
discharged from Navy 242
promotions 5–6, 8, 20, 60, 83, 123
character 4, 6–7, 26, 28–9, 29, 56, 61–2, 71, 81–3, 90, 96–7, 100–1, 110–11, 134–5, 154, 172–3, 174, 176–8, 180, 182, 229, 246, 258
engagement and marriage 48
health 8, 29, 61–2, 71–2
decorations 7, 25, 169
diaries 251–2, 256
with Freikorps 38–42, 44, 47–8, 53, 61, 78–9, 82
appointed head of Abwehr 89–91, 93
suspended from Abwehr and restored 214
relieved of office 241–2
transferred to OKW 242–3
attitude to Hitler and Nazis 88–90, 110–11, 112, 117, 123–4, 160
contacts with Allies 220–2, 234–6, 242–3, 243, 254
resistance to Hitler 115–16, 124–6, 131–2, 136, 145, 148–51, 154, 158, 161, 165–6, 169, 172–7, 179–80, 194–5, 208, 224–6, 233
forbids Abwehr involvement in plots 177
use and protection of Jews 170–1, 209–14, 226–8
downfall of 208, 220–2, 227–41, 244–58
arrested 244–5, 251
interrogated 245–7, 254–5
trial and execution 256–8
Canaris, Auguste Amelie (mother) 3, 5, 14
Canaris, Brigitte (daughter) 242
Canaris, Carl (brother) 3, 30, 32
Canaris, Carl (father) 3–5
Canaris, Constantin 218, 231
Canaris, Erika (wife) 61, 242
Canaris, Eva (daughter) 242
Cap Frio (Ger) 6
Carnarvon, HMS 15–16
Casablanca Conference 220–1
Castro, President Cipriano 7
Cattaro 24, 26–8, 30–2
Cave Brown, Anthony 242–3
Chamberlain, Neville 135–7, 139, 145, 150–1, 172
Chiang Kai-shek 109
Chile 6, 12–17, 19
China 108–9
Churchill, Winston 15, 131–2
Ciano, Count 106, 147–8, 186, 190, 195
Cincar-Marcovic, Foreign Minister of Bulgaria 201
Communism 39, 41, 60, 80, 83, 104–5, 107–8, 125, 131, 138, 157, 160, 181, 200, 202, 235
concentration camps 109–10, 125, 150, 160, 213, 255
Condor Legion 106–7, 120, 189, 194
Conway, HMS 16
Cornwall, HMS 15
Coronel, Battle of 12–15
Corrientes (Ger) 11
Corsica 190
Costa Rica 7
Coulondre, Robert 153, 155
Cradock, Admiral Christopher 13–14
Croatia 213
Cuevas, Admiral 16
Cuxhaven 39
Cvetkovic, President 201

Czechoslovakia 97, 103, 110, 127–31, 181
  Sudeten crisis 123, 127–40, 146, 160

da Fonseca, Hermes 7
Dahlerus a Swedish businessman 155
Daladier 139, 145, 155–6
Daluege, Kurt 100, 138
d'Arcy Osborne, Sir Francis 180–1, 184
DDP 49
de Magaz, Admiral 67
Delbrück, Erwin 244–5
Denmark 46, 59–60, 182, 184, 209, 256
  invasion of 183
Dieckhoff, Ambassador 238–41
Dirksen, Ambassador von 108–9
Dissel, Werner 108
Dohnanyi, Christine von 115, 231, 233
  arrested 226
Dohnanyi, Hans von 115–16, 125, 136, 171, 173, 180–3, 185, 206, 212, 224–5, 227–31, 241, 243, 245, 252–3, 255–7
  arrested 226, 230
Dönitz, Admiral Karl 82, 241–2
Donner, Captain 70–3, 81
Donovan, William J 220–1, 235
Dresden (Ger) 8–20
Drumcliffe (GB) 11
Du Faur, Moritz Faber 103–4
Duesterberg, Georg and Theodor 125
Duke, Florimond 221
Dulles, Allen Welsh 221, 254

Earle, Captain George H 221, 234–5
Ebert, President Friedrich 32, 37, 39–41, 44, 46, 51–2, 54–6, 58
Echevarrietta, Horacio 23, 65–72, 76–7, 80–2

Eden, Anthony 98, 103, 235
Edler von Vivremont, General Erwin 109
Eggerstadt, Deputy 58–60
Ehrhardt, Captain Hermann 45, 51–4, 57, 59–61
Eichhorn, Emil 39–41
Elser, Georg 177
Engel, Gerhard 214
Erzberger, Matthias 47, 57, 83
Etsdorf, Hasso von 173

Falklands, battle of the 15
'Fall Gelb' plan 172–3
Federation of Former Ehrhardt Officers 57
Fegelein, SS-Brigadeführer 241
Fiedler, Werner 166, 223
Finland 199, 202
Fischer, Hermann 258
Fisher, Admiral Jackie 15
Flossenburg 256–8
France 3, 65, 80, 97–8, 102–3, 121–2, 127, 131, 137, 139
  assistance to Spanish Republicans 104–5
  French-Soviet Pact 102–3, 105
  in WW I 10, 12, 21–4
  in WW II 145–56, 159, 161, 165, 170, 172, 174–6, 179, 183–4, 187–90, 192–3, 218, 222, 242–3
Franco, General Francisco 104–6, 186–95, 240
Frank, Hans 170
Frank, Karl Hermann 127–8, 131–3, 138
Freikorps 38–9, 41–3, 45, 56–9, 134, 136, 152
Freikorps Maercker 61
Freytag-Loringhoven, Oberst 233, 239, 243
Frick, Admiral 170, 203
Fricke, Carlos 65, 203
Frisch, Rittmeister Achim von 114, 117–18
Frisia (Neth) 20
Fritsch, General von 93–4, 102, 112

dismissal of 97–8, 113–14, 116–18, 121, 126, 129, 245, 252, 255
  death of 168
Fritze, Ulrich 76
Fromm, General 173

Gagern, Freiherr Captain Ernst von 55, 62
Gamm, Major von 204–5
Garcia, Captain Don Mateo 65–7
Gehre, Ludwig 136, 225, 253, 255, 257
General Church (GB) 28
German Army and OKH 37–40, 45, 49–56, 59, 116, 123, 133, 145–6, 152, 161–2, 179, 188, 199–200, 202–3, 225, 232, 243, 252
  relations with SS 138, 163, 200–1
  resistance 126, 173
German Navy and OKM 3–5, 10, 12, 16, 39, 54–60, 63–4, 64, 88–90, 105–6, 242
Gessler, Dr Otto 55, 58, 63, 74–6, 79, 81
Gestapo 89, 94–5, 100, 104, 108, 113–17, 123–5, 131, 138, 140, 152, 154, 160, 163, 166, 185, 205, 210, 213, 229, 234–5, 244–5, 252, 255
  involved in 1939 plot 176
GFP (Geheime Feldpolizei) 107, 152–3, 156, 166–7
Gibraltar 8, 27, 186–95, 223, 232
Gilsa, Major von 48–50, 53–5
Gisevius, Hans 114–17, 134–6, 144, 154, 156, 158, 173, 175–7, 221, 224, 254
GKS-Corps 45, 51–2
GKSD (Garde-Kavallerie-Schützen-Division) 39, 42–5, 47–8, 124–5
Glaise-Hortenau, Edmund 120

Glasgow, HMS 12–17, 19
Gneisenau (Ger) 13–14
Goebbels, Joseph 87–8, 113,
121, 130, 157, 211, 241
Goeben (Ger) 8
Goerdeler, Carl 115–16, 156,
169, 174, 177, 224
Goering, Hermann 88–9, 92,
95, 98, 102–3, 106–8,
112–13, 117–18, 121–4,
132–3, 143, 163, 165,
168, 173, 176, 184
Goltz, Rüdiger von der
117–18
Gomez, President Juan
Vicente 7
Good Hope, HMS 12–14
Goss, Dr Ritter von 81
Grabowsky, Fritz 44, 47, 52,
125
'Graf Group' 126, 134
Gramatzki, Archibald von
228
Greece 8, 190–2, 201
Groener, General Wilhelm
31–2, 45, 49–51, 60, 76,
81–2, 87–8, 91
Groscurth, Helmuth 123,
125, 129–34, 136–40,
144, 150, 152–3, 155–8,
161, 163, 165–6, 168–70,
172–6, 179–81, 218–19
death of 179
Grote, Freiherr von 239–40
Guatemala 7
Günther, Albrecht 136
Gürtner, Franz 115–16, 171
Guttenberg, Freiherr von und
zu 245, 254

Haag, Inge 175, 218
Haase, Hugo 39, 41, 47
Hack, Friedrich Wilhelm 108
Haeften, Werner von 251
Halder, General Franz 124,
129, 134–6, 139, 145,
148–9, 154, 157, 160,
163, 165–6, 169, 172–80,
182, 188–92, 199, 252,
256
Halifax, Lord 122, 135, 139
Hammerstein, General Kurt
von 53

Hansen, Oberst 244
HAPAG line 11–12
'Harlequin' 222–3
Harnack, Ernst von 171
Hase, Paul 135
Hassell, Ulrich von 69, 102,
107, 169, 179, 194
Heil, Hermann 10
Heinkel, Gerhard 100
Heinz, Friedrich Wilhelm
51–2, 109–10, 124, 126,
128, 135–6, 138, 200,
246, 252–3
Helldorf, Graf von 87, 125,
136, 156, 177
Hendaye meeting 189–91,
194
Henderson, Sir Neville 122–
3, 136, 139, 148, 150–1,
153, 157–8
Henlein, Konrad 127, 132–3,
137
'Herman' plan 235
Herzlieb, Walter 227–9
Herzner, Hans-Albrecht 136,
146, 155
Hess, Rudolf 105, 170
Heydrich, Reinhard 60–1, 89,
92, 95–7, 99–101, 110,
114–15, 122–3, 138, 145,
148, 150, 152–3, 157,
160, 163, 166–8, 181,
184–5, 200, 202–3, 209,
211, 215–18, 230
assassinated 218–19
Heydt, Eduard von der 227,
229
Himmler, Heinrich 94–5,
100, 109, 114–15, 118,
122, 134, 137, 145,
148–9, 154, 157, 160,
162, 166, 168, 170, 176,
180–1, 200, 210, 214–18,
221, 230–1, 233, 239,
241–3, 245, 253, 255
Hindenburg, President Paul
von 44, 67, 70, 87, 89,
91, 112
Hirschmann, Obermaat 38
Hitler, Adolf 57, 59, 61, 88–9,
91–2, 95, 98, 102–4, 106,
108–10, 112–13, 115–16,
118, 120–4, 127–9, 132–

4, 138, 143–4, 147–8,
152–7, 159–60, 162–3,
165–8, 172, 176, 184,
186, 188–91, 193, 195,
200, 208, 211–12, 214,
218, 225, 238–9, 241,
247, 253, 256
Munich putsch (1923) 57,
59–60, 77
runs for Presidency 87
seizes power as Chancellor
89, 91
takes command of
Wehrmacht 94, 112
and attack on the West
170–8
plots against
in 1938 124–6, 129–30,
134–9, 224–5
Elser, 1939 177
Vatican, 1939 180
Zossen, 1939 154–8,
173–7, 180
in 1943 224–6
20 July 1944 114–15,
243–4, 246, 251–2, 254
Hoepner, General Erich 135,
159
Hoffmann, General Heinrich
von 39, 44, 46
Holland 20, 32, 47, 64, 66,
182–4
Höllein, Emil 78
Holmwood (GB) 12
Hopman, Admiral 6–7, 31
Horthy, Admiral von 131
Hossbach, Friedrich 94, 98,
113, 118, 124, 129
Höttl, Wilhelm 213
Hoyningen-Huene, Baron
Oswald von 235
Huerta, President Victoriano
8–9
Hummel, Hauptmann 239
Hungary 98–9, 108, 131, 137,
201, 214, 225
and Komintern Pact 109
Huppenkothen, Walter 96,
184–5, 185, 215–16,
230, 241, 243–5, 251–4,
257–8
Hyades, HMS 11–12

Ickrath, Hauptmann 228
Inflexible, HMS 15
Invincible, HMS 15
Ireland 163
Iron Brigade, The 38–9, 41–2
Isenberg, Sally 74–5
Italy 22, 65, 76, 80, 97–9,
    102–3, 121, 123, 128,
    132, 139, 148, 152–3,
    156, 181, 186, 188, 191,
    193, 195, 201, 223, 226,
    231–3, 237–8
  assistance to Franco in
    Spanish Civil War
    105–7
  and Komintern Pact 109
  Pact of Steel 147

Jaenicke, Günther 205
Jamaica 9
Jansa, General 120
Janschkow, Hermann 47
Japan 63–4, 108–9, 156, 186,
    188, 211–12
Jary, Ryko 164, 167, 204
Jews and anti-Semitism 61,
    113, 160, 163–4, 164–5,
    167–8, 170, 191, 202,
    204–5, 207–8, 208–9,
    214, 228, 255
  'Operation Seven' 226–7
Jodl, General 121, 126, 133,
    164–5, 184, 186, 188,
    211, 215, 241
John, Otto 171
Jorns, Kriegsgerichtsrat Paul
    44–8, 82–3
Jost, Heinz 95, 137–8, 148–9
Juhlin-Dannfeldt, Curt 210
Jung, Kapitän 57–8
Jung, Lt-Col Helge 210

Kalle, Major 21
Kaltenbrunner, Ernst 238,
    243–7, 253, 256
Kapp, Wolfgang 51–2, 54–5
  Kapp-Lüttwitz putsch
    50–6, 59, 65, 82
Kauder, Richard 209
Kaulbars, Baron von 243–4,
    254–5
Kautschke, Fritz 191–2

Keitel, General 109, 114,
    116–17, 120–1, 126, 128,
    132–3, 149–50, 154–7,
    164–5, 170, 179, 181,
    188, 193–4, 201, 205–6,
    214–15, 217, 226, 230–1,
    231, 239, 241–2
Kent, HMS 15–17
Kern, Leutnant Erwin 57
Kerstenhahn, Kurt 252
Kessel, Albrecht von 139
Kesselring, General 223
Kiel 5, 8, 20, 29, 31–3, 37–42,
    48, 55, 57–61, 63, 66–7,
    89–90, 107
Kiep, Dr Otto 220, 235
Kirk, Alexander 145, 235
Klatt, Richard 213–14
Klaus, Edgar 209–10, 211,
    214
Kleist, Field-Marshal 131–2
Klintzsch, Hans-Ulrich 59
Kluge, General von 116
Knaak, Hans-Wolfram 136
Knobelsdorff, Freda von 226
Köhler, Fregattenkapitän
    Erich 8–9
Kollantai, Alexandra 210–11
Köln (Ger) 88–9
Komintern Pact 108–9
Kordt, Erich 134, 139, 148,
    154, 173, 175
Kordt, Theo 134–5, 148
Köstring, General 199
KPD 41, 76, 79, 125
Kraell, Alexander 230
Kraneck, Wolfgang 105
Kreisau resistance circle 220,
    234
Krichbaum, Wilhelm 152–3,
    156, 166–7
Kriwitzi, General 107
Krohn, Captain von 21, 23

Lahousen, General Erwin
    121–3, 125, 130–1, 146,
    148–9, 152, 155, 160–1,
    164–7, 174, 192, 194–5,
    199, 201, 204–5, 207–8,
    223–5, 231, 233
Lahousen, Stephanie 258
Lammel, Richard 128
Langenheim, Adolf P 105

Langhaeuser, Major Rudolf
    165–6
Langkau, Major 187
Latvia 209, 211
League of Nations 102–3
Leeb, Ritter von 172–3,
    176–7
Leiber, Peter 181, 183
Leipzig (Ger) 12–14
Leissner, Captain Wilhelm
    187, 192, 239
Lequis, General Arnold 40
Lersner, Kurt Freiherr von
    221
Leuschner, Wilhelm 171
Leverkühn, Dr Paul 122,
    220–1, 234, 236
Libya 188
Liebknecht, Karl 39–41
  murder of 43–4, 47, 79,
    82–3
Liebmann, General Kurt 94
Lieder, Kurt 57, 59–60
Liedig, Franz-Maria 124,
    136, 138, 182–3, 253,
    255
Liepmann, Rudolph 45
Liessner, Captain Wilhelm
    107
Lietzmann, Captain 105
Lissner, Ivar 209, 211–12,
    214
Lissner, Percy and Robert
    211–12
Lissner, Sigrid 212
List, General 116
Lithuania 204, 209–10
Lloyd of Dolobran, Lord 131
Locarno Treaty 98, 102–3
Loehr, General 201
Loewenfeld, Captain
    Wilfried von 38–9,
    41–2, 57, 59–60
Loewenthal, Captain 56–7,
    82
Lohmann, Captain Walther
    63–4, 68–77
London Naval Treaty 1935
    126
Lossberg, General von 51
Lossow, Hans-Ludwig von
    210
Luce, Captain John 17

Lüdecke, Captain Emil 8–14, 16–19, 46
Lüdecke, Frau Else 29
Ludendorff, General Erich 39, 51, 61
Luftwaffe 106, 121, 188–9, 192–3, 201
Lunding, Hans 256–8
Luther, Reich Chancellor 69
Lüttwitz, General Walther von 42, 44, 46, 50–2, 54–5
  see also Kapp-Lüttwitz pusch under Kapp
Luxemburg, Rosa 39–41
  murder of 43–8, 79, 82–3
Lyushkov, General 109

Maas, Hermann 126
Macedonia, HMS 15
MacFarland, Lanning 234
Madero, President Francisco 8
Maercker, General 15, 50–1, 54, 61
Magaz, Almirante 67–8
Magistrati, Massimo 148
Maizar (GB) 27–8
Malta 8, 31
Manchuria 212
Manstein, General 149, 210
Marogna-Redwitz, General 122–3, 125
Martinez Anido, General Severiano 80
Marz, Wilhelm 75
Mas-a-Tierra Island 17, 19
Mauer, Max 54
Maurer, Helmut 243–4
Mayrhofer, Kapitänleutnant 64–5
Medina y Morris, Captain 65
Mehring, Kapitän 11
Meisinger, Josef 212
Melnyk, Andrej 164, 199, 203
Menzel, Hermann 192
Menzies, Stewart 235
Messerschmidt, Oberleutnant 70, 81
Meusel, Korvettenkapitän 56
Mexico 8–10

Meyer, Conrad 65
Michaelis, Konteradmiral 56
Miklas, President Wilhelm 122
Mikosch, Oberst 187
Minsk 225
Mola, General 104–5
Molotov, Vyacheslav 151
Moltke, Helmut Graf von 205, 220, 234–5
Mommsen, Vizeadmiral 69
Monmouth, HMS 12–14
Montenegro 8
Morocco 31, 64, 67–8, 71, 105, 190, 193, 222, 232
Moses, Dr Julius 77–8, 78–9
MSDP party 56
Müller, Heinrich 149, 230, 244–5, 253, 255–6
Müller, Josef 180–5, 195, 205, 215–16, 226, 228–30, 245, 252–3, 254–5, 258
  arrested 226
Müller, Oberst Vincenz 176–7
Munich bomb plot 177
Munich Conference 135–9, 143, 151
Munich putsch (1923) 57, 59–60, 77
Mussolini, Benito 102–3, 107, 122, 128, 139, 147–8, 150, 153–4, 156–7, 190
  arrested 233

Naval Brigades 45, 52–3, 125
  Naval Brigade Ehrhardt 52–4, 57, 124, 152
  Naval Brigade Loewenfeld 38, 41–2, 45, 48, 52, 56, 65
Nebe, Arthur 114, 117, 136
Neilung, Leutnant 12–13
Neurath, Konstantin von 102, 116
Nieden, First Officer 9, 19
Niemöller, Martin 30, 32–3, 37
NKVD 107, 109
Nockeburg, Hans 202
Noots, Hubert 181, 184

Norddeutsche Lloyd line 11–12, 19
North Africa 192, 201, 222–3, 231, 241
Norway 8, 29, 32, 90, 182
  invasion of 183
Noske, Gustav 32, 37–42, 44–55, 83, 116
NSDAP (Nazi Party) 87–8, 91–2, 95, 110–11, 112, 114, 117, 123, 126, 211–12, 215, 245, 255
  organisation 92, 105, 108
Nürnberg (Ger) 14

OKH see German Army and OKH
OKM see German Navy and OKM
Olbricht, Friedrich 224, 244, 246, 251
Oldershausen, General von 53
Operation Felix 186–95, 199
Operation Marita 201
Operation Pastorius 227
Operation Sealion 186, 188, 190–1
Operation Seven 228–31
Operation Torch 222
Oppenheim, Waldemar von 214
Orama, HMS 19
Org-C 57–61, 77, 79, 124–5, 152
Ortega, HMS 12
Oshima, Hiroshi 108–9
Oster, Hans 110, 114–15, 115–17, 124–6, 128–31, 134–6, 138–9, 144–5, 154–8, 161, 171, 173–7, 180–5, 199–200, 212, 224, 226–30, 241, 243, 252–8
  arrested 226, 245
  interrogated 245–6
Ostrecht, Hauptmann 187
Otranto, HMS 12–14
Oven, General von 53

Pabst, Waldemar 39–48, 50–2, 125

Papen, Franz von 88–9, 91, 120, 221, 234–7
Pardo, Colonel 187, 191
Pariani, General 132, 155
Patagonia 11–12
Patschowski, Günther 95–6
Patzig, Conrad 89–93, 95, 110–11, 124
Paul, Elfriede 108
Paul VI, Pope 184
Paulus, General 172
Persia (Ger) 11
Pétain, Marshal 184
Pflugk-Harttung, Elli 48, 82
Pflugk-Harttung, Heinz von 39, 43, 48
Pflugk-Harttung, Horst von 39, 43–6, 48, 82–3
Pfuhlstein, Alexander von 223, 246, 254
Philipp, Albrecht 78
Phoebus Film Company 73–6
Piekenbrock, Hans 160–1, 167, 187, 206, 208
Pius XII, Pope 181
Pius XXII, Pope 180
Poland 97, 108, 137, 168–70, 203, 254, 256
  Bromberg 161–3
  invasion of 143–71, 172, 176, 178–9, 199, 209, 255
  provocateurs 145, 148–50, 153, 160
  police 94–5, 96, 100, 108, 160, 167–8, 170
  see also Gestapo, GFP
Pöllnitz, Gisela von 108
Popoff, Dusko 227–8
Portugal 20, 184, 223, 226, 232, 237
Primo de Rivera, General Miguel 66–71, 80
Protze, Richard 5, 58, 99, 112
Pruck, Erich 121–2
Prussia 40–1, 45, 49, 54, 59, 76, 87, 95
Prussia (Ger) 11–12
Püllen, Captain Theodor 26–7

Quisling, Vidkun 183

Raeder, Admiral 59–60, 81–2, 90–1, 93, 115, 118, 143, 188
Rathenau, Walther 57, 77
Ratibor, Prince 23
Rattenhuber, Hans 256
Reichenau, General Walther von 92, 120, 172, 183, 252
Reinhardt, General Georg 41, 45, 49–54
Reinhold, Peter 74, 76
Reinicke, General Hermann 205
Republican People's Militia 40
Rheinland (Ger) 63
Rhineland, occupation of 102–3
Ribbentrop, Joachim von 102, 108–9, 116, 120, 126–7, 131, 145, 147–8, 150–1, 153–4, 157–8, 164, 173, 180, 190, 234, 238–40
Richthoven, Wolfram von 189, 194–5
Rio de Janeiro 7, 11
Ritgen, Ulrich 45–6
Roatta, General 106, 147–8, 155, 240
Roeder, Manfred 226, 229–31
Rohleder, Major Joachim 107, 184–5
Röhm, Ernst 92–3
Roma (Ger) 23
Romania 190, 192, 201, 205, 213
Rome *see* Vatican
Rommel, General 223
Ronge, General 122
Roosevelt, President F D 220–1
Rosenberg, Alfred 79, 202–3
'Rota Kapelle' ring 107–8
RSHA 213, 215–17, 230, 242, 251, 253, 255
Ruge, Ludwig 228
Ruhr, occupation of in 1924 63

Runciman, Lord 132, 136–7
Rundstedt, General von 115, 166, 169, 172–4
Runge, Otto 43, 45–6
Russia 3, 10, 62, 73–4, 97, 102, 106–8, 110, 127–8, 131, 146–7, 152, 164, 166, 179, 186, 199–200, 209–11, 213–14, 224–5, 235–6, 255
  attempt to assassinate Hitler 225
  German-Soviet Pact 150–1, 156–7, 168–9, 210
  German treatment of POWs 205–8
  Kursk Offensive 225
  Operation Barbarossa 188, 194, 199–208, 210, 212, 223, 254
  Military Law Order 201–2

SA 57, 59, 87–8, 91–3, 108, 130, 134
Saar plebiscite 97
Sachsenhausen concentration camp 109
Sachsenwald (Ger) 7
Sack, Judge Karl 125, 136, 230–1, 243–4, 253, 257
Sacro-Lirio, Baron del 66, 69, 80, 82
Saemisch, Friedrich 75
Sanjurjo, General 104
Santa Isabel (Ger) 12–13
Sardinia 27
Sas, G J S 182–5
Schacht, Hjalmar 115, 134–6, 154, 156, 177
Schäfer, Emanuel 166
Schäfer, Karl 99–100
Scharnhorst (Ger) 13–15, 183
Scheer, Admiral Reinhard von 29, 32
Scheidemann, Philipp 41, 44, 48–50, 57, 59
Schellenberg, Walter 122, 177, 181, 184–5, 202, 209, 215, 233, 242, 244–5
Schenk, Leutnant Otto 10
Schindler, Oskar 128

Schlabrendorff, Fabian von
224–5, 254
Schleicher, General Kurt von
44, 87–8, 91, 93, 245
Schlesien (Ger) 81–2, 89–90
Schmidhuber, Major
Wilhelm 184, 226,
228–30
Schmidt, Guido 121
Schmidt, interpreter 147–8,
154, 158
Schmidt, Otto 113, 118
Schmidt-Richberg, Major
Erich 167
Schneerson, Joseph Isaak
170–1
Schneller, Ernst 76
Schoen, Walter 229
Schrader, Werner 125, 243,
252
Schubert, Carl von 68, 70
Schulenburg, Graf von der
125–6, 139
Schulz, Werner 212
Schulze, Bruno 45–6
Schulze-Boysen, Harro and
Libertas 107–8
Schussnig, Karl 256
Schussnigg, Karl 120–2
Schuster, Captain Otto
58–60
Schweppenburg, Geyr von
103
SD 92, 95, 99–100, 104, 110,
123, 138, 148–9, 149,
160, 163, 177, 203, 205,
207, 209, 213, 215, 218,
231, 236–9
SDF (Sudeten-Deutsches
Freikorps) 137–8
Seeckt, General Hans von
51–3, 58–9, 79
Seewald, Heinrich 46
Seyss-Inquart, Arthur 120–2
Sicily 8, 31
Allied invasion of 232–3
Sierra Cordoba 16
Sierra Salvada (Ger) 11
Sievers, Leutnant zur See
23–4
Simon, Lord 98, 132
Sipo (Sicherheitspolizei)
100, 123, 138, 149, 160,

167, 178, 200–1, 205,
213, 215–16, 218, 231
Sklobin, Nikolai 110
Slovakia 201, 213
Sodenstern, General von 208
Soennecken,
Oberwachtmeister 207
Solf, Hanna 220
Sonderegger, Franz 226,
229–30, 245, 251–4, 257
Souchon, Leutnant zur See
48
Spain 7, 20–4, 31, 64–72, 80,
82, 104–5, 112, 186–95,
214, 223, 232–3, 238–41
assistance to from
Germany 64–72, 76–82,
104–8
and Komintern Pact 109
SIPM 107
in WW II 187–8
Spartacus League 39–42, 48
SPD (Social Democrats)
32, 39–42, 46, 58–9, 81,
125–6, 160, 171
Spee, Admiral Graf
Maximilian von 13–15
Spellman, Archbishop 234
Spengler, Oswald 126
Sperrle, General Hugo 106,
120
SS 92–4, 100, 104, 109, 112,
114, 122, 125, 128, 134,
138, 140, 145, 149, 157,
160–1, 166–70, 184–5,
209, 211–12, 218
Einsatzgruppen 123, 160–1,
162–3, 166–8, 178,
200–4, 213
organisation 137–8
and 'Ten Commandments'
209, 215
Waffen-SS 245
SS-RSHA 209–11
SSD 201
Stahlhelm, the 125, 136
Stalin, Josef 107, 110, 151,
157, 169, 199, 209, 213
Stalingrad, battle of 179, 223
Stang, Ulrich 183
Stauffenburg, Graf von
243–4, 251–2
Stein, SMS (Germany) 5

Steinbart-Real High School,
Duisberg 4
Stephani, Major 42
Stevens, Major RH 177
Stiege, Heinrich 45–6
Stöckler, Christian 11–12, 19
Stolze, Erwin 128
Strasser, Otto 126, 252
Streckenbach 215–16
Stresemann, Gustav 71
Strünk, Theodor 221
Stülpnagel, Karl-Heinrich
von 156–7, 172–4, 177,
180
Sturdee, V/A 15
Sudetendeutsche Partei
(SdP) 127–8, 131, 133
Suffolk, HMS 10
Suñer, Serrano 189–90, 192,
194–5
Sweden 90, 183, 210, 243,
256
Swinemünde 90
Switzerland 173, 180, 207,
226–8

Talcahuano 12–13, 19
Thomas, General Georg 116,
150, 154–7, 172–3, 182,
203, 252–3, 256
Thorbeck, Otto 257–8
Tippelskirch, General von
152, 179–80, 199
Tirpitz, Admiral Alfred von
3, 29, 107
Toeppen, Johannes 227–8
Treckow, Oberst von 224
Trendelenburg, Ernst 68
Tresckow, Hening von 135,
224–5, 251
Trotha, Admiral von 40, 50,
52–5
Trotsky, Leon 28
Trott zu Sulz, Adam von
126, 220, 234, 236
Tukhachevsky, Marshal
Mikhail 110
Tunis 190, 222–3, 231, 233
Turkel, General Anton 213
Turkey 8, 220–1, 234–8
Twardowski, Dr Fritz von
234

U-boats 20, 22–3, 23–4,
    26–38, 63–4, 71, 76, 80
'unrestricted U-boat
    warfare' in WW I 26,
    29–30
Ukraine 28, 152, 163–4, 166,
    199, 202–4
Ulex, General 116
Uruguay 10
USA 7, 9–10, 26, 31, 49,
    74, 150, 170, 188, 214,
    220–1, 223, 232, 234–7,
    254
'Dogwood-Cereus Circle'
    234
USPD (Independent Social
    Democratic Party) 32,
    39–41, 47, 78
Üxküll, Graf 126

Valparaiso 12–14, 19
Vansittart, Sir Robert 131–2,
    134
Vatican 180–2, 184–5, 226,
    229–30, 253–4
'X-Report' 182, 253
Veltjens, Josef 104
Venlo incident 177, 181, 184
Vermehren affair 234–8, 241
Versailles Treaty 49–51, 56–
    8, 63–4, 66, 68, 88, 102
abrogated 98
Viebahn, General Max von
    116
Vigón, General Juan 186–7,
    189, 192–5
Villa, Pancho 9
Ville de Verdun (Fr) 28
Vittorio Emmanuel, King of
    Italy 150
VMD (People's Naval
    Division) 39–41
Vogel, Kurt 44–8, 78–9, 82–3
Vormann, Nikolaus von 165

Voss, Hans-Erich 192
Voss, Werner 57

Waetjen, Eduard 221
Wagner, Eduard 160, 167,
    239
Wagner, Otto 175–6, 213–
    14, 217
Wahl-Welskirch, Roland
    von 213
Warlimont, General 149,
    183, 188
Wartenburg, Yorck von 126
Wehrmacht and OKW 4–5,
    112, 116–18, 123–4,
    130, 134, 143, 149, 156,
    160–1, 162, 166, 170,
    172, 183, 186, 188,
    201, 205, 208, 212–13,
    215–17, 228–9, 231,
    236, 242, 245, 254
and conscription 99
politicisation of 114 and sev
    way back
rearmament of 97–8
relations with Abwehr 126
relations with Gestapo 115,
    118–19 and back, 119,
    164
relations with Hitler and
    NDASP 92–3, 112–16,
    118–19, 126, 143–4
relations with SD 138
relations with Sipo 138
relations with SS 112, 119,
    126, 129, 164, 167–8
resistance 98, 133–4, 139,
    149–50, 158, 160, 170,
    172–7, 175, 177–80, 224
see also GFP and individual
    campaigns
Weimar Republic 37–87, 245
Weizsäcker, Ernst von 44,
    128, 131–2, 134–5, 148,

158–9, 171–2, 180–1,
    183, 194, 220
Welczeck, Johannes Graf
    von 69–70, 80
Wels, Otto 39–40
Wende, Kapitänleutnant
    Kurt 57
Weygand, General 193
Wiking-Bund, the 60, 79,
    124
Wilbrandt, Hans 234–5
Wilhelm, Prince of Prussia
    136
Wilhelm II, Kaiser 3–5, 8–9,
    17–18, 25, 31–2
Wilson, President Woodrow
    49
Winter, General Paul 242
Winzer, Oberinspektor Paul
    104
Wittenau, Rittmeister
    Schack von 200
Witzig, Hauptmann Richard
    187
Witzleben, General Erwin
    von 126, 134–6, 138,
    173, 176–7, 252
World War I 3, 9–18, 65, 161
Armistice terms 31–2,
    49–50
World War II 143–258
Woyrsch, Udo von 162

'X-Report' see under Vatican

Yugoslavia 201, 213

Zenker, Admiral Hans 55,
    63–4, 66–7, 68, 73–4,
    74–6, 81
Zossen 152, 159, 167, 173–4,
    178, 180, 182, 192, 247,
    252–4, 256–7